BOOKS IN
THE IRWIN SERIES IN ACCOUNTING

THE IRWIN SERIES IN ACCOUNTI

Consulting Editor

WILLARD J. GRAHAM, Ph.D., C.P.A.
University of North Carolina

FUNDAMENTAL ACCOUNTING PRINCIPLES

Fundamental

1959 • REVISED EDITION

Accounting Principles

By WILLIAM W. PYLE

School of Business Administration
University of Oregon

and JOHN ARCH WHITE

College of Business Administration
University of Texas

RICHARD D. IRWIN, INC. • HOMEWOOD, ILLINOIS

REVISED EDITION
First Printing, March, 1959

Library of Congress Catalogue Card No. 59–7828

PRINTED IN THE UNITED STATES OF AMERICA

PREFACE

THIS revised edition of *Fundamental Accounting Principles*, like the previous edition, is designed for use in a first-year accounting course at the college level. It presents a graded, accurate, and realistic approach to the study of accounting that is as nearly self-teaching as is possible. It was written to meet the needs of those students who will make accountancy a career as well as those who will use accounting as a tool in some other field of specialization or in carrying on their personal affairs.

The primary objective of the text is to present the subject matter of accounting in an easily understood manner that emphasizes both principles and the whys of each accounting process. This is the primary objective because students who are grounded in principles and who understand the whys of accounting have no difficulty with the subject and are prepared both for more advanced accounting courses and the application of their knowledge in other fields.

The revision of the material of the previous edition has been extensive. More than half of the chapters have been completely rewritten; the remainder have been given close editorial attention; and four new chapters, Chapter 26, *Management's Use of Accounting Data;* Chapter 27, *Budgets and Budgeting;* Chapter 29, *Statement of Sources and Applications of Funds;* and Chapter 30, *Fundamental Accounting Conventions, Concepts, and Standards,* have been added. All present the subject matter of accounting in such a manner that nothing is learned in one way and then later unlearned so that it may be relearned in a different way.

In addition to the materials presented in Chapters 26 and 27 which deal primarily with management's use of accounting data, the uses of accounting are pointed out and discussed at every opportunity from the first chapter to the last.

The latest of accepted terminology is employed throughout the text; however, older terms are introduced and discussed as a matter of historical interest and because a knowledge of the older terms is needed in the reading of accounting literature.

The number of completely different problems in this revised edition is more than twice that offered in the previous edition. All are closely co-ordinated with the text material, and as a rule are given in the order of the degree of their difficulty. The supplementary problems are separated from the regular problems because they are of a more thought-provoking nature. The problems listed as class exercises are short, require no special paper, and are usually ideal for either testing or drill.

In addition to the many users of the previous edition who offered valuable suggestions for its improvement, the authors owe a special debt of gratitude to Professor Robert B. Wetnight of Western Michigan University, Professor Clarence L. Dunn of Louisiana State University, Professor Raymond L. Mannix of Boston University, Professor L. H. Malchman of Northeastern University, Professor Richard M. Colwell of Pennsylvania State University, and Professor Willard J. Graham of the University of North Carolina for their critical reviews and helpful comments.

William W. Pyle
John Arch White

February, 1959

TABLE OF CONTENTS

Chapter 1

INTRODUCTION THROUGH ACCOUNTING EQUAT

ACCOUNTING is the art of recording and summarizing business tra
tions and of interpreting their effects on the affairs and activities
economic unit. A business transaction is an exchange of property or
ices; and the institution we call business is a never-ending cycle of
exchanges. The taxicab owner who exchanges money for a taxicab,
line, oil, and tires so that he may exchange transportation to the publ
money to meet his own personal needs and to buy more equipment and
plies is said to be in business. For the taxicab owner, and others, acc
ing is the art used to record the many transactions of a business, to
marize the recorded transactions, and to interpret their effects upo
affairs and activities of the business.

Accounting has received its greatest development in the field of
ness; however, accounting is not limited to business. Accounting is a
cable to every unit that makes up our economic society. These units in
not only business units, where this text will place its emphasis, but
political units, such as school districts, cities, states, and the federal
ernment; and social units, such as clubs, fraternities, and churche

Use of Accounting Data

When business transactions are recorded, accounting data are accu
lated. These data when summarized and interpreted answer for the o
or manager of a business such questions as: What property is ow
What debts are owed? Were there earnings? Are expenses too large in
tion to sales? Is too little or too much merchandise being kept?
amounts owed by customers being collected as rapidly as they bec
due? Will the business be able to meet its own debts when they mat
Should the plant be expanded? Should a new product be introdu
Should selling prices be increased?

Beyond the foregoing, grantors of credit such as banks, whole
houses, and manufacturers use accounting data in answering such a
tional questions as: Are the customer's earning prospects good? Wha
his debt-paying ability? Has he paid his debts promptly in the past?

Likewise, governmental units make use of accounting data in regu
ing businesses and in collecting taxes; labor organizations use accou
ing data in negotiating working conditions and wage agreements;
investors make wide use of accounting data in deciding where and in w
to invest.

Accounting and Bookkeeping

Many people confuse accounting and bookkeeping and look upon them as one and the same—in effect, they identify the whole with one of its parts. Actually bookkeeping is only one phase of accounting, the record-making phase. A comparison of the work of the bookkeeper with that of the accountant illustrates this. A bookkeeper records business transactions; he must know a system for recording transactions and be able to follow it. An accountant practices the art of accounting. An accountant must have a comprehensive knowledge of the systems for recording transactions; but his knowledge must go far beyond this. He must be able to survey a business as to the number and kinds of its transactions, the uses to be made of its accounting records, its outlook for growth, and so on. Then from his survey he must be able to design an accounting system to fit the needs of the business. After designing and installing the system, he must be able to supervise the bookkeepers of the business in their recording of the transactions of the business and in the preparation of summaries of the recorded transactions, called financial reports. After this, and most important, he must be able to interpret the financial reports and the information they give as to the financial progress and position of the business.

Accountancy as a Profession

Men devote their lives to accounting just as men devote their lives to law or medicine. Accountancy, like law or medicine, is a profession; one for which the training is as long and thorough as the training for other professions. Like all professions, accountancy tends toward specialization. Some of the specialized fields of accounting are:

Commercial Accounting. This is the accounting of a business enterprise that periodically seeks to show the gain or loss from operations. All economic units that exist for profit use this kind of accounting.

Cost Accounting. The objective of cost accounting is to find the unit cost of manufacturing a product, or the unit cost of selling a product, or the unit cost of providing a service.

Tax Accounting. Tax accounting has for its objective the preparation of the tax returns that are required by state and federal governments. In addition to the preparation of the returns, the tax accountant attempts to tell a businessman how to conduct his business in such a manner as to incur the smallest amount of tax. Tax accounting requires in addition to a knowledge of accounting a thorough understanding of the laws and regulations which underlie the assessment of taxes.

Auditing. Auditing stresses the verification of accounting records. It enables the accountant to render an opinion as to the probable accuracy of the reported gain or loss and the reported financial position of a business. The verification of the accounting records of a business by a *Certified Public Accountant* is often required by banks before loans are granted.

Verification of the accounting records is always required of companies whose stocks are sold on a stock exchange. A certified public accountant is one who has passed an examination of his knowledge of accounting and related subjects. In addition to passing the examination, he must also meet certain experience requirements. Only those who pass the examination and meet the experience requirements may use the title "Certified Public Accountant," or C.P.A. The certified public accountant examination is given by the various states.

Budgeting. Planning business transactions before they occur is budgeting. The objective of budgeting is to provide management with an intelligent plan of estimated future operations. Presumably, if the plan is achieved, maximum earnings will be made.

Governmental Accounting. The accounting of a governmental unit differs from the accounting of a commercial enterprise because the objectives of business and government differ. Business exists for earnings, while the objective of government is to provide services. Governmental accounting has as its main objective an accounting for the stewardship of public property.

Each of these fields offers many opportunities for employment with compensations that compare favorably with those of other professions.

Property and Property Rights

A business enterprise, to operate, must own and use property. A place of business in a building that is either owned or rented must be provided. Equipment suitable to the needs of the business is required. If merchandise is bought and sold, items of merchandise must be purchased and kept available until sold. All of this requires the use and exchange of property; and the use and exchange of property provides the raw material of accounting. Accounting is concerned with recording and reporting the changes that take place when property is used and exchanged by a business.

If a satisfactory record of the property owned, used, and exchanged by a business is to be kept, some common unit of measure for the property is required. The best possible unit of measure for property is the monetary unit. In the United States, this is the dollar. The value of any property may be measured in dollars. For example, a businessman owns a store building worth $20,000. The value of the building is measured in dollars. Suppose this man lists all of his property and its dollar values as follows:

Store building	$20,000
Store equipment	5,000
Merchandise for sale	15,000
Money in the cash register	200
Total Property	$40,200

By assigning a dollar value to each piece of property, all of the property is reduced to a common denominator. The dollar value of each kind of property is measured in the common denominator; and by addition it is possible to secure the total dollar value of all the property. By using the dollar as the unit of measure for all property, it is possible to secure statistical data and financial facts that would be otherwise unobtainable. In accounting, property is measured and accounted for by using its dollar value.

Property may be defined as something of value that is owned. All property has value, and all property is owned. It is the purpose of accounting to account not only for the changes that take place in the property of a business but also for the changes that take place in the ownership rights in that property.

The store building in the list of property previously given has a monetary value of $20,000. The building is assigned this value because its owner gave $20,000 in money for it. The owner was willing to give $20,000 for the building because owning the building gives him rights that he considers are worth $20,000. These rights include the rights of possession, of use, and of exchange. The owner may possess the building, he may use the building, and he may exchange the building for other property. These rights have value. The value of the rights is equal to the value of the building. This may be expressed in equation form as follows:

VALUE OF THE PROPERTY, $20,000   =   VALUE OF THE OWNERSHIP RIGHTS, $20,000

The building is the thing of value that is owned. The building is property. The value of the property is $20,000. The rights to possess, to use, and to exchange this building are the ownership rights in the building. These ownership rights are also valued at $20,000.

The Accounting Equation

In accounting, a unit of property is called an *asset*, and the ownership rights in property are known as *equities*. If the word "asset" is substituted for the word "property" and the word "equities" is substituted for "ownership rights," then the equation showing the relationship between property and the ownership rights in the property will read:

VALUE OF THE ASSET   =   VALUE OF THE EQUITIES
or
ASSET   =   EQUITIES

The owner of a business is known as the *proprietor.* The owner's equity in the business, the ownership rights of the owner in his assets, is known as *proprietorship.* If there are no rights in the assets of the business other than those of the owner, then

ASSETS   =   PROPRIETORSHIP

To illustrate, assume that Frank Jones buys a store building for which he pays $75,000 in cash. The store building is property; it is an asset. The value of the store building is $75,000. Frank Jones owns the store building. He has all the rights of ownership: he may possess the building; he may use the building; and he may exchange the building. The value of the ownership rights of Frank Jones is equal to the value of the building. This may be expressed in equation form as follows:

ASSETS	=	PROPRIETORSHIP
STORE BUILDING, $75,000	=	FRANK JONES, CAPITAL, $75,000

The ownership rights of the proprietor in the assets of his business are usually shown under the name of the proprietor followed by the word *capital*. This is illustrated in the equation just given.

Most businessmen find it to their advantage to use in their business more assets than they are able to provide with their own resources. They obtain these additional assets either (1) by borrowing money from others and using the money to buy additional assets, or (2) by buying the additional property *on account* or *on credit*. Buying on account or buying on credit means buying with a promise to pay at a later date. Those from whom businessmen borrow or from whom they buy on account are known as *creditors*. The creditors of a business have a claim against the assets or a right in the assets of the business. The right of the creditors of a business is the right to receive payment of their claims. Law recognizes the right of the creditor to receive payment from the assets of the *debtor*. Furthermore, if the debtor does not pay the claims of his creditors, law gives the creditors the right to force the sale of the assets of the debtor. Money from the sale of the assets is then used first to pay the creditor claims. By law the claims of the creditors come before the claim of the proprietor. In accounting, the rights of the creditors are known as *liabilities*.

It is evident then that the assets of a business are subject to two types of claims. They are the claims of the owner and the claims of the creditors. To show both types of claims the original equation must be expanded and expressed as follows:

$$ASSETS = LIABILITIES + PROPRIETORSHIP$$

Note that this equation still preserves the original hypothesis: *Value of the property equals the value of the rights in the property.*

To illustrate that the value of property is equal to the value of the rights in the property, assume that Paul Becker buys a store building priced at $45,000. He pays $30,000 of his own cash and borrows the balance from Coast Mortgage Company by placing a mortgage on the property in the amount of $15,000. A mortgage is a legal document that involves a promise to pay at a later date. The equation that illustrates this situation is:

ASSETS	=	LIABILITIES	+	PROPRIETORSHIP
STORE BUILDING, $45,000	=	COAST MORTGAGE CO., $15,000	+	PAUL BECKER, CAPITAL, $30,000

The dollar value of the store building, $45,000, is equal to the dollar value of the rights of both Coast Mortgage Company and Paul Becker. Paul

Becker has the right to possess and use the building. His equity in the building is measured at $30,000. This is $15,000 less than the full dollar value of the building because he must pay $15,000 to Coast Mortgage Company at a later date. Coast Mortgage Company has a claim against the building measured at $15,000. This claim is the right to receive money in the amount of $15,000. If Becker pays $15,000 to Coast Mortgage Company, the right of the company is ended. If Becker does not pay the amount when due, then Coast Mortgage Company has the additional right to force the sale of the building to secure its money.

The equation, *Assets = Liabilities + Proprietorship, is the fundamental equation upon which all double-entry accounting is based.* A thorough understanding of it is necessary.

Like any mathematical equation the elements may be transposed and the equation may be expressed:

$$\text{ASSETS} \quad - \quad \text{LIABILITIES} \quad = \quad \text{PROPRIETORSHIP}$$

The equation in this form illustrates that the equity of the proprietor is secondary to the claims of the creditors. While the owner or proprietor of assets has the right of possession and use, his right continues only if he pays the claims of his creditors. This has led to the expression of the fundamental accounting equation in the form of:

$$\text{ASSETS} \quad - \quad \text{LIABILITIES} \quad = \quad \text{NET WORTH}$$

"Net worth" is synonymous with "proprietorship." It is the net amount left after subtracting the claims of the creditors from the total of the assets.

Business Transactions and Accounting Values

When a business transaction is to be recorded, it is the transaction price that sets the accounting value for the asset or service purchased and sets the amount to be used in recording the asset or service. For example, when a building is purchased, the agreed price between the buyer and the seller measures the amount to be used in recording the transaction. If the building is purchased for $25,000, then the building is valued at $25,000 in the accounting records. The seller may have acquired the building for $18,000; it may have been assessed for tax purposes at $12,500; and it may have been appraised for sale as being worth $27,500. The buyer may have received an offer of $30,000 for the building on the same day that he purchased it. The offer of $30,000 strongly indicates that the building is worth more than $25,000. Nevertheless, the agreed exchange price of $25,000, the cost of the building, sets the amount to be used in recording the purchase.

In accounting, all assets and services acquired are accounted for at their cost. This is a fundamental principle of accounting and is known as the principle of cost. The need for such a principle is obvious. If amounts other than costs were used in recording transactions, for example, amounts established by estimates, judgments, and appraisals, then accounting records would lose much of their usefulness. When cost is used as the basis for recording a transaction, a buyer and a seller dealing at arms' length determine the amount to be used in recording the transaction. It is usually a fair measure of value.

Effect of Transactions on the Accounting Equation

Business transactions affect the elements of the accounting equation. For example, on the first day of July, Paul Allen invested $11,000 in a taxicab business. After the investment, the assets of the taxicab business and the equity of Allen in the assets of the business are shown by the following equation:

$$\text{ASSETS} = \text{PROPRIETORSHIP}$$
$$\text{CASH, \$11,000} = \text{PAUL ALLEN, CAPITAL, \$11,000}$$

Note carefully the foregoing equation. It shows the one asset of the Paul Allen Taxicab Company: cash, $11,000. There are no liabilities; therefore, the equity of Allen in the one asset of the company is $11,000. The $11,000 equity in the taxicab company may not be all of Allen's assets. In addition to his equity in the taxicab company, he may own a clothing store, a farm, a service station, and many personal assets. The foregoing equation does not show these; it shows only the one asset of a single business, the Paul Allen Taxicab Company; and it shows Allen's equity in the one asset of the business.

The discussion of the preceding paragraph seems elementary; yet it emphasizes a fundamental accounting concept, the business entity concept. Because of this concept, in accounting and for accounting purposes, every business is a separate entity, separate from all other businesses and separate from the person or persons that own it. This concept results for each business in a separate set of records in which the assets of the business are equal to the equities of its creditors and its owner or owners.

To continue the illustration of the effect of transactions on the equation, after investing the $11,000, Allen used $300 of his invested cash to pay the rent for three months in advance on a building to be used as an office and garage, and he used $10,000 to buy four taxicabs. These two transactions changed the nature of the assets of the business. The equation that shows the change in the assets is:

$$\text{ASSETS} = \text{PROPRIETORSHIP}$$

CASH, $700	+	PREPAID RENT, $300	+	TAXICABS, $10,000	=	ALLEN, CAPITAL, $11,000

The nature of the assets of the business was changed by the two transactions. Only $700 of the original $11,000 in cash remains; but the business has acquired four taxicabs valued at their cost, $10,000, and the right to occupy a building as an office and garage for the next three months. The transactions altered the nature of the assets; but they did not alter the total amount of the assets. Likewise, the equity of Allen in the assets remained unchanged at $11,000.

To conduct his business properly, assume that Allen found it necessary to have some equipment in the taxicab garage. He did not have sufficient cash with which to buy this equipment; consequently, he purchased $800 worth of equipment from West Supply Company on account or on credit. After this transaction was completed, the equation that shows the assets of the business and the equities in the assets is:

ASSETS				=	LIABILITIES	+	PROPRIETORSHIP
CASH,	PREPAID RENT,	EQUIPMENT,	TAXICABS,	=	WEST SUPPLY CO.,	+	ALLEN, CAPITAL,
$700	$300	$800	$10,000		$800		$11,000

or

ASSETS, $11,800 = LIABILITIES, $800 + PROPRIETORSHIP, $11,000

The assets were increased by the purchase of the equipment. However, even though the assets increased, the proprietorship remained unchanged because the West Supply Company acquired a claim against the assets equal to the increase in the assets.

Increasing the Proprietorship

The primary objective of a business is to increase the proprietorship by earning profits or a net income. Mr. Allen will accomplish this objective by exchanging transportation for money. Of course, he will earn a profit or a net income and increase his proprietorship only if the amount of money received for the transportation supplied is greater than all the expense of supplying the transportation. For example, by July 15, the cab drivers collected and turned in fares totaling $890. At that time, for their services Mr. Allen paid them $445 as commissions; and he also paid the cab despatcher a salary of $120 for the first two weeks of July. The effect of these three transactions on the accounting equation of the Allen Taxicab Company is:

ASSETS				=	LIABILITIES	+	PROPRIETORSHIP
CASH	PREPAID RENT	GARAGE EQUIPMENT	TAXICABS	=	WEST SUPPLY CO.	+	ALLEN, CAPITAL
$ 700	$300	$800	$10,000	=	$800	+	$11,000
+890							+890
−445							−445
−120							−120
$1,025	$300	$800	$10,000	=	$800	+	$11,325

The $890 of taxicab fares collected by Mr. Allen's cab drivers are an example of what is known in accounting as *revenue*. A revenue is an inflow of cash or other assets in exchange for goods or services. A revenue can also be in the form of rent or interest. Here the inflow is in exchange for services.

The handling of the $890 in taxicab fares in the equation of Allen demonstrates the effect of revenue on the assets and proprietorship. Revenue increases both assets and proprietorship. Likewise the handling of the drivers' commissions and the despatcher's salary illustrate the effect of expenses. Expenses always decrease proprietorship and either decrease assets or increase liabilities.

Whether or not Mr. Allen actually made a profit or a net income and increased his proprietorship during the first half of the month of July depends upon the amount of his expenses for this period in addition to the commissions paid the drivers and the salary of the despatcher. If the additional expenses, gas, oil, tires, insurances, taxes, etc., were less than $325 ($890 minus $445 and $120 equals $325), then there was a net income and an increase in proprietorship.

QUESTIONS FOR CLASS DISCUSSION

1. List several ways in which a businessman may use accounting data.
2. Differentiate between accounting and bookkeeping.
3. Many labor leaders are returning to school to take courses in accounting. Why?
4. Define the terms: (1) asset, (2) liability, (3) proprietorship, and (4) equity.
5. Give a synonym for "proprietorship."
6. Name ten assets owned by a business with which you are familiar. Name five liabilities that this business may owe.
7. Which of the assets named in Question 6 is money? May all of the assets and liabilities named be measured in money? Is there a unit of measure that will better measure all of these items than money?
8. What is the fundamental accounting equation? Why is an understanding of the fundamental accounting equation essential to the student of accounting?
9. Is it possible for a transaction to affect one asset item without affecting any other asset, liability, or proprietorship item? Is it possible for a transaction to increase or decrease a single liability without affecting any other asset, liability, or proprietorship item?
10. Fred Smith owns: cash in the bank, $650; a United States savings bond, $375; a house, $12,500; a car, $1,200; and household furniture, $3,000. He owes a savings and loan association $5,000, the balance due on the mortgage on his house. What are the values of Mr. Smith's (1) assets, (2) liabilities, and (3) proprietorship?
11. What is a business transaction? Name five transactions that you have completed.
12. Why are "costs" used in recording transactions?
13. Dennis Forbes owns and operates a grocery store; and in addition he owns a half interest in a drugstore. Should Forbes show one half the value of each asset of the drugstore in the accounting records of the grocery store? If Forbes made a list of his assets, what would be some of the assets listed?

14. Which of the following are business transactions and which are not?
   a) Gave $400 in payment of the October rent.
   b) Hired a salesclerk, agreeing to pay him $50 per week.
   c) Purchased merchandise for cash.
   d) Sold merchandise for cash.
   e) Sold merchandise on credit.
   f) Paid the clerk's salary.
   g) Asked the clerk to place an order for merchandise with a traveling salesman.
   h) Transferred cash from the cash register to the office safe.
15. Give a transaction that will—
   a) Increase an asset and decrease an asset.
   b) Increase an asset and increase a liability.
   c) Decrease an asset and decrease a liability.
   d) Increase an asset and increase proprietorship.
   e) Decrease an asset and decrease proprietorship.

PROBLEMS

Problem 1–1

Dean Beck has decided to enter the moving and storage business. He plans to call his firm Inter-City Moving and Storage Company. During a short period of time he completed the following transactions for the firm.
   a) Cashed eight mature $1,000 United States savings bonds and deposited the $8,000 in the First National Bank to the account of the Inter-City Moving and Storage Company.
   b) Paid the rent for three months in advance on a building to be used as an office and for storage, $450.
   c) Purchased a truck for cash, $3,600.
   d) Purchased $400 of office equipment from Town Equipment Company on credit.
   e) Purchased $50 of office supplies for cash.
   f) Collected $300 for moving the household furniture of customers.
   g) Paid the truck driver's wages, $60.
   h) Paid Town Equipment Company $200 on account.
   i) Purchased an additional truck for $4,200 by giving $1,200 in cash and a promissory note payable for $3,000. (See the first page of Chapter 11 for an illustration of a promissory note.)
   j) Paid for newspaper advertising that had appeared in the local paper, $25.

Required:

   1. Arrange the following asset, liability, and proprietorship titles in an expanded accounting equation such as that shown in Exercise 1–1 on page 12: Cash; Prepaid Rent; Office Supplies; Office Equipment; Trucks; Promissory Note Payable (a liability); Town Equipment Company; and Dean Beck, Capital.
   2. Show by additions and subtractions, as in Exercise 1–1, the effect of each transaction on the assets, liabilities, and proprietorship of Inter-City Moving and Storage Company. Show new totals for all items after each transaction.

Problem 1–2

John Reed opened a real estate office which he called the Cascade Realty Company. During a month he completed the following business for the firm:

a) Withdrew $10,000 from his personal savings account and deposited it in the bank to the account of the Cascade Realty Company.

b) Purchased for the business a small office building for $15,000 by paying $7,000 cash and signing a mortgage contract promising to pay the balance over the next ten years.

c) Purchased office supplies for cash, $100.

d) Purchased $500 of office equipment from the Ace Equipment Company on credit.

e) Paid for advertising that had appeared in the local paper, $25.

f) Collected a $750 commission for the sale of real estate.

g) Hired a stenographer, agreeing to pay her $50 per week.

h) Took his personal automobile, which had a fair market value of $2,000, for permanent and exclusive use in the business.

i) Paid the Ace Equipment Company $250 of the amount owed.

j) Paid the stenographer's salary, $50.

k) Withdrew $200 from the bank account of the business to be used for personal living expenses.

Required:

1. Arrange the following asset, liability, and proprietorship titles in an expanded accounting equation like that shown in Exercise 1-1 on page 12: Cash; Office Supplies; Office Equipment; Automobile; Building; Ace Equipment Company (a creditor); Mortgage Payable; and John Reed, Capital.

2. Show by additions and subtractions, as in Exercise 1-1, the effect of each transaction on the assets, liabilities, and proprietorship of the Cascade Realty Company. Show new totals for all items after each transaction.

Problem 1-3

James Baker is the owner and operator of the Quick Service Company, a package delivery firm. At the beginning of the current month the firm had the following assets: cash, $500; office supplies, $75; office equipment, $700; and delivery equipment, $5,500. The firm owed the Apex Garage $110. During the month the firm completed the following transactions:

a) Mr. Baker invested an additional $3,000 in the business.

b) Purchased $50 of office supplies for cash.

c) Gave $1,000 in cash and an old delivery truck, which was carried in the accounting records at $1,500, for a new $2,500 delivery truck.

d) Received $200 from customers (stores) for delivering packages.

e) Paid the truck driver's wages, $60.

f) Paid the Apex Garage $50 of the amount owed.

g) Sold for $40 some office equipment carried in the accounting records at $60.

h) Mr. Baker took from his home for permanent use in the office of the delivery firm a typewriter having a fair market value of $100.

i) Purchased at a price of $1,500 a motorcycle for delivering packages. Gave $500 in cash and a promissory note for $1,000. (See the first page of Chapter 11 for an illustration of a promissory note.)

j) Purchased $200 of office equipment on credit from the ABC Equipment Company.

k) Paid the Service Garage $75 for repairs to a delivery truck.

l) Received $375 from customers for delivering packages.

m) Mr. Baker withdrew $250 from the bank account of the firm to be used for his personal living expenses.

Required:

1. Arrange the following asset, liability, and proprietorship titles in an expanded accounting equation like that shown in Exercise 1–1 below: Cash; Office Supplies; Office Equipment; Delivery Equipment; Apex Garage (a creditor); ABC Equipment Company (a creditor); Promissory Note Payable; and James Baker, Capital.
2. Enter the assets and liabilities of the Quick Service Company under the titles of the equation. Determine the equity of James Baker in the company and enter under the title James Baker, Capital.
3. Show by additions and subtractions, as in Exercise 1–1, the effect of each of the transactions on the elements of the accounting equation. Show new totals for all items after each transaction.

CLASS EXERCISES

Exercise 1–1

The effects of five transactions on the assets and equities of Snappy Service Laundry are shown in the following equations with each transaction identified by a letter. Write a short sentence or phrase that tells the probable nature of each transaction.

	CASH	+	LAUNDRY SUPPLIES	+	LAUNDRY EQUIPMENT	+	DELIVERY EQUIPMENT	=	LAUNDRY SUPPLY Co.	+	SAM SMALL, CAPITAL
					ASSETS			=	LIABILITIES	+	PROPRIETORSHIP
	$ 500 +		$ 50	+	$5,500	+	$1,500	=	$100	+	$7,450
a)			+50						+50		
	$ 500 +		$100	+	$5,500	+	$1,500	=	$150	+	$7,450
b)	+200										+200
	$ 700 +		$100	+	$5,500	+	$1,500	=	$150	+	$7,650
c)	+350				−500						−150
	$1,050 +		$100	+	$5,000	+	$1,500	=	$150	+	$7,500
d)	−100								−100		
	$ 950 +		$100	+	$5,000	+	$1,500	=	$ 50	+	$7,500
e)	−500				+1,200				+700		
	$ 450 +		$100	+	$6,200	+	$1,500	=	$750	+	$7,500

Exercise 1–2

On October 1 of the current year Thomas Stark began a business known as the Fairview Garage. The following accounting equation of the garage was prepared after Mr. Stark completed the fourth transaction of the garage. Analyze the equation and list the four transactions with their amounts.

CASH,	+	REPAIR PARTS AND SUPPLIES,	+	OFFICE FURNITURE,	+	LAND AND BUILDING,	=	AUTOMOBILE SUPPLY Co.,	+	MORTGAGE PAYABLE,	+	THOMAS STARK, CAPITAL,
$3,400		$2,000		$600		$18,000		$2,000		$10,000		$12,000

SUPPLEMENTARY PROBLEMS

Problem 1–A

Craig C. Dent has owned and operated the Service Shoe Repair Shop for the past year without keeping separate business and personal records. The following information about Mr. Dent's business and personal affairs is available:

a) Mr. Dent has two checking accounts. In one, which has a balance of $480, the revenues of the shop are deposited. On this account checks upon which the shop name, Service Shoe Repair Shop, is printed are drawn to pay shop bills. The other checking account has a balance of $118. Ordinary checks supplied by the bank are drawn on this account to pay Mr. Dent's personal expenses. Mr. Dent signs his name, Craig C. Dent, on the checks written on both accounts.

b) There is $5,540 worth of shoe repair equipment in the shop, which is leased from the United Shoe Repair Equipment Company for an annual rental of $600. On the current date three month's rent is paid in advance.

c) Mr. Dent's residence has a fair market value of $12,500. Cascade Mortgage Company holds a mortgage on the residence upon which there is a balance payable of $7,500.

d) Shop supplies having a fair market value of $130 are on hand in the shop.

e) Of the $130 of shop supplies on hand, $50 worth was received from Shoe Repair Supply Company two days ago and has not been paid for as yet.

f) The shelves, chairs, and showcases in the shop have a fair market value of $450. Mr. Dent purchased and paid for these items of shop furniture and fixtures when he first opened his shop.

g) Mr. Dent has a personal automobile that has a value of $800.

h) On the current date Mr. Dent owes the Town and Travel Shop $45 for a dress purchased by his wife.

i) The furnishings in Mr. Dent's house have a fair market value of $3,200.

Required:

Construct two accounting equations. (*a*) In the first show the assets, liabilities, and the equity of Mr. Dent in the Service Shoe Repair Shop. (*b*) In the other list the personal assets, personal liabilities, and the personal net worth of Mr. Dent. (Be sure to list his equity in the shoe shop as one of his personal assets.)

Problem 1–B

David Burket is a practicing attorney, and in addition he owns the Rio Theatre. On October 1 of the current year he had the following assets, liabilities, and net worth: cash in personal checking account, $850; residence, $22,000; household effects, $7,000; automobile, $4,200; equity in Rio Theatre, $49,350; equity in the assets of his law firm, $13,410; stocks and bonds, $9,500; mortgage payable on residence, $9,000; and net worth, $97,310.

On October 1 the assets, liabilities, and proprietorship of the Rio Theatre were: cash in theatre bank account, $300; theatre supplies, $250; furniture and equipment, $7,700; land and building, $41,450; Lion Films (a liability), $350; and David Burke, capital, $49,350.

On October 1, the assets, liabilities, and proprietorship of the law firm were: cash, $4,500; prepaid rent, $300; office supplies, $150; law library, $5,000; office equipment, $3,600; Legal Publishing Company (a liability), $140; and David Burke, capital, $13,410.

During a short period of time Mr. Burke completed the following transactions:

a) Used $600 of his personal funds to buy a color television set for his home.

b) Transferred $1,000 of law firm cash to his personal bank account.

c) Transferred $2,500 of law firm cash from the law firm bank account to the bank account of the theatre.

d) Paid $800 of theatre cash for new theatre equipment.

e) Paid the Legal Publishing Company $140 from the cash of the law firm.

f) Purchased additional law books from the Legal Publishing Company on credit, $300.

g) Used theatre cash to pay Lion Films, $200.

h) Sold $4,000 of the personally owned bonds for $5,000.

i) Earned and collected legal fees totaling $1,500 and incurred and paid law office expenses amounting to $800.

j) The theatre collected $2,000 in admissions and incurred and paid $2,300 of expenses.

Required:

1. Prepare three expanded accounting equations. (*a*) In the first show the assets, liabilities, and proprietorship of the Rio Theatre after the foregoing transactions were recorded. (*b*) In the second show the assets, liabilities, and proprietorship of the law firm after the transactions were recorded. And (*c*) in the last show the personal assets (include the equities in the law firm and theatre), liabilities, and total net worth of David Burke.

2. Answer the following questions: (*d*) How many accounting entities are represented in this problem? (*e*) How many sets of accounting records in which assets equal liabilities plus proprietorship would you recommend that David Burke keep? (*f*) Why?

Chapter

2

ACCOUNTS AND THE TRIAL BALANCE

ACCOUNTING is the art of recording, summarizing, and interpreting the effects of business transactions. In the previous chapter, the effects of transactions on the elements of the accounting equation were shown by placing amounts in columns and adding or subtracting each amount. Such a system gave the detailed effects of each transaction; however, it required a great many additions and subtractions and would not be satisfactory for a business. A business requires a better system; and the first requirement of such a better system is that it make possible the recording of many transactions in such a way that they can be easily summarized and the total of their effects calculated.

The cash transactions of Paul Allen from the previous chapter may be used to illustrate what is meant by summarizing transactions and calculating the total of their effects. In the previous chapter, Paul Allen began his business by investing $11,000. He then rented a building, purchased four taxicabs, received the fares of his drivers, paid the drivers' commissions, and paid the despatcher two weeks' wages. Each of these transactions affected the cash of Allen. After their completion, to summarize them and learn their total effect on the cash, three calculations are necessary. The three calculations are:

1. Group together and add the items that increased cash.

Investment	$11,000
Receipt of fares	890
Sum of the Increases	$11,890

2. Group together and add the items that decreased cash.

Payment for rent	$ 300
Payment for cabs	10,000
Payment of the despatcher's wages	120
Payment of commissions	445
Sum of the Decreases	$10,865

3. And then subtract the sum of the decreases from the sum of the increases.

Sum of the increases	$11,890
Sum of the decreases	10,865
Balance of Cash Remaining	$ 1,025

The three calculations, when completed, indicate that the total effect of all of the cash transactions was a reduction in Allen's invested cash from $11,000 to $1,025.

The three calculations also demonstrate that if many transactions affecting an item are to be easily summarized so that the total of their effect may be seen, a device is needed that makes it possible to record together in one group the increases in the item and to record together in another group the decreases in the item. Such a grouping together of increases and grouping together of decreases makes it possible at any time to (1) quickly add the increases, and (2) quickly add the decreases, so that (3) the total of the decreases may be subtracted from the total of the increases and the summarized effect of all of the increases and decreases calculated. The *account* is such a device.

The Account

The account is a bookkeeping device that makes it possible to quickly summarize the effect of many transactions. In its most simple form an account looks like the letter "T" and is called a "T-account." Note in Illustration 1, which shows a "T-account," that the "T" gives the account a left side, a right side, and a place for the name of the item recorded therein.

Illustration 1

(Place for the Name of the Item Recorded)

(Left side)	(Right side)

When an account is used in recording the increases and decreases in an item, the increases are placed on one side and the decreases are placed on the other. For example, if the increases and decreases in the cash of Paul Allen are recorded in a"T-account,"the account appears as follows:

Cash

Investment	11,000	Payment for rent	300
Receipt of fares	890	Payment for cabs	10,000
		Despatcher's wages	120
		Drivers' commissions	445

After transactions are recorded in an account, they may be summarized at any time and the total of their effect calculated by adding (called "footing") the items on the increases' side, adding ("footing") the items on the decreases' side, and subtracting the sum of the decreases from the sum of the increases. This is called securing the *balance* of an account. The balance of an account is the difference between the sum of the increases and the sum of the decreases recorded in the account.

The Ledger

When transactions are recorded by a business, a separate account is required for each asset, each liability, and each proprietorship item for which an individual record is desired. Consequently, a large number of accounts, often several hundred, is required by even a small business in recording its transactions. Each account is on a separate page in a bound or a loose-leaf book, or is on a separate card in a tray of cards.

A group of accounts used by a business in recording its transactions is called a *ledger*. If the accounts are kept in a book, the book containing the accounts is also known as a ledger; and if the accounts are kept on cards in a file tray, the tray of cards is likewise known as a ledger.

Accounts Commonly Used

The particular accounts used by a business in recording its transactions vary from one business to another. In any business, the accounts used depend upon the kinds of assets owned, the kinds of debts owed, and the information to be secured from the accounting records. Nevertheless, although the particular accounts used vary, the following accounts are commonly used.

Asset Accounts.   If useful records of the assets of a business are to be kept, an individual account is needed for recording the increases and decreases in each kind of asset owned. Some of the more common kinds of assets for which accounts are maintained are:

Cash.   Increases and decreases in the cash of a business are recorded in an account called "Cash." The cash of a business consists of money or any media of exchange that a bank will accept at face value for deposit. Cash usually includes coins, currency, checks, postal and express money orders, and bank drafts. Increases and decreases in both the cash on hand in the store or office and the cash on deposit in the bank are recorded in a single Cash account.

Notes Receivable.   A formal written promise to pay a definite or determinable sum of money at a fixed future date is called a promissory note. (Promissory notes are illustrated and discussed in detail in Chapter 11.) When amounts due from others are evidenced by promissory notes, the notes are known as *notes receivable*. Since the amount due from each debtor on each note is evidenced by a written promise to pay, all increases and decreases in notes receivable are recorded in a single Notes Receivable account.

Accounts Receivable.   Goods and services are commonly sold to customers or clients upon the basis of oral or implied promises of future payment. Such sales are known as "sales on credit" or "sales on account" or "sales on open account"; and the oral or implied promises to pay are known as accounts receivable. Individual accounts receivable are increased by sales on credit and are decreased by the customer's payments. Since it is necessary to know the amount currently owed by each individual customer or client, a separate account must be kept for each. Each account carries the name of the customer or client whose purchases and payments are recorded therein.

Merchandise Inventory. The merchandise of a business consists of the products for sale by the business. Shoes offered for sale in a shoe store and clothing offered for sale in a clothing store are examples of merchandise. The amount of merchandise that is on hand at a given time is normally determined by a physical count or inventory and is recorded in an account called "Merchandise Inventory."

Prepaid Insurance. Fire, liability, workmen's compensation, and other types of insurance protection are normally paid for in advance. The amount paid for protection is called a "premium" and it may give protection from loss for from one to five years. As a result, a large portion of each premium paid is an asset for a considerable period of time after payment. When insurance premiums are paid, the asset "prepaid insurance" is increased by the amount of the premium paid. The increase is normally recorded in an account called "Prepaid Insurance." Day by day insurance premiums expire. Consequently, at intervals the insurance policies of a company are examined; the amount of insurance that has expired is calculated; and the balance of the Prepaid Insurance account is reduced by the amount of the expired insurance.

Office Supplies. Stamps, stationery, paper, pencils, adding machine tapes, and like items are known as office supplies. These items are assets at the time they are purchased, and they continue to be assets until they are consumed. As they are consumed, the amounts consumed become expenses. Increases and decreases in the asset "office supplies" are commonly recorded in an account called "Office Supplies."

Store Supplies. Wrapping paper, cartons, sacks, string, and similar items used by a store are known as store supplies. Increases and decreases in store supplies are usually accounted for in an account of that name.

Other Prepaid Expenses. Prepaid expenses are items that are assets at the time they are purchased but that become expenses as they are consumed or are used. Prepaid insurance, office supplies, and store supplies are examples of prepaid expenses that have already been discussed. Not all companies have the same kinds of prepaid expenses; but other examples of prepaid expenses are prepaid rent, prepaid taxes, prepaid wages, factory supplies, and laundry supplies. Each type of prepaid expense is normally accounted for in a separate account which carries the name of the item, the increases and decreases of which are recorded therein.

Equipment Accounts. Increases and decreases in such things as typewriters, desks, chairs, and other office machinery and equipment of a permanent nature are commonly recorded in an account called "Office Equipment." Likewise, changes in the amount of counters, showcases, shelves, cash registers, and like items used by a store are recorded in an account called "Store Equipment." And a company that owns and uses such things as lathes, drill presses, boring machines, and like equipment records the increases and decreases in these items in an account called "Machinery and Equipment."

Buildings. A building used by a business in carrying on its operations may be a store, garage, warehouse, or factory. Regardless of the use to which buildings are put, an account called "Buildings" is commonly used to record the increases and decreases in the buildings owned by a business and used in carrying on its operations.

Land. An account called "Land" is commonly used to record the increases and decreases in the land owned by a business. Although land and the buildings placed upon it are inseparable in physical fact, it is usually desirable to account for land and its buildings in separate accounts. This is because buildings depreciate or wear out, but land does not.

Liability Accounts. Most companies do not have as many liability accounts in their ledgers as asset accounts. However, the following liability accounts are common.

Notes Payable. Increases and decreases in amounts owed because of promissory notes given to creditors are accounted for in a single account called "Notes Payable." Normally, accepted time drafts and trade acceptances are treated as forms of promissory notes and are also recorded in the Notes Payable account.

Accounts Payable. An account payable is an amount owed to a creditor which resulted from either an oral or implied promise to pay. Most accounts payable grow out of the purchase on credit of merchandise, supplies, equipment, and services. Since it is necessary to know the amount owed each creditor, an account bearing the name of each creditor must be kept.

Other Short-Term Payables. Wages payable, taxes payable, and interest payable are additional short-term liabilities for which individual accounts must be kept.

Mortgage Payable. A mortgage payable is a long-term debt owed by a business for which the creditor has a secured prior claim against some one or more of the assets of the business. Ordinarily a mortgage payable is represented by two legal documents. These are a promissory note and a mortgage. To mortgage property, a business executes both the note and the mortgage. The note is a written promise to pay money at a future date. The mortgage is given to secure the note. It gives the holder of the mortgage note the right to force the sale of the mortgaged assets through a foreclosure, if the note is not paid when due. If the mortgage debt is not paid when due and the mortgage holder forecloses and forces the sale of the mortgaged property, the proceeds of the sale go first to pay the mortgage note. Any balance remaining after the payment of the mortgage note reverts to the original owner of the property.

An account called "Mortgage Payable" is commonly used in recording the increases and decreases in the amount owed on a mortgage.

Proprietorship Accounts. Many transactions affect the proprietorship of a business, either increasing it or decreasing it. These transactions include the investment of the proprietor, his withdrawals of cash and other assets for personal use, the earning of revenues, and the incurring of expenses. Of these transactions, the more numerous and, from a managerial viewpoint, the more important are the revenue and expense transactions.

In the previous chapter, where the effects of transactions on the elements of the accounting equation were shown, all increases and decreases in proprietorship, including revenues and expenses, were placed in a single column under the name of the proprietor. The single column helped to simplify the material of the chapter, but it did not readily provide information as to the total amount of each kind of proprietorship increase and decrease. A single proprietorship account would have the same disadvantage; it too would summarize transactions and would not readily supply information as to the total amount of each kind of increase and decrease recorded therein. Consequently, in order that information as to the amounts of the various kinds of increases and decreases in proprietorship can readily be secured, numerous proprietorship accounts are used, a different one for each kind of increase or decrease. Among the many proprietorship accounts used are the following:

Capital Account. When a person invests in a business of his own, his investment is recorded in an account carrying his name and the word "Capital." For example, an account called "Paul Allen, Capital" is used in recording the investment of Paul Allen in his taxicab business. In addition to providing a place for recording the original investment, the Capital account is also used in recording any permanent increases or decreases in proprietorship.

Withdrawals Account. Usually a man invests in a business in order to earn profits or a net income. Normally, he expects the net income to be large enough to pay his personal living expenses. Often, before a net income is earned or before it is known that a net income has been earned, a businessman finds it necessary to withdraw money or other assets from his business for his personal living expenses. These withdrawals reduce in like amounts both the assets and the proprietorship of the business. However, since, at the time of the withdrawals, it is expected that sufficient income will be earned to make good the withdrawals, such withdrawals are called "withdrawals in anticipation of income" and are commonly recorded in an account carrying the name of the proprietor and the word "Withdrawals." For example, an account called "Paul Allen, Withdrawals" is used to record Paul Allen's withdrawals in anticipation of income. The Withdrawals account is also known as the "Personal" account or the "Drawing" account, and it often appears in ledgers as "George Hayes, Personal" or "James Ford, Drawing."

Revenue and Expense Accounts. Revenues increase and expenses decrease proprietorship. Actually, over a period of time, proprietorship is increased or decreased by the difference between revenues earned and expenses incurred. Proprietorship is increased when revenues exceed expenses, and it is decreased when expenses exceed revenues. When revenues exceed expenses, a profit or a net income is said to be earned; and when expenses exceed revenues, a loss or a net loss is said to be incurred.

Earning a net income and avoiding a net loss is the primary objective of a business; and if a business is to earn a net income and avoid a loss, the owner or manager must normally have rather detailed information as to the amounts of each kind of revenue earned and each kind of expense incurred. This information is secured by providing in the ledger a separate account for each kind of revenue earned and each kind of expense incurred and then, as revenue and expense transactions are completed, by recording in the separate accounts the amounts of each kind of revenue received and the amounts of each kind of expense incurred.

Recording revenues and expenses in separate revenue and expense accounts requires numerous accounts in any business. In addition, all businesses do not have the same revenues and expenses. Consequently, it is impossible to list all the revenue and expense accounts found in business ledgers. However, Revenue from Repairs, Commissions Earned, Fees Earned, Rent Earned, and Interest Earned are common examples of revenue accounts; and Advertising Expense, Store Supplies Used, Depreciation of Store Equipment, Office Salaries, Office Supplies Used, Rent Expense, Heating and Lighting Expense, Utilities Expense, Insurance Expense, and Miscellaneous Expenses are common examples of expense accounts. It should be noted that in each case the kind of revenue or expense recorded in each of the above-mentioned accounts is evident from its title. This is generally true of all revenue and expense accounts.

Accounts as a Sorting Device

A group of accounts is a sorting device that may be expanded or contracted as the need for information expands or contracts. For example, in a department store all sales salaries can be recorded in a single Sales Salaries expense account, or the ledger can be expanded and a separate Sales Salaries expense account provided for each department. If the single account is used, its balance will reveal the sales salaries of the entire store; but if the several accounts are used, their individual balances will give the sales salaries of each of the departments.

Obviously, there is no limit as to how far the system of accounts of a business can be expanded in order to secure more detailed information. However, a practical limit is reached when the cost of the more detailed information exceeds its value.

Debit and Credit

In bookkeeping, the left side of any account is called the *debit* side, abbreviated "Dr."; and the right side is called the *credit* side, abbreviated "Cr." When amounts are recorded on the left side, they are called *debits*, and the account is said *to be debited*. When items are recorded on the right side of an account, they are called *credits*, and the account is said *to be credited.* The difference between the total debits and the total credits recorded in an account is called the *balance* of the account. The balance of an account may be a *debit balance* or it may be a *credit balance.* An account has a debit balance when the sum of the debits entered in the account exceeds the sum of the credits. Likewise, an account is said to have a credit balance when the sum of the credits exceeds the sum of the debits; and it is said to be *in balance* when the sums of its debits and credits are equal.

The terms "to debit" and "to credit" should not be confused with "to increase" and "to decrease." To debit means simply to enter an amount on the left-hand side of an account, to credit means to enter an amount on the right-hand side, and either may be an increase or a decrease. This may readily be seen by examining the way in which the $11,000 investment of Paul Allen is recorded in his Cash and Capital accounts which follow:

Cash	Paul Allen, Capital
Investment 11,000	Investment 11,000

When Paul Allen invested $11,000 in his taxicab business, both the cash of the business and Paul Allen's proprietorship were increased. Observe in the foregoing accounts that one increase, the increase in cash, is recorded on the left or debit side of the Cash account; while the other increase, the increase in proprietorship, is recorded on the right or credit side. This results from the mechanics of *double-entry bookkeeping.*

Mechanics of Double-Entry Bookkeeping

The mechanics of double-entry bookkeeping are such that every transaction affects and is recorded in two or more accounts with equal debits and credits.

Reason for Equal Debits and Credits. The reason for recording transactions with equal debits and credits in a double-entry system is that equal debits and credits offer a proof of the recording accuracy. The proof is, if all transactions are recorded with equal debits and credits, the sum of the debits in the ledger must equal the sum of the credits. At intervals, when a double-entry bookkeeping system is in use, a test of the equality of the debits and credits in the ledger is made by preparing a *trial balance.* If, when the trial balance is prepared, the debits equal the credits, it is assumed that errors have not been made. The trial balance and its preparation are discussed in more detail later in this chapter.

Reason Equal Debits and Credits Are Possible. Equal debits and credits in recording transactions are possible under a double-entry system of bookkeeping because the system is based on an algebraic equation $A = L + P$, and the rules of algebra apply. The person who first devised the system recognized this. In devising the system he assigned the recording of increases $(+)$ in assets to the debit side of asset accounts. He then applied the algebraic rule that signs must change when the equal (=) sign is crossed and got the following results:

ASSETS		=	LIABILITIES		+	PROPRIETORSHIP	
+	−		−	+		−	+

Observe in the foregoing T-accounts that the increases (+) side of an asset account is the left or debit side; consequently, because of the algebraic rule of changing signs when the equal sign is crossed, the right or credit side becomes the increases (+) side of liability and proprietorship accounts.

When the foregoing is applied in recording transactions, rules of debit and credit are possible. The rules are:

1. Increases in assets are debited to asset accounts; consequently, decreases in assets must be credited.
2. Increases in liabilities and proprietorship items are credited to liability and proprietorship accounts; consequently, decreases must be debited.

Transactions Illustrating the Application of the Rules of Debit and Credit

The following transactions of Paul Allen are used to illustrate the application of the rules of debit and credit and to show how transactions are recorded in the accounts. The number preceding each transaction is used throughout the illustration to identify the transaction as it appears in the accounts. Note that seven of the first eight transactions are the same transactions that were used in Chapter 1 to illustrate the effect of transactions on the elements of the accounting equation.

1. Paul Allen invested $11,000 in a taxicab business.
2. He paid three months' rent in advance on a garage and office, $300.
3. Paid $10,000 for four taxicabs.
4. Purchased on credit from West Supply Company a gasoline storage tank and other garage equipment priced at $800.
5. Purchased 500 gallons of gasoline from the Coast Oil Company on credit, $135.
6. Paid the cab despatcher's wages for the first two weeks of July, $120.
7. Received $890 in cab fares during the first half of July.
8. Paid the cab drivers $445 as commissions earned during the first half of July.
9. Paid West Supply Company $400 of the amount owed to them.
10. Paid the despatcher's wages for the third and fourth weeks of July, $120.
11. Received $1,260 in additional cab fares during the last half of July.
12. Paid the drivers $630 additional commissions.
13. Paid the telephone and other utilities for July, $40.
14. Paul Allen withdrew $200 for his personal living expenses.

Before a transaction can be recorded, it must be analyzed into its debit and credit elements. The process of analysis consists of: (1) determining what asset, liability, or proprietorship items are increased or decreased by the transaction; and then (2) applying the rules of debit and credit to determine the debit and credit effect of the increases or decreases. An analysis of each of the following transactions of Paul Allen is given in order to demonstrate the process.

1. On July 1 of the current year, Paul Allen invested $11,000 in a taxicab business.

Analysis of the transaction: The transaction increased the cash of the Paul Allen Taxicab Company, and at the same time, it increased the equity of Paul Allen in the assets of the company. Increases in assets are debited, and increases in proprietorship are credited. Consequently, Cash should be debited and Paul Allen, Capital should be credited for $11,000.

Cash		Paul Allen, Capital	
(1) 11,000			(1) 11,000

2. Paid the rent for three months in advance on the garage and office, $300.

Cash	
(1) 11,000	(2) 300

Prepaid Rent	
(2) 300	

Analysis of the transaction: The asset, prepaid rent, the right to occupy the building for three months, is increased, and cash is decreased. Increases in assets are debited, and decreases in assets are credited. Therefore, debit Prepaid Rent and credit Cash for $300.

3. Purchased four taxicabs for $10,000.

Cash	
(1) 11,000	(2) 300
	(3) 10,000

Taxicabs	
(3) 10,000	

Analysis of the transaction: The asset, taxicabs, is increased, and the asset, cash, is decreased. Debit Taxicabs and credit Cash for $10,000.

4. Purchased on credit from West Supply Company a gasoline storage tank and garage equipment priced at $800.

Analysis of the transaction: This transaction increased the asset, garage equipment; but it also increased the liabilities by granting West Supply Company a claim against the assets. Increases in assets are debited, and increases in liabilities are credited. Consequently, Garage Equipment is debited and an account carrying the name of West Supply Company is credited for $800.

Garage Equipment		West Supply Company	
(4)	800	(4)	800

5. Purchased 500 gallons of gasoline on credit from Coast Oil Company, $135.

Analysis of the transaction: This transaction, like the preceding one, increased both the assets and the liabilities. Therefore, the asset account, Gasoline, is debited to show the asset increased; and the liability account, Coast Oil Company, is credited to show the liability increased.

Gasoline		Coast Oil Company	
(5)	135	(5)	135

6. Paid the cab despatcher's wages for the first two weeks of July, $120.

Analysis of the transaction: Both the assets and the proprietorship were decreased in equal amounts. Decreases in proprietorship are debited, and decreases in assets are credited. Consequently, the proprietorship account, Despatcher's Wages (the name of the account shows the nature of the expense that decreased proprietorship), is debited and the Cash account is credited.

Cash				Despatcher's Wages	
(1)	11,000	(2)	300	(6)	120
		(3)	10,000		
		(6)	120		

7. Received $890 in cab fares during the first half of July.

Analysis of the transaction: The assets and the proprietorship were both increased. Increases in assets are debited, and increases in proprietorship are credited. Therefore, Cash is debited; and in order to show the nature of the increase in proprietorship, the proprietorship account, Taxicab Fares, is credited.

Cash				Taxicab Fares	
(1)	11,000	(2)	300	(7)	890
(7)	890	(3)	10,000		
		(6)	120		

8. Paid the cab drivers $445 as commissions earned during the first half of July.

Analysis of the transaction: This transaction decreased in equal amounts both the assets and the proprietorship. Debit the account, Drivers' Commission, to show the decrease and the nature of the decrease in proprietorship; and credit the Cash account to show the decrease in the asset.

Cash				Drivers' Commissions	
(1)	11,000	(2)	300	(8)	445
(7)	890	(3)	10,000		
		(6)	120		
		(8)	445		

9. Paid West Supply Company $400 of the amount owed.

Analysis of the transaction: Payments to creditors decrease in like amounts both the assets and the liabilities. Decreases in liabilities are debited, and decreases in assets are credited. Debit West Supply Company and credit Cash.

Cash				West Supply Company			
(1)	11,000	(2)	300	(9)	400	(4)	800
(7)	890	(3)	10,000				
		(6)	120				
		(8)	445				
		(9)	400				

10. Paid the despatcher's wages for the third and fourth weeks of July, $120.

Analysis of the transaction: This expense decreased both the assets and the proprietorship. Debit Despatcher's Wages to show the decrease in proprietorship and credit Cash to show the decrease in assets.

Cash				Despatcher's Wages	
(1)	11,000	(2)	300	(6)	120
(7)	890	(3)	10,000	(10)	120
		(6)	120		
		(8)	445		
		(9)	400		
		(10)	120		

11. Received $1,260 in additional cab fares during the last half of July.

Analysis of the transaction: This revenue increased both the assets and the proprietorship. Debit Cash to show the increase in the assets and credit Taxicab Fares to show the increase in proprietorship.

Cash				Taxicab Fares	
(1)	11,000	(2)	300	(7)	890
(7)	890	(3)	10,000	(11)	1,260
(11)	1,260	(6)	120		
		(8)	445		
		(9)	400		
		(10)	120		

12. Paid the drivers $630 of additional commissions.

Analysis of the transaction: This expense decreased the assets and proprietorship in like amounts. Debit Drivers' Commissions and credit Cash.

Cash				Drivers' Commissions		
(1)	11,000	(2)	300	(8)	445	
(7)	890	(3)	10,000	(12)	630	
(11)	1,260	(6)	120			
		(8)	445			
		(9)	400			
		(10)	120			
		(12)	630			

13. Paid the telephone and other utilities expenses for July, $40.

Analysis of the transaction: Debit the expense account, Telephone and Utilities, to show the nature and amount of the expense that decreased proprietorship; credit Cash to show the decrease in assets.

Cash				Telephone and Utilities	
(1)	11,000	(2)	300	(13)	40
(7)	890	(3)	10,000		
(11)	1,260	(6)	120		
		(8)	445		
		(9)	400		
		(10)	120		
		(12)	630		
		(13)	40		

14. Paul Allen withdrew $200 for his personal living expenses.

Analysis of the transaction: This transaction reduced in equal amounts both the assets and the proprietorship. However, since the withdrawal is a withdrawal in anticipation of income, a withdrawal of a temporary nature, it is debited to the Withdrawals account rather than the Capital account. Consequently, debit Paul Allen, Withdrawals and credit Cash.

Cash				Paul Allen, Withdrawals	
(1)	11,000	(2)	300	(14)	200
(7)	890	(3)	10,000		
(11)	1,260	(6)	120		
		(8)	445		
		(9)	400		
		(10)	120		
		(12)	630		
		(13)	40		
		(14)	200		

The Relationship of the Accounts and the Equation Illustrated

In Illustration 2 on the following page the transactions of Paul Allen are shown in the accounts, with the accounts brought together and clas-

Illustration 2

ASSETS = LIABILITIES + PROPRIETORSHIP

ASSETS

Cash

(1)	11,000	(2)	300
(7)	890	(3)	10,000
(11)	1,260	(6)	120
		(8)	445
		(9)	400
		(10)	120
		(12)	630
		(13)	40
		(14)	200

Prepaid Rent

| (2) | 300 | | |

Gasoline

| (5) | 135 | | |

Taxicabs

| (3) | 10,000 | | |

Garage Equipment

| (4) | 800 | | |

LIABILITIES

West Supply Company

| (9) | 400 | (4) | 800 |

Coast Oil Company

| | | (5) | 135 |

PROPRIETORSHIP

Paul Allen, Capital

| | | (1) | 11,000 |

Paul Allen, Withdrawals

| (14) | 200 | | |

Taxicab Fares

| | | (7) | 890 |
| | | (11) | 1,260 |

Despatcher's Wages

| (6) | 120 | | |
| (10) | 120 | | |

Drivers' Commissions

| (8) | 445 | | |
| (12) | 630 | | |

Telephone and Utilities

| (13) | 40 | | |

sified under the elements of the accounting equation. The illustration shows the relationship of the accounts and the equation.

Preparing a Trial Balance

As previously stated, when a double-entry bookkeeping system is in use, every transaction is recorded with equal debits and credits so that the equality of the debits and credits may be tested as a proof of the recording accuracy. In a double-entry system the equality of the debits and credits is tested at intervals by preparing a trial balance.

A trial balance is prepared by (1) securing the balance of each account in the ledger, (2) listing the accounts in their ledger order with the debit balances in one column and the credit balances in another (as in Illustration 3), (3) adding the debit balances, (4) adding the credit balances, and then (5) comparing the sum of the debit balances with the sum of the credit balances.

Illustration 3

PAUL ALLEN TAXICAB COMPANY
Trial Balance, July 31, 1959

Cash	$ 895	
Prepaid rent	300	
Gasoline	135	
Taxicabs	10,000	
Garage equipment	800	
West Supply Company.		$ 400
Coast Oil Company.		135
Paul Allen, capital.		11,000
Paul Allen, withdrawals.	200	
Taxicab fares.		2,150
Despatcher's wages	240	
Drivers' commissions	1,075	
Telephone and utilities.	40	
	$13,685	$13,685

In Illustration 3, the two columns of the trial balance of Paul Allen are equal. When the columns of a trial balance are equal, as in this illustration, the trial balance is said to be "in balance."

The Proof Offered by a Trial Balance

If when a trial balance is prepared the trial balance does not balance—the two columns are not equal—errors have been made either in recording transactions, in securing the balances of the accounts, in copying the balances on the trial balance, or in adding the trial balance columns. On the other hand, if a trial balance balances, it is assumed that no errors have been made. However, a trial balance that balances is not absolute proof of accuracy. Errors may have been made that did not affect the balance of the trial balance. For example, an error in which a correct debit amount is debited to the wrong account or a correct credit amount is credited to the wrong account will not show up on a trial balance. Likewise, an error in which a wrong amount is both debited and credited to the right accounts will not cause a trial balance to be out of balance. Consequently, a trial balance in balance is considered only presumptive proof of recording accuracy.

QUESTIONS FOR CLASS DISCUSSION

1. What is an account?
2. How do a firm's accounts act as a sorting device?
3. What is a ledger? Is a ledger always a book?
4. Explain the meanings of the words and terms: (1) debit, (2) to debit, (3) credit, and (4) to credit.
5. If increases in assets were recorded as credits rather than as debits, how would increases in liabilities and proprietorship be recorded? Why?
6. Does debit always mean increase and credit always mean decrease?
7. A transaction is to be entered in the accounts. How do you determine the accounts in which amounts are to be entered? How do you determine whether a particular account is to be debited or credited?
8. Most business firms use a double-entry system of bookkeeping. Why is it called a double-entry system?
9. An accounting student in his first lessons confused the words "debit" and "credit." He consistently recorded debits on the right side of accounts and credits on the left side. What difficulty, if any, did he experience in recording transactions and making a trial balance? Would you recommend that he change his procedure? Why?
10. Give the rules of debit and credit for (1) asset accounts, and (2) liability and proprietorship accounts.
11. Why is the rule of debit and credit the same for both liability and proprietorship accounts?
12. If in a single transaction only two accounts are involved, would it be possible to have:
    a) An increase in an asset and an increase in a liability?
    b) An increase in an asset and an increase in an expense?
    c) An increase in an asset and a decrease in an expense?
    d) An increase in an asset and a decrease in a liability?
    e) A decrease in an asset and an increase in an expense?
    f) A decrease in an asset and an increase in a liability?
13. List the steps in the preparation of a trial balance.
14. What is the reason for preparing a trial balance?
15. Why is the trial balance considered to be only presumptive proof of recording accuracy? What types of errors are not revealed by a trial balance?
16. Give a transaction that will result in—
    a) A debit to an asset and a credit to a liability.
    b) A debit to an asset and a credit to proprietorship.
    c) A debit to an asset and a credit to an asset.
    d) A debit to a liability and a credit to an asset.
17. Joe Smallhead records increases in all accounts on the debit side and decreases in all accounts on the credit side. Will the debits equal the credits in Joe's ledger? Suggest a better method.

18. For the following transactions tell whether the account named in the paren-
thesis is debited or credited and why it is debited or credited:
   a) Purchased equipment for cash (Cash).
   b) Sold un-needed equipment on credit (Equipment).
   c) Purchased supplies from the Ajax Supply Company on credit (Ajax
   Supply Company).
   d) Paid the Ajax Supply Company the amount owed (Ajax Supply Company).
   e) Paid the clerk's salary (Cash).
   f) Sold merchandise for cash (Cash).

19. Which of the following accounts normally have debit balances and which
normally have credit balances?
   a) Cash.
   b) Ajax Supply Company (a creditor).
   c) Store Equipment.
   d) Frank Smith, Capital.
   e) Joe Small (a customer).
   f) Store Supplies.
   g) Revenue from Fees.
   h) Salaries Expense.

20. Suppose that you are given the name of an account with which you are not
familiar and are asked whether it normally has a debit balance or a credit
balance. What one fact about the account would you wish to know in order to
tell whether the balance of the account is normally a debit balance or a credit
balance?

PROBLEMS

Problem 2–1
1. Open the following T-accounts: Cash; Prepaid Rent; Office Supplies; Office Equipment; Trucks; Notes Payable; Town Equipment Company;
Dean Beck, Capital; Moving and Trucking Revenue; Wages Expense;
and Advertising Expense.
2. Record in the accounts the transactions of Problem 1–1 which you will
find at the end of Chapter 1. Use the letters before each transaction to
identify the transaction amounts in the accounts.
3. Prepare a trial balance. Use the current date.

Problem 2–2
Bruce Hankins opened a plumbing shop and began business by (*a*) investing
cash in the amount of $500, a truck having a fair market value of $300, land
valued at $800, a building at $4,500, and tools worth $250. He called his business
the BH Plumbing Shop. During a short period of time he completed the following transactions:
   b) Bought additional tools from Bix Wholesale Company on credit, $125.
   c) Completed work for William Peek and received $150 cash in full pay-
   ment.
   d) Traded the truck for additional tools.
   e) Purchased a secondhand truck for cash, $500.
   f) Completed repair work and billed Roy K. Rice for $235. (Debit the ac-
   count receivable, Roy K. Rice, and credit Revenue from Repairs.)
   g) Paid the Evening Sentinel for newspaper advertising that had appeared,
   $10.

h) Completed repair work and billed Richard Tuttle for $175.
i) Received a check from Roy K. Rice in full payment of his account.
j) Paid the telephone bill and other utilities, $15.
k) Paid George Holmes, a plumber's helper who had worked from time to time during the previous two weeks, $80.
l) Mr. Hankins withdrew $100 from the business to be used in paying his personal living expenses.
m) Paid Bix Wholesale Company $75 of the amount owed.

Required:

1. Set up the following T-accounts: Cash; Roy K. Rice; Richard Tuttle; Tools; Truck; Land; Building; Bix Wholesale Company; Bruce Hankins, Capital; Bruce Hankins, Withdrawals; Revenue from Repairs; Advertising Expense; Wages Expense; Utilities Expense.
2. Record the transactions in the accounts. Identify the amounts in the accounts with the letters preceding the transactions.
3. Prepare a trial balance. Use the current date.

Problem 2–3

Craig Duncan began a real estate agency which he called Northwest Realty Company. During a short period of time he completed the following transactions:

a) Invested $15,000 in the firm.
b) Purchased the small office building and the office equipment of the Pacific Company which included: land, $5,000; building, $20,000; and office equipment, $2,000. Gave $9,000 in cash and signed a mortgage promising to pay the balance over a period of five years.
c) Took his personal automobile, which had a fair market value of $2,500, for permanent and exclusive use in the business.
d) Purchased additional office equipment on credit from the West Equipment Company, $500.
e) Purchased office supplies for cash, $55.
f) Collected a commission from the sale of property, $600.
g) Paid the office clerk's salary, $65.
h) Billed George Stanley for property management services, $50. (Debit the account receivable, George Stanley, and credit Property Management Fees.)
i) Purchased additional office supplies on credit from Royal Supply Company, $40.
j) Paid for advertising that had appeared in the local paper, $25.
k) Collected a commission from the sale of property, $750.
l) Paid Royal Supply Company in full.
m) Billed Dean Fuller for property management services, $50.
n) Received a $50 check from George Stanley in payment of the amount owed.
o) Paid the salary of the office clerk, $65.
p) Paid the telephone and other utilities, $20.
q) Paid for advertising that had appeared in the local paper, $35.
r) Withdrew $400 to be used for personal living expenses.

Required:

1. Open the following T-accounts: Cash; George Stanley; Dean Fuller; Office Supplies; Office Equipment; Automobile; Land; Building; Royal Supply Company; West Equipment Company; Mortgage Payable; Craig Duncan, Capital; Craig Duncan, Withdrawals; Commissions Earned;

Property Management Fees; Advertising Expense; Salaries Expense; and Telephone and Utilities Expense.

2. Record the transactions in the accounts. Use the letters preceding the transactions to identify the amounts placed in the accounts.

3. Prepare a trial balance. Use the current date.

CLASS EXERCISES

Exercise 2–1

The following accounts contain seven transactions keyed together with numbers.

ASSETS			LIABILITIES			PROPRIETORSHIP		
Cash			**City Furniture Company**			**Rapp, Capital**		
(1)	500	(3)	100	(7)	200	(4)	600	
(2)	300	(6)	120					(1) 500
(5)	200	(7)	200					

Furniture		**Bank Loan**		**Rapp, Withdrawals**	
(4)	600		(5) 200	(6) 120	

Revenue	
	(2) 300

Expenses	
(3) 100	

Required:

Write a short explanation of each transaction.

Exercise 2–2

List the account or accounts to be debited and the account or accounts to be credited, together with the amount of each debit and credit, required in recording each of the following transactions:

a) John R. Smith invested $10,000 cash in a radio repair business called High Fidelity Radio Shop.

b) Purchased a small building for $5,000, paying $3,000 in cash and giving two notes in equal amounts to the seller, Frank Owen, for the balance.

c) Bought two display cases for electrical equipment for $600 cash.

d) Bought radio repair equipment from the Austin Supply House on open account, payment to be made in thirty days. Cost of equipment, $700.

e) Mr. Smith had a small truck which he had purchased for $800. He transferred this truck to the High Fidelity Radio Shop for use in the business.

f) Purchased radio tube testing equipment from the Austin Supply House for $1,500, on open account, payment due in thirty days.
g) Paid one of the notes given to Frank Owen in transaction (*b*).
h) Mr. Smith withdrew $500 cash from the business for his personal use.
i) Paid the Austin Supply House for the equipment bought on open account in transaction (*d*).
j) Sold the old delivery truck for $800 cash.

SUPPLEMENTARY PROBLEMS

Problem 2–A

New Service Cleaners cleans garments at wholesale for retail cleaning firms. On October 1, 19—, the firm's trial balance appeared as follows:

NEW SERVICE CLEANERS
Trial Balance, October 1, 19—

Cash	$ 850	
Eastside Cleaners	90	
Prepaid insurance	150	
Cleaning supplies	410	
Office supplies	85	
Office equipment	1,200	
Cleaning equipment	8,500	
Delivery truck	2,400	
Land	4,000	
Building and improvements	22,000	
Mortgage payable		$10,000
Gary Sturgis, capital		29,685
	$39,685	$39,685

During a period of time the firm completed the following transactions:
a) Purchased cleaning supplies for cash, $50.
b) Paid the premium on a public liability insurance policy, $110.
c) Bought office equipment from Garrett Equipment Company on credit, $230.
d) Delivered cleaning to customers and collected cash, $650.
e) Billed Rose Cleaners for cleaning delivered, $140.
f) Collected $90 from Eastside Cleaners.
g) Purchased cleaning equipment on credit from Apex Equipment Company, $800.
h) Paid employees' wages, $300.
i) Mr. Sturgis gave his personal automobile to a paving contractor in exchange for the paving of a parking lot at the rear of the cleaning plant. The automobile had a fair market value of $2,800.
j) Billed Eastside Cleaners $60 for cleaning delivered.
k) Paid the Apex Equipment Company $300 on account.
l) Paid Garrett Equipment Company in full.
m) Paid the electricity and water bill, $45.
n) Received and recorded a bill from United Motors for repairs to the delivery truck, $65.
o) Paid the employees' wages, $290.
p) Delivered cleaning to customers and collected cash, $680.
q) Mr. Sturgis withdrew $300 to be used for his personal living expenses.

Required:

1. Open T-accounts as required. Enter the October 1, 19—, trial balance amounts in the T-accounts. Identify each trial balance amount by writing the abbreviation "Bal." before each trial balance amount.
2. Enter the transactions in the accounts. Use the transaction letters to identify the transaction amounts in the accounts.
3. Prepare a trial balance. Use October 31 and the current year as the date.

Problem 2–B

The following alphabetically arranged accounts and their balances were taken from the ledger of the Corner Grocery on December 31 of the current year. Without changing the alphabetical arrangement of the accounts, prepare a trial balance for the Corner Grocery.

Accounts payable (total)	$ 4,000	Office equipment	$ 600
Accounts receivable (total)	3,500	Office supplies	35
Building	27,000	Prepaid insurance	60
Cash	2,500	Prepaid interest	15
Delivery equipment	1,500	Rent expense	1,200
Interest payable	50	Revenue from sales	30,240
James Tucker, capital	19,700	Store equipment	5,400
James Tucker, withdrawals	4,200	Store supplies	80
Land	3,000	Taxes payable	210
Merchandise inventory	8,500	Telephone expense	120
Mortgage payable	5,000	Truck repairs	140
Notes payable	1,500	Wages expense	2,400
Notes receivable	500	Wages payable	50

Problem 2–C

Roy Mills has completed six transactions since beginning business as a real estate agent. The six transactions are reflected in the trial balance that follows. Analyze the trial balance and prepare a list of the six transactions.

MILLS AGENCY
Trial Balance, October 15, 19—

Cash	$2,195	
Office supplies	55	
Office equipment	1,200	
Fox Equipment Company		$1,200
Roy Mills, capital		2,000
Roy Mills, withdrawals	300	
Commissions earned		650
Rent expense	100	
	$3,850	$3,850

Chapter 3

THE GENERAL JOURNAL AND POSTING

IN THE preceding chapter, transactions were recorded by making debits and credits directly in the accounts. Transactions could be recorded in this manner. However, in actual practice, they seldom are because recording transactions directly in the ledger accounts has three obvious objections. They are:

1. *The information that can be recorded in an account is not great.* The primary purpose of an account is to classify and summarize information. If the account is expanded to show details, it does not serve as well as a classifying and summarizing device.
2. A ledger may have hundreds of accounts, with each account located on a different page. At least two accounts, located on different pages, are required to record each transaction. Consequently, *entries in the accounts fail to provide in one place a complete record of each transaction, and the transactions of any one day are scattered over many pages of the ledger.*
3. If transactions are recorded directly in the accounts, *errors are easily made and are difficult to locate.* For example, any interruption may cause the bookkeeper to record the debit of a transaction and to forget to record the credit.

The General Journal

In order to overcome these objections, it is the universal practice to record chronologically all transactions first in a record called a *journal.* After being recorded in a journal, the information of the transactions is copied from the journal to the ledger accounts. Because transactions are recorded first in a journal, the journal is often called a *book of original entry.* Likewise, since transaction information is copied from the journal to the ledger, the ledger is often called a *book of final entry.*

Various kinds of journal records are kept. In every business, size and needs normally determine the kind or kinds of journals used. However, the simplest and most flexible type of journal record is a single book called a *General Journal.* The General Journal provides for each transaction places for recording: (1) the date of the transaction; (2) the names of the accounts involved; (3) an explanation of the transaction; (4) the page numbers of the ledger pages to which the debit and the credit of the transaction are copied; and (5) the debit and credit effect of the transaction on the accounts named. A standard form of the ruling of a General Journal page is shown in Illustration 4.

Illustration 4

GENERAL JOURNAL   PAGE /

DATE	ACCOUNT TITLES AND EXPLANATION	FO-LIO	DEBIT	CREDIT
1959 July 3	Cash		120000	
	Automobile		270000	
	Frank Wilson, Capital			390000
	Began a real estate agency by			
	investing cash and an auto-			
	mobile.			
3	Rent Expense		12500	
	Cash			12500
	Paid one month's rent.			

Recording Transactions in a General Journal

To record transactions in the General Journal:

1. The year is written in small figures at the top of the first column.
2. The month of the first transaction is written on the first line in the first column. The year and the month are not repeated except at the top of a new page or at the beginning of a new month or year.
3. The day of each transaction is written in the second column on the first line of the transaction. When several transactions occur on the same day, many bookkeepers repeat the date for each. Other bookkeepers leave the date blank with the implication that the date is the same as the date of the transaction above. Regardless of whether the date is repeated or left blank, a single line is skipped between each transaction to set the transactions apart.
4. The names of the accounts to be debited and credited and an explanation of the transaction are written in the Account Titles and Explanation column. The name of the account debited is written first, beginning at the left margin of the column. The name of the account credited is written on the following line, indented about one inch. The explanation is placed on the next line. It is commonly indented about one-half inch from the left margin of the column. The explanation should be short but sufficient to explain the transaction and set it apart from every other transaction.
5. The amount debited is written in the debit column opposite the name of the account to be debited. The amount credited is written in the credit column opposite the account to be credited.

At the time transactions are recorded in the General Journal, nothing is entered in the Folio column. However, when the debits and credits of the transactions are copied from the journal to the ledger, the page numbers of the ledger accounts in which the debits and credits are copied are entered in the Folio column. The use of the Folio column is discussed in more detail later in this chapter.

Compound Journal Entries

The first of the two entries in Illustration 4 records the investment of Frank Wilson. Mr. Wilson invested both cash and an automobile in his real estate agency. The investment could have been recorded with two separate entries, each having a debit to an asset account and a credit to Frank Wilson, Capital. However, since both entries would have had credits to the same account, Frank Wilson, Capital, time and effort in journalizing and posting were saved by combining the two entries and recording the investment as in Illustration 4 with a *compound entry.* A compound entry is an entry involving three or more accounts.

Standard Form of the Account

"T-accounts" like the ones used in Chapter 2 are commonly used in teaching accounting, and they are also commonly used by accountants in solving problems. In either case they are used because they eliminate details and enable the student or the accountant to concentrate on ideas. Nevertheless, although "T-accounts" are extensively used in teaching and in solving problems, it should be understood that they are not used in business for recording transactions. In business, one of the standard rulings of the account, such as that shown in Illustration 5, is normally used when transactions are to be recorded.

Illustration 5

Cash | PAGE 1

DATE	EXPLANATION	FO-LIO	DEBIT	DATE	EXPLANATION	FO-LIO	CREDIT
1959 July 1		1	11000 00	1959 July 1		1	300 00
				3		1	1000 00
				13		2	120 00

The standard form of the account as shown in Illustration 5 is like a "T-account" in that it has two sides and a place for the name of the item recorded therein. It is also like a "T-account" in that increases are placed on one side and decreases on the other. However, it differs from a "T-account" in that each side of the account is divided into columns for the recording of specific information. With the exception of the Folio columns, the information that is placed in each of the columns is more or less evident.

Copying Transaction Information from the Journal to the Ledger

Transactions are recorded first in a journal as journal entries. After being recorded, the information of the journal entries is copied in a ledger. The process of copying journal entry information and transferring it from the journal to the ledger is called *posting.* Normally, at the end of each day, all of the transactions that were recorded in the journal that day are posted to the ledger. In the posting procedure, journal debits are copied and recorded as ledger account debits and journal credits are copied and recorded as ledger account credits. To minimize errors, most bookkeepers follow a set posting procedure. The four most common types of posting errors are: (1) posting a debit as a credit or posting a credit as a debit; (2) posting the wrong amount; (3) omitting a posting; and (4) posting to the wrong account.

The first type of error, posting to the wrong side of an account, is minimized if all the debit items of all the transactions to be posted are posted first, followed by the posting of all the credit items.

To reduce the second type of error, posting the wrong amount, the posting procedure for each debit and each credit is:

1. Find in the ledger the account named in the journal entry.
2. Write into the spaces provided:
   a) *First,* the amount of the debit or credit. Entering the amount first reduces the chances of entering the wrong amount.
   b) *Second,* the date of the entry.
   c) *Third,* a word of explanation if needed. With most transactions, no explanation is needed because it is easy to refer back to the journal explanation.
   d) *Last,* in the Folio column, the journal page from which the debit or credit of the entry was posted.
3. Then, when the individual posting of an item is completed in the ledger, insert in the Folio column of the journal the page number of the account to which the debit or the credit was posted. The insertion of the ledger page number in the journal Folio column serves two purposes: (1) The ledger page number in the journal and the journal page number in the ledger act as a cross reference when it is desired to trace an amount from one record to the other. (2) Writing the ledger page number in the journal as the last step in posting indicates that posting is completed. When posting is interrupted, the bookkeeper, by examining the Folio column of the journal, can easily see where the posting stopped. Also, by scanning the Folio column of the journal, the bookkeeper can see any items omitted in the posting. This last step, scanning the Folio, minimizes the third type of error, omission of postings.

Journalizing and Posting Illustrated

Illustration 6, which follows on the next four pages, shows the transactions of Paul Allen, the illustrative transactions of Chapter 2, recorded in Allen's General Journal and posted to his ledger accounts. In this illustration, in order to conserve space, the ledger accounts are reproduced several to a page. The student should realize that in actual practice each account would be placed on a separate page or, if the ledger were a tray of ledger cards, on a separate ledger card.

Note the folio numbers, or as they are often called, *posting reference numbers,* as they appear in the Folio columns of Allen's journal and ledger.

Observe also that in posting to the account of the Coast Oil Company, the credit was transposed and written as $153 rather than the correct amount of $135. This error was discovered and corrected by drawing a single line through the incorrect amount and writing in the correct amount above. A bookkeeper never erases an amount entered in error such as this. Corrections are always made in such a manner that the exact correction can be seen. An erasure seems to imply an effort to conceal what actually occurred.

Illustration 6

GENERAL JOURNAL   PAGE 1

DATE	ACCOUNT TITLES AND EXPLANATION	FO-LIO	DEBIT	CREDIT
1959 July 1	Cash	1	1100 00	
	Paul Allen, Capital	11		1100 00
	Invested in a taxicab business			
1	Prepaid Rent	2	300 00	
	Cash	1		300 00
	Paid rent three months in advance			
3	Taxicabs	4	1000 00	
	Cash	1		1000 00
	Bought four taxicabs			
5	Garage Equipment	7	800 00	
	West Supply Company	8		800 00
	Purchased equipment on credit.			
7	Gasoline	3	135 00	
	Coast Oil Company	9		135 00
	Purchased gasoline on credit.			
13	Despatcher's Wages	14	120 00	
	Cash	1		120 00
	Paid despatcher's wages for two weeks			
15	Cash	1	890 00	
	Taxicab Fares	13		890 00
	Fares of the first half of July.			
15	Drivers' Commissions	15	445 00	
	Cash	1		445 00
	Paid drivers' commissions.			

Illustration 6—Continued

GENERAL JOURNAL PAGE 2

DATE		ACCOUNT TITLES AND EXPLANATION	FO-LIO	DEBIT	CREDIT
1959 July	23	West Supply Company	8	400 00	
		Cash	1		400 00
		Paid on account.			
	27	Despatcher's Wages	14	120 00	
		Cash	1		120 00
		Wages for third and fourth weeks of July.			
	31	Cash	1	1260 00	
		Taxicab Fares	13		1260 00
		Fares of the last half of July.			
	31	Drivers' Commissions	15	630 00	
		Cash	1		630 00
		Paid drivers' commissions.			
	31	Telephone and Utilities	16	40 00	
		Cash	1		40 00
		Paid telephone and utilities.			
	31	Paul Allen, Withdrawals	12	200 00	
		Cash	1		200 00
		Withdrew cash for personal use.			

Cash PAGE 1

DATE		EXPLANATION	FO-LIO	DEBIT	DATE		EXPLANATION	FO-LIO	CREDIT
1959 July	1		1	1100 00	1959 July	1		1	30 00
	15	13,150.00	1	89 00		3		1	1000 00
	31	13,255.00	2	126 00		13		1	12 00
		895.00		1315 00		15		1	445 00
						23		1	400 00
						27		1	120 00
						31		2	630 00
						31		2	40 00
						31		2	200 00
									1 2255 00

Prepaid Rent PAGE 2

DATE		EXPLANATION	FO-LIO	DEBIT	DATE	EXPLANATION	FO-LIO	CREDIT
1959 July	1		1	30 00				

Illustration 6—Continued

Gasoline · PAGE 3

DATE	EXPLANATION	FO-LIO	DEBIT	DATE	EXPLANATION	FO-LIO	CREDIT
1959 July 7		1	135 00				

Taxicabs · PAGE 4

DATE	EXPLANATION	FO-LIO	DEBIT	DATE	EXPLANATION	FO-LIO	CREDIT
1959 July 3		1	10000 00				

Garage Equipment · PAGE 6

DATE	EXPLANATION	FO-LIO	DEBIT	DATE	EXPLANATION	FO-LIO	CREDIT
1959 July 5		1	800 00				

West Supply Company · PAGE 8

DATE	EXPLANATION	FO-LIO	DEBIT	DATE	EXPLANATION	FO-LIO	CREDIT
1959 July 23		1	400 00	1959 July 5		1	800 00

Coast Oil Company · PAGE 9

DATE	EXPLANATION	FO-LIO	DEBIT	DATE	EXPLANATION	FO-LIO	CREDIT
				1959 July 7		1	135 00 / 153 00

Paul Allen, Capital · PAGE 11

DATE	EXPLANATION	FO-LIO	DEBIT	DATE	EXPLANATION	FO-LIO	CREDIT
				1959 July 1		1	11000 00

Illustration 6—Continued

Paul Allen, Withdrawals   PAGE 12

DATE	EXPLANATION	FO-LIO	DEBIT	DATE	EXPLANATION	FO-LIO	CREDIT
1959 July 31		2	200 00				

Taxicab Fares   PAGE 14

DATE	EXPLANATION	FO-LIO	DEBIT	DATE	EXPLANATION	FO-LIO	CREDIT
				1959 July 15		1	890 00
				31		2	1260 00

Despatcher's Wages   PAGE 15

DATE	EXPLANATION	FO-LIO	DEBIT	DATE	EXPLANATION	FO-LIO	CREDIT
1959 July 13		1	120 00				
27		1	120 00				

Drivers' Commissions   PAGE 16

DATE	EXPLANATION	FO-LIO	DEBIT	DATE	EXPLANATION	FO-LIO	CREDIT
1959 July 15		1	445 00				
31		2	630 00				

Telephone and Utilities   PAGE 17

DATE	EXPLANATION	FO-LIO	DEBIT	DATE	EXPLANATION	FO-LIO	CREDIT
1959 July 31		2	40 00				

Bookkeeping Techniques

Periods and Commas in Dollar Amounts. When amounts are entered in a journal or a ledger, commas to indicate thousands of dollars and periods to separate dollars and cents are not necessary because the ruled lines accomplish this purpose. However, when statements are prepared on unruled paper, the periods and commas are necessary.

Dollar Signs. Dollar signs are not used in journals or ledgers, but they are required on the financial reports. On the reports, a dollar sign is placed (1) before the first amount in each column of figures, and (2) before the first amount appearing after a ruled line that indicates an addition or a subtraction. Examine Illustration 7 on Page 55 for illustrations of the uses of dollar signs on a financial report.

Omission of Zeros in the Cents Columns. When an amount to be entered in a ledger or a journal is an amount of dollars and no cents, some bookkeepers will use a dash in the cents column in the place of two zeros to indicate that there are no cents. They feel that the dash is easier and more quickly made than the two zeros. This is a matter of choice in journal and ledger entries. However, on financial reports the two zeros are preferred because they are neater in appearance.

Often in this text, where space is limited, exact dollar amounts are used in order to save space. Obviously, in such cases, neither zeros or dashes are used to show that there are no cents involved.

Preparing the Trial Balance from the Ledger Accounts

When a trial balance is prepared, many students have found that its preparation and checking are facilitated if account balances that are not apparent at a glance are determined and entered in the accounts in the following manner. First, in each account having several debits and credits, the debit and credit columns are each added and the totals are written in small pencil figures just below the last item on either side; for example, see the Cash account in Illustration 6. These pencil totals, often called "footings," are made small enough so that the space in which they appear may be used for the next amount to be posted to or entered in the account. Next, after the columns of an account are footed, if the balance of the account is a debit balance, the subtraction to determine the balance is made in the debit explanation column of the account, as in the Cash account of Illustration 6. Or, if the balance is a credit balance, the subtraction is made in the credit explanation column. After the balance of an account is determined in this manner, it is entered on the trial balance along with the account name. Students have found that footing accounts and making in the accounts the subtractions to determine balances retains these figures and calculations for later checking in case their trial balances fail to balance.

Locating Errors

Frequently the bookkeeper, and more often the accounting student, must spend a great deal of time in looking for errors. Consequently, following are some procedures that are helpful in locating errors. It should be pointed out that these suggestions for finding errors assume that in each case there is only one error. This is often not true. In many cases, the difference in the totals of a trial balance is the net of several errors. In such cases the suggestions will help. However, imagination plus a trial-and-error procedure are necessary to find a combination of errors.

If when a trial balance is prepared the trial balance does not balance, the first step in locating the error or errors is to check the addition of the trial balance columns. Frequently, the error is one of addition. When a trial balance fails to balance by 1 or 2 cents, 10 or 20 cents, $1 or $2, $10 or $20, or some other small even amount, the error is often one of addition or subtraction. When re-adding the trial balance, in order to locate such an error, it is a good procedure to re-add the columns in the opposite direction from that in which they were first added.

If the error is not one of addition in the trial balance columns, it is next wise to determine the exact amount of the error. The amount of the error is found by subtracting the smaller of the two column totals from the larger. The amount of an error often offers a clue as to where the error may be found. For example, suppose that the sum of the debit column of a trial balance is $2,442 and the sum of the credit column is $2,468. The difference is a $26 excess of credits. This means that the credit total is too large by $26; or the debit total is too small by $26; or there is a combination of errors, the net effect of which is a $26 excess of credits.

At this point, if the number of transactions is not great, it is usually wise to scan the transactions for a transaction of exactly $26. A transaction of $26 in which the credit is recorded twice will cause the trial balance to be out of balance by exactly $26. Likewise, a transaction of $26 in which the credit is recorded and the debit omitted will cause the trial balance to be out of balance by $26.

If the error is not a transaction of $26, look for a transaction of $13. A transaction of $13 recorded as two credits of $13 each, rather than as a debit to one account and a credit to another, will cause the trial balance to be out of balance by $26.

If scanning the transactions does not locate the error, it is then usually necessary to check the entire accounting procedure step by step. It is usually best to check the steps in the opposite manner from which they were originally performed. If this suggestion is followed, the listing of the account balances on the trial balance is checked first. Each of the account balances as it appears on the trial balance is compared with the balance of that account as it appears in the ledger. Care should be taken to see that a debit account balance of $26 has not been omitted. This will cause an excess of credits. Likewise, a debit account balance of $13 entered on the trial balance as a credit will cause a $26 excess of credits.

If an error in listing the accounts has not been made, then the computation of the account balances is checked. After this the posting is checked, and then the original recording of each transaction is examined. Normally the error or errors are found before this point is reached.

Transposition Errors and Slide Errors

Knowing the type of error made often aids in locating the error. A trial balance out of balance by 1, 2, 10 or 20 cents, or some other small even amount, is usually an indication of an error in addition or subtraction. Just as an error in addition or subtraction may leave its evidence, a slide or a transposition will do likewise. A slide is an error where, for example, $5.00 is recorded as $50, or $100 is recorded as $10 or $1.00. A transposition is an error in which figures are transposed, for example, $72 is recorded as $27. Either of these types of errors will cause the trial balance to be out of balance by an amount that is exactly divisible by nine.

To illustrate, cash in the amount of $72 is paid for equipment. In recording the transaction, Equipment is debited for $72, but the credit to Cash is transposed and recorded as a credit of $27. If only this error is involved, the trial balance will be out of balance by $45. The debits will exceed the credits by exactly $45. Nine will go into $45 exactly five times. The amount of the difference in the trial balance totals is exactly divisible by nine. The error has left its evidence; it is a transposition. The one looking for the error is alerted to the probable type of error for which he is looking.

Correcting Errors

When an error is discovered in either the journal or the ledger, it must be corrected. As previously stated, an amount entered in error is never erased; however, the exact method of correction will vary with the nature of the error.

If an error is discovered in a journal entry before the error is posted, the error may be corrected by ruling a single line through the incorrect amount or account name and writing in above the correct amount or account name. Likewise, an error in posting in which only the amount is wrong may be corrected in the same manner. However, when a posted error involves a wrong account, it is considered best to correct the error with a correcting journal entry. For example, the following journal entry to record the purchase of office supplies was made and posted:

Oct.	14	Office Furniture and Fixtures............	15.00	
		Cash............................		15.00
		To record the purchase of office supplies.		

Obviously, the debit of the entry is to the wrong account; consequently, the following entry is needed to correct the error:

Oct.	17	Office Supplies........................	15.00	
		Office Furniture and Fixtures........		15.00
		To correct the entry of October 14 in which the Office Furniture and Fixtures account was debited in error for the purchase of office supplies.		

The debit of the second entry correctly records the purchase of supplies, and the credit cancels the error of the first entry. Note the full explanation of the correcting entry. The explanation of a correcting entry should always be full and complete in order that anyone can see exactly what has occurred.

QUESTIONS FOR CLASS DISCUSSION

1. Is it possible to record transactions directly in the ledger accounts? What is gained by first recording transactions in a journal and then posting the journal entries to the ledger accounts?
2. In recording transactions in a journal, where is the name of the account debited written? The name of the account credited? The explanation?
3. How do compound entries save labor?
4. Define or describe each of the following:
   a) Journal.   e) Folio column.
   b) Ledger.   f) Posting.
   c) Book of original entry.   g) Footing.
   d) Book of final entry.   h) Posting reference numbers.
5. Describe how a transaction is recorded in a journal.
6. Name four common types of posting errors.
7. Outline a posting procedure that will help to eliminate posting errors.
8. The entry in the Folio column of the journal of the ledger page number to which an amount was posted is the last step in posting the amount. What is gained by making this the last step?
9. How may the balance of each account be calculated in such a manner as to aid in the preparation of the trial balance?
10. How should each of the following errors be corrected if discovered before being posted?
    a) A purchase of office supplies entered in the journal as a debit to the Office Equipment account.
    b) A $500 sale on account to Richard Tuttle entered in the journal as a $50 sale on account.
11. How should each of the foregoing errors be corrected if they were not discovered until after they were posted?
12. In recording a $32.50 check received from a customer in payment of his account, Cash was debited and Sales was credited for $32.50. Would this error keep the trial balance from balancing? Would the error probably be discovered? When?

PROBLEMS

Problem 3-1

On November 2 of the current year Larry Perkins began the operation of the Northside Cabinet Shop. During November he completed the following transactions:

Nov. 2 Cashed four mature United States savings bonds and deposited the $4,000 proceeds to the account of the Northside Cabinet Shop.
      2 Paid the rent for the month on the shop building, $60.
      3 Purchased $3,000 of shop machinery, giving $1,000 cash and a promissory note payable for the balance.
      4 Purchased $2,000 of shop supplies from the A and B Planing Mill on credit.

Nov. 8 Collected cash on delivery for $300 of cabinet work.
12 Billed Ralph Dubin for $425 of cabinet work delivered today.
15 Paid Motor Delivery Service $24 for delivery services during the first half of the month.
15 Paid the wages of the workmen, $250.
18 Mr. Perkins took $50 of shop supplies home for use in repairing his carport.
22 Paid the A and B Planing Mill $1,000 on account.
26 Collected $410 for cabinet work delivered to Thomas Mann.
28 Mr. Perkins withdrew $100 for personal living expenses.
30 Paid the wages of the workmen, $250.
30 Paid the electric light and power bill, $45.
30 Paid Motor Delivery Service $32 for delivery service during the last half of the month.

Required:

1. Open the following ledger accounts: Cash; Ralph Dubin; Shop Supplies; Shop Machinery; Notes Payable; A and B Planing Mill; Larry Perkins, Capital; Larry Perkins, Withdrawals; Revenue from Cabinet Work; Rent Expense; Delivery Expense; Wages Expense; and Light and Power Expense. Assign the accounts page numbers beginning with 1.
2. Prepare general journal entries to record the transactions, post to the ledger accounts, and prepare a trial balance.

Problem 3–2

On October 3 of the current year George Hunter began business as a building and excavating contractor under the firm name of Inter-City Construction Company. During the month he completed the following transactions for the firm:

Oct. 3 Transferred $10,000 from his personal bank account to the account of the Inter-City Construction Company, a firm of which he is sole owner.
3 Purchased land to be used as an office site and for parking excavating equipment, $2,000.
4 Paid the premiums on several insurance policies, $240.
5 Purchased $12,000 of excavating equipment by giving $4,000 cash and signing a promissory note payable for the balance.
5 Purchased for $2,500 in cash and moved onto the equipment parking lot a small office building.
6 Completed an excavating job and collected cash in payment, $680.
10 Purchased office equipment on credit from the Stillman Equipment Company, $400.
12 Billed Cascade Contractors for an excavation job completed today, $460.
14 Paid cash for repairs to equipment, $60.
15 Paid the wages of the equipment operators, $650.
17 Billed Pacific Construction Company for an excavation job completed today, $850.
21 Received a $460 check from Cascade Contractors in payment of their account.
23 Received and recorded a bill from Crawler Equipment Company for special equipment rented and used on the Pacific Construction job, $120.
25 Purchased additional excavating equipment from Crawler Equipment Company on credit, $470.

Oct. 25 Received an $850 check from Pacific Construction Company in pay-
ment of their account.

26 Billed Cascade Contractors $600 for a job completed today.

27 Mr. Hunter withdrew $250 for his personal use.

31 Paid the wages of the equipment operators, $630.

31 Paid the telephone, water, and electricity bills, $10.

31 Paid Stillman Equipment Company in full.

Required:

1. Open the following ledger accounts: Cash; Prepaid Insurance; Cascade
Contractors; Pacific Construction Company; Office Equipment; Exca-
vating Equipment; Land; Building; Notes Payable; Stillman Equipment
Company; Crawler Equipment Company; George Hunter, Capital;
George Hunter, Withdrawals; Excavating Revenue; Equipment Repairs;
Wages Expense; Rent of Equipment Expense; and Utilities Expense.
Assign the accounts page numbers beginning with 1.

2. Prepare and post general journal entries to record the transactions.

3. Prepare a trial balance.

Problem 3–3

Nov.	10	Cash.................................	2,000.00		
		Robert Maxwell, Capital...........		2,000.00	
	11	Rent Expense.......................	150.00		
		Cash............................		150.00	
	12	Dental Equipment...................	5,400.00		
		Cash............................		1,000.00	
		Notes Payable...................		4,400.00	
	15	Dental Equipment...................	210.00		
		Professional Supply Company.......		210.00	
	16	Cash...............................	80.00		
		Revenue from Professional Fees.....		80.00	
	17	Dental Supplies....................	50.00		
		Professional Supply Company.......		50.00	
	21	Prepaid Insurance..................	65.00		
		Cash............................		65.00	
	22	David McKeen.......................	40.00		
		Revenue from Professional Fees.....		40.00	
	24	Professional Supply Company..........	210.00		
		Cash............................		210.00	
	25	Cash...............................	350.00		
		Revenue from Professional Fees.....		350.00	
	27	Cash...............................	40.00		
		David McKeen....................		40.00	
	28	Robert Lyons.......................	75.00		
		Revenue from Professional Fees.....		75.00	
	29	Robert Maxwell, Withdrawals...........	100.00		
		Cash............................		100.00	
	30	Salaries Expense...................	60.00		
		Cash............................		60.00	

Required:

1. Write a general journal explanation for each of the foregoing entries.
2. Post the entries to the following ledger accounts: Cash; Prepaid Insurance; Dental Supplies; David McKeen; Robert Lyons; Dental Equipment; Notes Payable; Professional Supply Company; Robert Maxwell, Capital; Robert Maxwell, Withdrawals; Revenue from Professional Fees; Rent Expense; and Salaries Expense.
3. Prepare a trial balance.

CLASS EXERCISES

Exercise 3–1

During one month the bookkeeper of a small firm made the following errors:
1. An item of $7.92 for office supplies purchased was entered as a debit to Office Supplies of $9.72.
2. A customer paid his account. The customer was debited, and cash was credited for $15 paid.
3. A credit of $7.50 to Cash was entered as a debit to Office Equipment.
4. A credit of $12 to Office Equipment was entered as a credit to Office Supplies.
5. The debit side of a creditor's account totaled $34, and the credit side totaled $56. The two sides were added, and the sum of $90 was entered as the debit balance of the account.

Tell the effect of each error on the trial balance.

Exercise 3–2

The following accounts and trial balance of Services Unlimited have several errors that keep the trial balance from balancing:

Cash			Land			Joel Bond, Capital	
Bal. 1,900	1,000		Bal. 1,500				Bal. 8,950
450	200						
	600						

Office Supplies		Building		Revenue from Services	
Bal. 50		Bal. 5,500			450

Office Equipment		Notes Payable	
1,000		600	2,000
2,000			
200			

SERVICES UNLIMITED
Trial Balance, October 31, 19—

Cash	$ 550	
Office equipment	3,300	
Land		$ 1,500
Building	5,500	
Notes payable	1,500	
Joel Bond, capital		9,850
Revenue from services	450	
	$11,300	$11,350

Required:

Make a list of the errors that were made in preparing the trial balance.

SUPPLEMENTARY PROBLEMS

Problem 3–A

On November 27 of the current year a trial balance of the ledger of the Grand Theatre appeared as follows:

GRAND THEATRE
Trial Balance, November 27, 19—

Cash	$ 1,500	
Advertising supplies	210	
Prepaid insurance	140	
Theatre furniture and equipment	17,300	
Simplex Equipment Company		$ 700
Fox Films		230
Sentinel Publishing Company		40
Catherine Jones, capital		13,620
Catherine Jones, withdrawals	5,600	
Admissions revenue		54,000
Salaries and wages	17,500	
Film rentals	19,900	
Theatre rent	4,400	
Advertising expense	960	
Heat, light, and power	870	
Equipment repairs	210	
	$68,590	$68,590

During the last three days of November the business completed the following transactions:

Nov. 28　Purchased advertising supplies for cash, $40.

　　　28　Admissions revenue for the day was $250.

　　　29　Paid the weekly salaries and wages, $510.

　　　29　Purchased theatre equipment from the Simplex Equipment Company on credit, $130.

　　　29　Catherine Jones withdrew $300 for her personal use.

　　　29　Paid Fox Films $200 on account.

　　　29　Admissions revenue for the day was $280.

　　　30　Received and recorded a bill from Fox Films for rentals on movies already shown, $110.

Nov. 30 Paid $15 for repairs to equipment.
    30 Received and recorded a bill from the Sentinel Publishing Company for advertising that had appeared, $35.
    30 Paid the premium on a liability insurance policy, $60.
    30 Paid the electric bill, $55.
    30 Paid Simplex Equipment Company $500 on account.
    30 Admissions revenue for the day was $310.

Required:

1. Open the accounts listed in the trial balance of the theatre and enter the November 27 amounts. Write the date and the word "balance" on the line with each trial balance amount.
2. Prepare and post general journal entries to record the transactions.
3. Prepare a November 30 trial balance.

Problem 3–B

19—					Page 1
Oct.	10	Cash...........................	15,000.00		
		Phillip Gardner, Capital...........		15,000.00	
	10	Automobile.......................	3,100.00		
		Phillip Gardner, Capital...........		3,100.00	
	10	Land............................	5,000.00		
		Building........................	27,000.00		
		Office Supplies...................	100.00		
		Office Equipment.................	3,000.00		
		Cash........................		10,100.00	
		Mortgage Payable..............		25,000.00	
	14	Cash............................	900.00		
		Commissions Revenue...........		900.00	
	15	Office Salaries...................	50.00		
		Cash........................		50.00	
	21	Office Supplies...................	60.00		
		Apex Supply Company...........		60.00	
	23	Advertising Expense..............	35.00		
		Cash........................		35.00	
	25	Phillip Gardner, Withdrawals.......	400.00		
		Cash........................		400.00	
	27	Office Equipment.................	220.00		
		Royal Equipment Company........		220.00	
	27	Apex Supply Company.............	60.00		
		Cash........................		60.00	
	28	Cash............................	800.00		
		Commissions Revenue...........		800.00	
	31	Office Salaries...................	150.00		
		Cash........................		150.00	
	31	The Estate of James Glass.........	80.00		
		Property Management Revenue.....		80.00	
	31	Water and Lighting Expense........	12.00		
		Cash........................		12.00	

Required:

1. Write a descriptive general journal entry explanation for each of the fore-going entries of the Commonwealth Realty Company.
2. Open ledger accounts and post the entries to the accounts.
3. Prepare a trial balance of the ledger.

Chapter

4

ADJUSTING THE ACCOUNTS AND PREPARING THE STATEMENTS

ALTHOUGH a business has earnings when its revenues exceed its expenses, it is impossible to learn the exact earnings of a business until after it has completed its last transaction and all of its assets have been converted into cash. This is because it is impossible to measure precisely over a short period of time some of the items that enter into the calculation of earnings, for example, depreciation. Nevertheless, although earnings cannot be exactly measured over a short period of time, it is also impractical to wait until the life of a business is ended in order to learn its exact earnings. It is impractical to wait because successful companies continue to operate for a long period of years, because income tax regulations require the payment at least once each year of taxes on earnings, and because of the need of management for information. Consequently, it has become universal practice to divide the life of a business into accounting periods of equal length, a year being the most common length, and to measure, as accurately as possible, the earnings of each of these periods.

It has also become common practice to prepare for a business at the end of each accounting period in its life at least two financial reports or statements. The first of these statements is called an *income statement.* It reports, as nearly as it can be measured, the gain or the loss incurred by the business during the accounting period. The second of the statements is called a *balance sheet*. It reports as of the end of an accounting period the amounts of the assets owned, the liabilities owed, and the proprietorship of the owner or owners. Both statements are prepared primarily from information contained in the ledger accounts.

The Income Statement

The income statement is perhaps the more important of the two statements. This is because it shows how the business accomplished or failed to accomplish its primary objective of earning a "profit," or, as an accountant would say, earning a net income. As is demonstrated in Illustration 7, an income statement shows how a net income was earned or a net loss was incurred by (1) listing the amount of revenue earned during the accounting period, (2) listing with their total the expenses incurred during the period, and (3) showing, by subtracting the expenses from the revenue, the amount of net income or net loss.

The Committee on Terminology of the American Institute of Certified Public Accountants recommends that when revenues exceed expenses, the excess be listed on the income statement as "net income."[1] This excess also sometimes appears on income statements as "net profit." However, since it is difficult to measure exactly the profit or loss of a business over a short period of time, many accountants prefer to use the term "net income" when revenues exceed expenses and to use the term "net loss" when expenses exceed revenues. These accountants reserve the word "profit" for

Illustration 7

SNOWHITE LAUNDRY
Income Statement for Year Ended December 31, 1959

Revenue:			
Laundry receipts			$14,407
Operating expenses:			
Laundry expenses:			
Laundry supplies used	$ 960		
Water and electricity	384		
Rent expense	1,200		
Depreciation of laundry equipment.	360		
Total Laundry Expenses		$2,904	
Delivery expenses:			
Delivery salaries.	$4,200		
Gas, oil, and repairs.	720		
Depreciation of delivery equipment	480		
Total Delivery Expenses.		5,400	
Total Operating Expenses . . .			8,304
Net Income			$ 6,103

use in describing the gain on a particular transaction, for instance, the sale of an asset.[2]

Heading of the Income Statement

An income statement is always prepared for a specific business and covers a specific period of time. The name of the business for which the income statement is prepared and the period of time covered are always given in the statement's heading. Normally the heading of an income statement is written on two lines: the name of the business for which the statement is prepared is placed on the first line and the name of the statement and the period of time covered by the statement are shown on the second.

The period of time covered by an income statement is of extreme significance. This is because the items on the statement have no importance except when interpreted in connection with a period of time. For example, the item "Laundry receipts, $14,407," on the income statement of the

---

[1] *Accounting Terminology Bulletin No. 2*, "Proceeds, Revenue, Income, Profit, and Earnings" (New York: American Institute of Certified Public Accountants, 1955), pp. 3 and 4.

[2] *Ibid.*, pp. 3 and 4.

Snowhite Laundry of Illustration 7 has little significance until it is known that the amount represents the laundry receipts of one year and not the receipts of a week, a month, or six months.

Classification of Income Statement Items

The sale of a service or the sale of a product normally requires the performance of several functions. For example, the Snowhite Laundry of Illustration 7 performs at least two main functions. They are: (1) laundering, and (2) delivering the finished laundry. Notice in Illustration 7 how the expenses are classified as either laundry expenses or delivery expenses. An income statement on which expenses are classified by functions is known as a *classified income statement.* A classified income statement is more useful than an unclassified statement because the classified statement sets out the cost of each function performed and enables management to better observe the variations in the costs of each function when income statements of successive accounting periods are compared.

The Balance Sheet

A balance sheet is a statement prepared to show the financial position of a business. It shows financial position by listing the amounts of the various assets of the business for which it is prepared and the claims against these assets. In addition to listing the various assets and claims, a balance sheet, by classification and arrangement, also attempts to show the probability of an adequate supply of funds being available to pay each claim as it becomes due.

A balance sheet is closely related to the fundamental accounting equation. Actually, it is an elaboration of the equation in which the assets, liabilities, and proprietorship are individually listed, and the sum of the assets is shown to be equal to the sum of the liabilities and proprietorship. This may be seen by examining Illustration 8.

Heading of the Balance Sheet

A balance sheet is prepared to show the financial position of a specific business on a specific date. The name of the business for which the balance sheet is prepared and the date of the balance sheet are always shown in the heading of the statement. Since transactions change the amounts of the individual balance sheet items, the heading must show the exact date on which the statement is prepared. The date indicates that the balance sheet shows the amounts of the assets, liabilities, and proprietorship at the close of business on the day of the balance sheet date. The heading of a balance sheet is usually written on two lines. The first line gives the name of the business; the second gives the name of the statement and the date.

Illustration 8—An Account Form Balance Sheet

VALLEY HARDWARE STORE
Balance Sheet, December 31, 1959

ASSETS

Current Assets:

Cash	$ 1,050	
Notes receivable	300	
Accounts receivable. . . .	3,961	
Merchandise inventory. . .	10,248	
Prepaid insurance.	109	
Office supplies.	46	
Store supplies	145	
Total Current Assets .		$15,859

Fixed Assets:

Office equipment	$ 1,500		
Less: Accumulated depr..	300	$ 1,200	
Store equipment.	$ 3,200		
Less: Accumulated depr..	800	2,400	
Buildings.	$25,000		
Less: Accumulated depr..	7,400	17,600	
Land		4,200	
Total Fixed Assets . .			25,400

Total Assets $41,259

LIABILITIES

Current Liabilities:

Notes payable	$3,000	
Accounts payable.	2,715	
Accrued wages payable . .	112	
Total Current Liabilities		$ 5,827

Long-Term Liabilities:

First-mortgage payable, secured by mortgage on land and buildings. . .		10,000
Total Liabilities . .		$15,827

PROPRIETORSHIP

Samuel Jackson, capital, January 1, 1959.		$23,721
Net income for year ended December 31, 1959 . .	$7,711	
Less: Withdrawals	6,000	
Excess of income over withdrawals		1,711
Samuel Jackson, capital, December 31, 1959. . .		25,432
Total Liab. and Prop. .		$41,259

Classification of Balance Sheet Items

A balance sheet showing a number of items becomes more useful when the items are classified into significant groups of assets and significant groups of liabilities. This is because the reader of a *classified balance sheet* can better see the adequacy of the different kinds of assets used in the business. He can also better estimate the probable availability of funds to meet the various liabilities as they become due.

Accountants are not in full agreement as to the best way in which to classify balance sheet items. Consequently, balance sheet items are classified in several ways. One common method classifies assets into (1) current assets, (2) long-term investments, (3) fixed assets, (4) intangible assets, (5) deferred charges. It classifies liabilities into (1) current liabilities, and (2) long-term or fixed liabilities.

Of the five asset classifications listed in the preceding paragraph, only two, current assets and fixed assets, appear on the balance sheet of the Valley Hardware Store of Illustration 8. This is because the Valley Hardware Store is a small company and does not have long-term investments, intangible assets, or deferred charges. For a balance sheet showing items of all five classifications, examine Illustration 124 in Chapter 22.

Current Assets

When a balance sheet is prepared, the assets listed under the current asset caption are primarily those assets to which the current creditors (current liabilities) may look for payment of their claims. As they are presently defined, current assets consist of two kinds of assets: (1) cash and assets that will be realized in cash within a short period of time, usually one year; and (2) prepaid expenses. The American Institute of Certified Public Accountants through its Committee on Accounting Procedure has defined current assets as: "cash and other assets or resources commonly identified as those which are reasonably expected to be realized in cash or sold or consumed during the normal operating cycle of the business."[3] The words "or consumed" place prepaid expenses within the current asset classification. The Committee on Accounting Procedure classifies prepaid expenses as current assets because, as it says: "Prepaid expenses are not current assets in the sense that they will be converted into cash but in the sense that, if not paid in advance, they would require the use of current assets during the operating cycle."

Notice in Illustration 8 that the sum of all the accounts receivable of the Valley Hardware Store is shown in one amount, "Accounts receivable, $3,961." Retail companies selling on credit normally have from several dozen to several thousand different accounts receivable, one for each credit

---

[3] *Accounting Research Bulletin No. 43,* "Restatement and Revision of Accounting Research Bulletins" (New York: American Institute of Certified Public Accountants, 1953), p. 20.

customer. It is the usual practice to show only the sum of their balances on the balance sheet. The same practice is also commonly followed with accounts payable; and since the sum of all of the prepaid expenses is often not material in amount when compared with the other current assets, the practice of showing only the total of all the prepaid expenses is not uncommon.

Long-Term Investments

The second classification of balance sheet items is long-term investments. Several items are placed on the balance sheet under this caption. Among them are items that will be realized in cash but not for a long period of time; and also items that will be realized in cash but, when realized, the cash will not be available to meet current debts. A more complete discussion of long-term investments is not needed at this time and is deferred until a later chapter.

Fixed Assets

Fixed assets are the third balance sheet classification of assets. Fixed assets are items of a more or less permanent nature that are used in carrying on the normal functions of the business and are not for sale. From this definition it can be seen that an item to be classed as a fixed asset must have three characteristics. It must be: (1) of a more or less permanent nature, (2) used in carrying on the normal functions of the business, and (3) not for sale. Normally it is expected that fixed assets will be worn out or consumed in the operations of the business. However, a fixed asset may be sold before it wears out if it is no longer needed in the business operations. The order of listing the individual fixed assets within the fixed asset classification is not uniform. Often the order of listing is from the ones of the least permanent nature to the ones of the most permanent nature.

Some of the more common kinds of fixed assets are such things as office equipment, store equipment, factory machinery and equipment, buildings, and land.

Intangible Assets

Intangible assets are assets having no physical nature, their value being dependent upon the rights conferred upon their owner by their possession. Goodwill, patents, and trade-marks are examples of intangible assets. A full discussion of such assets is unnecessary at this point and is deferred until a future chapter.

Deferred Charges

Long-term prepaid expenses are known as "deferred charges." They are the last balance sheet classification of asset items. A full discussion of deferred charges is also unnecessary at this point, and it is delayed until a future chapter.

Liability Classifications

Most companies do not have as many different liability items on their balance sheets as asset items. The two most common liability classifications found on balance sheets are: (1) current liabilities, and (2) long-term liabilities.

Current Liabilities. Current liabilities are obligations that will become due within a short period of time, usually one year, and that will normally be paid when due from current assets. The order of listing current liabilities is not uniform. Often notes payable are listed as the first current liability because notes receivable are listed first after cash in the current asset section. Common current liabilities are notes payable, accounts payable, wages payable, taxes payable, interest payable, and unearned revenues.

Unearned revenue items are normally the last items in the current liability section of a balance sheet. Unearned items commonly grow out of transactions in which money is received for goods or services to be delivered at a future date. Subscriptions received in advance by a publisher, rent received in advance by a landlord, and payments received for the future delivery of merchandise are examples of unearned revenues. Each is a liability. Each is an obligation to deliver goods or services at a future date. Each is classified as a current liability because current assets will normally be required in its liquidation. Payments for the future delivery of merchandise will be earned and the obligation for the delivery of the merchandise will be liquidated by delivering merchandise. Merchandise is a current asset. Likewise, payment for services to be performed at a future date will be earned and the obligation liquidated by performing the services. The performance of services normally requires the payment of cash for wages and other expenses. Cash is a current asset.

Unearned revenues are sometimes called "deferred credits to income." A deferred credit is a delayed credit. When unearned revenue items are called "deferred credits to income," they are so called because their credit to income or revenue is delayed or put off until earned.

Long-Term Liabilities. The second main balance sheet liability classification is long-term liabilities. Liabilities that are not due and payable for a comparatively long period of time, usually more than one year, are listed on the balance sheet under the long-term liability classification. Common long-term liability items are mortgages payable and bonds payable.

Proprietorship on the Balance Sheet

Proprietorship, net worth, and capital are synonymous terms in accounting. All three are used to indicate the equity, in the assets, of the owner or owners of a business. Of the three terms, proprietorship and capital are considered the better terms. This is because net worth seems to indicate that the amount shown as the equity of the owner is the net value of that equity. The amount shown as the equity of the owner may or may not be the exact value of his equity. It is true that the equity of the owner in the assets of a business is the net amount remaining after the equity of the creditors is deducted. However, balance sheet amounts for some assets are always estimated amounts and do not necessarily represent their current value. Cost of fixed assets less their estimated depreciation is an example. Consequently, since the amounts of some of the assets are always estimated amounts, the amount of the equity of the owner is also always an estimated amount rather than a net amount or a net worth.

The manner of reporting the ownership equity on the balance sheet depends upon the type of business organization for which the balance sheet is prepared. A business may be organized as a sole proprietorship, a partnership, or a corporation. If a business is organized as a sole proprietorship, the proprietorship is commonly reported:

PROPRIETORSHIP

James Gibbs, capital, January 1, 1959. . .		$13,152
Net income for year ended December 31, 1959	$3,753	
Withdrawals.	4,800	
Excess of withdrawals over earnings· · ·		1,047
James Gibbs, capital, December 31, 1959. .		$12,105

The preceding illustrated method of showing proprietorship on the balance sheet gives the details of the increases and decreases resulting from earnings and withdrawals. Some accountants prefer to show these details on a supplementary schedule called a "statement of proprietorship." When such a supplementary schedule is used, proprietorship is shown on the balance sheet as follows:

PROPRIETORSHIP

James Gibbs, capital, December 31, 1959 . . . $12,105

If two or more people own a business as a partnership, the changes in the equity of each resulting from earnings and withdrawals are normally reported on a statement of proprietorship and only the total proprietorship of each partner on the balance date is shown on the balance sheet as follows:

PROPRIETORSHIP

James Smith, capital	$ 6,534
Robert Jones, capital.	8,506
Total Proprietorship	$15,040

If a business is organized as a corporation, the ownership rights are vested in the stockholders of the corporation. The owners or stockholders of some corporations number in the thousands, and the individual stockholders change daily. These changes result from the sale and purchase by different individuals of ownership rights as evidenced by shares of stock. Consequently, because of the great number of stockholders of some corporations and the constant change in stockholders, the individual equity of each stockholder is not reported on a corporation balance sheet. Rather the combined equity of all the stockholders is reported in two amounts as follows:

PROPRIETORSHIP

```
Capital stock  . . . . . . . . . . . . . . . . . $100,000
Retained earnings. . . . . . . . . . . . . . . .   53,506
       Total Proprietorship . . . . . . . . . . $153,506
```

Arrangement of Balance Sheet Items

The items appearing on a balance sheet may be arranged in several ways. The two more common ways are the *account form balance sheet* (Illustration 8) and the *report form balance sheet* (Illustration 9). In an account form balance sheet, with the assets on the left and the liabilities and proprietorship on the right, the arrangement follows that of an account. In a report form balance sheet a vertical arrangement of the items is used. Either form is satisfactory. The account form is said to have the advantage of making easier a comparison of groups of related items, for example, current assets and current liabilities. However, this is offset by the fact that it is easier to place a report form balance sheet on a single sheet of typing paper or columnar paper.

Need for Adjustments before the Statements Are Prepared

An income statement prepared at the end of an accounting period should reflect as nearly as it can be measured the exact amount of revenue earned during the period and the exact amount of each expense incurred in earning the revenue. Likewise, a balance sheet prepared at that time should show as accurately as possible the amounts of the various assets and liabilities and the owner's equity.

Occasionally, at the end of a period, statements reflecting the proper amounts of revenue, expenses, assets, liabilities, and proprietorship may be prepared directly from the ledger accounts just as soon as all of the transactions are recorded. However, this is unusual. Normally, several of the account balances as they appear on the end-of-the-period trial balance do not show the proper amounts for the preparation of the statements. This is because the balances of some accounts become inaccurate for statement purposes simply because of the expiration of costs brought about by the passage of time. For example, the second item on the trial balance

Illustration 9—A Report Form Balance Sheet

VALLEY HARDWARE STORE
Balance Sheet, December 31, 1959

ASSETS

Current Assets:			
Cash		$ 1,050.00	
Notes receivable		300.00	
Accounts receivable.		3,961.00	
Merchandise inventory.		10,248.00	
Prepaid insurance.		109.00	
Office supplies.		46.00	
Stores supplies.		145.00	
Total Current Assets			$15,859.00
Fixed Assets:			
Office equipment	$ 1,500..00		
Less: Accumulated depreciation	300.00	$ 1,200.00	
Store equipment.	$ 3,200.00		
Less: Accumulated depreciation	800.00	2,400.00	
Buildings.	$25,000.00		
Less: Accumulated depreciation	7,400.00	17,600.00	
Land		4,200.00	
Total Fixed Assets			25,400.00
Total Assets			$41,259.00

LIABILITIES

Current Liabilities:			
Notes payable.		$ 3,000.00	
Accounts payable		2,715.00	
Accrued wages payable.		112.00	
Total Current Liabilities.		$ 5,827.00	
Long-Term Liabilities:			
First-mortgage payable, secured by a mort-			
gage on land and buildings		10,000.00	
Total Liabilities.			$15,827.00

PROPRIETORSHIP

Samuel Jackson, capital, January 1, 1959 . . .		$23,721.00	
Net income for the year ended December 31,			
1959	$ 7,711.00		
Less: Withdrawals.	6,000.00		
Excess of income over withdrawals.		1,711.00	
Samuel Jackson, capital, December 31, 1959 . .			25,432.00
Total Liabilities and Proprietorship			$41,259.00

of Paul Allen, as presented in Chapter 2 and reproduced again as Illustration 10 on the next page, is "Prepaid rent, $300." This $300 represents the amount of rent paid for three months in advance on July 1. On July 31 the $300 is not the correct amount of the asset, prepaid rent; one month's rent, or $100, has expired and only $200 of prepaid rent remains as an asset. Likewise, a portion of the 500 gallons of gasoline as represented by the $135 debit balance in the Gasoline account has been used; and the taxicabs and garage equipment have begun to wear out and depreciate. Obviously, then, the end-of-the-period balances of the Prepaid Rent, Gasoline, Taxicabs and Garage Equipment accounts, as they appear on the trial balance, simply do not reflect the proper amounts for the preparation of the July 31 statements. The balance of each and the balance of the Despatcher's Wages account must be *adjusted* before they will show the proper amounts for the July 31 statements.

Illustration 10

PAUL ALLEN TAXICAB COMPANY
Trial Balance, July 31, 1959

Cash	$ 895	
Prepaid rent	300	
Gasoline	135	
Taxicabs	10,000	
Garage equipment	800	
West Supply Company.		$ 400
Coast Oil Company.		135
Paul Allen, capital.		11,000
Paul Allen, withdrawals.	200	
Taxicab fares.		2,150
Despatcher's wages	240	
Drivers' commissions	1,075	
Telephone and utilities.	40	
	$13,685	$13,685

Adjustment of the Accounts Illustrated

Prepaid Expenses. As the name implies, a prepaid expense is an expense that has been paid for in advance of its use. At the time of payment an asset is acquired that will be used or consumed and, as it is used or consumed, it will become an expense. For example:

On July 1 Paul Allen paid three months' rent in advance. This payment gave him the right to occupy the rented building for the following three months. On July 1 this right was an asset valued at its exchange price of $300; but day by day Paul Allen occupied the building; and each day a portion of the prepaid rent was consumed or expired and became an expense. On July 31 one month's rent, valued at one third of $300, or $100, had expired. Consequently, if Paul Allen's July 31 accounts are to reflect the proper asset and expense amounts, the following adjusting entry is required:

July	31	Rent Expense..........................	100.00	
		Prepaid Rent......................		100.00
		To record the expired rent.		

Posting the adjusting entry has the following effect on the accounts:

Prepaid Rent				**Rent Expense**		
July 1	300	July 31	100	July 31	100	

After the entry is posted, both the Prepaid Rent and the Rent Expense accounts show the proper statement amounts.

Early in the month of July, Paul Allen purchased 500 gallons of gasoline and placed it in a gasoline storage tank. Each day his drivers filled the tanks of their cabs, and each day a portion of the gasoline was consumed. The amount consumed each day was an expense that daily reduced the assets and Allen's proprietorship. However, the daily reductions were not recognized in Allen's accounts because day-by-day information as to the amounts used and remaining was not needed in the accounts and because bookkeeping labor could be saved if only a single amount, the total amount used during the month, was recorded.

Consequently, if on July 31, Paul Allen's accounts are to reflect proper statement amounts, it is necessary for him to record the amount of gasoline consumed during the month. To do this, it is first necessary for him to learn the amount consumed. He can learn the amount consumed by measuring the amount of gasoline remaining in the tank and deducting this amount from the amount purchased. If, for example, 200 gallons of the original 500 remain, then 300 gallons, or three fifths of the $135, of gasoline has been consumed. Three fifths of $135 is $81; and the following entry is required to record the gasoline consumed:

July	31	Gasoline Consumed...................	81.00	
		Gasoline.........................		81.00
		To record the amount of gasoline consumed.		

The effect of the adjusting entry on the accounts is:

Gasoline				Gasoline Consumed	
July 7	135	July 31	81	July 31	81

Note again that the adjustment serves a twofold purpose. It adjusts the asset account and it records the expense.

Often, unlike in the two previous examples, items that are prepaid expenses at the time of purchase are both bought and fully consumed within a period of time between the beginning and end of a single accounting period. For example, a company that operates with annual accounting periods pays its rent in advance on the first day of each month. Each month the amount paid results in a prepaid expense that is entirely consumed before the end of the month and before the end of the accounting period. In such cases, it is best to ignore the fact that an asset results from each prepayment. In such cases bookkeeping labor, an end-of-the-accounting-period adjustment, can be saved if each amount paid is recorded as an expense at the time of payment.

Other prepaid expenses that are handled in the same manner as prepaid rent and gasoline are prepaid insurance, office supplies, store supplies, and factory supplies.

Depreciation.   When a business purchases a fixed asset, it in effect purchases a "fund of usefulness." Day by day, as the asset is used in carrying on the operations of the business, a portion of this "fund of usefulness" is consumed or expires. In accounting, this expiration of an asset's "fund of usefulness" is known as *depreciation*.

The depreciation of an asset is an expense just like the decline through use of the amount of gasoline in a storage tank is an expense. The only difference is that over a short period of time depreciation is more difficult to measure. Actually, because of the difficulty of exactly foretelling how long a fixed asset will last, the amount that a fixed asset depreciates each accounting period cannot be precisely measured at the time the depreciation takes place; it can only be estimated.

A more complete discussion of the nature of depreciation and its estimation is not necessary at this time and is deferred until Chapter 13. However, for purposes of illustration, assume that:

On July 31 Paul Allen estimated the depreciation of his four taxicabs for the month at $200 and the depreciation of his garage equipment at $10. In both cases the depreciation reduced Allen's assets and increased his expenses. To record the depreciation the following adjusting entries are required:

July	31	Depreciation Expense, Taxicabs........	200.00	
		Accumulated Depreciation, Taxicabs.		200.00
		To record the July depreciation.		
	31	Depreciation Expense, Garage Equipment.	10.00	
		Accumulated Depreciation, Garage Equipment.....................		10.00
		To record the July depreciation.		

The effect of the entries on the accounts is:

Taxicabs			Depreciation Expense, Taxicabs		
July 1	10,000		July 31	200	

Accumulated Depreciation, Taxicabs		
	July 31	200

Garage Equipment			Depreciation Expense, Garage Equip.		
July 5	800		July 31	10	

Accumulated Depr., Garage Equipment		
	July 31	10

Two important points should be observed in regard to the depreciation entries just given: (1) note that separate expense accounts are used in recording the depreciation on each kind of fixed asset; and (2) note that the estimated depreciation is not credited directly to the fixed asset accounts.

Separate depreciation expense accounts are used because they make it possible on the income statement to classify the various depreciation expenses according to the functions performed by the business in carrying on its operations. For example, a firm that owns and uses store equipment, office equipment, and delivery equipment should provide a Depreciation Expense, Store Equipment account; a Depreciation Expense, Office Equipment account; and a Depreciation Expense, Delivery Equipment account. The balance of the Depreciation Expense, Store Equipment account can then be placed on the firm's income statement in the selling expense section, the office equipment depreciation expense can be placed in the administrative expense section, and the delivery equipment depreciation expense can be placed in the delivery expense section.

Depreciation is recorded at the end of each accounting period of a fixed asset's life. For example, in this illustration, at the end of the fourth month in the life of Paul Allen's taxicabs the Taxicabs account and its related Accumulated Depreciation, Taxicabs account will appear as follows:

Taxicabs		Accumulated Depreciation, Taxicabs	
July 1 10,000		July 31	200
		Aug. 31	200
		Sept. 30	200
		Oct. 31	200

And the taxicabs will appear on Allen's October 31 balance sheet as:

```
Taxicabs . . . . . . . . . . . . . . . $10,000
     Less: Accumulated depreciation . . .      800
                                            $9,200
```

Normally, a decrease in an asset is recorded as a direct credit to the asset account. However, as the Taxicabs and its related Accumulated Depreciation, Taxicabs accounts show, this procedure is not followed in recording depreciation. The depreciation of a fixed asset, as in the examples just given, is normally recorded in a *contra account* such as "Accumulated Depreciation, Taxicabs." (A contra account is an account the balance of which is subtracted from the balance of a second account to show a more proper amount for the items recorded in the second account.) There are good reasons for using contra accounts in recording depreciation. First, at its best, depreciation is only an estimate; and, second, the use of a contra account better preserves the facts of an asset's life. In this case the asset account, Taxicabs, preserves the historical cost of the cabs, and the Accumulated Depreciation, Taxicabs account shows the accumulated depreciation to date.

Accumulated depreciation accounts are commonly found in ledgers and on statements under titles such as "Allowance for Depreciation, Store Equipment" or "Reserve for Depreciation, Office Equipment." However, the newer terminology for these accounts is "Accumulated Depreciation, Store Equipment" and "Accumulated Depreciation, Office Equipment." The newer terminology is better because it is more descriptive.

Accrued Expenses. Most expenses are normally recorded during an accounting period at the time they are paid. However, at the end of a period there are almost always expenses that have been incurred but that have not been paid and recorded because payment is not yet due. These unpaid and unrecorded expenses for which payment is not yet due are called *accrued expenses*. Earned but unpaid wages are a common example of an accrued expense. To illustrate:

The Paul Allen Taxicab Company has a cab despatcher who is paid $10 per day or $60 per week for a six-day week that begins on Monday and ends on Saturday. Her wages are due and payable every two weeks on Saturday night; and during July they were paid on the 13th and 27th and recorded as follows:

Cash			Despatcher's Wages	
	July 13	120	July 13	120
	27	120	27	120

If the calendar for the month of July appears as illustrated and the despatcher worked on Monday, Tuesday, and Wednesday, July 29, 30, and 31, then, at the close of business on Wednesday, July 31, the despatcher has earned three days' wages that are not paid and recorded because they are not yet due. However, this $30 of earned but unpaid wages is just as much a part of the expenses of the month of July as the $240 of wages that have been paid. Furthermore, on July 31, the $30 of unpaid wages is a liability. Consequently, if Allen's accounts are to show the correct amount of despatcher's wages expense for July and if the accounts are to show all of the liabilities owed on July 31, then an adjusting entry like the following must be made:

JULY

S	M	T	W	T	F	S
	1	2	3	4	5	6
7	8	9	10	11	12	13
14	15	16	17	18	19	20
21	22	23	24	25	26	27
28	29	30	31			

July	31	Despatcher's Wages....................	30.00	
		Wages Payable....................		30.00
		To record the earned but unpaid wages.		

The effect of the entry on the accounts is:

Despatcher's Wages			Wages Payable	
July 13	120		July 31	30
27	120			
31	30			

Note that the adjustment again accomplishes a twofold purpose: it adjusts the expense account, Despatcher's Wages; and it records the liability for the unpaid wages.

The Adjusted Trial Balance

A trial balance prepared before adjustments are recorded is known as an *unadjusted trial balance,* or simply as a trial balance. A trial balance prepared after adjustments are recorded and posted is known as an *adjusted trial balance.* If, after the adjustments are posted to the accounts, an adjusted trial balance of the ledger of Paul Allen is prepared, the adjusted trial balance will appear as in Illustration 11.

Illustration 11

PAUL ALLEN TAXICAB COMPANY
Adjusted Trial Balance, July 31, 1959

Cash	$ 895	
Prepaid rent	200	
Gasoline	54	
Taxicabs	10,000	
Accumulated depreciation, taxicabs .		$ 200
Garage equipment	800	
Accumulated depr., garage equipment.		10
West Supply Company.		400
Coast Oil Company.		135
Wages payable.		30
Paul Allen, capital.		11,000
Paul Allen, withdrawals.	200	
Taxicab fares.		2,150
Despatcher's wages	270	
Drivers' commissions	1,075	
Telephone and utilities.	40	
Rent expense	100	
Gasoline consumed.	81	
Depreciation expense, taxicabs . . .	200	
Depr. expense, garage equipment. . .	10	
	$13,925	$13,925

Preparing the Statements from the Adjusted Trial Balance

At the end of an accounting period the items on an adjusted trial balance show proper balance sheet and income statement amounts; and, consequently, the adjusted trial balance may be used in preparing the statements. To prepare the statements from the adjusted trial balance is an easy task. All that is required is a rearrangement of the revenue and expense items into the income statement and a rearrangement of the items representing assets, liabilities, and owner's equity into the balance sheet. To demonstrate the ease with which this may be accomplished, the revenue and expense items from the adjusted trial balance of Paul Allen are rearranged into an income statement in Illustration 12 on page 70; and the items representing the assets, liabilities, and owner's equity are rearranged into a formal balance sheet in Illustration 13 on page 71.

When the statements are prepared from an adjusted trial balance, the income statement is normally prepared first. This is because the amount

Illustration 12

PAUL ALLEN TAXICAB COMPANY
Adjusted Trial Balance, July 31, 1959

Cash	$ 895	
Prepaid rent	200	
Gasoline	54	
Taxicabs	10,000	
Accumulated depr., taxicabs. .		$ 200
Garage equipment . . .	800	
Accum. depr., garage equip. .		10
West Supply Company. . .		400
Coast Oil Company. . . .		135
Wages payable.		30
Paul Allen, capital. . . .		11,000
Paul Allen, withdrawals. .	200	
Taxicab fares.		2,150
Despatcher's wages. . .	270	
Drivers' commissions . .	1,075	
Telephone and utilities. .	40	
Rent expense	100	
Gasoline consumed . . .	81	
Depr. expense, taxicabs. .	200	
Depr. expense, garage equip.	10	
	$13,925	$13,925

PREPARING THE INCOME STATEMENT
FROM THE ADJUSTED TRIAL BALANCE

PAUL ALLEN TAXICAB COMPANY
Income Statement for Month Ended July 31, 1959

Temporary accounts

Revenue:		
Taxicab fares		$2,150
Operating expenses:		
Despatcher's wages. . .	$ 270	
Drivers' commissions. . .	1,075	
Telephone and utilities . .	40	
Rent expense.	100	
Gasoline consumed . . .	81	
Depreciation expense, taxicabs. . .	200	
Depreciation expense, garage equipment.	10	
Total Operating Expenses. . .		1,776
Net Income.		$ 374

Illustration 13

PAUL ALLEN TAXICAB COMPANY
Adjusted Trial Balance, July 31, 1959

Account	Debit	Credit
Cash	$ 895	
Prepaid rent	200	
Gasoline	54	
Taxicabs	10,000	
Accumulated depr., taxicabs		200
Garage equipment	800	
Accum. depr., garage equip.		10
West Supply Company		400
Coast Oil Company		135
Wages payable		30
Paul Allen, capital		11,000
Paul Allen, withdrawals	200	
Taxicab fares		2,150
Despatcher's wages	270	
Drivers' commissions	1,075	
Telephone and utilities	40	
Rent expense	100	
Gasoline consumed	81	
Depr. expense, taxicabs	200	
Depr. expense, garage equip.	10	
	$13,925	$13,925

PAUL ALLEN TAXICAB COMPANY
Balance Sheet, July 31, 1959

ASSETS

Current Assets:
Cash	$ 895	
Prepaid rent	200	
Gasoline	54	
Total Current Assets		$ 1,149

Fixed Assets:
Taxicabs	$10,000		
Less: Accumulated depreciation	200	$ 9,800	
Garage equipment	$ 800		
Less: Accumulated depreciation	10	790	
Total Fixed Assets			10,590
Total Assets			$11,739

LIABILITIES

Current Liabilities:
West Supply Company	$ 400	
Coast Oil Company	135	
Wages payable	30	
Total Liabilities		$ 565

PROPRIETORSHIP

Paul Allen, capital, July 1, 1959			$11,000
July net income		$ 374	
Less: Withdrawals		200	
Net increase in capital			174
Paul Allen, capital, July 31, 1959			11,174
Total Liab. and Prop.			$11,739

July net income from the July income statement

of the net income, as calculated on the income statement, is needed in completing the proprietorship section of the balance sheet. Observe on the balance sheet in Illustration 13 how the net income from the income statement is combined with the withdrawals and the excess of the net income over the withdrawals, $174, is added to Allen's July 1 capital to secure the amount of his July 31 capital.

Arrangement of the Accounts in the Ledger

In the first part of this chapter it was shown that asset, liability, proprietorship, revenue, and expense accounts are classified and arranged on the statements in such a manner as to make the statements more useful. Likewise, accounts are classified and logically arranged in the ledger. A logical arrangement of the ledger accounts has two purposes: (1) It aids in locating any account, and (2) it aids in the preparation of the statements. Obviously, statements can be prepared with the least difficulty if the accounts are arranged in the ledger in the order of their appearance on the statements. Arranging accounts in the ledger in the order of their statement appearance causes the accounts to appear on the adjusted trial balance in the order of their statement arrangement. This aids in rearranging the adjusted trial balance items into a balance sheet and an income statement. Consequently, the balance sheet accounts beginning with the first current asset, cash, and ending with the proprietorship accounts appear first in the ledger. These are followed by the revenue and expense accounts in the order of their appearance on the income statement.

QUESTIONS FOR CLASS DISCUSSION

1. Is the item "net income" as reported on an income statement the exact amount of income earned? Why?
2. Why is the period of time covered by an income statement of extreme significance?
3. What is a classified income statement?
4. What is the advantage of an account form balance sheet? A report form balance sheet?
5. What are the characteristics of a current asset? A fixed asset?
6. If a current asset is an item that will be realized in cash or consumed within one year, how would you classify a note receivable that the owner intends to hold to its maturity which is three years hence?
7. Why are prepaid expenses classified as current assets?
8. Why are adjustments usually necessary before statements can be prepared at the end of an accounting period?
9. If at the end of an accounting period an asset account called "Postage" has a debit balance of $235 and there is $45 worth of postage stamps on hand, what adjustment is required?
10. Would it be possible to keep accounting records in such a manner that end-of-the-period adjustments of the accounts were not necessary? Explain.
11. What is a contra account?

12. If a firm's sales employees are paid a total of $250 per weekly pay period beginning on Monday and ending on Friday, what adjustment is required if the accounting period ends on Tuesday? On Thursday?

13. Under what sort of a situation might it be wise to record the payment of a prepaid expense as an expense? Why?

14. On October 1 the Grand Theatre debited Prepaid Insurance for $360. This was the amount of the premium on a three-year liability policy paid that day. What adjustment is required when the accounting period ends on December 31? What are the effects on the balance sheet and income statement prepared on December 31 if the adjustment is not made?

15. On January 1 of the current year the balance of the Advertising Supplies account of the Grand Theatre was $172. During the year $312 of advertising supplies were purchased. On December 31 an inventory showed $154 of advertising supplies on hand. What adjustment is required? What are the effects on the balance sheet and income statement if the adjustment is not made?

PROBLEMS

Problem 4-1

The Downtown Realty Company operates with annual accounting periods that end each December 31. On December 31 of the current year, after the year's transactions were recorded, a trial balance of the firm's ledger appeared as follows:

DOWNTOWN REALTY COMPANY
Trial Balance, December 31, 19—

Cash	$ 800	
Office supplies	140	
Prepaid insurance	180	
Office equipment	1,650	
Accumulated depreciation, office equipment		$ 330
Automobile	2,850	
Accumulated depreciation, automobile		750
Merit Publishing Company		120
Martin Gibbs, capital		3,410
Martin Gibbs, withdrawals	4,800	
Commissions earned		10,600
Salaries expense	3,100	
Advertising expense	380	
Rent expense	1,200	
Telephone expense	110	
	$15,210	$15,210

Required:

1. Open the ledger accounts of the trial balance plus these additional accounts: Office Supplies Used; Expired Insurance; Depreciation of Office Equipment; Depreciation of Automobile; and Salaries Payable. Enter the trial balance amounts in the accounts.

2. Use the following information to prepare and post adjusting entries to the accounts:

   a) An inventory of office supplies showed $35 of office supplies on hand.

   b) An examination of the insurance policies showed that $120 of the prepaid insurance had expired.

c) Estimated depreciation on the office equipment amounted to $165 and on the automobile, $300.

d) Two days' wages amounting to $20 had been earned by the office clerk but were unpaid on December 31 because they were not due.

3. Prepare an adjusted trial balance, income statement, and a classified report form balance sheet.

Problem 4–2

Deluxe Cleaners operate with accounting periods that are one year in length. On December 31 of the current year their accounting period ended and the following trial balance was taken from their ledger:

DELUXE CLEANERS

Trial Balance, December 31, 19—

Cash	$ 780	
Hoffman Hotel	140	
Cleaning supplies	368	
Prepaid insurance	174	
Cleaning equipment	6,130	
Accumulated depreciation, cleaning equipment		$ 1,610
Delivery equipment	3,200	
Accumulated depreciation, delivery equipment		1,350
Building	18,000	
Accumulated depreciation, building		4,000
Land	3,000	
Cleaning Supply Company		280
Mortgage payable		8,000
Charles Jenkins, capital		9,742
Charles Jenkins, withdrawals	4,200	
Cleaning and pressing receipts		21,200
Cleaning plant wages	6,240	
Heat, light, and power	340	
Delivery wages	3,100	
Gas, oil, and repairs	510	
	$46,182	$46,182

Required:

1. Open the accounts of the trial balance plus these additional accounts: Cleaning Supplies Used; Insurance Expense, Cleaning Plant; Insurance Expense, Delivery Equipment; Depreciation Expense, Cleaning Equipment; Depreciation Expense, Delivery Equipment; Depreciation Expense, Building; and Wages Payable. Enter the trial balance amounts in the accounts under the date of December 31.

2. Use the following information to prepare and post adjusting journal entries:

a) Cleaning supplies on hand, $54.

b) An examination of the insurance policies showed that $70 of insurance on the cleaning plant and $65 of insurance on the delivery equipment had expired.

c) Estimated depreciation on the cleaning equipment, $580; on the delivery equipment, $340; and on the building, $420.

d) There were earned but unpaid wages due the cleaning plant employees of $25 and the delivery truck driver of $15.

3. After posting the adjusting entries prepare an adjusted trial balance, a classified income statement, and a classified report form balance sheet.

Problem 4–3

Placed side by side in the columns below are the trial balance and the adjusted trial balance of the Alhambra Theatre:

ALHAMBRA THEATRE

Trial Balance and Adjusted Trial Balance, December 31, 19—

	Trial Balance		Adjusted Trial Balance	
Cash.....................................	$ 1,500	$.....	$ 1,500	$......
Advertising supplies.....................	450	.....	75	......
Prepaid insurance.......................	310	.....	70	......
Office supplies..........................	160	.....	50	......
Office equipment........................	1,350	.....	1,350	......
Accumulated depreciation, office equipment..	.....	680	......	815
Projection and sound equipment...........	5,400	.....	5,400	......
Accumulated depreciation, projection and sound equipment.....................	.....	1,600	......	2,200
Theatre furniture.......................	3,600	.....	3,600	......
Accumulated depreciation, theatre furniture .	.....	600	......	960
Building................................	53,000	.....	53,000	......
Accumulated depreciation, building........	.....	23,000	......	23,860
Land...................................	5,000	.....	5,000	......
Notes payable..........................	.....	2,000	......	2,000
Fox Films..............................	.....	250	......	250
Blair Sound Equipment Company...........	.....	2,400	......	2,400
Wages payable..........................	.....	.....	......	250
Mortgage payable........................	.....	14,000	......	14,000
Robert Knott, capital....................	.....	16,655	......	16,665
Robert Knott, withdrawals................	5,200	.....	5,200	......
Admissions revenue......................	.....	38,200	......	38,200
Salaries and wages......................	14,600	.....	14,850	......
Office supplies used......................	.....	.....	110	......
Depreciation of office equipment...........	.....	.....	135	......
Film rentals............................	5,350	.....	5,350	......
Advertising............................	2,300	.....	2,675	......
Heat, light, and power...................	615	.....	615	......
Depreciation of building..................	.....	.....	860	......
Expired insurance.......................	.....	.....	240	......
Depreciation of projection and sound equip..	.....	.....	600	......
Depreciation of theatre furniture..........	.....	.....	360	......
Equipment repairs......................	210	.....	210	......
Interest expense........................	350	.....	350	......
	$99,395	$99,395	$101,600	$101,600

Required:

Analyze the foregoing trial balances and prepare in general journal form the adjusting entries that were made by the Alhambra Theatre.

CLASS EXERCISES

Exercise 4–1

1. What was the balance of the Prepaid Insurance account after the 1959 adjusting entries were posted if: (a) the balance of the account on January 1, 1959, was $154; (b) insurance premiums totaling $96 were paid during the year; and (c) $178 of insurance expired during the year?

2. How much prepaid insurance did a firm's December 31, 1958, balance sheet show if: (a) its December 31, 1959, balance sheet showed $310 of prepaid insurance; (b) the firm paid $215 of insurance premiums during 1959; and (c) during 1959 $235 of insurance expired?

3. How many dollars of office supplies were bought during a year if: (a) the balance of the Office Supplies account at the beginning of the year was $114; (b) the balance of the account at the end of the year was $134; and (c) $197 of office supplies were used during the year?

4. How many dollars of store supplies were used during a year if: (a) the balance of the store supplies account at the beginning of the year was $187; (b) store supplies costing $248 were purchased; and (c) $143 of store supplies were on hand at the end of the year?

Exercise 4–2

A business the annual accounting period of which ends on December 31 has one employee who is paid $20 per day and who works a five-day week which ends on Friday. The last Friday of the current year fell on December 27, and the employee was paid in full on that date; however, he worked the following Monday and Tuesday, December 30 and 31.

Required:

1. Give in general journal form the adjusting entry to record the accrued wages.
2. Assume the foregoing adjusting entry was not made and tell the effect of the omission on the current year's income statement and balance sheet.
3. Assume that the omission of the foregoing adjusting entry was not discovered during the succeeding accounting period. Tell the effect on the succeeding year's income statement.

SUPPLEMENTARY PROBLEMS

Problem 4–A

An inexperienced bookkeeper prepared the first of the following two income statements, but he forgot to adjust the ledger account balances before preparing the statement. However, the oversight was discovered and the second correct statement was prepared. Analyze the two statements and prepare the entries in general journal form for the adjustments that were made between the construction of the two statements.

WESTERN COMPANY

Income Statement for Year Ended December 31, 19—

Revenue:		
Commissions earned..............................		$11,904.25
Operating expenses:		
Salaries expense.................................	$3,050.00	
Rent expense.....................................	900.00	
Advertising expense..............................	320.12	
Water and electricity.............................	88.06	
Telephone expense................................	121.51	
Gas, oil, and repairs.............................	237.65	
Total Operating Expenses......................		4,717.34
Net Income......................................		$ 7,186.91

WESTERN COMPANY
Income Statement for Year Ended December 31, 19—

Revenue:		
Commissions earned...............................		$11,904.25
Operating expenses:		
Salaries expense...................................	$3,081.50	
Rent expense......................................	900.00	
Advertising expense...............................	320.12	
Water and electricity..............................	96.38	
Telephone expense.................................	121.51	
Gas, oil, and repairs...............................	237.65	
Office supplies used................................	142.12	
Expired insurance.................................	82.18	
Depreciation of office equipment....................	157.00	
Depreciation of automobile.........................	315.50	
Total Operating Expenses......................		5,453.96
Net Income.......................................		$ 6,450.29

Problem 4–B

At the close of business on the last day of an annual accounting period the following trial balance was taken from the ledger of the Gem Laundry:

GEM LAUNDRY
Trial Balance, December 31, 19—

Cash..	$ 1,340	
City Barber Shop..................................	62	
Tower Hotel.......................................	106	
Laundry supplies..................................	604	
Prepaid insurance.................................	380	
Laundry equipment................................	11,300	
Accumulated depreciation, laundry equipment.............		$ 2,540
Delivery trucks....................................	4,900	
Accumulated depreciation, delivery trucks................		2,170
Scott Supply Company..................................		160
Ralph Graham, capital..............................		13,242
Ralph Graham, withdrawals.........................	7,200	
Laundry receipts..................................		29,592
Laundry wages....................................	11,512	
Rent expense......................................	2,400	
Utilities expense..................................	480	
Truck drivers' wages...............................	6,802	
Gas, oil, and repairs...............................	618	
	$47,704	$47,704

The following information for adjusting entries was available:

a) Inventory of unused laundry supplies, $111.
b) Expired insurance, laundry equipment, $88; and expired insurance, delivery trucks, $124.
c) Depreciation of laundry equipment, $530.
d) Depreciation of delivery trucks, $540.
e) Wages payable to the laundry workers, $168; and to the truck drivers, $22.

f) On the trial balance date there were unpaid and unrecorded personal property taxes on the laundry equipment amounting to $204. The taxes were applicable to the year ended on the trial balance date.

Required:

1. Open the ledger accounts of the trial balance plus these additional accounts: Laundry Supplies Used; Insurance Expense, Laundry; Insurance Expense, Delivery Trucks; Depreciation of Laundry Equipment; Depreciation of Delivery Trucks; Wages Payable; Property Taxes, Laundry Equipment; and Property Taxes Payable.
2. Enter the trial balance amounts in the accounts.
3. Prepare and post adjusting entries.
4. Prepare an adjusted trial balance, a classified income statement, and a report form balance sheet.

Chapter 5

THE WORK SHEET; CLOSING THE ACCOUNTS

In the problems of the previous chapter, at the end of an accounting period, after all transactions were recorded:

1. Adjusting entries were entered in the journal and posted to the ledger accounts.
2. After this, an adjusted trial balance was prepared and used in the construction of a formal income statement and a formal balance sheet.

Recording and posting adjusting entries before the statements are prepared is a satisfactory procedure for a small business. However, if a company has more than a very few ledger accounts and a very few adjustments, errors in adjusting the accounts and constructing the statements are less apt to be made if a *work sheet* is prepared and the statements are constructed from it before the adjusting entries are actually entered in the journal and posted.

The Work Sheet

A work sheet is a columnar tool of the accountant upon which he (1) achieves the effect of adjusting the accounts without entering the adjustments in the accounts, (2) sorts the adjusted account balances into columns according to whether they are used in preparing the income statement or the balance sheet, and (3) calculates and proves the mathematical accuracy of the net income. Actually, the work sheet is a tool for bringing together in an orderly manner the information used in preparing the statements, the adjusting journal entries, and the closing entries. (Closing entries will be discussed later in this chapter.)

Preparation of the Work Sheet

The Paul Allen Taxicab Company of the previous chapters does not have a sufficient number of accounts or adjustments to actually warrant the preparation of a work sheet. However, since its transactions and adjustments are familiar, they may be used to illustrate the preparation and use of a work sheet.

During July, Paul Allen completed the following transactions:

1. Invested $11,000 in a taxicab business.
2. Paid three months' rent in advance, $300.
3. Paid $10,000 for four taxicabs.
4. Purchased on credit from the West Supply Company equipment valued at $800.

5. Purchased 500 gallons of gasoline from Coast Oil Company on credit, $135.
6. Paid the cab despatcher's wages for the first two weeks of July, $120.
7. Received $890 in cab fares.
8. Paid the drivers' commissions of $445.
9. Paid the West Supply Company $400 on account.
10. Paid the despatcher's wages for the second two weeks of July.
11. Received $1,260 in additional cab fares during the last half of July.
12. Paid the drivers' commissions amounting to $630.
13. Paid the telephone and other utilities, $40.
14. Withdrew $200 for his personal living expenses.

On July 31, after these transactions were recorded, but BEFORE ANY ADJUSTING ENTRIES WERE PREPARED AND POSTED, a trial balance of the ledger of Paul Allen appears as in Illustration 14. Notice

Illustration 14

PAUL ALLEN TAXICAB COMPANY
Trial Balance, July 31, 1959

Cash	$ 895	
Prepaid rent	300	
Gasoline	135	
Taxicabs	10,000	
Garage equipment	800	
West Supply Company.		$ 400
Coast Oil Company.		135
Paul Allen, capital.		11,000
Paul Allen, withdrawals.	200	
Taxicab fares.		2,150
Despatcher's wages	240	
Drivers' commissions	1,075	
Telephone and utilities.	40	
	$13,685	$13,685

that the illustrated trial balance is an UNADJUSTED TRIAL BALANCE. The accounts have not been adjusted for rent expired, gasoline consumed, depreciation, and the accrued despatcher's wages. Nevertheless, this unadjusted trial balance is the starting point in the preparation of a work sheet, and it is copied in the first two money columns of the work sheet.

The Work Sheet Illustrated

Note that the work sheet shown in Illustration 15 has five pairs of money columns. The first pair of money columns is labeled "Trial Balance." In this first pair of columns is copied the unadjusted trial balance of the Paul Allen ledger. Often in the construction of a work sheet the trial balance is prepared for the first time in the first two money columns of a work sheet.

The second pair of columns is labeled "Adjustments"; and the adjustments are entered in this second pair of columns. In the work sheet shown in Illustration 15, the adjustments used are the same adjustments for

Illustration 15

Paul Allen Taxicab Company
Work Sheet for Month Ended July 31, 1959

ACCOUNT TITLES	TRIAL BALANCE DR.	TRIAL BALANCE CR.	ADJUSTMENTS DR.	ADJUSTMENTS CR.	ADJUSTED TRIAL BALANCE DR.	ADJUSTED TRIAL BALANCE CR.	INCOME STATEMENT DR.	INCOME STATEMENT CR.	BALANCE SHEET DR.	BALANCE SHEET CR.
Cash	895 00				895 00				895 00	
Prepaid rent	300 00			(a) 100 00	200 00				200 00	
Gasoline	135 00			(b) 81 00	54 00				54 00	
Taxicabs	10,000 00				10,000 00				10,000 00	
Garage equipment	800 00				800 00				800 00	
Test Supply Co.		400 00				400 00				400 00
Coast Oil Company		135 00				135 00				135 00
Paul Allen, capital		11,000 00				11,000 00				11,000 00
Paul Allen, withdrawals	200 00				200 00				200 00	
Taxicab fares		2,150 00				2,150 00		2,150 00		
Dispatcher's wages	240 00		(a) 30 00		270 00		270 00			
Drivers' commissions	1,075 00				1,075 00		1,075 00			
Telephone & utilities	40 00				40 00		40 00			
Rent expense			(a) 100 00		100 00		100 00			
Gasoline consumed			(b) 81 00		81 00		81 00			
Depr. expense, taxicabs			(c) 200 00		200 00		200 00			
Accum. depr., taxicabs				(c) 200 00		200 00				200 00
Depr. exp., garage equip.			(d) 10 00		10 00		10 00			
Accum. depr., garage equip.				(d) 10 00		10 00				10 00
Wages payable				(a) 30 00		30 00				30 00
	13,685 00	13,685 00	421 00	421 00	13,925 00	13,925 00	1,776 00	2,150 00	12,149 00	11,775 00
Net income							374 00			374 00
							2,150 00	2,150 00	12,149 00	12,149 00

which adjusting journal entries were prepared and posted in the previous chapter, prior to the construction of the statements. Note that the adjustments on the illustrated work sheet are keyed together with letters. When a work sheet is prepared, after it and the statements are completed, the adjusting entries still have to be recorded in the journal and posted to the ledger. At that time the key letters of the work sheet adjustments help to identify the related debits and credits of each adjustment. Explanations of the adjustments on the Paul Allen work sheet are:

Adjustment (a) To adjust for the amount of rent expired.
Adjustment (b) To adjust for the amount of gasoline consumed.
Adjustment (c) To adjust for the depreciation of the taxicabs.
Adjustment (d) To adjust for the depreciation of the garage equipment.
Adjustment (e) To adjust for the accrued despatcher's wages.

Each adjustment on the Paul Allen work sheet required the writing in of one or two additional account names below the original trial balance. These accounts did not have balances when the original trial balance was prepared; and, consequently, were not listed in the original trial balance. Often, when a work sheet is prepared, the effects of the adjustments are anticipated; and any additional accounts required by the adjustments are provided, without amounts, in the body of the trial balance.

When a work sheet is prepared, after the adjustments are entered in the Adjustments columns, the Adjustment columns are totaled to prove the equality of the adjustments.

The third set of work sheet columns is labeled "Adjusted Trial Balance." In constructing a work sheet each individual amount in the Trial Balance columns is combined with its adjustment in the Adjustments columns, if there is an adjustment, and is entered in the Adjusted Trial Balance columns. For example, the Prepaid Rent account has a $300 debit balance in the Trial Balance columns. This $300 debit in the Trial Balance columns is combined with the $100 credit in the Adjustments columns to give the Prepaid Rent account a $200 debit balance in the Adjusted Trial Balance columns. Rent Expense has no balance in the Trial Balance columns, but it has a debit of $100 in the Adjustments columns. Therefore, no balance combined with a $100 debit gives Rent Expense a $100 debit in the Adjusted Trial Balance columns. Cash, West Supply Company, and several other accounts have trial balance amounts but no adjustments. As a result, their trial balance amounts are carried unchanged into the Adjusted Trial Balance columns. Notice that the result of combining the amounts in the Trial Balance columns with the amounts in the Adjustments columns is an adjusted trial balance in the Adjusted Trial Balance columns.

After the amounts in the Trial Balance columns are combined with the amounts in the Adjustments columns and carried to the Adjusted Trial Balance columns, the Adjusted Trial Balance columns are added to prove their equality. After the equality of the Adjusted Trial Balance columns is proved, the amounts in these columns are sorted to the proper Balance Sheet and Income Statement columns. The assets are transferred to the Balance Sheet debit column. The liabilities and the balance of the Capital account go to the Balance Sheet credit column. The balances of the accumulated depreciation accounts represent subtractions from assets; consequently, they are placed in the Balance Sheet credit column. Likewise, the balance of the Withdrawals account represents a subtraction from proprietorship and is placed in the Balance Sheet debit column. The revenues are placed in the Income Statement credit column and the expenses in the Income Statement debit column.

After the amounts are sorted to the proper columns, the columns are totaled. After the columns are totaled, the difference between the debit total and the credit total of the Income Statement columns is the net income or net loss. The difference is the net income or net loss because revenues are entered in the credit column and expenses are entered in the debit column. If the credit column total exceeds the debit column total, the difference is a net income. If the debit column total exceeds the credit column total, the difference is a net loss. In the Paul Allen work sheet, the credit column total exceeds the debit column total, and the result is a net income of $374.

On the Paul Allen work sheet, after the net income is determined in the Income Statement columns, it must be added to the total of the Balance Sheet credit column. The reason for this is that with the exception of the balance of the Capital account, the amounts appearing in the Balance Sheet columns are "end-of-the-period" balances. Therefore, it is necessary to add the net income to the total of the Balance Sheet credit column to make the Balance Sheet columns equal. Adding the net income to the Balance Sheet credit column has the effect of adding the net income to the Capital account. This is necessary because the "end-of-the-period" assets in the Balance Sheet debit column are not equal to the "end-of-the-period" liabilities plus the "beginning-of-the-period" proprietorship of $11,000 in the credit column. The "end-of-the-period" proprietorship, $11,000 plus $374, is required in balancing the columns. If a net loss had been incurred, it would have been necessary to add the amount of the loss to the debit column. This is because losses decrease proprietorship. Adding the loss to the debit column has the effect of subtracting the amount from the Capital account.

Balancing the Balance Sheet columns of a work sheet with the net income or net loss is a proof of the accuracy with which the work sheet has been prepared. If the net income or the net loss of the Income Statement columns balances the Balance Sheet columns, it is assumed that no errors have been made. However, if the net income or net loss does not make the Balance Sheet columns balance, it is proof that an error or errors have been made. The error or errors may have been either a mathematical error or errors, or an amount may have been sorted to a wrong column.

Although balancing the Balance Sheet columns with the net income or net loss is a proof of the accuracy with which the work sheet has been prepared, it is not an absolute proof. The Balance Sheet columns will balance even when errors have been made if the errors are of a certain type. For example, an expense carried into the Balance Sheet debit column or an asset carried into the debit column of the income statement section will cause both the Balance Sheet debit column and the Income Statement debit column to have incorrect totals. Likewise, the net income will be incorrect. However, when such an error is made, the Balance Sheet columns will still balance, but with the incorrect amount of net income. Because of this, when a work sheet is prepared, care must be taken to accurately sort the amounts in the Adjusted Trial Balance columns into the correct Income Statement or Balance Sheet columns.

Work Sheet and the Financial Statements

After a work sheet is completed, the items in its Income Statement columns are rearranged into a formal income statement, and the items in its Balance Sheet columns are rearranged into a formal balance sheet. Then, after the statements are completed, the adjustments in the work sheet Adjustments columns are used in preparing the adjusting entries.

The Work Sheet and Adjusting Entries

When a work sheet is used in the preparation of the statements, both the work sheet and the statements are prepared before the ledger accounts are adjusted. As a result, after the work sheet and the statements are completed, it is still necessary to prepare and post adjusting journal entries. Fortunately, when a work sheet is prepared, this is an easy task. It is easy because the adjusting journal entries may be taken directly from the Adjustments columns of the work sheet. When the adjusting journal entries are taken from the Adjustments columns, an adjusting journal entry is made for each adjustment in the Adjustments columns simply by debiting the account debited and crediting the account credited by each adjustment. To make the preparation of the entries still easier, at the time the work sheet is prepared each adjustment's debits and credits are keyed together with a letter.

Need for Closing Entries

In the first chapter of this text transactions were recorded by placing in columns increases and decreases in assets, liabilities, and proprietorship. In that chapter all increases and decreases in proprietorship, including revenues and expenses, were placed in a single column under the name of the proprietor. Actually, this is their effect. Revenues increase proprietorship and expenses decrease proprietorship; or, more accurately, over a period of time proprietorship is increased by the amount that revenues exceed expenses or decreased by the amount that expenses exceed revenues. However, as it was first pointed out in Chapter 2, although revenues and expenses increase and decrease proprietorship, they are not recorded in the proprietor's Capital account. Rather, numerous revenue and expense accounts are used to sort and classify these items so that the proprietor can have information as to the total amount of each individual kind of revenue and expense.

Information as to the total amounts of the various kinds of revenues and expenses is essential in the operation of business; but accumulating this information in numerous revenue and expense accounts makes it necessary periodically to close these accounts and to summarize and transfer their balances to the proprietor's capital account. Revenue and expense accounts are closed and their summarized balances are transferred to the Capital account at the end of each accounting period by means of *closing entries*.

Closing entries accomplish a dual purpose:

1. They transfer the net income or net loss accumulated in the revenue and expense accounts from the revenue and expense accounts to the proprietor's Capital account.
2. And they clear these accounts of their balances in preparation for recording the revenues and expenses of the next accounting period. (This point is discussed in more detail later in this chapter under the topic of ruling accounts.)

Effect of Closing Entries

Revenue and expense accounts are closed by means of closing entries that are entered in the General Journal and posted to the ledger accounts. Normally compound entries are used. However, the effects of closing entries are more readily apparent if each revenue and expense account is closed with a separate entry. Consequently, in the next few pages, separate entries are used to close the familiar accounts of Paul Allen; after which, compound closing entries are discussed.

At the end of July before his accounts were closed, but after his work sheet and statements were prepared and the adjusting entries were entered in the journal and posted, Paul Allen's proprietorship accounts had balances as shown in Illustration 16 on the next page.

Observe in Illustration 16 that Allen's Capital account shows only its July 1 balance of $11,000. This is not the amount of Allen's July 31 proprietorship; closing entries are required to make this account show the July 31 proprietorship.

Note also the third account in Illustration 16, the Income Summary account. This proprietorship account is used only at the end of the accounting period in summarizing and closing the revenue and expense accounts.

Closing the Revenue Accounts.   Before closing entries are made, revenue accounts have credit balances. To close and clear a revenue account of

Illustration 16

Paul Allen, Capital		
	July 1	11,000

Drivers' Commissions		
July 15	445	
31	630	

Paul Allen, Withdrawals		
July 31	200	

Telephone and Utilities		
July 31	40	

Income Summary	

Rent Expense		
July 31	100	

Gasoline Consumed		
July 31	81	

Taxicab Fares		
	July 15	890
	31	1,260

Depreciation Expense, Taxicabs		
July 31	200	

Despatcher's Wages		
July 13	120	
27	120	
31	30	

Depreciation Expense, Garage Equip.		
July 31	10	

its balance, a closing entry debiting the account and crediting Income Summary is required. Paul Allen has only one revenue account, and the entry to close and clear it is as follows:

July	31	Taxicab Fares..........................	2,150.00	
		Income Summary...................		2,150.00
		To close the Taxicab Fares account.		

Posting this entry has the following effect on the accounts:

Taxicab Fares			
July 31	2,150	July 15	890
		31	1,260

Income Summary			
		July 31	2,150

Note that the closing entry has a dual effect: (1) it transfers the balance of the revenue account to the credit side of the Income Summary account, and (2) it clears the Taxicab Fares account of its balance.

Closing the Expense Accounts. Before closing entries are prepared and posted, expense accounts have debit balances. Consequently, to close and clear an expense account of its balance, a closing entry debiting Income Summary and crediting the expense account is required. Paul Allen has seven expense accounts, and the entries to close and clear them are:

July	31	Income Summary............................ Despatcher's Wages.................. To close the Despatcher's Wages account.	270.00	270.00
	31	Income Summary............................ Drivers' Commissions.............. To close the Drivers' Commissions account.	1,075.00	1,075.00
	31	Income Summary............................ Telephone and Utilities............. To close the Telephone and Utilities account.	40.00	40.00
	31	Income Summary............................ Rent Expense..................... To close the Rent Expense account.	100.00	100.00
	31	Income Summary............................ Gasoline Consumed............... To close the Gasoline Consumed account.	81.00	81.00
	31	Income Summary............................ Depreciation Expense, Taxicabs...... To close the Depreciation Expense, Taxicabs account.	200.00	200.00
	31	Income Summary............................ Depreciation Expense, Garage Equipment............................. To close the Depreciation Expense, Garage Equipment account.	10.00	10.00

Posting these entries has the effect shown in Illustration 17. Note again that the effect is a dual effect: (1) the entries transfer the balances of the expense accounts to the debit side of the Income Summary account, and (2) they clear the expense accounts of their balances.

Closing the Income Summary Account. After all revenue and expense accounts are closed to Income Summary, the balance of the Income Summary account is equal to the amount of the net income or the net loss. If the revenues exceed the expenses, there is net income and the Income Summary account has a credit balance. On the other hand, if the expenses exceed revenues, there is a net loss and the account has a debit balance.

When there is net income, the credit balance of the Income Summary account is closed to the Withdrawals account with a closing entry that has a debit to Income Summary and a credit to the Withdrawals account.

Illustration 17

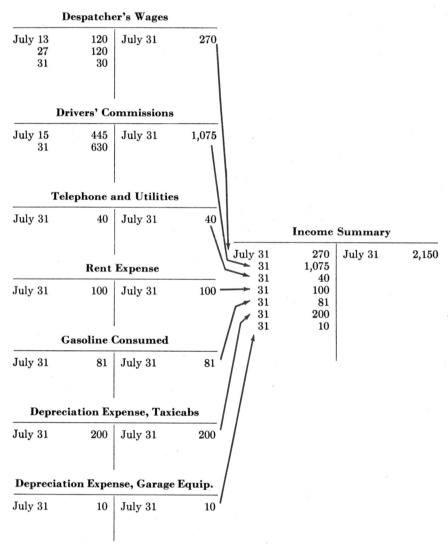

Despatcher's Wages			
July 13	120	July 31	270
27	120		
31	30		

Drivers' Commissions			
July 15	445	July 31	1,075
31	630		

Telephone and Utilities			
July 31	40	July 31	40

Rent Expense			
July 31	100	July 31	100

Gasoline Consumed			
July 31	81	July 31	81

Depreciation Expense, Taxicabs			
July 31	200	July 31	200

Depreciation Expense, Garage Equip.			
July 31	10	July 31	10

Income Summary			
July 31	270	July 31	2,150
31	1,075		
31	40		
31	100		
31	81		
31	200		
31	10		

Likewise, when there is a loss and a debit balance in the Income Summary account, the Income Summary account is closed with an entry having a debit to the Withdrawals account and a credit to Income Summary.

The Paul Allen Taxicab Company earned $374 during July. Consequently, after all of its revenue and expense accounts are closed, the balance of its Income Summary account is a credit balance of $374 and is closed to Paul Allen's Withdrawals account with an entry like the following:

July	31	Income Summary......................	374.00	
		Paul Allen, Withdrawals............		374.00
		To close the Income Summary account.		

Posting this entry has the following effect on the accounts:

Income Summary				Paul Allen, Withdrawals			
July 31	270	July 31	2,150	July 31	200	July 31	374
31	1,075						
31	40						
31	100						
31	81						
31	200						
31	10						
31	374						

Note again that the closing entry serves a dual purpose: (1) it closes and clears the Income Summary account of its balance, and (2) it transfers the amount of the net income to the Withdrawals account.

Closing the Withdrawals Account. Withdrawals from a business by the proprietor of cash and other assets for his personal use are called "withdrawals in anticipation of income" and are recorded on the debit side of his Withdrawals account. Consequently, after the Income Summary account is closed to the Withdrawals account, the balance of the Withdrawals account shows the excess or deficiency of income over withdrawals.

If there is an excess of income over withdrawals, the excess may be left in the Withdrawals account on the assumption that the proprietor will withdraw this amount for his personal use during the next accounting period. However, if the proprietor does not desire to withdraw the excess of income and plans to leave the amount permanently invested in the business, then the Withdrawals account is closed to the Capital account with an entry like the following:

July	31	Paul Allen, Withdrawals................	174.00	
		Paul Allen, Capital.................		174.00
		To close the Withdrawals account.		

Posting the entry has this effect on the accounts:

Paul Allen, Withdrawals				Paul Allen, Capital		
July 31	200	July 31	374		July 1	11,000
31	174				31	174

As previously stated, there are two reasons for closing entries. They are: (1) closing entries, by transferring the net income or net loss from the revenue and expense accounts through the Withdrawals account and on to the Capital account, bring the balance of the Capital account up to date; and (2) at the end of an accounting period, closing entries clear the revenue and expense accounts of their balances in preparation for the re-cording of the revenues and expenses of the new accounting period. An examination of the proprietorship accounts of Allen as shown above and on the previous few pages will reveal that both of these objectives have been accomplished as soon as his Withdrawals account is closed to his Capital account.

The Work Sheet and Closing Entries

In the previous few pages, in order better to show the effects of closing entries, a separate entry was used to close each revenue and expense account. This is not the normal practice. Normally, compound entries are used and the compound entries are taken from the Income Statement columns of the work sheet.

If the work sheet of Paul Allen on page 81 is examined, it will be seen that every account that has its balance extended into the Income Statement debit column has a debit balance in the ledger. In closing these accounts, Income Summary must be debited and the individual accounts credited. Consequently, time and effort are saved if, in the place of separate entries, a compound entry like the following is used:

July	31	Income Summary......................	1,776.00	
		Despatcher's Wages...............		270.00
		Drivers' Commissions..............		1,075.00
		Telephone and Utilities.............		40.00
		Rent Expense....................		100.00
		Gasoline Consumed...............		81.00
		Depreciation Expense, Taxicabs.....		200.00
		Depreciation Expense, Garage Equip-ment............................		10.00
		To close the temporary proprietorship accounts having debit balances.		

Note in the entry just given that each account that has its balance extended into the Income Statement debit column is credited and Income Summary is debited for the sum of all of the credits. In making the entry it is not necessary to add the individual credit amounts in order to secure the amount of the debit to Income Summary. The debit to Income Summary may be taken from the total of the Income Statement debit column (see page 81) on the work sheet.

The Paul Allen work sheet has only one amount in the Income Statement credit column. If there were more than one amount, a compound closing entry to close the amounts normally would be used.

Temporary Proprietorship Accounts

Revenue and expense accounts plus the Income Summary and Withdrawals accounts are called "temporary proprietorship accounts." A moment's thought will reveal the reason for this is that, in a sense, the items recorded in these accounts are only temporarily recorded therein. At the end of each accounting period the items, through their balances, are transferred out and on to the proprietor's Capital account.

Ruling the Temporary Proprietorship Accounts

After the closing entries are posted, the amounts appearing in the debit and credit columns of the temporary proprietorship accounts represent revenues, expenses, and withdrawals of an accounting period ended and closed. It is important that these amounts be set apart in the accounts from the revenues, expenses, and withdrawals of the next accounting period. Setting these amounts apart insures that they will not be included on the income statement of the new period. Closing entries are a step in setting the amounts apart. As a further step, all temporary proprietorship accounts are ruled after they are closed.

When the last closing entry is posted, the debit and credit amounts entered in each of the temporary proprietorship accounts are equal. To rule these temporary proprietorship accounts: (1) both the debit and credit sides of each account are totaled, and the totals are entered opposite each other on the first available full line. For example, see the Taxicab Fares account as it appears on page 94. If only one amount appears on each side of an account, the totals are not necessary. Note the Rent Expense account on page 95. (2) After the totals are entered where necessary, each account is ruled with double ruled lines across all columns except the Explanation columns. These double ruled lines are notice to the bookkeeper that the amounts above the rulings need not be considered in any future balance of the account.

Balancing and Ruling Open Accounts

After closing entries are posted, all temporary proprietorship accounts are in balance and are known as "closed accounts." However, at that time, most of the asset and liability accounts plus the proprietor's Capital account have balances and are said to be "open accounts."

At the time temporary proprietorship accounts are ruled, any open accounts the balances of which are not readily apparent at a glance may be balanced and the balances brought down as a convenience to the bookkeeper. To balance an open account:

1. The balance of the account with the word "balance" and the date is written on the side having the smaller total. When this balance is added to the smaller side, the total of the smaller side is then equal to the larger side.
2. Next, the totals of both sides are brought down opposite each other on the first available full line.
3. After the totals are brought down, the account is ruled with double ruled lines through all columns except the Explanation columns. (Again the double ruled lines are notice to the bookkeeper that he need consider nothing above the lines when calculating the new balance of the account.)
4. Then, the word "balance" and the amount of the balance is written on the next line below the rulings on the side that had the larger total. For example, see the Cash account shown below. Note the check marks in the

Cash — PAGE 1

DATE	EXPLANATION	FO-LIO	DEBIT	DATE	EXPLANATION	FO-LIO	CREDIT
1959				1959			
July 1		1	11,000.00	July 1		1	300.00
15	13,150.00	1	890.00	3		1	10,000.00
31	12,255.00	2	1,260.00	13		1	120.00
	895.00		13,150.00	15		1	445.00
				23		1	400.00
				27		1	120.00
				31		2	630.00
				31		2	40.00
				31		2	200.00
				31	Balance	✓	12,255.00
							895.00
			13,150.00				13,150.00
aug 1	Balance	✓	895.00				

Prepaid Rent — PAGE 2

DATE	EXPLANATION	FO-LIO	DEBIT	DATE	EXPLANATION	FO-LIO	CREDIT
1959				1959			
July 1		1	300.00	July 31		2	100.00

Gasoline — PAGE 3

DATE	EXPLANATION	FO-LIO	DEBIT	DATE	EXPLANATION	FO-LIO	CREDIT
1959				1959			
July 7		1	135.00	July 31		2	81.00
				31	Balance	✓	54.00
			135.00				135.00
aug. 1	Balance	✓	54.00				

Taxicabs   PAGE 4

DATE	EXPLANATION	FO-LIO	DEBIT	DATE	EXPLANATION	FO-LIO	CREDIT
1959 July 3		1	1 0 0 0 00				

Accumulated Depreciation, Taxicabs   PAGE 5

DATE	EXPLANATION	FO-LIO	DEBIT	DATE	EXPLANATION	FO-LIO	CREDIT
				1959 July 31		2	20 00

Garage Equipment   PAGE 6

DATE	EXPLANATION	FO-LIO	DEBIT	DATE	EXPLANATION	FO-LIO	CREDIT
1959 July 5		1	80 00				

Accumulated Depreciation, Garage Equipment   PAGE 7

DATE	EXPLANATION	FO-LIO	DEBIT	DATE	EXPLANATION	FO-LIO	CREDIT
				1959 July 31		2	1 00

West Supply Company   PAGE 8

DATE	EXPLANATION	FO-LIO	DEBIT	DATE	EXPLANATION	FO-LIO	CREDIT
1959 July 23		1	40 00	1959 July 5		1	80 00

Coast Oil Company   PAGE 9

DATE	EXPLANATION	FO-LIO	DEBIT	DATE	EXPLANATION	FO-LIO	CREDIT
				1959 July 7		1	1 35 00

Wages Payable   PAGE 10

DATE	EXPLANATION	FO-LIO	DEBIT	DATE	EXPLANATION	FO-LIO	CREDIT
				1959 July 31		2	3 00

Paul Allen, Capital — PAGE 11

DATE	EXPLANATION	FOLIO	DEBIT	DATE	EXPLANATION	FOLIO	CREDIT
				1959 July 1		1	11000 00
				31		3	174 00

Paul Allen, Withdrawals — PAGE 12

DATE	EXPLANATION	FOLIO	DEBIT	DATE	EXPLANATION	FOLIO	CREDIT
1959 July 31		2	200 00	1959 July 31		3	374 00
31		3	174 00				
			374 00				374 00

Income Summary — PAGE 13

DATE	EXPLANATION	FOLIO	DEBIT	DATE	EXPLANATION	FOLIO	CREDIT
1959 July 31		3	1776 00	1959 July 31		3	2150 00
		3	374 00				
			2150 00				2150 00

Taxicab Fares — PAGE 14

DATE	EXPLANATION	FOLIO	DEBIT	DATE	EXPLANATION	FOLIO	CREDIT
1959 July 31		3	2150 00	1959 July 15		1	890 00
				31		2	1260 00
			2150 00				2150 00

Despatcher's Wages — PAGE 15

DATE	EXPLANATION	FOLIO	DEBIT	DATE	EXPLANATION	FOLIO	CREDIT
1959 July 15		1	120 00	1959 July 31			270 00
31		1	120 00				
31		2	30 00				
			270 00				270 00

Drivers' Commissions — PAGE 16

DATE	EXPLANATION	FOLIO	DEBIT	DATE	EXPLANATION	FOLIO	CREDIT
1959 July 15			445 00	1959 July 31		3	1075 00
31			630 00				
			1075 00				1075 00

Telephone and Utilities　　　　PAGE 17

DATE	EXPLANATION	FO-LIO	DEBIT	DATE	EXPLANATION	FO-LIO	CREDIT
1959 July 31		2	40 00	1959 July 31		3	40 00

Rent Expense　　　　PAGE 18

DATE	EXPLANATION	FO-LIO	DEBIT	DATE	EXPLANATION	FO-LIO	CREDIT
1959 July 31		2	100 00	1959 July 31		3	100 00

Gasoline Consumed　　　　PAGE 19

DATE	EXPLANATION	FO-LIO	DEBIT	DATE	EXPLANATION	FO-LIO	CREDIT
1959 July 31		2	81 00	1959 July 31		3	81 00

Depreciation Expense, Taxicabs　　　　PAGE 20

DATE	EXPLANATION	FO-LIO	DEBIT	DATE	EXPLANATION	FO-LIO	CREDIT
1959 July 31		2	200 00	1959 July 31		3	200 00

Depreciation Expense, Garage Equipment　　　　PAGE 21

DATE	EXPLANATION	FO-LIO	DEBIT	DATE	EXPLANATION	FO-LIO	CREDIT
1959 July 31		2	10 00	1959 July 31		3	10 00

Folio columns of the lines on which the balances are entered. These check marks indicate that the amounts were not posted from the journal.

After adjusting and closing entries are posted and the accounts are balanced and ruled, the accounts of Paul Allen appear as just shown. (Note in the Income Summary account that a compound entry was used in closing the expense accounts.)

The Post-Closing Trial Balance

It is not difficult to make errors in adjusting and closing the accounts. Consequently, after all adjusting and closing entries are posted and the accounts are balanced and ruled, a new trial balance is prepared to retest the equality of the open accounts. This new, after-closing trial balance is called a *post-closing trial balance;* and for Paul Allen it appears as follows:

PAUL ALLEN TAXICAB COMPANY
Post Closing Trial Balance, July 31, 1959

Cash	$ 895	
Prepaid rent	200	
Gasoline	54	
Taxicabs	10,000	
Accumulated depreciation, taxicabs		$ 200
Garage equipment	800	
Accumulated depr., garage equipment		10
West Supply Company.		400
Coast Oil Company.		135
Wages payable.		30
Paul Allen, capital.		11,174
	$11,949	$11,949

The Accounting Cycle

The life of every business is divided into accounting periods. Each accounting period is a re-occurring accounting cycle, beginning with transactions recorded in a journal and ending with a post-closing trial balance. All of the steps in the cycle have now been presented. A knowledge of accounting requires that each step be understood and that the relationship of each step to the others be seen. The steps of the accounting cycle in the order of their occurrence are:

1. *Journalizing* . . . . Analyzing and recording transactions in a journal.
2. *Posting* . . . . Transferring the debits and credits of journal entries to debits and credits in the ledger.
3. *Preparing a trial balance* . . . . Summarizing the ledger accounts and testing the accuracy of the recording procedure.
4. *Constructing a work sheet* . . . . Affecting the adjustment of the accounts without the necessity of making entries in the ac-

counts. Then sorting the account balances into balance sheet and income statement accounts to obtain the income or loss.

5. *Preparing the statements* .... Rearranging the information of the work sheet into a balance sheet and an income statement.

6. *Adjusting the ledger accounts* .... Preparing adjusting journal entries from information in the Adjustments columns of the work sheet and posting the entries in order to bring the account balances up to date.

7. *Closing the temporary proprietorship accounts* .. Preparing and posting entries that close the temporary proprietorship accounts and transfer the net income or net loss to proprietorship.

8. *Balancing and ruling accounts* .... Separating the entries of one accounting period from the entries of the next.

9. *Preparing a post-closing trial balance* .... Proving the accuracy of the adjusting and closing procedure.

Accounting Periods and the Natural Business Year

In order to shorten the material presented, textbooks commonly use problems and illustrations in which businesses operate with accounting periods one month in length. In actual practice monthly accounting periods are seldom if ever used. An occasional business will close its books every three or every six months. However, almost all businesses operate with annual accounting periods or accounting periods one year in length.

Any accounting period of twelve consecutive months is known as a *fiscal year*. A fiscal year or annual accounting period may coincide with the calendar year, or it may follow the *natural business year*. The natural business year of a company begins and ends when the business activity of the company is at its lowest point. For example, in the automobile sales business the natural business year begins October 1, just before the new models are brought out, and ends the following September 30. When accounting periods follow the natural business year, the books are closed when inventories of goods for sale are at their lowest point and when the pressure of business activity is at its lowest ebb.

QUESTIONS FOR CLASS DISCUSSION

1. Is it possible to complete the work of statement preparation and of adjusting and closing the accounts without preparing a work sheet? What is gained by the preparation of a work sheet?

2. At what stage in the accounting process is a work sheet prepared?

3. From where are the amounts that are entered in the Trial Balance columns of a work sheet obtained?

4. Why are the adjustments in the Adjustments columns of a work sheet keyed together with letters?

5. What is the result of combining the amounts in the Trial Balance columns with the amounts in the Adjustments columns of a work sheet?

6. Why must care be exercised in sorting the items in the Adjusted Trial Balance columns to the proper Income Statement or Balance Sheet columns?

7. In extending the items in the Adjusted Trial Balance columns of a work sheet, what would be the result of extending: (a) an expense into the Balance Sheet debit column; (b) a liability into the Income Statement credit column; and (c) a revenue into the Balance Sheet debit column? Would each of these errors be automatically detected on the work sheet? Which would be automatically detected? Why?

8. Why are revenue and expense accounts called "temporary proprietorship accounts"?

9. What two purposes are accomplished by recording closing entries?

10. What accounts are affected by closing entries? What accounts are not affected?

11. Explain the difference between adjusting and closing entries.

12. What is the purpose of the Income Summary account?

13. Why are temporary proprietorship accounts ruled at the end of each accounting period?

14. Which ledger accounts may be balanced, ruled, and the balances brought down? Why are such ledger accounts balanced and ruled and their balances brought down?

15. Why is a post-closing trial balance prepared?

16. A bookkeeping student's post-closing trial balance listed "Depreciation expense, building, $672." What did this indicate?

PROBLEMS

Problem 5–1

Jefferis Repair Service operates with annual accounting periods that end on September 30. On September 30 of the current year a trial balance of their ledger appeared as follows:

JEFFERIS REPAIR SERVICE

Trial Balance, September 30, 19—

Cash	$ 953	
Repair supplies	825	
Prepaid insurance	203	
Repair equipment	8,426	
Accumulated depreciation, repair equipment		$ 2,303
Wadman Wholesale Company		112
Leland Jefferis, capital		5,786
Leland Jefferis, withdrawals	4,800	
Repair receipts		14,240
Salaries expense	4,980	
Rent expense	1,800	
Advertising expense	454	
	$22,441	$22,441

Required:

1. Enter the trial balance amounts in the Trial Balance columns of a work sheet and complete the work sheet using the following information:

  a) An inventory of repair supplies showed $215 of supplies on hand.

   b) Insurance premiums expired, $161.
   c) Estimated depreciation of repair equipment, $804.
   d) Wages earned by the employees but unpaid on the trial balance date, $60.
2. From the work sheet prepare a report form balance sheet and an income statement.
3. From the work sheet prepare adjusting entries and compound closing entries.

Problem 5–2

On November 1 of the current year Delbert Wade opened the Quick Service Shoe Repair Shop. During the month he completed the following transactions:

Nov. 1   Withdrew $1,000 from his personal bank account and deposited in the account of the shop.
     1   Paid the Joyce Realty Company $100, the rent on the shop space for one month.
     1   Paid the premium on a one-year insurance policy, $96.
     2   Signed a lease with National Equipment Company for the installation and use of shoe repair equipment. The lease called for a monthly rental of $40; Mr. Wade paid the first month's rent.
     4   Purchased on credit from Warner Equipment Company a showcase, chairs for the shop, and other shop furniture, $500.
     5   Purchased shop supplies on credit from Ajax Supply Company, $90.
     8   Paid for advertising on the local radio station, $25.
   15   Cash shoe repair receipts for the first half of the month, $72.
   20   Paid Warner Equipment Company $100 on account.
   25   Paid Ajax Supply Company in full.
   30   Cash shoe repair receipts for the last half of the month, $134.

Required work for November:

1. Open the following ledger accounts: Cash; Prepaid Insurance; Shop Supplies; Shop Furniture; Accumulated Depreciation, Shop Furniture; Warner Equipment Company; Ajax Supply Company; Delbert Wade, Capital; Delbert Wade, Withdrawals; Income Summary; Shoe Repair Receipts; Shop Rent; Equipment Rent; Advertising Expense; Expired Insurance; Shop Supplies Used; and Depreciation of Shop Furniture.
2. Prepare and post journal entries to record the November transactions.
3. Prepare a trial balance in the Trial Balance columns of a work sheet. Complete the work sheet using the following information:
   a) One month's insurance has expired.
   b) An inventory of shop supplies showed $40 of shop supplies on hand.
   c) Estimated depreciation on shop furniture, $10.
4. Prepare a November income statement and a balance sheet as of November 30.
5. From the work sheet prepare and post adjusting and compound closing entries.
6. Rule the temporary proprietorship accounts. Balance, rule, and bring down the balances of the open accounts, the balances of which are not readily apparent.
7. Prepare a post-closing trial balance.

During December Delbert Wade completed the following additional transactions for the Quick Service Shoe Repair Shop:

Dec. 1 Paid the Joyce Realty Company $100 rent on the shop space.
    1 Paid National Equipment Company the December rent on the shop equipment.
    4 Purchased on credit from Warner Equipment Company some additional chairs for the shop, $125.
    8 Purchased shop supplies on credit from Ajax Supply Company, $160.
   15 Cash shoe repair receipts for the first half of the month, $280.
   18 Paid for newspaper advertising that had appeared, $40.
   23 Paid Warner Equipment Company $400 on account.
   30 Withdrew $200 to be used for personal living expenses.
   31 Cash shoe repair receipts for the second half of the month, $305.

Required work for December:

1. Prepare and post journal entries to record the December transactions.
2. Prepare a trial balance in the Trial Balance columns of a work sheet. Complete the work sheet using the following information:
   a) One month's insurance has expired.
   b) An inventory of shop supplies showed $65 of shop supplies on hand.
   c) Estimated depreciation of shop furniture, $12.
3. Prepare a December income statement and a balance sheet as of December 31.
4. From the work sheet prepare and post adjusting and compound closing entries.
5. Rule the temporary proprietorship accounts. Balance, rule, and bring down the balances of the open accounts, the balances of which are not readily apparent.
6. Prepare a post-closing trial balance.

Problem 5–3

The following trial balance was taken from the ledger of the Gem Automatic Laundry at the end of its current annual accounting period:

GEM AUTOMATIC LAUNDRY
Trial Balance, December 31, 19—

Cash.	$ 1,780	
Laundry supplies.	422	
Prepaid insurance.	168	
Laundry equipment.	8,670	
Accumulated depreciation, laundry equipment.		$ 3,430
Packer-Scott Company.		120
Harvey Bell, capital.		6,000
Harvey Bell, withdrawals.	4,200	
Laundry receipts.		13,400
Salaries expense.	6,100	
Rent expense.	1,200	
Utilities expense.	362	
Miscellaneous expenses.	48	
	$22,950	$22,950

Required:

1. Open the ledger accounts of the trial balance plus these additional accounts: Income Summary; Laundry Supplies Used; Expired Insurance;

Depreciation of Laundry Equipment; Salaries Payable; and Rent Payable. Enter the trial balance amounts in the accounts.

2. Enter the account balances in the Trial Balance columns of a work sheet. Complete the work sheet using the following information:
   a) Laundry supplies inventory, $74.
   b) Expired insurance, $136.
   c) Estimated depreciation of laundry equipment, $515.
   d) Salaries payable, $82.
   e) The lease contract for the laundry building provides for a yearly rental equal to 10 per cent of the gross laundry receipts with a minimum of $100 per month, payable monthly, and the balance payable at the end of each year.

3. From the work sheet prepare an income statement and a report form balance sheet.

4. From the work sheet prepare and post adjusting entries and compound closing entries.

5. Rule the temporary proprietorship accounts. Balance, rule, and bring down the balances of the open accounts having two or more amounts.

6. Prepare a post-closing trial balance.

CLASS EXERCISES

Exercise 5–1

At the end of this exercise is a list of trial balance accounts and their balances. To simplify the problem and to save time the account balances are in numbers of not more than two integers. However, in order to increase your skill in sorting adjusted trial balance amounts to the proper columns, the accounts are listed in alphabetical order.

Required:

1. Prepare a work sheet form on ordinary notebook paper and enter the trial balance accounts and amounts on the work sheet in their alphabetical order.

2. Complete the work sheet using the following information:
   a) The supplies inventory shows $1.00 of supplies on hand.
   b) Wages earned but unpaid amount to $1.00.
   c) Prepaid rent expired, $4.00.
   d) Estimated depreciation on shop equipment, $1.00.

Trial Balance Accounts and Amounts

Accumulated depreciation on shop equipment............$ 4		Miscellaneous expenses..........$ 2	
Advertising expense.............	2	Notes payable..................	5
Cash.........................	5	Prepaid rent...................	6
Customer accounts..............	4	Revenue from service...........	24
George Cole, capital.............	10	Shop equipment................	11
George Cole, withdrawals........	1	Supplies......................	4
		Wages expense.................	8

SUPPLEMENTARY PROBLEMS

Problem 5–A

The Rex Theatre operates with annual accounting periods that end each December 31. On December 31 of the current year a trial balance of the firm's ledger appeared as follows:

REX THEATRE
Trial Balance, December 31, 19—

Cash	$ 1,520	
Advertising supplies	680	
Prepaid insurance	410	
Prepaid rent	3,000	
Theatre furniture	9,450	
Accumulated depreciation, theatre furniture		$ 3,130
Projection equipment	7,470	
Accumulated depreciation, projection equipment		1,960
Simplex Equipment Company		650
Lion Films		80
Larry Buttler, capital		17,130
Larry Buttler, withdrawals	4,800	
Admissions receipts		32,740
Rent of popcorn concession		1,200
Salaries and wages	13,520	
Film rentals	8,310	
Advertising expense	2,790	
Heat, light, and power	2,380	
Equipment repairs	560	
Theatre rent	2,000	
	$56,890	$56,890

Required:

1. Enter the trial balance amounts in the Trial Balance columns of a work sheet and complete the work sheet using the following information:
    a) An inventory of advertising supplies showed $110 of advertising supplies on hand.
    b) Insurance premiums amounting to $280 had expired.
    c) The theatre building rents for $500 per month. On January 1 of the current year six months' rent was paid in advance. July, August, September, and October rents were paid monthly as they became due on the first day of each of these months. The rent for November and December has not been paid.
    d) Estimated depreciation on the theatre furniture, $640; and (*e*) on the projection equipment, $510.
    f) Salaries and wages amounting to $170 have been earned by the employees but have not been paid.
2. Prepare an income statement and a balance sheet.
3. Prepare adjusting and closing entries.

Problem 5–B
O. K. Janitorial Service operates with annual accounting periods that end each October 31. On October 31 of the current year a trial balance of their ledger appeared as follows:

O. K. JANITORIAL SERVICE
Trial Balance, October 31, 19—

Cash	$ 1,218
Accounts receivable	1,397
Prepaid insurance	284
Cleaning supplies	347

Cleaning equipment..	$ 2,896	
Accumulated depreciation, cleaning equipment.............		$ 1,284
Trucks...	3,989	
Accumulated depreciation, trucks........................		2,146
Building...	12,600	
Accumulated depreciation, building......................		2,440
Land...	2,800	
Accounts payable.......................................		627
Mortgage payable.......................................		4,000
Richard Harmon, capital................................		12,299
Richard Harmon, withdrawals...........................	4,800	
Janitorial receipts......................................		23,623
Wages expense...	14,712	
Advertising expense....................................	324	
Gas, oil, and truck repairs..............................	798	
Miscellaneous expenses.................................	94	
Interest expense.......................................	160	
	$46,419	$46,419

Required:

1. Open the ledger accounts of the trial balance plus any additional accounts required. Enter the trial balance amounts in the accounts.
2. Enter the trial balance on a work sheet form and complete the work sheet using the following additional information:
   a) Expired insurance, $171.
   b) The cleaning supplies inventory showed $138 of cleaning supplies on hand. However, when this amount was subtracted from the balance of the Cleaning Supplies account, the amount remaining was not sufficiently large as to represent the amount of supplies used. (c) Consequently, the bookkeeper examined his records and found that a $215 purchase of cleaning supplies had been recorded as a purchase of cleaning equipment. (Make an adjustment to correct the error before making the adjustment to record the supplies used.)
   d) Depreciation was estimated at $310 on the cleaning equipment; (e) $804 on the trucks; and (f) $252 on the building.
   g) Wages amounting to $118 had been earned by the employees but were unpaid on the trial balance date.
   h) The $324 debit balance of the Advertising Expense account resulted from $198 of payments for newspaper advertising that had appeared and from a payment of $126 for advertising desk calendars that were to be distributed to customers and prospective customers beginning on December 15 of the new accounting period.
   i) Interest on the mortgage is at the rate of 6 per cent annually and is paid semiannually on each December 31 and June 30. The last interest payment was June 30, and consequently on the trial balance date there was an unrecorded liability for four months' interest.
3. From the work sheet prepare and post adjusting entries and compound closing entries.
4. Rule the temporary proprietorship accounts. Balance, rule, and bring down the balances of the open accounts, the balances of which are not readily apparent.
5. Prepare a post-closing trial balance.

Chapter

6

ACCOUNTING FOR A MERCHAN-
DISING BUSINESS

A SERVICE-TYPE enterprise depends upon sales of services for its earnings; a merchandising business differs in that it depends upon sales of goods or merchandise. However, although the two types differ as to the nature of their sales, the general principles presented in previous chapters as applicable to a service-type business apply to a merchandising business. The general principles apply, but since a merchandising business must account for the purchase, handling, and sale of a stock of merchandise, a merchandising business makes use of accounts and methods not previously discussed.

Merchandising Accounts

The accounts and methods used to record the transactions connected with purchasing, handling, and selling merchandise are:

The Purchases Account. When merchandise is purchased for later resale, its cost is debited to an account called *Purchases*, as follows:

Oct.	2	Purchases.............................	850.00	
		Eastlake Wholesale Company........		850.00
		Purchased merchandise on credit.		

The Purchases account has as its sole purpose the accumulation and summarization of the cost of all merchandise purchased during an accounting period. The account does not at any time show whether the merchandise purchased is on hand or has been disposed of through sale or other means.

The Purchases Returns and Allowances Account. Merchandise received from suppliers sometimes and for a variety of reasons is not acceptable to the purchaser and must be returned or, if kept, is kept only because the supplier grants an allowance or reduction in its price.

When merchandise is purchased and returned, or an allowance on its cost is received, the situation is the opposite of a purchase and could be recorded by a credit to the Purchases account. However, if returns and allowances are recorded in this manner, the entries in the Purchases account must be analyzed in order to learn the amount of returns and allowances. Consequently, in order to make such information readily available, returns and allowances on purchases are recorded in an account called *Purchases Returns and Allowances* with entries similar to the following:

Oct.	9	Eastgate Wholesale Company...........	54.00	
		Purchases Returns and Allowances....		54.00
		Returned merchandise previously purchased on credit.		

The Freight-In Account. Sometimes a manufacturer or wholesaler pays the freight, express, or other transportation costs on merchandise he sells, and the total cost of the goods to the purchaser is the amount paid the manufacturer or wholesaler. Other times the purchaser must pay transportation costs. When the purchaser pays the transportation charges on goods he has purchased, such charges are a proper addition to the cost of the goods and may be recorded by a debit to the Purchases account. However, more complete information is obtained if such costs are debited to an account called *Freight-In*, as follows:

Dec.	11	Freight-In...........................	24.50	
		Cash............................		24.50
		Paid express charges on merchandise purchased.		

When an income statement is prepared at the end of an accounting period, the balance of the Purchases Returns and Allowances account is subtracted from the balance of the Purchases account to secure *net purchases;* and then the balance of the Freight-In account is added to secure *net cost of purchases,* as follows:

```
Purchases . . . . . . . . . . . . .    $49,400
   Less: Purchases returns and allow-
      ances . . . . . . . . . . . . .       275
   Net purchases . . . . . . . . . . .  $49,125
      Add: Freight-in . . . . . . . . .    1,100
   Net Cost of Purchases . . . . . . .           $50,225
```

The Sales Account. When merchandise is sold, the transaction is recorded in most stores simply by debiting an asset account and crediting the *Sales* account for the selling price of the goods sold. For example, Nelson Hardware Company sold for $50 merchandise that cost $32. The company records the sale as follows:

Nov.	1	Cash (if the sale is for cash).............	50.00	
		Sales.............................		50.00
		Sold merchandise for cash.		
		or		
	1	Frank Smith (if the sale is on credit).....	50.00	
		Sales.............................		50.00
		Sold merchandise on credit.		

Each of the debits in the entries just given records an increase in an asset; the credits to Sales record the revenue from the merchandise sold.

The foregoing entries illustrate the methods of recording sales used in a *periodic inventory system* of accounting for merchandising transactions. Observe that in neither entry is the cost of the goods sold recorded. This is a distinguishing characteristic of the periodic inventory system. When such a system is used, cost of goods sold is not recorded at the time of a sale; rather, cost of goods sold is ignored in the accounts until the end of each accounting period when a periodic physical inventory or count of the unsold goods remaining is made and the cost of all of the goods sold during the period is calculated. (Both periodic inventories and the calculation of cost of goods sold are discussed in more detail later in this chapter.)

In passing it should be said that another system of accounting for merchandising transactions called the *perpetual inventory system* is sometimes used by companies that sell a limited variety of items having a rather high individual value. However, since the periodic inventory system is the more common, it is made the subject of this chapter, and a discussion of the perpetual inventory system is deferred until Chapter 12.

The Sales Returns and Allowances Account. Since a merchandising company depends for its earnings upon sales of merchandise, it is important that such a company watch carefully for signs of dissatisfaction among its customers with the merchandise they have purchased. Normally, a dissatisfied customer is permitted to return unsatisfactory merchandise and is either given a refund of his money or credit on his account for the merchandise returned. Sometimes a customer is permitted to keep the unsatisfactory merchandise and is granted a reduction in the sales price or an allowance on the sales price. Either a return or an allowance has the reverse effect of a sale and could be recorded by means of debits in the Sales account. However, as in the case of purchases returns and allowances, it is important that the amounts of returns and allowances be accumulated in such a manner that their total is readily available. Consequently, returns and allowances are commonly recorded and accumulated in an account called *Sales Returns and Allowances*, with entries like the following:

Dec.	15	Sales Returns and Allowances...........	35.00	
		Frank Welch.....................		35.00
		Customer returned merchandise.		

When an income statement is prepared, sales returns and allowances are deducted on it from sales to show *net sales,* as follows:

NELSON HARDWARE COMPANY
Income Statement for Year Ended December 31, 19--

Revenue:
Gross sales $79,300
Less: Sales returns and allowances. . . .   650
Net Sales $78,650

The Merchandise Inventory Account.   In order to satisfy the needs of its customers, a merchandising business must keep a stock of merchandise on hand at all times. Consequently, such a company begins and ends an accounting period with merchandise on its shelves and in its stock room. The merchandise on hand at the beginning of a period is known as *the beginning inventory* and that on hand at the end of a period is known as *the ending inventory.* Furthermore, since accounting periods follow one after another, the ending inventory of one period is always the beginning inventory of the next.

When a periodic inventory system is in use, no effort is made throughout an accounting period to keep a record of the merchandise on hand. Rather, periodically, at the end of each accounting period, the cost of the merchandise on hand is determined by (1) physically counting the items of merchandise on the shelves in the store and in the stock room, and (2) multiplying the count for each item by its cost. After the dollar amount of all the ending inventory is determined in this manner, it is used in calculating the cost of goods sold and is entered in an account called *Merchandise Inventory,* where it remains as the record of the amount of the inventory at the end of the period ended and of the beginning of the new period.

It should be emphasized at this point that entries are made in the Merchandise Inventory account only at the end of each accounting period; that during a period the Merchandise Inventory account does not show the amount of merchandise on hand; and that, after a period begins, the Merchandise Inventory account becomes a historical account, the balance of which shows only the cost of the merchandise that was on hand at the beginning of the period.

Calculating Cost of Goods Sold

As previously stated, a company using a periodic inventory system makes no effort to keep track of the cost of the goods it sells. Consequently, at the end of an accounting period, when such a company wishes to learn its net income for the period, it must first calculate the cost of the goods it has sold during the period. To make this calculation, information must be available as to:

1. The cost of the beginning inventory of merchandise.
2. The net cost of goods purchased.
3. The cost of the ending inventory of merchandise.

At the end of an accounting period (1) the balance of the Merchandise Inventory account shows the cost of the beginning inventory; (2) the balances of the Purchases, Purchases Returns and Allowances, and Freight-In accounts carry the information as to the net cost of purchases; and (3) a physical inventory or count of the unsold merchandise on hand is made to learn the ending inventory.

At the end of an accounting period, as soon as the ending inventory of unsold goods is completed, the information as to the beginning inventory, net cost of purchases, and the ending inventory are combined as follows to compute the cost of goods sold during the period:

Cost of goods sold:

Merchandise inventory, January 1, 19--		$ 7,750
Purchases	$49,400	
Less: Purchases returns and allowances	275	
Net purchases	$49,125	
Add: Freight-in	1,100	
Net cost of purchases		50,225
Goods available for sale		$57,975
Merchandise inventory, December 31, 19--		8,950
Cost of Goods Sold		$49,025

A merchandising business has available for sale and may sell during an accounting period the goods it had on hand at the beginning of the period plus any goods purchased during the period. If it sells all of these goods, then its cost of goods sold is equal to the cost of the goods that were available for sale. However, if any goods remain on hand unsold at the end of an accounting period, then the cost of goods sold is equal to the cost of the goods available for sale less the cost of the ending inventory of unsold goods. Observe that this is the essence of the cost of goods sold calculation just illustrated.

Merchandising Accounts on the Income Statement

A classified income statement of a merchandising firm has three sections: (1) the revenue section, (2) the cost of goods sold section, and (3) the operating expenses section. Each of these sections appears on the income statement of Nelson Hardware Company in Illustration 18.

Observe in the income statement of Illustration 18 how cost of goods sold is subtracted from net sales to secure *gross profit from sales*. Gross profit from sales is the amount of "profit" before operating expenses are subtracted.

In the income statement of Nelson Hardware Company, Illustration 18, note how the operating expenses are classified as either "Selling expenses" or "General and administrative expenses." Selling expenses include the expenses of storing and preparing goods for sale, promoting sales, actually making sales, and, if there is not a delivery department separate from the selling departments, the expenses of delivering goods to customers. General and administrative expenses include the general office, accounting, personnel, and credits and collections expenses.

Sometimes an expenditure should be divided or prorated part to selling expenses and part to general and administrative expenses. Nelson Hardware Company divided the rent on their store building in this manner, as an examination of Illustration 18 will reveal. However, it did not prorate its insurance expense because the amount involved was so small that the company felt the extra exactness did not warrant the extra work. (The prorating of expenses is discussed in more detail in Chapter 9.)

Illustration 18

NELSON HARDWARE COMPANY

Income Statement for Year Ended December 31, 19--

Revenue:			
Gross sales			$79,300
Less: Sales returns and allowances. .			650
Net sales			$78,650
[new section]			
Cost of goods sold:			
Merchandise inventory, January 1, 19--		$ 7,750	
Purchases	$49,400		
Less: Purchases returns and allowances	275		
Net purchases	$49,125		
Add: Freight-in	1,100		
Net cost of purchases		50,225	
Goods available for sale.		$57,975	
Merchandise inventory, December 31, 19--		8,950	
Cost of goods sold.			49,025
Gross profit from sales			$29,625
Operating expenses:			
Selling expenses:			
Sales salaries	$ 8,200		
Rent expense, selling space	· 4,800		
Advertising expense	900		
Freight-out and delivery expense. . .	1,350		
Store supplies used	425		
Depreciation expense, store equipment	775		
Total Selling Expenses.		$16,450	
General and administrative expenses:			
Office salaries	$ 3,100		
Rent expense, office space.	600		
Expired insurance	65		
Office supplies used.	125		
Depreciation expense, office equipment	160		
Total General and Administrative			
Expenses.	4,050		
Total Operating Expenses.		20,500	
Net Income.		$ 9,125	

Merchandising Accounts on the Work Sheet

In many respects the accounting records and accounting methods of a merchandising business are just like those of a service-type business. Both types of companies record transactions in journals and post to ledger accounts. Both balance their accounts and enter the account balances on work sheets. Both complete their work sheets and use them in the preparation of their financial statements. Both record and post adjusting and closing entries, and both prepare post-closing trial balances. However, because of its merchandising operations, a merchandising business does use accounts that are not used by a service-type business, and these accounts do require special work sheet treatment.

The special work sheet treatment of the merchandising accounts is

demonstrated in Illustration 19 where the handling of the Sales, Sales Returns and Allowances, Purchases, Purchases Returns and Allowances,
Freight-In, and Merchandise Inventory accounts is emphasized by showing these accounts and their amounts in color.

The accounts of a merchandising business, other than the merchandising accounts, are treated on the work sheet in the same manner as are the
accounts of a service-type business. This treatment was discussed in
Chapter 5 and needs no further discussion here.

Trial Balance Columns. The Trial Balance columns of the Nelson
Hardware Company's work sheet, Illustration 19, shows the balances of
the company's accounts as of December 31, 19—. The account balances
were taken from the company's ledger of that date. The balances of the
merchandising accounts indicate that:

1. The January 1 beginning of the year merchandise inventory was $7,750.
2. Sales totaling $79,300 were made during the year.
3. Customers returned $650 worth of the merchandise they had purchased.
4. The year's purchases of merchandise amounted to $49,400.
5. Merchandise purchases totaling $275 were returned.
6. Freight, express, and postage amounting to $1,100 was paid on shipments
   of merchandise purchased.

Adjustments Columns and Adjusted Trial Balance Columns. Generally none of the merchandise accounts require adjustments. Consequently, no adjustments appear opposite these accounts in the Adjustments columns and the unadjusted trial balance amounts are carried
directly into the Adjusted Trial Balance columns.

Cost of Goods Sold Columns. In preparing a work sheet for a merchandising business, many accountants like to add an additional pair of
money columns. These are the "Cost of Goods Sold" columns. They are
added between the Adjusted Trial Balance columns and the Income
Statement columns and are used in summarizing and calculating the cost
of goods sold.

The calculation of cost of goods sold is the same whether it is made on
a work sheet or on an income statement. On the income statement of
Nelson Hardware Company, as shown in Illustration 18, the calculation
appears as follows:

```
Cost of goods sold:
  Merchandise inventory, January 1,
    19--  . . . . . . . . . . . . . .              $ 7,750
  Purchases. . . . . . . . . . . .    $49,400
    Less: Purchases returns and
      allowances . . . . . . . . .        275
  Net purchases. . . . . . . . .     $49,125
    Add: Freight-in. . . . . . . .     1,100
  Net cost of purchases. . . . . .                 50,225
  Goods available for sale . . . .               $57,975
  Merchandise inventory, December
    31, 19--  . . . . . . . . . . .                 8,950
      Cost of goods sold . . . . .               $49,025
```

Illustration 19

NELSON HARDWARE COMPANY
Work Sheet for Year Ended December 31, 19—

Account Titles	Trial Balance Dr.	Trial Balance Cr.	Adjustments Dr.	Adjustments Cr.	Adjusted Trial Balance Dr.	Adjusted Trial Balance Cr.	Cost of Goods Sold Dr.	Cost of Goods Sold Cr.	Income Statement Dr.	Income Statement Cr.	Balance Sheet Dr.	Balance Sheet Cr.
Cash	2,400				2,400						2,400	
Accounts receivable	3,300				3,300						3,300	
Merchandise Inventory	**7,750**				**7,750**		7,750					
Prepaid insurance	195			(a) 65	130						130	
Store supplies	590			(b) 425	165						165	
Office supplies	185			(c) 125	60						60	
Store equipment	7,910				7,910						7,910	
Accumulated depreciation, store equipment		3,200		(d) 775		3,975						3,975
Office equipment	1,590				1,590						1,590	
Accumulated depreciation, office equipment		250		(e) 160		410						410
Accounts payable		1,700				1,700						1,700
George Nelson, capital		14,095				14,095						14,095
George Nelson, withdrawals	4,800				4,800						4,800	
Sales		79,300				79,300				79,300		
Sales returns and allowances	650				650				650			
Purchases	49,400				49,400		49,400					
Purchases returns and allowances		275				275		275				
Freight-in	1,100				1,100		1,100					
Sales salaries	8,200				8,200				8,200			
Rent expense, selling space	4,800				4,800				4,800			
Advertising expense	900				900				900			
Freight-out and delivery expense	1,350				1,350				1,350			
Office salaries	3,100				3,100				3,100			
Rent expense, office space	600				600				600			
	98,820	98,820										
Expired insurance			(a) 65		65				65			
Store supplies used			(b) 425		425				425			
Office supplies used			(c) 125		125				125			
Depreciation expense, store equipment			(d) 775		775				775			
Depreciation expense, office equipment			(e) 160		160				160			
			1,550	1,550	99,755	99,755						
Merchandise inventory to Balance Sheet Columns **Cost of goods sold to Income Statement Columns**								8,950 · 49,025	49,025		8,950	
							58,250	58,250	70,175	79,300	29,305	20,180
Net Income									9,125			9,125
									79,300	79,300	29,305	29,305

Observe in the foregoing calculation of cost of goods sold that beginning inventory, purchases, and freight-in are added and that purchases returns and allowances and the ending inventory are subtracted. Or, in other words, that cost of goods sold is equal to:

1. The sum of:
   Beginning inventory.........................$ 7,750.00
   Purchases.................................. 49,400.00
   Freight-in................................. 1,100.00
                                                           $58,250.00
2. Minus the sum of:
   Purchases returns and allowances..............$ 275.00
   Ending inventory.......................... 8,950.00   9,225.00
                                                           $49,025.00

Keep this last calculation in mind and observe that it is the same calculation that is effected in the Cost of Goods Sold columns of the work sheet in Illustration 19.

1. Observe in the Cost of Goods Sold columns of Illustration 19 that the amounts of the beginning inventory, purchases, and freight-in are carried into the Cost of Goods Sold debit column where their sum becomes the column total. Remember that these are the "addition items" of the cost of goods sold calculation.
2. Notice that the balance of the Purchases Returns and Allowances account and the amount of the ending inventory are placed in the Cost of Goods Sold credit column. Remember that these items are the "subtraction items" of the cost of goods sold calculation.
3. And then note that the difference between (1) the sum of the items in the Cost of Goods Sold debit column, and (2) purchases returns and allowances and ending inventory in the Cost of Goods Sold credit column is equal to cost of goods sold. Observe that this difference, the cost of goods sold, is entered in the Cost of Goods Sold credit column and the Income Statement debit column.

Direct Entry of the Ending Inventory. At the end of an accounting period, before closing entries are posted, the dollar amount of the ending inventory does not appear in any account. As previously stated, this dollar amount is determined at the end of each period by counting the number of items of each kind of merchandise on hand and multiplying the count of each item by its cost. Commonly the accounting department is given the inventory sheets showing the counts of each item of merchandise, and it is the duty of the accounting department to apply the cost prices and complete the multiplications and additions to learn the total dollar amount of the ending inventory.

When the total dollar amount of the ending inventory is learned, it is entered directly on the work sheet in the Cost of Goods Sold credit column and the Balance Sheet debit column, as in Illustration 19. This direct entry on the work sheet accomplishes two purposes. First, entering the ending inventory in the Cost of Goods Sold credit column effects the subtraction of the ending inventory, along with purchases returns and allowances, from the "addition items" in the Cost of Goods Sold debit column. And, second, since the ending inventory is an end-of-the-period asset, entering it in the Balance Sheet debit column places this item in position to be added to the other assets and to appear on the balance sheet.

Cost of Goods Sold on the Work Sheet.   When a work sheet like that of Illustration 19 is being prepared, after the amount of the ending inventory is entered directly in the Cost of Goods Sold credit column and the Balance Sheet debit column, the difference between the items in the Cost of Goods Sold debit column and the amounts shown for the ending inventory and purchases returns and allowances in the Cost of Goods Sold credit column is equal to the cost of goods sold. As a last step in handling the items in the Cost of Goods Sold columns, this difference, the cost of goods sold, is entered in both the Cost of Goods Sold credit column and the Income Statement debit column. This step also accomplishes two purposes. First, placing the amount of the cost of goods sold in the Cost of Goods Sold credit column makes the two Cost of Goods Sold columns equal. Second, since cost of goods sold is subtracted from net sales to secure the gross profit from sales, entering the cost of goods sold in the Income Statement debit column effects this subtraction on the work sheet.

Income Statement Columns.   On the formal income statement prepared for a merchandising business, sales returns and allowances are subtracted from sales to secure net sales. After this, the cost of goods sold is subtracted from net sales to secure gross profit. These same subtractions are made on the work sheet of a merchandising firm. They are effected by entering the balance of the Sales account in the Income Statement credit column and entering both the balance of the Sales Returns and Allowances account and the cost of goods sold in the Income Statement debit column. In effect, sales in the Income Statement credit column less sales returns and allowances in the Income Statement debit column equal net sales. Likewise, sales in the Income Statement credit column less both sales returns and allowances and cost of goods sold in the income Statement debit column equal gross profit.

Balance Sheet Columns.   No new techniques are required in completing the Balance Sheet columns of a merchandising company's work sheet; consequently, no additional discussion of these columns is required here.

Preparing the Statements; Adjusting Entries

In any business, after the work sheet is completed, the statements are prepared and adjusting and closing entries are entered in a journal and are posted. The financial statements of a merchandising business are prepared from the work sheet just as are the financial statements of a service-type business. When Cost of Goods Sold columns are used, the income statement is prepared from the information in the Cost of Goods Sold and Income Statement columns; the balance sheet is prepared from the information in the Balance Sheet columns; and no essentially new techniques are required in the preparation of either. Likewise, no new techniques are required in the preparation of a merchandising company's adjusting entries. Each adjustment in the Adjustments columns of its work sheet requires an adjusting entry just as in a service-type company. However, although there are no essential differences in the preparation of the statements and adjusting entries for the two types of companies, there are differences in the closing entries when Cost of Goods Sold columns are used.

Closing Entries *for work sheet pg 111*

A company that uses a work sheet having Cost of Goods Sold columns may also, and probably will, use a Cost of Goods Sold account in closing its accounts, the balances of which enter into the calculation of the cost of goods sold.

When such columns and such an account are used, closing entries like the following are prepared and posted. The entries given were prepared from the work sheet of Illustration 19.

Notice that the first of the illustrated closing entries closes the Mer-

Dec.	31	Cost of Goods Sold......................	58,250.00	
		Merchandise Inventory.............		7,750.00
		Purchases........................		49,400.00
		Freight-In		1,100.00
		To close the cost of goods sold accounts having debit balances.		
	31	Purchases Returns and Allowances.......	275.00	
		Merchandise Inventory................	8,950.00	
		Cost of Goods Sold...............		9,225.00
		To close the Purchases Returns and Allowances account and to set up the ending inventory.		
	31	Income Summary......................	70,175.00	
		Sales Returns and Allowances.......		650.00
		Sales Salaries....................		8,200.00
		Rent Expense, Selling Space.........		4,800.00
		Advertising Expense..............		900.00
		Freight-Out and Delivery Expense...		1,350.00
		Office Salaries...................		3,100.00
		Rent Expense, Office Space.........		600.00
		Expired Insurance................		65.00
		Store Supplies Used...............		425.00
		Office Supplies Used..............		125.00
		Depr. Expense, Store Equipment....		775.00
		Depr. Expense, Office Equipment....		160.00
		Cost of Goods Sold...............		49,025.00
		To close the temporary proprietorship accounts having debit balances.		
	31	Sales................................	79,300.00	
		Income Summary.................		79,300.00
		To close the Sales account.		

Dec.	31	Income Summary...................... To close the Income Summary account.	9,125.00	
		George Nelson, Withdrawals........		9,125.00
	31	George Nelson, Withdrawals........... To close the Withdrawals account.	4,325.00	
		George Nelson, Capital.............		4,325.00

chandise Inventory, Purchases, and Freight-In accounts and transfers their balances to the debit side of the Cost of Goods Sold account, as is shown in Illustration 20.

Illustration 20

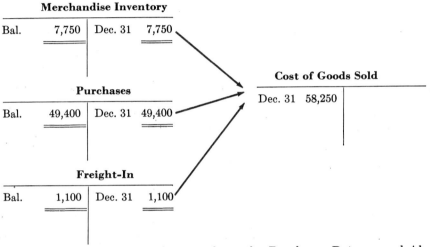

Observe that the second entry closes the Purchases Returns and Allowances account and also, in effect, subtracts the ending inventory from the other cost of goods sold items, setting up this ending inventory in the Merchandise Inventory account where it is a record of the merchandise on hand at the end of the period ended and also of the beginning of the new period.

Illustration 21

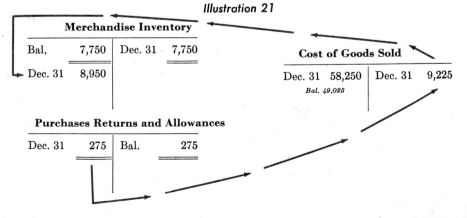

The effects of this second entry on the accounts is shown in Illustration 21. Notice in Illustration 21 that after the second entry is posted, the balance of the Cost of Goods Sold account is equal to the cost of the goods sold.

Finally, observe the last credit in the third closing entry. This credit closes the Cost of Goods Sold account and transfers its balance to the Income Summary account as follows:

Cost of Goods Sold			Income Summary	
Dec. 31 58,250	Dec. 31	9,225		
	31	49,025 ⟶ ⟶		
58,250		58,250		

Alternate Method for Handling the Cost of Goods Sold Accounts

As has just been demonstrated, when Cost of Goods Sold columns are placed on a work sheet, the balances of the accounts that enter into the calculation of cost of goods sold are summarized in these columns and their summarized amount, the cost of goods sold, is then carried into the Income Statement debit column of the work sheet. Likewise, when a Cost of Goods Sold account is used, the balances of the Merchandise Inventory, Purchases, Purchases Returns and Allowances, and Freight-In accounts are closed to and are summarized in the Cost of Goods Sold account, after which their summarized amount, the balance of the Cost of Goods Sold account, is closed to the Income Summary account. These are satisfactory procedures and are commonly used. However, some accountants prefer to shorten somewhat their end-of-the-period work by omitting these summarizing steps.

When the foregoing described summarizing steps are omitted, Cost of Goods Sold columns are not placed on the work sheet and the balances of the cost of goods sold accounts are carried directly into the Income Statement columns. Likewise, when the foregoing described summarizing steps are omitted, the Cost of Goods Sold account is not used and the cost of goods sold accounts are closed directly to the Income Summary account. Obviously the effect is the same whether the accounts are carried and closed directly or are first summarized and their summarized amount is carried and closed to the Income Statement columns and the Income Summary account. This may be readily seen by examining the work sheet of Illustration 22 which does not have Cost of Goods Sold columns and comparing this work sheet with the one shown in Illustration 19 which does have Cost of Goods Sold columns.

When a work sheet like that of Illustration 22 is used, the accounts are closed with compound closing entries like the following:

Illustration 22

NELSON HARDWARE COMPANY
Work Sheet for Year Ended December 31, 19—

Account Titles	Trial Balance Dr.	Trial Balance Cr.	Adjustments Dr.	Adjustments Cr.	Adjusted Trial Balance Dr.	Adjusted Trial Balance Cr.	Income Statement Dr.	Income Statement Cr.	Balance Sheet Dr.	Balance Sheet Cr.
Cash	2,400				2,400				2,400	
Accounts receivable	3,300				3,300				3,300	
Merchandise inventory	7,750				7,750		7,750			
Prepaid insurance	195			(a) 65	130				130	
Store supplies	590			(b) 425	165				165	
Office supplies	185			(c) 125	60				60	
Store equipment	7,910				7,910				7,910	
Accumulated depreciation, store equipment		3,200		(d) 775		3,975				3,975
Office equipment	1,590				1,590				1,590	
Accumulated depreciation, office equipment				(e) 160		410				410
Accounts payable		1,700				1,700				1,700
George Nelson, capital		14,095				14,095				14,095
George Nelson, withdrawals	4,800				4,800				4,800	
Sales		79,300				79,300		79,300		
Sales returns and allowances	650				650		650			
Purchases	49,400				49,400		49,400			
Purchases returns and allowances		275				275		275		
Freight-in	1,100				1,100		1,100			
Sales salaries	8,200				8,200		8,200			
Rent expense, selling space	4,800				4,800		4,800			
Advertising expense	900				900		900			
Freight-out and delivery expense	1,350				1,350		1,350			
Office salaries	3,100				3,100		3,100			
Rent expense, office space	600				600		600			
	98,820	98,820								
Expired insurance			(a) 65		65		65			
Store supplies used			(b) 425		425		425			
Office supplies used			(c) 125		125		125			
Depreciation expense, store equipment			(d) 775		775		775			
Depreciation expense, office equipment			(e) 160		160		160			
			1,550	1,550	99,755	99,755	79,400	88,525	29,305	20,180
Merchandise inventory to Balance Sheet Columns								8,950	8,950	
							88,525	88,525	29,305	29,305
Net Income							9,125			9,125
							88,525	88,525	29,305	29,305

Dec.	31	Income Summary......................	79,400.00	
		Merchandise Inventory.............		7,750.00
		Sales Returns and Allowances.......	)	650.00
		Purchases.........................		49,400.00
		Freight-In........................		1,100.00
		Sales Salaries.....................		8,200.00
		Rent Expense, Selling Space........		4,800.00
		Advertising Expense...............		900.00
		Freight-Out and Delivery Expense...		1,350.00
		Office Salaries....................		3,100.00
		Rent Expense, Office Space........		600.00
		Expired Insurance.................		65.00
		Store Supplies Used...............		425.00
		Office Supplies Used..............		125.00
		Depreciation Expense, Store Equip...		775.00
		Depreciation Expense, Office Equip...		160.00
		To close the temporary proprietorship accounts having debit balances.		
	31	Sales................................	79,300.00	
		Purchases Returns and Allowances.......	275.00	
		Merchandise Inventory.................	8,950.00	
		Income Summary.................		88,525.00
		To close the temporary proprietorship accounts having credit balances and to set up the ending inventory.		
	31	Income Summary......................	9,125.00	
		George Nelson, Withdrawals........		9,125.00
		To close the Income Summary account.		
	31	George Nelson, Withdrawals............	4,325.00	
		George Nelson, Capital.............		4,325.00
		To close the Withdrawals account.		

The foregoing closing entries were taken directly from the work sheet of Illustration 22. Compare these entries with the ones used when Cost of Goods Sold columns and a Cost of Goods Sold account are used. In the comparison observe that the method of the Cost of Goods Sold columns and account have the extra summarizing steps but that the effects are the same with either method.

QUESTIONS FOR CLASS DISCUSSION

1. How and when is cost of goods sold determined in a store using a periodic inventory system?

2. May a firm sell goods at a price above their cost and still suffer a loss? How?

3. Why should a firm be interested in the amount of its sales returns and allowances?

4. Since the total sales returns and allowances are subtracted from the balance of the Sales account on the income statement, why not save the effort of

this subtraction by debiting each sales return or allowance to the Sales account?

5. If a firm has the priviledge of returning for full credit all unsatisfactory merchandise purchased, why should it be interested in the amount of merchandise returned?

6. Which of the following are debited to the Purchases account of a grocery store: (a) the purchase of a cash register; (b) the purchase of a roll of wrapping paper; (c) the purchase of advertising space in a newspaper; and (d) the purchase of a case of tomato soup?

7. At the end of an accounting period which inventory, the beginning inventory or the ending, appears on the trial balance?

8. During a year a company purchased merchandise costing $25,000. What was the company's cost of goods sold if there were:
a) No beginning or ending inventories?
b) A beginning inventory of $11,000 and no ending inventory?
c) A beginning inventory of $8,000 and an ending inventory of $9,500?
d) No beginning inventory and an ending inventory of $7,000?

9. In counting the merchandise on hand at the end of an accounting period, a clerk failed to count, and consequently omitted from the inventory, all the merchandise on one shelf. If the cost of the merchandise on the shelf was $214, what was the effect of the omission on (a) the balance sheet, and (b) the income statement?

10. Suppose that the omission of the $214 of merchandise from the inventory (Question 9) was not discovered. What would be the effect on the balance sheet and income statement prepared at the end of the next accounting period?

11. What is summarized in the Cost of Goods Sold account? Is it necessary to use a Cost of Goods Sold account?

12. Copy the following tabulation and fill in the missing amounts. Indicate a loss by placing a minus sign before the amount. Each horizontal row of figures is a separate problem situation.

Sales	Begin- ning In- ventory	Purchases	Ending Inventory	Cost of Goods Sold	Gross Profit	Expenses	Net Income or Loss
80,000	50,000	40,000	35,000	55,000	45,000	20,000	2,000
90,000	35,000	60,000	45,000	50,000	?	25,000	15,000
125,000	50,000	60,000	40,000	70,000	55,000	35,000	20,000
16?	40,000	70,000	35,000	7,500	30,000	35,000	?
100,000	40,000	65,000	?	60,000	?	25,000	?
70,000	30,000	?	35,000	40,000	?	?	10,000
?	40,000	50,000	30,000	?	40,000	?	−5,000
75,000	?	50,000	35,000	43,000	30,000	?	10,000

PROBLEMS

Problem 6–1

Prepare general journal entries to record the following transactions:

Nov. 3   Sold merchandise to Jessie M. Smith for cash, $407.

     4   Purchased merchandise on credit from Abbot and Mason, $1,034.

4 Wrote a check to Western Railroad Company in payment of the freight charges on the merchandise purchased from Abbot and Mason, $78.

5 Sold merchandise on credit to James Carter, $183.

5 Paid freight charges on the shipment to James Carter, $18.

6 Returned for credit $205 of the merchandise purchased from Abbot and Mason on December 4.

7 James Carter returned for credit $22 of the merchandise purchased on December 5.

8 Purchased on credit from Valley Equipment Company a typewriter for use in the office, $205.

10 Sold merchandise for cash, $53.

11 Purchased office supplies from Office Supply Company on credit, $76.

12 The cash customer who purchased merchandise for cash on December 10 returned $10 worth of the merchandise and was refunded his money.

Problem 6–2

The following condensed trial balance was taken from the ledger of The Man's Shop at the end of its annual accounting period:

THE MAN'S SHOP
Trial Balance, December 31, 19—

Cash	$ 1,800	
Merchandise inventory	8,000	
Other assets	12,000	
Other liabilities		$ 4,400
A. L. Peiterson, capital		14,500
A. L. Peiterson, withdrawals	4,000	
Sales		52,300
Sales returns and allowances	500	
Purchases	30,000	
Purchases returns and allowances		300
Freight-in	200	
Selling expenses	10,000	
Administrative expenses	5,000	
	$71,500	$71,500

Required:

1. Copy the trial balance onto a twelve-column work sheet having Cost of Goods Sold columns. Complete the work sheet under the assumption that there are no adjustments and the ending inventory is $10,000.

2. Prepare an income statement from the work sheet.

3. Prepare compound closing entries from the work sheet. (A Cost of Goods Sold account should be used.)

4. After completing the foregoing, copy the trial balance onto a ten-column work sheet that does not have Cost of Goods Sold columns. Complete the work sheet.

5. Prepare compound closing entries from the ten-column work sheet. (A Cost of Goods Sold account should not be used.)

Problem 6–3

Valley Sports Center operates with annual accounting periods that end each December 31. On December 31 of the current year a trial balance of their ledger appeared as follows:

VALLEY SPORTS CENTER

Trial Balance, December 31, 19—

Cash..	$ 2,870	
Merchandise inventory...............................	15,245	
Store supplies......................................	810	
Prepaid insurance...................................	195	
Store equipment....................................	10,865	
Accumulated depreciation, store equipment..............		$ 3,340
Accounts payable...................................		3,110
Douglas Murphy, capital..............................		16,120
Douglas Murphy, withdrawals..........................	6,000	
Sales..		75,225
Sales returns and allowances..........................	1,875	
Purchases..	40,540	
Purchases returns and allowances......................		865
Freight-in..	970	
Sales salaries......................................	11,890	
Rent expense.......................................	6,000	
Advertising expense.................................	825	
Utilities expense....................................	575	
	$98,660	$98,660

Required:

1. Copy the trial balance into the Trial Balance columns of a twelve-column work sheet (Cost of Goods Sold columns) and complete the work sheet using the following information:
    a) Inventory of store supplies, $225.
    b) Expired insurance, $120.
    c) Estimated depreciation of store equipment, $1,150.
    d) Sales salaries payable, $145.
    e) Ending merchandise inventory, $17,860.
2. Prepare the trading section (net sales less cost of goods sold) of an income statement for the firm.
3. Prepare compound closing entries.

Problem 6–4

Required:

1. Copy the trial balance of the Valley Sports Center (Problem 6–3) into the Trial Balance columns of a ten-column work sheet (no Cost of Goods Sold columns) and complete the work sheet using the adjustments information of Problem 6–3.
2. Prepare the trading section of an income statement for the firm. (Skip this requirement if Problem 6–3 has also been assigned.)
3. Prepare compound closing entries.

Problem 6–5

The Town and Travel Shoppe operates with annual accounting periods that end each year on the last day of February. On February 28 of the current year a trial balance of their ledger appeared as follows:

TOWN AND TRAVEL SHOPPE
Trial Balance, February 28, 19—

Cash.	$ 3,735	
Accounts receivable.	6,430	
Merchandise inventory.	18,780	
Store supplies.	1,160	
Office supplies.	354	
Prepaid insurance.	246	
Office equipment.	2,570	
Accumulated depreciation, office equipment.		$ 953
Store equipment.	12,850	
Accumulated depreciation, store equipment.		4,357
Notes payable.		5,000
Accounts payable.		6,905
Catherine Jones, capital.		28,723
Catherine Jones, withdrawals.	5,400	
Sales.		91,323
Sales returns and allowances.	2,129	
Purchases.	57,932	
Purchases returns and allowances.		620
Freight-in.	642	
Sales salaries.	12,564	
Rent expense, selling space.	6,600	
Advertising expense.	758	
Delivery expense.	856	
Office salaries.	3,657	
Rent expense, office space.	600	
Telephone and utilities.	618	
	$137,881	$137,881

Required:

1. Enter the trial balance in the Trial Balance columns of a ten-column work sheet (no Cost of Goods Sold columns.) Complete the work sheet using the following information:
   a) Store supplies inventory, $185.
   b) Office supplies inventory, $127.
   c) Expired insurance, $174.
   d) Estimated depreciation on the office equipment, $251.
   e) Estimated depreciation on the store equipment, $1,325.
   f) Sales salaries amounting to $84 and office salaries amounting to $26 were earned but unpaid on the trial balance date.
   g) Merchandise inventory, $17,164.
2. From the work sheet prepare a classified income statement and a classified balance sheet.
3. From the work sheet prepare adjusting and closing entries.

CLASS EXERCISES

Exercise 6–1

At the end of this exercise is a list of trial balance accounts and their balances. To simplify the problem and to save time, the account balances are in numbers of not more than two integers. However, in order to increase your skill in sorting adjusted trial balance amounts to the proper columns, the accounts are listed in alphabetical order.

Required:

1. Prepare a twelve-column work sheet form (Cost of Goods Sold columns) on ordinary notebook paper.

2. Enter the trial balance accounts and their amounts on the work sheet in the order of their alphabetical listing.
3. Complete the work sheet using the following information:
   a) Rent expense for the period is $5.00.
   b) Inventory of store supplies, $1.00.
   c) Earned but unpaid salaries, $3.00.
   d) Estimated depreciation on the store equipment, $1.00.
   e) Ending merchandise inventory, $5.00.

Trial Balance Accounts and Amounts

Accumulated depreciation, store equipment	$ 1	Merchandise inventory	$ 4
		Prepaid rent	6
Advertising expense	4	Purchases	10
Cash	5	Purchases returns	1
Creditor accounts	2	Salary expense	5
Customer accounts	3	Sales	33
Freight-in	1	Sales returns	2
John Lear, capital	17	Store equipment	9
John Lear, withdrawals	2	Store supplies	3

Exercise 6–2

Prepare a ten-column work sheet form (no Cost of Goods Sold columns) on ordinary notebook paper. Enter the trial balance accounts and amounts of Exercise 6–1 on the ten-column work sheet. Complete the work sheet using the inventory and adjustments information of Exercise 6–1.

SUPPLEMENTARY PROBLEMS

Problem 6–A

Following are the unadjusted trial balance, income statement, and post-closing trial balance of the Duncan Sales Company as they appeared at the end of the 1959 accounting period. From the information on these statements reproduce the 1959 adjusting and compound closing entries of the company.

DUNCAN SALES COMPANY

Unadjusted Trial Balance, December 31, 1959

Cash	$ 1,437	
Merchandise inventory	16,714	
Store supplies	1,482	
Office supplies	365	
Prepaid insurance	283	
Office equipment	2,162	
Accumulated depreciation, office equipment		$ 1,274
Store equipment	14,740	
Accumulated depreciation, store equipment		5,905
Accounts payable		7,324
Earl Duncan, capital		20,513
Earl Duncan, withdrawals	4,800	
Sales		93,604
Sales returns and allowances	1,842	
Purchases	59,746	
Purchases returns and allowances		627
Freight-in	544	
Sales salaries	15,014	
Rent expense, selling space	4,950	
Advertising	1,253	
Office salaries	3,144	
Rent expense, office space	550	
Telephone and utilities	221	
	$129,247	$129,247

DUNCAN SALES COMPANY

Post-Closing Trial Balance, December 31, 1959

Cash	$ 1,437	
Merchandise inventory	15,426	
Store supplies	231	
Office supplies	118	
Prepaid insurance	76	
Office equipment	2,162	
Accumulated depreciation, office equipment		$ 1,484
Store equipment	14,740	
Accumulated depreciation, store equipment		6,725
Accounts payable		7,324
Salaries payable		132
Rent payable		500
Earl Duncan, capital		18,025
	$34,190	$34,190

DUNCAN SALES COMPANY

Income Statement for Year Ended December 31, 1959

Revenue:			
Gross sales		$93,604	
Less: Sales returns and allowances		1,842	
Net sales		$91,762	
Cost of goods sold:			
Merchandise inventory, January 1, 1959		$16,714	
Purchases	$59,746		
Less: Purchases returns and allowances	627		
Net purchases	$59,119		
Add: Freight-in	544		
Net cost of purchases		59,663	
Goods available for sale		$76,377	
Merchandise inventory, December 31, 1959		15,426	
Cost of goods sold			60,951
Gross profit from sales			$30,811
Operating expenses:			
Selling expenses:			
Sales salaries	$15,122		
Rent expense, selling space	5,400		
Advertising	1,253		
Store supplies used	1,251		
Depreciation of store equipment	820		
Total Selling Expenses		$23,846	
Administrative expenses:			
Office salaries	$ 3,168		
Rent expense, office space	600		
Telephone and utilities	221		
Office supplies used	247		
Expired insurance	207		
Depreciation of office equipment	210		
Total Administrative Expenses		4,653	
Total Operating Expenses			28,499
Net Income			$ 2,312

Problem 6–B

Morgan Supply Company operates with annual accounting periods that end each October 31. On October 15 of the current year, after all transactions had been recorded, the account balances in the firm's ledger were as follows:

MORGAN SUPPLY COMPANY
Trial Balance, October 15, 19—

Cash...	$ 3,310	
George Fox...	160	
Carl Gibson..	280	
Merchandise inventory..............................	14,950	
Store supplies.....................................	490	
Prepaid insurance..................................	185	
Store equipment....................................	8,770	
Accumulated depreciation, store equipment..........		$ 2,420
Pioneer Wholesale Company..........................		540
Northwest Manufacturing Company....................		395
Paul Morgan, capital...............................		15,165
Paul Morgan, withdrawals...........................	5,500	
Sales..		75,720
Sales returns and allowances.......................	1,130	
Purchases..	44,380	
Purchases returns and allowances...................		515
Freight-in...	440	
Sales salaries.....................................	10,120	
Rent expense.......................................	4,800	
Telephone and utilities............................	240	
	$94,755	$94,755

During the last half of October Morgan Supply Company completed:

Oct. 17 Purchased merchandise on credit from Pioneer, $360.
18 Sold merchandise on credit to George Fox, $80.
19 Paid the Northwest Manufacturing Company account in full.
21 George Fox returned for credit $20 of the merchandise purchased on December 18.
22 Cash sales for the week ending October 22 were $1,430.
24 Purchased merchandise on credit from Northwest, $560.
24 Paid freight on the merchandise purchased from Northwest, $40.
26 Returned for credit $60 of the merchandise purchased from Northwest on December 24.
27 Purchased store supplies for cash, $15.
29 Cash sales for the week ending October 29, $1,820.
29 Paid the biweekly sales salaries, $365.
31 Paid telephone and utilities expense, $25.
31 Paul Morgan withdrew $500 for his personal use.

Required:

1. Open the required accounts and enter the October 15 trial balance amounts directly in the accounts.
2. Prepare and post journal entries to record the transactions.
3. Prepare a trial balance in the Trial Balance columns of a work sheet. Complete the work sheet using the following information: *a*) Store supplies inventory, $85; *b*) Expired insurance, $115; *c*) Estimated depreciation of store equipment, $620; *d*) Sales salaries payable, $30; *e*) October 31, 19—, merchandise inventory, $13,810.
4. From the work sheet prepare an income statement and a balance sheet.
5. From the work sheet prepare and post adjusting and closing entries.
6. Rule the temporary proprietorship accounts; and balance, rule, and bring down the balances, of the open accounts, the balances of which are not readily apparent.
7. Prepare a post-closing trial balance.

Chapter 7

BUSINESS PAPERS AND PROCEDURES FOR PURCHASES AND SALES

THUS far in the discussion, emphasis has been placed on the accounting procedures used in recording and reporting business transactions. Accounting has been presented primarily as a tool for recording and reporting the effects of business transactions. This is one of the uses of accounting, but accounting has another important use. Accounting is also a tool of management that is used to control the operations of a business. For example, management uses accounting to control the sales procedure of a business so that every customer gets the goods he orders and every sale is recorded. It also uses accounting to control the purchasing procedure so that only properly requisitioned goods are ordered and paid for.

Need for Business Papers and Procedures

To insure that all transactions are properly completed and recorded, systematic business and accounting procedures are designed for handling transactions. These systematic procedures often require that business papers be prepared to record and report the steps of each transaction as the steps are completed. The transaction is then controlled, and recording is insured by providing within the procedure a systematic method for collecting and recording the papers prepared.

The procedures and business papers discussed in this chapter for handling purchases and sales are illustrative of those found in many companies. However, all companies do not use the same procedures and papers in completing identical transactions. Procedures and papers vary from company to company because both procedures and business papers are designed to meet particular needs. Among companies of the same size, procedures and papers are very similar. However, the procedures of a large company often vary greatly from those of a small company. This is because the owner or manager of a small company is usually actively engaged in all phases of his company's operations. His active participation helps to control the operations. In a large company, duties and responsibilities must be divided and delegated to various employees. When duties and responsibilities are divided and delegated, there is a greater need for business papers to co-ordinate and control the operations carried on by the business.

Sales Procedures of a Small Business

In a small retail store many sales are for cash. The customers of such a store select, with the aid of a salesclerk, the items of merchandise desired. The clerk wraps the merchandise and rings up the sale on a cash register. It is a common practice to require the salesclerk to record each sale on the cash register before the merchandise is wrapped. This helps to insure that each sale is recorded. By placing the cash register in such a position that the customer can see the amount "rung up," the customer will help insure that the proper amount is recorded. At the end of each day, the total sales as shown by the cash register or registers are recorded by a single journal entry debiting Cash and crediting Sales.

A small retail firm makes use of sales tickets when goods are sold on credit. Each clerk is issued a book of prenumbered sales tickets. When goods are sold on credit, the credit customer selects the merchandise desired. The salesclerk fills out a sales ticket in duplicate, secures approval of the customer's credit standing from the store office, wraps and gives the merchandise to the customer. The original copy of the sales ticket is wrapped with the merchandise. Since the customer will usually check his copy of the sales ticket, this helps to insure that the sales ticket is made out for the proper amount. The carbon copy of the sales ticket is sent to the store office where it is used to make a journal entry debiting the customer and crediting sales. Accounting for all sales ticket numbers helps to insure that every credit sale is recorded.

Purchases Procedure of a Small Business and Sales Procedure of a Large Business

A small retail business orders most of its merchandise from traveling sales representatives of wholesalers and manufacturers. These sales representatives call upon the retailer at set intervals to take orders. Some sales representatives display samples of merchandise; others sell from catalogues.

The owner of a small business, from his close contact and familiarity with his business, usually knows the items of merchandise in need of restocking. Often he keeps an informal "want book." This is often an ordinary notebook. In the "want book" the owner writes down, as they come to his attention, items in need of restocking. When the sales representative calls, orders are placed for the merchandise needed. The sales representative usually writes up the order in his order book, listing the items and quantities desired. The store owner signs the order blank and is given a copy for his files. The salesman transmits the original copy of the order to his home office.

Most wholesale companies reserve the right to review and either to accept or to reject the orders obtained by their salesmen. Occasionally a credit order is rejected because of the poor credit reputation of the buyer, and occasionally part or all of an order is rejected because the merchandise is temporarily not available. If the wholesaler does not consider the taking of an order to be a sale, it is not a transaction in the accounting sense of the term. A transaction is an exchange of goods or services; and since an exchange of goods or services does not occur, no formal debit and credit record of the order is made by either party.

Upon receipt of the order from its salesman, the wholesaler begins the processing of the order. The wholesaler processes hundreds of orders daily; consequently, to do so efficiently, he must divide the processing procedure into parts and assign each part to a specialized department. With a division of the procedure there is a division of responsibility. Yet, the whole procedure must be controlled and co-ordinated in such a manner as to insure that the buyer receives the merchandise ordered and is charged for the sale. Co-ordination and control of the work of the various departments responsible for processing the order is often obtained by use of several copies of an *invoice*.

Illustration 23—An Invoice

THE EUGENE MANUFACTURING COMPANY
2590 Chula Vista Street
Eugene, Oregon

Invoice No.
3216

Sold to

Date_____

Purchase Order_____

Shipped Via_____

Shipped to_____ Number of Packages_____

Terms_____

Quantity	Description	Unit Price	Amount

The Invoice. An invoice is an itemized statement of goods bought or sold. It is prepared by the seller who is often called the *vendor*. To the seller it is known as a *sales invoice*. A copy of the same invoice, when received by the buyer or *vendee*, is known to the buyer as a *purchase invoice*. In manufacturing and wholesaling, invoices are of the general type shown in Illustration 23.

An invoice such as the one in Illustration 23 sets forth the quantity, description, and unit prices of the goods sold, plus the total amount charged. It also commonly shows to whom the goods were sold, the terms of the sale, the seller's invoice number, the date of the invoice, the purchase order number, the manner in which the goods were shipped, the number of packages, where the goods were shipped, and often other data.

Processing the Order. The processing of an order by a large wholesaler begins with the preparation of several duplicate copies of the sales invoice. The duplicate copies are prepared from information contained in the order sent in by the traveling salesman or from a purchase order or a letter sent by the prospective buyer. The sales department produces all copies in one operation by the use of carbon paper. The copies are usually made on different colors of paper to facilitate their identification. Co-ordination and control of the processing of an order is best illustrated by a chart showing the movement of the different copies of the invoice. Such a chart is shown in Illustration 24. An examination of the chart will show that:

Copies 2 and 3 The sales department starts the processing of the order by sending copies 2 and 3 of the invoice to the credit department for approval of the credit standing of the buyer. In wholesaling, almost all sales are made on credit; therefore, care must be exercised to see that goods are not sold to customers who cannot pay. The duty of granting credit is normally assigned to a credit department rather than to the sales department, because the sales department might be swayed in its judgment of the customer's ability to pay by a desire to make a sale. The credit department approves or rejects the credit standing of the customer and returns the sales department copy of the invoice with its decision shown thereon. Rejections are not too numerous, and in each case the sales department attempts to arrange a cash sale.

When the approval of the customer's credit standing is received from the credit department, the sales department distributes the remaining copies of the invoice.

Copies 4 and 5 Copies 4 and 5 are sent to the stock room. In the stock room the merchandise is assembled and sent to the shipping department with copy 4, the bookkeeping copy of the invoice. In the shipping department, the merchandise is packed for shipment and dispatched to the customer. After this, copy 4, the bookkeeping copy of the invoice, is sent to the accounting department as a notification that the goods have been shipped.

Copy 6 Copy 6 is sent directly to the shipping department so that it may be used to check back, if the goods do not arrive in the shipping depart-

Illustration 24—Copies of the Invoice Used to Control the Procedure for Processing a Customer's Order

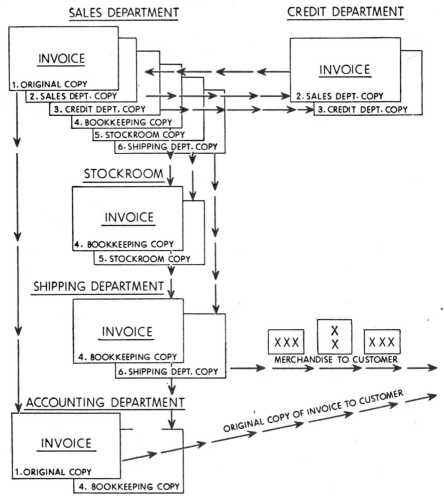

ment. Copy 1 may be used by the accounting department to check back, if the bookkeeping copy does not arrive from the shipping department as notification that the shipment has been made.

Copy 1 Copy 1 is sent directly to the accounting department where it awaits the arrival of the bookkeeping copy. Upon receipt of the bookkeeping copy notifying that the goods have been shipped, the accounting department mails copy 1 of the invoice to the customer. It then uses the bookkeeping copy to record the sale by an entry debiting the customer and crediting Sales.

Receipt of the Invoice by the Buyer. Upon receipt of the invoice and the merchandise, the buyer first examines the invoice for clerical errors. He then compares the invoice with the copy of the order left by the salesman or with a copy of his own letter or purchase order to see that all items were ordered. Next, the items of merchandise received are compared with the invoice to see that all items listed were received. If the invoice is correct and the goods were ordered and received in good condition, the invoice is then used by the buyer to make a journal entry recording the purchase.

Purchasing Procedure of a Large Business

In a large business it is necessary to delegate duties and responsibilities to many employees. However, the duties and responsibilities delegated must be co-ordinated and controlled in such a manner as to insure a smoothly functioning business whole. Business papers are commonly used to co-ordinate and control the operations of a large business. The papers used by a large business to co-ordinate and control its purchasing activities are listed in Illustration 25. An examination of each of these

Illustration 25

Business Paper	Prepared by	Sent To
1. Purchase requisition	Selling department manager desiring that merchandise be purchased	Purchasing department
2. Purchase order	Purchasing department	Company selling the desired merchandise
3. Invoice	Company selling the merchandise	Purchasing department
4. Receiving report	Receiving department	Purchasing department
5. Invoice approval form	Purchasing department	Attached to invoice and sent to the accounting department

forms and its use will illustrate the purchasing procedure of a large business.

Purchase Requisition. A large merchandising company is normally divided into selling departments and service departments. Each department is under the supervision of a department manager. The selling departments each sell a different type of merchandise, and the service departments perform services for the selling departments. For example, the purchasing department is a service department responsible for buying for all departments.

In a large business the purchasing department cannot know, first hand, the merchandise needs of all the selling departments; therefore, the responsibility of keeping an adequate supply of the right kind of merchandise in each department is often delegated to each department manager. However, the various department managers cannot be permitted to purchase directly from the sources of supply because if each department manager were permitted to deal directly with wholesalers and manufacturers, the amount of merchandise purchased and the resulting liabilities incurred could not be controlled. Consequently, in order to secure control over purchases and their resulting liabilities, department managers are commonly required to place all orders for merchandise through the purchasing department. In such cases the function of the various department managers in the purchasing procedure is to inform the purchasing department of the merchandise needed by their departments. Each department manager performs this function by preparing in duplicate a purchase requisition listing the merchandise desired. A purchase requisition is shown in Illustration 26.

Illustration 26—A Purchase Requisition

PURCHASE REQUISITION Eugene Manufacturing Company	Requisition No. **2613**

Date_____ Department_____

Date Wanted_____

Quantity	Description

Requisitioned by_____ Approved by_____

Purchase Order No._____ Date Ordered_____

Ordered from_____

The original copy of the purchase requisition is sent to the purchasing department. The duplicate copy is retained by the department issuing the requisition as a check on the purchasing department. All requisitions are prenumbered so that each may be accounted for. Requisitioning merchandise is not a transaction in the accounting sense of the term. Therefore, no formal debit and credit record of a requisition is made.

Ordinarily, the purchasing department does not make purchases except upon requisition. However, the purchasing department may call the attention of interested department managers to any attractively priced articles normally required by their departments.

Purchase Order. The purchase order is a business form used by the purchasing department in placing an order with a manufacturer or wholesaler. It authorizes the supplier to ship the merchandise ordered, and it takes the place of a typewritten letter placing the order. A sample purchase order is shown in Illustration 27.

On receipt of a purchase requisition from a selling department, the

Illustration 27—A Purchase Order

PURCHASE ORDER	Purchase Order No. **4238**

EUGENE MANUFACTURING COMPANY
2590 Chula Vista Street
Eugene, Oregon

Date_____

To_____

_____

_____

Please enter our order for the following:

Quantity	Description	Unit Price	Total

Do not enclose invoice with merchandise. Mark order number on all packages.

DELIVER NO MERCHANDISE WITHOUT
A WRITTEN ORDER ON THIS FORM

EUGENE MANUFACTURING COMPANY

By_____

purchasing department prepares four copies of the purchase order. More copies may be made if needed. The four copies are distributed as follows:

Copy 1 Copy 1, the original copy, is sent to the supplier as a request to purchase and as authority to ship the merchandise listed.

Copy 2 Copy 2 is sent to the department issuing the requisition as an acknowledgement of the requisition and as a notification of the action taken.

Copy 3 Copy 3 is sent to the receiving department as authority to receive the merchandise. The receiving department is a service department responsible for receiving, unpacking, and checking all merchandise received. Usually the receiving department copy of the purchase order does not list the quantities ordered. The quantities ordered are omitted to insure that the receiving department will record on the receiving report an independent count of the items received. The reason for the statement "Do not enclose invoice with merchandise," which is commonly printed on purchase order forms, is to avoid making available to the receiving department a list of the merchandise shipped.

Copy 4 Copy 4 of the purchase order is retained on file by the purchasing department until the merchandise is received.

When a purchase results from the call of the supplier's salesman, the original copy of the purchase order may be attached to the salesman's order blank for transmission to the supplier. The copy of the salesman's order left with the buyer is then attached to the copy of the purchase order retained on file in the purchasing department.

Invoice. The original copy of the purchase order is sent to the supplier. Upon its receipt, the manufacturer or wholesaler processes the order. As previously explained, this results in the shipment of the merchandise and the mailing of the invoice covering the shipment. The goods are delivered to the receiving department of the buyer, and the invoice is sent to the purchasing department of the buyer.

Receiving Report. Most large companies maintain a special department assigned the duty of receiving all merchandise purchased. It is the duty of this department to open all cartons and packages and to check the merchandise received as to quantity and condition.

Illustration 28—A Receiving Report

RECEIVING REPORT   No. **4383**

The Eugene Manufacturing Company

Received from _____   Date_____

Purchase Order No._____

Supplier's Invoice No._____

Received Via_____

Quantity	Description	Condition

Counted and Inspected by_____

As each shipment is received, counted, and checked, the receiving department prepares a receiving report in triplicate. The receiving report lists the quantity, description, and condition of the items received. The original copy of the receiving report is sent to the purchase department; the second copy is sent to the department that requisitioned the merchandise; and the third copy is retained on file in the receiving department. The copies sent to the purchasing department and the requisitioning department act as a notification of the arrival of the goods. An example of a receiving report is shown in Illustration **28**.

Invoice Approval Form.   When the receiving report arrives in the purchasing department, the purchasing department then has in its possession:

1. A copy of the requisition listing the items requested by the requisitioning department.
2. A purchase order that lists the merchandise ordered.
3. An invoice showing the quantity, description, unit price, and the total of the goods shipped by the seller.
4. A receiving report that lists the quantity and condition of the items received.

With the information on these business papers, the purchasing department is in position to approve the invoice for entry on the books and ultimate payment. In approving the invoice, the purchasing department checks and compares the information on all of these papers. To facilitate the checking and to insure that no step in the checking procedure is omitted, an invoice approval form (Illustration **29**) is used. The invoice ap-

Illustration 29

INVOICE APPROVAL FORM

Purchase Order No._____

Requisition Check_____

Purchase Order Check_____

Receiving Report Check_____

Invoice Check
   Price Approval_____

   Calculations_____

   Terms_____

   Transportation_____

Accounting Distribution_____

_____

Final Approval_____

proval form may be a separate business paper that is attached to the invoice, or the information shown on the illustrated form may be stamped directly on the invoice by means of a rubber stamp.

As each step in the checking procedure is completed, the clerk making the check initials the invoice approval form. Initials in each space on the form indicate:

1. Requisition Check ...... The items on the invoice agree with the requisition and were requisitioned.
2. Purchase Order Check ... The items on the invoice agree with the purchase order and were ordered.
3. Receiving Report Check . The items on the invoice agree with the receiving report and were received.
4. Invoice Check
   Price Approval ...... The invoice prices are the agreed prices for the items listed.
   Calculations .... The invoice has no mathematical errors.
   Terms .... The terms are the agreed terms for the transaction.
   Transportation ...... The seller followed the shipping instructions of the purchasing department. This is important because failure to follow instructions may result in additional transportation costs.
5. Accounting Distribution . The purchasing department is responsible for buying for all departments. An invoice, therefore, may contain items of supplies, equipment, or merchandise. The account or accounts to be debited in recording the invoice are indicated under accounting distribution.

Recording the Invoice. After the invoice is checked and approved, the purchase requisition, purchase order, receiving report, and invoice approval form, if a stamp is not used, are attached to the invoice. All of the papers are then sent to the accounting department for recording. In the accounting department an entry is made debiting purchases, if merchandise was purchased, and crediting the creditor. The papers are then filed.

The entire purchasing procedure is presented in Illustration 30 by a chart showing the movement of the business papers used in purchasing.

Debit Memorandum and Credit Memorandum

(1) Invoice errors, (2) goods received in a damaged condition, (3) goods received that were not ordered, and (4) goods received short of the amount ordered and billed are points for adjustment between the buyer and the seller. In some cases the buyer can make the adjustment, and in other cases the adjustment is a subject for negotiation between the buyer and the seller. When goods are received that were not ordered or when there are errors on the invoice, the buyer may make the adjustment. If the buyer makes an adjustment, he must notify the seller of his action. The buyer notifies the seller by sending a *debit memorandum* or a *credit memorandum.*

Illustration 30—Use of Business Papers to Control Purchases

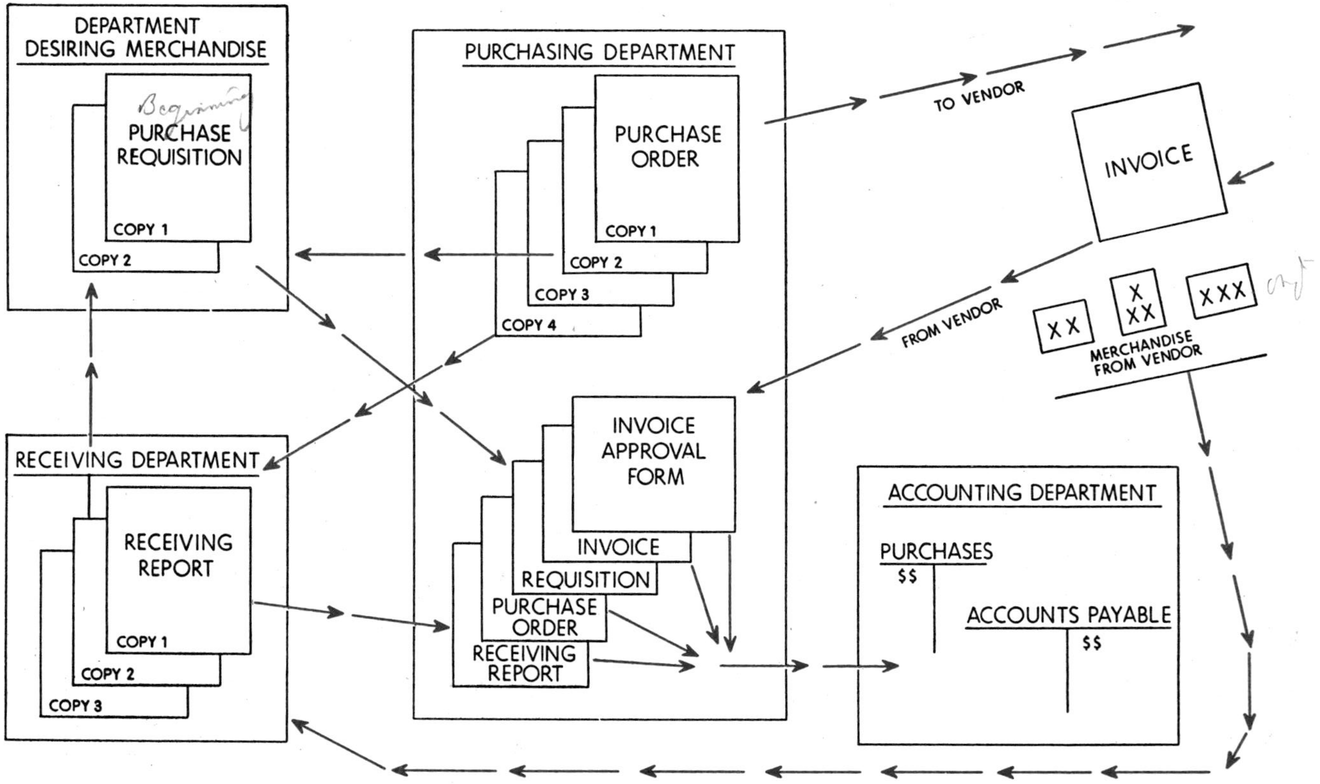

For instance, the Salem Department Store, in checking an invoice for merchandise purchased from the Acme Wholesale Company, discovers an invoice error that increases the total amount of the invoice. This causes the Salem Department Store to increase the amount credited to its account payable with Acme Wholesale Company. The Salem Department Store notifies the Acme Wholesale Company of the adjustment by sending a credit memorandum indicating that it is crediting and increasing its account payable. This credit memorandum is shown in Illustration 31. The Salem Department Store should discover an error such as this before the invoice is recorded. If it does so, the Purchases account is debited, and

Illustration 31

CREDIT MEMORANDUM

SALEM DEPARTMENT STORE
SALEM, OREGON

DATE December 3, 19 —

To: Acme Wholesale Company
1234 N.W. First Avenue
Portland Oregon

WE *CREDIT* YOUR ACCOUNT AS FOLLOWS:

Your invoice No. 72-245, dated 12-1-—, error in calculations. Invoice should total $135 not $125 $10.00

SALEM DEPARTMENT STORE

Frank Hatts

Manager, Purchasing Department

the Acme Company account payable is credited for the correct larger amount of $135. A copy of the memorandum is attached to the recorded invoice to indicate the adjustment. On receipt of the memorandum, the Acme Wholesale Company will debit the Salem Department Store account receivable and credit its Sales account for an additional $10.

If in checking another invoice, the Salem Department Store discovers an error that decreases the amount of the invoice, it notifies the seller with a debit memorandum. This debit memorandum, shown in Illustration 32, indicates that the Salem Department Store is debiting and decreasing the amount payable to the Eugene Manufacturing Company. The Salem Department Store records the invoice to which this debit memorandum applies by debiting Purchases and crediting Eugene Manufacturing Company for $25 less than the original invoice amount.

Some adjustments, such as merchandise received in a damaged condition or merchandise that does not meet specifications, normally require negotiations between the buyer and the seller. In such cases the buyer may debit Purchases for the full amount of the invoice and enter into negotiations with the seller for the return of the merchandise or for an adjustment. If the seller agrees to the return of the merchandise or to an adjustment of the invoice price, he notifies the buyer with a credit memorandum. This memorandum is a credit memorandum to the seller because the return or the adjustment reduces the amount of the account receivable with the buyer. For example, the Salem Department Store purchased a

Illustration 32

DEBIT
MEMORANDUM

SALEM DEPARTMENT STORE
SALEM, OREGON

DATE___December 5, 19___

To:
Eugene Manufacturing Company
2590 Chula Vista Street
Eugene, Oregon

WE *DEBIT* YOUR ACCOUNT AS FOLLOWS:

Your invoice No. C-1113. Two dozen Highlight
Window Shades--not ordered and returned to
you collect. $25.00

SALEM DEPARTMENT STORE

Frank Hatts
Manager, Purchasing Department

number of items from the Novelty Supply Company. The invoice for this merchandise totaled $100. When the merchandise arrived, five ceramic figurines were found to have been improperly packed and were consequently damaged in transit. The Salem Department Store recorded the full amount of the invoice by debiting Purchases and crediting the Novelty Supply Company for $100. It then entered into negotiations for an adjustment equal to the value of the broken figurines. The Novelty Supply Company agreed to the adjustment and notified the Salem Department Store with the credit memorandum shown in Illustration 33.

Since the Salem Department Store debited Purchases and credited the Novelty Supply Company for the full amount of the original invoice, it records the credit memorandum by a debit to the Novelty Supply Company and a credit to Purchases Returns and Allowances for $18.

A debit memorandum or credit memorandum may originate with either party to a transaction. The memorandum secures its name from the action of the party originating it. If the originator of the memorandum debits, he sends a debit memorandum. If the originator of the memorandum credits, he sends a credit memorandum. Therefore, the receipt of a credit memorandum causes the receiver of the memorandum to debit the originator of the memorandum. Likewise, the receipt of a debit memorandum causes the receiver to credit the account of the originator of the memorandum.

A debit memorandum form and a credit memorandum form are often very similar in physical appearance. The similarity in appearance creates the possibility of errors. This is because, for example, the clerk responsible for preparing the required form may use a debit memorandum form

Illustration 33

CREDIT MEMORANDUM
L-364

NOVELTY SUPPLY COMPANY
PORTLAND, OREGON

To:
Salem Department Store
1451 High Street
Salem, Oregon

DATE December 12, 19——

WE *CREDIT* YOUR ACCOUNT AS FOLLOWS:

5 ceramic figurines damaged in transit and returned	$18.00

NOVELTY SUPPLY COMPANY

T. A. Briggs
Sales Manager

when a credit memorandum form is required. To reduce errors of this nature and to facilitate the ready identification of the two forms, most companies print debit memoranda on one color of paper and credit memoranda on a different color.

Credit Terms and Cash Discounts

Most manufacturers and wholesalers find that sales are increased by granting a period of time in which the buyer may make payment for merchandise purchased. Sales are increased because the buyer is enabled by the credit period to carry a larger stock of merchandise and thereby increase his own sales. The buyer is able to carry a larger stock of merchandise because part of the merchandise in his store is placed there for a period of time without a cash investment on his part. In many cases the storekeeper is able to buy merchandise and sell it before payment must be made to the manufacturer or wholesaler.

In extending credit, business firms make the terms of payment definite so that there will be no disagreement as to the amount and time of payment. The terms always appear on the invoice and are part of the sales agreement. The exact terms granted usually depend upon the custom of the trade. In some trades it is customary for invoices to become due and payable within ten days after the end of the month in which the sale took place. Invoices in these trades carry the terms, "10 E.O.M." In other trades, it is customary for invoices to become due and payable thirty days after the date of the invoice. Invoices in these trades carry the terms "n/30." This means that the net amount of the invoice is due thirty days after the date of the invoice.

When credit periods are long, creditors usually grant discounts for early payments. These are called *cash discounts*. The practice of granting cash discounts has two favorable results for the creditor. It tends to reduce the amount invested in accounts receivable, and it tends to decrease losses from uncollectible accounts. When discounts for early payment are granted, they are made part of the credit terms and appear on the invoice as, for example, "Terms 2/10, n/60." Terms of 2/10, n/60 mean that the credit period is sixty days but that the debtor may deduct 2 per cent from the amount of the invoice if payment is made within ten days after the date of the invoice.

Although cash discounts may be recorded at the time of the sale or purchase (discussed in Chapter 15), they are more commonly recorded at the time payment is made and received. For example, on November 15, the Valley Hardware Company received merchandise priced at $1,000 from Foster Wholesale Company. The invoice for this merchandise was dated November 12, and the terms were 2/10, n/60. The purchase was recorded by the Valley Hardware Company with the following entry:

Nov.	15	Purchases..............................	1,000.00	
		Foster Wholesale Company............		1,000.00
		Purchased merchandise, terms 2/10, n/60.		

The Valley Hardware Company may pay the full amount of this invoice any time before November 22 by mailing a check for $980 to Foster Wholesale Company. Or, if the Valley Hardware Company so wishes, it may wait until January 11 and pay the full $1,000. If the company chooses to pay by November 22 and to take advantage of the cash discount, it records the payment with the following entry:

Nov.	22	Foster Wholesale Company............	1,000.00	
		Purchases Discounts.............		20.00
		Cash........................		980.00
		Paid the invoice of November 12 less 2 per cent discount.		

Businesses find it advantageous to take cash discounts even if money must be borrowed to do so. For instance, in the above example the interest on $980 at 6 per cent for fifty days is $8.17. This is less than one half of the 2 per cent discount on the $1,000.

The series of transactions previously illustrated between the Valley Hardware Company and Foster Wholesale Company are a sale and the collection of an account to Foster Wholesale Company. It records the transactions with entries like the following:

Nov.	12	Valley Hardware Company............	1,000.00	
		Sales........................		1,000.00
		Sold merchandise, terms 2/10, n/60.		
Nov.	24	Cash.......................	980.00	
		Sales Discounts...................	20.00	
		Valley Hardware Company........		1,000.00
		Received full payment of the invoice of November 12 less a 2 per cent discount.		

Discounts on the Income Statement

Until within the last few years cash discounts were commonly shown on the income statement as separate items of revenue and expense. Today, the more common practice is to show purchases discounts as a deduction from the cost of the goods purchased and sales discounts as a deduction from the revenue from sales, as in Illustration 34.

Illustration 34

HASKIN LUMBER COMPANY
Income Statement for Year Ended February 28, 19--

Revenue:
Gross sales $153,710
    Less: Sales returns . . . . $ 2,450
           Sales discounts   2,510   4,960
Net sales $148,750

Cost of goods sold:
Merchandise inventory, March 1, 19-- $17,205
Purchases $104,300
    Less: Purchases returns . $2,250
          Purchases discounts   1,910   4,160
Net purchases $100,140

Transportation Terms

The terms of an invoice commonly designate the party who is to pay the transportation charges. Commonly, terms are either "F.O.B. Shipping Point" or "F.O.B. Destination."

F.O.B. Shipping Point. These terms mean "free on board" freight cars or other means of transportation at the factory, and that the buyer must pay the freight. For example, Maley Wholesale Company of St. Louis received a purchase invoice from Trenton Manufacturing Company of Chicago, amount $1,000, freight terms F.O.B. Chicago.

Freight Is Paid by Buyer upon Receipt of Goods. If freight is paid by the buyer upon receipt of the goods, Maley's entries, without explanations, for the purchase and payment of freight are:

Nov.	3	Purchases...............................	1,000.00	
		Trenton Manufacturing Company....		1,000.00
	3	Freight-In............................	90.00	
		Cash............................		90.00

Freight Is Prepaid by Shipper. Sometimes the shipper prepays the freight on the F.O.B. factory shipment, either because the regulations require prepayment on that class of merchandise or because the customer has requested it. In this event the shipper adds on the prepaid freight at the bottom of the invoice. If Trenton prepaid the freight on the above shipment in spite of the freight terms, Maley would record the invoice as follows:

Nov.	3	Purchases...............................	1,000.00	
		Freight-In............................	90.00	
		Trenton Manufacturing Company....		1,090.00

If a cash discount is allowed for the early payment of the above invoice, the amount of the discount must be based on the merchandise purchased only. For example, if this invoice is paid in time to take a 2 per cent cash discount, the entry for payment in this case would be:

Nov.	9	Trenton Manufacturing Company.......	1,090.00	
		Cash............................		1,070.00
		Purchases Discounts (2 per cent of $1,000)............................		20.00

F.O.B. Destination. This means "free on board" cars to destination of the shipment and that the seller agrees to pay the freight.

Freight Is Paid by Buyer upon Receipt of Goods. If the terms on the Trenton Manufacturing Company invoice were F.O.B. St. Louis, the shipper is responsible for payment of the freight. Therefore, if the freight is not prepaid by the shipper, Maley should deduct the amount of freight paid from the amount of the invoice before paying Trenton, and Maley's entries for the purchase and for payment of the freight are:

Nov.	3	Purchases..............................	1,000.00	
		Trenton Manufacturing Company.....		1,000.00
	3	Trenton Manufacturing Company (for freight).............................	90.00	
		Cash...............................		90.00

Any cash discount allowed should be based on the merchandise purchased (net of any returns or allowances, of course). Maley would record payment, less 2 per cent discount in this case as follows:

Nov.	9	Trenton Manufacturing Company.......	910.00	
		Cash...............................		890.00
		Purchases Discounts (2 per cent of $1,000).............................		20.00

Freight Is Prepaid by Shipper. Since the shipper is responsible for the freight under terms of F.O.B. destination, he should prepay it. Where this is done, Maley needs only to record the full amount of the purchase invoice, $1,000, as a debit to Purchases and a credit to Trenton Manufacturing Company.

Trade Discounts

Cash discounts, which have been previously discussed, are granted for the prompt payment of an invoice. Trade discounts have no relation to payments. A trade discount is a deduction from a list price that is used in determining the actual selling price of goods. Trade discounts are commonly used by manufacturers and wholesalers to avoid the frequent republication of catalogues when selling prices change. If selling prices change, the prices of a catalogue can be adjusted by merely issuing a new list of discounts to be applied to the catalogue prices.

Trade discounts may be stated as a single percentage or as a chain of percentages. For example, a single discount of 40 per cent off of the listed catalogue price may be granted or discounts of 20 per cent, 10 per cent, and 10 per cent may be granted. If a single discount of 40 per cent is granted, the selling price of the goods is calculated:

List or catalogue price.....................................	$1,000
Less: Trade discount of 40 per cent.........................	400
Selling price...	$ 600

If a chain of discounts such as 20 per cent, 10 per cent, and 10 per cent is given, the selling price of goods is calculated:

```
List or catalogue price.....................................$1,000
     Less: First discount of 20 per cent..........................  200
Amount remaining............................................$  800
     Less: Second discount of 10 per cent........................   80
Amount remaining............................................$  720
     Less: Third discount of 10 per cent.........................   72
Selling Price...............................................$  648
```

Trade discounts are not entered in the accounts; only selling prices are used. For example, the sale of the chain discount calculation just given is recorded:

Dec.	10	University Supply Company............ Sales........................... Sold merchandise on account.	648.00	648.00

QUESTIONS FOR CLASS DISCUSSION

1. Explain why there is a greater need in a large business than in a small business for business papers to control transactions.
2. How does the requirement that clerks record each cash sale on a cash register before wrapping the merchandise help to insure that all cash sales are correctly recorded?
3. An order taken by a traveling salesman is usually not considered an accounting transaction. Why?
4. Why is the granting of credit usually assigned to a credit department rather than to the department responsible for sales?
5. How are the several copies of an invoice used to control the processing of an order by a large wholesaler?
6. In a large store, why are the department managers not permitted to deal directly with the sources of supply in the purchase of merchandise?
7. What are the duties of the selling department managers in the purchasing procedure of a large company?
8. Why is the statement: "Do not include invoice with merchandise," printed on many purchase orders?
9. As the term is used in this chapter, what is a "service" department? Name several "service" departments found in large companies.
10. What is the difference between a debit memorandum and a credit memorandum? When a debit memorandum is issued, who debits, the one originating the memorandum or the one receiving it?
11. An invoice is dated July 18. What is the last day of the credit period if the terms are: (1) 10 E.O.M.; (2) 2/10, n/30; and (3) 2/20, n/60?
12. Tell (1) who prepares, (2) who receives, and (3) the purpose of each of the following business papers:
    a) Purchase requisition.
    b) Purchase order.
    c) Invoice.
    d) Receiving report.
    e) Invoice approval form.
13. Robert Short purchased $1,000 worth of merchandise, terms 2/10, n/60. If Mr. Short borrowed sufficient money to pay this invoice on the last day of

the discount period at 6 per cent interest, how much did he save by borrowing to take advantage of the discount?

14. George Long purchased $545 worth of merchandise from Blue and White Supply Company, terms 2/10, n/30. He paid for the purchase within the discount period. Give the general journal entries to record: (1) the purchase and the payment on the books of Long; and (2) the sale and the collection on the books of Blue and White Supply Company.

15. Robert Short received from Blue and White Supply Company an invoice totaling $45 and the merchandise covered by the invoice. In checking the invoice, Mr. Short found the correct total of the invoice to be $49. Mr. Short sent Blue and White a memorandum pointing out the error.
   a) Was this a debit memorandum or a credit memorandum?
   b) Give the entry or entries made by Short to record the purchase.
   c) Give the entry made by Blue and White to record the memorandum.

16. Frank Brown purchased $50 worth of merchandise from Ajax Supply Company. Upon receipt and examination of the merchandise, Mr. Brown felt that $20 worth did not meet specifications. Nevertheless, he recorded the entire purchase of $50 and entered into negotiations to return the unsatisfactory portion. He received permission from Ajax to make the return. Mr. Brown returned $20 worth of unsatisfactory merchandise and received a memorandum showing that Ajax had entered the return in his account.
   a) Was this a debit memorandum or a credit memorandum?
   b) Give the journal entries to record the purchase and return on the books of Brown.
   c) Give the entries in general journal form to record the sale and return on the Ajax books.

17. Can you give a logical reason for deducting sales discounts from gross sales and deducting purchases discounts from gross purchases?

18. Distinguish between a cash discount and a trade discount.

PROBLEMS

Problem 7–1

On November 16 of the current year McBee Sales Company sent a purchase order to Ritter Manufacturing Company for merchandise having a catalogue list price of $2,500, less trade discounts of 20 per cent, 10 per cent, and 10 per cent, F.O.B. factory, terms 2/10, n/30. On November 18 Ritter Manufacturing Company shipped the entire order of merchandise, prepaying the freight charges of $108, which they added to the invoice price of the goods.

On November 20 McBee Sales Company received the shipment of goods. Upon inspection they found that one fourth of the goods did not meet specifications. Nevertheless, they recorded the entire purchase and entered into negotiations to return the unsatisfactory portion. Ritter Manufacturing Company agreed to the return of the unsatisfactory goods with the understanding that they would pay the freight charges on the goods returned and grant full credit for the goods returned plus one fourth of the freight charges on the original shipment. The unsatisfactory goods were returned with freight charges of $28.50, C.O.D.

On November 26 a credit memorandum dated November 24 and granting full credit for the goods return plus one fourth the freight charges on the original shipment was received. On November 27 McBee Sales Company mailed Ritter Manufacturing Company a check in full of the amount owed.

Required:

Prepare general journal entries to record the transaction on the books of McBee Sales Company.

Problem 7–2

On the last day of February of the current year, the end of an annual accounting period, a trial balance of the ledger of The Outdoor Store appeared as follows:

THE OUTDOOR STORE
Trial Balance, February 28, 19—

Cash	$ 3,560	
Merchandise inventory	14,610	
Store supplies	645	
Prepaid insurance	225	
Store equipment	11,420	
Accumulated depreciation, store equipment		$ 2,685
Accounts payable		2,710
David Rankin, capital		22,295
David Rankin, withdrawals	7,200	
Sales		69,230
Sales returns and allowances	855	
Sales discounts	1,390	
Purchases	43,380	
Purchases returns and allowances		615
Purchases discounts		785
Freight-in	635	
Sales salaries	13,420	
Heating and lighting expenses	980	
	$98,320	$98,320

Required:

1. Copy the trial balance onto a ten-column work sheet form (no Cost of Goods Sold columns) and complete the work sheet using the following information:

   a) The inventory of store supplies showed $170 of store supplies on hand. However, (b) when this amount was subtracted from the balance of the Store Supplies account, the bookkeeper realized the amount shown as store supplies used was too small when compared with the amounts used in previous years. Consequently, he examined his records and found that $245 of store supplies had been charged in error to the Store Equipment account. (Make an adjustment on the work sheet to correct the error before making the adjustment to record the store supplies used.)

   c) Expired insurance, $180.

   d) Estimated depreciation of store equipment, $1,250.

   e) Ending merchandise inventory, $16,570.

2. Prepare the trading section (completed through the calculation of gross profit) of the firm's income statement.

3. Prepare adjusting, correcting, and compound closing entries from the work sheet.

Problem 7–3

The adjusting and closing entries without explanations and the post-closing trial balance of the Rapp Mercantile Company follow:

Dec.	31	Store Supplies Used..................	965.00	
		Store Supplies...................		965.00
	31	Insurance Expense..................	215.00	
		Prepaid Insurance...............		215.00
	31	Depreciation of Store Equipment......	1,835.00	
		Accumulated Depreciation, Store Equipment....................		1,835.00
	31	Depreciation of Store Building.........	900.00	
		Accumulated Depreciation, Store Building.....................		900.00
	31	Sales Salaries.....................	230.00	
		Sales Salaries Payable...........		230.00
	31	Income Summary....................	145,355.00	
		Merchandise Inventory..........		22,920.00
		Sales Returns and Allowances.....		1,430.00
		Sales Discounts.................		2,420.00
		Purchases......................		83,380.00
		Freight-In.....................		2,370.00
		Sales Salaries.................		26,645.00
		Advertising Expense............		1,335.00
		Heating and Lighting Expenses....		940.00
		Store Supplies Used.............		965.00
		Insurance Expense..............		215.00
		Depreciation of Store Equipment..		1,835.00
		Depreciation of Store Building.....		900.00
	31	Sales...........................	141,955.00	
		Purchases Returns and Allowances.....	1,235.00	
		Purchases Discounts.................	1,660.00	
		Merchandise Inventory...............	18,765.00	
		Income Summary................		163,615.00
	31	Income Summary....................	18,260.00	
		Andrew Rapp, Withdrawals.......		18,260.00
	31	Andrew Rapp, Withdrawals...........	11,660.00	
		Andrew Rapp, Capital...........		11,660.00

RAPP MERCANTILE COMPANY
Post-Closing Trial Balance, December 31, 19—

Cash...	$ 7,210	
Accounts Receivable.................................	10,580	
Merchandise inventory...............................	18,765	
Store supplies......................................	280	
Prepaid insurance...................................	145	
Store equipment.....................................	14,395	
Accumulated depreciation, store equipment..............		$ 6,560
Store building.......................................	45,000	
Accumulated depreciation, store building...............		4,500
Land..	5,000	
Accounts payable....................................		15,775
Sales salaries payable................................		230
Andrew Rapp, capital................................		74,310
	$101,375	$101,375

Required:

Reproduce the original, unadjusted, December 31, 19—, trial balance.

CLASS EXERCISES

Exercise 7–1

Blue Company received quotations on an item of merchandise from two different suppliers. The quotations were:

From Taylor and Berg: List price $1,200; less 20 per cent, 20 per cent, and 10 per cent, F.O.B. destination; terms 2/10, n/30.

From Zee Mfg. Company: List price $1,200; less 25 per cent and 25 per cent, F.O.B. destination; terms 1/10, n/30.

Blue Company accepted the best offer including the cash discount and completed the following transactions:

Nov. 18 Received the merchandise and an invoice dated November 15.

    18 Paid $62 of freight charges on the shipment which the supplier had failed to pay; charged the amount paid to the account of the supplier.

    25 Sent the supplier a check in full payment of the amount due, less the discount.

Required:

1. General journal entries to record this series of transactions on the books of Blue Company.
2. General journal entries to record the transactions on the books of the vendor.

Exercise 7–2

A store paid the following invoices which had terms offering cash discounts. Calculate and list the amount of the payment in each case.

Date of Invoice	Terms	Amount	Date of Payment
a) March 3	2/10, n/30	$400	March 12
b) March 5	2/10, 1/30, n/60	800	March 14
c) March 8	2/10, 1/30, n/60	900	April 1
d) March 10	1/15, n/60	700	April 1
e) March 18	2/10, n/30	500	March 30

SUPPLEMENTARY PROBLEMS

Problem 7–A

The following information was taken from the income statement of Duncan Sales Company on December 31, 1959, the end of its annual accounting period:

Gross profit	$49,355	Purchases discounts	$ 1,640
Freight-in	1,850	Purchases returns	1,235
Merchandise inventory, December 31, 1959	25,780	Sales	138,340
		Sales discounts	2,510
Purchases	82,960	Sales returns	1,845

Required:

From the foregoing information determine the January 1, 1959, merchandise inventory.

Problem 7–B

Following are the unadjusted trial balance and a portion of the closing entries of the X-L Company as they appeared at the end of the firm's annual accounting period. Prepare a work sheet for the firm from the information supplied.

X-L COMPANY

Trial Balance, December 31, 19—

Cash..	$ 2,725	
Merchandise inventory.................................	14,265	
Store supplies..	780	
Prepaid insurance......................................	210	
Store equipment..	11,240	
Accumulated depreciation, store equipment................		$ 4,795
Notes payable...		4,000
Accounts payable.......................................		8,530
David Ryan, capital.....................................		17,240
David Ryan, withdrawals...............................	4,800	
Sales...		62,865
Sales returns and allowances...........................	1,370	
Sales discounts...	1,080	
Purchases...	41,390	
Purchases returns and allowances.......................		820
Purchases discounts....................................		495
Freight-in...	780	
Sales salaries...	12,960	
Rent expense..	6,000	
Heating and lighting expense...........................	1,085	
Interest expense..	60	
	$98,745	$98,745

Dec.	31	Income Summary......................	80,915.00	
		Merchandise Inventory.............		14,265.00
		Sales Returns and Allowances.......		1,370.00
		Sales Discounts....................		1,080.00
		Purchases.........................		41,390.00
		Freight-In........................		780.00
		Sales Salaries.....................		13,190.00
		Rent Expense......................		6,000.00
		Heating and Lighting Expense.......		1,085.00
		Interest Expense...................		90.00
		Store Supplies Used................		545.00
		Insurance Expense.................		160.00
		Depreciation of Store Equipment....		960.00
	31	Sales................................	62,865.00	
		Purchases Returns and Allowances.......	820.00	
		Purchases Discounts..................	495.00	
		Merchandise Inventory...............	15,180.00	
		Income Summary.................		79,360.00

Chapter 8

/

SPECIAL JOURNALS AND SUBSIDIARY LEDGERS

WHEN a company's transactions are few, a two-column General Journal similar to the one described in previous chapters can be used in recording all of its transactions. However, when transactions become numerous, a considerable saving in posting labor plus the possibility of a division of labor may be achieved by classifying the transactions into classes of like transactions and providing a special columnar journal for the recording of each class. When this is done, the particular journals provided depend upon the number of like transactions a company has in a given class. A special journal may be provided for any class of like transactions in which there are within the class a sufficient number of transactions to warrant a special journal. For example, if the transactions of an average mercantile company are examined, it will be seen that the great majority fall into four distinct classes. If a special journal is provided for each, the classes and special journals provided are:

Classes of Transactions	Special Journal
1. Sales on account	Sales Journal
2. Purchases on account	Purchases Journal
3. Receipts of cash	Cash Receipts Journal
4. Payments of cash	Cash Payments Journal

While the four journals listed are the more common, other special journals are also commonly used. Also, most of the transactions of a business using special journals are recorded in one of its special journals. However, regardless of the special journals provided, there are always a few miscellaneous transactions plus adjusting, closing, and correcting entries which cannot be recorded in any of the special journals. For these, a General Journal must be provided.

Advantages Gained from the Use of Special Journals

The primary advantage gained from the use of special journals is that the number of postings to the ledger accounts is reduced. How this is achieved is discussed in the next section of this chapter.

A second advantage is that special journals make possible a division of labor. Only one clerk, at one time, can record transactions in a General Journal. However, if transactions are classified and recorded by classes in five different journals, five clerks may work on the journals at the same time. Such a division of labor is often necessary in a large company.

A third advantage gained from the use of special journals is that less experienced, and therefore, less expensive, labor may be employed. Much training and experience is required by a bookkeeper who is capable of recording any transaction that may occur. However, a clerk without previous knowledge of bookkeeping may be taught in a matter of hours to record transactions in any one of the special journals.

How Special Journals Save Posting Labor

When like transactions are classified and each class is recorded in a special journal, it is possible to save posting labor by taking advantage of

Illustration 35

SALES JOURNAL

Date		Account Debited	Address	Invoice No.	Amount
Oct.	1	James Henry	205 N.W. First St.	307	—200.00
	6	Albert Smith	106 W. 22nd St.	308	—100.00
	12	John Wright	22nd and Elm	309	—150.00
	15	Paul Roth	1314 S. Elm St.	310	—225.00
	22	Sam Moore	1006 N. Oak St.	311	—125.00
	25	Frank Booth	306 S.W. First St.	312	— 50.00
	28	James Henry	205 N.W. First St.	313	—175.00
	31	Total—Sales Credit			1,025.00

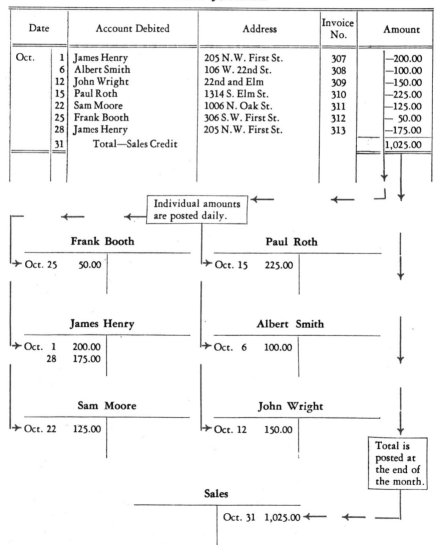

Individual amounts are posted daily.

Frank Booth
Oct. 25   50.00

Paul Roth
Oct. 15   225.00

James Henry
Oct. 1   200.00
28   175.00

Albert Smith
Oct. 6   100.00

Sam Moore
Oct. 22   125.00

John Wright
Oct. 12   150.00

Total is posted at the end of the month.

Sales
Oct. 31   1,025.00

the fact that in any one class of transactions either the debit or the credit is always to the same account. For example, when charge sales are recorded, each sale results in a credit to Sales; the customer accounts debited differ, but each sale results in a credit to Sales. In a Sales Journal these repetitive credits to Sales are taken advantage of and posting labor is saved by placing the amounts in a column and posting to the credit side of the Sales account only the column total. This is graphically shown in Illustration 35.

Observe in Illustration 35 (1) how each charge sale is recorded on a single line, (2) how the amount of each sale is individually debited to a customer's account, and (3) how only the column total, the sum of all the sales, is credited to the Sales account. The Sales Journal of Illustration 35 has recorded therein only seven charge sales. If it is assumed that these seven sales represent seven hundred or seven thousand sales, the tremendous amount of posting labor saved by the single credit to Sales can be better visualized.

The single-column Sales Journal is one of the more simple of the special or columnar journals. It has been used to introduce the subject of columnar special journals and to demonstrate the savings in posting labor that may be achieved by recording like transactions in a column and posting the column total. Before additional columnar journals are discussed, the subject of subdividing the ledger should be introduced.

Need for Subdividing the Ledger

If a company has a large number of accounts, placing all of its accounts in a single ledger has several disadvantages, among which are that a ledger with many accounts is large and awkward, a division of posting labor is difficult, the trial balance of such a ledger is long, and if errors are made, they are hard to find because they cannot be localized. To overcome these disadvantages, many companies subdivide their ledgers.

Basis for Subdividing the Ledger

When the original ledger of a firm is subdivided, it is subdivided by removing from it any one or more large classes of like accounts. Each large class of like accounts removed is placed in a separate ledger called a *subsidiary ledger*. The original ledger is then called the *General Ledger*. When a ledger is subdivided by removing a class of like accounts, it is necessary to substitute in the original ledger or General Ledger a summary account, the balance of which is equal to the sum of the balances of the accounts removed. This is necessary because the original or General Ledger will not balance with a portion of its accounts removed. The summary account, the balance of which takes the place of the balances of the accounts removed, is called a *controlling account* or a *control account*.

In most companies the largest two classes of like accounts are the accounts receivable and the accounts payable. These are usually the first two classes of accounts removed from a ledger. When the accounts receivable are removed from the General Ledger, they are placed in a subsidiary ledger called the *Accounts Receivable Ledger* and a controlling account called *Accounts Receivable* is substituted in their place in the General Ledger. Likewise, when the accounts payable are removed from the General Ledger, they are placed in a subsidiary ledger called the *Accounts Payable Ledger* and a controlling account called Accounts Payable is substituted in their place.

Accounts receivable and accounts payable are the most common classes of accounts placed in subsidiary ledgers. However, it should be understood that any large class of accounts may be removed from the General Ledger and placed in a subsidiary ledger. For example, a company operating a national chain of stores usually has money on deposit in a bank in each city in which it has a store. Often such a company will maintain a Cash controlling account in its General Ledger and a subsidiary ledger with an account for each bank in which it has money on deposit. Another example: A company with many operating expense accounts may place an Operating Expenses controlling account in its General Ledger and place the individual expense accounts in a subsidiary ledger.

Establishing a Subsidiary Ledger Illustrated

The Sloan Novelty Company, a firm that has previously kept all of its accounts in one ledger, decides to subdivide its ledger by removing therefrom all of its customer accounts. The accounts with customers are to be placed in a subsidiary Accounts Receivable Ledger. Since the ledger of the Sloan Novelty Company, like that of most companies, is a loose-

Illustration 36

SLOAN NOVELTY COMPANY

Trial Balance

December 31, 19—

Cash	$ 1,600	
Notes receivable	400	
A. B. Dean	75	
Frank Fish	125	
T. M. Johnson	250	
W. C. Nagle	160	
John Roak	100	
Sam Warren	140	
Store supplies	125	
Prepaid insurance	75	
Land	1,000	
Building	14,900	
Equipment	2,000	
Acme Mfg. Company		$ 450
Horn Supply Company		600
Mortgage payable		5,000
C. Sloan, capital		14,900
	$20,950	$20,950

SLOAN NOVELTY COMPANY

Trial Balance

December 31, 19—

Cash	$ 1,600	
Notes receivable	400	
Accounts receivable	850	
Store supplies	125	
Prepaid insurance	75	
Land	1,000	
Building	14,900	
Equipment	2,000	
Acme Mfg. Company		$ 450
Horn Supply Company		600
Mortgage payable		5,000
C. Sloan, capital		14,900
	$20,950	$20,950

leaf ledger, this is a simple task. To accomplish the task, it is only necessary to:

1. Remove from the loose-leaf General Ledger all of the pages containing accounts with customers.
2. Place these customer account pages in a separate ledger binder.
3. Place in the General Ledger a summary controlling account, the balance of which equals the sum of the balances of the customer accounts removed.

In Illustration 36, on the left, is shown the trial balance of the Sloan Novelty Company's ledger before the accounts receivable were removed; and on the right is shown the trial balance of the company's General Ledger after the accounts receivable were removed. In Illustration 36, there are only six accounts receivable. If it is assumed that these six accounts with customers represent six hundred accounts receivable, the tremendous reduction in the length of the trial balance may be appreciated.

A subsidiary Accounts Payable Ledger or a subsidiary Operating Expense Ledger would be established in the same manner.

Preparing Schedules of Subsidiary Ledgers

After a group of like accounts, such as the accounts receivable, are removed from the General Ledger, the equality of the accounts remaining in the General Ledger is still tested by preparing a trial balance. Also,

Illustration 37

SLOAN NOVELTY COMPANY
Schedule of Accounts Receivable
December 31, 19--

A. B. Dean	$ 75
Frank Fish	125
T. M. Johnson.	250
W. C. Nagle.	160
John Roak.	100
Sam Warren	140
Total Accounts Receivable.	$850

normally at the time the equality of the General Ledger is tested, each of the subsidiary ledgers is proved. This is accomplished by preparing a list or a schedule of the balances of the accounts in each subsidiary ledger and seeing, for example, that the sum of the balances on the schedule of accounts receivable is equal to the balance of the Accounts Receivable controlling account. A schedule of the Accounts Receivable Ledger of the Sloan Novelty Company appears as in Illustration 37. Note that the total of this schedule, $850, is equal to the balance of the Accounts Receivable controlling account in the trial balance on the right in Illustration 36.

Posting Principle of Controlling Accounts and Subsidiary Ledgers

As previously stated, any class of accounts taken from the General Ledger is removed to reduce the number of accounts in the ledger. Since the trial balance of the General Ledger will not balance with part of its accounts removed, a controlling account having a balance equal to the sum of the balances of the accounts removed is substituted in the General Ledger. Thereafter, the posting principle upon which the subsidiary ledger and its controlling account operate requires that (1) the controlling account must be debited periodically for an amount or amounts equal to the sum of the debits to its subsidiary ledger accounts, and (2) the controlling account must be credited periodically for an amount or amounts equal to the sum of the credits to its subsidiary ledger accounts. Debiting the controlling account for the sum of the debits to the subsidiary ledger accounts and crediting the controlling account for the sum of the credits to the subsidiary ledger accounts brings the balance of the controlling account up to date and, if no errors have been made, makes it equal to the sum of the balances of the subsidiary ledger accounts.

Accounts Receivable Ledger and the Sales Journal

When a subsidiary Accounts Receivable Ledger is used, the individual debits recording sales in the Sales Journal are posted daily to the customer accounts in the Accounts Receivable Ledger. Consequently, at the end of the month, in line with the posting principle under which controlling accounts and their subsidiary ledgers operate, the column total of the journal must be posted not only to the credit side of the Sales account but also to the debit side of the Accounts Receivable account. Posting the total of the Sales Journal to both the debit side of the Accounts Receivable account and to the credit side of the Sales account accomplishes two purposes: (1) Since both the Sales account and the Accounts Receivable account are in the General Ledger, the posting keeps the General Ledger in balance. (2) The posting also provides a debit to the Accounts Receivable controlling account that is equal to the sum of the debits to the customer accounts in the subsidiary ledger. The posting of the Sales Journal when a subsidiary ledger is used is demonstrated in Illustration 38.

Note the check marks in the Folio column of the Sales Journal shown in Illustration 38. The Accounts Receivable Ledger is generally a loose-leaf ledger or a tray of ledger cards; and its accounts are arranged alphabetically to aid in locating any account. Furthermore, new accounts are placed in the ledger in their proper alphabetical position as required. Consequently, since the accounts are arranged alphabetically and new accounts are added in their proper alphabetical position, it is impossible to number the accounts. Therefore, when posting the individual amounts from the Sales Journal, a check mark, rather than a page number, is

Illustration 38—Posting the Sales Journal to the Accounts Receivable Ledger and to the General Ledger

SALES JOURNAL

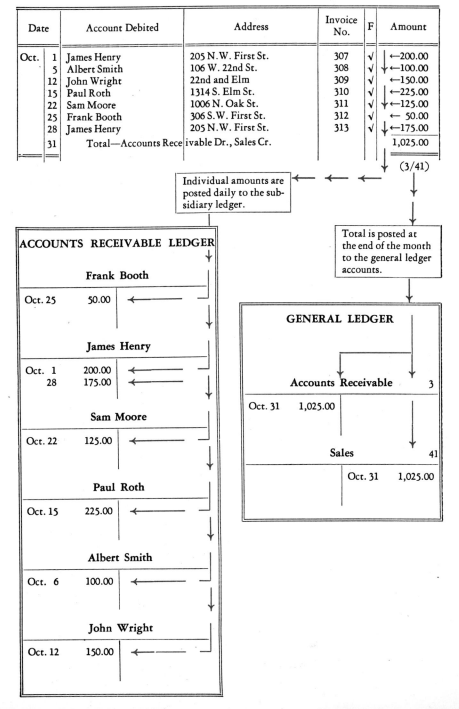

Date	Account Debited	Address	Invoice No.	F	Amount
Oct. 1	James Henry	205 N.W. First St.	307	√	←200.00
5	Albert Smith	106 W. 22nd St.	308	√	←100.00
12	John Wright	22nd and Elm	309	√	←150.00
15	Paul Roth	1314 S. Elm St.	310	√	←225.00
22	Sam Moore	1006 N. Oak St.	311	√	←125.00
25	Frank Booth	306 S.W. First St.	312	√	← 50.00
28	James Henry	205 N.W. First St.	313	√	←175.00
31	Total—Accounts Receivable Dr., Sales Cr.				1,025.00

(3/41)

Individual amounts are posted daily to the subsidiary ledger.

Total is posted at the end of the month to the general ledger accounts.

ACCOUNTS RECEIVABLE LEDGER

Frank Booth

Oct. 25	50.00

James Henry

| Oct. 1 | 200.00 |
| 28 | 175.00 |

Sam Moore

Oct. 22	125.00

Paul Roth

Oct. 15	225.00

Albert Smith

Oct. 6	100.00

John Wright

Oct. 12	150.00

GENERAL LEDGER

Accounts Receivable   3

Oct. 31	1,025.00

Sales   41

Oct. 31	1,025.00

placed in the Folio column of the journal to indicate that the amount has been posted.

As previously stated, when the Sales Journal is posted, the debits to customer accounts are posted daily. These daily postings make it possible to determine the current balance of a customer's account at any time. This is important because the total amount of credit granted to any one customer is usually limited, and before a decision as to granting further credit can be made, the person responsible for granting credit must know the amount currently owed by the customer seeking credit. He must also know the customer's promptness in meeting past obligations. This information is obtained from an examination of the account of the customer. If all postings have not been made, the one responsible for granting further credit is deceived.

Sales Taxes

Many cities and states require retailers to collect sales taxes from their customers and periodically to remit these taxes to the city or state treasurer. When a columnar Sales Journal is used, a record of the taxes collected can be obtained by the addition of special columns as shown in Illustration 39.

Illustration 39
SALES JOURNAL

Date	Account Debited	Inv. No.	F	Accounts Receivable Debit	Sales Taxes Payable Credit	Sales Credit
Dec. 1	D. R. Horn	7–1698		103.00	3.00	100.00

In posting a journal like that in Illustration 39, the individual amounts entered in the Accounts Receivable column are posted daily to the customer accounts in the Accounts Receivable Ledger and the column total is posted at the end of the month to the Accounts Receivable controlling account. The individual amounts in the Sales Taxes Payable and the Sales columns are not posted. However, at the end of the month the columns are totaled; the total of the Sales Taxes Payable column is credited to the Sales Taxes Payable account; and the total of the Sales column is credited to the Sales account.

A firm making cash sales upon which sales taxes must be collected may add a special Sales Taxes Payable column in its Cash Receipts Journal.

Sales Invoices as a Sales Journal

Many large companies do not record their sales in a Sales Journal. These companies post each sales invoice directly to the customer's account

in a subsidiary Accounts Receivable Ledger. The sales invoices are
then bound in numerical order in a binder. At the end of the month, all
of the invoices of that month are totaled on an adding machine; and a
general journal entry is made debiting the Accounts Receivable control
account and crediting Sales for the total. In effect, the bound copies
of the sales invoices act as a Sales Journal. Such a procedure eliminates
the labor of entering each invoice in a Sales Journal and is known as
direct posting of the sales invoices.

Cash Receipts Journal

Two important accounting techniques have been presented thus far in
this chapter. They are: (1) a technique for reducing posting labor by
placing, for example, the many repetitive credits to an account in a journal
column and posting them in one amount, the column total; and (2) a technique for reducing the number of accounts in the General Ledger and the
length of the trial balance by placing portions of the accounts in subsidiary ledgers.

Both of these techniques affect the design of the Cash Receipts Journal, causing it to be a multicolumn journal such as that shown in Illustration 40 on page 161. A multicolumn journal is necessary because, although
all cash receipts are alike in that they result in debits to the Cash account, cash receipts differ as to their sources and, consequently, as to
the accounts credited when cash is received. If the cash receipts of the
average mercantile company are classified as to sources, they fall into
three groups: (1) cash received from customers in payment of their accounts; (2) cash from cash sales; and (3) cash received from miscellaneous sources. Note in Illustration 40 that a special column is provided
for the credits resulting when cash is received from each of these sources.

Cash from Charge Customers.   A company having numerous receipts
from customers in payment of their accounts saves considerable posting
labor by recording these receipts in a Cash Receipts Journal like that
shown in Illustration 40. Posting labor is saved because columns are provided for the repetitive debits and credits. The repetitive debits and
credits are: (1) debits to Cash; (2) debits to Sales Discounts; and (3)
credits to the Accounts Receivable controlling account.

When a receipt from a charge customer in payment of his account is
recorded in a columnar Cash Receipts Journal like that of Illustration 40,
the customer's name is entered in the Account Credited column; the
amount credited to his account is entered in the Accounts Receivable
credit column; and the debits to Sales Discounts and Cash are entered
in the Sales Discounts and Cash debit columns.

Give close attention to the Accounts Receivable credit column of the
Cash Receipts Journal of Illustration 40. Observe (1) that only credits to
customer accounts are entered in this column; (2) that the individual
credits are posted daily to the customer accounts in the subsidiary Accounts Receivable Ledger; and (3) that the column total is posted at

the end of the month to the credit of the Accounts Receivable controlling account. This is the normal recording and posting procedure when controlling accounts and subsidiary ledgers are maintained. When controlling accounts and subsidiary ledgers are maintained, transactions are normally entered in a journal column; the individual amounts are posted to the subsidiary ledger accounts; and the column total is posted to the controlling account. Note that this recording and posting procedure keeps the balance of the controlling account equal to the sum of the balances in its subsidiary ledger.

Cash Sales. In the average company that sells for cash, cash sales are accumulated each day on one or more cash registers and their total is recorded by means of a journal entry at the end of the day. All of these journal entries are alike; all have repetitive debits to Cash and repetitive credits to Sales.

When cash sales are recorded in a Cash Receipts Journal like that of Illustration 40, the repetitive debits to Cash are entered in the Cash debit column and a special column headed "Sales credit" is provided for the repetitive credits to Sales. By entering the amounts of the daily cash sales in the Sales column, all of the cash sales of a month may be posted at the end of the month as a single amount, the column total. (Although cash sales are normally recorded daily from the cash register reading, the cash sales of Illustration 40 are recorded only once each week in order to shorten the illustration.)

At the time daily cash sales are recorded in the Cash Receipts Journal, many bookkeepers, as in Illustration 40, place a check mark in the Folio column of the journal to indicate that no amount is individually posted from that line of the journal.

Miscellaneous Receipts of Cash. The major share of all cash receipts come from customer collections and cash sales. However, cash is occasionally received from other sources such as, for example, a cash sale of an unneeded fixed asset or a promissory note given to a bank in order to borrow money. For transactions such as these the Sundry Accounts credit column is provided in the Cash Receipts Journal.

Posting the Cash Receipts Journal

The individual items in the Accounts Receivable column of the Cash Receipts Journal are posted daily to the credit sides of the customer accounts named in the Account Credited column. These items must be posted daily so that the accounts receivable ledger accounts show the current balance of each customer's account.

In the average company, the items in the Sundry Accounts credit column of the Cash Receipts Journal are few and are posted to a variety of general ledger accounts. Normally, postings are less apt to be omitted if these items are also posted daily. Furthermore, if the individual items in both the Sundry Accounts and the Accounts Receivable columns are

Illustration 40—Posting the Cash Receipts Journal to the Accounts Receivable Ledger and to the General Ledger

CASH RECEIPTS JOURNAL

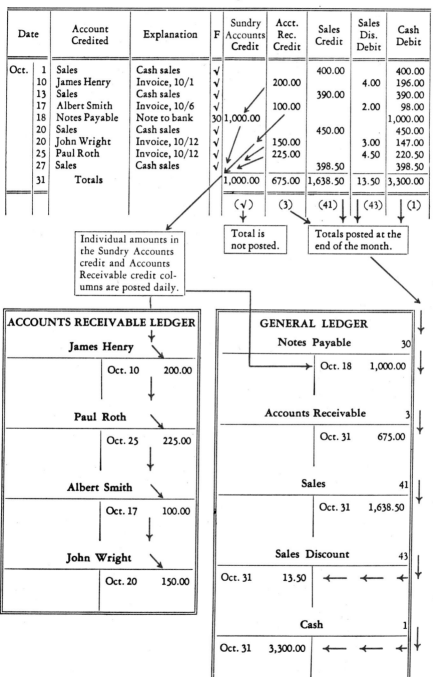

Date	Account Credited	Explanation	F	Sundry Accounts Credit	Acct. Rec. Credit	Sales Credit	Sales Dis. Debit	Cash Debit
Oct. 1	Sales	Cash sales	√			400.00		400.00
10	James Henry	Invoice, 10/1	√		200.00		4.00	196.00
13	Sales	Cash sales	√			390.00		390.00
17	Albert Smith	Invoice, 10/6	√		100.00		2.00	98.00
18	Notes Payable	Note to bank	30	1,000.00				1,000.00
20	Sales	Cash sales	√			450.00		450.00
20	John Wright	Invoice, 10/12	√		150.00		3.00	147.00
25	Paul Roth	Invoice, 10/12	√		225.00		4.50	220.50
27	Sales	Cash sales	√			398.50		398.50
31	Totals			1,000.00	675.00	1,638.50	13.50	3,300.00
				(√)	(3)	(41)	(43)	(1)

Individual amounts in the Sundry Accounts credit and Accounts Receivable credit columns are posted daily.

Total is not posted.

Totals posted at the end of the month.

ACCOUNTS RECEIVABLE LEDGER

James Henry

	Oct. 10	200.00

Paul Roth

	Oct. 25	225.00

Albert Smith

	Oct. 17	100.00

John Wright

	Oct. 20	150.00

GENERAL LEDGER

Notes Payable   30

	Oct. 18	1,000.00

Accounts Receivable   3

	Oct. 31	675.00

Sales   41

	Oct. 31	1,638.50

Sales Discount   43

Oct. 31	13.50	

Cash   1

Oct. 31	3,300.00	

posted daily, only the column totals of the journal remain to be posted at the end of the month.

The totals of the Accounts Receivable, Sales, Sales Discounts, and Cash columns are posted at the end of the month. However, since the transactions recorded in a journal must result in equal debits and credits to the general ledger accounts, the equality of the debits and credits in a columnar journal such as the Cash Receipts Journal is proved before these totals are posted. This is accomplished by *crossfooting* or cross adding the column totals. The debit column totals are added together, the credit column totals are added together, and the two sums are compared for equality. For example, if the debit column totals of the Cash Receipts Journal of Illustration 40 are added together and the credit column totals are added together, the two sums appear as follows:

Debit Columns		*Credit Columns*	
Sales discounts debit	$ 13.50	Sundry accounts credit	$1,000.00
Cash	3,300.00	Accounts receivable credit	675.00
		Sales credit	1,638.50
Total	$3,313.50	Total	$3,313.50

Since the two sums are equal, the debits recorded in the journal are assumed to equal the credits.

After the equality of the debits and credits is proved by crossfooting, the totals are posted. The total of the Accounts Receivable column is posted to the credit side of the Accounts Receivable controlling account in the General Ledger; the total of the Sales column is posted to the credit side of the Sales account; the total of the Sales Discounts account is posted to the debit of the Sales Discounts account; and the total of the Cash column is posted to the debit side of the Cash account. Since any individual items in the Sundry Accounts column are posted daily, the total of this column is not posted. This posting procedure is demonstrated in Illustration 40.

Posting items daily from the Sundry Accounts column of the Cash Receipts Journal with a delayed posting of the offsetting totals causes the ledger to be out of balance throughout the month. This is of no consequence because the offsetting totals are posted before a trial balance is prepared.

The Folio column of the Cash Receipts Journal is used only for the daily postings from the Sundry Accounts and Accounts Receivable columns. The numbers appearing in the Folio column indicate items posted to the General Ledger from the Sundry Accounts column; and the check marks indicate either that an item like a day's cash sales was not posted or that an item was posted to the subsidiary Accounts Receivable Ledger. The total of the Sundry Accounts column is not posted. Note in Illustration 40 the check mark below this column. The check mark indicates that when the journal was posted, this column total was not posted. The page numbers of the General Ledger to which the totals of the Accounts Receivable, Sales, Sales Discounts, and Cash columns of Illustration 40 were posted are indicated in parentheses below each column.

Miscellaneous Credits to Accounts Receivable

Credits to accounts receivable occur when merchandise previously sold on credit is returned. A company having a few such returns records them in a General Journal with an entry like the following.

Oct.	17	Sales Returns and Allowances.......	42	17.50	
		Accounts Receivable—Geo. Ball	3/ √		17.50
		Returned defective merchandise.			

The debit of the entry is posted to the debit side of the Sales Returns and Allowances account; and the credit is posted to both the Accounts Receivable controlling account and to the customer's account. Note the page number and the check, 3/✔, in the Folio column on the credit line. This indicates that both the Accounts Receivable controlling account in the General Ledger and the Geo. Ball account in the Accounts Receivable Ledger were credited for $17.50.

Companies having a sufficient number of sales returns can save posting labor by recording these returns in a special Sales Returns and Allowances Journal like that of Illustration 41. Note that this is in keeping with the idea that a company can design and use a special journal for any class of like transactions in which there are within the class a sufficient number of like transactions to warrant the journal. When a Sales Returns and Allowances Journal is used to record sales returns, the individual amounts entered in the journal are posted daily to the credit side of each affected customer account. At the end of the month, the total of the journal is posted to both the debit side of the Sales Returns and Allowances account and to the credit side of the Accounts Receivable controlling account. A Sales Returns and Allowances Journal and its posting are shown in Illustration 41 on the next page.

Occasionally a customer is unable to pay his account when it is due. In such cases, a promissory note is sometimes given by the customer in settlement of the account. The note does not pay the debt, but it does change the form of the debt from an informal promise to pay to a formal written promise to pay, and the change must be reflected in the accounting records. This is because informal promises appear on the balance sheet as accounts receivable, while formal written promises appear as notes receivable. A general journal entry to record the receipt of a note in settlement of an account appears as follows:

Oct.	19	Notes Receivable.................	2	239.50	
		Accounts Receivable—D. A. Root	3/ √		239.50
		Received a sixty-day, 6 per cent			
		note in settlement of the account.			

Illustration 41—Posting the Sales Returns and Allowances Journal

SALES RETURNS AND ALLOWANCES JOURNAL

Date	Account Credited	Address	Explanation	Credit Memo No.	F	Amount
Oct. 7	Robert Moore	106 E. 1st	Defective mdse.	203	√	←10 00
14	James Warren	10th and Oak	Defective mdse.	204	√	←12.00
18	T. M. Jones	134 W. 6th	Not ordered	205	√	← 6.00
23	Sam Smith	Salem, Ore.	Defective mdse.	206	√	←18.00
31	Sales Returns and Allowances Dr.,		Accounts Receivable Cr.			46.00
						(42/3)

Posted as individual amounts each day.

Total posted at the end of the month.

ACCOUNTS RECEIVABLE LEDGER

T. M. Jones

Oct. 18   6.00

Robert Moore

Oct. 7   10.00

Sam Smith

Oct. 23   18.00

James Warren

Oct. 14   12.00

GENERAL LEDGER

Accounts Receivable   3

Oct. 31   46.00

Sales Returns and Allowances 42

Oct. 31   46.00

The debit of the entry is posted to the Notes Receivable account in the General Ledger. The credit is posted to both the Accounts Receivable controlling account in the General Ledger and to the account of the customer in the subsidiary ledger.

In some companies where the receipt of notes from customers is common, a special Notes Receivable Journal is used. In other companies, if the receipt of notes is common, a special column is added to the General Journal. If a special column is added to the General Journal, all debits to Notes Receivable are entered in this column. This makes it possible to post the total of the debits to Notes Receivable in one amount. The use of a Notes Receivable Journal or the addition of a Notes Receivable debit column to the General Journal follows the principle that a special column may be added to a journal or a special journal may be added to the accounting system whenever like transactions are sufficient to warrant the addition.

Establishing a Subsidiary Accounts Payable Ledger

The Accounts Receivable Ledger and the journals which are posted to it have been used thus far in demonstrating the principles of special journals and of controlling accounts. However, these principles apply equally well to an Accounts Payable Ledger and the journals that affect it. For example, a firm wishing to establish a subsidiary Accounts Payable Ledger does so by following steps similar to those previously outlined for establishing an Accounts Receivable Ledger. Then, after establishing the ledger, it normally makes use of a Purchases Journal, a Cash Payments Journal, and perhaps a Purchases Returns and Allowances Journal in recording the majority of the transactions that affect the ledger. These journals operate in the same manner as the journals described thus far in this chapter.

The Purchases Journal and Its Posting

The form of the Purchases Journal is very similar to that of the Sales Journal, and both journals operate in the same manner. The information recorded in the Purchases Journal usually includes the date of each entry, the name of the creditor, his address, the date of the invoice, the terms, and the amount of the purchase. This information is recorded from approved purchase invoices; and its use, in the main, is apparent. The date of the invoice and the terms together indicate the date on which payment is due.

The Purchases Journal is posted in the same manner as the Sales Journal: (1) The individual amounts in the Amount column are posted daily to the subsidiary Accounts Payable Ledger to the credit side of each creditor's account named in the Account Credited column. (2) The total of the Amount column is posted at the end of the month to the debit side of the Purchase account and the credit side of the Accounts Payable controlling account. The posting of the Purchases Journal is demonstrated in Illustration 42 on page 166.

The Cash Payments Journal and Its Posting

The Cash Payments Journal, like the Cash Receipts Journal, has columns that make it possible to post repetitive debits and credits in column totals. The repetitive debits and credits of cash payments are debits to the Accounts Payable controlling account and credits to both Purchases Discounts and Cash. In most companies the purchase of merchandise for cash is not common; therefore, a Purchases column is not needed; and a purchase of merchandise for cash is recorded as on line 3 of Illustration

Illustration 42—Posting the Purchases Journal
PURCHASES JOURNAL

Date		Account Credited	Address	Date of Invoice	Terms	F	Amount
Oct.	3	Horn Supply Co.	1455 S. Elm St.	10/2	n/30	√	←350.00
	5	Acme Mfg. Co.	127 E. 10th St.	10/5	2/10, n/30	√	←200.00
	13	Wycoff & Company	Portland, Ore.	10/10	n/30	√	←150.00
	20	Smith and Company	2332 E. 9th St.	10/19	2/10, n/30	√	←300.00
	25	Acme Mfg. Co.	127 E. 10th St.	10/24	2/10, n/30	√	←100.00
	27	A. Evans and Son	1586 E. 12th St.	10/27	1/10, n/30	√	← 50.00
	29	H. A. Green Co.	1009 S. Oak St.	10/28	2/10, n/60	√	←175.00
	31	Total—Purchases Dr., Accounts Payable Cr.					1,325.00
							(46/21)

Individual amounts are posted daily.

Total is posted at the end of the month.

ACCOUNTS PAYABLE LEDGER

Acme Mfg. Co.

Oct. 5	→200.00
25	→100.00

A. Evans and Son

Oct. 27	50.00

H. A. Green Co.

Oct. 29	175.00

Horn Supply Co.

Oct. 3	350.00

Smith and Company

Oct. 20	300.00

Wycoff & Company

Oct. 13	150.00

GENERAL LEDGER

Purchases 46

Oct. 31	1,325.00

Accounts Payable 21

Oct. 31	1,325.00

43. However, although cash purchases of merchandise are commonly treated as on line 3, it should be pointed out that any company having many cash purchases would find it advantageous to place a Purchases column in its Cash Payments Journal.

In posting the Cash Payments Journal the individual amounts in the Sundry Accounts column are posted daily to the debit side of the general ledger account named in the Account Debited column; and the individual amounts in the Accounts Payable column are posted daily to the subsidiary Accounts Payable Ledger to the debit of the creditors named in the Account Debited column. At the end of the month, after the column totals are crossfooted to prove the equality of the debits and credits, the total of the Accounts Payable column is posted to the debit side of the Accounts Payable controlling account in the General Ledger; the total of the Purchases Discounts column is posted to the credit of the Purchase Discounts account; and the total of the Cash column is posted to the credit of the Cash account. Since the items in the Sundry Accounts column are posted individually each day, the total of this column is not posted. Posting of the Cash Payments Journal is demonstrated in Illustration 43.

When several special journals are used and are posted to the accounts, it is necessary to indicate in the account Folio column before each posted amount the journal as well as the page number of the journal from which the amount was posted. The journal from which an item was posted is indicated by using its initial or initials. Because of this, items posted from the Cash Payments Journal carry the initials "CP" before their journal page number in the Folio columns. Likewise, items from the Sales Journal carry the initial "S," items from the Purchases Journal carry the initial "P," and so on.

Miscellaneous Debits to Creditor Accounts

A company that has a sufficient number of purchases returns and allowances may use a Purchases Returns and Allowances Journal like that shown in Illustration 44. If such a journal is used, the individual amounts entered in the journal are posted daily as debits to creditor accounts in the Accounts Payable Ledger. At the end of the month the total of the journal is posted to both the debit side of the Accounts Payable controlling account and to the credit side of the Purchases Returns and Allowances account.

A company having but few purchases returns and allowances records each with a general journal entry like the following:

Oct.	23	Accounts Payable—Medford Mfg. Company........................	21/ √	32.00	
		Purchases Returns and Allow-ances........................	47		32.00
		Returned defective merchandise.			

Illustration 43—Posting the Cash Payments Journal
CASH PAYMENTS JOURNAL

Date	Account Debited	Explanation	F	Sundry Accounts Debit	Accts. Pay. Debit	Pur. Dis. Credit	Cash Credit
Oct. 3	Freight-In	Freight on purchase	49	← 4.50			4.50
10	Misc. General Expense	Utilities	53	←14.00			14.00
12	Purchases	Cash purchase	46	←25.00			25.00
15	Acme Mfg. Co.	Invoice, 10/5	√	←	200.00	4.00	196.00
15	Salaries Expense	Salaries	52	←86.00			86.00
20	Horn Supply Co.	Invoice, 9/20	√	←	75.00		75.00
29	Smith and Company	Invoice 10/9	√	←	300.00	6.00	294.00
31	Totals			129.50	575.00	10.00	694.50
				(√)	(21)	(48)	(1)

Individual amounts in the Sundry Accounts debit column and Accounts Payable debit column are posted daily.

Totals posted at the end of the month.

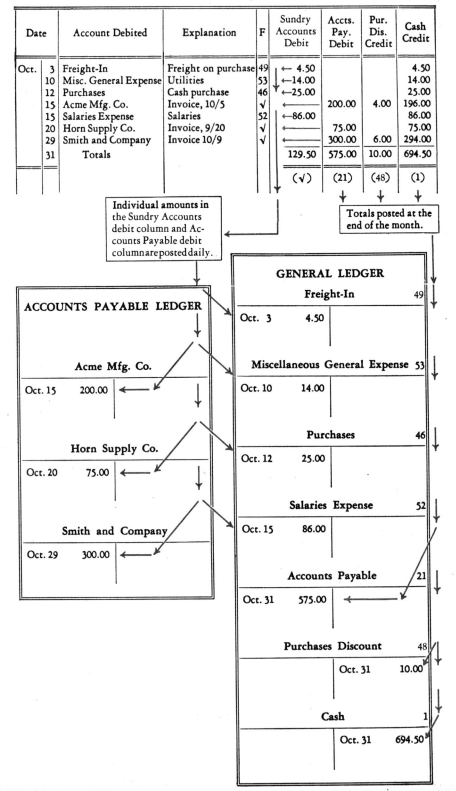

ACCOUNTS PAYABLE LEDGER

Acme Mfg. Co.

Oct. 15   200.00

Horn Supply Co.

Oct. 20   75.00

Smith and Company

Oct. 29   300.00

GENERAL LEDGER

Freight-In   49

Oct. 3   4.50

Miscellaneous General Expense   53

Oct. 10   14.00

Purchases   46

Oct. 12   25.00

Salaries Expense   52

Oct. 15   86.00

Accounts Payable   21

Oct. 31   575.00

Purchases Discount   48

Oct. 31   10.00

Cash   1

Oct. 31   694.50

Illustration 44

PURCHASES RETURNS AND ALLOWANCES JOURNAL

Date	Account Debited	Address	Explanation	F	Amount
Oct. 8	Medford Mfg. Co.	Medford, Ore.	Defective mdse.	√	← 32.00
12	Towne & Shell	10th and Pine	Below specifications	√	←110.00
23	Sports Weavers	Van Ness, Ore.	Defective mdse.	√	← 23.00
28	Short Novelty Co.	Portland, Ore.	Damaged in transit	√	← 14.00
31	Accounts Payable Dr., Purchases Returns and Allowances Cr.			21/47	179.00

> Individual amounts are posted daily to the Accounts Payable Ledger.

> Total is posted at the end of the month to the General Ledger.

Note the posting of the debit of the entry to both the Accounts Payable controlling account and to the creditor's account.

Sometimes a note is issued in payment of an account with a creditor. The note changes the form of the liability from an informal promise to pay to a formal written promise to pay. Such a transaction is recorded with a general journal entry like the following:

Oct.	24	Accounts Payable—Springfield Company.........................	21/ √	500.00	
		Notes Payable................	30		500.00
		Gave a thirty-day, 5 per cent note in settlement of the account.			

Purchase and Sale of Assets Used in the Business

When a single-column Purchases Journal and a single-column Sales Journal are used, only purchases and sales of merchandise may be recorded in these journals. This is because the column total of the Purchases Journal is debited to the Purchases account; the column total of the Sales Journal is credited to the Sales account; and purchases and sales of assets other than merchandise do not result in debits and credits to these accounts. However, every company must purchase assets for use in the business; and when these assets are no longer needed, they are sold. If the purchase or sale of an asset other than merchandise is for cash, the transaction is recorded in one of the cash journals. But if the purchase or sale is on credit, the transaction must be recorded in either the General Journal or, in cases where assets are purchased and such a journal is used, a multicolumn Purchases Journal similar to that shown in Illustration 45.

Illustration 45
PURCHASES JOURNAL

Date		Account Credited	Address	F	Accts. Payable Credit	Pur- chases Debit	Store Supplies Debit	Office Supplies Debit
Oct.	2	Marsh Wholesale Co.	876 10th St.		154.10	154.10		
	2	Office Supply Co.	344 13th St.		18.75			18.75

Some companies save posting labor by using a multicolumn Purchases Journal like the one shown in Illustration 45. Note that the journal has one credit column and, in this case, three debit columns; more debit columns could be used. The credit column is used to record the amounts credited to each creditor; and the items purchased are recorded in the debit columns. Such a journal is sometimes known as an "Accounts Payable Register."

Many companies do not use a multicolumn Purchases Journal. In companies using an ordinary one-column Purchase Journal, purchases of assets for use in the business are recorded in the General Journal with an entry like the following:

Oct.	29	Office Supplies......................	9	23.75	
		Accounts Payable—Ace Supply Co.	21/ √		23.75
		Bought office supplies.			

Balance Form of Ledger Account

The two-column form of ledger account used thus far in this text may be used for all types of accounts. Furthermore, for accounts other than those with customers and creditors, such an account form is very satisfactory. This is because the balances of accounts other than those with customers and creditors generally need to be known only at the time a trial balance is taken. However, although the two-column account form may be used with customer and creditor accounts, the *balance form of ledger account* is usually more satisfactory. This is because the balance form of ledger account provides a Balance column for recording the current balance of a customer or creditor account as each transaction is posted. A balance column account for a customer is shown at the end of this paragraph. It provides a column for debits, a column for credits, and a column for the current balance of the account. As each debit or credit is posted to the account, the new balance is entered in the Balance column. Often the Balance column does not indicate whether the account balance is a debit or a credit. However, since all accounts receivable normally have debit balances, any account in the Accounts Receivable Ledger is assumed to have a debit balance. Likewise, any account in the Accounts Payable

Ledger is assumed to have a credit balance. In those few cases where an overpayment causes an account to have a balance opposite from its normal balance, such a balance is entered in red ink, or is entered in black ink and encircled. A credit balance in an account receivable account or a debit balance in an account payable account is entered in red or is entered in black and encircled.

James Henry 205 N. W. First St.						
Date		Explanation	F	Debit	Credit	Balance
Oct.	1		S-1	200.00		200.00
	10	.	CR-2		200.00	—
	28		S-1	175.00		175.00
Nov.	4		S-2	50.00		225.00
	7		CR-3		175.00	50.00

Since the balance column form of ledger account is better adapted to machine posting, this form is commonly used for all accounts when posting is done by machine.

Special Journals for a Particular Business

It should be noted that the special journals of this chapter are only illustrative of those in use. In most cases special journals are designed with the needs of a particular business in mind. As a result the columns provided and the placement of the columns are such as to fit the needs of the business for which they are designed.

Special Journal for a Small Business

The journals and ledgers of a business should always be designed to fit its needs. In a large company where a division of labor is required to handle the recording of many transactions, five or more special journals may be used. In such a company the five or more special journals make it possible to divide the labor of recording transactions between five or more bookkeepers. In a small business having relatively few transactions such a division of labor is not necessary, and, as a result, five or more separate books of original entry are not needed. However, a small business does need the laborsaving benefits of special journals, and it commonly secures these benefits by using a type of columnar journal called a *Combination Journal* or a *Combined Cash Journal*. This journal is described and discussed in more detail in the next chapter.

QUESTIONS FOR CLASS DISCUSSION

1. What may a business gain by the use of special journals?
2. How do special journals save posting labor?

3. How is it possible to tell from which journal a particular amount in a ledger was posted?

4. How do special journals take advantage of the fact that for any single class of transactions either the debit or the credit of each transaction is always to the same account?

5. How is a multiple-column journal crossfooted? Why is a multiple-column journal crossfooted?

6. A business uses a Cash Receipts, a Cash Payments, a single-column Sales, a single-column Purchases, and a General Journal. In which journal will it record each of the following transactions?
   a) Sale of merchandise on credit.
   b) Purchase of office supplies on credit.
   c) Purchase of merchandise on credit.
   d) Purchase of office equipment for cash.
   e) Sale of unneeded office equipment on credit.
   f) Return of a charge sale.
   g) Return of a cash sale.
   h) Return of a credit purchase.
   i) Payment of a creditor.
   j) Correction of a posted error, wrong account.
   k) Adjusting entries.
   l) Closing entries.

7. What is gained by the use of subsidiary ledgers and controlling accounts?

8. A company has the following number of accounts with balances in its General Ledger:

   a) Asset accounts (not including customer accounts)........................ 25
   b) Accounts with customers... 500
   c) Liability accounts (not including creditor accounts)..................... 5
   d) Accounts with creditors... 50
   e) Proprietorship accounts (including income statement accounts)............ 20
         Total..600

   How many items appear on the trial balance of this company? If the accounts with customers and creditors are removed from the General Ledger and placed in subsidiary ledgers, how many items will appear on the trial balance?

9. Why must an Accounts Receivable controlling account be substituted in the General Ledger in the place of the customer accounts when the customer accounts are removed and placed in a subsidiary ledger?

10. You have been asked to establish a subsidiary Accounts Receivable Ledger and an Accounts Receivable controlling account for a firm that has previously kept all of its customer accounts in its General Ledger. Explain how you propose to accomplish this.

11. How is the equality of a controlling account and its subsidiary ledger maintained?

12. How is a schedule of accounts receivable prepared when the accounts receivable are kept in a subsidiary ledger? Why is such a schedule prepared?

13. Why are postings to customer accounts made daily?

14. After all posting is completed, the balance of the Accounts Receivable controlling account does not agree with the sum of the balances in the Accounts Receivable Ledger. If the trial balance is in balance, where is the error apt to be? Why?

15. When a general journal entry is used to record a returned charge sale, the credit of the entry must be posted twice. Does this cause the trial balance to be out of balance? Why or why not?

16. Both credits to customer accounts and credits to miscellaneous accounts are individually posted from a Cash Receipts Journal like that of Illustration 40. Why not place both kinds of credits in the same column and thus save journal space?

17. A company uses a Sales Journal, an Accounts Receivable controlling account, and a subsidiary Accounts Receivable Ledger similar to the ones described in this chapter. If it makes the following errors, when will each error be apt to be first discovered?

a) A $10 sale on account is recorded in the Sales Journal as a $100 sale.

b) A $10 sale is correctly recorded in the Sales Journal but is posted to the customer's account as a $100 sale.

c) An error is made in securing the balance of a customer's account.

d) An error is made in totaling the Amount column in the Sales Journal.

18. Is a "red ink" balance in an accounts receivable ledger account a debit balance or a credit balance?

PROBLEMS

Problem 8–1

The following sales, cash receipts, and miscellaneous transactions were completed by Ballard Automotive Supply Company during December of the current year:

Dec.   2   Sold merchandise on credit to Robert Nance, Roseburg, Oregon, Invoice No. 878, $1,200. (Terms of all sales are 2/10, n/30.)

4   William Ballard, the proprietor of Ballard Automotive Supply Company, invested an additional $1,500 in the business.

6   Sold merchandise on credit to Scott Taylor, Redmond, California, Invoice No. 879, $1,600.

8   Robert Nance returned $200 of merchandise for credit because it did not meet specifications.

10   Sold merchandise on credit to Carl Gordon, Bend, Oregon, Invoice No. 880, $2,200.

12   Received a check from Robert Nance in full payment of Invoice No. 878, less the return and the discount.

13   Sold merchandise on credit to Carl Gordon, Bend, Oregon, Invoice No. 881, $900.

13   Sold $250 of unneeded office equipment to Scott Taylor on credit.

15   Cash sales for the first half of the month were $2,350. (Cash sales are commonly recorded daily from the cash register reading. They are recorded only twice monthly in this problem in order to shorten the problem.)

15   *Make the individual postings from the journals. Normally, items that are posted as individual amounts from the journals are posted daily. Since the number of such items in this problem is few, you are asked to post them on only two occasions.*

16   Gave the First National Bank a sixty-day promissory note in order to borrow $2,000.

18   Sold merchandise on credit to Robert Nance, Roseburg, Oregon, Invoice No. 882, $1,300.

20 Received a check from Carl Gordon in full payment of Invoice No. 880, less the discount.

22 Sold merchandise on credit to Robert Nance, Roseburg, Oregon, Invoice No. 883, $1,700.

23 Received a check from Carl Gordon in full payment of Invoice No. 881, less the discount.

25 Received a check from Scott Taylor in full payment of Invoice No. 879.

28 Received a check from Robert Nance in full payment of Invoice No. 882, less the discount.

31 Cash sales for the last half of the month were $2,675.

31 *Make the individual postings from the journals.*

31 *Make the month-end postings from the journals.*

Required:

1. Open the following general ledger accounts: Cash; Accounts Receivable; Office Equipment; Notes Payable; William Ballard, Capital; Sales; Sales Returns and Allowances; and Sales Discounts.

2. Open the following accounts receivable ledger accounts: Carl Gordon; Robert Nance; and Scott Taylor. Use balance column accounts.

3. Prepare a Sales Journal similar to Illustration 38, a Cash Receipts Journal similar to Illustration 40, and a General Journal. Enter the transactions in the journals and post at the points where you are instructed to do so in the narrative of transactions.

4. Prepare a month-end trial balance and a schedule of accounts receivable. (An asset account will have a credit balance in the trial balance. This is because you have not been asked to record all of the transactions of the business.)

Problem 8–2

The following purchases, cash disbursements, and miscellaneous transactions were completed by Central Sales Company during December of the current year:

Dec. 3 Received merchandise and an invoice dated November 30, terms 2/10, n/60, from Bigbee Manufacturing Company, Seattle, Washington, $2,800.

5 Paid advertising expense, $210.

6 Received merchandise and an invoice dated December 4, terms 2/10, n/60, from Robert McBroom, Inc., Eugene, Oregon, $1,800.

8 Received merchandise and an invoice dated December 6, terms 2/10, n/60, from Joslin and Kerns, Dallas, Oregon, $2,300.

10 Sent Bigbee Manufacturing Company a check in payment of the invoice of November 30, less the discount.

13 Sent Robert McBroom, Inc., a check in payment of the invoice of December 4, less the discount.

13 Purchased $400 of store equipment from West Equipment Sales, 1081 High Street, terms 10 E.O.M.

16 Paid the sales salaries for the first half of the month, $750.

16 Sent Joslin and Kerns a check in payment of the invoice of December 6, less the discount.

16 *Make the individual postings from the journals. Normally, items that are posted as individual amounts from the journals are posted daily. Since the number of such items in this problem is few, you are asked to post them on only two occasions.*

18 Purchased $50 of store supplies for cash.

19 Received merchandise and an invoice dated December 18, terms 2/10, n/60, from Robert McBroom, Inc., Eugene, Oregon, $1,700.

22 Received a credit memorandum from Robert McBroom, Inc., for defective merchandise received from them on December 19 and returned for credit, $300.

25 Received merchandise and an invoice dated December 23, terms 2/10, n/60, from Robert McBroom, Inc., Eugene, Oregon, $600.

27 Sent a check to Robert McBroom in payment of the invoice of December 18, less the return and the discount.

31 Paid the sales salaries for the last half of the month, $750.

31 Gary Bolton, the owner of Central Sales Company withdrew $500 for his personal use.

31 *Make the individual postings from the journals.*

31 *Make the month-end postings from the journals.*

Required:

1. Open the following general ledger accounts: Cash; Store Supplies; Store Equipment; Accounts Payable; Gary Bolton, Withdrawals; Purchases; Purchases Returns and Allowances; Purchases Discounts; Advertising Expense; and Sales Salaries.

2. Open the following accounts payable ledger accounts: Bigbee Manufacturing Company; Joslin and Kerns; Robert McBroom, Inc.; and West Equipment Sales. Use balance column accounts.

3. Prepare a Purchases Journal similar to Illustration 42, a Cash Payments Journal similar to Illustration 43, and a General Journal. Enter the transactions in the journals and post at the points where you are instructed to do so in the narrative of transactions.

4. Prepare a trial balance and a schedule of accounts payable.

Problem 8–3

Munzel Sales Company completed the following transactions during February of the current year:

Feb. 2 Sold merchandise on credit to Tyler and Vance, Grandview, Oregon, $1,250. (Terms of all sales are 2/10, n/30. Number sales invoices beginning with 758.)

2 Sold merchandise on credit to Bruce Sawyer, Inc., Dale, Oregon, $1,500.

3 Received merchandise and an invoice dated January 31, terms 2/10, n/60, from Globe Manufacturing Company, Portland, Oregon, $2,800.

4 Paid advertising expense, $185.

5 Sold unneeded store equipment for cash, $140.

7 Cash sales for first week of February, $1,200.

7 *Make the individual postings from the journals. Normally items that are posted as individual amounts are posted daily. You are asked to post such items only once each week in this problem in order to shorten the problem.*

8 Issued a credit memorandum to Bruce Sawyer, Inc., for defective merchandise purchased on February 2 and returned for credit, $400.

10 Sold merchandise on credit to Rice and Son, Salem, Oregon, $800.

10 Received merchandise and an invoice dated February 6, terms 1/10, n/60, from Western Supply Company, Denver, Colorado, $1,850.

10   Sent a check to Globe Manufacturing Company in full of the invoice of January 31, less the discount.

12   Received a check from Tyler and Vance in full payment of the sale of February 2, less the discount.

12   Received a check from Bruce Sawyer, Inc., in full payment of the sale of February 2, less the return and the discount.

14   Cash sales for the week ended February 13, $1,450.

14   *Make the individual postings from the journals.*

15   Sold merchandise on credit to Rice and Son, Salem, Oregon, $900.

15   Paid the sales salaries for the first half of the month, $600.

17   Issued a credit memorandum to Rice and Son, Salem, Oregon, for defective merchandise purchased on February 15 and returned, $150.

18   Sold merchandise to Bruce Sawyer, Inc., Dale, Oregon, $1,300.

18   Received merchandise and an invoice dated February 15, terms 2/10, n/30, from F. M. Pope, Portland, Oregon, $3,500.

19   Received store equipment and an invoice dated February 18, terms 10 E.O.M., from Ryan Equipment Company, 210 Main Street, $650.

20   Received a check from Rice and Son in full of the sale of February 10, less the discount.

20   Cash sales for the week ended February 20, $1,550.

21   *Make the individual postings from the journals.*

22   Received merchandise and an invoice dated February 18, terms 1/10, n/60, from Western Supply Company, Denver, Colorado, $1,250.

22   Received merchandise and an invoice dated February 18, terms 2/10, n/60, from Globe Manufacturing Company, Portland, Oregon, $2,650.

23   Received a credit memorandum from F. M. Pope, Portland, Oregon, $350. The merchandise covered by the memorandum did not meet specifications and had been returned.

24   Received a check from Rice and Son in full of the invoice of February 15, less the return and the discount.

24   Sent F. M. Pope a check in full of the invoice of February 15, less the return and the discount.

25   Sold merchandise on credit to Tyler and Vance, Grandview, Oregon, $1,175.

27   Borrowed $5,000 from the United States National Bank by giving them a sixty-day, 6 per cent note payable.

28   Sent Globe Manufacturing Company a check in full of the invoice of February 18, less the discount.

28   Paid the sales salaries for the last half of the month, $600.

28   Cash sales for week ended February 28, $1,225.

28   *Make the individual postings from the journals.*

28   *Crossfoot and make the month-end postings.*

Required:

1. Open the following general ledger accounts: Cash; Accounts Receivable; Store Equipment; Notes Payable; Accounts Payable; Sales; Sales Returns and Allowances; Sales Discounts; Purchases; Purchases Returns and Allowances; Purchases Discounts; Advertising Expense; and Sales Salaries.

2. Open the following subsidiary accounts receivable ledger accounts using

balance column accounts: Bruce Sawyer, Inc., Dale, Oregon; Rice and Son, Salem, Oregon; and Tyler and Vance, Grandview, Oregon.

3. Open the following subsidiary accounts payable ledger accounts using balance column accounts: Globe Manufacturing Company, Portland, Oregon; F. M. Pope, Portland, Oregon; Ryan Equipment Company, 210 Main Street; and Western Supply Company, Denver, Colorado.

4. Prepare a Sales Journal similar to Illustration 38, a Sales Return and Allowances Journal similar to Illustration 41, a Purchases Journal similar to Illustration 42, a Cash Receipts Journal similar to Illustration 40, a Cash Payments Journal similar to Illustration 43, and a General Journal.

5. Enter the transactions in the journals and post to the ledger accounts when instructed to do so in the narrative of transactions.

6. Prepare a trial balance of the General Ledger and schedules of accounts receivable and accounts payable.

Problem 8–4

S. M. Coe began a business called S. M. Coe Equipment Company on October 1 of the current year. Following are his special journals as they appeared after the first month's operations:

SALES JOURNAL

Date		Account Debited	Address	Invoice No.	F	Amount
Oct.	4	H. A. Clark	1210 Moss Street	1		80.00
	5	A. V. Kirk	1400 Columbia Street	2		72.00
	11	Robert Price	201 East 10th Street	3		120.00
	13	H. A. Clark	1210 Moss Street	4		40.00
	18	John Biggs	2202 Agate Street	5		46.00
	20	A. V. Kirk	1400 Columbia Street	6		105.00
	22	John Biggs	2202 Agate Street	7		78.00
	25	Robert Price	201 East 10th Street	8		41.00
	29	John Biggs	2202 Agate Street	9		26.00
						608.00

PURCHASES JOURNAL

Date		Account Credited	Address	Date of Invoice	Terms	F	Amount
Oct.	4	M. A. Berry Co.	Portland, Ore.	10/1	2/10, n/30		500.00
	6	Sunbeam, Inc.	Seattle, Wash.	10/2	1/10, n/60		150.00
	10	Long Supply Co.	12th and Oak Sts.	10/9	2/10, n/30		250.00
	11	Sunbeam, Inc.	Seattle, Wash.	10/7	1/10, n/60		105.00
	15	M. A. Berry Co.	Portland, Ore.	10/12	2/10, n/30		350.00
	20	Valley Sales Co.	Harrisburg, Ore.	10/18	2/10, n/30		300.00
	26	M. A. Berry Co.	Portland, Ore.	10/22	2/10, n/30		575.00
							2,230.00

CASH RECEIPTS JOURNAL

Date		Account Credited	Explanation	F	Sundry Accounts Credit	Accts. Rec. Credit	Sales Credit	Sales Dis. Debit	Cash Debit
Oct.	1	S. M. Coe, Capital	Investment		2,000.00				2,000.00
	5	Store Supplies	Sold supplies		5.00				5.00
	6	Cash Sales	Week 10/6				200.00		200.00
	8	H. A. Clark	Sale of 10/4			80.00		1.60	78.40
	13	Cash Sales	Week 10/13				350.00		350.00
	15	A. V. Kirk	Sale of 10/5			72.00		1.44	70.56
	20	Robert Price	Sale of 10/11			120.00		2.40	117.60
	20	Cash Sales	Week 10/20				475.00		475.00
	23	H. A. Clark	Sale 10/13			40.00		.80	39.20
	27	Cash Sales	Week of 10/-27				550.00		550.00
	29	John Biggs	Sale of 10/18			46.00		.92	45.08
	30	A. V. Kirk	Sale of 10/20			105.00		2.10	102.90
	31	Cash Sales	Last three days				200.00		200.00
					2,005.00	463.00	1,775.00	9.26	4,233.74

CASH PAYMENTS JOURNAL

Date		Account Debited	Explanation	F	Sundry Accounts Debit	Accts. Pay. Debit	Pur. Dis. Credit	Cash Credit
Oct.	2	Rent Expense	October rent		200.00			200.00
	2	Store Supplies	Purchased supplies		52.00			52.00
	11	M. A. Berry Co.	Invoice of 10/1			500.00	10.00	490.00
	15	Salaries Expense	Paid salaries		150.00			150.00
	19	Long Supply Co.	Invoice 10/9			250.00	5.00	245.00
	22	M. A. Berry Co.	Invoice 10/12			350.00	7.00	343.00
	27	Valley Sales Co.	Invoice 10/18			300.00	6.00	294.00
	31	Salaries Expense	Paid salaries		150.00			150.00
					552.00	1,400.00	28.00	1,924.00

Required:

1. Open the following general ledger accounts: Cash; Accounts Receivable; Store Supplies; Accounts Payable; S. M. Coe, Capital; Sales; Sales Discounts; Purchases; Purchases Discounts; Rent Expense; and Salaries Expense.
2. Open the following accounts receivable ledger accounts: John Biggs; H. A. Clark; A. V. Kirk; and Robert Price.
3. Open the following accounts payable ledger accounts: M. A. Berry Company; Long Supply Company; Sunbeam, Inc.; and Valley Sales Company.

4. Post the special journals and prepare a trial balance of the General Ledger and schedules of the accounts receivable and accounts payable.

CLASS EXERCISES

Exercise 8–1

At the end of this exercise are the special journals of a small business. The column headings of the journals are incomplete in that whether the columns are debit columns or credit columns is not shown.

Required:

1. Prepare T-accounts on a sheet of ordinary notebook paper for the following general ledger and subsidiary ledger accounts. Separate the accounts of each ledger into groups.

General Ledger Accounts
Cash
Accounts Receivable
Prepaid Insurance
Equipment
Accounts Payable
Robert Small, Capital
Sales
Sales Returns
Sales Discount
Purchases
Purchases Returns
Purchases Discount

Accounts Receivable Ledger Accounts
W. Wall
D. Dale
M. Morris

Accounts Payable Ledger Accounts
ABC Co.
LMN Co.
XYX Co.

2. Without referring to illustrations showing complete column headings for special journals, post the following special journals to the proper T-accounts:

CASH RECEIPTS JOURNAL

Account	Sundry Accounts	Accts. Rec.	Sales	Sales Discount	Cash
Robert Small, Capital	24,000.00				24,000.00
Cash Sales			800.00		800.00
D. Dale		400.00		8.00	392.00
M. Morris		1,400.00		28.00	1,372.00
	24,000.00	1,800.00	800.00	36.00	26,564.00

CASH PAYMENTS JOURNAL

Account	Sundry Accounts	Accts. Payable	Purchases Discount	Cash
Equipment	3,000.00			3,000.00
ABC Company		5,800.00	58.00	5,742.00
Prepaid Insurance	600.00			600.00
LMN Company		3,000.00	60.00	2,940.00
	3,600.00	8,800.00	118.00	12,282.00

SALES JOURNAL		SALES RETURNS AND ALLOWANCES JOURNAL		PURCHASES JOURNAL		PURCHASES RETURNS AND ALLOWANCES JOURNAL	
Account	Amount	Account	Amount	Account	Amount	Account	Amount
W. Wall	1,000.00	D. Dale	100.00	ABC Co.	6,000.00	ABC Co.	200.00
D. Dale	500.00	W. Wall	30.00	LMN Co.	3,000.00	XYZ Co.	20.00
M. Morris	1,400.00		130.00	XYZ Co.	600.00		220.00
	2,900.00				9,600.00		

Exercise 8–2

Pension Company maintains controlling accounts and subsidiary ledgers for both accounts receivable and accounts payable. How would each of the following errors (a) affect the company's trial balance, (b) affect the proof of the subsidiary ledgers, and (c) how would you correct each error?

1. An error was made in footing the purchases journal, the incorrect total being $6,926 instead of the correct amount of $6,826.
2. A sale made in exchange for a note receivable, $800, was entered in the Sales Journal, Notes Receivable being entered as the account debited. In making the daily postings, Notes Receivable was debited for the $800.
3. Cash sales totaling $1,200 were entered in the Sales Journal. The amount of cash received for cash sales was also entered in the Cash Receipts Journal, the amounts being entered in the "Sundry Accounts, credit" column and the "Cash, debit" column. The entries in both journals were checked in the journal Folio columns, and no amounts were posted individually.
4. A sale to J. R. Jones was posted from the Sales Journal to J. C. Jones' account, amount $50.

Exercise 8–3

In the records of Northwest Supply Company on November 30 of the current year the account payable to Gem Manufacturing Company had a credit balance of $510. The balance of the account on November 1 had been $1,040. During November $210 of defective merchandise had been returned to Gem Manufacturing Company, and during the month the company was paid a total of $2,499 for merchandise purchased. Each payment was made within the discount period and took advantage of a 2 per cent discount. How much merchandise was purchased from Gem Company during November?

SUPPLEMENTARY PROBLEMS

Problem 8–A

Inter-City Sales completed the following transactions:

Dec. 3 Purchased from Best Supply Company, Albany, Oregon, $1,200 of merchandise.
5 Purchased from Dale and Ross, Eugene, Oregon, $800 of merchandise.
6 Purchased from Best Supply Company, Albany, Oregon, $55 of store supplies and $175 of office supplies.
9 Purchased from Western Jobbers, Eugene, Oregon, $750 of merchandise and $110 of store supplies.
11 Purchased $350 of office equipment from Dawson Equipment Company, Eugene, Oregon.

15 Purchased from Best Supply Company, Albany, Oregon, $85 of office supplies and $600 of merchandise.

22 Purchased from Dale and Ross, Eugene, Oregon, $1,300 of merchandise.

28 Purchased from Western Jobbers, Eugene, Oregon, $525 of merchandise.

Required:

1. Prepare a General Journal and also a multicolumn Purchases Journal having the same columns as that shown in Illustration 45.
2. Enter the transactions in the journals.
3. Under the assumption that the firm maintains a subsidiary Accounts Payable Ledger, describe in your own words the manner in which you would post the multicolumn Purchases Journal.

Problem 8–B

On page 182 is one of the special journals used by Midway Sales Company. In the journal cents are omitted to conserve space.

Required:

1. Open general ledger and subsidiary accounts payable ledger accounts as required and then make use of the knowledge acquired in this chapter to post the special journal.
2. Prepare a trial balance of the general ledger accounts and a schedule of the accounts payable.

CASH DISBURSEMENTS, PURCHASES, AND PURCHASES RETURNS JOURNAL

	Debit Columns				Date	Account Titles and Explanations	F	Credit Columns			
Store Supplies	Sales Salaries	Pur-chases	Accts. Payable	Sundry Accts.				Sundry Accts.	Accts. Payable	Pur. Discount	Cash
				500	Dec. 1	Rent expense					500
75		525			2	Horn Supply Company			600		
		850			5	Whitney Company			850		
			600		10	Horn Supply Company				12	588
			100		13	Whitney Company—Purchases Returns		100			
			750		14	Whitney Company				15	735
		1,200			15	Swing Wholesale Company			1,200		
	750				15	Salaries for the first half of month					750
				175	18	Store equipment					175
50		1,100			23	Horn Supply Company			1,150		
			1,200		24	Swing Wholesale Company				24	1,176
	750				31	Salaries for last half of month					750
125	1,500	3,675	2,650	675				100	3,800	51	4,674

Chapter

9

MODIFICATION OF THE JOURNALS: THE COMBINATION JOURNAL; DEPARTMENTAL ACCOUNTING

THE JOURNALS and ledgers used by a particular business should be designed to fit its needs. To stress this point the first portion of this chapter shows how the special journals introduced in Chapter 8 are combined into the *Combination Journal* or *Combined Cash Journal*, the journal used by a large number of small businesses. After this, the chapter explains how the special journals may be expanded in order to secure easily information in more detail as is required in departmental accounting.

The Combination Journal

A large business often requires the services of several bookkeepers in recording its many transactions. In such a business separate special journals like those described in Chapter 8 are commonly necessary in order to enable more than one bookkeeper to work on the accounting records at the same time. For example, in such a business, in order to handle the volume of work, it may be necessary for one bookkeeper to record cash receipts in a Cash Receipts Journal while another bookkeeper is recording sales in a Sales Journal and a third bookkeeper is posting from the Cash Payments Journal.

Although separate special journals are often necessary in a large business, in a small business, one having no more than a sufficient number of transactions as to require the services of just one bookkeeper, several separate special journals are something of a handicap to the bookkeeper. They are a handicap because the bookkeeper must put aside one special journal and pick up another each time a different kind of transaction is to be recorded.

Nevertheless, any business, large or small, needs the laborsaving benefits of columnar journals; and in order to secure these benefits, many small companies make use of a journal that combines the columns of the five or more special journals of a large business into a single columnar journal called a Combination Journal or a Combined Cash Journal. Such a journal is illustrated at the top of the following two pages.

The Combination Journal shown at the top of the following two pages, Illustration 46, is a combination Sales Journal, Purchases Journal, Cash Receipts Journal, Cash Payments Journal, and General Journal. Transactions are entered in the columns of this journal in much the same manner

Illustration 46
COMBINATION JOURNAL

Page 14

Cash		Check No.	Date		Account Titles and Explanation	F	Sundry Accounts		
Debit	Credit						Debit	Credit	
	100.00	108	Oct.	1	Rent Expense	51	100.00		1
				4	James Henry	√			2
				6	Acme Mfg. Company	√			3
	98.00	109		6	Horn Supply Company	√			4
	160.00	110		6	Weekly Salaries	√			5
49.00				10	James Henry	√			6
				11	Store Supplies—Ace Company	8/√	31.00		7
2,213.00 (1)	1,468.00 (1)						160.00 (√)	78.00 (√)	40

as transactions were entered in the columns of the special journals described in Chapter 8. Likewise, the individual amounts and column totals are posted in a similar manner. A comparison of the Combination Journal with the special journals of Chapter 8 will show:

SPECIAL JOURNAL OF CHAPTER 8

COMBINATION JOURNAL EQUIVALENT

Sales Journal

The Accounts Receivable debit column and the Sales credit column of the Combination Journal are the equivalent of a single-column Sales Journal. The amount of each credit sale is entered in the Sales credit column. The name of the customer debited is entered in the Account Titles column, and the amount debited is entered in the Accounts Receivable debit column. Daily, the individual debits to customer accounts are posted to the Accounts Receivable Ledger. The totals of the Accounts Receivable debit column and the Sales credit column are posted to these general ledger accounts at the end of the month.

Illustration 46—Continued

FOR MONTH OF *October*____, 19—

Page 14

	Accounts Receivable		Accounts Payable		Sales Credit	Pur-chases Debit	Sales Dis-count Debit	Pur-chases Dis. Cr.	Office Salaries Expense Debit	Sales Salaries Expense Debit
	Debit	Credit	Debit	Credit						
1										
2	50.00				50.00					
3				150.00		150.00				
4			100.00					2.00		
5									50.00	110.00
6		50.00					1.00			
7				31.00						
40	650.00 (2)	410.00 (2)	843.00 (21)	891.00 (21)	2,451.00 (41)	795.00 (46)	12.00 (62)	15.00 (61)	200.00 (52)	440.00 (53)

SPECIAL JOURNAL
OF CHAPTER 8

Purchases Journal

COMBINATION JOURNAL EQUIVALENT

The Accounts Payable credit column and the Purchases debit column of the Combination Journal are the equivalent of a single-column Purchases Journal. The amount of each credit purchase is entered in the Purchases debit column. The name of the creditor is entered in the Account Titles column, and the amount credited is entered in the Accounts Payable credit column. Daily, the individual amounts entered in the Accounts Payable credit column are posted to the creditor accounts in the Accounts Payable Ledger. At the end of the month, the totals of the Accounts Payable credit column and the Purchases debit column are posted to these accounts in the General Ledger.

SPECIAL JOURNAL OF CHAPTER 8	COMBINATION JOURNAL EQUIVALENT
Cash Receipts Journal	The Cash debit, Sundry Accounts credit, Accounts Receivable credit, Sales credit, and Sales Discount debit columns of the Combination Journal are the equivalent of a special Cash Receipts Journal. Cash receipts are entered in these columns in the same manner as they are entered in a special Cash Receipts Journal. Posting of the individual amounts in these columns and the column totals is accomplished in the same manner as posting the special Cash Receipts Journal.
Cash Payments Journal	The Cash credit, Sundry Accounts debit, Accounts Payable debit, and Purchases Discount credit columns of the Combination Journal are the equivalent of a special Cash Payments Journal. Transactions are entered in these columns, and the posting of the individual amounts and column totals is accomplished in the same manner as in a special Cash Payments Journal.
General Journal	The Account Titles column, the Sundry Accounts debit column, and the Sundry Accounts credit column are the equivalent of a General Journal. The transactions that do not fit into the other columns of the Combination Journal are entered in the Sundry Accounts debit and credit columns. The amounts entered in these columns are posted in the manner of a General Journal.

Special Columns in the Combination Journal

Many of the transactions of a small business affect the same account. This is particularly true of cash payments. Consequently, to avoid many individual postings to the same ledger account, special columns for these repetitive transactions are placed in the Combination Journal. The journal illustrated in this chapter has special columns for sales salaries expense and office salaries expense. Other special columns to fit the needs of a particular business may be used.

The use of the Combination Journal by small companies is most common. Almost all ready-made, small business, bookkeeping systems provide such a journal. The column headings are printed in to meet the needs of the type of business for which the ready-made system is designed. A small business that is unable to find a ready-made journal with column headings that meet its needs may design its own journal. In such cases, the column headings are written in on blank forms secured from a printer or stationery store.

Departmental Accounting

When a store sells several different kinds of merchandise, the store may be divided into departments based upon the different kinds of merchandise sold. For example, a men's and boys' clothing store may be divided into departments as follows: men's clothing department, boys' clothing department, and shoe department. When a store is departmentalized in this manner, and its accounting system is properly designed, it is possible to account for the revenue from the sale of each kind of merchandise and to know the profit of each department. This in turn makes it possible to push the sales of profitable departments, and to understand why unprofitable departments do not earn a profit. When it is known why certain departments do not earn a profit, measures may be taken to make them profitable; or if the unprofitable departments cannot be made to earn a profit, they may be discontinued. Unprofitable departments are often discontinued when they cannot be made profitable. However, although unprofitable departments are often discontinued when they cannot be made profitable, they are also commonly continued at a loss either because of the business they bring to the profitable departments or because they make a contribution toward payment of the overhead and to the over-all profitableness of the business.

Basis of Departmentalization

In every departmentalized business there are always two basic kinds of departments. They are *productive departments* and *service departments*. In a merchandising business the productive departments are the sales departments; they produce sales. The service departments of a store are such departments as the general office department, the purchasing department, and the building maintenance department. The service departments are the departments that assist or perform services for the sales departments.

When a store is divided into sales departments, the exact division is usually based upon the kinds of merchandise sold. However, several principles should be observed in the division. First, the goods to be included in each sales department should be related in nature and so located as to be convenient for one person to supervise and control. In addition, all the goods of any one department should have approximately the same percentage of markup or gross profit. If the last principle is not observed, one kind of merchandise with a high profit margin may carry another kind of merchandise that produces little or no profit.

Problems of Departmental Accounting

If a merchandising business is to determine earnings by departments, the sales, cost of goods sold, and expenses of each department must be known. It is not too difficult to keep a record of sales and to determine cost of goods sold by departments. Most of the difficult problems of departmental accounting are problems of expense allocation. Expense allocation problems are problems of how to allocate fairly expenses to the several departments of a firm. For example, how much of the total rent expense of a store should be borne by each of its departments? Should the share of the total rent expense that is allocated to each department be determined entirely on the basis of the number of square feet of floor space occupied by each department? Or, should consideration be given to such things as, for example, that floor space directly in front of the main entrance is more valuable than floor space in an out-of-the-way corner? Often questions such as these cannot be exactly answered; and, consequently, the share of an expense that should be borne by each department cannot be exactly measured. Often in such cases an allocation, if made, must be based upon judgment; and the result is only as accurate as the judgment is good.

Since the problems of determining sales, cost of goods sold, and gross profits by departments are the least difficult of the problems of departmental accounting, these problems will be considered first in this chapter. After this, some of the problems of departmentalizing expenses will be discussed.

Departmentalizing the Merchandise Accounts

There are many combinations of methods and procedures that may be used in accounting for the merchandise transactions of a departmentalized company. Normally the size of a company and the number of its departments determine the exact methods and procedures to be followed.

In a small departmentalized company, one having not more than four or five departments, a practice is to provide in the General Ledger separate sales, sales returns, purchases, purchases returns, and merchandise inventory accounts for each department. For example, a departmentalized store having a men's clothing department, a boys' clothing department, and a shoe department commonly provides in its ledger three separate sales accounts: Men's Clothing Department Sales, Boys' Clothing Department Sales, and Shoe Department Sales. Such a store also commonly provides three sales returns accounts, three purchases accounts, three purchases returns accounts, and three merchandise inventory accounts. In short, such a store commonly provides a separate set of merchandise accounts for each of its departments. It then records the merchandise transactions of each of its departments in the department's merchandise accounts. At the end of each accounting period, it takes inventories by departments and, using the information in the several department merchandise accounts, it calculates cost of goods sold and gross profits by departments.

Changes in the Books of Original Entry

As previously stated, in a departmentalized store having not more than four or five departments, separate sales, sales returns, purchases, purchases returns, and merchandise inventory accounts may be opened in the General Ledger for each department. Likewise, in such a store special columns may be added to the books of original entry so that the merchandise transactions of the several departments may be more easily recorded.

For example, the Valley Haberdashery which has three departments, men's clothing, boys' clothing, and shoes, maintains separate merchandise accounts for each of its departments. Also, to record the merchandise transactions of each of its departments, the store provides special columns in its journals. The Purchases Journal of the store with its special columns for recording purchases by departments is shown in Illustration 47.

Illustration 47
PURCHASES JOURNAL

Date	Account Credited	Address	F	Accounts Payable Credit	Purchases Debit		
					Men's Dept.	Boys' Dept.	Shoe Dept.
Feb. 1	Acme Mfg. Co.	Seattle, Wash.		250.00	250.00		
1	N. A. Green Co.	Portland, Ore.		110.00			110.00
2	Horn Supply Co.	Portland, Ore.		275.00	200.00	75.00	

The Valley Haberdashery records each of its purchase invoices on a single line in its special departmentalized Purchases Journal as each invoice is received. The amount of each invoice is entered in the Accounts Payable credit column and distributed to the proper department purchases debit columns according to the items purchased. The credits to each of the individual creditor accounts are posted daily; the column totals are posted to the Accounts Payable controlling account and the proper department purchases accounts at the end of the month.

The Sales Journal of the Valley Haberdashery is expanded in the same manner as its Purchases Journal with special department sales columns as in Illustration 48. The posting of the Sales Journal is similar to the posting of the Purchases Journal. The individual debits to customer accounts are posted daily; the column totals are posted at the end of the month.

Illustration 48
SALES JOURNAL

Date	Account Debited	Invoice No.	Accounts Receivable Debit	Sales Credit		
				Men's Dept.	Boys' Dept.	Shoe Dept.
Feb. 2	John Wright	3–345	78.00	78.00		
2	Sam Moore	3–346	37.00		30.00	7.00
3	Paul Roth	3–347	10.50			10.50

Since the Valley Haberdashery has but three departments, its Cash Receipts Journal is also expanded by the addition of a cash sales column for each department. The cash sales of each department, as shown by the various department cash register totals, are entered in the proper cash sales column at the end of each day. At the end of the month the total of each of the cash sales columns is posted to the sales account of the proper department. The special cash sales columns of the Cash Receipts Journal of the Valley Haberdashery appear as in Illustration 49.

· **Illustration 49**
CASH RECEIPTS JOURNAL

Date	Account Credited		F	Sundry Accounts Credit		Cash Sales Credit		
						Men's Dept.	Boys' Dept.	Shoe Dept.

If a company such as the Valley Haberdashery has a sufficient number of returns to warrant special returns and allowances journals, it may also departmentalize these journals by adding additional columns for each department.

Departmental Analysis Sheets

A store with only a few departments may expand its special journals by adding columns for recording transactions by departments. However, a store with more than four or five departments finds its journals unnecessarily large and awkward if it adds special columns for each department. Consequently, a store having more than four or five departments often secures information as to each of its department's sales, sales returns, purchases, and purchases returns by the use of *departmental analysis sheets*. When a store uses departmental analysis sheets, its journals and ledgers are the same as those of an undepartmentalized firm. No special departmental columns are added in the journals, and only one general ledger account each for Sales, Sales Returns, Purchases, and Purchases Returns is maintained in the ledger. In the place of numerous accounts and special journal columns, a separate departmental analysis sheet having a column for each department is provided for the transactions affecting each of the merchandise accounts. The merchandise transactions of all departments are then recorded in the undepartmentalized journals and general ledger accounts as though the store was not departmentalized. However, in addition to recording the sales, sales returns, purchases, and purchases returns in the undepartmentalized journals and ledger accounts, summaries of each day's merchandise transactions are also entered on the departmental analysis sheets. For example, in addition to entering the total charge sales of all departments in the Sales Journal, each day's charge sales tickets are sorted by departments, and the total for each department is entered in the proper department column of a *departmental sales analysis sheet*. Likewise, in addition to recording the total cash sales of all departments in the Cash Receipts Journal, the cash sales of each department are also entered at the end of each day in the proper department column of the sales analysis sheet. At the end of the month, the totals of the various sales analysis sheet columns give the total sales of the departments, and the grand total of all of the columns should equal the balance of the Sales account in the ledger. A departmental analysis sheet for the analysis of sales is shown in Illustration 50.

Illustration 50

DEPARTMENTAL SALES ANALYSIS SHEET

Date		Type of Sales	Men's Wear Dept.	Boys' Wear Dept.	Men's Shoe Dept.	Men's Hat Dept.	Women's Wear Dept.
May	1	Cash sales	257.00	110.00	155.00	37.00	197.00
		Charge sales	102.00	82.00	58.00	76.00	105.00
	2	Cash sales	138.00	97.00	127.00	58.00	222.00
		Charge sales	127.00	103.00	82.00	62.00	189.00
	3	Cash sales	152.00	72.00	97.00	73.00	205.00

When a store uses departmental analysis sheets, it uses a separate analysis sheet for the items recorded in each of its merchandise accounts. Such a store uses a departmental sales analysis sheet, a departmental sales returns analysis sheet, a departmental purchases analysis sheet, and a departmental purchases returns analysis sheet. At the end of each accounting period, the several analysis sheets give a breakdown by departments of the store's sales, sales returns, purchases, and purchases returns. This breakdown is used in calculating the cost of goods sold and gross profit of each of the store's departments.

Allocation of Freight-In

Freight-in is a factor in the calculation of cost of goods sold. When a store is departmentalized, if possible, payments for freight on merchandise purchased should be analyzed and charged to the individual departments so that a more accurate gross profit may be calculated for each department.

Some stores maintain a separate freight-in account for each of their departments. Other stores use a departmental freight-in analysis sheet to accumulate the freight charges applicable to each of their departments. When either method is used, each freight bill is analyzed at the time of payment and charged to the responsible departments. Sometimes this is easy, and sometimes it is not so easy. If all of a shipment of merchandise is consigned to a single department, the entire amount of freight on the shipment may be charged to the single responsible department. However, often items of merchandise for several departments are included in a single shipment having a single freight bill. When this happens, the freight charges on the shipment must be allocated in some manner to the responsible departments. Often in such cases, if possible, freight charges are allocated on the basis of the size and weight of the items of merchandise received by each department.

Although in some companies each freight bill is allocated at the time of payment on the basis of the size and weight of the items received, in other companies because of the nature of the freight shipments, it is difficult if not impossible to determine and assign freight charges to departments in this manner. Often in these latter companies freight charges are accumulated in a single undepartmentalized freight-in account without any effort being made to allocate the charges at the time of payment to the responsible departments. When freight charges are accumulated in this manner, they are accumulated in the single freight-in account until the end of each accounting period. At the end of each accounting period the balance of the freight-in account is allocated to the various departments on the basis of, for example, the dollar value of the purchases of the departments. When this is done, a department with $\frac{1}{8}$ of the total purchases is charged with $\frac{1}{8}$ of the freight-in, and a department with $\frac{1}{6}$ of the purchases is charged with $\frac{1}{6}$ of the freight-in. While this is not as accurate as allocating each freight payment at the time of payment on the basis of size and weight of the merchandise received, it is often deemed satisfactory.

Income Statement with Only the Trading Section Departmentalized

Many small companies do not attempt to departmentalize any but their merchandise accounts. These companies calculate gross profits by departments; but, because of the difficulties involved, make no attempt to assign operating expenses to their various departments.

When a company that departmentalizes only its merchandise accounts prepares an income statement, the income statement normally shows gross profits by departments but is otherwise undepartmentalized. Such a statement appears somewhat as in Illustration 51.

Departmentalization of Expenses

Small companies often departmentalize only their merchandise accounts and make no effort to assign operating expenses to their depart-

Illustration 51

VALLEY HABERDASHERY
Income   Statement
For Year Ended December 31, 19--

	Men's Clothing	Boys' Clothing	Shoes	Combined
Revenue from sales:				
Sales	$46,000	$34,000	$20,000	$100,000
Less: Sales returns . .	750	425	350	1,525
Net sales	$45,250	$33,575	$19,650	$ 98,475
Cost of goods sold:				
Inventory, Jan. 1	$ 7,400	$ 4,200	$ 3,350	$14,950
Purchases	30,000	21,700	11,800	63,500
Freight-in. . . .	150	125	75	350
Goods for sale. .	$37,550	$26,025	$15,225	$78,800
Inventory, Dec. 31	8,100	3,500	4,150	15,750
Cost of goods sold. . . .	29,450	22,525	11,075	63,050
Gross profits	$15,800	$11,050	$ 8,575	$ 35,425

Operating expenses:

Selling expenses:

Sales salaries	$7,000	
Sales commissions.	5,000	
Advertising.	550	
Sales supplies used.	200	
Depreciation of store equipment.	700	
Total Selling Expenses		$13,450

General and administrative expenses:

Office salaries.	$3,800	
Office suppies used.	250	
Expired insurance	300	
Bad debts.	210	
Depreciation of office equipment	150	
Depreciation of building	1,200	
Property taxes	900	
Total General and Administrative Expenses.		6,810
Total Operating Expenses		20,260
Net Income		$ 15,165

ments. However, large companies commonly assign and allocate operating expenses to their departments. When expenses are assigned to departments, several methods or combinations of methods may be followed in accumulating and recording the expenses applicable to each department. One method is to open in the General Ledger an account for each expense of each department. When this is done, expenses are charged to department expense accounts in the books of original entry and are posted to the proper department expense accounts in the General Ledger. A variation of this procedure is to keep only one Operating Expense controlling account in the General Ledger and to maintain a subsidiary ledger having separate department expense accounts for each of the various departments.

If a controlling account for operating expenses and a subsidiary Operating Expense Ledger are used, the controlling account and subsidiary ledger are handled in much the same manner as controlling accounts and subsidiary ledgers for customers and creditors. Usually, expenses are recorded in a special column in a book of original entry. The individual amounts are then posted from the column to the individual expense accounts in the subsidiary ledger, and the column total is posted to the expense controlling account. This is similar to the procedure previously illustrated for customer and creditor transactions.

Assigning Code Numbers to Accounts

When expenses are charged to numerous department expense accounts a system of code numbers to identify each expense account becomes almost a necessity. If code numbers are not used, identifying the many individual expense items entered in the books of original entry and posting these items to the proper department expense accounts is almost impossible.

When expense accounts are assigned code numbers as a means of identification, normally all accounts are assigned identifying code numbers. In one account numbering system three-digit numbers with each digit having a significant meaning are used. In this system the first digit of each account number signifies the major balance sheet or income statement classification of the account to which it is assigned. For example, account numbers with a first digit of 1, numbers 111 to 199, are assigned to asset accounts. Liability accounts are assigned account numbers with first digits of 2, numbers 211 to 299. When this numbering system is used, the main balance sheet and income statement classifications of accounts are assigned the following numbers:

111 to 199 are assigned to asset accounts.
211 to 299 are assigned to liability accounts.
311 to 399 are assigned to proprietorship accounts.
411 to 499 are assigned to sales or revenue accounts.
511 to 599 are assigned to cost of goods sold accounts.
611 to 699 are assigned to operating expense accounts.
711 to 799 are assigned to other revenue and expense accounts.

When accounts are assigned code numbers having several digits, all of the digits have a significant meaning. In the system under discussion where the first digit indicates the main balance sheet or income statement classification of each account, the second and third digits further classify the account. For example, the second digits under each of the following main classifications indicate the subclassification shown:

111 to 199.   Asset accounts
    111 to 119.   Current asset accounts (second digits of 1)
    121 to 129.   Long-term investment accounts (second digits of 2)
    131 to 139.   Fixed asset accounts (second digits of 3)
    141 to 149.   Intangible asset accounts (second digits of 4)
    151 to 159.   Deferred charges (second digits of 5)

211 to 299.   Liability accounts
    211 to 219.   Current liability accounts (second digits of 1)
    221 to 229.   Long-term liability accounts (second digits of 2)

611 to 699.　Operating expense accounts
    611 to 629.　Selling expense accounts (second digits of 1 and 2)
    631 to 649.　Delivery expense accounts (second digits of 3 and 4)
    651 to 669.　General administrative expense accounts (second digits of 5 and 6)

The third digit in each account number further classifies the account. For example, in the numbering system under discussion, all selling expense accounts which have account numbers with first digits of 6 and second digits of 1 and 2 are further classified as follows:

611 to 699.　Operating expense accounts
    611 to 629.　Selling expense accounts
        611.　Sales salaries (third digit of 1)
        612.　Advertising (third digit of 2)
        613.　Depreciation of store equipment (third digit of 3)

When this system is used with departmental expense accounts, a decimal point and a fourth digit are often used to identify an expense with a department. For example:

611 to 699.　Operating expense accounts
    611 to 629.　Selling expenses
        611.　Sales salaries
            611.1.　Sales salaries, Department 1
            611.2.　Sales salaries, Department 2
            611.3.　Sales salaries, Department 3
            611.4.　Sales salaries, Department 4

Commonly, when account code numbers are used, the code numbers are used in the place of page numbers in the ledgers.

Allocation of Expenses

When expenses are allocated and charged to departments, great care and judgment must be used in their allocation. If care and judgment are not used and expenses are incorrectly allocated and charged, the resulting departmental income statements are at least misleading.

The need for care and judgment in the allocation of expenses is obvious in the following paragraphs in which the allocations of an illustrative group of expenses are discussed. In the discussions no hard-and-fast rules are set forth. On the contrary, in some cases, more than one suggestion for the allocation of a particular expense is offered. The reason for this is obvious. In the allocation of certain expenses several factors are commonly involved, and the importance of the factors vary from one situation to another. Consequently, if the expenses are to be fairly allocated, judgment must be used in each case as to the weight to be given the various factors.

Salaries. The salaries of most employees are a direct departmental expense and are usually easy to allocate. The payroll records show the amount paid each employee and the department to which he is assigned and to which his salary should be charged. If an employee works in more than one department, the expense of his salary should normally be divided, and a share should be charged to each department in which he works according to the time worked in each department.

Sometimes a supervisory employee supervises several departments. In such cases it is often difficult to exactly charge the expense of his salary to the several departments. In some companies the salary of a supervisory employee is charged to the several departments he supervises on the basis of the number of employees in each. In other companies the salary of a supervisory employee is charged to the departments he supervises on the basis of the sales made by each. When the salary of a supervisory employee is charged to his departments on the basis of the number of employees in each department, the assumption is made that the supervisory employee is supervising other employees and the amount of time he spends in each department is related to the number of employees in each department. When the salary of a supervisory employee is charged to the departments he supervises on the basis of sales, it is assumed that the time he spends in each department is related to the productiveness of each department.

Rent. Rent expense is normally allocated to the various sales and service departments upon the basis of the amount and value of the floor space occupied by each. Obviously, ground floor space is more valuable for retail purposes than is basement or upper floor space, and space near the front entrance is more valuable than space in an out-of-the-way corner. Yet, because there is no exact measure of floor space values, all floor space values must be based upon judgment. In every case the very best judgment plus any statistics as to customer traffic or any other information available should be used in determining the values to be assigned to the various parts of a building.

In allocating rent expense to the various departments, the space occupied by stairs, aisles, and show windows is often disregarded, and rent is allocated on the basis of the net remaining space.

Advertising. When a store advertises, if the advertising is at all effective, people are induced to come into the store to buy the advertised products. However, often at the time these people buy advertised products they also buy other unadvertised products. Consequently, advertising is often assumed to benefit all departments, even those the products of which are not advertised. Because advertising is often assumed to benefit all departments, many stores allocate advertising costs to their departments on the basis of sales. When this is done, a department producing $\frac{1}{15}$ of the total sales is charged with $\frac{1}{15}$ of the total advertising and a department producing $\frac{1}{6}$ of the sales is charged with $\frac{1}{6}$ of the advertising.

Although in many stores advertising is allocated to the departments on the basis of sales, in other stores it is charged directly to the departments on the basis of, for example, newspaper space used. When this is done, each advertisement is analyzed and the cost of the number of column inches of space devoted to the products of each department is charged to the proper department.

Insurance, Taxes, and Depreciation. Insurance, taxes, and depreciation on equipment are normally allocated to the various departments upon the basis of the value of the equipment in each department. Insurance, depreciation, and taxes on the building, if the building is owned, are normally allocated on the same basis as rent expense.

Lights. Lighting expense is normally assigned to the various departments on the basis of the number, size, and burning time of the lights in each department.

Heat. Heat costs are normally allocated to the various floors of a building on the basis of the amount of radiation on each floor. Usually the first floor requires more radiation because of the heat lost through the doors as customers enter and leave. After heat expense is allocated to the various floors, the heat expense of each floor is assigned to the departments on each floor according to the floor space occupied by each.

Delivery Expense. The cost of delivering packages depends upon the number, size, and weight of the packages delivered. Usually, it is impossible to consider all three of these factors in one single basis of allocation. Consequently, the most important one of the three is often used as the allocation basis. Sometimes all three factors, number, size, and weight, are ignored, and delivery expense is allocated on the basis of the sales of each department. Often, too, in for example a grocery store where the number, size, and weight of packages are closely related to sales, an allocation based upon sales is fair.

Departmental Expense Analysis Sheet

Some companies analyze and charge operating expenses to numerous department expense accounts as the expenses are recorded. Other companies are of the opinion that such a procedure requires too much recording and posting labor. In order to save recording and posting labor, these latter companies record their expenses in undepartmentalized operating expense accounts and allocate the expenses recorded in this manner to the proper departments in a single operation at the end of each accounting period.

Normally, companies that record their expenses in undepartmentalized expense accounts and allocate these expenses to the proper departments in a single operation at the end of each accounting period use a *departmental expense analysis sheet* in making the allocation. A form of a departmental expense analysis sheet is shown in Illustration 52. The form illustrated lists each undepartmentalized expense account and its balance and shows the basis on which each expense is allocated. In addition it provides a column for the collection of each department's share of the expenses allocated.

When a departmental expense analysis sheet is used, operating expenses

Illustration 52
DEPARTMENTAL EXPENSE ANALYSIS SHEET

Undepartmentalized Expense Accounts	Basis of Allocation	Expense Account Balance	Allocation of Expenses to Departments					
			General Office Dept.	Purchasing Dept.	Cleaning Dept.	Men's Clothing Dept.	Boys' Clothing Dept.	Furnishings Dept.
Salaries expense	Payroll records	$14,150	$ 800	$ 950	$1,200	$5,100	$3,700	$2,400
Advertising expense	Sales	1,030				460	340	230
Rent expense	Amount and value of floor space	3,600	180	180	20	1,600	407	1,213
Expired insurance	Value of equipment	160	25	15	6	66	12	36
Depreciation of equipment	Value of equipment	500	79	47	19	197	37	121
Lighting expense	Wattage of lights	226	18	18	5	90	40	55
Heating expense	Floor space	480	24	24	4	212	72	144
Supplies used	Requisitions	586	103	63	85	133	54	148
Total Expenses by Departments		$20,732	$1,229	$1,297	$1,339	$7,858	$4,662	$4,347

are recorded throughout each accounting period in undepartmentalized expense accounts. At the close of each accounting period the balances of the undepartmentalized expense accounts are copied into the Expense Account Balance column of the departmental expense analysis sheet and are allocated to the departments on the bases shown. The expense amounts in the several columns are then used in the construction of the department income statements.

Allocation of Service Department Expenses

A departmentalized business normally has productive departments and service departments. When a store is departmentalized and earnings are to be calculated for each of its selling departments, each selling department must bear a fair share of the expenses of operating the service departments, such as the general office, purchasing, and cleaning departments. This is logical. The service departments perform services for the selling departments. If each selling department were a separate store or business, each would have to provide and pay for these services for itself.

Although it is logical that each selling department bear its share of the expenses incurred in the operation of the service departments, it is normally impossible at the time the expenses of the service departments are paid and first recorded to allocate directly and charge these expenses to the selling departments served by the service departments. Consequently, service department expenses are normally accumulated first by service departments. The service department expenses may be accumulated in numerous service department expense accounts as they are paid and recorded, or they may be allocated to the service departments at the end of an accounting period by means of a departmental expense analysis sheet. Either way the total of the expenses incurred in the operation of each of the service departments is first determined. Then, after the expenses incurred in the operation of each of the service departments are determined, a *service department expense allocation sheet* is used to allocate to the selling departments the cost of operating each of the service departments. A service department expense allocation sheet is shown in Illustration 53.

When a service department expense allocation sheet is used to allocate service department expenses to the productive departments, the total of the expenses incurred in the operation of each individual service department and each individual productive department is entered in the proper department column on the first line of the allocation sheet. After this the total of the expenses incurred in the operation of each service department is in turn allocated to the productive or selling departments it serves. Generally the allocation is based in each case upon the amount of services performed for each of the productive departments by the service department whose expenses are being allocated. For example, the expenses of operating the general office are usually allocated to the selling departments on the basis of sales. The assumption is that the selling departments re-

Illustration 53

SERVICE DEPARTMENT EXPENSE ALLOCATION SHEET

Service Departments	Basis of Allocation	Allocation of Expenses to Departments					
		Gen. Office Dept.	Pur-chas-ing Dept.	Clean-ing Dept.	Men's Cloth-ing Dept.	Boys' Cloth-ing Dept.	Fur-nish-ings Dept.
Total department expenses..............		$1,229	$1,297	$1,339	$7,858	$4,662	$4,347
General office department	Sales	1,229			557	421	251
Purchasing department..	Purchases		1,297		601	347	349
Cleaning department....	Floor space			1,339	655	294	390
Total Selling Department Expenses...					$9,671	$5,724	$5,337

quire services from the general office in proportion to their sales. Likewise, the purchasing department expenses are allocated to the selling departments on the basis of the purchases made for each department, and the cleaning department expenses are allocated on the basis of the square feet of floor space in each department. In each case the allocation base is considered a fair measure of the services performed for each of the departments.

Sometimes service departments perform services for other service departments. However, this is often ignored in allocating service department expenses because the major share of the services performed by each service department is normally performed for the productive departments.

Combined Expense Analysis and Service Department Expense Allocation Sheet

A company that collects its department expenses in numerous department expense accounts secures the cost of operating each of its departments from the department expense accounts in its ledger. Likewise, a company that records its operating expenses in undepartmentalized expense accounts and allocates these expenses to its departments by means of a departmental expense analysis sheet secures the cost of operating each of its departments from the expense analysis sheet. Both types of companies may use a service department expense allocation sheet similar to the one shown in Illustration 53 in allocating their service department expenses to their productive departments. However, although a firm that records its expenses in undepartmentalized expense accounts may use a service department expense allocation sheet similar to the one in Illustration 53, such a firm commonly combines its departmental expense analysis sheet and its service department expense allocation sheet into a combination form similar to the one shown in Illustration 54.

Illustration 54

EXPENSE ANALYSIS AND SERVICE DEPARTMENT EXPENSE ALLOCATION SHEET

Undepartmentalized Expense Accounts and Service Departments	Basis of Allocation	Expense Account Balance	Allocation of Expenses to Departments					
			General Office Dept.	Purchasing Dept.	Cleaning Dept.	Men's Clothing Dept.	Boys' Clothing Dept.	Furnishings Dept.
Salaries expense	Payroll records	$14,150	$ 800	$ 950	$1,200	$5,100	$3,700	$2,400
Advertising expense	Sales	1,030				460	340	230
Rent expense	Amount and value of floor space	3,600	180	180	20	1,600	407	1,213
Expired insurance	Value of equipment	160	25	15	6	66	12	36
Depreciation of equipment	Value of equipment	500	79	47	19	197	37	121
Lighting expense	Wattage of lights	226	18	18	5	90	40	55
Heating expense	Floor space	480	24	24	4	212	72	144
Supplies used	Requisitions	586	103	63	85	133	54	148
Total Expense by Departments		$20,732	$1,229	$1,297	$1,339	$7,858	$4,662	$4,347
General office department	Sales		1,229			557	421	251
Purchasing department	Purchases			1,297		601	347	349
Cleaning department	Floor space				1,339	655	294	390
Total Expenses Applicable to Selling Departments		$20,732				$9,671	$5,724	$5,337

Department Income Statements

A departmentalized store having more than three or four departments normally prepares an income statement that shows only the combined sales, costs, expenses, and earnings for all departments. This statement is similar to the undepartmentalized statements illustrated in the first chapters of this text. In addition, for the use of its executives, such stores normally attach to their undepartmentalized income statement a separate income statement for each department. The information for these department income statements comes from the department accounts and the analysis and allocation sheets.

Closing Entries for a Departmentalized Business

No essentially new procedures are required in closing the books of a departmentalized business. If only undepartmentalized merchandising accounts and undepartmentalized expense accounts or an expense controlling account are maintained in the General Ledger, these accounts are closed in the usual manner through a single income summary account. This is true whether subsidiary ledgers are maintained or expense analysis sheets are used. If subsidiary ledgers are maintained, the accounts in the subsidiary ledgers are closed at the same time their controlling accounts are closed. Of course, if analysis sheets are used, new analysis sheets are prepared each accounting period and a closing of the analysis sheets is unnecessary.

A store that maintains in its General Ledger separate merchandise and expense accounts for each of its departments also often maintains a separate income summary account for each of its departments. The separate department income summary accounts, one for each department, are in addition to a general income summary account. When department income summary accounts are maintained, the revenues, costs, and expenses of each department are summarized in each department's income summary account. Then only the net income or loss of each department is closed to a general income summary account.

Eliminating an Unprofitable Department

Departmental accounting makes it possible to account for the revenues, costs, and expenses and to know the earnings of each department of a departmentalized firm. This in turn makes it possible to push the sales of profitable departments and to know why unprofitable departments do not earn a profit. When it is known why certain departments do not earn a profit, measures may often be taken to make them profitable. However, sometimes unprofitable departments cannot be made profitable. When a department cannot be made profitable, it may either be discontinued or continued at a loss. Unprofitable departments that cannot be made profitable are often discontinued. They are also commonly continued at a loss either because of the business they bring to profitable departments or because they contribute to the total net income of the business. For example, the Joe M. Hardt Company is contemplating the elimination of Department A of its store. A departmental income statement of the store for 19— appears as shown in Illustration 55.

Illustration 55

JOE M. HARDT COMPANY
Department Income Statement
For Year Ended December 31, 19--

		Department A	Department B	Combined
Sales		$42,100	$63,150	$105,250
Cost of goods sold.		31,400	37,800	69,200
Gross profits		$10,700	$25,350	$ 36,050
Operating expenses:				
Selling expenses:				
Sales salaries.	$6,000	$10,000	$16,000	
Advertising	600	900	1,500	
Store supplies used	150	280	430	
Depreciation of store equip..	240	410	650	
Rent expense	1,600	3,200	4,800	
Delivery expense.	1,200	1,800	3,000	
Total Selling Expenses. .	$9,790	$16,590	$26,380	
General and admin. expenses:				
Office salaries	$1,280	$ 1,920	$ 3,200	
Expired insurance	200	350	550	
Bad debts expense	150	225	375	
Misc. office expenses	100	150	250	
Total Gen. and Admin. Ex.	$1,730	$ 2,645	$ 4,375	
Total Operating Expenses		11,520	19,235	30,755
Net Income or Loss (*).		$ 820*	$ 6,115	$ 5,295

Department A of the Joe M. Hardt Company incurred a net loss of $820 for the year. However, an examination of the situation revealed that the elimination of Department A would have the following results:

1. The department's sales of $42,100 and gross profit of $10,700 would be lost.
2. The following Department A expenses would be eliminated: sales salaries, $6,000; advertising, $600; and store supplies used, $150.
3. The store equipment of Department A consists of shelving and built-in display cases. Their sale would result in a large loss. Consequently, Mr. Hardt is of the opinion that if the department is eliminated it would be wise to keep this equipment and make some use of it in the operation of Department B.
4. There would be no savings in rent because the entire space occupied would have to be retained under the terms of the lease.
5. The "Delivery expense" item consists of the salary of the delivery truck driver, depreciation of the delivery truck, and repairs. The truck would have to be operated for the deliveries of Department B. Consequently, there would be no appreciable savings here.
6. The item "Office salaries" consists of the salary of one office girl. She would have to be retained for the work of Department B.
7. Insurance expense on the merchandise inventory of Department A amounting to $180, bad debts of $150, and $25 of the miscellaneous office expenses would be eliminated.

The net effect of the elimination of Department A may be summarized as follows:

ESTIMATED EFFECT OF ELIMINATING DEPARTMENT A

Combined net incomes of Departments A and B......		$5,295
Reduction in gross profit that would result from the elimination of Department A....................	$10,700	
Expense reductions that would result from the elimination of Department A:		
Sales salaries.................................$6,000		
Advertising...................................... 600		
Store supplies used............................. 150		
Expired insurance.............................. 180		
Bad debts expense.............................. 150		
Miscellaneous expense......................... 25		
Total Reductions.............................	7,105	
Reduction in net income that would result from the elimination of Department A....................		3,595
Net Income with Department A Eliminated..........		$1,700

The statement summarizing the estimated effect of the elimination of Department A shows that Department A contributes to the over-all profitableness of the firm, even though it operates at a loss.

The expense item, bad debts expense, that appears in the foregoing calculations represents the losses from uncollectible accounts receivable. This expense is discussed in more detail in Chapter 12.

QUESTIONS FOR CLASS DISCUSSION

1. Why would a company having only one bookkeeper use a Combination Journal in preference to using five or more of the special journals described in Chapter 8?
2. Will an amount entered in the wrong column of a Combination Journal and posted to the ledger cause the trial balance to be out of balance?
3. As the terms are used in departmental accounting, distinguish between productive departments and service departments.
4. Name several of the productive departments and several of the service departments of (a) a merchandising company, and (b) a manufacturing company.
5. For several years, Clinton Mullen has operated a small retail store having five departments. Mullen's accounting records consist of undepartmentalized special journals, a General Ledger, and customer and creditor ledgers. He would like to redesign his books of original entry and his General Ledger so that he can determine gross profits by departments. (a) What changes would you suggest that he make? (b) How could he secure the information necessary in determining departmental gross profits without making any changes in his journals and ledgers?
6. What is a departmental sales analysis sheet? How is a departmental sales analysis sheet used to determine sales by departments?
7. What different kinds of analysis sheets may be used by a departmentalized store?

8. Gilbert Ridley operates a shoe store having two departments: men's shoe department and women's shoe department. Freight shipments to the store commonly have both men's and women's shoes packed indiscriminately in large shipping cartons. Ridley would like to assign freight charges to the proper departments. Can you suggest a fair method that he may use?

9. How reliable are the amounts shown as net incomes for the various departments of a store when expenses are allocated to the departments?

10. Why are code numbers assigned to accounts?

11. Suggest a basis for allocating the following expenses to departments: (a) salaries of supervisory employees, (b) rent, (c) heat, (d) electricity used for lighting, (e) janitor service, (f) advertising, (g) expired insurance, and (h) taxes.

12. What is a departmental expense analysis sheet?

13. What is a service department expense allocation sheet?

14. Explain how an unprofitable department, although unprofitable, may make a contribution to the overhead and to the over-all profitableness of a firm.

15. When may it be unwise to discontinue an unprofitable department?

PROBLEMS

Problem 9–1

1. Open the general ledger and subsidiary ledger accounts required in the solution of Problem 8–3 on page 175.

2. Prepare a Combination Journal similar to the one of Illustration 46.

3. Enter the transactions of Problem 8–3 in the Combination Journal and post to the ledger accounts when instructed to do so in the narrative of transactions.

4. Prepare a trial balance of the General Ledger and schedules of the accounts receivable and accounts payable.

Problem 9–2

On January 31 of the current year, at the end of its annual accounting period, the bookkeeper of the Pioneer Hardware Store prepared the adjusted trial balance that follows on page 206.

PIONEER HARDWARE STORE
Adjusted Trial Balance, January 31, 19—

Cash	$ 8,900	
Accounts receivable	12,800	
Merchandise inventory, hardware department	11,040	
Merchandise inventory, paint department	2,400	
Merchandise inventory, appliance department	4,100	
Store supplies	120	
Office supplies	75	
Store equipment	6,500	
Accumulated depreciation, store equipment		$ 2,760
Office equipment	2,300	
Accumulated depreciation, office equipment		480
Accounts payable		7,160
Scott Moyer, capital		24,685
Sales, hardware department		42,560
Sales, paint department		12,500
Sales, appliance department		22,060
Sales returns, hardware department	440	
Sales returns, paint department	160	
Sales returns, appliance department	320	
Purchases, hardware department	26,000	
Purchases, paint department	8,200	
Purchases, appliance department	12,100	
Freight-in, hardware department	420	
Freight-in, paint department	110	
Freight-in, appliance department	225	
Sales salaries	9,000	
Advertising	450	
Store supplies used	175	
Depreciation of store equipment	650	
Rent, selling space	3,600	
Taxes, selling equipment	210	
Office salaries	3,000	
Office supplies used	140	
Expired insurance	230	
Depreciation of office equipment	210	
Rent expense, office space	300	
Taxes, office equipment	30	
	$112,205	$112,205

The departmental inventories at the end of the accounting period were:

Hardware department	$11,340
Paint department	2,500
Appliance department	4,200

Required:
Prepare an income statement for the Pioneer Hardware Store in which only the trading section is departmentalized.

Problem 9–3
Design an account numbering system for the Pioneer Hardware Store of Problem 9–1. List on a sheet of notebook paper each of the accounts of the firm's trial balance, along with the account number you would assign to it.

Problem 9–4
The Superior Jewelry Store has three sales departments: (1) jewelry, (2) china, and (3) silver. It also has two service departments: (1) general office, and (2) purchasing department.

The store charges all merchandise transactions directly to department merchandise accounts. It charges all expenses to undepartmentalized expense accounts. At the end of each accounting period the store uses an expense analysis and service department expense allocation sheet similar to the one shown in Illustration 54 to allocate expenses to departments and to allocate service department expenses to the sales departments.

On December 31, 1959, the accountant of the firm secured the following information from the store:

1959 MERCHANDISE TRANSACTIONS AND INVENTORIES:

	Jewelry	China	Silver
December 31, 1958, inventory	$ 27,100	$14,800	$12,700
December 31, 1959, inventory	31,400	12,700	13,600
Sales	108,500	31,000	46,500
Purchases	72,300	13,200	24,500

UNDEPARTMENTALIZED EXPENSES:

Accounts	Amount	Basis of Distribution
Rent Expense	$ 8,500	Amount and value of floor space
Salaries	35,630	Payroll records
Advertising Expense	7,440	Sales
Expired Insurance	500	Value of equipment
Lighting Expense	630	Floor space
Heating Expense	1,080	Floor space
Depreciation of Equipment	2,500	Value of equipment
Supplies Used	834	Requisitions
Janitor Services	1,800	Floor space
Total	$58,914	

ADDITIONAL INFORMATION:

Floor Space Occupied		Value of Equipment	
General office	600 sq. ft.	General office	$ 3,500
Purchasing department	400 sq. ft.	Purchasing department	1,800
Jewelry department	4,000 sq. ft.	Jewelry department	10,000
China department	2,500 sq. ft.	China department	6,000
Silver department	1,500 sq. ft.	Silver department	3,700
Total	9,000 sq. ft.	Total	$25,000

The general office and purchasing department occupy a balcony at the rear of the store. This floor space is not as valuable as space on the main floor. Consequently, the executives of the store feel that $500 of the rent expense should be charged to these two departments and the balance to the sales departments.

The payroll records indicate that salaries should be charged to the departments as follows: general office, $8,200; purchasing department, $5,900; jewelry department, $14,280; china department, $3,900; and silver department, $3,350.

Requisitions for supplies indicated the following amounts should be charged to the departments for supplies used: general office, $146; purchasing department, $128; jewelry department, $290; china department, $112; and silver department, $158.

It was felt that sales were a fair basis for allocating the general office department expenses to the sales departments and that purchases were a fair basis for allocating the purchasing department expenses.

Required:

1. Prepare an expense analysis and service department expense allocation sheet.
2. Prepare an income statement for the china department.

Problem 9–5

At the end of the current annual accounting period a departmental income statement for John H. Beale and Son appeared as follows:

JOHN H. BEALE AND SON
Departmental Income Statement
For Year Ended December 31, 19—

	Department 1	Department 2	Combined
Sales...............................	$91,050	$45,525	$136,575
Cost of goods sold..............	51,820	32,225	84,045
Gross profits...................	$39,230	$13,300	$ 52,530
Operating expenses:.............			
Selling expenses:			
Rent expense...............$ 4,200	$ 1,800	$ 6,000
Sales salaries............. 10,320	7,165	17,485
Advertising............... 1,125	935	2,060
Depreciation of store equip-			
ment.................... 1,540	680	2,220
Store supplies used........ 470	210	680
Insurance expense......... 320	190	510
Delivery expense.......... 2,440	1,115	3,555
Total Selling Expenses....$20,415	$12,095	$32,510
Gen. and admin. expenses:			
Office salaries.............$ 3,600	$ 1,800	$ 5,400
Bad debt losses............ 910	455	1,365
Misc. office expenses........ 420	210	630
Total General and Ad-			
ministrative Expenses. .$ 4,930	$ 2,465	$ 7,395
Total Operating Ex-			
penses..............	25,345	14,560	39,905
Net Income (Loss*)...........	$13,885	$ 1,260*	$ 12,625

The management of John H. Beale and Son is considering the elimination of its Department 2. Upon investigation the management found that:

a) The amount of rent paid by the store and the total amount of depreciation of store equipment would not be affected by the elimination of the department.

b) One half of the insurance expense and 80 per cent each of the office salaries and miscellaneous office expense presently charged to Department 2 would be eliminated if the department were to be discontinued.

c) All of the sales salaries, advertising, store supplies used, delivery expense, and bad debts expense presently charged to Department 2 would be eliminated if the department were to be discontinued.

Required:

Prepare a statement showing the effect of the elimination of Department 2.

CLASS EXERCISES

Exercise 9–1

The following information was taken from the records of Becker Supply Company at the end of their accounting period just ended:

Beginning inventory	$ 6,820	Purchases	$57,830
Cost of goods sold	54,300	Purchases returns	630
Ending inventory	8,640	Sales	87,200
Gross profit	30,510	Sales returns	820

If the firm did not pay any freight on merchandise purchased, what were the amounts of its sales and purchases discounts? (Hint: The construction of an income statement will aid in the solution of this exercise.)

Exercise 9–2

From the following information prepare an expense analysis and service department expense allocation sheet allocating all operating expenses to the sales departments, Departments A and B:

| | Totals | Departments | | | | |
		A	B	1	2	3
Sales	$ 80,000	$20,000	$60,000			
Purchases	50,000	15,000	35,000			
Expenses charged directly	7,800	2,000	3,000	$ 600	$1,200	$1,000
Indirect expenses:						
Property taxes	330					
Repairs and maintenance	220					
Telephone	160					
Miscellaneous general expense	780					
Assessed valuation of property	110,000	20,000	30,000	50,000	6,000	4,000
Floor space occupied (percentage of total)		30%	50%	......	10%	10%
Number of telephone instruments	16	5	6	1	3	1

Department 1 is the occupancy department (rent, cleaning, etc.); Department 2 is the general management department; and Department 3 is the purchasing department.

Allocate repairs and maintenance and property taxes on the basis of the value of the property (assessed) in each department. Allocate miscellaneous general expenses on the basis of direct departmental expenses. Make other allocations of indirect expenses as needed.

Allocate Department 1 expenses on the basis of floor space occupied by the other departments; allocate Department 2 expenses on the basis of sales; and allocate Department 3 expenses on the basis of purchases. (In case of fractions carry to the nearest dollar.)

SUPPLEMENTARY PROBLEMS

Problem 9–A

The operations of the Rollins Sales Company are carried on in two selling departments and an office department. On December 31, at the end of an annual accounting period, the bookkeeper of the company prepared the following adjusted trial balance:

ROLLINS SALES COMPANY

Adjusted Trial Balance, December 31, 19—

Cash.	$ 5,860	
Merchandise inventory, Department A	5,625	
Merchandise inventory, Department B	9,860	
Supplies	280	
Equipment	15,900	
Accumulated depreciation, equipment		$ 3,615
Accounts payable		2,820
James Rollins, capital		20,335
James Rollins, withdrawals	4,000	
Sales, Department A		56,700
Sales, Department B		87,500
Purchases, Department A	34,250	
Purchases, Department B	51,340	
Salaries expense	29,582	
Advertising	4,326	
Rent	6,000	
Heating and lighting expense	1,200	
Supplies used	680	
Insurance expense	477	
Depreciation of equipment	1,590	
	$170,970	$170,970

Required:

1. Prepare a combined expense analysis and service department expense allocation sheet for Rollins Sales Company, making use of the following information and bases for allocating expenses to the firm's office department and two selling departments:

   a) Salaries expense should be allocated to the departments on the basis of the payroll records. The payroll records show that of the $29,582 of salaries expense, $4,507 should be allocated to the general office department, $9,450 should be allocated to Department A, and $15,625 to Department B.

   b) Advertising expense should be allocated on the basis of sales.

   c) Rent expense and the heating and lighting expense should be allocated on the basis of floor space. The general office department occupies 10 per cent of the floor space, and of the remaining space, Department A occupies one half as much as Department B.

   d) Supplies used should be allocated on the basis of requisition records. The records show that the general office requisitioned $145 of supplies, Department A requisitioned $220 of supplies, and Department B requisitioned supplies valued at $315.

   e) Insurance expense should be allocated on the basis of the assets insured. Examination of the policies and other records indicate that two thirds of the insurance expired was insurance on the merchandise inventory and should be allocated to the selling departments on the basis of the average inventories in the departments. The remaining one third was insurance on the equipment. Equipment records indicate that of all the insured equipment, $3,600 is in the office, $5,100 is in Department A, and $7,200 is in Department B.

   f) Depreciation should be allocated on the basis of the value of the equipment in each department.

   g) The general office department expenses should be allocated to the two selling departments on the basis of sales.

2. Use the information of the trial balance and the expense analysis and service department expense allocation sheet to prepare a departmental income statement showing the net income of each of the selling departments based upon allocated expenses. The ending departmental inventories are: Department A, $4,575; and Department B, $11,740.

Problem 9–B

The Norbert Kranz Company has two selling departments: Department A and Department B. Department B is not profitable, and Mr. Kranz is considering its elimination. The firm's departmentalized income statement for the year just ended appears as follows:

NORBERT KRANZ COMPANY

Departmentalized Income Statement
For Year Ended December 31, 19—

	Department A	Department B
Sales..................................	$60,500	$36,300
Cost of goods sold.'.....................	36,225	27,225
Gross profit...........................	$24,275	$ 9,075
Operating expenses:		
Selling expenses:		
Sales salaries.........................$ 8,450		$5,070
Advertising expense................... 1,200		930
Store supplies used.................... 320		240
Depreciation of store equipment........ 925		410
Rent expense......................... 2,250		1,350
Total Selling Expenses..............$13,145		$8,000
General and administrative expenses:		
Office salaries.......................$ 2,160		$1,220
Expired insurance.................... 500		300
Bad debts expense.................... 250		150
Miscellaneous office expenses........... 300		180
Total Gen. and Admin. Expenses......$ 3,210		$1,850
Total Operating Expenses..........	16,355	9,850
Net Income (Loss*)......................	$ 7,920	$ 775*

Mr. Kranz is of the opinion that the elimination of Department B will have the following results:
1. The elimination of Department B will cause a 10 per cent decline in the sales of Department A; but this will not effect the rate of gross profit in the department.
2. The 10 per cent decline in the sales of Department A will result in the following reductions in the expenses of Department A:
   a) Store supplies used, 10 per cent.
   b) Insurance expense, 8 per cent.
   c) Bad debt losses, 10 per cent.
3. The Kranz Company has an office clerk and four salesclerks, each of whom earns $65 per week, or $3,380 per year. At the present the salaries of two and one-half salesclerks are charged to Department A and the salaries of one and one-half salesclerks are charged to Department B. Mr. Kranz is of the opinion that two salesclerks may be dismissed if Department B is eliminated. This will leave only two full-time clerks in Department A; however, the elimination of Department B will reduce the work of the

office clerk to a point where she can work half time as a salesclerk in Department A.

4. The elimination of Department B will:

a) Eliminate the Department B advertising expense, losses from uncollectible accounts, and store supplies used.

b) Cause a 90 per cent reduction in the insurance expense charged to Department B and cause a 25 per cent reduction in the miscellaneous office expenses charged to Department B.

Required:

Prepare a statement showing the estimated effect of the elimination of Department B.

Chapter

10

ACCOUNTING FOR CASH

CASH has universal usefulness, small bulk for high value, and no special identification marks by which its ownership may be established. These characteristics plus the great number of cash transactions completed by the average company make the procedures for the control of cash important. Obviously, the control of cash is very important to a business owner. However, its control is equally as important to the employees responsible for handling cash. It is equally important to the employees because an adequate system for the control of cash enables the employees, at all times, to prove that their work has been completed accurately and honestly.

No effort will be made here to present a complete discussion of procedures for safeguarding cash. However, an adequate system of internal check and control should be set up for handling all cash receipts and disbursements, and in this system two basic principles should be observed. First, there should be a separation of duties so that the people responsible for handling cash are not the same people that make entries in the cash journals or that post to the accounts in which sources and uses of cash are recorded. Second, all receipts of cash should be deposited in the bank, intact; and all payments of cash should be made by check. The one exception to this last principle is that small disbursements may be made in cash from a petty cash fund. This exception will be discussed later in this chapter.

The reason for the first basic principle is obvious. As for the second, requiring that all receipts be deposited intact and that all payments be made by check provides in the records kept by the bank a separate and external record of cash transactions. This external record is in addition to a company's own records, and it may be used to check and prove the records kept by the company. A summary of the bank's record of the cash transactions of a company is submitted to the company at the end of each month in a bank statement. The individual items on the bank statement are supported by duplicate deposit tickets and canceled checks.

The Deposit Ticket

All cash received each day should be deposited in the bank at the end of that day or early the next morning. When a deposit is made, the depositor lists the items being deposited on a form provided by the bank. This form is called a *deposit ticket,* and appears as in Illustration 56. On it the depositor enters the name of the company making the deposit, the address of the company, and the date. The depositor then lists the total amounts of currency and coins, and the amount of each individual check being deposited. Opposite the amount of each check is written the name of the local bank or the address of the out-of-town bank on which each check is drawn. Some banks prefer that the depositor list all checks by the American Bankers' Association number of the bank on which each check is drawn. Every bank has a different American Bankers' Association number that readily identifies it. Most banks print this number on their checks following the name of the bank.

Illustration 56—Deposit Ticket

Deposited for		
in the **MERCHANTS NATIONAL BANK** Eugene, Oregon		
_____19___ Please list each check separately.		
	Dollars	Cents
Currency_____		
Coin _____		
Checks_____		
Total		

Items listed above are accepted for deposit subject to collection.

When a deposit is made, most companies present the deposit, an original deposit ticket, and a duplicate carbon copy of the deposit ticket to the receiving teller of the bank. The deposit and the original copy of the deposit ticket are kept by the bank. The duplicate deposit ticket is stamped by the teller and returned to the depositor as an acknowledgment of the deposit. At any time thereafter, if all receipts are deposited, it is possible to compare the individual cash receipts of each day as shown by the Cash Receipts Journal with the individual items deposited. This comparison makes it possible to prove that every item recorded in the Cash Receipts Journal actually reached the bank. Each check received and entered in the Cash Receipts Journal appears on a duplicate deposit ticket as a check deposited. The total currency and coin receipts of each day appear as currency and coin deposited on that day.

Deposits and the Cash Receipts Journal

In a business that deposits its cash receipts intact and makes all payments by check, after all cash items are recorded and posted, the balance of the Cash account should be the same as the amount of money on deposit in the bank. Because of this, many such companies change the name of their Cash account to the name of the bank in which cash is deposited. They also change the names of the Cash columns in their journals. In the

Cash Receipts Journal the Cash debit column is changed to, for instance, "Merchants National Bank debit," and in the Cash Payments Journal the Cash credit column is changed to, for example, "Merchants National Bank credit."

Some companies that deposit all cash intact each day place a double "cash" column in their Cash Receipts Journal in order to show the amount of each day's deposit. Such a double "cash" column appears as in Illustration 57.

Illustration 57

CASH RECEIPTS JOURNAL

Date		Account Credited			Sales Credit	Sales Discounts Debit	1st National Bank	
							Memo	Debit
Nov.	1	Michael Doran				6.00	294.00	
	1	James McBroom				12.00	588.00	
	1	Henry Fleck				2.50	122.50	
	1	Cash Sales			1,200.00		1,200.00	2,204.50

When a double "cash" column like the one shown in Illustration 57 is used, each day's receipts, a day's cash sales are treated as one receipt, are individually entered in the Memo column. At the end of each day, the amounts entered in the Memo column that day are totaled, the cash is deposited, and the amount deposited is entered in the Debit column. The individual amounts entered in the two columns are not posted. However, at the end of the month the total of the Debit column is posted to the debit side of the "Cash" or "1st National Bank" account.

Checks

Everyone is familiar with ordinary checks. A check is a written order, signed by a depositor, directing the bank to pay a specified sum of money to the person designated on its face, or to his order. The widespread use of checks is one of the distinguishing characteristics of modern business. Checks are widely used by businesses not only because they may be safely sent through the mails but also because each check acts as a receipt. Too, companies using checks for all payments secure a double record of cash payments, their own record and the record of the bank. An ordinary check with stub attached is shown in Illustration 58.

The bank balance is recalculated on the check stub as each check is drawn. This is shown in Illustration 58. To arrive at the new bank balance, all deposits made since the last check was drawn are added to the old balance. The amount of the check being drawn is then deducted. When a check with stub attached is used, the stub should be filled out first. This prevents making a check and overlooking the entries on the stub until after the check has been sent out and the data for the stub are no longer available. Many companies use a type of check in which a carbon copy of each check takes the place of the check stub.

Illustration 58—Check with Stub Attached

| No. 46 | $196.00 | | No. 46 | EUGENE, OREGON | October 15 | 19 59 |
| Oct. 15 | 1959 | | | | | |

To Acme Mfg. Co.

Merchants National Bank 96-71

For Invoice 10/5

Balance	$ 687.00
Deposited	110.00
Deposited	
Total	797.00
Amt. Check	196.00
Balance	601.00

PAY TO THE ORDER OF Acme Mfg. Co. $196.00

--Exactly one hundred and ninety-six------------------DOLLARS

F. A. Spoke

Certified Check. A certified check is like an ordinary check in every way with the exception that it has been certified by the bank upon which it was drawn. In certifying a check, an officer of the bank upon which it is drawn certifies that the maker of the check has on deposit funds sufficient to pay the check. He stamps the word "certified" and the name of the bank on the check, signs his name, returns the check to its maker, and immediately orders a deduction of funds equal to the amount of the check from the account of the maker of the check. Thereafter, the bank guarantees the payment of the check. Any creditor will readily accept a certified check.

Cashier's Check. A cashier's check is a bank's own check drawn by its cashier on itself. Cashier's checks are purchased from a bank and are used in making payments in cases where a company's own check might not be acceptable.

Bank Draft. A bank draft, like a cashier's check, is purchased from a bank and is also used in cases where a company's own check might not be acceptable. A bank draft is like a cashier's check in that it is drawn by the bank from which it is purchased; but it differs in that it is drawn upon funds that the bank has on deposit in another bank.

Indorsements

Checks received by a business are normally deposited in the bank on the day they are received. However, checks are also commonly transferred from person to person. Normally, when a check is transferred to a new owner, the check is indorsed by the person transferring it. An indorsement consists of the signature of the owner of the check on the back thereof. When the owner of a check indorses it, he not only effects the transfer of the check but he also, if the indorsement is not qualified, guarantees payment of the check. Indorsements, like the following indorsements of John W. Evans, are of several kinds:

Blank. A blank indorsement consists of only the signature of the indorser. For example:

John W. Evans

Such an indorsement makes a check or other negotiable instrument payable to bearer.

Special or Full. A special or full indorsement consists of the signature of the indorser preceded by the words "Pay to the order of" and the name of the indorsee. For example:

Pay to the order of Joel E. Freeman
John W. Evans

If the indorsement illustrated is used, Joel E. Freeman must indorse the check before title to it can be transferred again. Such an indorsement is used when a check that has already been indorsed in blank is to be sent through the mail.

Qualified. A qualified indorsement consists of the signature of the indorser preceded by the words "Without recourse," or other words having the same meaning. For example:

Without recourse
John W. Evans

Such an indorsement is used when an indorser wishes to limit his liability for payment of a check or other negotiable instrument.

Restrictive. A restrictive indorsement ends further transfer of a check or other negotiable instrument and appears, for example:

Pay to the order of
Allen W. Oaks only
John W. Evans
or
Pay to the order of
the U.S. National
Bank for deposit
John W. Evans

The Check Register

Most companies require the printer to number their checks consecutively as the checks are printed. This makes it possible to account for each check. Checks are commonly accounted for in a *Check Register*. When checks are prenumbered and when all payments are made by check, the Cash Payments Journal may be altered slightly to make it a Check Register. When a Check Register is used, it takes the place of a Cash Payments Journal. An examination of the Check Register in Illustration 59 will show that it differs but slightly from a Cash Payments Journal. The differences are:

1. The Explanation column is omitted. Any explanation of a transaction that is needed is placed on the check stub or the carbon copy of the check.
2. A column is added for the name of the payee of each check. This aids in comparing canceled checks with check register entries.
3. A column is added for check numbers; and each check is entered in numerical order. This makes it possible to scan the numbers for omitted checks.
4. The name of the Cash credit column is changed to the name of the bank in which the cash is deposited.

Illustration 59—A Check Register

CHECK REGISTER

Page 32

Date	Check No.	Payee	Account Debited	F	Sundry Accounts Debit	Accts. Pay. Debit	Pur. Dis. Credit	Merchants Bank Credit
Oct. 3	42	L. & Y. Co.	Freight-In		4.50			4.50
10	43	Eugene Electric	Misc. Gen. Ex.		14.00			14.00
12	44	Voided check	Voided check					
12	45	Frank Hyatt	Purchases		25.00			25.00
15	46	Acme Mfg. Co.	Acme Mfg. Co.			200.00	4.00	196.00

All checks are entered in the Check Register in numerical order. If a check is spoiled in writing, many firms require an entry such as the one on line three of the register illustration. The spoiled check is then marked void and attached to its stub.

The Check Register is posted in exactly the same manner as a Cash Payments Journal.

The Bank Statement

At the end of each month, banks furnish to each depositor a statement of his account. The bank statement shows: (1) the amount on deposit at the beginning of the month, (2) the checks and any other amounts deducted from the account, (3) the deposits and any other amounts added to the account, and (4) the balance of the account at the end of the month, according to the records of the bank. If all receipts are deposited and all payments are made by check, the bank statement becomes a device for checking and proving the cash records of the depositor. A bank statement is shown in Illustration 60.

Most banks mail statements to their depositors soon after the end of each month. Included in the envelope with the statement are the depositor's *canceled checks* and any debit or credit memoranda that have affected the depositor's account. The checks returned are the ones that the bank has paid during the month. They are called "canceled checks" because they are canceled by stamping or punching to show that they have been paid. During any month, in addition to the checks that the depositor has drawn, the bank may deduct from the depositor's account amounts for service charges, for printing checks, for items deposited that are uncollectible, or for errors. The bank notifies the depositor of each such deduction with a debit memorandum. A copy of the memorandum is always included with the monthly statement. The bank may also add amounts to the depositor's account for errors and for amounts collected for the depos-

Illustration 60—Bank Statement

Valley Hardware Company 10th and Pine Sts. Eugene, Oregon			Statement of Account with **MERCHANTS NATIONAL BANK OF EUGENE, OREGON**	
Checks in Detail		Deposits	Date	Balance
Balance Brought Forward Sept. 30 '59				1,578.00
58.00			Oct. 2 '59	1,520.00
120.00	200.00		Oct. 5 '5 9	1,200.00
		240.00	Oct. 6 '5 9	1,440.00
25.00	75.00	150.00	Oct. 10 '5 9	1,490.00
		180.00	Oct. 18 '59	1,670.00
10.00	50.00		Oct. 23 '59	1,610.00
	135.00	100.00	Oct. 25 '59	1,575.00
	9.00		Oct. 28 '59	1,566.00
		198.50	Oct. 30 '59	1,764.50
				Last amount in this column is your balance.

If no error is reported within ten days this account will be considered correct.   Vouchers Returned 9

itor. The bank uses a credit memorandum to notify the depositor of any such additions to his account.

Need for Reconciling the Bank Account

Normally, the balance of cash at the end of the month as shown by the bank statement does not agree with the balance of cash as shown by the accounting records of the depositor. In order to prove the accuracy of both the records of the depositor and the records of the bank, it is necessary to reconcile any differences between the two balances and to bring the balances into agreement.

Numerous things may cause the bank statement balance to differ from the depositor's book balance of cash. Some of the more common are:

1. *Outstanding Checks.* These are checks that have been drawn by the depositor and deducted on his records but have not been presented to the bank for payment.
2. *Unrecorded Deposits.* Companies often make deposits at the end of each business day, after the bank has closed for that day. These deposits

are made in the night depository of the bank and are not recorded by the bank until the next business day. Consequently, the deposit of the last day of a month, if it is placed in the night depository, does not appear on the bank statement of that month.

3. *Charges for Service and Uncollectible Items.* The bank often deducts amounts from a depositor's account for services rendered. The bank also deducts for items deposited that it is unable to collect. Insufficient funds checks are the most common of the latter. The bank notifies the depositor of each such deduction with a debit memorandum. If the item is material in amount, the debit memorandum is mailed to the depositor on the day of the deduction. In a well-managed company, each of these deductions is entered in the Cash Payments Journal or the Check Register on the day the memorandum is received. However, occasionally there are unentered amounts near the end of the month.

4. *Collections.* Banks often act as collecting agents for their depositors. For a small fee a bank will collect promissory notes and other items. When an item such as a promissory note is collected, the bank usually adds the proceeds to the account of the depositor and sends a credit memorandum as notification of the transaction. As soon as the memorandum is received, an entry should be made in the Cash Receipts Journal. Occasionally there are unentered amounts near the end of the month.

5. *Errors.* Regardless of care and of systems of internal control for the automatic detection of errors, both the bank and the depositor make errors that affect the bank balance. Occasionally, these errors are not discovered until the bank balance is reconciled.

Reconciling the Bank Balance

The steps in reconciling the bank balance are:

1. Compare each deposit listed on the bank statement with deposits shown in the accounting records. Note any discrepancies and discover which is correct. List any errors or unrecorded items.

2. When canceled checks are returned by the bank, they are in a stack in the order in which the bank paid them and also in the order of their listing on the bank statement. While the checks are in this order, compare each check with its listing on the bank statement. List any discrepancies or errors.

3. Rearrange the returned checks in numerical order, the order in which they were written. Secure the previous month's bank reconciliation and determine if any checks listed as outstanding at the end of the previous month are still outstanding. If there are any, list them. Also, see that any deposits that were unrecorded by the bank at the end of the previous month have been recorded.

4. Insert among the canceled checks any bank memorandum according to their dates. Compare each check with its entry in the Check Register. If a register is not maintained, compare each check with its stub. Note for correction any discrepancies, and list any unpaid checks or unrecorded memorandum.

5. Prepare a statement reconciling the bank statement balance with the book balance of cash. Such a statement is shown in Illustration 61.

6. Determine if any debits or credits appearing on the bank statement are unrecorded in the books of account. Make journal entries to record the unrecorded items.

Illustration of a Bank Reconciliation

To illustrate a bank reconciliation, assume that the Valley Hardware Company found the following items when it attempted to reconcile its bank balance of October 31.

The bank balance as shown by the bank statement was $1,764.50, and the balance of cash as shown by the accounting records was $1,370. Check No. 124 for $150 and Check No. 126 for $200 were outstanding and unpaid by the bank. A deposit of $120, placed in the night depository of the bank

Illustration 61—Bank Reconciliation

VALLEY HARDWARE COMPANY
Bank Reconciliation
As of October 31, 19—

Book Balance of Cash.		$1,370.00	Bank Statement Balance.............			$1,764.50
Add:			Add:			
Proceeds of note. .	$200.00		Deposit of 10/31. .	$120.00		
Less: Collection			Valley Haberdashery check			
fee..........	1.50	198.50	charged in			
		$1,568.50	error......		25.00	145.00
						$1,909.50
Deduct:			Deduct:			
N.S.F. check of			Outstanding checks:			
Frank Jones.		9.00	No. 124........	$150.00		
			No. 126........	200.00		350.00
Adjusted Balance.....		$1,559.50	Adjusted Balance.....			$1,559.50

after banking hours on October 31, was unrecorded by the bank. Among the returned checks was a credit memorandum showing that the bank had collected a note receivable for the company. The proceeds of the note, $200 less a collection fee of $1.50, had been credited to the company account on October 30. Also returned with the bank statement was an N.S.F. (not sufficient funds) check for $9.00. This check had been received from a customer, Frank Jones, on October 25. It had been included in the deposit of that day. The collection of the note and the return of the N.S.F. check were unrecorded on the company books. In addition to these two items, a check for $25 drawn by the Valley Haberdashery was among the canceled checks returned. This check had been charged in error to the account of the Valley Hardware Company. The statement reconciling these amounts is shown in Illustration 61.

The bank reconciliation helps to locate any errors made by either the bank or the depositor. It also discloses any items which have been entered on the company books but have not come to the attention of the bank. Likewise, it discloses items that should be recorded on the company books but are unrecorded on the date of the reconciliation. For example, in the Valley Hardware Company bank reconciliation illustrated, the adjusted cash balance, $1,559.50, is the true cash balance. However, at the time the reconciliation is completed, the accounting records show a book balance of cash of $1,370.00. Consequently, entries must be made to adjust the book balance and to increase it to the true cash balance. This requires two entries, the first in general journal form is:

Nov.	2	Cash..	198.50	
		Collection Expense......................	1.50	
		Notes Receivable..................		200.00
		To record the proceeds and collection charge of a note collected for us by the bank.		

The entry is self-explanatory. The bank collected a note receivable, deducted a collection fee, and deposited the balance to the account of the Valley Hardware Company. The entry increases the amount of cash on the books, records the collection expense, and reduces the amount of notes receivable.

The second entry required to adjust the book balance of cash to the true balance of cash is:

.	2	Accounts Receivable—Frank Jones.......	9.00	
		Cash............................		9.00
		To charge back the N.S.F. check received from Frank Jones in payment of his account.		

This entry records the N.S.F. check returned by the bank as uncollectible. The check was received from Jones in payment of his account and was deposited as cash. The bank, unable to collect the check, deducted $9.00 from the Valley Hardware account. The deduction makes it necessary for the company to reverse the original entry made when the check was received. After recording the returned check, the company will endeavor to collect the $9.00 from Frank Jones. If after all legal means of collection have been exhausted and the company is still unable to collect, the amount will be written off as a loss.

Need for a Petty Cash Fund

Proper control of cash requires that all receipts be deposited in the bank and that all payments be made by check. When this procedure is not followed, cash receipts are disbursed directly in paying obligations. This makes accounting for cash more difficult because cash receipts cannot be traced directly to the bank account and canceled checks are not available to prove cash payments. However, every business must make many small payments for items such as postage, express charges, telegrams, and small items of supplies. If each small payment is made by check, many checks for small amounts are written. To avoid writing many small checks, a *petty cash fund* is commonly used.

The Petty Cash Fund

When a petty cash fund is established, an estimate is made of the total of all small amounts that are likely to be disbursed during a short period of time, usually one month. A check is drawn and debited to the Petty Cash account for an amount slightly in excess of this estimate. The check

Illustration 62—Petty Cash Voucher

VALLEY HARDWARE COMPANY

PETTY CASH VOUCHER

NO. _1479_   DATE _Nov. 3, 19 —_

PAID TO _Western Union Telegraph Company_   _$1.65--_

FOR _Collect telegram_

Approved: Received Payment:

_B.Q.D._   _Bob Tone_

is cashed, and the money is turned over to a member of the office staff who is designated *petty cashier*. The petty cashier is responsible for the petty cash and for making payments therefrom.

The petty cashier usually keeps the petty cash money in a locked box in the office safe. As each disbursement is made from the box, a *petty cash voucher* or a *petty cash receipt* is completed. A petty cash voucher for a collect telegram is shown in Illustration 62. Each petty cash voucher acts as a receipt and is signed by the person receiving payment. As each payment is made, the paid voucher is entered in the *Petty Cash Record* and then placed with the remaining money in the petty cash box. Under this system, the petty cash box always contains paid vouchers and money equal to the amount of the petty cash fund.

Each disbursement reduces the amount of the money and increases the sum of the vouchers in the petty cash box. When the money in the box is nearly exhausted, the fund is reimbursed. To reimburse the petty cash fund, the petty cashier presents the paid petty cash vouchers to the company cashier. The company cashier stamps each voucher "paid," retains the vouchers, and gives the petty cashier a check for their sum. The entry to record the reimbursing check results in debits to expense accounts and a credit to general cash for the amounts paid from the fund. When this check is cashed and the proceeds returned to the petty cash box, the money in the box is restored to its original amount. Therefore, reimbursing the petty cash fund results (1) in restoring the amount of money in the petty cash box to the original amount of the fund, and (2) in charging the proper expense accounts for the amounts previously paid from the fund.

Only entries to reimburse the petty cash fund result in debits to the proper expense accounts for the amounts paid from the fund. Consequently, petty cash must be reimbursed at the end of each accounting period, as well as at any time the money in the fund is low. If the fund is not reimbursed at the end of each accounting period, the asset petty cash is overstated and the expenses are understated on the financial statements.

The Petty Cash account is debited when the fund is established. It is not debited or credited again unless the amount of the fund is changed. If the fund is exhausted and reimbursements occur too often, the fund should be increased. This results in an additional debit to the Petty Cash account and a credit to the regular Cash account for the amount of the increase. If the amount of petty cash is too large, part of the fund should be returned to general cash.

Petty Cash Fund Illustrated

To avoid writing numerous small checks, a company decides to establish a petty cash fund. One of its office clerks, Alice Smith, is designated petty cashier. A check for $20 is drawn, cashed, and the proceeds are

Illustration 63

CHECK REGISTER

Date	Chk. No.	Payee	Account Debited	F	Sundry Accts. Debit	Merchants Bank Credit
Nov. 3	58	Alice Smith, Petty Cashier	Petty cash		20.00	20.00

given to this clerk. The entry to record the check is shown in Illustration 63. The effect of the entry is to transfer $20 from the Cash account to the Petty Cash account.

During the first month of the fund's operation, the following petty cash payments are made:

Nov. 3	Collect telegram	$ 1.65
7	Purchased paper clips	.50
12	Express on purchases	3.75
18	Postage on sale	1.80
19	Dinner for employee working overtime	1.60
20	100 three-cent stamps	3.00
21	Express on purchases	2.80
24	Cleaning windows	1.00
27	Repair of typewriter	2.50
	Total	$18.60

As each amount is disbursed, a petty cash voucher is signed by the person receiving payment. Each paid voucher is then recorded in the Petty Cash Record and placed in the petty cash box. The Petty Cash Record with the paid vouchers entered is shown in Illustration 64.

Illustration 64—The Petty Cash Record

PETTY CASH RECORD

Date	Voucher No.	Explanation	Receipts	Payments	Postage	Freight-In	Misc. General Expense	Sundries Account	Amount
								Distribution of Payments	
Nov. 1	1	Established fund (check No. 58)	20.00						
1	1	Collect telegram		1.65			1.65		
7	2	Purchased paper clips		.50				Office supplies	.50
12	3	Express on purchases		3.75		3.75			
18	4	Postage on sale		1.80				Delivery expense	1.80
19	5	Overtime meals		1.60			1.60		
20	6	100 three-cent stamps		3.00	3.00				
21	7	Express on purchases		2.80		2.80			
24	8	Cleaning windows		1.00			1.00		
27	9	Repair of typewriter		2.50			2.50		
		Totals	20.00	18.60	3.00	6.55	6.75		2.30
		Balance		1.40					
			20.00	20.00					
Nov. 27		Balance	1.40						
Nov. 27		Replenishing check (No. 106)	18.60						

On November 27, after all of the payments just listed have been made, only $1.40 in money remains in the fund. Since only $1.40 in money remains in the fund, the petty cashier exchanges the paid vouchers for a check to replenish the fund. When the petty cash fund is replenished, the Petty Cash Record is balanced as shown in Illustration 64. The Petty Cash Record is usually a supplementary record and not a book of original entry; therefore, an entry must be made in the Check Register to record the reimbursement. The information for this entry is secured from the summarization of the Petty Cash Record. A check register entry to replenish the petty cash fund of Illustration 64 is shown in Illustration 65.

Illustration 65

CHECK REGISTER

Date	Chk. No.	Payee	Account Debited	F	Sundry Accts. Debit		Merchants Bank Credit
Nov. 27	106	A. Smith, Petty Cashier	Postage		3.00		
			Freight-In		6.55		
			Misc. Gen. Expenses		6.75		
			Office Supplies		.50		
			Delivery Expense		1.80		18.60

As previously stated, replenishing the petty cash fund serves two purposes. It restores the money in the fund and records, in the ledger accounts, the expenditures that have been made from the fund. After the petty cash fund is replenished, the cycle of its operations is ready to begin again.

Occasionally, at the time of a petty cash expenditure a petty cashier will forget to secure a receipt; and by the time the fund is reimbursed, she will have forgotten the expenditure. This causes the fund to be short. If at the time of reimbursement the petty cash fund is short and no errors or omitted entries can be found, the shortage is recorded as an expense in the reimbursing entry with a debit to the Cash Over and Short account.

Change Fund

Companies selling for cash that deposit all receipts intact should have a change fund to supply their cash registers at the beginning of each business day with cash from which to make change. A change fund is established in much the same way a petty cash fund is established. A check payable to the change fund cashier is drawn and recorded in the Check Register with an entry having a debit to the Change Fund Cash account and a credit to the general Cash account. The check is cashed and the proceeds are placed in the cash registers at the beginning of each day. Thereafter, at the end of each day, cash in the form of coins and small denomination bills equal to the amount of the change fund is removed from the cash registers and locked in the office safe over night. The money remaining in the cash registers after the change fund is removed is the proceeds of the day's cash sales and is deposited intact.

Cash Over and Short

Regardless of the care exercised in making change, customers are sometimes given too much change or are shortchanged. Consequently, at the end of a day the actual cash from a cash register is commonly not equal to the amount of cash sales "rung up" on the register. When this occurs and, for example, actual cash as counted is $557 but the cash register shows cash sales of $556, the entry in general journal form to record the sales and the overage is:

Nov.	23	Cash................................	557.00	
		Cash Over and Short..............		1.00
		Sales...........................		556.00
		Day's cash sales.		

If, on the other hand, cash is short, less actual cash than the amount of sales shown on the cash register, the entry to record the sales and the shortage is:

Nov.	24	Cash................................	621.00	
		Cash Over and Short..................	4.00	
		Sales...........................		625.00
		Day's cash sales.		

Over a period of time cash overages should about equal cash shortages. However, customers are more prone to report instances in which they are given too little change. Because of this the total amounts of cash short are apt to be greater than the total amounts of cash over; and, consequently, the Cash Over and Short account normally reaches the end of the accounting period with a debit balance. When the Cash Over and Short account has a debit balance, the balance of the account represents an expense. It may appear on the income statement, at the end of the statement, as one of the items in the other revenue and expense section; or if the amount is small, it may be combined with other miscellaneous expenses and appear as part of the item, miscellaneous expenses. When Cash Over and Short reaches the end of the accounting period with a credit balance, the balance of the account represents revenue and normally appears on the income statement as part of the item, miscellaneous revenues.

Internal Control

Depositing all receipts in the bank and making all payments by check will aid management in controlling cash transactions and safeguarding cash. However, this alone is not sufficient. Procedures for handling cash receipts must be so organized as to protect cash from its receipt until it is deposited in the bank. Additional procedures must be organized to insure that every payment is a proper payment and should be made. The organization of procedures for handling cash transactions in such a manner as to protect the cash is known as a system of *internal control* for cash. Such a system has for its purpose the automatic detection of errors and the prevention of fraud.

A system of internal control should be organized for all types of transactions and to protect all types of assets. However, because of the nature of cash, such a system for cash is most important. The essence of any system of internal control is a division between several employees of the duties and responsibilities for the completion and recording of each transaction. The division of duties and responsibilities must be made in such a manner that the work of one employee acts as a check on the work of another employee. This does not mean a duplication of work. Each employee performs an unduplicated portion of the whole transaction in such a manner that his portion acts as a check on the portion completed by a different employee.

For example, mail containing the payments of customers should be opened by a mail clerk. This mail clerk makes a list, in triplicate, of the money received. His list should give the name of the sender, the purpose for which the money was sent, and the amount. The mail clerk keeps one copy of the list for his own record, sends one copy to the cashier with the money, and sends the other copy to the bookkeeper. The cashier deposits the money in the bank. The bookkeeper uses his copy for entries in the Cash Receipts Journal. If the bank balance is reconciled by a fourth person, errors or fraud by the mail clerk, the cashier, or the bookkeeper will be detected. Errors will be detected because the cash deposited and the records of three different people must agree. Fraud is impossible, unless there is collusion on the part of the employees involved. The mail clerk must report all receipts or the customers will question their account balances. The cashier must deposit all receipts because the bank balance must agree with the cashbook balance of the bookkeeper. The bookkeeper and the person reconciling the bank account do not handle cash and therefore have no opportunity to withhold money.

The procedures listed above for the control of cash receipts are illustrative. The exact procedures involved in a complete system of internal control for all the cash transactions of a business depend upon the individual business. This is because the size of a business, the number of its employees, and the types of transactions completed will affect the organization of the system. It is true that every business needs some system of internal control. Also, the system should be extended beyond the mere protection of cash. It should protect and safeguard all assets and insure that every transaction is properly recorded. In a small business, because of the small number of employees, a division of duties is often impossible. This does not eliminate the need for internal control; it only makes internal control more difficult. A small business must often substitute the active participation of the owner in the affairs of the business for the protection gained by a division of duties.

It is the purpose of this text to point out the need for internal control, not to present a complete discussion of the subject. Such a discussion is reserved for a course in auditing or a course in accounting systems. However, Chapter 15, The Voucher System for Controlling Liabilities, will present some procedures for the control of cash payments.

QUESTIONS FOR CLASS DISCUSSION

1. Why is the control of cash important to (a) the owner of a business, and (b) the employees of a business?
2. Name and give the reason for two basic principles that should be observed in the control of cash.
3. What is meant by the phrase "all receipts should be deposited intact"?
4. Explain how a business that deposits all receipts intact can trace and prove that each cash item received actually was deposited in the bank.
5. What changes are made in the form of the Cash Payments Journal of earlier chapters in order to make it into a Check Register?
6. Name and describe several forms of indorsements.
7. What is a bank statement? What information appears on a bank statement?
8. Why are the bank statement balance of cash and the depositor's book balance of cash reconciled?
9. Explain how the following items cause the bank statement balance of cash to differ from the depositor's book balance of cash:
    a) Outstanding checks.
    b) Unrecorded deposits.
    c) Bank service charges.
    d) Charges for uncollectible items.
    e) Items collected for the depositor by the bank.
    In reconciling the bank balance, which of the above items is added to the bank statement balance? Which is added to the book balance of cash? Which require a journal entry on the books of the depositor?
10. Why does a firm with good cash control follow the practice of depositing receipts intact and making all payments either by check or from a petty cash fund?
11. Why are some cash payments made from a petty cash fund? Why are not all payments made by check?
12. What is a petty cash voucher? When a petty cash voucher is prepared, who signs it?
13. Explain how a petty cash fund operates.
14. Why must a petty cash fund be reimbursed at the end of each accounting period?
15. What are two results of reimbursing the petty cash fund?
16. Is the Petty Cash Record a book of original entry?
17. Which of the following statements are true? Which are false?
    a) The petty cash fund is kept in the bank.

b) Expenses paid from a petty cash fund are not recorded in the ledger accounts until the petty cash fund is replenished.

c) The amount of petty cash in the hands of the petty cashier should always be equal to the balance of the Petty Cash account.

d) The Petty Cash account is debited when the petty cash fund is reimbursed.

e) The amount of petty cash plus the petty cash vouchers should always equal the balance of the Petty Cash account.

f) Assets are overstated and expenses are understated if the petty cash fund is not replenished at the end of an accounting period.

18. What is the purpose of a system of internal control?

19. What is the essence of any system of internal control?

20. Why is a system of internal control important in the handling of cash transactions? Is internal control practiced only with cash transactions?

21. A company that receives remittances through the mails wishes to properly control cash transactions. Should the bookkeeper be permitted to open incoming mail? Should the mail clerk have access to the bookkeeping records? Why?

22. Is internal control important in a small business? Is a division of labor always possible in a small business? If a division of labor is not possible in a small business, what is often substituted to aid in controlling transactions?

PROBLEMS

Problem 10–1

The bookkeeper of Snappy Togs Store assembled the following information for use in reconciling the firm's November 30 bank statement balance with its book balance of cash as of that date:

a) The November 30 bank statement showed the firm's cash balance at $1,572.25, and the accounting records showed a cash balance of $1,435.00.

b) Checks No. 312 for $63 and No. 318 for $52 were outstanding when the bank balance was reconciled on October 31. Check No. 312 was returned by the bank with the November canceled checks, but No. 318 was not.

c) November checks No. 398 for $15, No. 399 for $36, and No. 403 for $107 were not among the canceled checks returned.

d) A deposit of $205 placed in the night depository of the bank on November 30 did not appear on the bank statement.

e) A debit memorandum with a $25 N.S.F. check signed by James Weston was included with the canceled checks.

f) A $5.00 debit memorandum for printing checks was included with the canceled checks returned.

g) Included among the canceled checks returned was a check for $36.25 drawn by Snappy Service Station and paid in error by the bank from the account of Snappy Togs Store.

h) On November 30 the bank had sent the Snappy Togs Store a credit memorandum in the amount of $198.50. The memorandum resulted from the collection by the bank for the store of a $200 note. The bank had deducted a $1.50 collection fee. The memorandum had not been recorded by the store.

Required:

1. Prepare a bank reconciliation for the Snappy Togs Store.

2. Prepare in general journal form the entries that the Snappy Togs Store would have to make to adjust its book balance of cash.

Problem 10–2

The bank account of Rapid Service Company was reconciled on December 31 with two checks, No. 812 for $157, and No. 813 for $93, outstanding. The following information was available for the January 31 bank reconciliation:

Rapid Service Company 1475 North Main Street		Statement of account with THE FIRST NATIONAL BANK	
Date	Checks and Other Debits	Deposits	Balance
Jan. 1	Balance brought forward		1,729.00
2	157.00		1,572.00
3	225.00	223.00	1,570.00
5	306.00		1,264.00
6	846.00		418.00
12		945.00	1,363.00
15	51.00 117.00		1,195.00
22		649.00	1,844.00
28	321.00	748.00	2,271.00
30	240.00 NSF		2,031.00
31	1.00 SC	498.00CM	2,528.00

Code: CM Credit Memorandum   NSF Not sufficient funds check
      DM Debit Memorandum   SC Service charge

From the Cash Receipts Journal

	First National Bank	
	Memo	Debit
Jan. 3	223.00	223.00
7	310.00	
9	405.00	
12	230.00	935.00
16	193.00	
20	206.00	
22	250.00	649.00
25	508.00	
28	240.00	748.00
31	319.00	319.00
		2,874.00

From the Check Register

Check Number	First National Bank Credit
814	306.00
815	225.00
816	846.00
817	51.00
818	117.00
819	321.00
820	129.00
821	163.00
	2,158.00

From the General Ledger

Cash

Jan. 1 Bal.	1,479.00	Jan. 31	2,158.00
31	2,874.00		

The deposit ticket given to the bank on January 12 was correct. The book-keeper prepared the deposit ticket by listing the items deposited. He did not discover his error of that date because he failed to compare the total of the deposit ticket with the amount shown in the Cash Receipts Journal as the amount deposited. Likewise, he failed to find this error before posting because at the end of the month he also made an offsetting error in totaling the Cash Sales column in his Cash Receipts Journal.

The N.S.F. check was received from a customer, James S. Jackson, in pay-ment of his account. Its return was unrecorded. The credit memorandum re-sulted from a $500 note which the bank had collected for Rapid Service Com-pany. The bank had deducted a $2.00 fee from the proceeds of the note. The collection was not recorded.

Required:

1. Prepare a statement reconciling the bank balance of Rapid Service Com-pany.
2. Prepare in general journal form the entries that would have to be made by the bookkeeper of the company.
3. The bookkeeper of the company also acted as cashier. List any changes that you would make in the firm's system of internal control for cash. Give your reason for each change.

Problem 10–3

Sales and Service, Inc., established a petty cash fund and appointed Mary Reed, one of its office clerks, petty cashier. A $20 check was drawn to establish the fund. During the first month in which the fund was in operation, Miss Reed completed the following petty cash transactions:

Jan. 2   Received and cashed check No. 786. Placed the $20 proceeds in the petty cash drawer of the office safe.
4   Paid $1.50 to have the windows washed.
7   Purchased 100 seven-cent air mail stamps.
8   Paid $2.50 for carbon paper.
10   Paid 60 cents for a collect telegram.
15   Purchased 50 four-cent stamps.
17   Paid $1.86 express on a purchase of merchandise.
23   Purchased paper clips, 50 cents.
27   Paid a boy 25 cents to deliver a package to a customer.
29   Paid $2.60 express on merchandise purchased.
31   Received replenishing check No. 897 in the amount of $18.81 from the company cashier in exchange for the paid petty cash vouchers.

Required:

1. Prepare a Petty Cash Record and a Check Register similar to the ones illustrated in this chapter.
2. Record the foregoing transactions in the Petty Cash Record and, where necessary, in the Check Register.
3. After recording the transactions in the Petty Cash Record, rule and bal-ance the record and enter the replenishing check in both the Petty Cash Record and the Check Register.

Problem 10–4

On September 30, Radio Supply Company established a petty cash fund and appointed Mary Green petty cashier. The following transactions involving petty cash were then completed during September, October, and November:

Sept. 30   Miss Green received check No. 725 in the amount of $10 to establish the fund.

Oct.   2   Paid $1.25 express on merchandise purchased.

      8   Bought 100 three-cent stamps.

    16   Paid $1.50 for repairs to an office chair.

    17   Paid $1.00 for washing windows.

    28   Purchased carbon paper, $2.00.

    31   Received check No. 787 to replenish the petty cash fund, $8.75.

Nov.   7   Paid 50 cents for the delivery of a package to a customer.

      9   Paid $1.40 express on merchandise purchased.

    15   Paid 65 cents for a collect telegram.

    21   Bought 100 three-cent stamps.

    25   Paid $2.10 express on merchandise purchased.

    29   Paid 15 cents postage due on a purchase of merchandise.

    30   Received check No. 853 to replenish the fund, $7.80.

Required:

1. Prepare a Petty Cash Record and a Check Register similar to the ones illustrated in this chapter. Open T-accounts for the following accounts: Cash; Petty Cash; Postage; Freight-In; Miscellaneous General Expense; Office Supplies; and Delivery Expense.

2. Record the check establishing the fund; and post the Check Register as of September 30. Rule the Check Register with double ruled lines.

3. Enter the October petty cash transaction in the Petty Cash Record. Balance the record, and enter the replenishing check in the Check Register and in the Petty Cash Record. Post the entries entered in the Check Register. Rule double ruled lines across the columns of the Check Register.

4. Enter the November petty cash transactions in the Petty Cash Record. Balance the record and post the replenishing entry from the Check Register.

CLASS EXERCISES

Exercise 10–1

Russell Sales Company, of which Dale Russell is sole owner, operates with annual accounting periods that end each December 31. On December 31 of the year just ended both the bookkeeper and the petty cashier forgot to reimburse the petty cash fund. At that time there were paid petty cash vouchers in the petty cash box as follows: office supplies, $5.65; postage, $12; freight on purchases, $7.35; and miscellaneous expenses, $2.10. The oversight was not discovered until the petty cash fund was reimbursed on February 3. By that time there were additional paid vouchers in the petty cash box as follows: office supplies, $8.50; and freight on purchases, $12.40. Give in general journal form the entry to reimburse the petty cash fund on February 3.

Exercise 10–2

The following information was taken from a company's bank statement and accounting records at the end of a month:

1. Balance per cash account.................................$2,860
2. Outstanding checks.. 820
3. Undeposited cash on hand................................. 180
4. Deposited unrecorded by bank............................. 208
5. Bank charges for safety box rental, collections, etc............ 18

Required:

Under the assumption that all transactions were properly recorded on the company's books, determine the amount shown on its bank statement as its balance of cash in the bank.

SUPPLEMENTARY PROBLEMS

Problem 10–A

On December 1 of the current year Hickman Company established a petty cash fund. During the month they completed the following petty cash transactions:

Dec. 1 Drew Check No. 518 to establish a $25 petty cash fund. Appointed Alice Cook petty cashier.

2 Paid express on merchandise purchased, $6.40.

4 Paid for advertising material delivered to the store by Custom Printing Company, $8.00.

7 Paid for meals of employees working overtime, $3.55.

9 Paid for a collect telegram, $1.35.

11 Paid express charges on merchandise purchased, $3.35.

11 Drew Check No. 584 to reimburse the petty cash fund; and because the fund had been so rapidly exhausted, made the check sufficiently large as to increase the size of the fund to $50.

13 Paid for cleaning of the office, $5.50.

15 Paid a college student $4.00 for delivering advertising circulars.

18 Paid express charges on merchandise purchased, $6.15.

23 Paid for meals of employees working overtime, $2.85.

28 Paid a sign painter to letter the company name on a door, $10.

31 Drew Check No. 635 to reimburse the fund at the end of the accounting period. The cash in the petty cash drawer amounted to $20.25 when it was counted.

Required:

From the foregoing transactions prepare in general journal form the entries that would appear in the Check Register of the Hickman Company as a result of the transactions.

Problem 10–B

From the following information prepare a bank reconciliation for the Reynolds Company as of November 30 of the current year. Present figures to prove deposits in transit and outstanding checks.

Information from the Reynolds Company Books:

Book balance of cash as of November 30..........................$ 3,380.22
Total of the daily deposits made during November (including one amounting to $423.60 which was mailed to the bank on November 28 and one amounting to $618.58 which was placed in the night depository on the night of November 30)...................... 11,240.00
Checks written during November............................... 10,196.42

Information from the Bank Statement of Reynolds Company:

Total deposits during the month (including a deposit of $798.20 placed
    by the company in the night depository on the night of October 31)..$10,996.02

Total checks paid (including $646.80 of checks written by the com-
    pany in October)... 9,882.34

November bank service charge................................ 8.17

Credit memorandum, representing the proceeds of a note less a collec-
    tion charge, mailed to the firm on November 30................ 1,521.94

Cash balance per bank statement.............................. 4,812.69

Other Information:

All checks written by Reynolds Company prior to November 1 were
    paid by the bank before November 30. The service charge and the
    credit memorandum were unrecorded on the firm's books.

ACCOUNTING FOR NOTES
AND DRAFTS

SOME companies sell merchandise on the installment plan and commonly secure promissory notes from their customers. Other companies in which the credit period is also long, such as dealers in farm machinery, likewise often secure notes from their customers. However, when companies in which the credit period is long are excepted, note transactions in comparison to other transactions are not too numerous. Nevertheless, many companies in which note transactions are not common will, at one time or another, accept a note from a customer in settlement of an account or will give a note to a creditor. Consequently, one interested in accounting must have some knowledge of note transactions.

Promissory Notes

A promissory note is an unconditional promise in writing to pay on demand or at a fixed or determinable future date a definite sum of money. In the note shown in Illustration 66, Hugo Brown promises to

Illustration 66—A Promissory Note

```
$100.00                    Eugene, Oregon                    March 9, 19__

_____Thirty days_____AFTER DATE____I____PROMISE TO PAY TO
THE ORDER OF_____Frank White_____
One hundred and no/100-----------------------------------------DOLLARS

FOR VALUE RECEIVED WITH INTEREST AT__6%____.

PAYABLE AT First National Bank of Eugene, Oregon
                              Hugo Brown
```

pay Frank White or his order a definite sum of money at a fixed future date. Hugo Brown is known as the *maker* of the note; Frank White is known as the *payee*.

Interest

The Hugo Brown note illustrated bears interest at the rate of 6 per cent. Interest is a charge for the use of money. To a borrower, interest is an expense; to a lender, it is a revenue. A note may be interest bearing or it

236

may be noninterest bearing. If a note bears interest, it must state the rate of interest or the amount of interest on its face. Interest is usually stated as a percentage of the face of the note. If a note is noninterest bearing, no interest is collected unless the note is not paid when due. If a noninterest-bearing note is not paid when due, interest at the full legal rate may be collected from the *date of maturity* until the date of final payment. The maturity date of a note is the date upon which the note is due and payable.

Calculating Interest

Unless otherwise stated, the rate of interest on a note is the rate charged for the use of the *principal* for one year. The principal of a note is the face of the note. The formula for calculating interest is:

$$\begin{array}{c}\text{PRINCIPAL} \\ \text{OF THE} \\ \text{NOTE}\end{array} \times \begin{array}{c}\text{RATE OF} \\ \text{INTEREST}\end{array} \times \begin{array}{c}\text{TIME OF THE} \\ \text{NOTE EXPRESSED} \\ \text{IN YEARS}\end{array} = \text{INTEREST}$$

For example, interest on a $1,000, 6 per cent, one-year note is calculated:

$$\$1,000 \times \frac{6}{100} \times 1 = \$60$$

In business, most note transactions involve a period of time that is less than a full year, and this period of time is usually expressed in days. When the time of a note is expressed in days, the actual number of days elapsing, not including the day of the date of the note but including the day on which the note falls due, is counted. For example, a ninety-day note, dated July 10, is due on October 8. The calculation of this October 8 due date is as follows:

The number of days in July..31
Minus the date of the note...10
Gives the number of days the note runs in July.....................21
Add the number of days in August...................................31
Add the number of days in September................................30
Total through September 30...82
Days in October needed to equal the time of the note, ninety days, also
   the due date of the note—October................................ 8
   Total Time the Note Runs in Days................................90

This calculation has the effect of not counting the day of the date of the note, but it does count the day on which the note is due.

Occasionally, the time of a note is expressed in months. In such cases, the note matures and is payable in the month of its maturity on the same day of the month as its date. For example, a note dated July 10 and payable three months after date is payable on October 10.

In calculating interest, banks and businessmen usually consider a year to have just 360 days. This simplifies most interest calculations. It makes the calculation of the interest on a ninety-day, 5 per cent, $1,000 note as follows:

$$\text{PRINCIPAL} \times \text{RATE} \times \frac{\text{EXACT DAYS}}{360} = \text{INTEREST}$$

or

$$\$1{,}000 \times \frac{5}{100} \times \frac{90}{360} = \text{INTEREST}$$

or

$$\$1{,}000 \times \frac{5}{100} \times \frac{90}{360} = \frac{25}{2} = \$12.50$$

Likewise, the calculation of interest on a $1,200, sixty-day, 6 per cent note is:

$$\$1{,}200 \times \frac{6}{100} \times \frac{60}{360} = \$12.00$$

Sixty-Day, 6 Per Cent Method

An examination of the preceding calculation shows the interest on $1,200 at 6 per cent for sixty days to be $12.00. Twelve dollars is 1 per cent, or 0.01, of $1,200. As in this case, the interest on any note that runs exactly sixty days and earns interest at exactly 6 per cent is always 1 per cent of the principal of the note. This is because sixty days are ⅙ of one year, and ⅙ of 6 per cent is 1 per cent. From this it is evident that to compute the interest on any given principal at exactly 6 per cent for exactly sixty days, it is only necessary to multiply the principal by 1 per cent, or 0.01. To multiply the principal by 0.01, the decimal point is moved two places to the left in the principal. For example, the interest on $757.00 for sixty days at 6 per cent is:

$$\$757.00 \times 0.01 = \$7.57$$

Six-Day, 6 Per Cent Method

Six days are ⅒ of sixty days. Because of this, the interest on a given principal for six days is ⅒ of 1 per cent, or 0.001. This means that to compute the interest on a given principal at 6 per cent for six days, it is only necessary to move the decimal point three places to the left in the principal. For example, the interest on $1,200 at 6 per cent for six days is:

$$\$1{,}200 \times 0.001 = \$1.20$$

The sixty-day, 6 per cent method or the six-day, 6 per cent method may be used for any combination of days. However, either has its greatest advantage when the time is either exactly sixty days, or exactly six days, or an even combination or fraction of one or the other. For example, the interest on $800.00 at 6 per cent for forty-five days is $6.00. The calculation of this is as follows:

Interest on $800 for sixty days at 6 per cent is (point off two places) $8.00.

Forty-five days are exactly ¾ of sixty days.

Therefore, the interest for forty-five days is ¾ of the interest for sixty days, or is: ¾ × $8.00 = $6.00.

Likewise, the interest on $500 at 6 per cent for forty-two days is $3.50, and it is calculated:

Interest on $500.00 for six days at 6 per cent is (point off three places) $0.50.

Forty-two days are the equivalent of seven periods of six days.

Therefore, the interest for forty-two days is seven times the interest for six days, or is: 7 × $0.50 = $3.50.

The sixty-day, 6 per cent method or the six-day, 6 per cent method of calculating interest may be used for other interest rates. For example, 8 per cent is 1 and ⅓ times 6 per cent. To calculate interest at 8 per cent, make the calculation at 6 per cent and add ⅓. Likewise, 4 per cent is ⅔ of 6 per cent. To calculate interest at 4 per cent, make the calculation at 6 per cent and take ⅔ of the result.

Actually, these short-cut methods can be used for any combination of days or for any rate of interest. However, any saving made by their use is lost when the calculation becomes complex.

Notes Payable

Notes payable may result from the purchase of an asset with a note or the settlement of an account payable with a note. Notes payable frequently arise when money is borrowed from a bank.

Giving a note in payment for an asset is not a common transaction. Occasionally, when the purchase price is high or the credit period is long, a note is given instead of making the purchase on open account. The entry for such a transaction is as follows:

Oct.	14	Store Equipment......................	1,600.00	
		Notes Payable....................		1,600.00
		Purchased display refrigerator with a one-year, 6 per cent note.		

Usually, all notes payable are recorded in a single Notes Payable account. If several notes are issued, each may be identified in the account by writing the name of the payee in the Explanation column on the line of the entry recording the issuance or payment of the note. If a company issues many notes, an unusual situation, a supplementary record called a Notes Payable Register may be kept. The details of each note are recorded in this Notes Payable Register.

Note Given to Secure an Extension of Time on an Account

Often, a note is given to secure an extension of time on an open account. For example, Frank Brown cannot pay his open account with the Ajax Company when it becomes due. The Ajax Company agrees to accept Brown's ninety-day, 4 per cent note for $350 in settlement of the account. Brown will record the transaction in his General Journal with the following entry:

Aug.	23	Accounts Payable—Ajax Company.......	350.00	
		Notes Payable....................		350.00
		Gave a ninety-day, 4 per cent note in settlement of our account.		

When the note becomes due, Brown gives the Ajax Company a check for $353.50 and records the payment of both the principal of the note and its interest with an entry as follows:

Nov.	21	Notes Payable.........................	350.00	
		Interest Expense......................	3.50	
		Cash.............................		353.50
		Paid our note with interest.		

The entry just given would normally be recorded by Brown in his Check Register or Cash Payments Journal. However, beginning at this point and continuing through the remainder of the text almost all entries will be given in general journal form in order to simplify the illustrations. The student should realize that a company would record such entries in its appropriate special journal if it made use of special journals.

Recording a Bank Loan

Banks distinguish between *loans* and *discounts*. A loan is an advance of money which is to be repaid with interest. With a loan an interest-bearing note is used, and the interest is paid when the note matures. A discount transaction differs from a loan transaction in that in a discount transaction the interest is deducted in advance at the time the loan is made. When money is advanced on a discount, a noninterest-bearing note is used because the interest is calculated and deducted from the face of the note at the time the loan is made. With the interest deducted in advance, the maker of the discounted note promises to repay only the principal. To illustrate loans and discounts, assume that Henry Green wishes to borrow $1,000 for sixty days at 6 per cent.

Borrowing Money with an Interest-Bearing Note

If Green gives the bank a $1,000, sixty-day, 6 per cent interest-bearing note, he will record the transaction as follows:

Sept.	10	Cash..................................	1,000.00	
		Notes Payable.....................		1,000.00
		Gave the bank a 6 per cent, sixty-day note.		

When the note and interest are paid, Green makes the following entry:

Nov.	9	Notes Payable........................	1,000.00	
		Interest Expense.....................	10.00	
		Cash............................		1,010.00
		Paid our sixty-day, 6 per cent note.		

Discounting a Note Payable

If, contrary to the situations of the previous paragraphs, it is the custom of Green's bank to collect interest in advance, the bank will take Green's noninterest-bearing note for $1,000; from the face of the note it will deduct 6 per cent interest for sixty days; and the bank will give Green $990. The $990 is $1,000 less the interest on $1,000 at 6 per cent for sixty days and is called the *proceeds* of the discounted note. The $10 interest collected in advance is known as *bank discount.* Bank discount is interest collected in advance by a bank. To record the discounted note, Green makes the following entry:

Sept.	10	Cash..................................	990.00	
		Interest Expense.....................	10.00	
		Notes Payable.....................		1,000.00
		Discounted at 6 per cent our noninterest-bearing note.		

When the note is paid at maturity, Green pays the bank only the face of the note, $1,000; and he records the transactions as follows:

Nov.	9	Notes Payable........................	1,000.00	
		Cash............................		1,000.00
		Paid our discounted note.		

Notice that Green does not pay interest when the discounted note is paid at maturity. No interest is due at maturity; the full amount of the interest was paid in advance when the loan was secured.

Notes Receivable

With the exception of companies selling on the installment plan and other companies in which the credit period is long, notes receivable are not common in retail enterprises. Many retail enterprises never take a note. Others occasionally take a note from a customer in settlement of a past-due account. Notes are more common in wholesaling and manufacturing. Here, when the credit period is long, notes are commonly taken in payment for merchandise or equipment. Also, in many wholesaling and manufacturing enterprises notes are often taken in settlement of past-due accounts.

In enterprises in which the credit period is long, notes are preferred to open accounts. This is because a note may be readily turned into cash before it is due. A note is converted to cash before maturity by discounting or selling it to a bank. Notes are also preferred to open accounts because the note represents a written acknowledgment by the debtor of both the debt and the amount of the debt. Too, notes are preferred because they generally earn interest.

Recording the Receipt of a Note

Notes receivable are recorded in a single Notes Receivable account. Each note may be identified in the account by writing the name of the maker in the Explanation column on the line of the entry recording its receipt or payment. Only one account is needed because the individual notes are on hand. The maker, rate of interest, due date, and other information may be secured by an examination of each note. However, if notes receivable transactions are numerous, a supplementary record may be maintained to record the details of each note. This supplementary record is called a Notes Receivable Register. As a supplementary record the Notes Receivable Register does not change the regular journal and ledger record of notes.

A note received at the time of a sale is recorded as follows:

Dec.	5	Notes Receivable......................	500.00	
		Sales............................		500.000
		Sold merchandise, terms six-month, 5 per cent note.		

When a note is taken in settlement of a past-due open account, the creditor usually attempts to collect part of the past-due account in cash. This reduces the amount of the debt and requires the acceptance of a smaller note. For example, Symplex Company agrees to accept cash in the amount of $132 and a $200, sixty-day, 6 per cent note from Joseph Cook in settlement of his past-due account. When Symplex receives the cash and the note, the following entry is made:

Oct.	5	Cash...................................	132.00	
		Notes Receivable......................	200.00	
		Accounts Receivable—Joseph Cook..		332.00
		Received cash and a note in settlement of an account.		

When Cook pays the note, this entry is made:

Dec.	4	Cash...................................	202.00	
		Notes Receivable.................		200.00
		Interest Earned....................		2.00
		Collected the Joseph Cook note.		

Dishonored Notes Receivable

Occasionally, the maker of a note either cannot or will not pay his note at maturity. When the maker of a note refuses to pay his note at maturity, the note is said to be *dishonored*. Dishonoring a note does not relieve the maker from his obligation, and every legal means should always be made to collect. However, collection may require lengthy legal proceedings.

The Notes Receivable account should show only notes that have not matured. Therefore, a dishonored, past-due note is always removed from the Notes Receivable account and charged back to the account of the maker. For example, the Symplex Company holds a $500, 6 per cent, sixty-day note of George Jones. At maturity, Mr. Jones dishonors the note. To remove the dishonored note from the Notes Receivable account, the Symplex Company makes the following entry:

Oct.	14	Accounts Receivable—George Jones......	505.00	
		Interest Earned..................		5.00
		Notes Receivable.................		500.00
		To charge the account of George Jones for his dishonored $500, 6 per cent, sixty-day note.		

Charging a dishonored note back to the account of the maker serves two purposes. It removes the note from the Notes Receivable account, leaving in the Notes Receivable account only notes that have not matured; and it records the dishonored note in the account of the maker. The second purpose is important because, in the future, if the maker of the dishonored note again applies for credit, his account will show all past dealings, including the dishonored note.

Observe in the foregoing entry which charged back the dishonored note of George Jones that the Interest Earned account is credited for interest earned even though the interest was not collected. The reason for this is that George Jones owes both the principal and the interest, and his account should reflect the amount owed.

Discounting Notes Receivable

Many businessmen prefer notes receivable to open accounts because a note may be discounted or sold to a bank. Discounting a note enables the businessman to turn the note into cash without waiting until the note matures. To discount a note, the owner of the note endorses and delivers the note to the bank. To endorse a note, the endorser signs his name on the back of the note in the same manner that a check is endorsed. A bank is frequently willing to accept and discount a note because the endorser of a note, by his endorsement, agrees to pay the note at maturity if it is not paid by the maker. This means that the endorser makes himself *contingently liable* for the payment of the note. His *contingent liability* depends upon the dishonor of the note by the maker. If the maker pays, the endorser has no liability. However, if the maker dishonors the note, then the contingent liability of the endorser becomes a real liability. Contingent liabilities, because they sometimes become actual liabilities, may affect the credit standing of the one contingently liable. Consequently, when a note is discounted, the contingent liability should appear in the accounts and on the balance sheet of the one discounting the note.

Aside from recording the contingent liability, discounting a noninterest-bearing note is similar to discounting one's own note payable. This is because the principal of a noninterest-bearing note is the same amount of money as its maturity value. The maker of a noninterest-bearing note pays only the principal at maturity. The bank discounting a noninterest-bearing note collects only the amount of the principal at maturity. Therefore, the discounting bank considers that it is lending the principal of the noninterest-bearing note from the *date of discount* until the date of maturity. The period of time from the date of discount to the date of maturity is called the *discount period*. The bank discounts or collects interest in advance for the discount period.

To illustrate, on February 4, Symplex Company receives a noninterest-bearing, sixty-day, $800 note, dated February 3, from Frank Brown in settlement of his account. The maturity date of this note is April 4, and it is calculated as follows:

Number of days in February	28
Date of note	3
Days note runs in February	25
Days note runs in March	31
Total days through March 31	56
Days in April needed to equal sixty and the maturity date of the note—April	4
Time of the Note in Days	60

If Symplex Company discounts this note at its bank on February 18, the bank must wait until April 4 to collect the $800 from Frank Brown. This is forty-five days and is calculated:

Number of days in February...................................28
Date of discount..18
Days note discounted in February.............................10
Days note discounted in March................................31
Days note discounted in April................................ 4
Days in Discount Period......................................45

The bank considers that it is lending $800 to Symplex Company for forty-five days. If the bank's rate of discount is 6 per cent, then the bank will deduct a $6.00 discount from the $800 maturity value of the note. ($800 × 0.01 × ¾ = $6.00.) This means that Symplex Company will receive $800 less $6.00, or $794, for the note. The $794 is called the "proceeds of the note." The $6.00 discount is interest expense to Symplex Company.

Symplex records the transaction:

Feb.	18	Cash.................................	794.00	
		Interest Expense.......................	6.00	
		Notes Receivable Discounted........		800.00
		Discounted the Brown note at 6 per cent.		

The credit to *Notes Receivable Discounted* records the contingent liability of Symplex. After the transaction is posted, the Notes Receivable and Notes Receivable Discounted accounts appear as follows:

Notes Receivable		Notes Receivable Discounted	
(Brown note) 800			(Brown note) 800
(Jones note) 500			

If a balance sheet is prepared before the maturity date of the discounted note, both the balance of the Notes Receivable account and the balance of the Notes Receivable Discounted account appear on the statement as follows:

Current Assets:

Cash..		$2,500
Notes receivable..............................	$1,300	
Notes receivable discounted...................	800	500
Accounts receivable...........................		4,000
Merchandise inventory.........................		8,000
Total Current Assets......................		$15,000

Showing "Notes receivable discounted" on the balance sheet as a subtraction from the "Notes receivable" indicates the contingent liability to a reader of the balance sheet.

Payment of a Discounted Note by the Maker

When a note is discounted at a bank, the bank takes possession of the note in exchange for money. The bank will then collect the note from the maker at maturity. If the maker pays at maturity, it is only necessary for the one who discounted the note to remove the discount liability from his books. If, for example, Frank Brown pays the note discounted by Symplex Company, Symplex will make the following entry:

April	7	Notes Receivable Discounted............	800.00	
		Notes Receivable.................		800.00
		To remove the discount liability of the		
		Brown note.		

The effect of this entry is to balance the Notes Receivable Discounted account and to remove the paid $800 note from the Notes Receivable account as follows:

Notes Receivable				Notes Receivable Discounted			
(Brown note)	800	(Brown note)	800	(Brown note)	800	(Brown note)	800
(Jones note)	500						

Dishonor of a Discounted Note

If it is able to do so, the bank always collects a discounted note directly from the maker. The one discounting the note will not hear from the bank if the discounted note is paid by the maker at maturity. However, if the discounted note is dishonored, the bank will notify, at once, the one who endorsed and discounted the note.

If the bank is unable to collect a discounted note from the maker at maturity, it will *protest* the note and look to the endorser or endorsers for payment. To protest a dishonored note is to fulfill one of the legal requirements necessary to hold endorsers liable. To protest a note, a *certificate of protest* is prepared and mailed to each endorser. A certificate of protest is a statement, usually attested by a notary public, indicating that the note was duly presented to the maker for payment and payment was refused. The cost of protesting a negotiable instrument is called a *protest fee*. The bank will look to the one who discounted the dishonored note for payment of both the maturity value of the note and the protest fee.

For example, suppose that instead of paying the $800 note previously illustrated, Frank Brown dishonors it. As soon as the note is dishonored, the bank notifies Symplex Company by mailing a copy of the certificate of protest and a letter asking payment of the maturity value of the note and the protest fee. Symplex Company must pay both. If the protest fee is $1.00, Symplex will pay the bank $801. In recording the payment, Symplex charges the note and protest fee back to the account of Frank Brown. The entry to record the payment of the note and protest fee is as follows:

Apr.	5	Accounts Receivable—Frank Brown......	801.00	
		Cash............................		801.00
		To charge the account of Brown with		
		his dishonored note and the protest fee.		

The dishonor of the note changed the contingent liability of Symplex to a real liability. Upon payment of the dishonored note both the real liability and the contingent liability are ended. The entry just given records the payment of the real liability. The following entry removes the contingent liability from the books:

April	5	Notes Receivable Discounted............	800.00	
		Notes Receivable..................		800.00
		To remove the contingent liability on the Frank Brown note dishonored today.		

Of course, upon receipt of the $801, the bank will deliver the dishonored note to Symplex. Symplex Company will then make every legal effort to collect from Brown. It will attempt to collect not only the maturity value of the note and protest fee but also interest on the maturity value and protest fee from the date of dishonor until the date of final settlement.

Discounting an Interest-Bearing Note

Discounting an interest-bearing note differs slightly from discounting a noninterest-bearing note. This is because when a bank discounts an interest-bearing note, it will collect from the maker at maturity both the principal of the note and interest. Because of this, the bank considers that it is lending the maturity value of the note for the discount period. Consequently, it calculates its discount on the maturity value. For example, on September 19, Symplex Company discounts the interest-bearing note of Carl Snow. The note is a $600, 4 per cent, ninety-day note and is dated August 20.

The maturity value of this note is $606. This is calculated:

$$\$600 \times \frac{4}{100} \times \frac{90}{360} = \$6.00$$

Principal of the note..	$600
Interest for ninety days at 4 per cent..........................	6
Maturity Value...	$606

The bank discounts the maturity value of the note for sixty days. The sixty days are calculated:

Time of the note in days..		90
Less: Time held by Symplex:		
Number of days in August.................................	31	
Date of note...	20	
Days held in August.......................................	11	
Days held in September...................................	19	
Total days held..		30
Discount Period..		60

This method of calculating the discount period differs from the method illustrated on page 245. However, either method gives the same result and is equally satisfactory.

The bank considers that it is lending Symplex Company the maturity value of the Carl Snow note for the discount period of sixty days. Therefore, it deducts its discount on the maturity value of $606 and gives Symplex the proceeds of $599.94. This is calculated:

```
Maturity value of the note................................$606.00
   Less: Interest on $606 at 6 per cent for sixty days ($606 × 0.01).   6.06
Proceeds................................................$599.94
```

Symplex Company may record this transaction as follows:

Sept.	19	Cash....................................	599.94	
		Interest Expense......................	6.06	
		Notes Receivable Discounted........		600.00
		Interest Earned....................		6.00
		Discounted the Carl Snow note for sixty days at 6 per cent.		

This method records as an expense the $6.06 interest deducted by the bank. It also records as revenue the amount of interest Symplex Company would have earned if it had held the note until maturity. A more common procedure is to offset the interest earned against the interest expense as follows:

```
Interest expense.......................................................$6.06
Interest earned........................................................ 6.00
Excess of Expense Over Revenue............................$0.06
```

Then, when the revenue and expense are offset, only the difference between them is recorded, in this manner:

Sept.	19	Cash....................................	599.94	
		Interest Expense......................	.06	
		Notes Receivable Discounted........		600.00
		Discounted the Carl Snow note for sixty days at 6 per cent.		

In the preceding example, the proceeds of the Carl Snow note, $599.94, are less than the principal. Since the proceeds are less than the principal, the difference is debited to Interest Expense. If the proceeds of a discounted note exceed the principal, the difference is credited to Interest Earned. For example, suppose that the Symplex Company held the Carl Snow note and discounted it on October 19 rather than on September 19. If the note is discounted on October 19, the discount period is thirty days. If the bank discounts the note for thirty days, at 6 per cent, it deducts a discount of $3.03. This is calculated by the sixty-day, 6 per cent method: $606 × 0.01 × ½ = $3.03. The proceeds of the note are then:

```
Maturity value of the note................................$606.00
   Less: The bank discount................................. 3.03
Proceeds................................................$602.97
```

In this case the proceeds are in excess of the principal, and the transaction is recorded as follows:

Oct.	19	Cash.................................	602.97	
		Notes Receivable Discounted........		600.00
		Interest Earned...................		2.97
		Discounted the Carl Snow note at 6 per cent for thirty days.		

In either case illustrated, the bank collects the maturity value of the discounted note from Carl Snow at maturity. If within a day or so after the maturity date of the note, Symplex does not receive notice of dishonor, it assumes that the note is paid. Symplex then makes a general journal entry to cancel its discount liability.

Discounted Interest-Bearing Note Dishonored at Maturity

If the Carl Snow note previously illustrated is dishonored at maturity, the bank will demand payment from Symplex of:

The maturity value of the note:
Principal...$600.00
Interest... 6.00 $606.00
Protest fee... 1.00
    Total... $607.00

Symplex must pay the $607. In recording the payment, it charges the $607 to the account of Carl Snow in the manner shown on page 243; in addition, it should cancel its discount liability.

When Symplex Company receives the dishonored note from the bank, it should make every legal effort to collect the maturity value of the note, the protest fee, and interest on both from the date of maturity. For example, if thirty days after the dishonor, Carl Snow pays the maturity value of the dishonored note, the protest fee, and interest, he should pay:

Maturity value...$606.00
Protest fee.. 1.00
Interest on $607 at 4 per cent for thirty days................. 2.02
    Total...$609.02

This is recorded by Symplex Company:

Nov.	18	Cash.................................	609.02	
		Accounts Receivable—Carl Snow....		607.00
		Interest Earned..................		2.02
		Dishonored note and protest fee collected with interest.		

Interest on the dishonored Carl Snow note illustrated is calculated at 4 per cent from the date of maturity. This is the rate of interest stated on the face of the dishonored note. In some cases, regardless of the rate stated, interest at the maximum legal rate is collected on the maturity value of a dishonored note and on the protest fee from the date of maturity. The maximum legal rate varies from 8 per cent to 12 per cent in the various states.

Collecting an Out-of-Town Note

A promissory note is a *negotiable instrument*. A negotiable instrument is a document to which title is readily changed, usually by endorsement, but sometimes by delivery only. Negotiable instruments readily pass from hand to hand without question because negotiable instrument laws have been written to encourage this. No effort will be made here to go into the legal aspects of negotiable instruments. That is reserved for a course in business law. For the purpose of this discussion, it is sufficient to point out that a *holder in due course* of a negotiable instrument, or one who receives a negotiable instrument from a holder in due course, has the legal right to collect the negotiable instrument without proving the existence of a debt. A holder in due course is one who gives something of value for a negotiable instrument before maturity without knowledge of defects in the title of previous holders. These legal aspects sometimes cause a problem in the collection of notes. The holder of a note will not part with the note without receiving payment. He does not wish to part with the evidence of indebtedness. The maker of a note will not pay his note without gaining possession of the note. This is because the maker must pay again if the original holder transfers the note, even after receiving payment, to a holder in due course or to one with the rights of a holder in due course.

No problem is involved in the collection of a note when both parties to the transaction live in the same city. The holder of a note can present the note directly to the maker for payment. However, when the parties live in different cities, a problem does arise in the exchange of cash for possession of a promissory note. This problem is overcome by using a bank as an agent to collect an out-of-town note. To illustrate, Symplex Company of Eugene, Oregon, holds the $1,000, 6 per cent, sixty-day note of Sam Small of Longview, Washington. When the note nears maturity, Symplex delivers the note to its Eugene bank for collection. The Eugene bank forwards the note to a Longview, Washington, correspondent bank. The Longview bank notifies Sam Small that it has the note for collection. When Small pays the Longview bank, he receives possession of the note. The Longview bank transmits the proceeds of the note to the Eugene bank. The Eugene bank credits the proceeds, less a collection fee, to the bank account of Symplex Company.

Only one entry is needed to record the collection of an out-of-town note through a bank acting as a collecting agent. This is made when the bank notifies that it has credited the proceeds less the collection fee. No entry is made when the note is delivered to the bank for collection. At that time it is not known if the note will be paid or dishonored. Until the note is paid, there is no change in the relationship of the parties. For example, when the Sam Small note is paid, the bank notifies Symplex that it has deposited the proceeds less the collection fee to Symplex's bank account. Symplex then makes the following entry:

Oct.	17	Cash.................................	1,009.00	
		Collection Expense.....................	1.00	
		Notes Receivable.................		1,000.00
		Interest Earned...................		10.00
		Proceeds of the Sam Small note less collection charge.		

Other Negotiable Instruments

Other negotiable instruments commonly used in the place of promissory notes are *commercial drafts* and *trade acceptances*. Commercial drafts are of two kinds, *sight drafts* and *time drafts*. A sight draft is payable on sight; a time draft is payable after the lapse of a period of time. Commercial drafts and trade acceptances differ from promissory notes in that drafts and trade acceptances arise with the creditor. Promissory notes read "I promise to pay"; they arise with the debtor or promisor. A commercial draft of trade acceptance reads "pay to the order of"; it arises with the creditor and is a written order drawn by the creditor which orders the debtor to pay a sum of money. A sight draft is shown in Illustration 67, and a time draft is shown in Illustration 68.

Illustration 67—A Sight Draft

$ 75.00   EUGENE, OREGON   October 10   19 59

At sight   PAY TO THE ORDER OF   Ourselves

--Seventy-five and no/100---DOLLARS

Symplex Manufacturing Company

TO   Thomas Black
          Portland, Oregon   BY W. A. Blue

Illustration 68—A Time Draft

$ 100.00   EUGENE, OREGON   October 15,   19 59

Thirty days after sight   PAY TO THE ORDER OF   Ourselves

One hundred and no/100---DOLLARS

Symplex Manufacturing Company

TO   Ralph Jones
          Cottage Grove, Oregon   BY W. A. Blue

Sight Draft as a Collection Device

A sight draft is often used as a device for collecting a past-due account. As such it is usually much more effective than a business letter. To illustrate, assume that the account of Thomas Black, in the amount of $75, is long past due on the books of Symplex Company. Symplex has written many letters to Black in an effort to collect. It has failed to do so. Now, in a final effort, before placing the account with an attorney for collection, Symplex notifies Black that it is drawing a sight draft to be presented for collection through a bank in Black's community. If at all possible, Symplex will present the draft through the bank Black offered as a credit reference when credit was first granted. This is usually the bank with which Black does business. After notifying Black, Symplex draws a sight draft for $75, as shown in Illustration 67, and sends it to the bank in Black's community. Since Black wishes to keep a good credit reputation with his local bank, he will usually honor the sight draft. To dishonor it is to admit to his local bank that he does not pay his debts. A sight draft is honored by payment.

Recording Sight Drafts

No entries are made by Symplex when the sight draft against Black is drawn. At that time it is not known if Black will honor the sight draft. Until the sight draft is honored, the relationship of the parties is unchanged. If Black honors the sight draft, he pays the face of the draft to the bank in his community. The bank sends the proceeds, less a collection charge, to Symplex. Receipt of the proceeds is Symplex's first notice of the honor of the draft. Upon receipt of the proceeds, Symplex makes the following entry:

Oct.	12	Cash..................................	74.50	
		Collection Expense.....................	.50	
		Accounts Receivable—Thomas Black		75.00
		Collected the account of Thomas Black with a sight draft.		

Aside from the collection expense, this is the entry that is made when any account receivable is collected.

Black records his payment of the sight draft in the same manner that he records the payment of any account payable. In effect, he has paid his account through the bank.

When a sight draft is dishonored, payment is refused. No entry is made by either party when a sight draft is dishonored because the relationship of the parties is unchanged.

Sight Drafts and C.O.D. Sales

Often when the credit reputation of an out-of-town buyer is unknown or is not good, the seller does not wish to sell on open account. In such cases the seller may use a sight draft and an order bill of lading to collect upon the delivery of the merchandise sold. A *bill of lading* is a special receipt for goods shipped by freight; it is issued by a transportation company. Bills of lading involve three people: (1) the transportation company, called the *carrier;* (2) the shipper, called the *consignor;* and (3) the person or firm to which the shipment is made, called the *consignee.* Bills of lading are of two kinds: (1) *straight bills of lading,* and (2) *order bills of lading.* A straight bill of lading reads, "Consigned to . . . ." It is used when the shipper sends goods consigned, or addressed, directly to the consignee. When it is used, title to the goods shipped passes to the consignee upon delivery of the goods by the shipper to the transportation company. The transportation company then delivers the goods directly to the consignee. An order bill of lading differs from a straight bill of lading in that it reads, "Consigned to the order of . . . ." It is a negotiable instrument. Often when it is used, the shipper sends the shipment consigned to himself at the address of the buyer. With an order bill of lading the shipper retains title to the goods shipped. Title is later transferred to the buyer by endorsement of the bill of lading. The transportation company will not deliver the consigned goods until the endorsed bill of lading is presented.

When the seller of merchandise wishes to collect on delivery, he uses an order bill of lading and a sight draft. The seller, with the order bill of lading, consigns the goods to himself at the address of the buyer. He then endorses the bill of lading to the buyer and attaches a sight draft for the full amount of the sale. Next he sends both the endorsed order bill of lading and attached sight draft to a bank in the town of the customer. The bank is instructed to deliver the bill of lading to the buyer only upon collection of the sight draft. To secure the shipment, the buyer must have the order bill of lading. To secure the bill of lading, he must pay the sight draft. If he pays, the collecting bank delivers the bill of lading to the customer. It then transmits the proceeds of the sight draft, less a collection fee, to the seller.

C.O.D. sales are accounted for in the same manner as sales on account. When the goods are shipped, the seller makes an entry in the Sales Journal debiting the customer and crediting sales. When the proceeds of the sight draft are received, cash and collection expense are debited, and the customer is credited. A collect on delivery purchase is a cash purchase to the buyer. It is recorded in the same manner as any cash purchase.

Time Drafts

A time draft differs from a sight draft in that a time draft is not payable until after the lapse of a period of time. Time drafts usually read:

Sixty days after date, pay to the order of. . . . . .

or

Thirty days after sight, pay to the order of. . . . . .

A draft payable sixty days after date is payable sixty days after the date of the draft. A draft payable thirty days after sight is payable thirty days after *acceptance*. A draft is accepted when the debtor agrees to pay it.

A time draft like a sight draft is drawn by the creditor; he is called the *drawer*. The draft orders the debtor to pay. A time draft has no effect until the debtor agrees to pay it. The debtor, called the *drawee*, agrees to pay by writing across the face of the draft the word "accepted" and his signature. When the drawee accepts a time draft, he agrees in writing to pay a definite sum of money at a fixed future date. Consequently, a time draft upon acceptance becomes a form of promissory note. In accounting, an accepted time draft is usually treated by both parties in the same manner as a promissory note.

For example, Symplex Company agrees to give Ralph Jones a thirty-day extension on his $100 account if Jones will accept a thirty-day time draft. Symplex draws the draft and sends it to Jones. This draft is shown in Illustration 68. No entry is made when the draft is drawn because it is not certain that Jones will accept it. Jones does accept the draft, and he returns the accepted draft to Symplex. The accepted draft is shown in Illustration 69.

Illustration 69—An Accepted Time Draft

Recording Time Drafts

Ralph Jones records his acceptance of the time draft with the following entry:

Oct.	16	Accounts Payable—Symplex Company...	100.00	
		Notes Payable....................		100.00
		Accepted a thirty-day time draft.		

When Symplex receives the accepted time draft from Jones, it makes the following entry:

Oct.	18	Notes Receivable......................	100.00	
		Accounts Receivable—Ralph Jones...		100.00
		Thirty-day time draft in settlement of account.		

Notice that these are the same entries that would have been made if Jones had given Symplex a promissory note. An accepted time draft is treated in the accounting records in the same manner as a promissory note.

Trade Acceptances

A trade acceptance is a time draft that arises from a current sale of goods or merchandise. It always has a statement to this effect printed on its face, as shown in Illustration 70.

Illustration 70—An Accepted Trade Acceptance

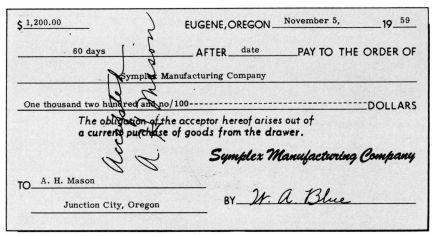

Because a trade acceptance grows out of a current sale of merchandise, and many notes result from the settlement of past-due accounts, trade acceptances have a better reputation than promissory notes. Bankers prefer trade acceptances because they feel that a trade acceptance is less apt to be dishonored at maturity. Trade acceptances are accounted for in the same manner as time drafts.

Interest, Notes, and Drafts on the Statements

Interest earned, interest expense, and collection expense appear on the income statement under the heading of "Other revenues and expenses." Because "Other revenues and expenses" are not revenues and expenses of the regular operations of a business, they appear as an addition to and a deduction from the income from operations, as follows:

```
Income from operation . . . . . . . .            $87,500
   Other revenues and expenses:
      Interest earned . . . . . . . . .   $1,200
      Interest expense. . . . . . . . .      900
      Addition to income from operations            300
Net Income. . . . . . . . . . . . . .            $87,800
```

Notes receivable, drafts receivable, and trade acceptances receivable all normally appear on the balance sheet in one amount under the caption of "Notes receivable." Likewise, notes, drafts, and trade acceptances payable all appear as one amount under the caption of "Notes payable."

QUESTIONS FOR CLASS DISCUSSION

1. Define:

   a) Promissory note.
   b) Payee of a note.
   c) Maturity date.
   d) Dishonored note.
   e) Certificate of protest.
   f) Holder in due course.
   g) Drawee of a draft.

   h) Maker of a note.
   i) Principal of a note.
   j) Maturity value.
   k) Contingent liability.
   l) Drawer of a draft.
   m) Straight bill of lading.
   n) Order bill of lading.

2. What distinction do banks make between discounts and loans?

3. Distinguish between bank discount and cash discount.

4. What are the due dates of the following notes:

   a) Ninety-day note dated July 10.
   b) Sixty-day note dated April 13.
   c) Ninety-day note dated December 12.

5. Calculate interest on the following amounts:

   a) $1,563 at 6 per cent for 60 days.
   b) $3,000 at 6 per cent for 24 days.
   c) $3,000 at 6 per cent for 72 days.

   d) $3,000 at 4 per cent for 60 days.
   e) $6,000 at 8 per cent for 30 days.
   f) $3,212 at 4 per cent for 90 days.
   g) $1,000 at 3 per cent for 120 days.
   h) $2,000 at 7 per cent for 54 days.

6. James Thumb borrows from two different banks. From the first bank he borrows by giving his $1,000, thirty-day, 6 per cent note. From the second bank he borrows by discounting his $1,000 note for thirty days at 6 per cent. (a) Give the entries in general journal form to record the two loans on the books of Thumb. (b) Give the entries in general journal form to record the payments of the loans. (c) How do the entries differ in the two situations? (d) Which method of making loans favors the bank?

7. B. A. Lee purchased $400 worth of merchandise from Noble Manufacturing Co., terms 2/10, n/30. Lee could not pay the account when due and secured an extension of time from Noble by giving a sixty-day, 6 per cent note in the amount of $400. Lee paid the note in full when due. Record this series of transactions in T-accounts (a) on the books of Lee, and (b) on the books of Noble.

8. On December 10, S. A. Starns received from a customer a $1,200, sixty-day, 6 per cent note dated December 8. On December 23, he discounted the note at 6 per cent. The note was not protested at maturity. Give the required entries in general journal form on the books of Starns.

9. If the following accounts and balances appear in a ledger:

Notes Receivable		Notes Receivable Discounted	
Bal. 8,500			Bal. 6,000

   a) How many dollars worth of notes receivable are in the hands of the company?

b) How many dollars worth of notes have been discounted?

c) What is the contingent liability of the company?

10. How does a commercial draft differ from a promissory note?

11. Tell how a sight draft is used to collect a C.O.D. sale.

12. Explain how a sight draft is used to collect a past-due account.

13. Why is a sight draft usually more effective as a collection device than a business letter?

14. Brown owes Green $300. The debt is past due, and Green draws a sight draft and sends it to Brown's bank for collection. Brown honors the draft. Give the required entries in general journal form (*a*) on the books of Green, and (*b*) on the books of Brown. The bank's fee was $1.50.

15. Why is a trade acceptance often considered more desirable than a time draft or a promissory note?

16. A trade acceptance is sometimes called "self-liquidating paper." Can you give a reason for this?

PROBLEMS

Problem 11–1

Prepare general journal entries to record the following transactions:

Dec. 12 Sold $1,200 of merchandise to Sidney Rodgers, terms 2/10, n/30.

Feb. 16 Accepted a $1,200, sixty-day, 6 per cent note dated February 14 in settlement of the open account of Sidney Rodgers.

Feb. 26 Discounted the Sidney Rodgers note at 6 per cent at the Second National Bank.

Apr. 18 Since a notice of protest of the Sidney Rodgers note had not been received, assumed the note had been paid and canceled the discount liability.

May 2 Sold $1,500 of merchandise to Allen Hale, terms 2/10, n/30.

July 5 Accepted a $1,500, sixty-day, 4 per cent note dated July 3 in settlement of the open account of Allen Hale.

July 9 Discounted the Allen Hale note at 6 per cent at the Second National Bank.

Sept. 2 Received a notice protesting the Allen Hale note. Paid the maturity value of the note plus a $1.00 protest fee. Canceled the discount liability.

Oct. 1 Received a check from Allen Hale in payment of the maturity value of his dishonored note plus the protest fee and plus interest at 4 per cent on both the maturity value of the note and the protest fee for the thirty days beyond maturity.

Oct. 3 Sold $1,800 of merchandise to James Berry, terms 2/10, n/60.

Dec. 10 Mailed an $1,800, 6 per cent, thirty-day time draft to James Berry who had agreed to accept the draft in order to secure a thirty-day extension on his account balance.

Dec. 14 Received the accepted time draft mailed to James Berry on December 10.

Jan. 8 Sent the accepted time draft of James Berry to the Second National Bank for collection.

Jan. 12 Received a credit memorandum from the Second National Bank. The memorandum represented the proceeds of the James Berry time draft less a $2.00 collection fee.

Problem 11–2

Prepare general journal entries to record the following transactions:

Jan. 3 Received a $2,400, sixty-day, 6 per cent note dated January 2 from James Foster in settlement of his past-due account.

5 Received $1,000 of merchandise from Drew and Ramsey, terms thirty-day, noninterest-bearing trade acceptance. Accepted the trade acceptance.

8 Sent Donald Porter an $800, thirty-day, noninterest-bearing time draft. Mr. Porter had agreed to accept the draft in order to secure an extension on the amount owed to us on his open account.

11 Drew a $500 sight draft on Richard Mann who has ignored numerous letters written in an effort to collect his past-due account. Sent the sight draft to the Shelbyville State Bank, Mr. Mann's bank, for collection.

12 Received the time draft sent to Donald Porter. The draft read, "Thirty days after sight, pay to the order of——." It had been accepted by Mr. Porter on January 10.

13 Received a $498 cashier's check from the Shelbyville State Bank. The check represented the proceeds of the Richard Mann sight draft less a $2.00 collection charge.

20 Discounted the James Foster note at 6 per cent at the Security State Bank.

22 Discounted at 6 per cent the thirty-day trade acceptance of Donald Porter.

Feb. 1 Received notice from the Security State Bank that they held for collection the Drew and Ramsey trade acceptance that we had accepted on January 5. Paid the accptance.

12 Since a notice protesting the Donald Porter time draft had not been reecived, assumed that the draft had been paid and canceled the discount liability.

Mar. 4 Received from the Security State Bank a notice protesting the James Foster note. Paid the bank the maturity value of the note plus a $1.00 protest fee. Canceled the discount liability.

15 Received a check from James Foster in payment of the maturity value of his dishonored note plus the protest fee and plus interest at 6 per cent on the maturity value and protest fee for twelve days beyond maturity.

Problem 11–3

Prepare general journal entries to record the following transactions:

Jan. 2 Received a $1,600, 6 per cent, sixty-day note dated December 30 from George Frank in settlement of his past-due account.

4 Received a $1,400, thirty-day, noninterest-bearing note dated January 2 from William Small in settlement of his past-due account.

6 Received $2,000 of merchandise from Lamer and Keane, terms sixty-day, noninterest-bearing trade acceptance. Accepted the trade acceptance.

8 Sent Roy Sherwood a $1,100, sixty-day, 6 per cent interest-bearing time draft for acceptance. The draft was dated January 8 and read, "Sixty days after date, pay to the order of." Mr. Sherwood had agreed to accept the draft in order to secure an extension on his past-due account.

8 Discounted the William Small note at 6 per cent at the First State Bank.

9 Sold and shipped $900 of merchandise to Bruce Hart, terms sixty-

day, noninterest-bearing trade acceptance dated January 9. Mailed
the trade acceptance.

12   Received the trade acceptance sent to Roy Sherwood on January 8.
It had been accepted.

12   Received from Bruce Hart the trade acceptance sent to him on
January 9. The instrument had been accepted.

12   Drew a $450 sight draft addressed to William King, a former
customer who had ignored numerous letters written in an effort
to collect his past-due account. Sent the draft to the Jacksonville
State Bank, Mr. King's bank, for collection.

14   Discounted the George Frank note at 6 per cent at the First State
Bank.

15   Received a $448 cashier's check from the Jacksonville State Bank.
The check represented the proceeds of the William King sight
draft less a $2.00 collection charge.

15   Discounted the Bruce Hart trade acceptance at 6 per cent at the
First State Bank.

26   Discounted the Roy Sherwood time draft at 6 per cent at the First
State Bank.

Feb. 3   Since a notice protesting the William Small note had not been
received, assumed that the note had been paid and canceled the
discount liability.

Mar. 1   Received a notice from the First State Bank protesting the
George Frank note. Paid the bank the maturity value of the note
plus a $1.00 protest fee. Canceled the discount liability.

7   Received notice from the First State Bank that they held for collection the Lamer and Keane trade acceptance. Paid the acceptance.

12   Since notices protesting the Roy Sherwood time draft and the
Bruce Hart trade acceptance had not been received, assume that
both had been paid and canceled the discount liabilities.

15   Received a check from George Frank for the maturity value of
his dishonored note and the protest fee plus interest on both at
6 per cent for fifteen days beyond maturity.

Problem 11–4

Prepare entries in general journal form to record the following draft transactions:

Oct. 5   Used an order bill of lading to sell and ship merchandise C.O.D.
to George Blank, Northport, Oregon. Sent the order bill of lading,
with a sight draft in the amount of $820 attached, to the First
State Bank in Northport for collection of the draft and delivery
of the bill of lading.

8   Drew a $200 sight draft addressed to George Smallwood who has
ignored numerous letters requesting payment of his account. Sent
the draft to the First National Bank of Harrisburg, Mr. Smallwood's bank, for collection.

9   Received a cashier's check from the First State Bank of Northport
in the amount of $817.50. The $817.50 is the proceeds, less a
collection charge, of the sight draft attached to the George Blank
order bill of lading.

11   Received a cashier's check in the amount of $198.50 from the First
National Bank of Harrisburg. The cashier's check represents the
proceeds, less a collection charge, of the George Smallwood sight
draft.

Oct. 12 Drew a $315, thirty-day, noninterest-bearing time draft addressed to William Sullivan. Sent the draft to Mr. Sullivan for acceptance.

16 Received the accepted time draft sent to William Sullivan. Mr. Sullivan attached a letter thanking us for using this method to grant him an extension on his open account.

22 Used a straight bill of lading to sell and ship $218 worth of merchandise to Paul Thompson, Seattle, Washington, terms sixty-day, noninterest-bearing, trade acceptance. Sent the $218 trade acceptance to Mr. Thompson for acceptance.

23 Received $450 worth of merchandise from the Ace Supply Company, terms thirty-day, noninterest-bearing, trade acceptance. Accepted the trade acceptance.

26 Received the accepted trade acceptance of Paul Thompson.

Nov. 9 Gave the accepted time draft of William Sullivan to the First National Bank for collection.

15 Received a credit memorandom from the First National Bank. The memorandum reported that the bank had collected the Sullivan draft, deducted a $1.50 collection fee, and deposited the balance in our account.

23 Received notice that the First National Bank held for collection the trade acceptance given the Ace Supply Company. Gave the bank a check in payment.

24 Discounted at 6 per cent, thirty days before maturity, the $218 trade acceptance received from Paul Thompson.

Dec. 27 Canceled the discount liability on the Paul Thompson trade acceptance.

CLASS EXERCISES

Exercise 11–1

On March 3 of the current year General Supply sold James Keller $3,000 of merchandise, terms 2/10, n/60. On May 14 the company accepted Keller's sixty-day, 6 per cent note dated that day in settlement of the past-due open account. On May 26 General Supply discounted Keller's note at 6 per cent. The note was paid at maturity.

Required:

Give entries in general journal form to record this series of transactions on the books of Keller and on the books of General Supply.

Exercise 11–2

On December 8, B. A. Day received a $500, 6 per cent, ninety-day note from Paul Sipe, a customer. On February 6, Day discounted the note at 6 per cent. On March 9, he received a notice of protest. He paid the bank the maturity value of the note plus a protest fee of $1.00. On April 7, Day received a check in full payment of the maturity value of the note, the protest fee, and interest at 6 per cent on both from the date of maturity. Give the required entries in general journal form.

SUPPLEMENTARY PROBLEMS

Problem 11–A

On September 11 General Manufacturing Company sold Thomas Darr goods having a catalogue price of $2,000, less 20 per cent and 10 per cent, terms 2/10, n/60. At the end of the credit period Darr was unable to pay and was granted an extension by General Manufacturing Company upon receipt of his sixty-day, 6 per cent note dated November 20. General Manufacturing Company held the note until December 5. On that date the firm discounted the note at 6 per cent at the First National Bank. The note was not protested at maturity. Answer the following questions:

1. How many dollars of trade discount were granted by General Manufacturing Company?
2. How much cash discount could Thomas Darr have obtained on this purchase?
3. What was the maturity date of the note?
4. How many days were in the discount period?
5. How much bank discount was deducted by the bank?
6. What were the proceeds of the note?
7. What was the last entry made by General Manufacturing Company as a result of this series of transactions?

Problem 11–B

Prepare entries in general journal form to record the following note transactions:

Oct. 2 Received a thirty-day, noninterest-bearing, $800 note, dated October 1, in settlement of the past-due account of Thomas Hill.

5 Gave Thompson Supply Company, a creditor, a $1,200, 4 per cent, sixty-day note to secure an extension of time on an open account.

16 Discounted the note of Thomas Hill at the First National Bank at 6 per cent.

16 Discounted at the First National Bank our own $1,000 note for thirty days at 6 per cent.

17 Received a thirty-day, 4 per cent, $900 note, dated October 15, from John Adams in settlement of a past-due account.

21 Discounted the John Adams note received on October 17 at the First National Bank at 6 per cent.

24 Received a 6 per cent, thirty-day, $200 note, dated October 23, and $150 in cash from F. M. Snare in settlement of his past-due account.

Nov. 3 Made an entry to cancel the contingent liability on the Thomas Hill note. This note was due on October 31. Since a notice of protest has not been received, it is assumed that Hill paid the note when due.

15 Sent the First National Bank a check in payment of our own note discounted on October 16.

15 Borrowed $500 from the U.S. National Bank. Gave the bank a $500, 6 per cent, thirty-day, interest-bearing note.

15 Received notice that John Adams had dishonored his note due yesterday. Gave the bank a check for the maturity value of the note, plus a $1.00 protest fee. Charged the amount to the account of Adams. Made an entry to cancel the contingent liability.

20 Sent the Snare note to the First National Bank for collection.

20 Received a check in the amount of $904.60 from John Adams. This amount is in full of the maturity value of Adams' dishonored note, the protest fee, and interest on both amounts from the date of maturity.

25 Received a credit memorandum from the First National Bank indicating that $199.75, the proceeds of the Snare note less a collection charge of $1.25, had been deposited to our account.

Dec. 4 Received notice that the First National Bank held for collection the note given to Thompson Supply Company. Gave the bank a check for $1,208 in full payment of the note and interest.

Chapter 12

BAD DEBTS AND ACCOUNTS RECEIVABLE: INVENTORIES AND COST OF GOODS SOLD

WHEN goods and services are sold on credit, some customers do not pay. The accounts of such customers are called *bad debts*. Keeping bad debts or uncollectible accounts to a minimum is an objective of good credit management.

Granting Credit

If losses from uncollectible accounts are to be held to a minimum, a business selling on credit must exercise the greatest care in selecting customers to whom credit is granted. Many companies have credit departments whose duty it is to investigate the debt-paying ability and the debt-paying habits of each prospective new customer and to decide how much credit, if any, can safely be granted. In making this investigation, a credit department examines the financial statements of the prospective customer, as well as credit reports secured from credit agencies. Almost every community of any size has a local credit agency that gathers and reports information about the debt-paying habits and abilities of local individuals and firms. On a national scale, Dun & Bradstreet publishes a credit-rating book containing information about the financial condition and debt-paying reputation of individuals and companies engaged in merchandising, manufacturing, and trading. This book is available to those subscribing for it. In addition to Dun & Bradstreet, there are several national credit agencies specializing in credit reports for particular lines of business. For example, the Lumbermen's Credit Association specializes in credit reports on companies producing and marketing lumber.

However, regardless of the care exercised in granting credit, there are always some accounts that can never be collected. The balances of these accounts are a loss and an expense of selling on credit. Determining the amount of this expense at the end of each accounting period is one of the problems of accounting for the revenue from charge sales.

Estimating Bad Debts Expense

When statements are prepared at the end of an accounting period, the amount of the uncollectible accounts should appear on the income statement as an expense and only the amount of the accounts receivable that will ultimately be collected should appear on the balance sheet as an asset.

This presents a problem because at the time the statements are prepared, it cannot be known exactly which of the accounts receivable will prove uncollectible. Normally the uncollectible accounts cannot be identified until sometime in the future after every effort to collect has resulted in failure.

However, although at the time the statements are prepared it is impossible to tell exactly which customers will not pay, it is usually possible to estimate with a reasonable degree of accuracy the probable amount of uncollectible accounts. This is because there is usually a close relationship, for example, between losses from bad debts and total charge sales or bad debts and total accounts receivable or bad debts and some other item. To illustrate, if a company, over a past period of years has experienced a loss on bad debts of 1 per cent of its charge sales, it is usually safe to assume that "history will repeat" and the company will experience a future loss from bad debts of 1 per cent of its charge sales.

To illustrate further, at the end of 1959 Atlas Company has accounts receivable totaling $7,500. This company has experienced in past years a loss from bad debts equal to 1 per cent of its charge sales. During 1959 the company's charge sales were $90,000. Consequently, if history repeats, the company may expect to lose 1 per cent of $90,000; or it may expect to lose approximately $900 of its $7,500 accounts receivable. Therefore, if Atlas Company presents a 1959 income statement that shows its best estimate of its 1959 net income, the company must deduct $900 of bad debts expense from its revenue from sales and show its accounts receivable on its balance sheet somewhat as follows:

ASSETS

Current Assets:		
Cash		$ 3,000
Accounts receivable.	$7,500	
Less: Allowance for bad debts	900	6,600
Merchandise inventory.		10,000
Total Current Assets		$19,600

The *allowance for bad debts* is an allowance for accounts that will not be collected. When the allowance for bad debts is subtracted from accounts receivable, the amount remaining reflects a more accurate balance sheet amount for the accounts receivable.

The item, allowance for bad debts, once commonly appeared on balance sheets under the heading of "reserve for bad debts." However, since the Committee on Terminology of the American Institute of Certified Public Accountants issued its *Research Bulletin No. 34* in which it ". . . recommended that the use of the term *reserve* in accounting be limited . . . and that the use of the term on the balance sheet, in describing deductions from assets . . . be discontinued," the term is not commonly seen.

Bad Debts in the Accounts

Estimated bad debts expense is recorded at the end of each accounting period by means of an adjustment on the work sheet and an adjusting journal entry. For example, Atlas Company with its $90,000 of charge sales and its bad debts loss experience of 1 per cent of charge sales records its bad debts expense with an adjusting entry as follows:

Dec.	31	Bad Debts Expense....................	900.00	
		Allowance for Bad Debts...........		900.00
		To record the estimated loss from bad debts.		

The debit of this entry is posted to the expense account, Bad Debts Expense, which is closed to Income Summary in the same manner as any other expense account. The credit is posted to a new account in the current asset section of the ledger called *Allowance for Bad Debts*. After the entry is posted, the Accounts Receivable and Allowance for Bad Debts accounts appear as follows:

Accounts Receivable	Allowance for Bad Debts
Dec. 31 Bal. 7,500	Dec. 31 900

The illustrated accounts show that the estimated amount of uncollectible accounts is not recorded by means of a credit to the Accounts Receivable account; rather the credit is to a new contra account called Allowance for Bad Debts. The contra account is necessary because at the time the adjustment is made, the particular customers who will not pay are unknown and their accounts cannot be removed from the subsidiary ledger. Consequently, since the accounts cannot be removed from the subsidiary ledger, the Accounts Receivable controlling account cannot be credited for the bad accounts, because to do so would cause the balance of the controlling account to differ from the sum of the balances in its subsidiary ledger.

Bad Debts Expense on the Income Statement

Bad debt losses result from unforeseen happenings and from errors of judgment in granting credit. Because it is usually feared that the sales department would be swayed in its judgment by the desire to make a sale, the granting of credit is not normally a responsibility of the sales department. Consequently, since the sales department is not responsible for granting credit, it is not responsible for bad debt losses; and, therefore, such losses appear on the income statement as an administrative expense rather than as a selling expense.

Writing off a Bad Debt

Occasionally, when a customer becomes bankrupt, it may be definitely known that his account is uncollectible. Otherwise, whether an account is collectible or not is usually a matter of judgment and opinion. Each account that is long past due must be individually judged. If an account is judged uncollectible, it is written off as a bad debt against the allowance for bad debts. To write off an uncollectible account, the Allowance for Bad Debts account is debited and both the Accounts Receivable controlling account and the customer's account are credited. For example, the credit department of Atlas Company decides that the $35 account of James Henry is uncollectible. To write off the account the following entry is made:

Jan.	14	Allowance for Bad Debts.	35.00		
		Accounts Receivable—James Henry. .		35.00	
		To remove the balance of the uncollectible account of James Henry from the ledgers.			

After this entry is posted, the Accounts Receivable controlling account and the Allowance for Bad Debts account appear as follows:

Accounts Receivable				Allowance for Bad Debts			
Dec. 31 Bal. 7,500	Jan. 14		35	Jan. 14	35	Dec. 31	900

An uncollectible account is one of the expenses of selling on credit. However, when it is decided that an account is uncollectible, the amount of the uncollectible account is charged against the Allowance for Bad Debts account rather than against an expense account, as in the foregoing entries. This is because the expense of the uncollectible account was recorded as an estimate at the end of the accounting period in which the sale occurred. The loss was foreseen, and the expense was recorded in the estimated bad debts adjusting entry.

Time of a Bad Debt Loss

A bad debt results from an error in judgment; the granting of credit and making a sale to a customer who will not pay. Consequently, a bad debt loss is incurred at the time credit is granted and the sale is made. Such a loss is usually not discovered until later; but it is incurred at the time of the sale. For example, if a sale is made in 1959 to a customer who will not pay, a loss is incurred in 1959. If the account is written off in 1960, the loss did not occur in 1960; it merely took until 1960 to discover the loss.

Matching Revenues and Expenses

A fundamental principle of accounting requires that on an income statement revenues must be matched with the expenses incurred in earning the revenues. By this is meant that when an income statement is prepared at the end of a year, the income statement should show all of the revenues earned during the year, and matched against (deducted therefrom) the revenues should be all of the expenses incurred in earning the revenues.

The procedure outlined in previous pages for accounting for losses from bad debts follows the principle of matching revenues and expenses. For example, providing at the end of 1959 an allowance for the estimated amount of bad debt losses that are expected to result from 1959 sales, and thereby charging the estimated losses from 1959 sales to a 1959 expense account, matches the 1959 expense with the 1959 sales.

Bad Debt Recoveries

Frequently an error of judgment is made in regard to a customer's ability to pay his past-due account. As a result, accounts written off as uncollectible are later often collected in full or in part. If an account is written off as uncollectible and later the customer pays a part or all of the amount previously written off, the payment should be shown in the customer's account. This places information as to the payment in the account for future credit action; and is desirable because when a customer fails to pay and his account is written off, the customer's credit standing is destroyed. Later, when the customer pays the amount previously written off, the payment helps to restore his credit standing. When an account previously written off as a bad debt is collected, two entries are made. The first is a general journal entry to reinstate the customer's account balance. It has the effect of reversing the original write-off. The second entry is the normal cash receipts journal entry to record the collection of an account receivable.

For example, James Henry, whose account was written off in January as a bad debt, pays in full on August 10. The entries to record the bad debt recovery are as follows:

Aug.	10	Accounts Receivable—James Henry......	35.00	
		Allowance for Bad Debts...........		35.00
		To reinstate the account of James Henry written off on March 31.		

CASH RECEIPTS JOURNAL

Date		Account Credited	Explanation	F	Sundry Accounts Credit	Accts. Receivable Credit		Cash Debit
Aug.	10	James Henry	Full of account			35.00		35.00

Other Methods of Estimating Bad Debts

As previously explained, the relationship between charge sales and past bad debt losses is often used in estimating losses from uncollectible accounts. Too, when the proportion of credit sales to cash sales remains about the same, total sales, rather than charge sales alone, may also be used. Likewise, in companies where about the same percentage of accounts receivable prove uncollectible each year, a percentage of the year-end balance of the Accounts Receivable account may be set up as the estimated bad debts expense.

Aging Accounts Receivable

In estimating bad debt losses, many companies age their accounts receivable. This consists of preparing a schedule of accounts receivable with the accounts listed and their balances entered in columns according to age. Such a schedule appears as in Illustration 71. After a schedule show-

Illustration 71

SCHEDULE OF ACCOUNTS RECEIVABLE BY AGE					
Customer's Name	Not Due	1 to 30 Days Past Due	31 to 60 Days Past Due	61 to 90 Days Past Due	Over 90 Days Past Due
Charles Abbot	45.00				
Frank Allen	53.00				
George Arden			14.00		
Paul Baum					27.00

ing the ages of the accounts receivable is prepared, responsible and experienced executives of the sales and credit departments examine each account listed thereon. These executives, from experience and by judgment, then decide which accounts are probably uncollectible. Normally, the majority of the accounts appearing on the schedule are current and not past due; these are examined for possible losses but receive less scrutiny than the past-due accounts. The older accounts are more apt to prove uncollectible; these receive the greatest attention. After decisions are made as to which accounts are probably uncollectible, the allowance for bad debts is adjusted to provide for them.

Correcting the Size of the Allowance for Bad Debts

Regardless of the method and care used in estimating losses from bad debts, errors in judgment occur. Often, too, unforeseen changes in economic and business conditions cause a change in the amount of uncollectible accounts. When either errors in judgment are made or changes in business conditions occur, the balance of the Allowance for Bad Debts account may become too large or too small. If losses are greater than anticipated, the allowance may become too small. If losses are less than anticipated, the allowance may become too large. Often, when the provision for bad debts is based on a fixed percentage of sales or accounts receivable, the passage of a number of accounting periods is required before it becomes apparent that the percentage used is either too large or too small. In such cases, when it becomes apparent that the percentage used is incorrect, an adjustment in the percentage should be made.

Sometimes, even though the amounts provided for bad debts over a number of accounting periods are approximately correct, during a single accounting period the allowance for bad debts may be exhausted by the write-off of an excessive number of uncollectible accounts. When this occurs, if additional losses are to be written off, the additional losses may be charged directly to the Bad Debts Expense account. This violates the principle of matching revenues and expenses; but it is acceptable if the amounts written off are not material in amount.

Occasionally a company will permit the credit balance of its Allowance for Bad Debts account to become much greater than the amount needed to provide for losses. This is particularly apt to happen when, without close attention to needs, a fixed percentage of sales or a fixed percentage of accounts receivable is set aside each year. Two errors result from permitting the allowance for bad debts to grow too large. First, in each year that the excessive allowance is provided, the expenses of that year are overstated and the net income is understated. In addition to this, after the allowance becomes too large, both the accounts receivable and the proprietorship are understated on the balance sheet.

When it is discovered that the balance of the Allowance for Bad Debts account has become too large because of excessive provisions for bad debts, an entry to correct the situation must be made. This entry appears as follows:

Jan.	22	Allowance for Bad Debts...............	500.00	
		Frank Jones, Capital...............		500.00
		To reduce the excessive allowance for bad debts.		

The debit to the Allowance for Bad Debts account corrects the understatement of accounts receivable. The credit to the Capital account corrects the understatement of proprietorship caused by the excessive past yearly debits to the Bad Debts Expense account.

Other Factors Affecting Accounts Receivable

Overpayment of an Account. Customers occasionally fail to take earned discounts or in some other manner overpay their accounts. Because of this, credit balances in the Accounts Receivable Ledger are not uncommon. When there are credit balances in the Accounts Receivable Ledger, the balance of the Accounts Receivable controlling account should not appear on the balance sheet as the amount of accounts receivable. In such cases, because assets and liabilities should not be offset, the accounts in the Accounts Receivable Ledger having debit balances should be added and their sum placed on the balance sheet as the amount of accounts receivable. At the same time the accounts having credit balances should be added and their sum placed on the balance sheet as a current liability under a heading such as, for example, "Credit balances in customer accounts."

Sales to and Purchases from the Same Firm. If goods are sold to and purchases are made from the same firm, two accounts should be kept, and the balances of the accounts should not be offset. In such cases the amount receivable should appear on the balance sheet as part of the accounts receivable; and the amount payable should appear as part of the accounts payable.

Miscellaneous Accounts Receivable. If the caption "Accounts receivable" appears on the balance sheet without any further descriptive words or limitations, only amounts due from regular trade debtors should be included under the heading. Accounts receivable from stockholders or company officers, in the case of a corporation, or from employees should be shown separately, unless the accounts arose from sales that are collectible in accordance with the company's regular selling terms. Loans and advances to stockholders, officers, and employees may be shown as current assets under a suitable descriptive title if there is evidence that the amounts receivable will be collected within the period normally allotted for the collection of current assets; otherwise, they should appear at the end of the asset section as, for example, "Other assets—accounts receivable from officers and employees."

INVENTORIES AND COST OF GOODS SOLD

Placing a proper accounting value on an ending inventory involves two distinct problems: (1) the problem of determining the quantity of each item on hand, and (2) the problem of pricing the items. Both problems are discussed in the following pages.

The Problem of Quantity

A merchandising company may find the amount of its unsold merchandise on hand in one of three ways. It may take a physical inventory, it may keep a perpetual or book inventory, or it may estimate the amount of its inventory. Of the three, a physical inventory is the most accurate. Obviously, the most accurate method of determining the exact amount of merchandise on hand is to count, weigh, or measure each item. In a physical inventory, each item is counted, weighed, or measured.

Physical Inventories

Counting the items of unsold merchandise on hand is a difficult task. Unless great care is exercised, items may be omitted from the count or they may be counted more than once. Because of this, physical inventories are commonly taken at night, on holidays, and on week ends; or the store is closed for business in order to take the inventory.

Illustration 72—An Inventory Ticket

INVENTORY TICKET
Ticket No._____ 786 _____
Item_____
_____
Quantity counted_____
Sales price_____
Cost price_____
Purchase date_____
Counted by_____
Checked by_____

The salesclerks who are familiar with the store and its merchandise are usually best equipped to make the count. Before the count is started, the merchandise should be straightened and arranged in an orderly fashion on the shelves and in the showcases. Items are less apt to be counted twice or omitted if prenumbered inventory tickets are used in making the count. An inventory ticket is shown in Illustration 72. At the start of the count, if inventory tickets are used, a sufficient number of tickets, at least one for each type of product on hand, is issued to each department in the store. When the inventory count is made, a clerk counts the quantity of each product on hand and, from the count and from the price tag attached to the merchandise, fills in the information on the inventory ticket. He then initials the ticket and attaches it to the counted items. A department head or other responsible person usually examines and recounts a sufficient proportion of the items to insure an accurate count. In each department, after the clerks complete the count, the department is examined for uncounted items. At this stage, inventory tickets are attached to all counted items. Consequently, any items without tickets attached are uncounted. After all items are counted and tickets attached, the tickets are removed and sent to the store office for completion of the inventory. To insure that no ticket is lost or left attached to the merchandise, all of the prenumbered tickets issued are accounted for when the tickets are returned to the office.

In the store office, the information of the tickets is copied on inventory sheets; and the summary sheets are completed by multiplying the number of units of each product by its cost. This gives the dollar amount of each product on hand, and the total for all products is the amount of the inventory.

For many years it has been a common practice to price inventory items at *cost or market, whichever is lower*. "Cost" is the actual price that was paid for an item when it was purchased. "Market" is the price that would have to be paid if the item were being purchased on the date of the inventory. In other words, "market" is the replacement cost of the item. For example, on the inventory summary sheet shown in Illustration 73, the Ajax

Illustration 73

INVENTORY SUMMARY SHEET

Item	Quantity on Hand	Date Purchased	Sales Price	Cost Price	Market Price	Inventory Value
Ajax claw hammers	4	12-12-59	1.50	1.00	1.25	4.00
Sharp hand saws	2	11-3-59	4.50	3.00	2.90	5.80
Danley 24-inch levels	2	9-14-59	5.50	3.50	3.50	7.00

claw hammers are valued at cost, because the cost price of $1.00 is below the market price of $1.25. Likewise, the Sharp hand saws are valued at market, because the market price of $2.90 is below the cost price of $3.00. Pricing an inventory at the lower of cost or market places an inventory on the balance sheet at a conservative figure.

Items Included on an Inventory

An inventory of merchandise should include all of the goods owned by a business and held for sale by it, regardless of where the goods may be located at the time of the inventory. In the application of this rule, there are generally no problems with respect to most of the items of an inventory. For most items all that is required is to see that they are counted, that nothing is omitted, and that nothing is counted more than once. However, goods in transit from a vendor, goods sold but not delivered, goods on consignment, and obsolete and damaged goods do require special attention.

When goods are in transit on the inventory date, the purchase should be recorded and the goods should appear on the purchaser's inventory if title has passed to the purchaser. The general rule as to the passing of title is: if goods are sold F.O.B. shipping point, title passes as soon as the goods are loaded aboard the means of transportation; if goods are sold F.O.B. destination, title passes when the goods arrive at their destination.

Sometimes a question arises as to the inclusion on the inventory of goods that have been segregated for delivery to a buyer but that have not been delivered. If a company has an order for goods, has segregated the goods, but has not delivered the goods, the question of title must still be answered. If title has passed to the buyer, the sale should be recorded and the goods should not appear on the seller's inventory. On the other hand, if title has not passed, the goods should appear on the inventory of the seller.

Goods on consignment are goods shipped by their owner (known as the consignor) to another person or firm (called the consignee) who is to sell the goods for the owner. Consigned goods belong to the consignor and should appear on his inventory.

Damaged goods and goods that have deteriorated or become obsolete should not be placed on the inventory if they are not salable. If such goods are salable but at a reduced price, they should be placed on the inventory at a conservative estimate of their realizable value (sale price less the cost of making the sale). This causes the accounting period in which the goods are damaged, deteriorate, or become obsolete to suffer the resultant loss.

Perpetual Inventories

In some types of business, where the number of different products involved is small or where the extra clerical work is worth its cost, perpetual inventories are kept. A perpetual inventory, or book inventory, makes use

Illustration 74

Item _¼ H.P. Electric Motors_   Location in stock room _Bin 8_
Maximum   _25_   Minimum   _5_

Date	Received			Sold			Balance		
	Units	Price	Total	Units	Price	Total	Units	Price	Balance
1/1							10	10.00	100.00
1/5				5	10.00	50.00	5	10.00	50.00
1/8	20	10.50	210.00				5	10.00	
							20	10.50	260.00
1/10				3	10.00	30.00	2	10.00	
							20	10.50	230.00

of a subsidiary inventory record card for each product in stock. On these individual cards, one for each product, the number of items received is recorded as items are received; the number of items sold is recorded as items are sold; and, after each receipt or sale, the balance of the product remaining on hand is recorded. (An inventory card for ¼ H.P. Electric Motors is shown in Illustration 74.) At any time, each perpetual inventory card tells the balance on hand of any one product. The total of all of the cards is the amount of the inventory.

Perpetual inventories not only tell the amount of inventory on hand at any time but they also aid in controlling the total amount invested in inventory. Each perpetual inventory card may have on it the maximum and minimum amounts of each item that should be kept in stock. By keeping the amount of each item within these limits, an oversupply or an undersupply of inventory is avoided.

Periodic and Perpetual Inventory Systems

A system of inventory accounting like that described in Chapter 6 is normally based upon periodic, physical inventories and is known as a periodic inventory system. As was explained in Chapter 6, cost of goods sold during an accounting period is determined under such a system by adding net cost of purchases to the beginning inventory and subtracting the ending inventory. When a system based upon periodic, physical inventories is used, a physical inventory is necessary in order to determine cost of goods sold.

Under a perpetual inventory system the cost of goods sold during a period, as well as the ending inventory, may be determined from the accounting records without a physical inventory. Under such a system an account called "Merchandise" takes the place of and is used for recording the information placed in the periodic inventory system accounts, "Purchases" and "Merchandise Inventory." The "Merchandise" account is a controlling account that controls the numerous perpetual inventory cards described in previous paragraphs.

When merchandise is purchased by a firm using a perpetual inventory system, the purchase is recorded as follows:

Dec.	14	Merchandise..........................	956.00	
		Accounts Payable—Blue Company....		956.00
		Purchased merchandise on account.		

In addition to the entry recording the purchase in the Merchandise account, entries are also made on the proper perpetual inventory cards in the Received columns to show the kinds of merchandise purchased.

When a sale is made, since the inventory cards show the cost of each item sold, it is possible to record both the sale and the cost of the goods sold. For example, if goods that according to the inventory cards cost $65 are sold for $100, the cost of the goods sold and the sale may be recorded as follows:

Dec.	16	Accounts Receivable—George Black......	100.00	
		Cost of Goods Sold....................	65.00	
		Sales............................		100.00
		Merchandise.....................		65.00
		Sold merchandise on account.		

In addition to the entry just given which credits the Merchandise account for the cost of the goods sold, the goods sold are entered in the Sold columns of the proper inventory cards.

Note the debit to Cost of Goods Sold in the entry just given. If this account is debited at the time of each sale for the cost of the goods sold, the debit balance of the account will show at the end of the accounting period the cost of all of the goods sold during the period.

Note also the Merchandise account as it appears in the two entries just given. If this account is debited for the cost of merchandise purchased and credited for the cost of merchandise sold, at the end of the accounting period its debit balance will show the cost of the unsold goods on hand, the ending inventory.

If cost of goods sold, as well as sales, is to be recorded in a columnar Sales Journal, an additional column is required.

Periodic inventory systems are more common than perpetual inventory systems in retail and wholsale firms. However, perpetual inventory systems are not uncommon in firms selling goods having a high unit cost.

The Problem of Inventory Pricing

The problem of pricing the items of an inventory is an important one because the dollar value placed on an ending inventory has a direct effect on cost of goods sold and reported net income.

Generally inventories are priced at cost.[1] However, a departure from cost is sometimes necessary when goods have been damaged or have deteriorated. Likewise, a departure from cost is sometimes necessary when the replacement costs for inventory items are less than the amounts actually paid for the items when they were purchased. This last point is discussed in more detail later in this chapter under the heading, "Cost or Market, the Lower."

---

[1] *Accounting Research Bulletin No. 43*, "Restatement and Revision of Accounting Research Bulletins" (New York: American Institute of Certified Public Accountants, 1953), p. 28.

Accounting for an Inventory at Cost

Accounting for an inventory at cost is not difficult when costs remain fixed. However, when identical items were purchased during an accounting period at different costs, a problem arises as to which costs apply to the ending inventory and which apply to the goods sold. There are at least four acceptable ways of assigning costs to goods in the ending inventory and to goods sold. They are: (1) specific invoice prices; (2) average invoice prices; (3) first-in, first-out; and (4) last-in, first-out.

To illustrate the four ways of assigning costs, assume that a company has on hand at the end of an accounting period twelve units of Article X. Also, assume that the company began the year and purchased Article X during the year as follows:

```
Jan.  1 Opening inventory............... 10 units @ $10.00 = $100.00
Mar. 13 Purchased...................... 15 units @ $11.50 =  172.50
Aug. 17 Purchased...................... 20 units @ $12.50 =  250.00
Nov. 10 Purchased...................... 10 units @ $12.00 =  120.00
         Total Purchases................ 55 units             $642.50
```

Specific Invoice Prices. When it is possible to identify each item of an inventory with a specific purchase and its invoice, specific invoice prices may be used to assign costs to the inventory and to the goods sold. For example, if for purposes of illustration it is assumed that six of the twelve remaining units of Article X were from the November purchase and six were from the August purchase, then costs are assigned to the inventory and goods sold by means of specific invoice prices as follows:

```
Total cost of 55 units available for sale.....................      $642.50
Less final inventory priced by means of specific invoices:
  6 units from the November purchase at $12.00 each....... $72.00
  6 units from the August purchase at $12.50..............  75.00
  12 units in ending inventory...........................           147.00
Cost of Goods Sold......................................            $495.50
```

Average Invoice Price. Under this method the several invoice prices weighted by the number of units on hand at the beginning and purchased on each of the invoices are averaged to find the average cost per unit, as follows:

```
                10 units at $10.00 = $100.00
                15 units at $11.50 =  172.50
                20 units at $12.50 =  250.00
                10 units at $12.00 =  120.00
                55                  $642.50
      $642.50 ÷ 55 = $11.682, average price per unit
```

After the average cost per unit is determined, this average cost is used to assign costs to the inventory and the units sold as follows:

```
Total cost of 55 units available for sale........................$642.50
Less ending inventory priced on an average cost basis:
  12 units at $11.682 each.................................. 140.18
Cost of Goods Sold.............................................$502.32
```

First-In, First-Out. In a merchandising business clerks are usually instructed to sell the oldest merchandise first. Consequently, when this instruction is followed, merchandise tends to flow out of a store on a first-in, first-out basis. When first-in, first-out is applied in pricing an inventory, it is assumed that costs also follow this pattern and, as a result, the costs of the last items received are assigned to the ending inventory and the remaining costs are assigned to goods sold. When first-in, first-out, or Fifo as it is often called from its first letters, is used, costs are assigned to the inventory and to the goods sold as follows:

Total cost of 55 units available for sale....................		$642.50
Less ending inventory priced on a basis of Fifo:		
10 units from the November purchase at $12.00 each......	$120.00	
2 units from the August purchase at $12.50 each.........	25.00	
12 units in the ending inventory........................		145.00
Cost of Goods Sold......................................		$497.50

Last-In, First-Out. This method of pricing, usually called Lifo, assumes that the flow of costs in relation to revenue receipts is more important to accurate income determination than is costing based on the flow of goods. Furthermore, this method holds that, for the going concern, as goods are sold, goods of approximately the same quantity must be purchased to replenish the stock of goods carried. Thus it is the sale that causes the purchase of the replacement goods. Therefore, the replacement costs should be matched against the sales, giving impetus to the new acquisitions.

Under Lifo, costs are assigned to the twelve remaining units of Article X and to the goods sold as follows:

Total cost of 55 units available for sale....................		$642.50
Less ending inventory priced on a basis of Lifo:		
10 units in the beginning inventory at $10.00 each........	$100.00	
2 units from the first purchase at $11.50 each...........	23.00	
12 units in the ending inventory........................		123.00
Cost of Goods Sold......................................		$519.50

Notice that this method of matching costs and revenue results in the final inventory being priced at the cost of the oldest twelve units.

Comparison of Methods. In a stable market where prices remain unchanged, the method of inventory pricing is of little importance. This is true because when prices are unchanged over a long period of time, all methods give the same cost figures. However, in a changing market where prices are rising and falling, each method may give a different result. This may be seen by a comparison of the cost of goods sold for Article X under each of the methods. The costs of goods sold as calculated on the previous pages were:

Based on specific invoice prices.............................	$495.50
Based on average invoice prices.............................	502.32
Based on Fifo...	497.50
Based on Lifo...	519.50

All four pricing methods are used; and each under certain circumstances has its advantages. Specific invoice prices exactly match costs and revenue; average invoice prices tend to smooth out price fluctuations; Fifo tends to associate costs and the merchandising ideal of selling the oldest merchandise first; and when prices are rising, as in the years following World War II, Lifo has certain tax advantages. However, since the method used may affect the amounts of the reported ending inventory and cost of goods sold, a company should show on its statements by means of footnotes or other manner the pricing method used. Also, accountants are of the opinion that a company should select for use the method that best reflects its periodic net income.

Consistency

Often a company's reported net income can be either increased or decreased simply by changing its inventory pricing method. For this reason, although accountants hold that a company may use any accepted inventory pricing method that fairly reflects its periodic income, they insist that the company consistently follow the chosen method.

Often there are several acceptable ways of handling any given transaction or accounting problem. Inventory pricing methods are one example, and the several methods of calculating depreciation as presented in the next chapter are another. Accountants hold that when there are several acceptable methods or procedures that may be followed in a given situation, a firm may choose any one so long as the chosen method or procedure fairly reflects periodic income and so long as the chosen method or procedure is consistently followed thereafter. Consistency is a fundamental principle of accounting. Accountants strive for consistency so that there will be a high degree of comparability in the statements prepared period after period.

In their desire for consistency, however, accountants do not hold that a method once chosen can never be changed. Rather, they agree that if upon additional consideration it is decided that a different acceptable method from the one in use will better reflect periodic net income, a change may be made. But, in such a case accountants insist that adequate disclosure of the change and its effects be reported in the company's statements.

Cost or Market, the Lower

Over the years, the traditional rule for pricing an inventory has been "the lower of cost or market." This rule gained its wide acceptance because it placed an inventory on the balance sheet at a conservative figure, the lower of cost or replacement cost on the balance sheet date.

The argument advanced in support of this conservatism was that if the replacement cost of an inventory item had declined, then its selling price would probably have to be reduced, and since this might result in a loss, the loss should be anticipated and taken in the year of the price decline. It was a good argument; however, since selling prices do not always exactly and quickly follow cost prices, the application of the rule often resulted in the misstatement of net income in the year of a price decline and again in the succeeding year. For example, suppose that a firm purchased $1,000 of merchandise; marked it up to a selling price of $1,500; and sold one half of the goods. The gross profit on the goods sold would be calculated as follows:

```
Sales...................................................$750
Cost of goods sold......................................  500
      Gross Profit......................................$250
```

However, if the replacement cost of the $500 of unsold goods had declined to $450 on the inventory date, an income statement based upon the traditional application of cost or market would show:

```
Sales......................................             $750
Cost of goods sold:
   Purchases.........................................$1,000
      Less: Ending inventory.........................   450    550
      Gross Profit.................................          $200
```

The $450 would be a conservative balance sheet figure for the unsold goods. However, if these goods were sold at their full price early in the following year, the $450 inventory figure would have the unconservative effect of deferring $50 of income to the second year's income statement as follows:

```
Sales...................................................$750
Cost of goods sold:
   Beginning inventory..................................  450
      Gross Profit......................................$300
```

Merchants are prone to be slow in marking down goods; they normally try to sell goods at their full price if possible. Consequently, the illustrated situation was not uncommon. For this reason the lower of cost or market rule has been modified in recent years as follows for situations in which replacement costs are below actual costs:[2]

1. Goods should be placed on an inventory at cost, even though replacement cost is lower, if there has not been and there is not expected to be a decline in selling price.
2. Goods should at times be placed on the inventory at a price below their cost but above their replacement cost. For example, suppose the cost of an item that is normally bought for $20 and sold for $30 declines from $20 to $16, and that its selling price declines from $30 to $27. The normal profit margin on this item is one-third of its selling price. If this normal margin is applied to $27, the item should be placed on the inventory at two-thirds of $27 or at $18. This is below cost but above replacement cost.
3. At times, goods should be placed on the inventory at a price below replacement cost. For example, assume that the goods described in the pre-

---
[2]*Ibid.,* pp. 30 and 31.

ceding paragraph can only be sold for $18.50 and that the disposal costs are estimated at $3. In this case the goods should be placed on the inventory at $15.50, a price below their replacement cost of $16.

Conservatism

Balance sheet conservatism was once considered one of the first principles of accounting. The objective of such conservatism was to place each item on the balance sheet at a conservative figure. This in itself was commendable; but it was often carried too far and resulted not only in the misstatement of asset values but also in unconservative income statements. For example, as shown in the foregoing paragraphs, when prices are falling, the blind application of the unmodified lower of cost or market rule to inventories may result in a conservative balance sheet figure for inventories; but it may also result in an improper deferring of net income and in inaccurate income statements. Likewise, the too rapid write-off of fixed assets to depreciation, not uncommon in the past, in order to place these assets on the balance sheet at conservative figures resulted not only in the misstatement of the asset values but also in the overstatement of expenses and in unconservative income statements. Consequently, today accountants recognize that balance sheet conservatism does not outweigh other factors. Today, accountants favor practices that result in the most accurate statement of net income.

Estimated Inventories

Retail Method. Retail firms commonly use the so-called retail inventory method in determining inventories for interim statements; and they also commonly take their end-of-the-accounting-period inventories at marked selling prices and later reduce the sum of these selling prices to a cost basis by an application of the retail inventory method.

When the retail method is used in determining an interim inventory, the information shown in Illustration 75 at both cost and retail (selling prices) is required. Also, when the retail inventory method is used, the calculations of Illustration 75 are made.

Illustration 75

	At Cost	At Retail
Beginning inventory	$11,500	$ 19,000
Net purchases	47,500	79,000
Freight-in	1,000	
Additional markups		2,000
Goods available for sale	$60,000	$100,000
(Observe that cost is 60 per cent of retail.)		
Sales		$ 77,000
Markdowns		3,000
Total		$ 80,000
Ending inventory at retail ($100,000 less $80,000)		$ 20,000
Ending inventory at cost (60 per cent of $20,000)	$12,000	

Most companies have a normal markup or a normal percentage that is added to the cost of merchandise purchased in order to arrive at its selling price. In addition to the normal markup, goods of outstanding quality or style are commonly given an additional markup; and slow-moving goods are commonly marked down if they are not sold at regular prices. Normal markups appear in Illustration 75 as the difference between "Net purchases" at cost and at retail.

It has long been customary in the use of the retail inventory method to consider additional markups but not markdowns in the computation of the percentage relationship between goods available for sale at cost and goods available for sale at retail. The justification for this was and is that a more conservative figure for the ending inventory, a figure that approaches "cost or market, the lower," results. A further discussion of this phase of the retail inventory method is reserved for a more advanced text.

In the previous paragraphs, the retail method of estimating an interim inventory was demonstrated. The retail inventory method is also used to reduce to its cost basis a physical inventory that has been taken at the marked retail prices of the inventoried goods. When this is done:

1. *The percentage relationship between goods available for sale during the period at cost and at retail is determined:*

	At Cost	At Retail
Beginning inventory	$18,000	$ 27,800
Net purchases	45,000	70,700
Freight-in	2,000	
Additional markups		1,500
Goods Available for Sale	$65,000	$100,000

(Relationship of cost to retail is 65 per cent.)

2. *A physical inventory of the unsold goods on hand is taken at the marked retail prices of the goods.*

Assume that the physical inventory of the unsold goods at their marked retail prices totals $30,000.

3. *The relationship of the goods available for sale at cost and at retail is applied to the inventory.*

$$\$30,000 \times 65\% = \$19,500$$

The ending inventory at cost is $19,500.

The use of the retail method in arriving at "cost" for an ending inventory eliminates the clerical work of costing the inventory items by referring to invoices and other data.

Gross Profit Method. Often retail price information about beginning inventory, purchases, and markups is not kept. In such cases the retail inventory method cannot be used. However, if a company knows its normal gross profit margin; has information at cost in regard to its beginning inventory, net purchases, and freight-in; and knows the amount of its sales and sales returns, the company can estimate its ending inventory by the gross profit method.

For example, on March 27, the inventory of a company was destroyed by a fire. The company's average rate of gross profit was estimated at 30 per cent of net sales, and on the date of the fire the company's accounts showed the following balances:

Sales...$31,500
Sales returns....................................... 1,500
Inventory, January 1, 19—........................ 12,000
Net purchases...................................... 20,000
Freight-in..   500

Since the inventory was totally destroyed by fire, it was necessary for insurance purposes to estimate the inventory by the gross profit method as shown in Illustration 76.

Illustration 76

Goods available for sale:		
Inventory, January 1, 19—........................		$12,000
Net purchases....................................	$20,000	
Freight-in.......................................	500	20,500
Goods available for sale.........................		$32,500
Less: Estimated cost of goods sold:		
Sales..	$31,500	
Sales returns....................................	1,500	
Net sales..	$30,000	
Less: Estimated gross profit (30% of $30,000)........	9,000	
Estimated cost of goods sold.....................		21,000
Estimated Ending Inventory.......................		$11,500

In addition to its use in insurance cases, the gross profit method of estimating an inventory is also commonly used by accountants in checking the probable accuracy of a physical inventory taken and priced in the normal way.

QUESTIONS FOR CLASS DISCUSSION

1. In estimating bad debt losses businesses commonly assume that "history will repeat." How is the assumption that "history will repeat" used in estimating bad debt losses?

2. A company has charge sales for a year amounting to $350,000. What amount of bad debt losses may the company expect to experience from these sales if its past record of bad debt losses shows losses equal to 1 per cent of charge sales? Give the entry the company would use to record its estimated bad debt losses.

3. What is a contra account? Why are estimated bad debt losses credited to a contra account rather than to the Accounts Receivable controlling account?

4. Classify the following accounts: (a) Accounts Receivable controlling account (b) Allowance for Bad Debts account, and (c) Bad Debts Expense account.

5. Why are bad debts estimated at the end of an accounting period and a bad debts adjusting entry made to record the expected losses? Why would it not be better to wait until actual losses occur and then record the amount of each loss by a debit to the Bad Debts Expense account?

6. The Ross Company estimated on December 31, 1959, that it would lose 1 per cent of its 1959 charge sales as bad debts. The Ross Company's 1959 charge sales were $162,000. Give the entry to record the estimated loss from bad debts.

7. On March 22, the Ross Company decided the account of George Thomas in the amount of $125 was uncollectible, and they wrote it off as a bad debt. On September 9, they received a $125 check from Thomas in full payment of the account. Give the general journal entries required to record these transactions.

8. In an audit of the accounts of James Huggins, the auditor found the balance of the Allowance for Bad Debts account to be $7,342. He thought this excessive. After a discussion with Mr. Huggins, it was decided to reduce the balance of the account to $2,500. Give the required journal entry.

9. What is the effect on the balance sheet and on the income statement of an excessive provision for bad debt losses?

10. What is the difference between a physical inventory and a perpetual inventory?

11. Outline a procedure for taking a physical inventory.

12. How do inventory tickets aid in the taking of a physical inventory?

13. Why are inventory tickets prenumbered?

14. The Ajax Company keeps perpetual inventory records of the merchandise in its store. In January of 1960 the company took a physical inventory. The physical inventory counts for many items differed from the amounts shown for these items in the perpetual inventory records. Give several reasons for the differences.

15. Explain the meanings of the terms "cost" and "market" as they are applied to inventory items.

16. What is the meaning of the phrase "cost or market, the lower" as it is applied to inventory items?

17. Outline the essential features in the operation of a perpetual inventory system.

18. In taking a year-end physical inventory at the end of 1959, the clerks failed to count the items on one whole shelf. The inventory value of the items was $150. What was the effect of the omission on the 1959 balance sheet and income statement? What was the effect on the 1960 statements?

19. What are the meanings of the terms "Fifo" and "Lifo"?

20. If prices are rising, will the "Lifo" or the "Fifo" method of inventory valuation result in the higher gross profit?

PROBLEMS

Problem 12–1

Philip A. Allison is the sole owner of Allison Wholesale Company. On December 31, 1958, the Allowance for Bad Debts account in the ledger of the company had a credit balance of $415. During 1958, 1959, 1960, and 1961, the company completed the following bad debt transactions:

1958

Dec. 31   Provided by means of a bad debt adjusting entry an additional allowance for bad debts equal to one half of 1 per cent of the $215,000 of 1958 charge sales.

      31   Closed the Bad Debts Expense account.

1959

Mar. 5   Wrote off as uncollectible the $268 account of Walter Ford.

Sept. 7   Wrote off as uncollectible the $305 account of John Marshall.

Dec. 31   Provided an additional allowance for bad debts equal to one half of 1 per cent of the $223,000 of 1959 charge sales.

      31   Closed the Bad Debts Expense account.

1960

Apr. 17   Wrote off as uncollectible the $450 account of Donald Thomas.

Aug.   5   Learned of the bankruptcy of Donald Thomas upon the receipt of a $45 check from his receiver in bankruptcy. A letter accompanying the check stated that the amount was a final payment on the amount owed and that no more would be paid. Recorded the receipt.

Oct. 19   Wrote off as uncollectible the $210 account of William Fall.

Dec. 31   Provided an additional allowance for bad debts equal to one half of 1 per cent of the $207,000 of 1960 charge sales.

      31   Closed the Bad Debts Expense account.

1961

Feb.   3   Upon completion of the 1960 audit, the auditor expressed an opinion that an allowance for bad debts of $1,000 would be adequate to take care of any losses from the December 31, 1960, balance of accounts receivable. Mr. Allison ordered the balance of the Allowance for Bad Debts account reduced to $1,000.

Required:

1. Open ledger accounts for Bad Debts Expense and Allowance for Bad Debts. Enter the $415 balance in the Allowance for Bad Debts account.
2. Make general journal entries to record the foregoing transactions.
3. Post the portions of the entries affecting the Bad Debts Expense account and the Allowance for Bad Debts account.

Problem 12–2

Automatic Sales maintains perpetual inventory records. During January of the current year the firm completed the following transactions involving Article ABA:

Jan.   1   A balance of 5 items of Article ABA each costing $5.00 were on hand.

      2   Received 10 items of Article ABA costing $5.40 each. (Two lines are required in the Balance columns to show the number of items at each price on hand.)

      6   Sold 3 items of ABA.

     10   Sold 8 items of ABA. (Two lines are required in the Sold columns to record the sale.)

     14   Received 8 items of ABA at a cost of $6.00 each.

     18   Sold 3 items of ABA.

     28   Sold 4 items of ABA.

Required:

1. Assume that Automatic Sales keeps its inventory records on a first-in, first-out basis, and on a perpetual inventory card similar to Illustration 74 record the foregoing transactions in Article ABA.
2. Assume that Automatic Sales keeps its inventory records on a basis of last-in, first-out, and on another perpetual inventory card record the foregoing transactions in Article ABA.
3. Prepare on a basis of last-in, first-out a general journal entry to record the sale and the cost of goods sold of the foregoing transaction of Jan-

uary 28. Assume that the four items of ABA were sold to Walter Slocum at a selling price of $10 each.

Problem 12–3

The Mellon Brick Company had a beginning inventory of common brick which consisted of 500 M of bricks with a cost of $14,000. (The inventory unit for bricks is 1,000 bricks; the symbol "M" is used to denote a 1,000.) The company's production and sales in chronological order were:

PRODUCTION		SALES
Units	Cost per M	
200 M	$25	220 M
250 M	24	200 M
300 M	23	310 M
320 M	26	300 M

Determine the cost of the inventory on:
1. A Fifo basis.
2. A Lifo basis.
3. An average cost basis.

Problem 12–4

On March 31 a retail firm wished to estimate its inventory of that date for an interim statement. The following information for the period January 1 through March 31 was available:

	At Cost	At Retail
January 1 inventory	$14,840	$ 21,680
Purchases	93,870	144,150
Freight-in	2,230	
Purchases returns	720	1,080
Sales		145,470
Sales returns		2,520
Additional markups		2,250
Markdowns		1,550

Required:

Prepare a statement showing the calculation of the firm's March 31 inventory by the retail method.

Problem 12–5

On the night of May 5 of the current year the store of John Reed burned. Everything except the accounting records, which were kept in a fireproof vault, was destroyed. Mr. Reed filed an insurance claim that listed an inventory loss of $26,300. As a fire insurance adjuster you are called upon to verify this claim. From the accounting records the following information is available:

1. Merchandise inventory on January 1 of the current year, $22,350.
2. Sales from January 1 through May 5, $95,380.
3. Sales returns for the same period, $3,120.
4. Purchases from January 1 through May 5, $62,470.
5. Purchases returns for same period, $1,240.
6. Freight-in from January 1 through May 5, $2,710.
7. Average gross profit on sales for past three years, 35 per cent.

Required:

Prepare a statement showing the estimated amount of John Reed's May 5 inventory.

CLASS EXERCISES

Exercise 12–1

During the current year Article BB was purchased as follows:

Jan. 12	12 items at $3.50
Mar. 2	20 items at $3.40
June 14	10 items at $3.75
Sept. 2	20 items at $3.80
Oct. 31	15 items at $4.00

On December 31 there were 18 units of Article BB on hand. What was the inventory valuation for these 18 units under each of the following assumptions:

a) The items were priced at actual invoice price. Assume that 7 of the 18 items in the final inventory were purchased on October 31, 3 on September 2, and the balance were purchased on June 14.

b) The items were priced at average invoice price.

c) The items were priced at cost on the basis of first-in, first-out.

d) The items were priced at cost on the basis of last-in, first-out.

Exercise 12–2

The following information is available for Department 59 of Maiton Store:

Inventory on May 1, $20,000 at cost and $32,600 at retail; net purchases for May, $13,000 at cost and $21,000 at retail; additional markups, $1,400; markdowns, $500; and sales for May, $15,000.

Compute the May 31 inventory at retail and at cost using the retail inventory method.

SUPPLEMENTARY PROBLEMS

Problem 12–A

Butler and Carter purchased 600 units of Article XYZ on December 3, 1959, at $20 per unit. They priced the units for sale at $30 each and sold 300 during the remainder of the month. On December 31, at the end of the firm's accounting period, the replacement cost for an item of XYZ was $15. However, regardless of the price decline, Butler and Carter did not reduce the selling price of Article XYZ, and during January, 1960, they sold the remaining 300 units of their December 3 purchase at $30 each.

Required:

1. Prepare 1959 and 1960 partial income statements for Butler and Carter which show sales, cost of goods sold, and gross profit from sales of Article XYZ under the assumption that the firm priced its 1959 inventory on the basis of cost or market, the lower.

2. Prepare 1959 and 1960 partial income statements for Butler and Carter which show sales, cost of goods sold, and gross profit from sales of Article XYZ under the assumption that the firm priced its 1959 inventory on the basis of cost.

3. Write a short statement telling which of the sets of statements is the more accurate and why.

Problem 12–B

On December 31, 19—, at the end of a yearly accounting period, a firm took an inventory of the merchandise in its store at marked selling prices. It found that it had $16,300 of merchandise, and it wished to use the retail inventory method to reduce this amount to a cost figure. The following information was available:

	At Cost	At Retail
January 1, 19—, inventory	$ 9,680	$ 14,710
Purchases	73,450	115,980
Purchases returns	1,860	2,790
Freight-in	3,880	
Additional markups		3,100
Markdowns		1,860

Required:

Prepare a statement showing the calculation of the firm's inventory at cost.

Problem 12–C

During a three-year period a firm purchased and sold Article M in successive purchases and sales as follows:

1958 Purchases		1958 Sales	
400 units @ $50 = $20,000		200 units @ $100 = $ 20,000	
200 units @ $55 = 11,000		300 units @ $110 = 33,000	
300 units @ $60 = 18,000		300 units @ $120 = 36,000	
300 units @ $65 = 19,500		200 units @ $130 = 26,000	
1,200 $68,500		1,000 $115,000	

1959 Purchases		1959 Sales	
500 units @ $60 = $30,000		300 units @ $125 = $ 37,500	
300 units @ $70 = 21,000		400 units @ $135 = 54,000	
200 units @ $70 = 14,000		300 units @ $140 = 42,000	
1,000 $65,000		1,000 $133,500	

1960 Purchases		1960 Sales	
200 units @ $70 = $14,000		300 units @ $140 = $ 42,000	
400 units @ $65 = 26,000		200 units @ $130 = 26,000	
200 units @ $65 = 13,000		200 units @ $135 = 27,000	
200 units @ $75 = 15,000		300 units @ $145 = 43,500	
1,000 $68,000		1,000 $138,500	

Required:

1. Prepare a series of income statements showing for each year the sales, the calculation of cost of goods sold, and the gross profit on the sales of Article M under the assumption that the firm priced its ending inventories on a Fifo basis. Assume that there was no beginning inventory of Article M in 1958.
2. Prepare another series of income statements under the assumption the firm prices its ending inventories on a Lifo basis.
3. Answer these two questions:
   a) Which method of inventory pricing results in the smaller income tax liability for the firm?
   b) Which method of inventory pricing better synchronizes costs and revenues?

Chapter

13

ACCOUNTING FOR FIXED ASSETS AND DEPRECIATION

FIXED assets are assets of a more or less permanent nature that are used by a business in carrying on its normal functions and are not for sale. From this definition it can be seen that fixed assets have three characteristics: (1) they are of a more or less permanent nature; (2) they are used in carrying on the normal functions of the business; and (3) they are not for sale.

Obviously, aside from land, few assets are absolutely permanent in nature. Sooner or later, all wear out or waste away. A building may be of service for fifty years, and a typewriter for five. Neither is absolutely permanent in nature. However, both are treated as assets of a more or less permanent nature. In accounting, assets are considered to be of a more or less permanent nature if they are to be used for a period of several years.

To be classed as a fixed asset, an item must be used in carrying on the normal functions of the business. For example, land is the most permanent of assets. Yet, it is not classed as a fixed asset unless it is used in carrying on the normal functions of the business. To illustrate, a company expects to expand its plant some five or ten years in the future. To expand, it will need the vacant land next to its present plant. Because this land is now vacant and available, and can be bought at a reasonable price, the company buys it for future expansion. The land is to remain unused and vacant for from five to ten years; it will then be used to expand the plant facilities. Until the plant is expanded and this land placed in use, the land is not classified as a fixed asset. Until the land is placed in use, it is classified as a long-term investment. This is because as long as the land is idle and vacant it is not used in the normal operations of the business. It is not classed as a fixed asset until placed in use.

Generally, with the exception of land which does not depreciate, it is expected that a fixed asset will be used in the business operations until it is no longer profitable to continue its use. However, any fixed asset may be sold while it is still useful if it is no longer needed.

Cost of a Fixed Asset

The acquisition of a fixed asset is recorded by debiting a fixed asset account for the cost of the asset acquired. The cost of a fixed asset includes the invoice price plus any additional expenditures incurred in getting the asset in place and ready to operate or use. For example, the cost of a factory machine includes the invoice price of the machine, less any discount for cash, plus freight, truckage, and unpacking. In addition, any special concrete bases or foundations, electrical or power connections, and adjustments needed to place the machine in operation are also part of its cost. In short, the cost of a fixed asset includes all normal costs incurred in getting the asset ready to produce. All of these costs are debited to the account of the fixed asset as they are incurred.

Nature of Depreciation

Accounting for fixed assets and accounting for prepaid expenses have much in common. This may be illustrated with prepaid insurance. When a businessman pays the premium on an insurance policy, he buys protection from future loss. He buys a supply of protection that may last several accounting periods. Day by day the insurance expires, or, in other words, each day the insurance protection is consumed in the operations of the business. At the end of each accounting period an adjusting entry is made to record the insurance expired. This entry is a debit to an expense account and a credit to the asset prepaid insurance. The debit records the cost of the insurance expired; or, in other words, it records the expense of the protection consumed during the accounting period. The credit reduces the balance sheet value of the prepaid insurance by the amount of the protection consumed. This reduction causes the balance sheet to show prepaid insurance at the cost of the protection that is yet unconsumed on the balance sheet date.

Accounting for fixed assets is similar to this. When a businessman buys a fixed asset, he buys a supply of future work or service. Any fixed asset is purchased because of the work or service it will produce. For example, a fixed asset such as a salesman's automobile may be thought of as a supply of prepaid transportation. The cost of the supply of prepaid transportation is the cost of the car minus its trade-in value. If a salesman's car costs $3,600 and in three years will have a trade-in value of $1,200, the cost of the prepaid transportation is $2,400. This $2,400 is the *service cost* of the car. The service cost of a fixed asset is the cost of the service it will produce during its *service life*. The service life of an asset is the period of time the asset is used by a business.

The $2,400 service cost of the salesman's car may be thought of as a $2,400 supply of prepaid transportation. Day by day, as the salesman drives the car in making his calls, a portion of this prepaid transportation is consumed. Each day a portion of the service cost of the car expires just as prepaid insurance expires. The day-by-day expiration in the service cost of a fixed asset is called *depreciation*. Depreciation is an expense of doing business just as expired insurance or the salary of an employee is an expense. At the end of each accounting period, the depreciation chargeable to that accounting period is recorded by means of an adjusting entry which causes the amount of the service cost that expired during the period to appear on the income statement as depreciation expense. It also causes the balance sheet value of the fixed asset to be reduced by the amount of the service cost expired, or the amount of the depreciation that occurred during the accounting period.

When a fixed asset is thought of as a supply of prepaid service and depreciation as an expiration of this prepaid service, then accounting for prepaid expenses, such as prepaid insurance, and accounting for fixed assets have much in common. However, there is one great difference. This difference is that depreciation is much more difficult to measure than expired insurance. Actually depreciation cannot be exactly measured in advance; it can only be estimated; and exactly estimating depreciation is difficult because both the service life and the service cost of the asset must be predicted in making the estimate.

Service Life of a Fixed Asset

The service life of a fixed asset is the period of time that the asset is used by a business. When a fixed asset is purchased, its service life must be predicted so that the depreciation chargeable to each accounting period may be estimated and recorded. Predicting or estimating the service life of an asset is sometimes difficult because several factors are often involved. Wear and tear and the action of the elements usually determine the useful life of an asset. However, two additional factors often need to be considered. These are *inadequacy* and *obsolescence*. When a business acquires fixed assets, it should acquire assets of a size and capacity to take care of its foreseeable needs. However, a business often grows more rapidly than anticipated. In such cases the fixed assets may become too small for the demands of the business long before they wear out. When fixed assets become inadequate for handling the increased demands of a business, inadequacy is said to have taken place. Inadequacy cannot be easily predicted. Obsolescence, like inadequacy, is also difficult to foretell. The exact occurrence of new inventions and improvements normally cannot be predicted. Yet new inventions and improvements often cause an asset to become obsolete. In such cases it is often desirable to discard the obsolete asset long before it wears out. Wear and tear and the action of the elements, along with inadequacy and obsolescence, determine the service life of a fixed asset. All are difficult to measure and foresee; yet all should be considered in estimating the service life of a new fixed asset.

When a fixed asset is purchased, its service life must be estimated so that depreciation may be recorded. A company that has previously used a particular type of asset may estimate the service life of a like new asset from its past experience. A company without previous experience with a particular asset must depend upon the experience of others or upon engineering studies and judgment. The Federal Bureau of Internal Revenue has published a booklet, *Bulletin F*, that gives the estimated service lives of hundreds of assets. Many businessmen refer to this bulletin in estimating the service life of a new asset.

Often the service life of an asset is not the same as its total potential life. For example, typewriters may have a potentially useful life of ten or twelve years. However, if a particular company uses its typewriters for three years and, at the end of that time, trades them in on new ones, typewriters in that company have a service life of three years.

Salvage Value

Depreciation is an expiration of the service cost of a fixed asset. The service cost of an asset is the cost of the asset minus its *salvage value.* The salvage value of a fixed asset is the portion of the asset's cost that is recovered at the end of its service life. Some assets such as typewriters, trucks, and automobiles are traded in on similar new assets at the end of their service lives. The salvage values of such assets are their trade-in values. Other assets may have no trade-in value and little or no salvage value. For example, at the end of its service life, some machinery can be sold only as scrap metal. The salvage value of such assets is the amount received from the sale of the scrap metal.

When the disposal of a fixed asset involves certain costs, as in the wrecking of a building, the salvage value is the net amount realized from the sale of the asset. The net amount realized is the amount received for the asset less the cost of its disposal.

Obviously, when a fixed asset is purchased, its exact salvage value is difficult to estimate. Yet, salvage value must be estimated so that depreciation can be estimated and recorded.

Apportioning Depreciation

Many methods of apportioning the total depreciation of a fixed asset to the several accounting periods of its service life have been suggested and are used. Four of the more common are the *straight-line method,* the *units of production method,* the *declining balance method,* and the *sum of the years' digits method.* Of the four, the straight-line method, because of its simplicity, is by far the most commonly used.

Straight-Line Method. When the straight-line method is used to calculate the amount a fixed asset depreciates each accounting period, the cost of the asset minus its salvage value is divided by the number of accounting periods the asset will be used. The result of this calculation is the amount the asset depreciates each accounting period. This calculation may be expressed in equation form as follows:

$$\frac{\text{Cost} - \text{Salvage Value}}{\substack{\text{Number of Accounting Periods} \\ \text{in the Asset's Service Life}}} = \substack{\text{Depreciation per} \\ \text{Accounting Period}}$$

The cost of a fixed asset minus its salvage value gives the service cost of the asset. The service cost of a fixed asset is the total amount the asset will depreciate during its service life. Obviously, the straight-line method allocates an equal share of an asset's service cost or an equal share of its

total depreciation to each accounting period of its life. For example, if a
machine cost $550, has an estimated service life of five years, and an
estimated salvage value of $50, its depreciation per year by the straight-
line method is $100. This is calculated as follows:

$$\frac{\text{COST} - \text{SALVAGE}}{\substack{\text{SERVICE LIFE} \\ \text{IN YEARS}}} = \frac{\$550 - \$50}{5} = \$100 \text{ PER YEAR}$$

Each year of the service life of this asset should be charged with $100
worth of depreciation expense, and each year the balance sheet value of
the asset should be reduced by the $100 of service cost expired.

Units of Production Method. The primary purpose of recording depreciation is to charge each accounting period in which an asset is used
with a fair share of the asset's depreciation. The straight-line method
charges an equal share to each accounting period of the asset's life. In
many businesses, fixed assets are used about the same amount in each
accounting period. Consequently, the straight-line method rather fairly
and accurately allocates their total depreciation. However, in some businesses the use of certain assets varies greatly from accounting period to
accounting period. For example, a building contractor may use a particular piece of equipment for a month and then not use it again for
many months. Normally the depreciation of an asset such as the contractor's equipment is related to its use. Consequently, if depreciation is related to use, and use varies from accounting period to accounting period,
then depreciation also varies from period to period. For such assets the
straight-line method of allocating depreciation usually does not fairly allocate depreciation. Often for such assets the units of production method
better measures and allocates depreciation.

In the units of production method of allocating depreciation, the service cost of an asset is divided by the estimated number of units of product the asset will produce during its entire service life. This division
gives the depreciation per unit of product. Then the amount the asset
depreciates in any one accounting period is found by multiplying the
number of units of product produced in that period by the depreciation
per unit of product. For example, a delivery truck costing $4,800 is esti-
mated to have a salvage value of $800. If it is also estimated that during
the truck's service life it will be driven 100,000 miles, the depreciation
per mile, or the depreciation per unit of product, is $0.04. This is cal-
culated as follows:

$$\frac{\text{COST} - \text{SALVAGE VALUE}}{\substack{\text{ESTIMATED UNITS OF} \\ \text{PRODUCTION}}} = \substack{\text{DEPRECIATION PER} \\ \text{UNIT OF PRODUCT}}$$

or

$$\frac{\$4,800 - \$800}{100,000 \text{ MILES}} = \$0.04 \text{ PER MILE}$$

If these estimates are correct, and the truck is driven 20,000 miles during its first year, the depreciation for the first year of the truck's operation is $800. This is 20,000 miles at $0.04 per mile. If the truck is driven 15,000 miles in the second year, the depreciation for the second year is 15,000 times $0.04, or $600.

Declining Balance Method. The Revenue Act of 1954 liberalized depreciation accounting by permitting methods of calculating depreciation which result in higher depreciation charges during the early years of a fixed asset's life. The declining balance method is one of these. Under the declining balance method, depreciation of up to twice the straight-line rate may be applied each year to the declining book value of a new fixed asset. If this method is followed and twice the straight-line rate is used, the amount charged each year as depreciation expense on a fixed asset is determined by: (1) calculating a straight-line depreciation rate for the asset without considering the asset's salvage value; (2) doubling this rate; and then (3) at the end of each year in the asset's life, applying this doubled rate to the asset's remaining book value. (The book value of a fixed asset is its cost less accumulated depreciation; it is the value shown for the asset on the books.)

If this method is used to charge depreciation on a $10,000 new asset that has an estimated life of five years: (Step 1) A straight-line depreciation rate is calculated by dividing $10,000 by five (years) to secure a straight-line amount of $2,000; and then dividing the $2,000 by $10,000 to secure a straight-line rate of 20 per cent. Next (Step 2) this rate is doubled; and then (Step 3) annual depreciation charges are calculated as in the following table:

Year	Calculation	Depreciation Expense	Remaining Book Value
1	40% of $10,000	$4,000.00	$6,000.00
2	40% of 6,000	2,400.00	3,600.00
3	40% of 3,600	1,440.00	2,160.00
4	40% of 2,160	864.00	1,296.00
5	40% of 1,296	518.40	777.60

Under this method the book value of a fixed asset never reaches zero; consequently, when the asset is disposed of, any remaining book value is used in determining the gain or loss on the disposal.

Sum of the Years' Digits Method. Under this reducing fraction method, the years in an asset's service life are added and their sum becomes the denominator of a series of fractions used in calculating the asset's annual depreciation. The numerators of the fractions are the years in the asset's life in their reverse order.

For example, if the sum of the years' digits method is to be used in calculating depreciation on a machine costing $7,000, having an estimated life of five years, and having an estimated salvage value of $1,000, the sum of the years' digits in the life of the asset is calculated:

$$1 + 2 + 3 + 4 + 5 = 15$$

and then annual depreciation charges are calculated as in the following table:

Year	Calculation	Depreciation Expense
1	5/15 of $6,000	$2,000
2	4/15 of 6,000	1,600
3	3/15 of 6,000	1,200
4	2/15 of 6,000	800
5	1/15 of 6,000	400
		$6,000

The reducing charge methods (both the declining balance and the sum of the years' digits methods) are advocated by an increasing number of accountants who claim that these give a more equitable "use charge" for long-lived fixed assets than do other methods. They point out, for example, that as assets grow older, repairs and maintenance increase. Therefore, smaller amounts of depreciation computed by a reducing charge method, when added to the increasing repair costs, give a somewhat more equitable expense charge to match against revenue than that produced by most other methods.

Also, they point out that as an asset grows older, in some instances its revenue production is materially reduced. For example, rentals from an apartment house are normally higher in the earlier years of its life but will decline as the building becomes less attractive and less modern. Certainly in this case, a more reasonable allocation of cost would provide heavier charges in the earlier years and lighter charges in the later years of the asset's life.

Recording Depreciation

Depreciation on the several classes of a firm's fixed assets is recorded at the end of each accounting period by means of adjusting entries. This subject was discussed in an earlier chapter and needs no further amplification here.

Depreciation on the Balance Sheet

In order to present as clearly as possible all the facts concerning the fixed assets of a business, both the cost of assets and their accumulated depreciation by functional classes are shown on the balance sheet. For example, the fixed assets of a merchandising concern are shown as follows:

```
Fixes Assets:
   Store equipment . . . . . . . . .      $ 4,000
      Less: Accumulated depreciation.       1,500   $ 2,500
   Office equipment. . . . . . . . .      $ 1,800
      Less: Accumulated depreciation.         600     1,200
   Building. . . . . . . . . . . .        $16,000
      Less: Accumulated depreciation.       1,820    14,180
   Land. . . . . . . . . . . . . . .                   3,000
          Total Fixed Assets. . . . . .                        $20,880
```

When fixed assets are presented in this manner, a reader of the balance sheet can see both the cost of the functional classes of assets and their accumulated depreciation to the date of the balance sheet. If both cost and depreciation are shown, a much better picture is obtained than if only net undepreciated costs are given. When both costs and accumulated depreciation are shown, the reader can tell not only something of the physical adequacy of the assets but also something of their age. For example, $50,000 of assets with accumulated depreciation of $45,000 are quite different from $5,000 of new assets. Yet, the net undepreciated cost is the same in both cases.

Balance Sheet Fixed Asset Values

From the discussion thus far the student should recognize that the recording of depreciation is not primarily a valuing process, rather it is a process of allocating the costs of fixed assets to the several accounting periods that benefit from their use.[1] Furthermore, he should recognize that because the recording of depreciation is an allocating process rather than a valuing process, balance sheets show for fixed assets unallocated costs or undepreciated costs rather than market values.

The fact that balance sheets show undepreciated costs rather than market values seems to disturb many beginning accounting students. It should not. When a balance sheet is prepared, normally the company for which it is prepared has no intention of selling its fixed assets; consequently, the market values of these assets are of no great significance. The student should recognize that when a balance sheet is prepared, the balance sheet is prepared under the assumption that the company for which it is prepared is a going concern that will continue in business long enough to recover the costs of its fixed assets through the sale of its products.

The assumption that a company is a going concern that will continue in business long enough to recover the costs of its fixed assets through the sale of its products is known in accounting as the *going concern concept*. It is a concept that the student or any balance sheet reader should bear in mind as he reads a balance sheet.

---

[1] *Accounting Terminology Bulletin No. 1*, "Review and Résumé" (New York: American Institute of Certified Public Accountants, 1953), p. 25.

Depletion

Natural resources such as timber lands, mineral deposits, and oil reserves, which are known as *wasting assets*, are carried in the accounts at cost less accumulated *depletion*. The amount such assets are depleted each year by cutting, mining, or pumping is commonly calculated on a "units of production" basis. For example, if a mine having an estimated 1,000,000 tons of available ore is purchased for $500,000, the depletion charge per ton of ore mined is $0.50 ($500,000 ÷ 1,000,000). If 150,000 tons of ore are mined during the first year, the depletion charge for the year is $75,000 (150,000 × $0.50) ; and the charge is recorded as follows:

Dec.	31	Depletion.............................	75,000.00	
		Accumulated Depletion, Mine.......		75,000.00
		To record depletion of ore body resulting from mining 150,000 tons of ore.		

On the balance sheet prepared at the end of the first year, the mine would appear at its $500,000 cost less the accumulated depletion of $75,000.

If all of the 150,000 tons were sold by the end of the year, the entire $75,000 depletion charge would appear on the income statement as the depletion cost of the ore sold. However, if a portion remained unsold and on hand at the end of the year, the depletion cost of the unsold ore would appear on the balance sheet as a portion of the cost of the inventory of unsold ore, a current asset.

Discarding and Selling a Fixed Asset

Sooner or later a fixed asset wears out, becomes obsolete, or becomes inadequate. When this occurs, the asset is discarded. If the service life and salvage value estimates were correct, the discarded asset may be sold for its salvage value. For example, a small drill press costing $900 and having an estimated service life of four years and an estimated salvage value of $100 depreciates $200 each year of its life. At the end of its fourth and last year of estimated service life, the drill press has a book value of $100; and the ledger accounts that show the history of this asset and its $100 book value appear as follows:

Machinery		Accumulated Depreciation, Machinery	
Jan. 2, '56 900			Dec. 31, '56 200
			Dec. 31, '57 200
			Dec. 31, '58 200
			Dec. 31, '59 200

If at the end of its fourth year the drill press is discarded and sold for its book value, the entry to record the sale is:

Jan.	2	Cash.....................................	100.00	
		Accumulated Depreciation, Machinery....	800.00	
		Machinery........................		900.00
		Sold machinery at book value.		

In the entry recording the sale of the drill press, the debit to the accumulated depreciation account and the credit to the Machinery account remove the machine from the accounts and end its accounting history.

Discarding and Selling Fixed Assets at a Gain or a Loss

Exactly estimating salvage value or exactly estimating service life is not easy. Normally the estimate of one or the other is incorrect. When a fixed asset is discarded and sold, and either its salvage value or its service life was incorrectly estimated, a book gain or a book loss is incurred. For example, if the drill press previously illustrated as having an estimated salvage value of $100 is sold at the end of its service life for only $60, a book loss of $40 is incurred. The entry to record the sale at a loss is:

Jan.	2	Cash.....................................	60.00	
		Loss on the Sale of Fixed Assets.........	40.00	
		Accumulated Depreciation, Machinery....	800.00	
		Machinery........................		900.00
		To record the sale of a drill press at a loss.		

Or assume that the drill press is sold at the end of its service life for $125. If the machine is sold for $125, a book gain of $25 is made. This is recorded:

Jan.	2	Cash.....................................	125.00	
		Accumulated Depreciation, Machinery....	800.00	
		Machinery........................		900.00
		Gain on the Sale of Fixed Assets......		25.00
		To record the sale of a drill press at a profit.		

To illustrate further, assume that an error is made in estimating service life and that the drill press previously illustrated wears out and must be discarded at the end of the third year of its estimated four-year service life. At this time the asset has a book value of $300; this is its $900 cost less three years' depreciation of $600. If the drill press is sold at the end of its third year for the estimated salvage value of $100, the entry to record the sale is:

Jan.	2	Cash...............................	100.00	
		Loss on the Sale of Fixed Assets.........	200.00	
		Accumulated Depreciation, Machinery....	600.00	
		Machinery.......................		900.00
		To record the sale of a drill press at a loss.		

If, on the other hand, the estimate of the service life of the drill press is too short, the machine will be in use after the end of its estimated service life. Normally, in such a situation, no depreciation is charged for the years after the end of the estimated service life, and the asset is carried on the books at its salvage value. When the asset is finally discarded, a gain or loss is recorded if the asset is sold for more or less than its salvage value.

Fixed Asset Gains and Losses on the Income Statement

Since it is difficult to estimate depreciation exactly in advance, when fixed assets are sold they are normally sold at either a gain or at a loss. As each asset is sold, the gain or the loss is recorded in either a loss or a gain account. At the end of the accounting period these loss and gain accounts are closed to Income Summary. Their balances then appear on the income statement, at the very end, in a section called "Extraneous gains and losses." Here gains are added and losses are subtracted from the income from operations.

Discarding Fixed Assets because of Damage

Occasionally, before the end of its service life, a fixed asset is wrecked by an accident or is destroyed by fire. In such cases a loss occurs. If an uninsured asset is totally destroyed in an accident such as a fire, the entry to record the loss is:

Jan.	3	Loss from Fire........................	500.00	
		Accumulated Depreciation, Machinery....	400.00	
		Machinery.......................		900.00
		To record the accidental destruction of machinery.		

If the asset is partially covered by insurance, the money received from the insurance company is debited to Cash and the loss is less. The entry to record an accidental loss that is partially covered by insurance is:

Jan.	3	Cash...............................	350.00	
		Loss from Fire.......................	150.00	
		Accumulated Depreciation, Machinery....	400.00	
		Machinery.......................		900.00
		To record the destruction of machinery and the receipt of insurance compensation.		

Depreciation for Partial Years

In all of the illustrations thus far the assumption has been that the assets were purchased and discarded at either the beginning or the end of an accounting period. This is an assumption that seldom occurs. Businessmen normally buy assets when they are needed and sell or discard these assets when they are no longer usable or no longer needed; and the purchases and sales are normally made without regard for time. Because of this, depreciation must often be calculated for partial years. For example, a truck costing $2,600 and having an estimated service life of five years and an estimated salvage value of $600 is purchased on October 8, 1955. If the yearly accounting period ends on December 31, depreciation for three months must be recorded for this truck. Three months are three twelfths of a year. Consequently, three months' depreciation on this truck is calculated as follows:

$$\frac{\$2,600 - \$600}{5} \times \frac{3}{12} = \$100.00$$

In the illustration, depreciation is calculated for a full three months, even though the asset was purchased on October 8. Depreciation is an estimate; therefore calculation to the nearest full month is usually considered sufficiently accurate. This means that depreciation is usually calculated for a full month on assets purchased before the fifteenth of the month. Likewise, depreciation for the month in which an asset is purchased is normally disregarded if the asset is purchased after the middle of the month.

The entry to record depreciation for three months on the truck purchased on October 8 is:

Dec.	31	Depreciation Expense, Delivery Equipment.................................	100.00	
		Accumulated Depr., Delivery Equipment............................		100.00
		To record depreciation for three months on the delivery truck.		

On December 31, 1956, and at the end of each of the following three years, a journal entry to record a full year's depreciation on this truck is made. This journal entry is:

Dec.	31	Depreciation Expense, Delivery Equipment...............................	400.00	
		Accumulated Depr., Delivery Equipment............................		400.00
		To record depreciation for one year on the delivery truck.		

After the December 31, 1959, depreciation entry is recorded, the accounts showing the history of this truck appear as follows:

Delivery Equipment		Accumulated Depreciation, Delivery Equipment	
Oct. 8, '55 2,600		Dec. 31, '55	100
		Dec. 31, '56	400
		Dec. 31, '57	400
		Dec. 31, '58	400
		Dec. 31, '59	400

If this truck is disposed of during 1960, two entries must be made to record the disposal. The first entry records the 1960 depreciation to the date of disposal, and the second records the actual disposal. For example, assume that the truck is sold for $900 on June 24, 1960. To record the disposal, depreciation for six months (depreciation to the nearest full month) must first be recorded. The entry for this is:

June	24	Depreciation Expense, Delivery Equipment...............................	200.00	
		Accumulated Depreciation, Delivery Equipment......................		200.00
		To record depreciation for one half of a year on the delivery truck.		

After making the entry to record depreciation to the date of sale, a second entry to record the actual sale is made. This entry is:

June	24	Cash....................................	900.00	
		Accumulated Depr., Delivery Equipment	1,900.00	
		Delivery Equipment................		2,600.00
		Gain on the Sale of Fixed Assets......		200.00
		To record the sale of a delivery truck.		

Exchanging Fixed Assets

Some fixed assets are sold at the ends of their useful lives. Others, such as machinery, automobiles, and office equipment, may be traded in on new, up-to-date assets of a like nature. When a fixed asset is traded in on a new fixed asset, normally either a book gain or loss on the trade is experienced. If the trade-in allowance received is greater than the book value of the traded asset, a book gain is experienced; and if the trade-in allowance is less than the book value of the traded asset, a book loss is incurred. When such gains and losses are material in amount, they should be entered in the accounts as gains and losses. Immaterial gains and losses may be absorbed into the cost basis of the new asset.

Recording Material Gains and Losses. When a material gain or loss is experienced on the exchange of a fixed asset, the gain or loss should be recognized in the accounts as a gain or a loss. For example, a machine which cost $18,000 and upon which depreciation of $15,000 has accumulated is traded in at $5,500 on the purchase of a like new machine having a cash price of $21,000. The book value of the old machine is $3,000. Therefore, if a trade-in allowance of $5,500 is received, there is a book gain of $2,500 on the transaction. The book value and gain are calculated:

Cost of old machine	$18,000
Less: Accumulated depreciation	15,000
Book value	$ 3,000
Trade-in allowance on new machine	$ 5,500
Book value of old machine	3,000
Book Gain on the Exchange	$ 2,500

When the exchange is completed, the entry to record it is:

Jan.	5	Machinery	21,000.00		
		Accumulated Depreciation, Machinery	15,000.00		
		Machinery		18,000.00	
		Gain on the Exchange of Fixed Assets		2,500.00	
		Cash		15,500.00	
		Exchanged old machine and cash for a like new machine.			

Or to illustrate further, assume that the old $18,000 machine with accumulated depreciation of $15,000 is traded in at $1,000 on the new machine having a cash price of $21,000. If the old machine is traded at $1,000, a book loss of $2,000 is incurred. The loss is calculated:

Book value of old machine	$3,000
Trade-in allowance on new machine	1,000
Book Loss on the Exchange	$2,000

If the old machine is traded at a loss, the entry to record the exchange is:

Jan.	5	Machinery.............................	21,000.00	
		Loss on the Exchange of Machinery.......	2,000.00	
		Accumulated Depreciation, Machinery....	15,000.00	
		Machinery.......................		18,000.00
		Cash............................		20,000.00
		Exchanged old machine and cash for a like new machine.		

Income Tax Method of Recording Fixed Asset Exchanges. Although
the exchange of a fixed asset usually results in either a book gain or loss,
the Internal Revenue Code does not recognize such gains and losses as
gains and losses for tax purposes. According to the Internal Revenue
Code, when an old asset is traded in on a like new asset, the cost basis of
the new asset is the sum of (1) the cash given plus (2) the undepreciated
book value of the old asset.

For example, if a typewriter which cost $180 and upon which deprecia-
tion in the amount of $150 has accumulated is traded in at $45 on the
purchase of a new $210 typewriter, the cost basis of the new typewriter is
calculated for tax purposes as follows:

Cash paid ($210 less the $45 trade-in allowance)................$165
Book value of old typewriter ($180 less $150)..................... 30
Income Tax Basis of the New Asset for Depreciation, Sale, or Disposal $195

If this tax basis is used in recording the exchange, the entry is:

New $210.00 typewriter

Jan.	5	Office Equipment......................	195.00	
		Accumulated Depr., Office Equipment....	150.00	
		Office Equipment................		180.00
		Cash............................		165.00
		Traded old typewriter and cash for a new typewriter.		

Or to illustrate further, if rather than a trade-in allowance of $45,
only a $20 allowance is received when the foregoing typewriter is ex-
changed, the cost basis of the new typewriter for tax purposes is calculated:

Cash paid ($210 less a $20 trade-in allowance)....................$190
Book value of old typewriter ($180 less $150)..................... 30
Income Tax Basis of the New Typewriter for Depreciation, Sale, or
  Disposal...$220

And if this basis is used in recording the typewriter exchange, the entry is:

New $210.00
typewriter

Jan.	5	Office Equipment.......................	220.00	
		Accumulated Depr., Office Equipment....	150.00	
		Office Equipment.................		180.00
		Cash.............................		190.00
		Exchanged old typewriter and cash for a		
		new typewriter.		

When an asset having a book value of $30 is traded at $45, there is a book gain of $15; likewise, there is a book loss of $10 when the asset is traded at $20. However, observe in the foregoing calculations and entries that the effect of the application of the tax rule is the nonrecognition of either the gain in the first instance or the loss in the second. The effect, when the tax rule is applied, is that the gain and the loss are absorbed into the cost of the new asset.

The reason for the tax rule is that it prevents a taxpayer from taking an unfair tax advantage by shifting taxable earnings from one year to the next by means of an arranged book gain or loss on an exchange. (A book loss for a taxpayer, for example, can be arranged if the dealer and the taxpayer agree to reduce by equal amounts both the normal trade-in allowance on the traded asset and the quoted price of the new asset.)

At first glance it might seem that nonrecognition of gains and losses works a hardship when errors in estimating depreciation are made. However, this is usually not true. For example, when an asset is exchanged at a loss, the loss may not be counted as a loss for tax purposes; it is in fact added to the cost of the new asset. This causes the new asset to be taken into the records at a higher price; the higher price results in greater depreciation expense throughout the life of the new asset; and the greater depreciation expense offsets the unrecognized loss on the exchange. In the end, through greater depreciation expense, proprietorship is reduced by the amount of the exchange loss. Likewise, in the end through reduced depreciation expense on the new asset, a book gain on an exchange increases proprietorship by the amount of the unrecognized gain.

Materiality and the Choice of Methods. When a fixed asset is traded in on a like new asset, there is normally either a book gain or loss on the exchange; but, as previously stated, the Internal Revenue Code does not recognize such gains and losses for tax purposes. Consequently, if a gain or a loss is recorded as such at the time of an exchange, two sets of depreciation expense records must be kept throughout the life of the new asset, one set for use in determining net income for accounting purposes and a different set for determining the depreciation deduction for tax purposes.

Obviously the keeping of two sets of records is more costly than the keeping of one. Yet, when an exchange results in a material gain or loss, the gain or loss should be recorded and the two sets of records should be kept. On the other hand, when an exchange results in an immaterial gain or loss, it is permissible to avoid the two sets of records by using the income tax method to record the transaction. The use of the income tax method when there is a minor exchange gain or loss is permissible under the accounting principle of materiality.

The principle of materiality holds that strict adherence to any accounting principle is not required if the cost to adhere is proportionally great and the lack of adherence will not materially affect the reported periodic net income. For example, if there is a $25 loss in trading an item of office equipment, using the income tax method to record the exchange would not materially affect the statements of the average company. On the other hand, recording the loss and thereafter keeping two sets of depreciations records would be costly. Consequently, the income tax method is commonly used in such cases.

Repairs and Replacements

Repairs and replacements of fixed assets fall into two classifications: (1) ordinary repairs and replacements, and (2) extraordinary repairs and replacements.

Expenditures for ordinary repairs and replacements are necessary to maintain an asset in good operating condition. A building must be painted and its roof repaired or a machine must be repaired and small parts replaced. Any expenditures made to maintain a fixed asset in its normal good state of repair are considered ordinary repairs and replacements. Expenditures for ordinary repairs are expenses and appear on the income statement as deductions from revenue. Consequently, they are known as *revenue expenditures*.

Expenditures for extraordinary repairs and replacements increase the value of an asset. They may increase value by increasing service life, salvage value, or efficiency. Expenditures for extraordinary repairs and replacements improve an asset. Consequently, they appear on the balance sheet as an increase in an asset and are called *capital expenditures*.

When extraordinary repairs are made, they may be recorded either as debits to an asset account or debits to an accumulated depreciation account. Extraordinary repairs that increase service life in effect cancel part of the depreciation that has been recorded. Consequently, repairs that increase service life, as well as those that increase salvage value, are commonly debited directly to an accumulated depreciation account. On the other hand, repairs and replacements that increase efficiency may reasonably be debited directly to the asset account.

It is often difficult to distinguish between ordinary repairs and replacements and extraordinary repairs and replacements. For example, the replacement of the motor in an automobile may be classed as ordinary repairs or it may be classed as extraordinary repairs. The classification depends upon whether or not replacement was anticipated when the service life of the automobile and its salvage value were originally estimated. If replacement was planned and the service life and salvage value estimates included replacement of the motor, then the replacement does not lengthen the estimated service life or increase the estimated salvage value. Since the estimated service life and salvage value are not increased, the replacement of the motor is an ordinary repair.

If, on the other hand, the motor replacement was not planned in the original estimates of service life and salvage value, and the replacement does increase the service life or salvage value, then the replacement is an extraordinary repair.

Even though it may be difficult to distinguish between ordinary repairs and extraordinary repairs, when possible it is important to do so. This is because ordinary repairs, an expense, recorded as extraordinary repairs not only overstate the assets and proprietorship on the current balance sheet but also understate expenses on the income statement. Nor does the error end here. The assets and proprietorship on the balance sheets and the depreciation expense on the income statements continue to be overstated for the life of the asset. Extraordinary repairs recorded as an expense have the opposite effect.

Fixed Asset Records

Fixed assets normally appear on a balance sheet in functional groups. For example, on the balance sheet of a store, the unrecovered cost of all store fixtures and equipment is normally listed as one amount, the unrecovered cost of all office equipment is listed as another amount, and the unrecovered cost of the delivery equipment is listed as still another amount. As a result, the General Ledger of such a store will normally have a separate fixed asset account and a separate accumulated depreciation account for each of its functional asset groups. It will normally have an Office Equipment account and an Accumulated Depreciation, Office Equipment account, and it will normally have a Store Equipment account and an Accumulated Depreciation, Store Equipment account. In short, the store will normally have a separate fixed asset account and a separate accumulated depreciation account for each functional group of assets that it owns. Furthermore, all of the transactions that affect any one of the functional groups are recorded in the asset and the accumulated depreciation accounts of that group. For example, the purchase, depreciation, exchange, or sale of all office equipment is recorded in the one office equipment and its related accumulated depreciation accounts.

Prior to 1934, the functional general ledger fixed asset accounts and their related accumulated depreciation accounts were often the only fixed asset records maintained by any but larger concerns. Since that time, federal income tax regulations have made more detailed records necessary. Today, any business that reports a deduction from income for depreciation or reports a gain or loss on the sale of a fixed asset must be able to substantiate such items with detailed records. No specific kind of records is required, but normally each general ledger fixed asset account and its related accumulated depreciation account become controlling accounts. These controlling accounts control detailed subsidiary records. For example, the Office Equipment account and the Accumulated Depreciation, Office Equipment account control a subsidiary ledger having a separate record for each individual item of office equipment. Likewise, the Store Equipment account and its related Accumulated Depreciation, Store Equipment account become controlling accounts controlling a subsidiary store equipment ledger. Often these subsidiary ledger records are kept on fixed asset record cards.

To illustrate controlling account, subsidiary ledger, fixed asset records, assume that the office equipment of a store consists of a desk and a chair. The general ledger record of these assets is maintained in the Office Equipment controlling account and the Accumulated Depreciation, Office Equipment controlling account. Since in this case there are only two assets, only two subsidiary records cards are needed. The general ledger and subsidiary ledger record of these assets appear as shown in Illustration 77 below and on the following two pages.

The information given on the subsidiary fixed asset record cards is in the main self-evident. Note how the balance of the general ledger account, Office Equipment, is equal to the sum of the balances in the asset record section of the two subsidiary ledger cards. The general ledger account controls this section of the subsidiary ledger. Note also how the Accumulated Depreciation, Office Equipment account controls the depreciation record section of the cards. The disposition section at the bottom of the card is used to record the final disposal of the asset. When the asset is discarded, sold, or exchanged, a note telling of the final disposition is entered here. The card is then removed from the subsidiary ledger and filed for future reference.

Illustration 77
OFFICE EQUIPMENT

Date		Explanation	F	Debit	Date	Explanation	F	Credit
1957 July	2	Desk and Chair	CP1	185.00				

ACCUMULATED DEPRECIATION, OFFICE EQUIPMENT

Date	Explanation	F	Debit	Date		Explanation	F	Credit
				1957 Dec.	31		G23	4.50
				1958 Dec.	31		G42	9.00
				1959 Dec.	31		G65	9.00

Illustration 77—Continued

SUBSIDIARY FIXED ASSET AND DEPRECIATION RECORD

Fixed Asset
No. *1*

Item *Office chair*

General Ledger
Account *Office Equipment*

Description *Solid oak office chair*

Mfg. Serial No.

Purchased
from *Office Equipment Co.*

Where Located *Office*

Person Responsible for the Asset *Office manager*

Estimated Life *12 years*   Estimated Salvage Value *$4.00*

Depreciation per Year *$3.00*   per Month *$0.25*

Date	Explanation	F	Asset Record			Depreciation Record		
			Dr.	Cr.	Bal.	Dr.	Cr.	Bal.
July 2, '57		*CP1*	40.00		40.00			
Dec. 31, '57		*G23*					1.50	1.50
Dec. 31, '58		*G42*					3.00	4.50
Dec. 31, '59		*G65*					3.00	7.50

Final Disposition of the Asset

Illustration 77—Continued

<table>
<tr><td colspan="2"></td><td colspan="2" align="right">Fixed Asset
No. 2</td></tr>
<tr><td colspan="4" align="center">SUBSIDIARY FIXED ASSET AND DEPRECIATION RECORD</td></tr>
</table>

Item *Desk*

General Ledger
Account *Office Equipment*

Description *Solid oak office desk*

Mfg. Serial No.

Purchased
from *Office Equipment Co.*

Where Located *Office*

Person Responsible for the Asset *Office manager*

Estimated Life *20 years*   Estimated Salvage Value *$25.00*

Depreciation per Year *$6.00*   per Month *$0.50*

Date	Explanation	F	Asset Record Dr.	Cr.	Bal.	Depreciation Record Dr.	Cr.	Bal.
July 2, '57		CP1	145.00		145.00			
Dec. 31, '57		G23					3.00	3.00
Dec. 31, '58		G42					6.00	9.00
Dec. 31, '59		G65					6.00	15.00

Final Disposition of the Asset_____

QUESTIONS FOR CLASS DISCUSSION

1. What is a fixed asset?
2. The cost of a machine includes its invoice price. What other items may be included in its cost?
3. Explain how accounting for fixed assets is similar to accounting for a prepaid expense such as prepaid insurance.
4. Define the following terms as they are used in accounting for fixed assets:
   a) Depreciation.   d) Trade-in value.   g) Inadequacy.
   b) Service life.   e) Market value.   h) Obsolescence.
   c) Service cost.   f) Book value.   i) Salvage value.
5. A machine costing $17,500 was installed. Its useful life was estimated at five years, after which it would have a trade-in value of $2,500. Its total life production was estimated at 60,000 units of product. During its second year the machine produced 10,000 units of product. What was the second-year charge for depreciation on the machine if depreciation were calculated on: (a) a straight-line basis; (b) units of production basis; (c) a reducing fraction basis; (d) a sum of the years' digits basis?

6. A building estimated to have a useful life of forty years was completed at a cost of $55,000. It was estimated that at the end of the building's life it would be wrecked at a cost of $1,000 and that materials salvaged from the wrecking operation would be sold for $800. How much depreciation should be charged on the building each year?

7. A mine having an estimated 1,000,000 tons of ore was purchased for $2,500,000. Under the assumption that 90,000 tons of ore were mined the first year, give the entry to record depletion.

8. Why do balance sheets normally show both the cost and the accumulated depreciation of each functional group of fixed assets?

9. Do balance sheets show market values for fixed assets? If not, what kind of values are shown?

10. Is it possible to keep a fixed asset in such an excellent state of repair that the recording of depreciation is unnecessary?

11. What is the purpose of recording depreciation at the end of each accounting period?

12. A machine was purchased new on January 3, 1954, at a cost of $2,600. The machine had an estimated service life of ten years and an estimated salvage value of $400. (a) What is the annual depreciation of the machine calculated by the straight-line method? (b) Give the entry to record the annual depreciation. (c) Assume that the machine was destroyed by fire on March 2, 1959, and that there was no insurance. Give the entries required to record the loss. (d) Assume that there was insurance and that $1,200 was received from the insurance company to cover the fire loss. Give the entries to record the loss.

13. A machine cost $3,600. It had an estimated service life of five years and an estimated salvage value of $600. Depreciation was correctly recorded at the end of each year of the asset's life. Give the entries required under each of the following assumptions:
    a) The machine was sold for $1,000 at the end of the fourth year of its life.
    b) The machine was sold for $1,500 at the end of its fourth year.
    c) The machine was traded at the end of its fourth year on a new machine with a list price of $4,000. A trade-in allowance of $1,000 was received. The loss on the exchange was recorded.
    d) The transaction just given (c) was recorded by the income tax method.
    e) The machine was traded in at the end of its fourth year on a new machine with a list price of $4,000. A trade-in allowance of $1,500 was received. The gain on the exchange was recorded.
    f) The transaction just given (e) was recorded by the income tax method.

14. When an old fixed asset is traded in at a book loss on a new fixed asset of a like nature, the loss is not recognized for tax purposes. In the end this normally does not work a great hardship on the taxpayer. Why?

15. What is the difference between a capital expenditure and a revenue expenditure? Give an example of each.

16. Classify the following expenditures as either capital expenditures or revenue expenditures:
    a) Repainted a building.
    b) Replaced the gears in a machine and thereby doubled its output.
    c) Replaced broken gears in a machine with like new gears.
    d) Replaced a worn-out wood shingle roof with a new tile roof that is guaranteed to last the life of the building.

17. In 1959 extraordinary repairs to a machine were recorded as a revenue ex-

penditure. What was the effect of this error on the 1959 financial statements? On the 1960 and later statements?

18. Frank Williams purchased land at the edge of a city with the intention of developing a high-class residential subdivision. Before Mr. Williams could complete his development a glue factory was erected next to his property. As a result Mr. Williams could not sell his land for the amount of his investment. Is this depreciation in the accounting sense of the term?

PROBLEMS

Problem 13–1

Walter Hansen organized a package deliver firm. During a three-year period he completed the following transactions:

1959

Sept. 3 Purchased a secondhand Mars truck paying $800 cash. The service life of the truck was estimated at three years with a trade-in allowance of $200 at the end of that time.

3 Paid Service Garage $90 for a new set of tires for the Mars truck, and paid them $30 for some minor repairs to the truck's motor.

Dec. 15 Paid Service Garage $15 for repairs to the bumper of the Mars truck. The bumper had been broken by the driver when he backed into a loading dock.

31 Recorded depreciation on the truck.

31 Closed the expense accounts involved.

1960

Mar. 28 Purchased a new Eclipse truck paying $2,400 cash. The service life of the truck was estimated at four years with a trade-in value of $900 at the end of that time.

30 Paid $100 for building special shelves and racks in the Eclipse truck. The additions did not increase the truck's trade-in value.

Oct. 24 Traded the Mars truck on a new Abar truck having a cash price of $2,800. Received a $700 trade-in allowance; paid the balance in cash. The service life of the Abar truck was estimated at four years with a $1,000 trade-in allowance at the end of that time. (Use income tax method.)

Dec. 15 Paid Service Garage $40 for a motor tuneup and minor repairs to the Eclipse truck.

31 Recorded depreciation on the trucks.

31 Closed the expense accounts.   *Accum Dep 290*

1961

June 29 Realized that the amount of business transacted did not warrant the use of two trucks. Sold the Abar truck for $2,200 cash.

Required:

Prepare general journal entries to record the foregoing transactions.

Problem 13–2

Early in January, 1951, Fall Creek Lumber Company purchased a new saw for its mill. The saw plus its concrete base cost $32,000. Its useful life was estimated at twenty years, and it was assumed that the saw would have no salvage value at the end of its useful life. During the first week in January, 1959, the saw was repaired and rebuilt at a cost of $5,400, of which $2,400 was considered ordinary repairs and $3,000 was considered extraordinary repairs. The extraordinary repairs increased the efficiency of the saw but did not extend its useful life or increase its salvage value. On March 30, 1960, the saw was destroyed by a fire. The lumber company collected $16,000 in insurance.

Required:

Prepare general journal entries to record the following:
1. The purchase of the saw.
2. The 1951 depreciation on the saw.
3. The expenditure for repairing and rebuilding the saw in 1959.
4. The 1959 depreciation on the saw.
5. The destruction of the saw and the receipt of the insurance payment.

Problem 13-3

The following four machines were owned by a firm whose accounting periods end each December 31.

Machine No. 1 was purchased on April 2, 1953, at an installed cost of $5,400. Its useful life was estimated at four years, and its trade-in value at $600. Depreciation on a straight-line basis was recorded on the machine on December 31, 1953, and on December 31, 1954. The machine was traded on Machine No. 2 on January 9, 1955. A trade-in allowance of $3,000 was received.

Machine No. 2 was purchased on January 9, 1955, at an installed cost of $6,500 less the trade-in allowance granted for Machine No. 1. The new machine's life was estimated at five years with a trade-in value of $800. Depreciation calculated by the sum of the years' digits method was recorded on the machine on each December 31 of its life. The machine was sold for $1,000 on January 6, 1960.

Machine No. 3 was purchased January 3, 1955, at an installed cost of $5,000. Its useful life was estimated at five years, after which it would have a trade-in value of $500. Depreciation calculated by the declining balance method was recorded on the machine at the end of 1955, 1956, 1957, and 1958. On January 10, 1959, the machine was traded on Machine No. 4. A trade-in allowance of $1,200 was received.

Machine No. 4 was purchased on January 10, 1959, at an installed cost of $6,552 less the trade-in allowance received for Machine No. 3. It was estimated that the new machine would produce 90,000 units of product during its useful life, after which it would have a trade-in value of $600. Depreciation calculated by the units of production method was recorded at the end of 1959. During 1959 the machine produced 12,000 units of product; and between January 1 and April 12, 1960, the machine produced 5,000 more units. On April 12, 1960, the machine was sold for $4,500.

Required:

Prepare general journal entries to record: (1) the purchase of each machine, (2) the depreciation recorded on the first December 31 of each machine's life, and (3) the disposal of each machine. Use the income tax method to record the exchanges. (Only one entry is required for both the purchase of a new machine and the disposal of an old machine when an old machine is traded on a new one.)

Problem 13-4

The Snappy Service Market completed the following transactions during a three-year period:

1958

Jan.   3   Purchased a Superior scale from the Store Equipment Company for $265. The serial number of the scale was B-23452, its service life was estimated at twenty years, and its trade-in value was estimated at $25.

       5   Purchased a Coldaire refrigerated display case from the Store Equipment Company for $3,200. The serial number of the display case was 00-23234, its service life was estimated at sixteen years, and its trade-in value was estimated at $800.

Apr.   7   Purchased a Regal cash register for $323 from the Woodson Equipment Company. The serial number of the cash register was 3-32564, its service life was estimated at sixteen years, and its trade-in value was estimated at $35.

Dec. 31   Recorded the 1958 depreciation on the store equipment.

1959

Oct. 28   Sold the Regal cash register to Thomas Seay for $275.

      28   Purchased a new Seashore cash register from the Uptown Equipment Company for $360. The serial number of the cash register was XXX-12435, its service life was estimated at twenty years, and its trade-in value was estimated at $48.

Dec. 31   Recorded the 1959 depreciation on the store equipment.

1960

May   28   Traded the Superior scale to the Rex Equipment Company on a new Rex scale having a list price of $298. Received a trade-in allowance of $200. The serial number of the new scale was MM-7678, its service life was estimated at twenty years, and its trade-in value was estimated at $34. (Use income tax method.)

Dec. 31   Recorded the 1960 depreciation on the store equipment.

Required:

1. Open general ledger accounts for Store Equipment and Accumulated Depreciation, Store Equipment. Prepare as needed a subsidiary fixed asset ledger card for each item of store equipment owned by Snappy Service Market.

2. Prepare general journal entries to record the fixed asset transactions completed by Snappy Service Market. Post the transactions to the proper general ledger and subsidiary ledger fixed asset accounts.

3. Prove the December 31, 1960, balances of the Store Equipment and the Accumulated Depreciation, Store Equipment accounts by preparing from the subsidiary fixed asset ledger cards a list showing the cost and the accumulated depreciation of each item of store equipment owned by Snappy Service Market on that date.

CLASS EXERCISES

Exercise 13–1

A machine was purchased for $800, 2/10, n/60, F.O.B. factory. The freight charges were $76, and the installation costs were $440. The invoice was paid within the discount period. It was estimated that the machine would last four years and would then have a trade-in value of $100. It was further estimated that the machine would produce 20,000 units of product during its four-year life. If the machine produced 6,000 units of product during its third year, what was the depreciation charge on the machine for the third year, if depreciation were calculated by the: (1) straight-line method; (2) units of production method; (3) declining balance method; and (4) sum of the years' digits method?

Exercise 13–2

In January of the current year, while making his initial audit of the accounting records of a new client, an auditor discovered an account called "Land and Buildings." The account had a debit balance of $60,000. An investigation showed the balance of the account had resulted from the purchase at $8,000 of the land on which the client's warehouse had been constructed at a cost of $52,000. Further investigation revealed that the warehouse site had been purchased ten years prior to the date of the audit and had been held two years before the warehouse building was erected. During this ten-year period property taxes in the amount of $9,730 had been paid on the land and its improvements and charged to an expense account called "Property Taxes." Of this amount, $270 applied to the years before the construction of the warehouse building. Examination of the expense account, Property taxes, revealed that three years before the date of the audit the street beside the warehouse had been paved by the city at a cost to the client of $820. The $820 tax assessment for the paving had been charged to the expense account, Property Taxes. In addition to the foregoing the client had not recorded any depreciation on the warehouse building during its eight-year life because "it was of concrete construction and should last forever." The building had an estimated service life of fifty years and no salvage value.

Required:

Prepare general journal entries to correct the client's accounting records through the year just ended.

SUPPLEMENTARY PROBLEMS

Problem 13–A

Blue and White Cab Company purchased three taxicabs at $3,200 each on January 7, 1959. The company planned to depreciate the cabs on a mileage basis. It estimated that the cabs would be driven 60,000 miles each, after which they would be traded on new cabs at an estimated $800 each. On November 14, 1959, after having been driven 19,300 miles, Cab No. 1 was totally destroyed in a wreck. The insurance company paid $2,100 in full settlement of the loss claim. The wrecked cab was not replaced. At the end of the 1959 accounting period, on December 31, Cab No. 2 had been driven 21,600 miles and Cab No. 3 had been driven 18,800 miles. On April 12, 1960, Cab No. 2 was sold for $1,900, after having been driven a total of 28,500 miles. On December 4, 1960, after having been driven a total of 43,500 miles, Cab No. 3 was traded on a new cab having a listed cash price of $3,000. A trade-in allowance of $1,500 was received.

Required:

Prepare general journal entries to record: (a) the purchase of the three cabs; (b) the destruction of the first cab and the insurance settlement; (c) the 1959 depreciation expense; (d) the sale of the second cab; and (e) the exchange of the third cab. (Use the income tax method in recording the exchange.)

Problem 13–B

The following machines were owned by a factory, the accounting periods of which end each December 31:

Asset	Pur-chased	Cost	Estimated Useful Life	Estimated Scrap Value	Method of Deprecia-tion	Disposal Date and Details
No. 1..	5-4-53	$1,750	5 years	$250	Straight-line	Traded on Asset No. 2, 1-3-55, trade-in allowance, $1,000
No. 2..	1-3-55	$2,150 less trade-in allowance	5 years	300	Sum of the years' digits	Sold for $400 on 1-5-60
No. 3..	1-2-55	$3,200	4 years	400	Declining balance	Traded on Asset No. 4, 1-7-59, trade-in allowance, $450
No. 4..	1-7-59	$3,500 less trade-in allowance	60,000 units of product	250	Units of produc-tion*	Sold for $2,500 on 3-15-60

* Asset No. 4 produced 10,000 units of product in 1959 and 3,000 before sale in 1960.

Required:

General journal entries to record: (1) purchase of each machine; (2) depreciation for each machine on the first December 31 of its life; and (3) the disposal of each machine. Use the income tax method to record exchanges. Only one entry is required to record the disposal of an old machine and the purchase of a new one when the old is traded in on the new.

Problem 13–C

Central Sales Company operates with annual accounting periods that end each December 31. On December 31 of the current year a trial balance of their ledger appeared as follows:

CENTRAL SALES COMPANY
Trial Balance, December 31, 19—

Cash	$ 3,240	
Petty cash	25	
Accounts receivable	5,210	
Allowance for bad debts		$ 120
Merchandise inventory	11,330	
Prepaid insurance	280	
Store supplies	440	
Office supplies	260	
Store equipment	5,355	
Accumulated depreciation, store equipment		1,575
Office equipment	2,100	
Accumulated depreciation, office equipment		910
Notes payable		2,500
Accounts payable		4,750
Walter Rink, capital		20,440
Walter Rink, withdrawals	4,200	
Sales		61,430
Sales returns and allowances	930	
Sales discounts	1,060	
Purchases	42,400	
Totals carried forward	$76,830	$91,725

Totals brought forward............................	$76,830	$91,725
Purchases returns and allowances........................		670
Purchases discounts....................................		790
Sales salaries..	6,420	
Rent expense, selling space............................	4,800	
Advertising expense...................................	1,170	
Office salaries..	3,230	
Rent expense, office space.............................	600	
Interest expense......................................	135	
	$93,185	$93,185

Required:

1. Enter the trial balance in the Trial Balance columns of a ten-column work sheet form (no Cost of Goods Sold columns). Complete the work sheet using the following information:
   a) Allowance for bad debts and additional 1 per cent of gross sales less sales returns and allowances.
   b) Expired insurance, $145.
   c) Store supplies inventory, $115.
   d) Office supplies inventory, $80.
   e) Depreciation of store equipment, $535.
   f) Depreciation of office equipment, $230.
   g) Sales salaries amounting to $60 and office salaries of $35 were earned but unpaid on the trial balance date.
   h) On December 7 a $2,500, sixty-day, noninterest-bearing note payable was discounted at the bank at a discount rate of 6 per cent.
   i) December 31 merchandise inventory, $9,960.
2. From the work sheet prepare a classified income statement and a classified balance sheet.

Chapter

14

ADJUSTMENTS, ADDITIONAL CONSIDERATIONS

THE LIFE of every business is divided into accounting periods. At the end of each period a balance sheet and an income statement are prepared. If these statements are to be useful and accurate, some system must be followed in assigning revenues and expenses to the proper periods. Normally the task of assigning revenues and expenses to the proper periods is quite simple. However, revenue is sometimes earned in one accounting period and collected in a different accounting period, and an expense is sometimes incurred in one accounting period and paid in another. When these situations occur, a problem arises as to which period the revenue or expense should be assigned. In each case the answer to the problem depends upon the *basis of accounting* in use. There are two bases of accounting in common use: the *cash basis* and the *accrual basis*.

The Cash Basis

Under the cash basis of accounting, revenues are considered to be earned at the time they are collected in cash and expenses are considered to be incurred at the time cash is disbursed in their payment. Under this system, the gain or loss of an accounting period is the difference between revenue receipts and expense disbursements.

The cash basis ignores (1) revenue represented by receivables, (2) expenses represented by payables, and (3) cost and expense reductions represented by inventories. Consequently, its use is generally restricted to individuals and to small firms in which inventories, receivables, and payables are not significant factors. Almost all individuals who file personal income tax returns use the cash basis for calculating income subject to tax. Here, where the sums involved are often small, the extra labor of deferring and accruing revenues and expenses is commonly not considered worthwhile. It is not considered worthwhile both because the sums involved are small and because, over several accounting periods, the results of the cash basis and the accrual basis tend to be the same.

In accounting for a business enterprise, the cash basis has the advantage of simplicity, but it has the great disadvantage of producing statements that are not comparable. Particularly is this true when accounting periods are short. For example, a firm that prepares monthly financial statements buys its entire winter's fuel supply in August and pays for it in September. Under the cash basis of accounting, this entire winter's fuel supply, which is used over several months, is unfairly recorded as an expense of the month of September. As a result, the September income statement shows a smaller income or a loss. Also, because of the extra burden of fuel expense, the September income statement is not comparable with the income statements of other months.

The Accrual Basis

If comparable statements are to be obtained, revenues must be allocated to the accounting period in which they are earned and expenses must be charged to the period in which they are incurred. This must be done regardless of when cash is received or disbursed. The accrual basis of accounting does this. Under the accrual basis, revenues are allocated to the accounting period in which they are earned regardless of when payments are received and expenses are allocated to the period in which they are incurred regardless of when cash is disbursed. As a result, under the accrual basis of accounting, the gain or loss of an accounting period is the difference between revenues earned and expenses incurred. Most business enterprises of any size use the accrual basis of accounting.

The obviously greater accuracy and usefulness of statements prepared under the accrual basis of accounting have been accepted from the beginning by this text. As a result, most of the recording procedures and adjustments necessary to allocate revenues and expenses to the proper accounting periods have already been discussed. For example, making adjustments for inventories of merchandise and supplies, prepaid expenses, depreciation, and bad debts result in allocating items to the proper accounting period. However, several additional factors need to be considered; and for purposes of discussion, these additional factors will be considered under five main headings. They are:

1. Accrued expenses.
2. Reversing entries.
3. Accrued revenues.
4. Prepaid expenses.
5. Unearned revenues.

Accrued Expenses

Normally, in recording the transactions of a business, expenses are recorded throughout each accounting period as they are paid. Consequently, at the end of each period, before adjustments are made, the ledger accounts of a business show all of the expenses that have been paid during the period. However, at the end of each period, these paid and recorded expenses are usually not all of the expenses that have been incurred during the period. Normally, at the end of each accounting period, there are expenses that have been incurred but that are not yet due and consequently have not been paid and recorded. These unpaid and unrecorded expenses that are not yet due are called *accrued expenses*.

When something accrues, it grows and accumulates with the passage of time. In accounting, accrued expenses are unpaid expenses which have grown and accumulated with the passage of time but which are not yet due. For example, on December 13, 1959, Beta Company borrows $18,000 from a bank by giving its sixty-day, 4 per cent, interest-bearing note. Interest expense in the amount of $2.00 accrues on this sixty-day note with the passage of each day; and by December 31, 1959, eighteen days' interest, or $36 of interest, has accrued. It is unpaid on December 31 because it is not due until the note is due on February 11.

Accrued Interest Expense, Cash Basis. In most businesses, accrued expenses such as accrued interest are accounted for on an accrual basis. However, accounting for such items on a cash basis is presented here for purposes of contrast.

Under the cash basis of accounting, it is almost correct to say that the method of handling accrued expenses is not a method of accounting at all. This is because under the cash basis of accounting all accrued expenses are ignored until they are paid. To illustrate, if the fiscal year of Beta Company ends on December 31, 1959, the eighteen days, or $36, of accrued interest expense on the $18,000 note previously described is rightfully an expense of the year ending on that date. This is because the year ending on December 31, 1959, received eighteen days' benefit from the use of the borrowed money. However, under the cash basis of accounting this is ignored. Under the cash basis of accounting all of the interest expense on this note is ignored until February 11, 1960, when both the note and interest are due. On that date the eighteen days of 1959 interest is added to the forty-two days of 1960 interest expense, and both are paid without any distinction being made between the two. When the note and interest are paid, the entry to record the payment under the cash basis of accounting is:

Feb.	11	Notes Payable........................	18,000.00	
		Interest Expense.....................	120.00	
		Cash............................		18,120.00
		Paid our $18,000, sixty-day, 4 per cent note.		

The $18,000 debit of this entry to the Notes Payable account records the payment of the note. The debit of $120 to the Interest Expense account records the payment of sixty days' interest expense. Since, under the cash basis, no notice is taken of accrued interest at the end of an accounting period, this debit records both the $36 of interest incurred in 1959 and the $84 of 1960 interest as an expense of 1960. Obviously this places an unfair burden on the 1960 accounting period.

Since, at the end of each accounting period, the cash basis of accounting ignores all accrued and deferred items, the remainder of this chapter is devoted to accounting for such items under the accrual basis.

Accrued Interest Expense, Accrual Basis. Although accrued expenses such as accrued interest are ignored under the cash basis of accounting, they are not ignored under the accrual basis. Under the accrual basis, all accrued expenses such as accrued interest, accrued taxes, and accrued wages are recorded at the end of each accounting period by means of adjusting entries. As a result these accrued items are shown as expenses of the accounting period which receives their benefit rather than as expenses of the accounting period in which they are paid.

To illustrate the accrual basis of accounting for accrued expenses such as accrued interest, assume that on December 20, 1959, the Ajax Company borrows $6,000 from a bank by giving its sixty-day, 6 per cent, interest-bearing note. When the accounting period of the Ajax Company ends on December 31, eleven days, or $11, of interest expense has accrued on this note. Under the accrual basis of accounting this accrued interest is recorded with the following adjusting entry:

Dec.	31	Interest Expense............................	11.00	
		Accrued Interest Payable............		11.00
		To record the accrued interest on a note payable.		

The debit of this entry to the Interest Expense account causes the eleven days of accrued interest to appear as an expense on the income statement of the accounting period ending on December 31, 1959. The credit of the entry causes the $11 of accrued interest payable to appear as a liability on the balance sheet of that date. After the adjusting entry recording the accrued interest expense is posted, the Interest Expense account and the Accrued Interest Payable account appear as follows:

INTEREST EXPENSE

Date		Explanation	F	Debit	Date	Explanation	F	Credit
Dec.	31	(Adjusting)		11.00				

ACCRUED INTEREST PAYABLE

Date	Explanation	F	Debit	Date		Explanation	F	Credit
				Dec.	31	(Adjusting)		11.00

After the December 31, 1959, statements are prepared, the Interest Expense account is closed in the usual manner. The closing entry to accomplish this is:

Dec.	31	Income Summary........................	11.00	
		Interest Expense....................		11.00
		To close the Interest Expense account.		

After this entry is posted, the Interest Expense account and the Interest Payable account appear as follows:

INTEREST EXPENSE

Date		Explanation	F	Debit	Date		Explanation	F	Credit
Dec.	31	(Adjusting)		11.00	Dec.	31	(Closing)		11.00

ACCRUED INTEREST PAYABLE

Date		Explanation	F	Debit	Date		Explanation	F	Credit
					Dec.	31	(Adjusting)		11.00

Observe that the Interest Expense account is closed and in balance but that the closing entry did not affect the Accrued Interest Payable account. The Accrued Interest Payable account still shows the liability for the $11 of accrued interest.

On February 18, 1960, the Ajax Company's $6,000, sixty-day, 6 per cent note of the previous illustrations becomes due. When it is paid, the company delivers a check for $6,060 to the bank. This pays the note and the sixty days of interest. The sixty days of interest include both the eleven days of 1959 interest and the 1960 interest. In recording the payment of the note and interest, the bookkeeper of the Ajax Company must remember that the eleven days, or $11, of 1959 accrued interest on this note was recorded on December 31, 1959. He must remember to divide the $60 payment for interest between current 1960 interest expense and the 1959 accrued interest recorded on December 31. As a result of the previously recorded accrued interest, the bookkeeper must record the payment of the note and interest with an entry as follows:

Feb.	18	Notes Payable.........................	6,000.00	
		Interest Expense......................	49.00	
		Accrued Interest Payable..............	11.00	
		Cash.............................		6,060.00
		Paid our sixty-day note.		

After the entry just given is posted, the Interest Expense and Accrued Interest Payable accounts appear as follows:

INTEREST EXPENSE

Date		Explanation	F	Debit	Date		Explanation	F	Credit
Dec.	31	(Adjusting)		11.00	Dec.	31	(Closing)		11.00
Feb.	18	(Payment)		49.00					

ACCRUED INTEREST PAYABLE

Date		Explanation	F	Debit	Date		Explanation	F	Credit
Feb.	18	(Payment)		11.00	Dec.	31	(Adjusting)		11.00

Observe that after the entry recording the payment of the note and interest is posted, the Accrued Interest Payable account is in balance and the Interest Expense account has a debit balance of $49. The $49 debit balance of the Interest Expense account is the 1960 interest expense on the borrowed $6,000.

Accrued Wages. Wages are earned and accrued each day that employees work. However, employees are seldom paid more often than once each week. Consequently, at the end of an accounting period, accrued wages are common. They make an additional good illustration of the accounting for accrued expenses.

For example, assume that the sales employees of Small Supply Company earn a total of $100 a day and that they work six days each week. Assume further that the employees are paid on a weekly basis and that the pay period ends on Saturday. Under these assumptions, Small Supply Company makes an entry as follows to record the payment of each full week's sales salaries:

Oct.	28	Sales Salaries Expense................	600.00	
		Cash............................		600.00
		Sales salaries for week ended October 28.		

If, in order to reduce the number of entries, it is assumed that Small Supply Company operates on the basis of monthly accounting periods, on October 28, after the employees have been paid for the fourth full pay period in the month, the Sales Salaries Expense account appears as follows:

SALES SALARIES EXPENSE

Date		Explanation	F	Debit	Date	Explanation	F	Credit
Oct.	7			600.00				
	14			600.00				
	21			600.00				
	28			600.00				

On Saturday, October 28, the Sales Salaries Expense account shows $2,400 of sales salaries expense. This is the amount of sales salaries paid during the first four weeks of October. However, by Tuesday, October 31, when the accounting period ends, this is no longer the full amount of the October sales salaries expense. By Tuesday, October 31, the employees have worked two additional days, Monday and Tuesday, and have earned two additional days' pay amounting to $200. Of course, they will not be paid for these two days until Saturday, November 4, which is in the next accounting period. However, payment in the next accounting period does not alter the situation. On Tuesday, October 31, Small Supply Company has had the benefit of its employees' services for these two days, and it has a liability to pay them. Consequently, under the accrual basis of accounting, since Small Supply Company has had the benefit of its employees' services for a total of four weeks and two days, it must show as an expense on its income statement the sum of both the $2,400 in wages that have been paid and the $200 of wages earned but unpaid. Likewise, under the accrual basis of accounting, since Small Supply Company has had the benefit of its employees' services on Monday and Tuesday, October 30 and 31, and has a liability to pay its employees for these two days' work, it must show the $200 of accrued wages on its October 31 balance sheet as a current liability. If the $200 of accrued wages are to be shown as a portion of the expenses and as a liability, the following adjusting entry must be made:

Oct.	31	Sales Salaries Expense..................	200.00	
		Accrued Salaries Payable..........		200.00
		To record the unpaid sales salaries of October 31.		

After this entry is posted, the Sales Salaries Expense account and the Accrued Salaries Payable account appear as follows:

SALES SALARIES EXPENSE

Date		Explanation	F	Debit	Date	Explanation	F	Credit
Oct.	7			600.00				
	14			600.00				
	21			600.00				
	28			600.00				
	31	(Adjusting)		200.00				

ACCRUED SALARIES PAYABLE

Date	Explanation	F	Debit	Date		Explanation	F	Credit
				Oct.	31	(Adjusting)		200.00

After the adjustment for accrued salaries is made, the $2,600 balance of the Sales Salaries Expense account appears on the income statement as an expense and the $200 balance of the Accrued Salaries Payable account appears on the balance sheet as a current liability.

Then, after the statements are prepared, the Sales Salaries Expense account is closed with a closing entry similar to the following:

Oct.	31	Income Summary......................	2,600.00	
		Sales Salaries Expense.............		2,600.00
		To close the Sales Salaries Expense account.		

When this closing entry is posted, the Sales Salaries Expense and the Accrued Salaries Payable accounts appear as follows:

SALES SALARIES EXPENSE

Date		Explanation	F	Debit	Date		Explanation	F	Credit
Oct.	7			600.00	Oct.	31	(Closing)		2,600.00
	14			600.00					
	21			600.00					
	28			600.00					
	31	(Adjusting)		200.00					
				2,600.00					2,600.00

ACCRUED SALARIES PAYABLE

Date		Explanation	F	Debit	Date		Explanation	F	Credit
					Oct.	31	(Adjusting)		200.00

After the October closing entries are posted, the Sales Salaries Expense account is closed and in balance. However, the closing entries do not affect the liability account, Accrued Salaries Payable. Consequently, it still shows a liability for the $200 of unpaid wages.

Under the assumptions presented thus far, when the sales salaries are paid on the first Saturday of the new accounting period, Small Supply Company makes the following entry to record the payment:

Nov.	4	Sales Salaries Expense.................	400.00	
		Accrued Salaries Payable..............	200.00	
		Cash...........................		600.00
		Sales salaries for week ended November 4.		

The $400 debit to Sales Salaries Expense records the wages earned during the first four days of the new accounting period. The $200 debit to Accrued

Salaries Payable cancels the liability for the wages earned during the last two days of the accounting period that ended on October 31. The $600 credit to Cash is the amount paid the employees. After this entry is posted, the two accounts appear as follows:

SALES SALARIES EXPENSE

Date		Explanation	F	Debit	Date		Explanation	F	Credit
Oct.	7			600.00	Oct.	31	(Closing)		2,600.00
	14			600.00					
	21			600.00					
	28			600.00					
	31	(Adjusting)		200.00					
				2,600.00					2,600.00
Nov.	4	(Payment)		400.00					

ACCRUED SALARIES PAYABLE

Date		Explanation	F	Debit	Date		Explanation	F	Credit
Nov.	4	(Payment)		200.00	Oct.	31	(Adjusting)		200.00

Reversing Entries

Many common transactions are exactly alike. If errors are to be avoided, a bookkeeper must be alert for the transaction that is similar to a common transaction but for some reason is different. If he is not careful, he will record the similar but different transaction in the same way he records the common transaction. Accrued expenses illustrate this point. Normally the payment of an expense is recorded with a single debit to an expense account. However, the payment of an expense incurred over a period of time extending into two accounting periods may be different. Such an expense is recorded with two debits if the amount of expense applicable to the first period has been recorded as an accrued expense and has not been reversed.

For example, four pay periods out of five the bookkeeper of Small Supply Company records the payment of sales salaries with an entry having a single debit as follows:

Oct.	14	Sales Salaries Expense.................	600.00	
		Cash............................		600.00
		Sales salaries for week ended October 14.		

One pay period out of five the bookkeeper must remember to divide the debit of his payroll entry between the expense for current salaries and the liability for salaries accrued at the end of the previous accounting period. One pay period out of five requires a payroll entry with two debits as follows:

Nov.	4	Sales Salaries Expense...............	400.00	
		Accrued Salaries Payable.............	200.00	
		Cash...........................		600.00
		Sales salaries for week ended November 4.		

Payments for interest offer another illustration of the need for care in recording common transactions. Generally, Interest Expense is debited for the amount of an interest payment. However, when the time of a note extends over two accounting periods, the payment for interest pays both current interest expense and the interest accrued at the end of the previous period. Here the final payment of interest previously recorded as accrued interest may offer a greater opportunity for an error than the payment of accrued salaries. This is because a longer period of time may elapse between the date of accrual and the date of final payment. Here a bookkeeper should be very careful not to record interest applicable to a previous accounting period as current interest expense.

When final payment of an accrued item is made, it is easy to forget to make a division between current expenses and the liability accrued at the end of the previous accounting period. Consequently, many bookkeepers prefer to handle accrued expenses in such a manner that a debit division is unnecessary. These bookkeepers prefer to make a *reversing entry* that eliminates the need of dividing the debit of the entry recording final payment of an accrued expense. This reversing entry reverses the adjusting entry that originally recorded the accrued expense. It is made after the closing entries are recorded and the post-closing trial balance prepared. Usually it is dated the first day of the new accounting period.

The accrued sales salaries of Small Supply Company may be used to illustrate reversing entries. In the Small Supply Company example beginning on page 320, sales salaries of $600 are paid and recorded at the end of each of four weekly pay periods. Then, at the end of the monthly accounting period, the following adjusting entry is made to record two days of accrued salaries:

Oct.	31	Sales Salaries Expense...............	200.00	
		Accrued Salaries Payable..........		200.00
		To record the unpaid sales salaries.		

After this adjusting entry is posted, the Sales Salaries Expense account is closed with a closing entry. After the closing entry is posted, the Sales Salaries Expense account and the Accrued Salaries Payable account of Small Supply Company appear as follows:

SALES SALARIES EXPENSE

Date		Explanation	F	Debit	Date		Explanation	F	Credit
Oct.	7			600.00	Oct.	31	(Closing)		2,600.00
	14			600.00					
	21			600.00					
	28			600.00					
	31	(Adjusting)		200.00					
				2,600.00					2,600.00

ACCRUED SALARIES PAYABLE

Date		Explanation	F	Debit	Date		Explanation	F	Credit
					Oct.	31	(Adjusting)		200.00

Thus far in the illustrated procedure there is nothing new. However, at this point, if the bookkeeper of Small Supply Company wishes to avoid a division of the debit in the entry that records the final payment of the $200 of accrued salaries, he must make the following reversing entry. Notice that the entry is dated the first day of the new accounting period:

Nov.	1	Accrued Salaries Payable..............	200.00	
		Sales Salaries Expense.............		200.00
		To reverse the accrued sales salaries		
		adjusting entry.		

Notice that this reversing entry is debit for credit and credit for debit, the reverse of the adjusting entry that originally recorded the accrued salaries. That is why it is called a "reversing entry." After this reversing entry is posted, the Sales Salaries Expense account and the Accrued Salaries Payable account appear as follows:

SALES SALARIES EXPENSE

Date		Explanation	F	Debit	Date		Explanation	F	Credit
Oct.	7			600.00	Oct.	31	(Closing)		2,600.00
	14			600.00					
	21			600.00					
	28			600.00					
	31	(Adjusting)		200.00					
				2,600.00					2,600.00
					Nov.	1	(Reversing)		200.00

ACCRUED SALARIES PAYABLE

Date		Explanation	F	Debit	Date		Explanation	F	Credit
Nov.	1	(Reversing)		200.00	Oct.	31	(Adjusting)		200.00

Notice that the reversing entry cancels the liability for the accrued salaries and it balances the Accrued Salaries Payable account. Notice that after the reversing entry is posted, the accrued salaries appear as a $200 *credit* in the Sales Salaries Expense account.

After the reversing entry places the accrued salaries in the Sales Salaries Expense account as a $200 credit, the entry that records the payment of both the current salaries and the accrued salaries needs only one debit. It is the common entry that is normally made when salaries are paid and appears in general journal form as follows:

Nov.	4	Sales Salaries Expense.................	600.00	
		Cash...........................		600.00
		Sales salaries for week ended November 4.		

The $600 debit of this November 4 payroll entry records the payment of the $200 of salaries earned in October and the $400 of salaries earned in November. The $200 was an expense of the month of October; the $400 is an expense of November. Yet, the entire $600 is recorded as a debit to the Sales Salaries Expense account. This is because, when the $600 debit is posted to the Sales Salaries Expense account, the $200 credit of the previously posted reversing entry reduces the debit balance of the account to $400. Thus, because of the reversing entry, the account shows only $400 in salaries expense. This is the correct expense for the four days of November. The Sales Salaries Expense account appears as follows after the reversing entry is posted. Note the $400 debit balance.

SALES SALARIES EXPENSE

Date		Explanation	F	Debit	Date		Explanation	F	Credit
Oct.	7			600.00	Oct.	31	(Closing)		2,600.00
	14			600.00					
	21			600.00					
	28			600.00					
	31	(Adjusting)		200.00					
				2,600.00					2,600.00
Nov.	4	(Payment)		600.00	Nov.	1	(Reversing)		200.00

Other Accrued Expenses

At the end of an accounting period, businesses may have other accrued expenses such as accrued advertising or accrued taxes. If the statements prepared at the end of an accounting period are to show all of the expenses and all of the liabilities, adjusting entries recording all of the accrued expenses must be made. The previously illustrated entries for accrued interest and accrued salaries show the proper methods for handling any accrued expense.

Accrued Revenue

Revenue that is earned during one accounting period but that will not be collected until a future accounting period because it is not due is called *accrued revenue*. Obviously, if revenue is actually earned during an accounting period, it is unfair to credit the revenue to a future period simply because it is collected in cash during the future period. The accrual basis of accounting recognizes this and requires that each period be given credit for the revenue actually earned during the period, regardless of when collection takes place.

Accrued Interest Earned. Accrued interest on notes receivable may be used to illustrate accounting for accrued revenue. For example, assume that on December 12, 1959, Gamma Company receives from a customer a $1,500, 6 per cent, thirty-day, interest-bearing note, dated December 11. By December 31, twenty days of interest is earned on this note. Of course, the interest will not be collected until the note is collected on January 10. Nevertheless, twenty days, or $5.00, of interest is earned by December 31 and is revenue of the month of December. Furthermore, if the Gamma Company income statement prepared on December 31 is to show all of the December revenue, this $5.00 of accrued interest must appear as part of the interest earned. Also, if the Gamma Company balance sheet of that date is to show all of the assets, the $5.00 of interest earned on this note must appear as a current asset called "accrued interest receivable." If the revenue and the asset are to be shown, the following adjusting entry must be made:

Dec.	31	Accrued Interest Receivable............	5.00	
		Interest Earned....................		5.00
		To record the accrued interest on a note receivable.		

This adjusting entry causes the $5.00 of accrued interest to appear on the December 31 income statement as part of the interest earned. It also causes the $5.00 of accrued interest to appear on the balance sheet of that date as a current asset. After the statements are prepared, the Interest Earned account is closed in the usual manner. After closing entries are made, the bookkeeper of Gamma Company may or may not choose to record reversing entries. Reversing entries are a matter of bookkeeping convenience. They permit a bookkeeper to forget an accrued item once it is reversed. If reversing entries are not made, the bookkeeper must remember to divide each entry, recording the final payment of a previously accrued item between the amount accrued and the amount applicable to the current period. If a bookkeeper chooses to make reversing entries, he should make reversing entries every period. This is because there is a much greater chance for errors if reversing entries are made one period and omitted the next.

If the bookkeeper of Gamma Company does not choose to make reversing entries, he must remember when the illustrated note and interest are paid to record the $7.50 of interest received with credits to both Interest Earned and Accrued Interest Receivable, as follows:

Jan.	10	Cash...............................	1,507.50	
		Accrued Interest Receivable.........		5.00
		Interest Earned...................		2.50
		Notes Receivable.................		1,500.00
		Note and interest due today.		

If, on the other hand, the bookkeeper of Gamma Company chooses to make reversing entries, he will make the following reversing entry to reverse the accrued interest adjusting entry:

Jan.	1	Interest Earned.......................	5.00	
		Accrued Interest Receivable.........		5.00
		To reverse the accrued interest adjusting entry.		

The reversing entry is made on the first day of the new accounting period. It is debit for credit and credit for debit the reverse of the adjusting entry it reverses. After the reversing entry is posted, the Accrued Interest Receivable and the Interest Earned accounts appear as follows:

ACCRUED INTEREST RECEIVABLE

Date		Explanation	F	Debit	Date		Explanation	F	Credit
Dec.	31	(Adjusting)		5.00	Jan.	1	(Reversing)		5.00

INTEREST EARNED

Date		Explanation	F	Debit	Date		Explanation	F	Credit
Dec.	31	(Closing)		5.00	Dec.	31	(Adjusting)		5.00
Jan.	1	(Reversing)		5.00					

If a reversing entry is made on January 1, the January 10th receipt of cash in payment of the note and interest is recorded with credits to Notes Receivable and Interest Earned only, as follows:

Jan.	10	Cash..	1,507.50	
		Interest Earned.....................		7.50
		Notes Receivable..................		1,500.00
		Notes and interest due today.		

The $7.50 credit to Interest Earned is the sum of the $5.00 of accrued interest earned during December and the $2.50 of interest earned during January. However, when the $7.50 credit is posted, the Interest Earned account shows only a $2.50 credit balance. This is the correct revenue for the month of January. The Interest Earned account shows only the January revenue of $2.50 because of the $5.00 reduction in the account balance caused by the reversing entry.

Prepaid Expenses

The cost of goods and services that have been consumed in the operations of a business are called expenses. The costs of goods and services that were purchased for consumption but that are unconsumed at the end of an accounting period are called *prepaid expenses*. Prepaid expenses are items whose charge to expenses is delayed or put off until they are consumed. Such items are purchased in one accounting period, but they are not entirely used or consumed until a future period. At the end of an accounting period, the unconsumed portions are assets that will become expenses when they are consumed.

Prepaid insurance, prepaid rent, prepaid taxes, prepaid interest, office supplies, store supplies, and factory supplies are examples of prepaid expenses. In accounting for such items, all may be treated in one of two ways. At the time of purchase, all may be recorded as either assets or as expenses. Prepaid insurance will be used in this chapter to illustrate the accounting for all prepaid expenses.

Fire, liability, workmen's compensation, and other types of insurance are paid for in advance. The amount paid for protection is called a *premium*, and premiums paying for protection for from one to five years are normally paid in one amount in advance. At the time of payment, the entire amount of each premium paid is an asset. However, the amount paid may be recorded as an asset or it may be recorded as an expense. It may be recorded either way because day by day as an insurance premium expires, the amount that expires becomes an expense. Normally, if premiums are paid several years in advance, at the end of each accounting period a part of each premium previously paid has become an expense and a part is still an asset. Therefore, regardless of whether a premium was originally recorded as an asset or as an expense, an adjustment must be made to separate the remaining asset and the expense. If a premium was originally recorded as an asset, the adjustment removes from the asset account the amount of the insurance expense. If a premium was originally recorded as an expense, the adjustment removes from the expense account the amount of the premium that is still an asset.

Recording a Prepaid Expense as an Asset. To illustrate the accounting for prepaid expenses such as prepaid insurance, assume that on August 1 a $360, three-year insurance premium is paid. If the payment of the premium is recorded as an asset, the following entry in general journal form is made to record the payment:

Aug.	1	Prepaid Insurance....................	360.00	
		Cash..........................		360.00
		Paid the premium on a three-year insurance policy.		

If the company making this entry operates with yearly accounting periods that end on each December 31, by that date $50 of this $360 insurance premium has expired and the following entry is made to remove from the asset account the $50 of expired insurance:

Dec.	31	Insurance Expense....................	50.00	
		Prepaid Insurance................		50.00
		To record the expired insurance.		

After the entry is posted, the Prepaid Insurance and the Insurance Expense accounts appear as follows:

Prepaid Insurance			Insurance Expense	
(Purchase) 360	(Adjusting)	50	(Adjusting) 50	

At the end of the accounting period, when the statements are prepared, the $310 debit balance of the Prepaid Insurance account appears on the balance sheet as an asset and the $50 balance of the Insurance Expense account appears on the income statement as an expense.

After the statements are prepared, in addition to the adjusting entry that removes the expired insurance from the asset account, the following closing entry is made:

Dec.	31	Income Summary.....................	50.00	
		Insurance Expense................		50.00
		To close the Insurance Expense account.		

After the entry is posted and the accounts are ruled, the Prepaid Insurance account and the Insurance Expense account appear as follows:

Prepaid Insurance				Insurance Expense			
(Purchase)	360	(Adjusting)	50	(Adjusting)	50	(Closing)	50
		Balance	310				
	360		360				
Balance	310						

When the purchase of a prepaid expense is recorded as an asset, a series of adjusting and closing entries similar to these is repeated at the end of each accounting period throughout the life of the prepaid expense.

Recording a Prepaid Expense as an Expense. Although a prepaid expense may be originally recorded as either an asset or as an expense, when a prepaid expense is to be charged to expenses over a number of accounting periods, this text favors the asset method. The asset method is favored because one less journal entry is required each accounting period.

However, although an additional entry is required each accounting period, prepaid expenses may be originally recorded as expenses. For example, if the payment of the $360 insurance premium previously illustrated is recorded as an expense, the following entry in general journal form is made to record the payment:

Aug.	1	Insurance Expense......................	360.00	
		Cash...........................		360.00
		To record the payment of an insurance premium as an expense.		

Then, at the end of the first accounting period, $310 of the balance of the Insurance Expense account is still an asset and only $50 is an expense. Consequently, the following adjusting entry is made:

Dec.	31	Prepaid Insurance....................	310.00	
		Insurance Expense................		310.00
		To remove the prepaid insurance from the expense account.		

This entry removes the $310 of prepaid insurance from the expense account. After it is posted the accounts appear as follows:

Prepaid Insurance			Insurance Expense			
(Adjusting)	310		(Purchase)	360	(Adjusting)	310

After the adjusting entry that removes the prepaid insurance from the Insurance Expense account is posted, the Insurance Expense account with a $360 debit and a $310 credit has a balance of $50. This $50 balance is the expired insurance for the accounting period and is closed to Income Summary with the following entry:

Dec.	31	Income Summary.....................	50.00	
		Insurance Expense................		50.00
		To close the Insurance Expense account.		

After the closing entry is posted and the accounts ruled, the Prepaid Insurance account and the Insurance Expense account appear as follows:

Prepaid Insurance		Insurance Expense			
(Adjusting) 310		(Purchase) 360	(Adjusting) 310		
			(Closing) 50		
		360	360		

At this point the $310 of unexpired insurance is recorded in the Prepaid Insurance account. If it is left in this account, the balance of the accounts are the same as if the purchase of the insurance was originally recorded as an asset. If it is desired to return the unexpired insurance to the Insurance Expense account, an additional entry is required. This entry is a reversing entry; it reverses the adjusting entry that originally removed the unexpired insurance from the Insurance Expense account. This entry is:

Jan.	1	Insurance Expense.....................	310.00	
		Prepaid Insurance................		310.00
		To reverse the unexpired insurance adjusting entry.		

After the reversing entry is posted, the accounts appear as follows:

Prepaid Insurance		Insurance Expense		
(Adjusting) 310	(Reversing) 310	(Purchase) 360	(Adjusting) 310	
			(Closing) 50	
		360	360	
		(Reversing) 310		

The reversing entry returns the remaining $310 of prepaid insurance to the Insurance Expense account.

When a prepaid expense is recorded as an expense, a series of adjusting, closing, and reversing entries similar to these three is made at the end of each accounting period.

Unearned Revenues

Revenue collected in one accounting period that is not earned until a future accounting period is called *unearned revenue*. An unearned revenue item is an item of revenue that is collected in one accounting period but that is not earned until a future accounting period. Unearned revenue items are liabilities until they are earned. Unearned subscriptions or subscriptions collected in advance by a publisher, unearned interest or interest collected in advance by a bank, and unearned rent or rent collected in advance by a landlord are examples of unearned revenues. Such items are received in one accounting period but are not entirely earned until a future accounting period.

For example, a building rents for $100 a month. On September 1, the building owner receives a $600 check from the tenant for six months' rent in advance. On the date of receipt, the entire $600 of unearned rent is a liability to the building owner. On that date the building owner has the liability to furnish the use of the building to the tenant for six months. Day by day as the tenant occupies the building, the liability is discharged and the rent is earned. If the building owner of this illustration operates with annual accounting periods that end on each December 31, by that date $400 of the $600 is earned and should appear on his income statement as revenue earned. The remaining $200 is unearned on that date and should appear on his balance sheet as a current liability.

Like a prepaid expense, the receipt of unearned revenue may be recorded in either of two ways. At the time of receipt, unearned revenue may be recorded as a liability or it may be recorded as revenue. Regardless of whether unearned revenue is recorded as revenue or as a liability, at the end of each accounting period an adjustment is made to separate the unearned liability portion and the earned revenue portion. If unearned revenue is recorded as a liability, the end of the period adjustment removes the earned revenue from the liability account. If unearned revenue is recorded as revenue, the adjustment removes the unearned liability portion from the revenue account. This text favors recording as liabilities all items of unearned revenue that will be earned during a period of time extending over several accounting periods. This is because the liability method requires one less journal entry at the end of each accounting period.

Unearned rent may be used to illustrate the recording of all unearned revenues. For example, assume that on September 1 a landlord receives $600 from a tenant in payment of six months' rent in advance.

Recording Unearned Revenue as a Liability. If the landlord records the unearned rent as a liability, the following entry in general journal form is made to record the receipt:

Sept.	1	Cash..................................	600.00	
		Unearned Rent...................		600.00
		To record the receipt of unearned rent as a liability.		

Recording the receipt in this manner places the entire $600 in a liability account. If the landlord's annual accounting period ends on December 31, when the end of the accounting period is reached, $400 of the $600 has been earned and the following adjusting entry is required to remove the earned rent from the liability account:

Dec.	31	Unearned Rent......................	400.00	
		Rent Earned....................		400.00
		To remove the earned rent from the Unearned Rent account.		

This adjusting entry causes the $400 of rent that was earned during the period to appear on the income statement as revenue. The balance remaining in the Unearned Rent account then appears on the balance sheet as a liability.

After the adjusting entry is posted, the Unearned Rent account and the Rent Earned account appear as follows:

Unearned Rent			**Rent Earned**	
(Adjusting) 400	(Receipt) 600		(Adjusting) 400	

At the end of the accounting period, in addition to the adjusting entry, the following entry to close the Rent Earned account is made:

Dec.	31	Rent Earned.......................	400.00	
		Income Summary................		400.00
		To close the Rent Earned account.		

When an unearned revenue is recorded as a liability, an adjusting entry and a closing entry similar to these two entries are made at the end of each accounting period.

Recording Unearned Revenue as Revenue. If the landlord of the previous illustration records the receipt of the unearned rent as revenue, the following entry in general journal form is made:

Sept.	1	Cash..................................	600.00	
		Rent Earned....................		600.00
		To record the receipt of unearned rent as revenue.		

This entry records the receipt of the entire $600 as revenue. At the end of the accounting period, only $400 of the amount is earned and only $400 should appear on the income statement as revenue. Consequently, the following adjusting entry is made:

Dec.	31	Rent Earned.......................... Unearned Rent.................... To remove the unearned rent from the Rent Earned account.	200.00	200.00

This entry removes from the Rent Earned account the amount that is unearned. After it is posted, the accounts appear as follows:

Unearned Rent			Rent Earned		
(Adjusting)	200	(Adjusting)	200	(Receipt)	600

After the statements are prepared and the adjusting entry is made, the Rent Earned account has a $400 credit balance. This is the rent earned and is closed to Income Summary with the following closing entry:

Dec.	31	Rent Earned.......................... Income Summary.................. To close the Rent Earned account.	400.00	400.00

At this point the $200 of unearned rent is recorded in the Unearned Rent account. If it is left in this account, the balances of the accounts are the same as if the receipt were originally recorded as a liability. If it is desired to return the unearned rent to the Rent Earned account, the following reversing entry is made:

Jan.	1	Unearned Rent........................ Rent Earned...................... To reverse the unearned rent adjusting entry.	200.00	200.00

This reversing entry reverses the adjusting entry that removed the unearned rent from the Rent Earned account. It returns the unearned rent to the revenue account. After it is posted the accounts appear as follows:

Unearned Rent				Rent Earned			
(Reversing)	200	(Adjusting)	200	(Adjusting) (Closing)	200 400	(Receipt)	600
					600	(Reversing)	600 200

When an unearned revenue is recorded as revenue, this series of adjusting, closing, and reversing entries is repeated at the end of each accounting period.

QUESTIONS FOR CLASS DISCUSSION

1. Distinguish between the cash basis of accounting and the accrual basis of accounting. What are the advantages and disadvantages of each?
2. Richard Snyder owns and operates a small weekly newspaper. The paper is operated with yearly accounting periods, and its receipts from subscriptions and advertising are about the same each year. Subscriptions are collected for a full year in advance, and both subscriptions and advertising receipts are considered revenue of the period in which they are collected in cash. Would you advise that Richard Snyder accrue and defer advertising and subscriptions revenue? Why?
3. Define and give an example of: (a) an accrued expense; (b) an accrued revenue; (c) a prepaid expense; and (d) an unearned revenue.
4. What is the difference between an accrued expense and a prepaid expense? An accrued revenue and an unearned revenue?
5. Classify the following items as: (a) a prepaid expense, (b) an accrued expense, (c) an accrued revenue, and (d) an unearned revenue.
   1. Wages paid an employee in advance.
   2. Interest received by a bank on a discounted note.
   3. Subscriptions payments received by a publisher.
   4. Unpaid interest on a note given to the bank.
   5. Unpaid interest on a customer's note.
   6. Insurance premiums received by an insurance company.
6. What is the purpose of: (a) an adjusting entry, (b) a closing entry, (c) a reversing entry, and (d) a correcting entry?
7. The following account is from the ledger of a firm that operates with monthly accounting periods. What is the nature of the entries marked (a), (b), (c), and (d) in the account?

Wages Expense

Jan. 7 (a)	60	Jan. 31 (c)	260
14 (a)	60		
21 (a)	60		
28 (a)	60		
31 (b)	20		
	260		260
		Feb. 1 (d)	20

8. Central Sales Company closes its books annually on each December 31. On December 11 the firm gave its $6,000, sixty-day, 6 per cent note to the bank in order to borrow money. (a) Assume that the firm keeps its books on a cash basis, and give in general journal form the entries that must be made because of this note from the time it is issued until it is paid. (b) Assume that the firm keeps its books on an accrual basis, and give the required entries.
9. The entries marked (a) in the following account resulted from interest payments, and the entries marked (b) and (c) were adjusting entries. What was

the nature of the entry marked (*b*)? The entry marked (*c*)? What was the nature of each of the entries marked (*d*), (*e*), and (*f*)?

Interest Expense

Apr. 17	(*a*)	40	Dec. 31	(*c*)	25
June 12	(*a*)	120	31	(*d*)	197
Dec. 1	(*a*)	50			
Dec. 31	(*b*)	12			
		222			222
Jan. 1	(*e*)	25	Jan. 1	(*f*)	12

10. Give in general journal form the entries to record the following:
   a) Nov. 16   Gave the bank a ninety-day, 4 per cent, $3,000 note.
   b) Dec. 31   Recorded the accrued interest.
   c) Jan.   1   Reversed the accrued interest adjusting entry.
   d) Feb. 14   Paid the note.
   If no reversing entry is made on January 1, what entry is required when the note is paid on February 14?

PROBLEMS

Problem 14–1

On December 31, 1959, at the end of an annual accounting period, the bookkeeper of Central Supply Company assembled the following information to be used in preparing his year-end adjusting entries:

   a) The Store Supplies account of the firm had been debited throughout the year with the cost of store supplies purchased. The year-end balance of the account was $438. An inventory showed that $116 of store supplies were on hand on that date.

   b) On December 11 the company's own sixty-day, 6 per cent, $6,000 note had been given to the bank.

   c) The company's own ninety-day, noninterest bearing, $5,000 note had been discounted at the bank on November 1 at a discount rate of 6 per cent. Interest Expense had been debited for the interest prepaid.

   d) On September 1, as a temporary proposition not expected to last more than six months, space had been rented in Central Supply Company's warehouse to General Wholesale Company. General Wholesale Company paid $1,200, six months' rent, in advance on that date. The Rent Earned account had been credited for the $1,200 received.

   e) John Sparks had been granted an extension on his account on November 25 in exchange for his sixty-day, 6 per cent, $2,000 note of that date.

   f) The warehouse building of the Central Supply Company cost $80,000 and has been depreciated under the assumption that it would have a forty-year life and no salvage value.

   g) On December 31, 1959, wages in the amount of $420 had been earned by the employees but had not been paid because they were not due.

Required:

   1. Prepare the adjusting entries required by this information.
   2. List by letter the entries you think it would be wise to reverse.
   3. Assume that the bookkeeper failed to make the adjustments required by the information given and failed to discover the omissions. State for each

omitted adjustment the effect of its omission on the 1959 net income and on the 1960 net income.

Problem 14–2

Following are seven errors that were made by a bookkeeper at the end of the 1959 accounting period:

1. Failed to record salaries earned but unpaid.
2. Failed to record an item of accrued revenue.
3. Failed to adjust the Interest Earned account to remove therefrom the unearned interest.
4. Failed to record an item of accrued expense.
5. Failed to record depreciation on an item of machinery.
6. The December 31, 1959, merchandise inventory was understated.
7. Failed to adjust the Interest Expense account to remove therefrom the prepaid interest.

Required:

Prepare a columnar form with headings and subheadings like in the following illustration. List each error by number in the column headed "Error Number." Then, under the assumption that none of the errors were discovered during 1960, list the effect of each error on the 1959 and 1960 income statements and on the 1959 balance sheet. In each case tell the effect of the error on the revenues, costs and expenses, net income, assets, liabilities, and proprietorship by writing in the proper column opposite each error the word "over" to indicate an overstatement of the item, "under" to indicate an understatement, and "none" to indicate no effect. For example, the effect of the first error is shown in the illustration.

Error Number	1959 Income Statement			December 31, 1959, Balance Sheet			1960 Income Statement		
	Revenues	Costs and Expenses	Net Income	Assets	Liab.	Prop.	Revenues	Costs and Expenses	Net Income
1	None	Under	Over	None	Under	Over	None	Over	Under

Problem 14–3

On the second Tuesday in July of the current year Northwest Publishing Company began publication of *The Second Tuesday Journal*, a monthly magazine. Cash was received for one-year subscriptions to the magazine as follows:

June	$ 1,800
July	3,600
August	4,200
September	3,900
October	6,300
November	4,500
December	4,800
	$29,100

Delivery of the magazine to a new subscriber was always begun in the month following the receipt of his subscription.

Required:

1. Under the assumption that the subscriptions were credited upon receipt to the Subscriptions Earned account, and that the firm's accounting period ends on December 31, give the required adjusting entry.
2. Give the required adjusting entry under the assumption that the subscriptions were credited upon receipt to the Unearned Subscriptions account.

Problem 14–4

Northwest Sales Company closes its books annually on December 31. On December 31 of the current year a trial balance of their ledger appeared as follows:

NORTHWEST SALES COMPANY

Trial Balance, December 31, 19—

Cash	$ 3,845	
Petty cash	50	
Notes receivable	2,500	
Accounts receivable	5,970	
Allowance for bad debts		$ 185
Merchandise inventory	10,445	
Prepaid insurance	280	
Store supplies	260	
Store equipment	9,435	
Accumulated depreciation, store equipment		1,820
Notes payable		3,500
Accounts payable		2,765
Stanley Sloan, capital		18,175
Stanley Sloan, withdrawals	6,000	
Sales		62,220
Sales returns and allowances	1,220	
Purchases	37,595	
Purchases returns		655
Purchases discounts		750
Sales salaries	6,770	
Rent expense	4,800	
Advertising	790	
Interest earned		125
Interest expense	235	
	$90,195	$90,195

Required:

1. Enter the trial balance in the Trial Balance columns of a ten-column work sheet form (no Cost of Goods Sold columns). Complete the work sheet using the following information:
   a) Allowance for bad debts, an additional 1 per cent of net sales.
   b) Expired insurance, $165.
   c) The inventory of store supplies showed $140 of store supplies on hand. However, when the bookkeeper subtracted this amount from the balance of the Store Supplies account, he recognized that the remainder represented an unusually small amount of store supplies used. Consequently, he investigated and discovered that an invoice for store supplies purchased had been charged in error to the Purchases account.

(d) The amount of the invoice was $230. (Handle the correction as an adjustment before recording the supplies used.)

e) Estimated depreciation of store equipment, $670.

f) Accrued interest on notes receivable, $5.00.

g) Unearned interest that had been collected on notes receivable, $15.

h) Interest prepaid on notes payable, $10.

i) Accrued interest on notes payable, $20.

j) December 31 merchandise inventory, $9,870.

2. Prepare from the work sheet adjusting and closing entries.

CLASS EXERCISES

Exercise 14–1

On November 1, as a short-term proposition, Central Sales rented space in its warehouse to Diamond Wholesale Company for six months. Diamond Wholesale Company paid in advance $600, the rent for the six months. The accounting periods of both firms end on December 31.

Required:

Prepare entries to record the rent receipt or payment and to adjust and close the accounts:

1. Of Central Sales:

   a) First, under the assumption that the receipt was credited to the Rent Earned account.

   b) And then, under the assumption that the receipt was credited to the Unearned Rent account.

2. Of Diamond Wholesale Company:

   a) First, under the assumption that the payment was debited to the Rent Expense account.

   b) And then, under the assumption that the payment was debited to the Prepaid Rent account.

Exercise 14–2

On December 31 of the current year, the following information is available in the accounts and records of an enterprise for use in determining the adjustments at the end of the annual fiscal period:

a) The Store Fixtures account has a balance of $5,200 composed of assets purchased on April 1 of the previous year, $4,000, and assets purchased on June 1 of the current year, $1,200. Depreciation is calculated at 5 per cent per year.

b) It has been determined that $270 of the total accounts receivable, $8,320, are uncollectible and are to be written off. The credit balance of the Allowance for Doubtful Accounts before any adjustments is $435. The allowance is to be adjusted to equal 4 per cent of the balance of accounts receivable after the charge-off.

c) Interest of $32 was prepaid on December 1 on a 120-day note receivable and credited to the account Interest Earned. Only one fourth of this amount has been earned.

d) The asset account, Trucks, has a balance of $5,400 and the account Accumulated Depreciation, Trucks has a credit balance of $540 before adjustment for the current year. The trucks were purchased on July 1 of the previous year.

e) The Interest Expense account includes a charge of $24 for interest prepaid on November 16 on a four months' note payable. There is accrued interest on a bank loan, $10.

 f) All office supplies purchased, $520, have been charged to the Office Supplies Expense account, and it has been found that there is an inventory of office supplies, $80, on hand at the end of the period.

 g) On October 1 of the current year, the company recorded the receipt of five months' rent paid in advance by crediting the account Unearned Rent. The rent is $120 per month.

 h) The building was purchased on May 1 of the current year for $30,000, and it is estimated that at the end of twenty years it will have a scrap value of $8,000.

 i) Accrued salaries are $750.

Required:

1. Prepare the current year's adjusting entries.
2. Indicate by letter which entries it might be wise to reverse.

SUPPLEMENTARY PROBLEMS

Problem 14–A

At the end of his 1959 accounting period, Charles Harris, a realtor and loan broker who has always kept his records and prepared his statements on a cash basis, prepared the following condensed income statement:

CHARLES HARRIS REALTOR

Income Statement for Year Ended December 31, 1959

Revenues	$42,400
Expenses	23,600
Net Income	$18,800

An examination of the accounting records revealed the following amounts of ignored deferred and accrued items at the ends of the 1958 and 1959 accounting periods:

	1958	1959
Prepaid expenses	$1,240	$ 870
Accrued expenses	2,410	3,100
Accrued revenues	1,040	1,230
Unearned revenues	1,780	1,640

Required:

Prepare a new 1959 condensed income statement for Charles Harris as it would appear if his records were kept and his statements were prepared on an accrual basis. Assume that all prepaid and unearned items that were not deferred at the end of 1958 became expenses or were earned during 1959, and that all the ignored 1958 accrued items were either received or paid during 1959.

Problem 14–B

Prepare adjusting, closing, and reversing entries as required for each of the following groups of data:

1. The Store Supplies account was debited throughout the accounting period for all store supplies purchased. On January 31, at the end of the accounting period, the balance of the account was $643. An inventory showed $178 of store supplies on hand on that date.

342 · FUNDAMENTAL ACCOUNTING PRINCIPLES [Ch. 14

2. The balance of the Interest Expense account was $873 at the end of the accounting period on January 31. The following notes payable were outstanding on that date:
   a) A ninety-day, noninterest-bearing, $3,000 note discounted at the bank on December 2 at a discount rate of 6 per cent. The Interest Expense account was debited for the discount.
   b) A sixty-day, 6 per cent, $5,500 note given to the bank on January 7.
3. The balance of the Interest Earned account was $367 on January 31, at the end of the accounting period. The following notes receivable were in the office strongbox on that date:
   a) A sixty-day, 6 per cent, $2,500 note, dated December 14.
   b) A ninety-day, 5 per cent, $3,600 note, dated January 1. Interest was collected in advance on this note and was credited at the time of collection to the Interest Earned account.
4. On January 31, at the end of the accounting period, the Prepaid Rent account had a debit balance of $3,000 and the Rent Expense account had a debit balance of $2,000. An examination of other records indicates that the balance of the Prepaid Rent account represents six months' rent that was prepaid on February 1, at the beginning of the accounting period. The rents for August, September, October, and November were paid on the first day of each of these months and were debited at the time of payment to the Rent Expense account. The rents for December and January were due but had not been paid.
5. At the close of business on January 31, before adjustments, the balance of the Sales Salaries Expense account was $15,200. The five sales employees are paid each Monday at the rate of $10 per day for a six-day week that ended the previous Saturday. The last Saturday in January fell on the 28th. One of the sales employees had had a financial emergency on Tuesday, January 31, and was paid his salary in advance for the week ending on February 4. The Sales Salaries Expense account was debited at the time of the payment for the $60 paid.

Chapter
15

THE VOUCHER SYSTEM FOR CON-TROLLING LIABILITIES

ACCOUNTING has two main uses. First, it is used in recording and reporting business transactions; and, second, it is used in supervising and controlling business operations. The mechanical recording and reporting phase is often emphasized, and little is said of accounting as a tool of management for controlling business operations. Yet, for many accounting students, understanding how accounting aids in controlling business operations is more important than learning to mechanically record transactions.

Accounting Systems

When accounting is approached from the broader viewpoint of management, an accounting system is more than business papers, journals, ledgers, and methods of journalizing and posting. From a broad viewpoint, an accounting system is all of this, plus an organized plan of procedures and practices for completing the various transactions of a business. From a broad viewpoint, the accounting system of a business is: (1) a series of organized procedures and practices for handling or performing each kind or type of transaction completed, (2) a division of the procedures and practices into steps and an assignment of the steps to departments and individuals for performance, (3) a series of business papers to record and report the steps of the procedures as they are performed, (4) a systematic method for collecting the papers prepared, and (5) a set of journals and ledgers together with a system for recording the information of the business papers. Actually, each type of transaction completed by a business is handled or completed in a different manner and requires a different set of business papers. Consequently, a complete accounting system may be thought of as a number of systems, one for each type or kind of transaction completed. For example, the complete accounting system of a store may be thought of as a system for handling cash receipts (see Chapter 10), another system for handling charge sales (see Chapter 7), a third system for handling petty cash (see Chapter 10), and so on. Of course, although a complete accounting system may be thought of as a number of systems, a complete accounting system makes use of but a single set of journals and ledgers.

Accounting systems vary from company to company. This is to be expected; the needs of different companies vary. All companies do not complete the same transactions; and, more important, all companies are not the same size. The size of a company has much to do with the design of its over-all accounting system. As long as a business is relatively small, the owner or manager can keep in close touch with all phases of its operations. His close association enables him to know the general condition of the business at all times and to exercise close control over its operations. In a small business, the accounting system may safely place its emphasis on the mechanical recording and reporting of transactions. Here, because of the personal contact of the owner or manager, supervision and control through accounting is not as important as in a large business. In a large business, duties and responsibilities are divided and delegated to a number of employees. With a division of duties and responsibilities, there is greater need for co-ordination and control. Consequently, the accounting system of a large business must emphasize control of transactions as well as mechanical recording and reporting.

This difference in emphasis is illustrated in the incurrence and payment of liabilities. In a small business the owner or manager is closely associated with all phases of the operations of his business. He often makes all purchases of goods and services, hires and closely supervises all employees, and personally negotiates all contracts. He normally signs all checks; and as he signs each check he knows from personal contact and observation that the assets, goods, or services for which the check pays were actually received by his business. This personal contact is not possible in a large business. In a large business several department heads or individuals are delegated the duty of requesting the purchase of assets or merchandise. The purchases are made by a purchasing department, and the goods are received by a receiving department from which they are forwarded on to the original requisitioning department. Likewise, the employees of a large business are hired by a personnel department, their working time recorded by a timekeeping department, and their pay calculated by a payroll department. Also, in a large business several executives may have the power to negotiate special contracts that result in liabilities. Finally, in a large business the checks in payment of the liabilities incurred by all of these departments and individuals are signed by a company treasurer or other disbursing officer. This company treasurer or other disbursing officer cannot possibly know from personal contact and observation that the assets, goods, or services for which the checks pay were received or if the items should have been purchased in the first place. If he cannot depend upon personal contact to tell him that each obligation is a proper obligation and should be paid, he must depend upon a system of internal control. In most large companies the system of internal control upon which the person who signs checks must depend is a *voucher system*.

The Voucher System

A voucher system is an accounting system for controlling the incurrence and payment of all obligations that require the disbursement of cash. Obligations that require the disbursement of cash normally arise from the purchase of the following:

Merchandise, Materials, and Supplies. A merchandising concern buys merchandise and sells it without modification; a factory buys materials and manufactures these materials into a salable product; both use supplies in their operations. In large enterprises these items are normally purchased through a purchasing department as outlined in Chapter 7.

Fixed Assets for Use in the Business. Every business uses such items as machinery, office equipment, land, and buildings. Small assets for use in the business are normally purchased through the purchasing department in the same manner as merchandise or supplies. Large assets often require special contracts that are negotiated by responsible officials of the company.

Services. All companies buy the services of their employees as well as services from outside tradesmen and professional people. In addition, all companies purchase such items as telephone, electricity, and water. In the accounting systems illustrated thus far, these service items have been handled as cash transactions. Under the voucher system, transactions that require the immediate disbursement of cash, so-called cash transactions, are recorded in the same manner as transactions requiring a later disbursement. Both are first recorded as liabilities. Then, those requiring immediate payment are paid at once, and the others are filed for later payment.

The voucher system aids in controlling the incurrence and payment of obligations arising from the purchase of items such as the ones just listed by providing a system:

1. That permits only selected departments and individuals to incur obligations, limits the type or kind of obligation that each may incur, and outlines the procedure to be followed in incurring each type or kind of obligation.
2. That requires the verification and approval for payment of all obligations at the time of their incurrence regardless of when payment is made, the verification and approval to be made by the department or individual responsible for incurring the obligation.
3. That requires the recording of all verified and approved obligations as liabilities at the time each is incurred. Each verified and approved obligation is recorded as a liability regardless of whether payment is made at once or at a later date.
4. That permits checks to be issued only in the payment of properly verified, approved, and recorded obligations.

The Voucher

The business paper around which the voucher system is organized is called a *voucher*. The dictionary defines the word "voucher" as a paper that certifies to the truthfulness of something. This is a satisfactory accounting definition of the term. In accounting, a voucher is a paper on which persons certify by their signatures the truthfulness of the facts stated thereon. It is a business form on which a transaction is summarized, its correctness certified, and its recording and payment approved.

Vouchers vary somewhat from company to company. In general, they are so designed that the invoice, bill, or other documents from which they are prepared are attached to and folded inside the voucher. This makes for ease in filing. The inside of a voucher, shown in Illustration 78, usually provides a space for (1) the date of the voucher, (2) the name of the payee and his address, (3) a brief summary of the transaction, and (4) the signatures of the persons verifying the transaction and approving it for recording and payment. The outside of the voucher usually shows a list of accounts commonly debited and provides a space for the amount of the debits and the amount of the credit to vouchers payable. It also provides

Illustration 78—Inside of a Voucher

VOUCHER NO.
767

VALLEY SUPPLY COMPANY
EUGENE, OREGON

DATE Oct. 1, 19 ___

PAY TO A. B. Seay Wholesale Company

CITY Salem STATE Oregon

FOR THE FOLLOWING: *(ATTACH ALL INVOICES AND SUPPORTING PAPERS)*

DATE OF INVOICE	TERMS	INVOICE NUMBER AND OTHER DETAILS	AMOUNT
Sept. 30, 19___	2/10,n/60	Invoice No. C-11756	800.00
		Less Discount	16.00
		Net Amount Payable	784.00

ACCOUNTING DISTRIBUTION AND RECORDING APPROVED

PAYMENT APPROVED

W. O. Jones

Chief Accounting Clerk

N. O. Neal

Treasurer

a space for (1) the due date of the voucher, (2) the payee, (3) a summary of the payment, (4) the date of payment, and (5) the paying check number. All of the information entered on the voucher, excepting the date of payment and the number of the paying check, is entered at the time the voucher is prepared. The information as to payment is written in later when the voucher is actually paid. The outside of a voucher is shown in Illustration 79.

Incurring, Recording, and Paying Obligations

When a voucher system is in use, control of liabilities begins with the incurrence of each obligation. Only specified people or departments are authorized to incur obligations, and the kind of obligation that each may incur is limited. For example, only the purchasing department may incur

Illustration 79—Outside of a Voucher

Voucher No.
767

ACCOUNTING DISTRIBUTION

Account Debited	Amount
Purchases	800.00
Freight-In	
Store Supplies	
Office Supplies	
Sales Salaries	
Office Salaries	
Delivery Salaries	
Advertising Expense	
Total Vouch. Pay. Cr.	800.00

Due Date   *October 10, 19___*

Pay to   *A. B. Seay Wholesale Co.*
City   *Salem*
State   *Oregon*

Summary of Charges:
    Total Charges_____ 800.00
    Discount_____ 16.00
    Net Payment_____ 784.00

Record of Payment:
    Paid_____
    Check No._____

obligations by purchasing merchandise, small assets, or supplies. Likewise, only the personnel, timekeeping, and payroll departments working together with the production departments may incur obligations for ordinary wages and salaries. Not only is the incurrence of each type of obligation assigned to a certain department or individual but also in each case the method to be followed in its incurrence is fixed. The method of incurrence is always planned in such a way that the transaction is controlled and that business papers are produced at each step to verify the transaction.

A final business paper called a "voucher" is then prepared, and copies of all the business papers produced at each step are attached to it and sent to the person responsible for payments. Here the voucher and the attached supporting papers tell the person responsible for payments that the transaction was a proper transaction, properly incurred, and should be paid.

An obligation incurred through the purchase of merchandise may be used to illustrate the operation of the voucher system. In the discussion of the control of purchases in Chapter 7 it was shown how the manager of a selling department desiring the purchase of merchandise completes a purchase requisition and sends it to the purchasing department. The purchasing department issues a purchase order to the proper vendor who ships the merchandise to the purchaser's receiving department and mails an invoice to the purchasing department. The receiving department counts and examines the merchandise and reports to the purchasing department on a receiving report. The purchasing department then has in its possession:

1. A copy of the requisition listing the items requested by the requisitioning department.
2. A purchase order listing the merchandise ordered.
3. An invoice showing the quantity, description, unit price and total of the goods shipped by the seller.
4. A receiving report listing the quantity and condition of the items received.

With the information contained on these business papers, the purchasing department is in a position to approve the invoice for entry on the books and ultimate payment. In approving the invoice, the purchasing department checks and compares the information on all of these papers. To facilitate the checking procedure, an invoice approval form is normally completed by the purchasing department. The invoice approval form provides a place for recording each step in the checking procedure and a place for recording a final approval of the purchase. After the invoice is checked and approved, the purchase requisition, purchase order, receiving report, and invoice approval form are attached to the invoice. All of the papers are then sent to the accounting department.

In the accounting department, the invoice and its attached supporting papers are used in the preparation of a voucher. This is a simple task demanding only that a clerk type the required information in the proper blanks on a voucher form. The information is taken from the invoice and its attached supporting documents. After the voucher is completed, the invoice and all of its supporting documents are attached to and folded inside the voucher. The voucher is then sent to the desk of the chief clerk or chief bookkeeper who makes an additional check of the voucher and its supporting papers. He then approves the accounting distribution of the voucher and approves the voucher for recording. The voucher is then recorded in the Voucher Register.

From this point, the treatment of vouchers for so-called cash transactions and the treatment of vouchers for credit transactions differ. If a voucher calls for immediate payment, a so-called cash transaction, after it is recorded in the Voucher Register, it is sent directly to the office of the company treasurer or disbursing officer for payment. If the voucher is to be paid at a later date, after it is recorded in the Voucher Register, it is filed in an unpaid voucher file until the date of payment. On the date of payment, the unpaid voucher is then taken from the files and sent to the office of the disbursing officer for payment.

Vouchers and the obligation they represent receive their final approval and checks are written for their payment in the office of the company treasurer or other disbursing officer. Here the person responsible for paying obligations bases the issuance of each check upon a voucher and its supporting papers. A voucher and its supporting papers tell the person responsible for issuing checks whether an obligation is a proper obligation and should be paid.

After payment is made, the paid voucher is filed in a permanent, paid voucher file. Normally paid vouchers are filed in the paid vouchers file in numerical order. This aids in locating any paid voucher.

The Voucher Register

In a sense the Voucher Register is an expanded purchase journal. It is an expanded journal because all purchases, with the exception of purchases in which a note is given in direct settlement, whether cash or open account, whether purchases of merchandise, assets, or services, are recorded therein. As an expanded purchases journal, when the voucher system is in use, it replaces the purchases journals illustrated thus far.

Every voucher is entered in the Voucher Register as soon as it is prepared and approved. Vouchers should always be prenumbered and entered in numerical order. If a voucher is spoiled in preparation, it should be marked void and entered without dollar amounts in its proper numerical order. In such cases the words "void" or "spoiled" are written in the register column provided for the creditor's name. Prenumbering vouchers and recording each voucher in numerical order helps eliminate unrecorded vouchers.

The exact form of the Voucher Register varies somewhat from company to company. In general, a Voucher Register provides columns for the date, the name of the creditor, the voucher number, and a record of voucher payments. In addition, a Voucher Register always has one Vouchers Payable credit column and a number of debit columns. Only one Vouchers Payable credit column is needed because every voucher recorded in the register is a credit to Vouchers Payable. The exact debit columns vary from company to company. In merchandising companies a debit column is always provided for recording purchases of merchandise; and in all companies, so long as space is available, in order that posting labor may be saved by posting column totals, special debit columns are provided for recording each type of expense that occurs sufficiently often to warrant a special column. In addition, a Sundry Accounts debit column is provided for those debits that do not occur often.

All of the information about each voucher that is entered in the register columns, with the exception of that entered in the columns used in recording the voucher's payment, is entered as soon as each voucher is approved for recording. The information as to the date of payment and the number of the paying check is entered later as each voucher is paid.

Sometimes a company, such as the company whose Voucher Register is shown in Illustration 80, places its expense accounts in subsidiary expense

Illustration 80

Page 32   **VOUCHER**

Date	Voucher No.	Payee	When and How Paid Date	Check No.	Vouchers Payable Credit	Pur- chases Debit	Freight- In Debit	
19— Oct. 1	767	A. B. Seay Co.	10/9	753	800 00	800 00		1
1	768	Daily Sentinel	10/9	754	53 00			2
2	769	Seaboard Supply Co.	10/12	756	235 00	155 00	10 00	3
4	770	Spoiled Voucher						4
6	771	George Smith	10/6	734	65 00			5
6	772	Frank Jones	10/6	735	62 00			6
6	773	George Roth	10/6	736	70 00			7
30	998	First National Bank	10/30	972	505 00			33
								34
30	999	Petty Cash	10/30	973	18 00	7 00	5 50	35
31	1000	Tarbell Wholesale Co.	Return—	GJ 38	235 00	235 00		36
31	1001	Office Equipment Co.	10/31	974	195 00			37
					5,079 00	2,435 00	156 00	38
					(213)	(511)	(514)	39
								40
								41

ledgers and maintains only expense controlling accounts in its General Ledger. When this is done, the usual controlling-account-subsidiary-ledger technique of posting column totals to the controlling accounts and posting the individual amounts from the columns to the subsidiary expense ledgers is followed.

If individual amounts are to be posted from voucher register expense columns such as those shown in Illustration 80, it is necessary to indicate in the Voucher Register at the time each expense voucher is recorded, the subsidiary ledger expense account to which the amount of the voucher is to be posted. The subsidiary ledger expense account to which an amount is to be posted could be indicated by placing the name of the account in an account name column. However, often there is not sufficient room for such a column; and, as in Illustration 80, the individual subsidiary ledger expense accounts to which amounts are to be posted are indicated by using account identifying code numbers. (It might be wise at this time for the student to review the discussion of account identifying code numbers on pages 194 and 195.) When an account identifying code number is used in the place of a name to identify the subsidiary ledger expense account to which an amount is to be posted, the code number is entered in the "Acct. Code" column at the time the amount is recorded.

A Voucher Register such as that shown in Illustration 80 is posted as follows. At the end of each month the columns are totaled and are then crossfooted to prove the equality of the recorded debits and credits. After

Illustration 80—Continued

REGISTER   Page 32

	Selling Expenses, Controlling Dr.			General Expenses Controlling Dr.			Sundry Accounts Debit		
	Acct. Code	Fo-lio	Amount Debit	Acct. Code	Fo-lio	Amount Debit	Account Name	Fo-lio	Amount Debit
1									
2	612	√	53 00						
3							Store Supplies	117	70 00
4									
5				651	√	65 00			
6	611	√	62 00						
7	611	√	70 00						
33							Notes Payable	211	500 00
34							Interest Expense	721	5 00
35							Office Supplies	118	5 50
36									
37							Office Equipment	134	195 00
38			837 00			716 00			935 00
39			(600)			(650)			(√)
40									
41									

this, the total of the Vouchers Payable column is posted to the credit side of the Vouchers Payable account, the total of the Purchases column is posted to the debit side of the Purchases account, and the total of the Freight-In column is debited to the Freight-In account. The individual amounts in these columns are not posted.

The totals of the Selling Expense and the General Expense columns are posted to the debit sides of these general ledger controlling accounts; and the individual amounts entered in the columns are debited to the subsidiary expense ledger accounts indicated by the account identifying code numbers in the "Acct. Code" columns.

The individual amounts in the Sundry Accounts column are debited to the accounts named; and the column total is not posted. If Voucher Register space is limited, account code numbers and an account code number column may be used in this section instead of account names and an Account Name column.

Although no amounts need be posted daily from the Voucher Register, the individual amounts in the Selling Expense, General Expense, and Sundry Accounts columns may be posted daily if the bookkeeper so wishes.

Filing Unpaid Vouchers

When a voucher system is in use, all purchases, both cash and credit, are recorded in the Voucher Register. Until after they are recorded in the Voucher Register, purchases requiring an immediate disbursement of cash, so-called cash transactions, are treated in the same manner as credit transactions. However, after recording is completed, their treatment differs. The difference in treatment, as previously explained, has to do with filing and payment. On one hand, a voucher for a transaction requiring an immediate disbursement is forwarded at once to the office of the treasurer or other disbursing officer for final approval and payment. On the other hand, a voucher for a credit transaction is filed in an *unpaid vouchers file* until due. On its due date, it is then taken from the unpaid vouchers file and forwarded for approval and payment.

An unpaid voucher may be filed under the date on which it will be paid, or it may be filed alphabetically under the name of the creditor. Each method has its advantages.

Generally unpaid vouchers are filed under the dates on which they will be paid. This method of filing aids in taking cash discounts because it automatically brings a voucher to the attention of the disbursing officer on its due date. Under this system a discount is never missed because of a voucher's due date being overlooked. In addition, filing vouchers by due dates aids in financial management. When vouchers are filed in this manner, it is easy for the person responsible for paying obligations to determine the total amount of obligations maturing in a short future period of time. This in turn aids in forecasting short-term cash needs. Filing vouchers by due dates has one disadvantage. Under this system it is difficult to locate a particular unpaid voucher.

Filing unpaid vouchers alphabetically under the names of each of the creditors aids in locating individual vouchers. It also makes it easier to know the total amount owed to each creditor. When vouchers are filed alphabetically by creditors, a supplementary record must be maintained to tell which vouchers are due each day. This supplementary record is often a file called a *tickler file*. A tickler file for unpaid vouchers is a file with a card for each day of the month. Individual vouchers are listed by creditors' names on the file card of their due date. The person responsible for paying vouchers must examine the tickler file each day to determine the vouchers due that day. He then removes these vouchers from the alphabetical file for payment.

All the advantages of both methods of filing without the undue complication of a tickler file may be obtained by making a carbon copy of each voucher as it is prepared. The original copies are then filed in the unpaid vouchers file by due dates and are used in making payments. After payment, the original copies are filed numerically in the paid vouchers file. The carbon copies are filed in a permanent file, alphabetically by creditors. Here they become a permanent record of purchases from each creditor.

Nature of the Unpaid Voucher File

When a voucher system is installed, the Voucher Register takes the place of the Purchases Journal. In addition, the Vouchers Payable account and the file of unpaid vouchers are substituted for the Accounts Payable controlling account and the subsidiary Accounts Payable Ledger. In effect the file of unpaid vouchers is a subsidiary ledger of creditors' accounts. Likewise, the Vouchers Payable account in the General Ledger is in effect a controlling account that controls both the unpaid vouchers file and the vouchers listed as unpaid in the Voucher Register.

All vouchers are entered in the Voucher Register and result in a credit to the Vouchers Payable account. Too, all vouchers are either paid at once or are filed in the unpaid vouchers file until they are paid. As each unpaid voucher becomes due, it is removed from the unpaid vouchers file and paid. It is then filed in a paid vouchers file. Checks drawn and entered in the Check Register in payment of vouchers result in a debit to the Vouchers Payable account. Consequently, when both the Voucher Register and the Check Register are posted, the balance of the Vouchers Payable account should equal the sum of the unpaid vouchers in the unpaid vouchers file.

This equality is verified after posting is completed each month by adding the amounts of the unpaid vouchers in the unpaid vouchers file and comparing the sum with the balance of the Vouchers Payable account. Likewise, the unpaid vouchers in the unpaid vouchers file are compared with the unpaid vouchers as shown in the record of payments column of the Voucher Register. Since the number of each paying check and the date of payment are entered in the payments column of the Voucher Register as each voucher is paid, the vouchers in the Voucher Register without check numbers and dates of payment should be the same vouchers as those in the unpaid vouchers file.

The Voucher System Check Register

Under the voucher system of controlling the incurrence and payment of obligations, no obligation is paid until a voucher is prepared and recorded. Furthermore, no check is drawn except in the payment of a specific voucher. As a result of these control procedures the Check Register used in a voucher system is materially simplified. Since checks are written only in payment of vouchers, all checks result in debits to Vouchers Payable and credits to Cash or to the bank. If the terms of an invoice being paid provide for a discount, there is an additional credit to discounts on purchases. Consequently, a voucher system Check Register needs only three money columns. It needs money columns for debits to Vouchers Payable, credits to Purchases Discounts, and credits to Cash or to the bank. Such a Check Register is shown in Illustration 81.

Illustration 81—The Voucher System Check Register

CHECK REGISTER

Date		Payee	Voucher No.	Check No.	Vouchers Payable Debit	Pur- chases Dis- counts Credit	Mer- chants National Bank Credit
19—							
Oct.	1	C. B. & Y. RR Co.	765	728	14.00		14.00
	3	Frank Mills	766	729	73.00		73.00
	3	Ajax Wholesale Co.	753	730	250.00	5.00	245.00
	4	Normal Supply Co.	747	731	100.00	2.00	98.00
	5	Thomas McGinnin	763	732	43.00		43.00
	6	Giant Equipment Co.	759	733	342.00		342.00
	6	George Smith	771	734	65.00		65.00
	6	Frank Jones	772	735	62.00		62.00
	30	First National Bank	998	972	505.00		505.00
	30	Petty Cash	999	973	18.00		18.00
	31	Office Equipment Co.	1001	974	195.00		195.00
					6,468.00	28.00	6,440.00
					(213)	(512)	(111)

Not only is the design of a Check Register used with a voucher system simplified, its posting is also easier. No amounts are posted individually; all amounts are posted in the column totals at the end of the month. In posting the Check Register used with a voucher system, the total of the Vouchers Payable debit column is posted to the debit side of the Vouchers Payable account. The total of the Purchases Discounts credit column is posted to the credit of the Purchases Discounts account, and the total of the Cash credit column is posted to the Cash account.

Recording Invoices at Their Net Amounts

Thus far in this text the illustrated method for handling invoices subject to cash discounts has been to enter all such invoices in the Purchases Journal, Voucher Register, or other book of original entry at their gross amounts and to record at the time of payment any discounts taken. This is a satisfactory procedure and is commonly used. However, companies that follow the practice of taking all offered discounts also commonly use a different procedure under which invoices are recorded upon receipt at their net amounts and any discounts not taken are recorded at the time of payment as discounts lost. Actually, under this system discounts taken are not formally recorded; but discounts missed are recorded as discounts lost. For example, if a company that records invoices at their net amounts purchases $1,000 of merchandise subject to terms of 2/10, n/30, the purchase is recorded in the company's Voucher Register with debits and credits as follows:

Dec.	17	Purchases...........................	980.00	
		Vouchers Payable..................		980.00
		Purchased $1,000 of merchandise subject to terms of 2/10, n/30.		

If the voucher for this purchase is paid within the discount period (all vouchers should be so paid), the check register entry recording the payment has a debit to Vouchers Payable and a credit to Cash or bank for $980. However, if payment is not made within the discount period and the discount is lost, an entry like the following must be made in the General Journal when the voucher is paid:

Jan.	15	Discounts Lost......................	20.00	
		Vouchers Payable..................		20.00
		To record a discount lost.		

In addition to the general journal entry, a notation in regard to the entry is placed in the When and How Paid column of the Voucher Register. The notation commonly reads "See General Journal, p. 35," or something of a similar nature. The reference makes it easy for a person examining the records to trace the entire transaction. Also, in addition to the journal entry and the voucher register notation, a notation as to the discount lost is placed on the voucher and a check for the full $1,000 amount of the invoice is drawn in its payment and entered in the Check Register.

When discounts are lost, the balance of the Discounts Lost account appears on the income statement as an expense and an indication of poor financial management.

The Voucher System and the Petty Cash Fund

Obviously a petty cash fund must be maintained when a voucher system is in use. This is because the issuance of a check under the voucher system is even more difficult, time consuming, and expensive than when a Cash Payments Journal or ordinary Check Register are in use. Fortunately, the voucher system does not materially affect the operation of the petty cash fund. (At this point it might be wise for the student to review the material of Chapter 10 in which the operation of the petty cash fund is explained.) If a petty cash fund is started after a voucher system is in operation, a voucher debiting Petty Cash is prepared and recorded. A check is then drawn and cashed in its payment, and the proceeds are turned over to the petty cashier. The fund then operates in the usual manner until it must be replenished. When the petty cash fund is replenished, a voucher is prepared for the amount of the replenishing check. The debits listed on the voucher are obtained in the usual manner from the petty cash receipts that were secured at the time each petty cash disbursement was made. These receipts are canceled by stamping or punching and are attached to the voucher. After the replenishing voucher is approved, a check is drawn in its payment and is cashed. The proceeds of the check are given to the petty cashier, and the fund is ready to begin anew the cycle of its operations.

Uncommon Voucher Transactions

The voucher system provides a more or less inflexible routine of procedures for handling obligations that result in the disbursement of cash. These inflexible procedures are designed to gain control over such transactions. As long as disbursement transactions follow the normal pattern, their handling and recording is a matter of routine. However, because of the inflexibility of the voucher system, uncommon transactions such as purchases returns, partial payments, notes payable, and transactions in which an error is made need special attention.

Errors. When a voucher system is in use, the procedures for checking invoices, payrolls, bills, and other data should be such that an undiscovered error is a most uncommon occurrence. Yet, regardless of care, errors will occur. An error involving the amount of a voucher that is discovered before the Voucher Register is posted may be corrected by ruling a single line through the incorrect amount. The correct amount is then written in above on the same line. Care must be exercised to see that the error is corrected both in the Voucher Register and on the voucher. An error in which the wrong account is debited is corrected both in the Voucher Register and on the voucher by ruling out the amount in the wrong column and on the wrong line. The amount is then written in the correct column of the Voucher Register and on the correct line of the voucher. If proper internal control is maintained, voucher corrections must be initialed on the voucher by the persons responsible for the approval of vouchers and their supporting documents.

An error discovered after the Voucher Register is posted must be corrected with a general journal entry. If, for example, the correction of the error decreases the amount of the voucher, the entry is a debit to Vouchers Payable and a credit to the account originally debited. Here again care must be taken to see that the correction is made on the voucher and that it is properly approved. In addition to the approved correction on the voucher, a reference to the general journal entry recording the correction is made in the Voucher Register. This reference is made in the payments column on the upper half of the line on which the corrected voucher is recorded. The reference normally reads "See General Journal, p. 34," or something of a similar nature. The reference makes it easy for a person examining the records to trace the entire transaction and to see that the amount of the general journal entry plus the amount of the paying check equal the amount of the original voucher.

Purchases Returns. A company with a well-organized and properly functioning routine for handling purchases finds most of its errors and makes most of its returns before vouchers are prepared. After all, finding mistakes is one of the reasons for the system. However, occasionally part of a purchase is returned after the voucher recording it is prepared and entered. Sometimes the return is even made after the Voucher Register is posted. In either case a return of merchandise is recorded with a general journal entry similar to the following:

Nov.	5	Vouchers Payable.....................	15.00	
		Purchases........................		15.00
		Credit memo No. 472 for merchandise purchased and entered on Voucher No. 1000.		

The entry is posted to the Vouchers Payable account and to the Purchases account in the General Ledger. In addition, in the payments columns of the Voucher Register, on the upper half of the line for the voucher on which the return is made, a reference is made to the general journal entry recording the return. This is illustrated with Voucher No. 1000 on the next to the last line of the Voucher Register shown in Illustration 80. Also, in addition to the general journal entry and the reference, the amount of the return is deducted on the voucher. The credit memorandum and other documents verifying the return are then attached to the voucher. When the voucher is paid, a check is drawn for the corrected amount shown on the voucher.

Notice that the purchases return recorded with the general journal entry just given is credited directly to the Purchases account. This is optional; a Purchases Returns and Allowances account may be maintained, and purchases returns may be credited to it. However, when a Purchases Returns and Allowances account is maintained, it should be maintained to gather information about all of the purchases returns and allowances. When a voucher system is in use, most errors are found and purchases returns are made before vouchers are prepared and approved. Consequently, in such cases, vouchers are normally prepared for the net amount purchased; and, as a result, each return is deducted from the amount of a purchase before the purchase is recorded. In such cases these returns are not recorded with formal debit and credit entries, and they do not appear in a Purchases Returns and Allowances account. Therefore, since the majority of the returns of a company using a voucher system are not recorded in a Purchases Returns and Allowances account, there is little gained in crediting such an account for those few returns made after vouchers are recorded. Consequently, many companies using a voucher system do not maintain a Purchases Returns and Allowances account. These companies maintain instead a memorandum record of all returns and allowances.

Partial Payments. Sometimes a company in a weak financial position temporarily cannot pay in full all of its obligations as they mature. Often in such cases a company will make partial payments on a number of invoices in order to help maintain its credit standing. The voucher system is not designed to meet easily such a situation. Under the voucher system every voucher is a unit to be paid in full as a unit with one check. If a business must make partial payments on its invoices, some form of records other than vouchers and a Voucher Register will reduce the complications of its accounting.

For example, assume that a company operating a voucher system has recorded a $1,500 obligation with a single voucher. When the obligation becomes due, the company decides to pay the debt in two equal installments. One $750 installment is to be paid at once, and the other is to be paid in thirty days. In such a case, two new vouchers for $750 each are prepared and entered in the Voucher Register. The amount of each voucher is entered in both the Vouchers Payable credit column and in the Sundry Accounts debit columns. In the Sundry Accounts debit columns, the name of the account debited is Vouchers Payable. Consequently, as a result of this recording procedure, the Vouchers Payable account is both debited and credited for the amounts of the new vouchers; and recording the new vouchers does not change either the number of dollars of vouchers payable or the balance of the Vouchers Payable account. In addition to the new vouchers, a reference to the new vouchers is made in the payments column of the Voucher Register on the line of the old voucher. Also the old voucher is marked "canceled," an explanation of the cancellation is written on it, and it is filed in the paid vouchers file. After all of this, the voucher that is to be paid at once is paid. The remaining voucher is filed until it is due.

If the payment of a liability in installments can be anticipated at the time the obligation is incurred, much of the difficulty of partial payments can be avoided. In such cases all that is necessary is the preparation of a number of vouchers, one for each installment.

Notes Payable. If a company borrows funds by giving a note to a bank, the note is recorded in the Cash Receipts Journal as a debit to Cash and a credit to Notes Payable. Likewise, if a company purchases assets and gives a note in payment, the transaction is recorded in the General Journal with a debit to the asset purchased and a credit to Notes Payable. In both cases the debt is represented by a note payable, and in both cases it is improper to classify the obligation as anything other than notes payable. Furthermore, neither transaction should be recorded in the Voucher Register. Recording the transactions in the Voucher Register is improper because all entries in the Voucher Register result in credits to Vouchers Payable. Transactions in which notes are given should result in credits to Notes Payable. However, when a note matures, a voucher for its payment is prepared. A voucher is prepared because no obligation is ever paid without a voucher verifying it as a proper obligation that should be paid. When a voucher prepared for the payment of a note is recorded in the Voucher Register, a debit to Notes Payable and a credit to Vouchers Payable results. The debit to Notes Payable and the credit to Vouchers Payable change the obligation in the accounting records only, from notes payable to vouchers payable. In the accounting records only, the obligation is a voucher payable for the length of time it takes to issue and record a check in payment of the voucher.

A company in a weak financial position may give a note to a creditor to secure an extension of time on an obligation. This situation, like a partial payment, is complicated to handle when a voucher system is in use. If, after a voucher is prepared and recorded, it is decided to secure an extension of time on an obligation by issuing a note, a general journal entry to change the obligation from a voucher payable to a note payable is made. Such an entry is similar to the following:

Nov.	24	Vouchers Payable.....................	700.00	
		Notes Payable....................		700.00
		To change the obligation of Voucher No. 983 to Notes Payable.		

In addition to making the journal entry, a reference to the entry is placed in the payments column of the Voucher Register. Also, the old voucher is marked "canceled," an explanation of the transaction is written on the voucher, and it is filed in the paid vouchers file. When the note becomes due, a new voucher for its payment is prepared and recorded in the Voucher Register. A check is then drawn in payment of the new voucher.

QUESTIONS FOR CLASS DISCUSSION

1. Is a voucher system a complete accounting system that may be used for recording all transactions?
2. What is the purpose of a voucher system?
3. Do all companies need a voucher system?
4. At what approximate point in a company's growth would you recommend that a voucher system be installed?
5. How does a voucher system aid in controlling the incurrence and payment of liabilities?
6. As it is used in a voucher system, what is the purpose of a voucher?

7. What information is usually shown (*a*) on the inside of a voucher, and (*b*) on the outside of a voucher?

8. What business papers in its support may be attached to a voucher for the purchase of merchandise? What does each of the papers tell the person responsible for signing checks?

9. A company using a voucher system prepares purchase requisitions, purchase orders, and receiving reports. Outline the steps that may be followed in this company in purchasing and paying for merchandise bought on account. Begin with the preparation of a purchase requisition and end with the mailing of a check.

10. Outline the steps followed in preparing, recording, and paying a voucher for (*a*) a so-called cash transaction, and (*b*) a so-called credit transaction. How do the steps differ in the two cases?

11. What is an unpaid vouchers file? What is a paid vouchers file?

12. When a company installs a voucher system, it no longer uses an Accounts Payable Ledger. What is substituted in the place of the Accounts Payable Ledger?

13. The Vouchers Payable account may be thought of as a controlling account. If the Vouchers Payable account is thought of as a controlling account, what does it control?

14. When a voucher system is installed, a Purchases Journal as described in previous chapters is no longer used. What is substituted in its place?

15. What effect, if any, does the installation of a voucher system have on the following: (*a*) Cash Receipts Journal, (*b*) Sales Journal, (*c*) Accounts Receivable Ledger, (*d*) Accounts Payable Ledger, (*e*) Check Register, (*f*) Purchases Journal (*g*) General Journal, and (*h*) General Ledger?

16. What is the purpose of a "tickler file" when used in a voucher system?

17. Why is it important that the person responsible for the approval of vouchers be required to initial all error corrections on vouchers?

18. An error in the Voucher Register discovered before the Voucher Register is posted may be corrected by ruling out the wrong account or amount and writing in the correct account or amount. An error in the Voucher Register discovered after the Voucher Register is posted must be corrected with a general journal entry. Why is there a difference?

19. Often a company operating a voucher system credits returns directly to the Purchases account rather than to a Purchases Returns and Allowances account. Why?

20. Would you recommend a voucher system for a firm that must often make partial payments on its invoices because it cannot meet its obligations in full when they are due? Why?

21. How many columns does the Check Register have in a firm that follows the practice of recording invoices at their net amounts?

PROBLEMS

Problem 15–1

The Quick Company uses a voucher system in which it records purchase invoices at their gross amounts. During January of the current year the firm completed, among others, the following transactions:

Jan. 2 Prepared Voucher No. 673 payable to Walker Company for the purchase of merchandise having an invoice price of $1,800, terms thirty days.

2   Prepared Voucher No. 674 payable to Northwest Realty Company for the January rent, $500. (Ten per cent of the rent is chargeable to the office, and the remainder to the store.) Issued Check No. 670 in payment of the voucher.

4   Prepared Voucher No. 675 payable to Pacific Wholesale Company for the purchase of merchandise having an invoice price of $800, terms 2/10, n/30.

8   Prepared Voucher No. 676 for $200 and Voucher No. 677 for $500. Both vouchers were payable to Apex Equipment Company and were for the purchase of a new calculator for use in the office. The terms of the purchase were $200 cash on delivery and $500 in thirty days if the machine proved satisfactory. Issued Check No. 671 in payment of Voucher No. 676.

10   Prepared Voucher No. 678 payable to Store Supply Company for the purchase of store supplies having an invoice price of $125, terms 10 E.O.M.

12   Prepared Voucher No. 679 payable to Pacific Wholesale Company for the purchase of merchandise having an invoice price of $1,250, terms 2/10, n/30.

13   Issued Check No. 672 in payment of Voucher No. 675.

18   Prepared Voucher No. 680 payable to Mary Nance, petty cashier, to reimburse the petty cash fund. Petty cash receipts showed payments for freight-in, $12; store supplies, $7.00; and advertising, $10. Issued Check No. 673 in payment of the voucher.

20   Issued Check No. 674 in payment of Voucher No. 679.

26   Prepared Voucher No. 681 payable to Pioneer Wholesale Company for the purchase of merchandise having an invoice price of $600, terms 2/10, n/30.

31   Walker Company agreed to accept $900 in cash and to grant a thirty-day extension on the balance of Voucher No. 673. Canceled Voucher No. 673, and prepared Vouchers Nos. 682 and 683 for $900 each. Issued Check No. 675 in payment of Voucher No. 682.

31   Prepared Voucher No. 684 payable to Payroll for sales salaries, $800; and office salaries, $300. Issued Check No. 676 in its payment. Cashed the check and paid the employees.

Required:

1. Prepare a Voucher Register and a Check Register similar to the ones shown in Illustrations 80 and 81. Enter the transactions in the registers. Use the following account code numbers:

115	Store Supplies	611	Rent Expense, Selling Space
133	Office Equipment	612	Sales Salaries
212	Vouchers Payable	618	Advertising
511	Purchase	651	Rent Expense, Office Space
512	Freight-In	652	Office Salaries

2. Open a Vouchers Payable account, crossfoot the registers, and post the register totals that affect the Vouchers Payable account.

3. Prepare a schedule of unpaid vouchers.

Problem 15–2

In their voucher system, Oakway Supply Company records at their net amounts all invoices carrying discounts. During a month the firm completed, among others, the following transactions:

Jan. 1 Prepared Voucher No. 956 payable to Gray Enterprises for the January rent, $600. (Charge one twelfth to Rent Expense, Office Space and the remainder to Rent Expense, Selling Space.) Issued Check No. 952 in payment of the Voucher.

1 Prepared Voucher No. 957 payable to Hydraulic Manufacturing Company for the purchase of merchandise having an invoice price of $1,200, terms 2/10, n/30.

1 Borrowed $5,000 from the First National Bank by giving a thirty-day, 6 per cent note. (Normally this transaction would be recorded in the Cash Receipts Journal. To simplify the problem you are asked to record it with a general journal entry.)

5 Prepared Voucher No. 958 payable to Newman Wholesale Company for the purchase of merchandise having an invoice price of $800, terms 2/10, n/60.

8 Prepared Voucher No. 959 payable to General Supply Company for the purchase of store supplies having an invoice price of $450, terms 2/10, n/30.

15 Issued Check No. 953 in payment of Voucher No. 958.

17 Prepared Voucher No. 960 payable to Jane Voss, petty cashier, to reimburse the petty cash fund. The paid vouchers of the petty cash fund showed expenditures of $18 for freight-in, $11 for store supplies, and $10 for advertising expenses. Issued Check No. 954 in payment of the voucher.

18 Discovered that the discount on Voucher No. 957 had been missed because the voucher had been filed in error for payment under a due date of January 18. Added to the voucher the amount of the discount lost, and refiled the voucher for payment on the last day of its credit period, January 31. Made an entry in the General Journal to record the discount lost.

18 Issued Check No. 955 in payment of Voucher No. 959.

20 Prepared Voucher No. 961 payable to Southern Sales Company for the purchase of merchandise having an invoice price of $1,400, terms 2/10, n/30.

23 Prepared Voucher No. 962 payable to North Equipment Company for the purchase of office equipment having an invoice price of $300, terms 10 E.O.M.

25 Prepared Voucher No. 963 payable to Swanson and Son. The invoice attached to the voucher was for $600 of merchandise, F.O.B. factory, terms 2/10, n/30. Swanson and Son had prepaid the freight amounting to $45 and had added it to the invoice which brought the total of the invoice to $645.

30 Issued Check No. 956 in payment of Voucher No. 961.

31 Prepared Voucher No. 964 payable to the First National Bank in payment of the note and interest due this day. Issued Check No. 957 in payment of the voucher.

31 Issued Check No. 958 in payment of Voucher No. 957 as adjusted for the discount lost.

31 Prepared Voucher No. 965 payable to Payroll for sales salaries of $850 and office salaries of $350. Issued Check No. 959 in payment of the voucher. Cashed the check and paid the employees.

Required:

1. Prepare a Voucher Register similar to Illustration 80. Prepare a Check Register similar to Illustration 81 with the exception that only one money column is needed. (Only one money column is needed because discounts

are not recorded in the register; consequently, the amounts debited to Vouchers Payable are the same as the amounts credited to Cash.) Use the following account code numbers:

115 Store Supplies	612 Sales Salaries
133 Office Equipment	618 Advertising
211 Notes Payable	651 Rent Expense, Office Space
212 Vouchers Payable	652 Office Salaries
511 Purchases	711 Interest Expense
512 Freight-In	712 Discounts Lost
611 Rent Expense, Selling Space	

2. Enter the transactions in the registers and, where necessary, in a two-column General Journal. Crossfoot and post the register column totals and the portions of the general journal entries that affect the Vouchers Payable account.
3. Prepare a schedule of unpaid vouchers.

Problem 15–3

Open T-accounts for Cash, Notes Payable, Vouchers Payable, Purchases, and Interest Expense. Prepare and post general journal entries to record the following transactions:

Jan. 1 Gave the First National Bank a thirty-day, 6 per cent, $1,500 note to secure a loan.

      5 Purchased $1,800 worth of merchandise, terms thirty-day, noninterest-bearing trade acceptance. Accepted the trade acceptance.

      7 Prepared and recorded a voucher for the purchase of $800 worth of merchandise, terms 2/10, n/30. (Record the gross amount.)

Jan. 31 Prepared a voucher payable to the First National Bank in payment of the note and interest due today. Issued a check in its payment.

Feb. 4 Received notice that the First National Bank held for collection the trade acceptance accepted by us on January 5. Prepared a voucher and issued a check in payment of the trade acceptance.

Feb. 6 Secured a sixty-day extension on the purchase of January 7 by giving a sixty-day, 6 per cent, interest-bearing note.

Apr. 7 Paid the sixty-day note and interest due today.

Problem 15–4

Westwood Sales uses a voucher system in which it records invoices at their gross amounts and records discounts at the time they are taken. On January 1 the firm's unpaid vouchers file showed the following unpaid vouchers:

Voucher No.	Payee	Invoice Date	Terms	Amount
292	General Supply Company	Dec. 1	30 days	1,500
298	Eugene Wholesale Company	Dec. 11	1/10, n/30	1,600
303	B. W. Webster Company	Dec. 15	30 days	825
				3,925

During January the company completed the following transactions affecting vouchers payable:

Jan. 2   Secured an extension of thirty days on the amount owed to General Supply Company, Voucher No. 292, by honoring a thirty-day, noninterest-bearing time draft.

     3   Prepared Voucher No. 333 payable to Johnson Company for the purchase of merchandise, $550, terms 2/10, n/30, invoice date December 31.

     5   Borrowed $2,000 from the bank by giving a fifteen-day, 6 per cent note. (The receipt of cash in this transaction would normally be recorded in the Cash Receipts Journal. To simplify the problem record in the General Journal.)

     6   Prepared Voucher No. 334 payable to the Emerald Supply Company for the purchase of store supplies, $78, terms thirty days.

     9   Prepared Voucher No. 335 payable to S. A. Towne Company for the purchase of merchandise, $1,360, terms 2/10, n/30.

   10   Issued Check No. 328 in payment of Voucher No. 333.

   10   Entered into an agreement with the Eugene Wholesale Company to pay at once $600 of the amount due on Voucher No. 298 and to pay the remaining $1,000 in thirty days. Canceled Voucher No. 298, and issued Vouchers Nos. 336 and 337 for $600 and $1,000, respectively. Issued Check No. 329 in payment of Voucher No. 336.

   12   Purchased $1,225 worth of new office equipment from the Office Equipment Company, terms $225 cash, $500 in thirty days, and $500 in sixty days. Prepared Voucher No. 338 for $225 and Vouchers Nos. 339 and 340 for $500 each. Issued Check No. 330 in payment of Voucher No. 338.

   14   Prepared Voucher No. 341 payable to the Circle Company for merchandise purchased, $860, terms 2/10, n/30.

   15   Issued Check No. 331 in payment of Voucher No. 303.

   15   Prepared Voucher No. 342 payable to Payroll for sales' salaries, $640; and office salaries, $85. Issued Check No. 332 in its payment. Cashed the check and paid the salaries.

   16   Spoiled in preparation Voucher No. 343.

   17   Prepared Voucher No. 344 payable to the Emerald Supply Company for the purchase of merchandise, $335, terms 2/10, n/30.

   19   Issued Check No. 333 in payment of Voucher No. 335.

   19   Received a $35 credit memorandum from the Emerald Supply Company for merchandise received on January 17 and returned on January 18. The merchandise of this credit memorandum was ordered in the wrong sizes. The error was not discovered until after the voucher for the original purchase was recorded.

   20   Prepared Voucher No. 345 payable to the First National Bank in payment of the note issued on January 5 and due today. Issued Check No. 334 in payment of the voucher.

   21   Prepared Voucher No. 346 payable to D. D. Brittsan Company. The voucher was for $435. The invoice of this shipment showed charges of $425 for merchandise and $10 for prepaid freight paid by the Brittsan Company. The terms were 2/10, n/30.

   24   Issued Check 335 in payment of Voucher No. 341.

   26   Prepared Voucher No. 347 payable to Joan Hardt, petty cashier. Petty cash receipts indicated that $12 of petty cash had been expended for freight on purchases, $4.50 for store supplies, $5.00 for advertising, and $1.50 for miscellaneous office expenses. Issued Check No. 336 in payment of the voucher.

Jan. 27 Issued Check No. 337 in payment of Voucher No. 344, less the return and less the discount.

   30 Prepared Voucher No. 348 payable to the General Supply Company in payment of the time draft due today. Issued Check No. 338 in payment of the voucher.

   31 Prepared Voucher No. 349 payable to Payroll in payment of sales salaries, $630; and office salaries, $85. Issued Check No. 339 in payment of the voucher. Cashed the check and paid the salaries.

   31 Issued Check No. 340 in payment of Voucher No. 346.

Required:

1. Prepare a Voucher Register and Check Register similar to the ones shown in Illustrations 80 and 81. In addition, a General Journal and a Vouchers Payable account are needed.

2. Enter the $3,925 balance in the Vouchers Payable account. Enter the three unpaid vouchers on the first three lines of the Voucher Register. Enter the amounts in the Vouchers Payable credit column only. These vouchers were recorded by Westwood Sales during December and were posted in the Voucher Register totals at the end of December. They are entered at this time on the first three lines of the Voucher Register so their payment may be marked in the When and How Paid column. To prevent their being posted a second time in the January totals, rule a double line after the third line of the Voucher Register.

3. Record the transactions of the month of January. Total and crossfoot the Voucher Register and the Check Register. Use the following code numbers where necessary:

115 Store Supplies	612 Sales Salaries
133 Office Equipment	618 Advertising
211 Notes Payable	652 Office Salaries
212 Vouchers Payable	659 Miscellaneous Office Expense
511 Purchases	711 Interest Expense
512 Freight-In	

4. Post those Voucher Register and Check Register totals that affect the Vouchers Payable account. Post those portions of the general journal entries that affect the Vouchers Payable account.

5. Prepare a schedule of unpaid vouchers as of January 31. Compare the schedule with the balance of the Vouchers Payable account.

CLASS EXERCISES

Exercise 15–1

A firm using a voucher system purchased $1,000 of office equipment. (a) Write a paragraph describing the firm's procedure for recording the purchase of the equipment and the payment for it under the assumption that the purchase was for cash. (b) Write another paragraph describing the recording procedure under the assumption that the purchase terms were 10 E.O.M. (c) Write a third paragraph under the assumption that the terms were a sixty-day, noninterest-bearing trade acceptance.

Exercise 15–2

The Keel Department Store has 108 accounts with creditors and is considering the installation of a voucher system. (a) What advantages will the store gain by the use of the voucher system? What disadvantages? (b) Give instructions to the accountant for the installation of the system.

SUPPLEMENTARY PROBLEMS

Problem 15–A

Smithfield Company uses a voucher system in which it records at their net amounts all invoices subject to discounts. During March of the current year the company completed the following transactions affecting vouchers payable:

Mar. 1 Prepared Voucher No. 981 payable to Baker, Inc., for the purchase of merchandise having an invoice price of $1,200, terms 2/10, n/30.

1 Prepared Voucher No. 982 payable to Brown Realty Company for the March rent, $800. (Charge 10 per cent of the rent to the office and the remainder to the store.) Issued Check No. 977 in payment of the voucher.

5 Prepared Voucher No. 983 payable to Valley Supply Company for the purchase of store supplies having an invoice price of $200, terms 2/10, n/30.

8 Received a credit memorandum from Baker, Inc., for merchandise having an invoice price of $150 which was received on March 1 and returned on March 5. This merchandise was defective but this was not discovered until after the voucher for the purchase was recorded.

12 Prepared Voucher No. 984 payable to Kimwood Manufacturing Company. The invoice attached to this voucher was for the purchase of $950 of merchandise, terms F.O.B. factory, 2/10, n/30. The vendor had prepaid $60 of freight on the purchase and had added this amount to the invoice.

14 Issued Check No. 978 in payment of Voucher No. 983.

18 Discovered that after adjusting Voucher No. 981 for the credit memorandum received on March 8, the voucher was refiled in error for payment on March 18. Adjusted the voucher for the discount lost and refiled it for payment on the last day of its credit period, March 31. Made a general journal entry to record the discount lost.

20 Issued Check No. 979 in payment of Voucher No. 984.

23 Prepared Voucher No. 985 payable to Litho Printers for advertising circulars printed and delivered this day. The invoice accompanying the circulars was for $45, terms 10 E.O.M.

27 Purchased a refrigerated display case from Commercial Refrigeration Company, terms $500 cash and $1,000 in thirty days. Prepared Voucher No. 986 for $500 and Voucher No. 987 for $1,000. Issued Check No. 980 in payment of Voucher No. 986.

31 Issued Check No. 981 in payment of Voucher No. 981 as adjusted for the return and the discount lost.

31 Issued Voucher No. 988 payable to Payroll for sales salaries, $1,100; and office salaries, $540. Issued Check No. 982 in payment of the voucher. Cashed the check and paid the employees.

Required:

1. Prepare a Voucher Register similar to Illustration 80. Prepare a Check Register like Illustration 81 with the exception that only one money column is needed. Enter the transactions in the registers and, where necessary, in a two-column General Journal. Use the following account code num-

bers: Rent Expense, Selling Space, 611; Advertising, 612; Sales Salaries, 613; Rent Expense, Office Space, 651; and Office Salaries, 652.

2. Total and crossfoot the registers and post to a Vouchers Payable account the column totals and the portions of the journal entries that affect this account.

3. Prepare a schedule of unpaid vouchers.

Problem 15–B

Western Supply Company uses a voucher system in which it records at their net amounts all invoices subject to discounts. On July 1 its unpaid vouchers file contained the following unpaid vouchers:

Voucher Number	Payee	Invoice Date	Terms	Amount
389	Northern Manufacturing Company	June 1	30 days	$1,600
394	General Wholesale Company	June 9	30 days	1,300
401	Brook Brothers	June 15	30 days	700
				$3,600

During July the company completed the following transactions affecting vouchers payable:

July   1   Prepared Voucher 424 payable to Southgate Company for the purchase of merchandise having an invoice price of $750, terms 2/10, n/30.

1   Secured an extension of thirty days on the amount owed Northern Manufacturing Company, Voucher No. 389, by giving them a thirty-day, 6 per cent note.

5   Prepared Voucher No. 425 payable to Store Supply Company for the purchase of store supplies having an invoice price of $300, terms 2/10, n/60.

6   Western Supply Company discounted at 6 per cent its own fifteen-day, noninterest-bearing $4,000 note at the bank. (Normally this transaction would be recorded in the Cash Receipts Journal. You are to make only a general journal entry.)

8   Purchased $1,400 worth of new office equipment from Office Equipment Company, terms $400 cash and $1,000 in sixty days. Prepared Voucher No. 426 for $400 and Voucher No. 427 for $1,000. Issued Check No. 409 in payment of Voucher No. 426.

9   Entered into an agreement with General Wholesale Company to pay at once $700 of the amount due on Voucher No. 394 and to pay the balance in thirty days. Canceled Voucher 394 and issued Vouchers Nos. 428 and 429 for $700 and $600, respectively. Issued Check No. 410 in payment of Voucher No. 428.

10   Prepared Voucher No. 430 payable to Hill Company for the purchase of merchandise having an invoice price of $1,450, terms 2/10, n/30.

12   Prepared Voucher No. 431 payable to Long-Bell Company for the purchase of merchandise having an invoice price of $950, terms 2/10, n/30.

13   Spoiled Voucher No. 432 in preparation.

July 13 Prepared Voucher No. 433 payable to Hill Company for the purchase of merchandise having an invoice price of $800, terms 2/10, n/30.

15 Issued Check No. 411 in payment of Voucher No. 401.

15 Issued Check No. 412 in payment of Voucher No. 425. Received a credit memorandum from Hill Company for merchandise having an invoice price of $50 which was received on July 10 and returned on July 12. The merchandise of this credit memorandum was ordered in the wrong sizes, and the error was not discovered until after the voucher was recorded.

18 Prepared Voucher No. 434 payable to Madison Company. The invoice of the voucher was for merchandise having an invoice price of $650, F.O.B. factory, terms 2/10, n/30. Madison Company had prepaid the freight charges of $40 and had added this amount to the invoice, bringing the total of the invoice to $690.

19 Issued Check No. 413 in payment of Voucher No. 430 as adjusted for the return.

20 Discovered that Voucher No. 424 had been filed in error for payment on July 20. Added to the voucher the amount of the discount lost, and refiled the voucher for payment on the last day of its credit period, July 31. Made a general journal entry to record the discount lost.

21 Prepared Voucher No. 435 payable to the First National Bank for the note due today. Issued Check No. 414 in payment of the voucher.

21 Issued Check No. 415 in payment of Voucher No. 431.

22 Issued Check No. 416 in payment of Voucher No. 433.

25 Prepared Voucher No. 436 payable to Judy Hale, petty cashier, to reimburse the petty cash fund. Petty cash vouchers showed payments of $22 for freight-in, $18 for store supplies, $10 for advertising, and $5.00 for miscellaneous office expenses. Issued Check No. 417 in payment of the voucher.

27 Issued Check No. 418 in payment of Voucher No. 434.

31 Issued Check No. 419 in payment of Voucher No. 424 as adjusted for the discount lost.

31 Prepared Voucher No. 437 payable to Northern Manufacturing Company in payment of the note and interest due this day. Issued Check No. 420 in payment of the voucher.

31 Prepared Voucher No. 438 payable to Payroll in payment of sales salaries, $1,410; and office salaries, $320. Issued Check No. 421 in payment of the voucher. Cashed the check and paid the employees.

Required:

1. Prepare a Voucher Register similar to Illustration 80. Prepare a Check Register similar to Illustration 81 with the exception that only one money column is needed. Enter the transaction in the registers and, where necessary, in a two-column General Journal.

2. Enter the $3,600 balance in the Vouchers Payable account. Also enter the three unpaid vouchers on the first three lines of the Voucher Register. Enter the amounts in the Vouchers Payable credit column only. These vouchers were recorded during June and were posted in the Voucher Register totals at the end of June. They are entered at this time on the first three lines of the Voucher Register so their payment may be marked in the When and How Paid column. To prevent their being posted a second

time in the July totals, rule a double line after the third line of the Voucher Register.

3. Record the transactions of the month of July. Total and crossfoot the Voucher Register and the Check Register. Use the following account code numbers as required:

116 Store Supplies	611 Advertising
133 Office Equipment	612 Sales Salaries
211 Notes Payable	651 Office Salaries
212 Vouchers Payable	659 Miscellaneous Office Expenses
511 Purchases	711 Interest Expense
512 Freight-in	712 Discounts Lost

4. Open a Vouchers Payable account. Post those totals of the Voucher Register and Check Register that affect the Vouchers Payable account. Post those portions of the general journal entries that affect the Vouchers Payable account.

5. Prepare a schedule of unpaid vouchers as of July 31. Compare the schedule with the balance of the Vouchers Payable account.

Chapter
16

AN UNDERSTANDING of payroll records and payroll accounting requires some knowledge of the state and federal laws that affect payrolls. Consequently, the more pertinent of these laws are discussed in the first portion of this chapter before the subject of payroll records is introduced.

The Federal Social Security Act

The Federal Social Security Act has two main provisions that materially affect payroll accounting. These are provisions for: (1) an old-age and survivors' benefits program, and (2) a federal unemployment tax program.

Federal Old-Age and Survivors' Benefits Program. The Social Security Act provides that a qualified worker in a covered industry who reaches the age of sixty-five, in some cases sooner, and retires shall receive monthly retirement benefits for the remainder of his life. It further provides benefits to the family of a worker covered by the act who dies either before or after reaching the age of sixty-five. The amount of the monthly benefits paid in either case is based upon the average earnings of the worker during the years of his employment in covered industries.

No attempt will be made here to list or discuss the requirements to be met by a worker or his family to qualify under the law for benefits. In general, any person who works for a company covered by the act for a sufficient length of time before his retirement or death qualifies himself and his family. All companies and individuals who employ one or more persons and are not specifically exempted are covered by the law.

Funds for the payment of old-age and survivors' benefits under the Social Security Act come from payroll taxes. These taxes are imposed under a law called the Federal Insurance Contributions Act and are often called "F.I.C.A. taxes." They are also often called "old-age benefit taxes" or just "social security taxes." These F.I.C.A. taxes are imposed in like amounts on both covered employers and their employees. As presently amended, the act provides for a 1959 tax on both employers and their employees of 2½ per cent of the first $4,800 paid each employee. The act also provides for increases in this rate as follows:

Years	Tax on Employees	Tax on Employers
1960 through 1962	3 %	3 %
1963 through 1965	3½	3½
1966 through 1968	4	4
1969 and after	4½	4½

The Federal Insurance Contributions Act, in addition to setting tax rates, requires that an employer:

1. During 1959, withhold each payday from each employee 2½ per cent of the wages earned. The withholding to continue during 1959 until 2½ per cent of $4,800 is withheld. (Observe in the table just given that this withholding rate increases to 3 per cent in 1960 and continues to increase until a rate of 4½ per cent is reached in 1969.)
2. Pay a payroll tax equal to the amount withheld from the wages of all employees.
3. Periodically pay both the amounts withheld from the employees and the employer's tax to the Director of Internal Revenue. (Times of payment are discussed later in this chapter.)
4. Within one month after the end of each quarter, file a tax information return known as Employer's Quarterly Federal Tax Return, Form 941. This return reports: (1) the employees' federal income taxes withheld, (2) wages subject to F.I.C.A. taxes, (3) the combined amount of employees' and employer's F.I.C.A. taxes, and (4) the name of each employee with wages subject to tax and the amount of his taxable wages. An Employer's Quarterly Federal Tax Return, Form 941, is reproduced as Illustration 82 on pages 372 and 373.
5. Furnish each employee before January 31 following each year a Withholding Tax Statement, Form W-2, which tells the employee the amounts of his wages subject to F.I.C.A. taxes and to federal income taxes and the amounts of F.I.C.A. and federal income taxes withheld. A Withholding Tax Statement, Form W-2, is reproduced as Illustration 83 on page 374.
6. Keep a record for each employee for four years after the tax is paid that shows: (1) the name, address, and social security number of the employee; (2) for each pay period the total amount of wages earned, the date of payment, and the period of time covered by the payment; (3) the amount of wages subject to F.I.C.A. tax; and (4) the amount of F.I.C.A. taxes withheld. The law does not specify the exact form of the records to be kept. Most employers keep individual employee earnings records similar to the one shown later in this chapter.

Federal Unemployment Insurance Program. The federal unemployment insurance phase of the social security program is supported by a tax levied under a law called the Federal Unemployment Tax Act. This tax is levied on employers only; employees pay nothing. Likewise, the funds raised by this tax are not used to pay unemployment benefits but are distributed to the states for use in the administration of the state unemployment compensation insurance programs.

Historically, in 1935 when the Federal Unemployment Tax Act was first passed by Congress, only one state had an unemployment compensation insurance program; consequently, Congress passed certain sections of the Social Security Act and the Federal Unemployment Tax Act with two purposes in view. The first purpose was to induce the individual states to pass laws creating satisfactory state unemployment compensation programs of their own. The acts were successful on this score; all states created satisfactory programs within two years after the passage of the federal acts. The second purpose was to provide funds to be distributed to

Illustration 82

FORM 941
U.S. Treasury Department
Internal Revenue Service

EMPLOYER'S QUARTERLY FEDERAL TAX RETURN

COPY FOR DISTRICT DIRECTOR

1. Federal Income Tax Withheld From Wages (If not required to withhold, write "None") . . . $

2. Adjustment for preceding quarter(s) of calendar year. (Attach explanation. See instructions) . . $

3. Income tax withheld, as adjusted . . . . **Enter Adjusted Total Here →** $

Federal Insurance Contributions Act Taxes (If no taxable wages paid, write "None")

4. Number of employees listed in Schedule A . . . . . . 5. Total taxable wages paid (from Item 21) $

6. 5% of wages in Item 5 (2½% employer tax and 2½% employee tax) . . . . $

7. Credit or adjustment. (Attach explanation. See instructions) . . . . $

8. F.I.C.A. taxes, as adjusted . . . . **Enter Adjusted Total Here →** $

9. Total taxes (Item 3 plus Item 8). If deposits of taxes are made, fill in Schedule B on other side $

I declare under the penalties of perjury that this return (including any accompanying schedules and statements) has been examined by me and to the best of my knowledge and belief is a true, correct, and complete return.

(Signed) _____ (Title) _____ (Date) _____ 195__
                                        (Owner, president, partner, member, etc.)

Make check
or money
order pay-
able to
Internal
Revenue
Service

10. Employer's identification number, name, and address of principal place of business.
(If incorrectly entered, make any necessary change.)

Return for Calendar Quarter
(Months and year)

T

P

I

Total

Schedule A—QUARTERLY REPORT OF WAGES TAXABLE UNDER THE FEDERAL INSURANCE CONTRIBUTIONS ACT (FOR SOCIAL SECURITY)

If wages were not taxable under the F.I.C.A., make no entries below except in Items 12 and 13. See instructions on back of this page.

12. If there has been a change of ownership or other transfer of the business during the quarter, give the name of the present owner (individual, partnership, or corporation) and the date change took place _____

13. Do you expect to pay taxable wages in the future to any employee (other than agricultural or household)? ☐ Yes ☐ No

If "No," write "Final Return" in Item 10, check appropriate block below and furnish the other information requested below:

14. Total pages of this return, including this page and any pages of Form 941a

15. Total number of

Records will be kept by _____ at _____

Do you expect to pay taxable wages within the next 6 months to a household employee? ☐ Yes ☐ No

List for each employee, except agricultural employees, the WAGES taxable under the Federal Insurance Contributions Act (for Social Security) which were paid during the quarter. If you pay an employee more than $4,800 in a calendar year, report ONLY THE FIRST $4,800 of such wages.

EMPLOYEE'S ACCOUNT NUMBER (If number is unknown, see Circular E) (17)			NAME OF EMPLOYEE (Please type or print) (18)	WAGES TAXABLE UNDER F.I.C.A. Paid to Employee in Quarter (Before deductions) (19)		State, Possession, or Territory of Employment (or "Outside U. S.") (20)
000	00	0000		Dollars	Cents	

If you need more space for listing employees, use Schedule A continuation sheets, Form 941a.

Total wages reported in column 19 on this page . . . . $

21. **TOTAL WAGES TAXABLE UNDER F.I.C.A., PAID DURING QUARTER**
(Total of such wages in column 19 of this page and on any continuation sheets) . . $ } Enter this total in Item 5 above.

THIS FORM MUST BE FILED WITH YOUR U. S. DISTRICT DIRECTOR OF INTERNAL REVENUE ON OR BEFORE THE LAST DAY OF THE FIRST MONTH FOLLOWING THE CLOSE OF THE QUARTER EVEN THOUGH NO TAX IS PAYABLE

c16—69832-8 Page 1

Illustration 83

WITHHOLDING TAX STATEMENT 1958
Federal Taxes Withheld From Wages

Copy A—For District Director

Type or print EMPLOYER'S identification number, name, and address above.

SOCIAL SECURITY INFORMATION		INCOME TAX INFORMATION	
$	$	$	$
Total F.I.C.A. Wages* paid in 1958	F.I.C.A. employee tax withheld, if any	Total Wages* paid in 1958	Federal Income Tax withheld, if any

EMPLOYER: See instructions on other side.

FOR USE OF INTERNAL REVENUE SERVICE	
Employee's Copy and Employer's Copy compared	

Type or print EMPLOYEE'S social security account no., name, and address above.

FORM W–2—U. S. Treasury Department, Internal Revenue Service

*Before payroll deductions.

c9—16—73608-1

the various states on the basis of population and employed workers. The funds were to be used in the administration of the various state unemployment insurance programs.

The Federal Unemployment Tax Act helped induce the various states to pass satisfactory unemployment compensation laws, and it also provides funds to be distributed to the states for the administration of their unemployment compensation programs by: (1) Levying a tax on employers of eight (since amended to four) or more employees equal to 3 per cent of the wages paid each employee. Only the first $3,000 in wages paid to each employee is taxed, amounts in excess of $3,000 are not taxed. (2) Permitting each employer to deduct from the federal tax levied, amounts paid in state unemployment compensation taxes or reductions in state unemployment taxes gained through merit ratings. In all cases the reduction in federal unemployment taxes may not exceed 90 per cent of the 3 per cent federal tax. This means that when the state tax rate is 2.7 per cent or more, 2.7 per cent of the state tax rate may be offset against the 3 per cent federal tax; the federal tax is thereby reduced to 0.3 per cent. This deduction feature of the federal tax act is the section of the law that helped induce all of the states to pass laws creating their own unemployment compensation programs. If any state had failed to create a satisfactory unemployment compensation program, its employees would have received no benefits from the amounts paid, and the state would have received no federal funds to be used in the administration of its unemployment compensation program.

The Federal Unemployment Tax Act requires nothing from employed workers, but it requires employers of four or more employees to:

1. Pay an excise tax equal to 3 per cent of the first $3,000 paid to each employee. The 3 per cent federal tax may be reduced to as little as 0.3 per cent by payments of state unemployment taxes and by state unemployment merit ratings. The tax is paid on an annual basis and is due before January 31 following the end of a taxable year.
2. Before January 31 following the close of a taxable year, file a tax return called an "Annual Return of Excise Tax on Employers of Four or More Individuals, Form 940." This return is reproduced in Illustration 84 on the following page and reports (1) the total taxable wages paid during the year (this is usually the total wages paid to all covered employees less amounts in excess of $3,000 paid to individual employees), (2) the full 3 per cent federal tax on taxable wages, (3) the deduction from the federal tax for state unemployment taxes, and (4) the federal unemployment tax due.
3. Keep records to substantiate the information on the tax return. In general the records required by other payroll laws and the regular accounting records satisfy this requirement.

State Unemployment Compensation Taxes

While the various state unemployment laws differ in several respects, all have three common objectives:

Illustration 84

Form 940
U.S. Treasury Department
Internal Revenue Service
(Revised Aug. 1956)

COPY FOR DISTRICT DIRECTOR

ANNUAL FEDERAL TAX RETURN OF EMPLOYERS
of 4 or more individuals under the Federal Unemployment Tax Act

1. Total taxable wages PAID during calendar year. *(From Schedule B, on back of page)* . . . . $

2. Gross Federal tax (3% of wages in Item 1) . . . . $

3. Less: Credit for contributions PAID into State funds, plus any additional credit, as shown in
   Schedule A. *(From Item 16.)* Total credit limited to 90 percent of tax shown in Item 2 . . . . $

4. Remainder of tax (Item 2 minus Item 3). This amount is payable with return. . . . . $
   (Make check or money order payable to "Internal Revenue Service")

I declare under the penalties of perjury that this return (including any accompanying schedules and statements) has been examined by me and to the best of my knowledge and belief is a true, correct, and complete return, and that no part of any payment made to a State unemployment fund which is claimed as a credit in Item 3 above was or is to be deducted from the remuneration of employees.

(Signed) _____ (Title) _____
(Date) _____, 195___   (Owner, president, partner, member, etc.)

Space below for Director's use

Penalty $ _____

Interest _____

Total . . $ _____

5. Employer's name, address of principal place of business, and identification
   number. (If incorrectly entered, make any necessary change.)   Return for calendar year

DO NOT DETACH AT THIS LINE

(Fill in Items 6 through 16, and Schedule B, before filling in Items 1 through 5, above. See instructions on back of this page.)
Schedule A—COMPUTATION OF CREDIT AGAINST FEDERAL UNEMPLOYMENT TAX

6. Employer's name, address of principal place of business, and identification number. (If incorrectly entered, make any necessary change.)

Return for calendar year

Name of State (7)	State reporting number as shown on employer's State contribution returns (8)	Taxable Payroll (As defined in State act) (9)	Experience rate period (10) From— To—	Experience rate (11)	Contributions had rate been 2.7% (col. 9×2.7%) (12)	Contributions payable at experience rate (col. 9 × col. 11) (13)	Additional credit (col. 12 minus col. 13) (14)	Contributions actually paid to State (15)
TOTALS....		$	xxx xxx	xxx	xxxx	xxxx	$	$

16. Total tentative credit (column 14 plus column 15)............$............

(That portion of Item 16 which is not in excess of 90 percent of gross tax liability as shown in Item 2 above should be entered in Item 3 above.)

EMPLOYERS—DO NOT USE SPACE BELOW

State reporting number as shown on employer's State contribution returns	Taxable Payroll (As defined in State act)	Experience rate period From— To—	Experience rate	Dates and amounts of contributions actually paid to State after January 31	Contributions actually paid to State before February 1

To the U. S. District Director of Internal Revenue:

I hereby certify that, except as noted above, the records of this office agree with the entries made by the employer in columns (8), (9), (10), (11), and (15) of Schedule A, and that all contributions were paid before February 1.

Name of State Officer ....

Name of State ....

THE EMPLOYER MUST FILE THIS RETURN WITH U. S. DISTRICT DIRECTOR OF INTERNAL REVENUE NOT LATER THAN JANUARY 31

1. The payment of limited amounts of unemployment compensation for limited periods of time to unemployed individuals. To be eligible for benefits under one of the various state laws, an unemployed individual must have a record of having worked for a taxpaying employer covered by the law. Employers covered by the various state laws vary with the states. In general the various state laws cover employers of from one to eight or more employees who are not specifically exempted.
2. The stabilization of employment by each employer subject to the payment of unemployment taxes. In all of the states this is accomplished by a so-called merit-rating plan. Under a merit-rating plan an employer who provides steady employment for his employees can gain a substantial reduction in state unemployment taxes. The amount of the merit-rating reduction, as well as the actual state unemployment tax paid, may be deducted from the federal unemployment tax until 90 per cent of the 3 per cent federal tax is deducted.
3. The establishment and operation of employment facilities to assist unemployed individuals in finding suitable employment and to assist employers in finding suitable employees.

Although the unemployment tax laws of the various states vary considerably, they have a number of points in common. All states levy a tax on employers to support their programs; only a very small number of states tax both employers and employees. The tax rate in all states is almost a uniform 2.7 per cent on the first $3,000 paid each employee. A few states provide for a higher rate if needed to meet unemployment compensation disbursements. The 2.7 per cent rate is more or less uniform among the states because the 3 per cent federal unemployment tax allows a deduction of 90 per cent for state unemployment taxes, and 90 per cent of 3 per cent is 2.7 per cent.

The state laws vary as to the number and type of reports that must be filed. In general, all require the filing of a tax return and the payment of the required tax within one month after the end of each calendar quarter Since the amount of benefits paid an eligible unemployed individual is based upon his earnings, the return usually must name and tell the amount of wages paid to each employee.

In addition to requiring reports and the payment of taxes, all states require employers to maintain certain payroll records. These, too, vary from state to state; but in general they require, among other things, a payroll record for each pay period that shows the date of the pay period and the hours worked and taxable earnings of all employees. An individual earnings record for each employee is also usually required. The individual employee earnings record generally must show about the same information as that required by the federal social security laws. In addition, information as to (1) the date the employee was hired, rehired, or reinstated after a layoff; (2) the date the employee quit, was discharged, or laid off; and (3) the reason for the termination of employment is also usually required.

Withholding of Federal Income Taxes

The first federal income tax law became effective in 1913, but it applied to only a few individuals with high earnings. It was not until the time of World War II that income taxes were levied on the great masses of wage earners. Since many of these wage earners could not be expected to save a sufficient sum of money with which to pay their income taxes once each year, a system of pay-as-you-go withholding of taxes each payday at their source was also instituted. Pay-as-you-go withholding of income taxes requires employers to act as tax collecting agents of the federal government. With few exceptions, employers of one or more persons are required to calculate, collect, and remit to the federal government the individual income taxes of each of their employees.

The amount of taxes withheld from an employee's wages is determined by the amount of his wages and the number of his exemptions. Each exemption exempts $600 of the employee's yearly earnings from income taxes. For example, an employee with five exemptions and earnings in one year of less than $3,000 pays no tax (5 × $600 = $3,000 exempted). An employee is allowed one exemption for himself, additional exemptions if he or his wife are over sixty-five or blind, and an exemption for each dependent. Each covered employee is required to furnish his employer an employee's withholding exemption certificate showing the number of exemptions to which he is entitled.

Illustration 85—Wage Bracket Withholding Table

If wages are paid Weekly:												
And the wages are:		And the number of withholding exemptions claimed is—										
		0	1	2	3	4	5	6	7	8	9	10 or more
At least	But less than	The amount of income tax to be withheld is:										
$80	$82	14.60	12.30	10.00	7.70	5.30	3.00	0.70	0	0	0	0
82	84	14.90	12.60	10.30	8.00	5.70	3.40	1.10	0	0	0	0
84	86	15.30	13.00	10.70	8.40	6.10	3.80	1.50	0	0	0	0
86	88	15.70	13.40	11.00	8.70	6.40	4.10	1.80	0	0	0	0

At the end of each pay period, employers are required to calculate and withhold income taxes from the wages of their employees. This applies to all except a very few employees in exempted occupations. The amount withheld in each case depends upon the amount of gross earnings and the number of exemptions to which each employee is entitled. In calculating amounts to be withheld from employees' gross earnings, most employers use wage bracket withholding tables similar to the one shown in Illustration 85.

The table shown in Illustration 85 is used when the pay period is one week in length. Different tables are provided for biweekly, semimonthly, and monthly pay periods. Finding the amount of tax to be withheld from an employee's gross wages is quite easy when a withholding table is used. First the employee's wage bracket is located in the first two columns of the table. Then the amount to be withheld is found on the line of the wage bracket in the column showing the number of exemptions to which the employee is entitled. The column heading numbers refer to the number of exemptions claimed by an employee on his exemption certificate.

In addition to calculating and withholding the proper amount of income tax from the wages of each employee every payday, employers are required to:

1. Remit the amounts of income taxes withheld from employees' wages to the Director of Internal Revenue.
2. Within one month after the end of each quarter, file a report showing income taxes withheld. This report is the Employer's Quarterly Federal Tax Return, Form 941, shown in Illustration 82. It is the same report required by the F.I.C.A. taxes and reports: (1) income tax withheld from employees; (2) total taxable wages paid; (3) F.I.C.A. taxes; and (4) the social security number, name, and wages paid to each employee.
3. On or before January 31 following each year, give each of his employees a Withholding Statement, Form W-2. This withholding statement tells each employee (1) his total wages for the preceding year, (2) wages subject to F.I.C.A. taxes, (3) income taxes withheld, and (4) F.I.C.A. taxes withheld. A copy of this statement must also be given to each terminated employee within thirty days after his last wage payment.
4. On or before January 31 following the end of each year, send to the Collector of Internal Revenue carbon copies of all W-2 forms given to employees.

Fair Labor Standards Act

The Fair Labor Standards Act, often called the Wages and Hours Law, sets minimum hourly wages and maximum hours of work per week for employees, with certain exceptions, of firms engaged either directly or indirectly in interstate commerce. As amended, the law at this writing sets a minimum wage of $1.00 per hour and a maximum workweek of forty hours. Although the acts sets a maximum workweek of forty hours, it does not prohibit an employee from working longer hours. However, it does provide that if an employee covered by the act works more than forty hours in one week, he must be paid for the hours in excess of forty at his regular pay rate plus an overtime premium of at least one half his regular pay rate. This gives an employee an overtime rate of at least one and one half times his regular hourly rate. The act also requires that employers subject to it must maintain records that show for each employee (1) the employee's name; (2) address; (3) date of birth (if under nineteen years of age); (4) occupation; (5) workweek; (6) regular hourly rate of pay or other basis on which wages are paid such as weekly rate, monthly rate, or piece rate; (7) hours worked each day; (8) total hours worked each week; (9) regular straight-time earnings; (10) overtime premium earnings; (11) additions to or deductions from wages; (12) net wages paid each pay period; and (13) date of payment and period covered by each wage payment.

Union Contracts

The Wages and Hours Law requires covered employers to pay time and one half for hours worked in excess of forty in any one week. Often employers operate under contracts with the employees' union that provide even better terms. Union contracts often provide for time and one half for work in excess of eight hours in any one day, time and one half for work on Saturdays, and double time for work on Sundays and holidays. If an employer is under such a contract with his employees' union, since the terms of the union contract are better than the terms of the Wages and Hours Law, the terms of the union contract take precedence over the Wages and Hours Law.

In addition to specifying working hours and wage rates, union contracts often provide for the collection of employees' union dues by the employer. Such a system for the collection of union dues is called a "check-off system." It provides that the employer shall deduct union dues from the wages of each employee and remit the entire amount deducted from all employees to the union. The employer is usually required to remit once each month and to report the name and amount deducted from the pay of each employee.

Other Payroll Deductions

In addition to the payroll deductions discussed thus far, employees may individually authorize additional deductions from their earnings. These additional deductions may include:

1. Deductions to accumulate funds for the purchase of United States savings bonds.
2. Deductions to pay group health, accident, hospital, or life insurance premiums.
3. Deductions to repay loans received from the company or the company credit union.
4. Deductions to pay for merchandise purchased from the company.
5. Deductions for donations to charitable organizations such as Boy Scouts, Girl Scouts, Community Chest, or Red Cross.

Timekeeping

Compiling a record of the time worked by each employee is called *time-keeping*. In each individual company the method of compiling such a record depends upon the nature of the business and the number of its employees. In a very small business, the recording of time may be a mere pencil notation of the working time of each employee made in a memorandum book by the manager or owner. In a larger company a time clock or several time clocks are often used to record on clock cards the time of arrival and departure of each employee. When time clocks are used, the clocks are placed at the entrances to the office, store, or factory. An "In" rack for clock cards is provided on one side of each clock, and an "Out" rack is placed on the other side. At the beginning of each payroll period a clock card for each employee similar to Illustration 86 is placed in the "Out" rack at the entrance to be used by each employee. An employee uses his clock card to record the time worked each day of the pay period. Each day, as an employee enters the plant, store, or office, he takes his card from the "Out" rack and places it in a slot in the time clock. This actuates the clock to stamp the date and time of arrival on the card. The employee

Illustration 86—A Clock Card

CLOCK No.		S. S. No.				
NAME						
	MORNING		AFTERNOON		OVERTIME	
	In	Out	In	Out	In	Out
Mon.						
Tues.						
Weds.						
Thurs.						
Fri.						
Sat.						
Sun.						
Pay Period Ending						
Regular Time		Hours		Rate		Earnings
Overtime						
Total Earnings for Period						

then places the card in the "In" rack and proceeds to his place of work. Upon leaving the plant, store, or office at noon or at the end of the day, the procedure is reversed. The employee takes the card from the "In" rack, places it in the clock, and stamps the time of departure. He then places the card in the "Out" rack and leaves the plant, store, or office.

The Payroll Register

Each pay period the information as to hours worked as compiled on the employee clock cards or otherwise is summarized in a Payroll Register.

Such a register is shown in Illustration 87. The column headings and the information recorded therein is in the main self-explanatory. The Payroll Register illustrated is for a payroll period of one week and shows the payroll data for each employee on a separate line.

The columns under the heading of "Daily Time" show the number of hours worked each day of the payroll period by each employee. The total of each employee's hours is entered in the column headed "Total Hours." If the hours worked include overtime hours, the number of these overtime hours is entered in the columns headed "O.T. Hours."

The column headed "Reg. Pay Rate" gives the hourly rate of pay of each employee. The total hours worked multiplied by the regular rate of pay gives the amount of regular pay. The overtime hours multiplied by the overtime premium rate gives the overtime premium pay. The sum of the regular pay and the overtime premium pay gives the gross pay of each employee.

Under the heading of "Deductions," the amounts withheld from the gross pay of each employee for social security or F.I.C.A. taxes are shown in the column marked "F.I.C.A. Taxes." The amounts of these taxes are found by multiplying the gross pay of each employee by the F.I.C.A. tax rate in effect. In this and the remaining illustrations of this chapter the 1959, 2½ per cent rate is used. Remember that as the law is presently amended, this rate becomes 3 per cent in 1960, 3½ per cent in 1963, 4 per cent in 1966, and 4½ per cent in 1969.

Observe in the F.I.C.A. Taxes column of Illustration 87 that there is no F.I.C.A. deduction for the last employee, George Tucker. This is because Tucker's cumulative earnings for the year have previously passed $4,800 and his wages are no longer subject to tax. (See the discussion for Illustration 91 on page 391.)

The amount of income tax withheld from each employee depends upon the amount of his gross pay and the number of his exemptions. The amount of tax withheld from each employee is usually determined by the use of a wage bracket withholding table and is entered in the column headed "Federal Income Taxes."

The column headed "U.S. Savings Bonds" shows the amounts withheld from those employees who are buying bonds through payroll deductions. The total amount withheld from all employees for this purpose is a current liability of the business. It is credited each payday to a current liability account called "Employees' Bond Deductions." When the total of the amounts deducted from any one employee is sufficient to purchase a bond, the bond is bought and delivered to the employee. At the same time the account Employees' Bond Deductions is debited, and Cash is credited for the cost of the bond.

Union contracts commonly require the employer to withhold the union dues of his employees and to periodically remit the amounts withheld to the union. The total amount withheld for employees' union dues is a current liability until paid to the union. The column marked "Union Dues" in the illustrated Payroll Register is used for this deduction.

Additional columns may be added to the Payroll Register for deductions that occur sufficiently often to warrant special columns. For example, a company that regularly deducts amounts from the pay of several of its employees for hospital insurance may add a special column to its Payroll Register for this deduction.

The gross pay of an employee less his total deductions gives his net pay. The amount of the net pay of each employee is entered in the column headed "Net Pay." The total of this column is the amount of money paid to all employees. The numbers of the checks used in paying the employees are entered in the column headed "Check No."

The three columns under the heading of "Distribution" are for sorting the salaries of the various employees into the proper salary expense accounts. Here the amount of each employee's salary is entered in the proper column according to the type of his work. The totals of the various columns then give the amounts to be debited to each salary expense account.

Recording the Payroll

Generally a Payroll Register such as the one shown in Illustration 87 is a supplementary memorandum record. As a supplementary record, the information recorded therein is not posted directly to the accounts. It is

Illustration 87

PAY
Week ending

Employee	Clock Card No.	M	T	W	T	F	S	S	Total Hours	O.T. Hours	Reg. Pay Rate	Regular Pay	O.T. Premium Pay	Gross Pay
Robert Austin	105	8	8	8	8	8			40		2.00	80.00		80.00
Charles Cross	97	8	8	8	8	8	4		44	4	2.00	88.00	4.00	92.00
John Cruz	89	8	8	8	8	8			40		1.80	72.00		72.00
Howard Keife	112	8	4	0	0	8			20		2.00	40.00		40.00
Guy Adams	76	8	8	8	8	8			40		2.00	80.00		80.00
Lee Miller	95	8	8	8	8	8			40		2.25	90.00		90.00
Dale Sears	53	8	8	8	8	8			40		2.00	80.00		80.00
Robert Smith	68	8	8	8	8	8	6		46	6	2.00	92.00	6.00	98.00
George Tucker	74	8	8	8	8	8			40		3.00	120.00		120.00
Totals														752.00

first recorded with a general journal entry, which is then posted to the ledger accounts. The general journal entry to record the payroll shown in Illustration 87 is:

Oct.	18	Sales Salaries........................	382.00	
		Office Salaries.......................	192.00	
		Delivery Salaries.....................	178.00	
		F.I.C.A. Taxes Payable............		15.80
		Employees' Federal Income Taxes		
		Payable.......................		79.60
		Employees' Bond Deductions........		27.50
		Employees' Union Dues Payable.....		11.25
		Accrued Payroll Payable...........		617.85
		To record the payroll of the week ended October 18.		

The debits of this entry are taken from the totals of the distribution columns of the payroll record. They record the gross earnings of the employees in the proper salary expense accounts. The credits to F.I.C.A. Taxes Payable, Employees' Federal Income Taxes Payable, Employees' Bond Deductions, and Employees' Union Dues Payable record these amounts as current liabilities. The credit to Accrued Payroll Payable records as a liability the amount to be paid to the employees.

Illustration 87—Continued

ROLL
October 18, 1959

Deductions					Payment		Distribution		
F.I.C.A. Taxes	Federal Income Taxes	U.S. Savings Bonds	Union Dues	Total Deductions	Net Pay	Check No.	Sales Salaries	Office Salaries	Delivery Salaries
2.00	5.30		1.25	8.55	71.45	893	80.00		
2.30	12.10	6.25	1.25	21.90	70.10	894	92.00		
1.80	3.90			5.70	66.30	895		72.00	
1.00	7.30	1.25	1.25	10.80	29.20	896	40.00		
2.00	12.30	1.25	2.50	18.05	61.95	897			80.00
2.25	7.10		1.25	10.60	79.40	898	90.00		
2.00	10.90	6.25	1.25	20.40	59.60	899	80.00		″
2.45	9.20	6.25	2.50	20.40	77.60	900			98.00
	11.50	6.25		17.75	102.25	901		120.00	
15.80	79.60	27.50	11.25	134.15	617.85		382.00	192.00	178.00

Paying the Employees

Almost all businesses pay their employees with checks. In a small firm having but few employees these checks are often drawn on the regular bank account. When this is done, each individual pay check is recorded in either the Check Register or the Cash Payments Journal. Since each

Illustration 88—An Ordinary Check Register with an Accrued Payroll Debit Column

Date		Check No.	Payee	Account Debited	F	Sundry Accounts Debit	Accts. Pay. Debit	Accr. Pay. Debit	Pur. Dis. Credit	Bank Credit
Oct.	18	893	Robert Austin	Accrued Payroll				71.45		71.45
	18	894	Charles Cross	"				70.10		70.10
	18	895	John Cruz	"				66.30		66.30
	18	896	Howard Keife	"				29.20		29.20
	18	897	Guy Adams	"				61.95		61.95
	18	898	Lee Miller	"				79.40		79.40
	18	899	Dale Sears	"				59.60		59.60
	18	900	Robert Smith	"				77.60		77.60
	18	901	George Tucker	"				102.25		102.25

check results in a debit to the Accrued Payroll Payable account, posting labor may be saved by adding an Accrued Payroll Payable debit column to the Check Register or Cash Payments Journal. For example, assume that a firm uses a Check Register like that described in Chapter 10; this was the Check Register similar to the Cash Payments Journal used in the chapters before the introduction of the voucher system. If a firm uses such a Check Register and adds an Accrued Payroll debit column, the entries to pay the employees of the payroll shown in Illustration 87 will appear somewhat like those in Illustration 88.

Although not required by law, most employers furnish their employees an earnings statement at the time of each wage payment. The objective of such a statement is to inform each employee, and to give him a record that may be retained, of his hours worked, gross pay, deductions, and net pay. The statement usually takes the form of a detachable pay check stub that is removed before the check is cashed. A pay check with a detachable stub showing deductions is reproduced in Illustration 89.

Payroll Bank Account

A business having a large number of employees normally makes use of a special payroll bank account in paying its employees. When a special payroll bank account is used, one check for the total amount of the payroll is drawn on the regular bank account. This check is then deposited in the special payroll bank account, and individual payroll checks are drawn on this special payroll account. Because only one check for the total of the payroll is drawn on the regular bank account each payday, the use of a special payroll bank account greatly simplifies the reconciliation of the regular bank account. When a special payroll bank account is used, the regular bank account is reconciled without considering the many payroll checks that may be outstanding. Likewise, when the payroll bank account is separately reconciled, only the outstanding payroll checks need be considered.

Illustration 89—A Payroll Check

EUGENE SUPPLY COMPANY
EUGENE, OREGON

EMPLOYEE ___*Charles Cross*___

STATEMENT OF EARNINGS AND DEDUCTIONS FOR EMPLOYEE'S RECORD——
DETACH BEFORE CASHING CHECK

TOTAL HOURS	O.T. HOURS	REG. PAY RATE	REG-ULAR PAY	O.T. PREM. PAY	GROSS PAY	F.I.C.A. TAXES	FEDERAL INCOME TAXES	U.S. SAVINGS BONDS	UNION DUES	TOTAL DEDUC-TIONS	NET PAY
44	4	2.00	88.00	4.00	92.00	2.30	12.10	6.25	1.25	21.90	70.10

EUGENE SUPPLY COMPANY
2590 Chula Vista Street   No. 894
Eugene, Oregon

DATE ___*October 18, 1959*___

PAY TO THE
ORDER OF ___*Charles Cross*___ $ 70.10

Seventy dollars and ten cents

EUGENE SUPPLY COMPANY

To: **Merchants National Bank**
EUGENE, OREGON

Often a company with a sufficient number of employees to have need of a special payroll bank account also uses a voucher system. Such a company in paying its employees completes the following steps:

1. First, the company records the information shown on its Payroll Register in the usual manner with a general journal entry similar to the one illustrated on page 385. This entry causes the sum of the net pay of all employees to be credited to the liability account Accrued Payroll Payable.
2. Next, a voucher for the amount of the accrued payroll payable is drawn and entered in the Voucher Register. This results in a debit to Accrued Payroll Payable and a credit to Vouchers Payable. It transfers the liability to a voucher payable.
3. Then a single check in payment of the payroll voucher is drawn, endorsed, and deposited in the payroll bank account. This transfers cash equal to

the amount of the net payroll from the regular bank account to the special payroll bank account.

4. Last, individual payroll checks for the amount of each employee's net pay are drawn on the special payroll bank account and delivered to the employees. This pays the employees; and, as soon as all of the employees cash their checks, exhausts the funds in the special account.

A special Payroll Check Register may be used in connection with a payroll bank account. However, most companies do not use such a register. They prefer to enter the numbers of the payroll checks in the Payroll Register. This in effect makes the Payroll Register act also as a Check Register.

Employee's Individual Earnings Record

As previously explained, the Payroll Register shown in Illustration 87 is usually a supplementary memorandum record. The information recorded in this Payroll Register is generally not posted directly to the ledger accounts but reaches these accounts through a summarizing general journal entry. The Employee's Individual Earnings Record shown in Illustration 90 is also a supplementary memorandum record. It provides for each employee in one record a full year's summary of his working time, gross earnings, deductions, and net pay. In addition it accumulates information:

1. That serves as a basis for the employer's state and federal payroll tax returns and reports.
2. That tells when an employee has earned $3,000, and his wages are no longer a basis for the employer's state and federal unemployment taxes.
3. That tells when an employee has earned $4,800, and his wages are no longer subject to deductions for F.I.C.A. taxes.
4. That supplies the data for the Withholding Statement, Form W–2, that must be given to the employee at the end of each year.

While both the Payroll Register and the Employee's Individual Earnings Record are supplementary memorandum records, the Payroll Register does in effect act as a book of original entry, and the earnings record does in effect act as a book of final entry. The Payroll Register acts as a book of original entry because the information as to each employee's earnings, deductions, and net pay is first recorded on a single line in the Payroll Register. After being recorded here, the information is then posted each pay period to the individual employees' earnings records which become the final record of the earnings of each employee.

Payroll Taxes Levied on the Employer

Under the previous discussion of the Federal Social Security Act, it was pointed out that F.I.C.A. taxes for the payment of employee old-age benefits are levied in like amounts on both employed workers and their employers. In every covered industry, each payday the employer is required by law to deduct from the pay of his employees the amounts of their F.I.C.A. taxes. In addition, a covered employer must himself pay a tax

Illustration 90

EMPLOYEE'S INDIVIDUAL EARNINGS RECORD

Employee's Name __Charles Gross__   S.S. Acct. No. __307-03-2195__   Employee No. __97__

Home Address __111 South Greenwood__   Notify in Case of Emergency __Margaret Gross__   Phone No. __4-9834__

Employed __6/7/52__   Date of Termination _____   Reason _____

Date of Birth __June 6, 1921__   Date Becomes 65 __June 6, 1986__   Male (X) Female ( )   Married (X) Single ( )   Number of Exemptions __4__   Pay Rate __$2.00 hr.__

Occupation __Press operator__   Place __Shop__

Date		Time Lost		Time Wk.				O.T. Prem. Pay	Gross Pay	Cumulative Pay	F.I.C.A. Taxes	Federal Income Taxes	U.S. Saving Bonds	Union Dues	Total Deductions	Net Pay	Check No.
Per. Ends	Paid	Hrs.	Reason	Total	O.T. Hours	Reg. Pay											
1/5	1/5			40		80.00			80.00	80.00	2.00	10.00	6.25	1.25	19.50	60.50	173
1/12	1/12			40		80.00			80.00	160.00	2.00	10.00	6.25	1.25	19.50	60.50	201
1/19	1/19			40		80.00			80.00	240.00	2.00	10.00	6.25	1.25	19.50	60.50	243
1/26	1/26	4	Sick	36		72.00			72.00	312.00	1.80	8.20	6.25	1.25	17.50	54.50	295
2/2	2/2			40		80.00			80.00	392.00	2.00	10.00	6.25	1.25	19.50	60.50	339
2/9	2/9			40		80.00			80.00	472.00	2.00	10.00	6.25	1.25	19.50	60.50	354
2/16	2/16			40		80.00			80.00	552.00	2.00	10.00	6.25	1.25	19.50	60.50	397
2/23	2/23			40		80.00			80.00	632.00	2.00	10.00	6.25	1.25	19.50	60.50	446
10/18	10/18	4		44	4	88.00		4.00	92.00	3,240.00	2.30	12.10	6.25	1.25	21.90	70.10	894

equal to the sum of his employees' F.I.C.A. taxes. Commonly, the tax levied on the employer is recorded at the same time the payroll to which it relates is recorded. Also, since both the employees' taxes and employer's tax are reported on the same tax return and are paid in one amount, the liability for both is normally recorded in the same liability account. Both are normally credited to a single F.I.C.A. Taxes Payable account.

Although F.I.C.A. taxes are levied in like amounts on both covered employers and their employees, employers only are required to pay federal and, usually, state unemployment taxes. Most employers record all three of these payroll taxes with one general journal entry. This entry is normally made at the same time the payroll to which the taxes relate is recorded. For example, the entry to record the employer's payroll taxes on the payroll shown in Illustration 87 is:

Oct.	18	Payroll Taxes Expense................	32.00	
		F.I.C.A. Taxes Payable............		15.80
		State Unemployment Taxes Payable..		14.58
		Federal Unemployment Taxes Payable		1.62
		To record the payroll taxes of the employer.		

The debit of this entry is to the expense account Payroll Taxes Expense. Often this one expense debit is broken into the amounts applicable to each type of salaries and is recorded in several expense accounts such as, for example, Payroll Taxes Expense on Sales Salaries, Payroll Taxes Expense on Office Salaries, and Payroll Taxes Expense on Delivery Salaries. A division such as this makes it possible to classify on the income statement the amount of taxes expense applicable to each type of salaries.

There are three current liability accounts credited in the foregoing entry recording the employer's payroll taxes. The credit to F.I.C.A. Taxes Payable is for $15.80. This amount is equal to and matches the amount shown as deducted from the employees' wages in the Payroll Register of Illustration 87. It is 2½ per cent, the 1959 rate, of $632. The total amount of the payroll is $752; but since the amount previously paid in wages to one employee, George Tucker, is in excess of $4,800, the $120 of his current wages is tax exempt. The fact that Tucker's current wages are not subject to F.I.C.A. taxes is determined by the person responsible for completing the Payroll Register by an examination of the Cumulative Pay column of Tucker's individual earnings record.

The $14.58 credit to State Unemployment Taxes Payable in the employer's payroll tax entry is based on the assumption that the employer's tax rate is a full 2.7 per cent of the first $3,000 paid each employee. As previously stated, it is the duty of the one responsible for completing the Payroll Register to check the Cumulative Pay columns of the employees' individual earnings records to see when the earnings of any employee reach $3,000 and are no longer subject to state and federal unemployment taxes, and when the earnings reach $4,800 and are no longer subject to F.I.C.A. taxes. In the illustrative payroll of this chapter it is assumed that the employees have cumulative earnings prior to this pay period as shown in Illustration 91.

If the employees have cumulative earnings as listed in Illustration 91, both George Tucker and Charles Cross have earned in excess of $3,000 and their pay is assumed, as it is in most states, to be exempt from unemployment taxes. If the $120 pay of Tucker and the $92 pay of Cross are tax exempt, the $14.58 credit to State Unemployment Taxes Payable in the entry recording the employer's payroll taxes is calculated as follows: Total wages of $752 less tax exempt wages of $212 equals $540 of wages subject to tax. Then, $540 of wages subject to taxes multiplied by the tax rate of 2.7 per cent gives $14.58 of state unemployment taxes payable.

Illustration 91

EMPLOYEES' CUMULATIVE EARNINGS
THROUGH THE OCTOBER 11 PAY PERIOD

Robert Austin	$2,860.00
Charles Cross	3,240.00
John Cruz	2,450.00
Howard Keife	2,840.00
Guy Adams	2,834.00
Lee Miller	2,610.00
Dale Sears	1,680.00
Robert Smith	2,210.00
George Tucker	4,920.00

Because the full 2.7 per cent of state unemployment tax rate may be deducted from the federal unemployment tax, the federal unemployment tax rate is 0.3 per cent. This tax also applies to only the first $3,000 paid to each employee. Therefore, the amount of federal unemployment tax liability in the illustrated journal entry is 0.3 per cent of $540, or $1.62.

Paying the Payroll Taxes

The federal income taxes and the F.I.C.A. taxes withheld each payday from the pay of the employees plus the F.I.C.A. tax imposed on the employer are current liabilities of the employer until paid to the Director of Internal Revenue. Both the employer's and the employees' F.I.C.A. taxes are credited to one F.I.C.A. Taxes Payable Account. Here they accumulate each payday until paid. Likewise, each payday, the liability for the employees' income tax is credited to an Employees' Federal Income Taxes Payable account where it accumulates until paid.

If the sum of these taxes exceeds $100 in any month, the amount of the taxes must be deposited in a federal depository bank to the credit of the United States Treasury Department. This deposit, for which the depositor receives a receipt, must be made within fifteen days after the end of the month to which the taxes apply. The entry to record the deposit of money equal to the amount of the taxes cancels the liability for the taxes on the books of the depositing employer. For example, assume that an employer is liable in one month for F.I.C.A. taxes of **$40** and employees' income taxes of **$115**. When he deposits a check for the sum of these amounts to the credit of the Treasury Department in a federal depository, he makes the following cash payments entry:

Nov.	14	F.I.C.A. Taxes Payable...............	40.00	
		Employees' Federal Income Taxes Payable	115.00	
		Cash.............................		155.00
		To record the deposit of an amount equal to the payroll taxes of October.		

If the employer's tax liability exceeds $100 each month of the quarter, after each month, he will deposit money equal to the amount of the tax liability of the month and make a journal entry similar to the one just given. Then, within one month after the end of the calendar quarter, he will file his Employer's Quarterly Tax Return, Form 941, reporting the amount of taxes. The employer will attach the depository receipts to the tax return to indicate that payment of the tax has been made by deposits in a federal depository bank. No journal entry is needed to record the filing of the return.

If the employer's tax liability is less than $100 each month, he may use the depository procedure in paying the taxes. However, if he chooses, he may accumulate the F.I.C.A. tax liability and employees' income tax liability until the end of each calendar quarter. The employer then files his Employer's Quarterly Tax Return and attaches a check to it in payment of the taxes. The check is recorded with debits to the F.I.C.A. Taxes Payable and Employees' Federal Income Taxes Payable and a credit to Cash.

The employer's liability for state unemployment tax is recorded in a current liability account called "State Unemployment Taxes Payable." It accumulates here each payday until paid to the state treasurer or other state official responsible for collecting the tax. Most states require a quarterly tax return to report the amount of the tax liability. Many states require the deposit in a state depository bank of an amount of money equal to the tax liability, if the tax exceeds $100 in a single month. These procedures are similar to the federal procedures; consequently, most employers account for state unemployment taxes in the same manner as F.I.C.A. and employee income taxes.

As previously stated, only employers pay a federal unemployment tax. The liability for this tax is recorded each payday in a current liability account called "Federal Unemployment Taxes Payable." The tax is paid only once each year; therefore, the liability accumulates each payday until the end of the year. Within one month after the end of the year, the employer files his tax return called an "Annual Federal Tax Return of Employers of Four or More Individuals Under the Federal Unemployment Tax Act, Form 940." He attaches a check to the return for the amount of his tax liability. The check is recorded with a debit to the account Federal Unemployment Taxes Payable and a credit to the Cash account.

Accruing Taxes and Wages

Payroll taxes are levied on wages actually paid. Consequently, since accrued wages are wages earned but unpaid, there is no legal liability for payroll taxes on accrued wages. Nevertheless, under the accrual basis of accounting both wages and the taxes on the wages are an expense of the accounting period in which the wages are earned by the employees. Therefore, since both wages and the payroll taxes on the wages are an expense of the period in which the wages are earned, if there are any accrued wages at the end of an accounting period, both the wages and the applicable payroll taxes should be recorded if all the expenses of the period are to appear on the income statement.

Many accountants record accrued payroll taxes in the same adjusting entry used to record accrued wages. To illustrate this entry, assume that the accounting period of a firm ends on December 31; that the last pay period of this firm ended on December 27; that the employees of the firm worked on December 29, 30, and 31; and that for these three days the employees earned $750 of sales salaries and $250 of office salaries. The adjusting entry to record the accrued wages and the payroll taxes on these wages is:

Dec.	31	Sales Salaries Expense.................	750.00	
		Office Salaries Expense................	250.00	
		Payroll Taxes Expense................	55.00	
		F.I.C.A. Taxes Payable............		25.00
		State Unemployment Taxes Payable..		27.00
		Federal Unemployment Taxes Payable		3.00
		Accrued Payroll Payable...........		1,000.00
		To record the accrued payroll.		

The $55 debit to Payroll Taxes Expense records the payroll taxes levied on the employer. The $55 is the sum of the $25 of F.I.C.A. taxes, $27 of state unemployment taxes, and $3.00 of federal unemployment taxes.

Although accrued payroll taxes on accrued wages are theoretically an expense of the accounting period in which the wages are earned, often such accrued taxes are not material in amount. Consequently, many accountants apply the rule of materiality (see page 302) and do not accrue such taxes at the time they record accrued wages.

QUESTIONS FOR CLASS DISCUSSION

1. What are F.I.C.A. taxes? Who pays these taxes and how much must be paid? For what purposes are the funds from F.I.C.A. taxes used?
2. Company A collects from its employees approximately $150 each month in F.I.C.A. taxes and federal income taxes; Company B collects approximately $73. When must each of these companies remit these amounts to the Director of Internal Revenue?

3. What amount of benefits is paid to unemployed workers by the Federal Unemployment Insurance Program? Why was the Federal Unemployment Insurance Act passed?

4. Who pays federal unemployment insurance taxes? What is the tax rate? When is the tax due?

5. What are the objectives of state unemployment insurance laws? Who pays state unemployment insurance?

6. What is a state unemployment merit rating? Why are such merit ratings granted?

7. What determines the amount that must be deducted from an employee's wages for federal income taxes?

8. What is a wage bracket withholding table? Use the wage bracket withholding table given in Illustration 85 to find the amount of income taxes to be withheld from the wages of an employee with three exemptions who earned $83.50 in a week.

9. What does the Fair Labor Standards Act require of a covered employer?

10. How is a clock card used in recording the time an employee is on the job?

11. How is a special payroll bank account used in paying the wages of employees?

12. At the end of an accounting period a firm's special payroll bank account has a balance of $162.35. The account has this balance because the payroll checks of two employees have not cleared the bank. Should this item appear on the firm's balance sheet? If so, where?

13. What information is accumulated on an employee's individual earnings record? Why must this information be accumulated? For what purposes is the information used?

14. What payroll taxes are levied on the employer? What taxes are deducted from the wages of an employee?

15. Paul O'Connor hires an employee and pays him $50 per week. How much do the services of the employee cost O'Connor if taxes are considered a part of the cost and O'Connor has a state unemployment merit rating that reduces his state unemployment taxes to 1.5 per cent?

PROBLEMS

Problem 16–1

On January 7 the column totals of a company's Payroll Register indicated that the company's sales employees had earned a total of $2,000 and its office employees had earned a total of $400 during the first payroll period of the current year. The employees were to have F.I.C.A. taxes withheld from their wages at the current rate; and they were to have $212 of federal income taxes withheld, $60 of United States savings bond deductions, and $15 of union dues withheld.

Required:

1. Use the current rate to calculate the total of the F.I.C.A. Taxes column in the foregoing register.

2. Prepare a general journal entry to record the information of the Payroll Register.

3. Assume that the company uses a voucher system and a special payroll bank account, and prepare entries in general journal form to record the payroll voucher and its payment.

4. Prepare a general journal entry to record the payroll taxes of the company under the assumptions that it has nine employees and a state unemploy-

ment tax merit rating that reduces its state unemployment tax rate to 1.5 per cent.

Problem 16–2

The Payroll Register of T. A. Swanson Company for the weekly pay period ended on October 15 of the current year and other records showed the following information:

Employees' Names	Clock No.	Daily Time							Pay Rate	Federal Income Taxes	U.S. Savings Bonds	Earnings to End of Previous Week
		M	T	W	T	F	S	S				
Harry Wingard	107	8	8	8	8	8	0	0	2.00	7.70	2.50	3,220.00
William Froman	108	8	8	8	8	8	8	8	2.25	9.20	2.50	4,880.00
Robert Sheppard	109	8	8	8	8	8	0	0	1.50	1.70	1.25	2,400.00
Carl Peterson	110	8	8	8	8	8	8	0	1.80	12.30	2.50	2,872.00

Required:

1. Enter the relevant information in the proper columns of a Payroll Register similar to the one shown in Illustration 87. Complete the register using the current F.I.C.A. tax rate in calculating F.I.C.A. taxes. Assume that the first two employees are sales employees, the third employee works in the office, and the fourth employee drives the delivery truck. Also, assume that the employees are subject to the terms of the Fair Labor Standards Act.
2. Prepare a general journal entry to record the column totals of the Payroll Register.
3. Assume that the company uses a voucher system and a special payroll bank account. Prepare entries in general journal form to record the payroll voucher and its payment. Enter the payroll check numbers in the Payroll Register; assume that the first payroll check number is 853.
4. Prepare the general journal entry to record the liabilities of the company for payroll taxes. Assume that the company pays a state unemployment tax of 2.7 per cent of the first $3,000 of each employee's wages.

Problem 16–3

The following information was taken from the Payroll Register and other records of Edom Sales Company for the weekly pay period ended December 8 of the current year:

Employees' Names	Clock No.	Daily Time							Pay Rate	Income Tax Exemptions	U.S. Savings Bonds	Union Dues	Earnings to End of Previous Week
		M	T	W	T	F	S	S					
James Baker	211	8	8	8	8	8	0	0	2.00	5	2.50	1.00	2,730.50
William Holmes...	212	8	8	8	8	8	0	0	2.00	3	2.50	1.00	4,010.50
Brian Peek........	213	8	8	8	8	8	0	0	2.50	5	2.50	1.00	4,740.00
Donald Watts.....	214	8	8	8	9	9	8	0	1.50	2	2.50	....	2,980.00

Required:

1. Enter the relevant information in the proper columns of a Payroll Register similar to the one shown in Illustration 87. Complete the register using the current F.I.C.A. tax rate in calculating F.I.C.A. taxes and the wage bracket withholding table of Illustration 85 in calculating amounts of federal in-

come tax to withhold from the wages of the employees other than Brian Peek. Assume that Peek's income tax withholding is $6.90. Assume that the first three employees are sales employees and that Donald Watts works in the office. Assume also that the company is subject to the Fair Labor Standards Act.

2. Prepare a general journal entry to record the information of the Payroll Register.
3. Assume that the company uses a voucher system and a special payroll bank account. Prepare entries in general journal form to record the payroll voucher and its payment. Enter the payroll check numbers in the Payroll Register; assume that the first payroll check number is 596.
4. Prepare a general journal entry to record the payroll taxes expense of the company that resulted from this payroll. Assume that the company has a merit rating that reduces its state unemployment tax rate to 1 per cent of the first $3,000 paid each employee.

Problem 16–4

Ryan Sales Company has eight employees to each of whom it pays $250 per month on the last day of each month. On December 1, 1959, the following accounts and balances appeared in the company's ledger:

a) F.I.C.A. Taxes Payable, $100. (Since the company's F.I.C.A. and employees' income taxes exceed $100 each month, the taxes must be paid each month. Consequently, the balance of this account represents the liability for both the employer and employees' F.I.C.A. taxes for the month of November only.)
b) Employees' Federal Income Taxes Payable, $163 (liability for month of November only).
c) Federal Unemployment Taxes Payable, $66 (liability for first eleven months of the year).
d) State Unemployment Taxes Payable, $48 (liability for October and November).
e) Employees' Bond Deductions, $65.
f) Employees' Group Insurance Premiums Payable, $72 (liability for October and November).

During December, the company completed the following payroll transactions:

Dec. 14 Prepared Voucher No. 645 payable to the First National Bank. The voucher was for $263 and was in payment of the November F.I.C.A. and employee income taxes. Issued Check No. 624 in payment of the voucher and received a federal depository receipt in return.

31 Prepared and posted a general journal entry to record the December Payroll Register. The column totals of the register were as follows:

Gross Pay	F.I.C.A. Taxes	Federal Income Taxes	U.S. Savings Bonds	Group Insurance Deductions	Total Deductions	Net Pay	Sales Salaries	Office Salaries
$2,000	$50.00	$163.00	$15.00	$36.00	$264.00	$1,736	$1,750	$250

31 Prepared Voucher No. 689 payable to Payroll in payment of the December payroll. Issued Check No. 671 in payment of the

voucher, deposited the check in the special payroll bank account, and issued payroll checks to the employees.

31 Prepared and posted a general journal entry to record the employer's liabilities for payroll taxes. (Use the 1959, 2½ per cent rate in calculating F.I.C.A. taxes.) Due to a merit rating, the company's state unemployment tax rate was 1.2 per cent.

Jan. 2 Prepared Voucher No. 692 payable to the First National Bank and issued Check No. 674 in its payment. The voucher and check were for $37.50 and were for the purchase of two $18.75, United States savings bonds. Delivered the bonds to the employees.

3 Prepared Voucher No. 698 payable to the Employees' Mutual Insurance Company and issued Check No. 682 in its payment. The voucher and check were for $108 and were in payment of the October, November, and December employees' group insurance premiums.

15 Prepared Voucher No. 752 payable to the State Tax Commission for the state unemployment taxes of October, November, and December. Issued Check No. 739 in its payment. Mailed the check along with the 1959 fourth-quarter tax return to the State Tax Commission.

15 Prepared Voucher No. 753 payable to the First National Bank and issued Check No. 740 in payment of the voucher. The voucher was in payment of the December F.I.C.A. and employee income taxes. Received a federal depository receipt.

28 Prepared Voucher No. 832 payable to the Director of Internal Revenue for the 1959 Federal Unemployment Taxes. Issued Check No. 818 in its payment. Mailed the check and the Annual Federal Unemployment Tax Return to the Director.

28 Mailed the Director of Internal Revenue the Employer's Quarterly Federal Tax Return reporting the F.I.C.A. taxes and the employee federal income tax deductions for the last quarter of 1959. Attached federal depository receipts to show that the tax liability had been paid.

Required:

1. Prepare a Check Register similar to the one shown in Illustration 81, and prepare a Voucher Register with the following columns:

Date	Voucher No.	Payee	When and How Paid		Vouchers Payable Credit	Sundry Accounts Debited		
			Date	Check		Account Name	F	Amount

2. Enter the payroll transactions in the Voucher Register, Check Register, and a General Journal.

CLASS EXERCISE

Exercise 16–1

The following information as to earnings and deductions for a pay period ended December 15 of the current year were taken from a company's Payroll Register and other payroll records:

Employees	Gross Pay	Earnings to End of Previous Period	Federal Income Taxes	U.S. Savings Bonds
Gary Hall................	84.00	2,930.00	3.00	2.50
John Hunt................	84.00	3,140.00	11.30	6.25
Keith Mills...............	96.00	4,760.00	7.70	5.00
Lyle Snow................	80.00	2,760.00	5.60	5.00

Required:

1. Use the current rate and calculate the F.I.C.A. taxes, total deductions, and net pay of the employees.
2. Prepare a general journal entry to record the information of the Payroll Register. (Assume that all employees are sales employees.)
3. Prepare a general journal entry to record the employer's payroll taxes. (Assume that the employer has a state unemployment tax merit rating that reduces his state unemployment tax rate to 2 per cent.)

SUPPLEMENTARY PROBLEMS

Problem 16–A

The accounting periods of Hatfield Company end each June 30. On June 30, 1959, the company made the following adjusting entry:

June	30	Sales Salaries Expense..................	1,200.00	
		Office Salaries Expense................	240.00	
		Employer's Payroll Taxes Expense.......	61.92	
		F.I.C.A. Taxes Payable............		36.00
		State Unemployment Taxes Payable..		21.60
		Federal Unemployment Taxes Payable.........................		4.32
		Accrued Payroll Payable...........		1,440.00
		To record the accrued payroll of the last three days of June.		

The adjusting entry was not reversed; and on July 2, when the June 28–July 2 pay period ended, the column totals of the Payroll Register for the pay period gave the following information:

Employees' F.I.C.A. Taxes Payable.........................$	60.00
Employees' Federal Income Taxes Payable..................	260.00
Employees' Bond Deductions.............................	75.00
Sales Salaries..	2,000.00
Office Salaries...	400.00

Required:

Under the assumption that no employee had earned $3,000 by July 2, give the general journal entries to record the June 28–July 2 payroll and the payroll taxes of the employer resulting from the payroll.

Problem 16–B

The following information was taken from a firm's payroll records for the weekly pay period ended November 4 of the current year:

| Employees' Names | Clock No. | Daily Time | | | | | | | Pay Rate | Federal In-come Taxes | U.S. Savings Bonds | Earnings to End of Previous Week |
		M	T	W	T	F	S	S				
Richard Blank	101	8	8	8	8	8	0	0	1.90	9.20	1.25	2,960.00
John Finan	102	8	8	8	8	8	4	0	2.00	6.80	2.50	3,204.00
Melvin King	103	8	8	8	8	8	8	0	2.00	14.80	5.00	4,624.00
James Partch	104	8	8	8	8	8	0	0	1.90	2.30	0	2,910.00
Thomas Reid	105	4	0	8	8	8	0	0	1.90	5.00	1.25	2,709.00
Jack A. Ripke	106	8	8	8	8	8	0	0	1.90	13.90	5.00	2,854.00
John Sullivan	107	8	8	8	8	8	4	0	2.00	9.10	2.50	3,164.00
Donald Vaaler	108	8	8	8	8	8	8	0	2.50	21.00	6.25	4,823.00

Required:

1. Enter the relevant information in the proper columns of a Payroll Register similar to Illustration 87, and complete the register using the current F.I.C.A. tax rate. Assume that the salaries of Richard Blank and James Partch are classified as delivery salaries, the salary of Melvin King is classified as office salaries, and the remaining salaries are classified as sales salaries.
2. Prepare the general journal entry to record the information of the Payroll Register.
3. Assume that the firm uses a special payroll bank account and a voucher system. Prepare entries in general journal form to record the payroll voucher and the check in its payment. Enter the payroll check numbers in the Payroll Register. Assume that the first payroll check number is 878.
4. Prepare a general journal entry to record the employer's payroll taxes expense resulting from the payroll. Assume that the firm has a merit rating that reduces its state unemployment tax rate to 1.2 per cent on the first $3,000 paid each employee.

Chapter 17

PARTNERSHIPS: NATURE AND SHARING OF EARNINGS

THERE ARE three common types of business organizations: single proprietorships, partnerships, and corporations. When a business enterprise is owned by a single individual, the business is said to be a *single proprietorship*. When two or more people enter into a contract to join their resources and abilities in the operation of a business, the business is called a *partnership*. A *corporation* joins the resources of three or more people in a more formal organization than a partnership. The business units illustrated thus far in this text have been single proprietorships. Corporations and their accounting are discussed beginning in Chapter **19**. This and the next chapter are devoted to a discussion of some of the problems of partnership accounting.

Characteristics of a Partnership

About one half of the states have adopted the Uniform Partnership Act to govern the formation and operation of partnerships. This act defines a partnership as "an association of two or more persons to carry on as co-owners a business for profit." A partnership has been further defined as "an association of two or more competent persons under a contract to combine some or all of their property, labor, and skill in the operation of a business, and to share the profits and losses of the business in certain proportions."

While both of these definitions point out the legal nature of a partnership, a better understanding of the partnership as a business enterprise may be gained by an examination of some of its characteristics.

A Voluntary Association. A partnership is a voluntary association of individuals. A person cannot be forced into a partnership. Members of a partnership have the right to select the people with whom they associate as partners. This is because each member of a partnership is responsible for the business acts of his partners that are within the scope of the partnership. Furthermore, each partner is unlimitedly liable for the debts of the partnership and should, therefore, be permitted to select as partners persons of his equal in financial responsibility.

Based upon a Contract. A partnership is formed by a contract between two or more people to associate themselves in a business for profit. The contract may be written, orally expressed, or implied. One of the advantages of the partnership form of organization is the ease with which a partnership may be started. All that is necessary is that two or more competent people agree to be partners. Their agreement should be in writing; however, it is just as binding if only expressed orally. Even beyond this, in the eyes of the law a partnership may be said to exist without an expressed agreement between the partners, if the partners so conduct themselves as to lead others to believe that they are partners.

Limited Life.   The life of a partnership is limited. A partnership is based upon a contract. If the partnership contract is for a fixed period of time, the partnership automatically dissolves at the end of the specified time. If the contract does not state a definite period of time, the partnership ends when the business for which it was created is completed. If no period of time is stated and if the business cannot be completed but goes on for an indefinite period, the partnership may be terminated at will by any one of the partners. In addition, since a partnership is based upon a contract, the death, bankruptcy, or anything that takes away the ability of one of the partners to enter into a contract automatically ends a partnership. Since some of these factors are unpredictable, a partnership may be ended at a financially inopportune time.

Co-ownership of Partnership Property.   A partner is co-owner with his partners of the partnership property. Partnership property belongs jointly to all of the partners. At times this may become important. For example, Smith, Jones, and Green form a partnership. Jones invests a building which he purchased several years previously for $20,000 and against which he has recorded depreciation of $5,000. Due to changing real estate values, of which Jones is not aware, the market value of the building at the time of the partnership formation is $25,000. Jones invests the building in the partnership at its book value of $15,000. One year later, the building is sold by the partners for $25,000. The $10,000 gain on the sale of the building belongs to all of the partners. Property once invested becomes partnership property and is jointly owned by all of the partners.

Co-ownership of Earnings.   One of the tests of the existence of a partnership is that the earnings are co-owned by the partners. This does not mean that earnings are shared equally. Earnings may be shared in any ratio; but if a partnership exists, each of the partners must have a true ownership right in the earnings. Although an ownership right in the earnings of a partnership is a test of the existence of a partnership, the sharing of earnings is not a conclusive test of such existence. For example, an employee may be given 10 per cent of earnings as a salary or bonus. This does not make him a partner; he has no ownership right in the earnings. The earnings are used merely to measure the amount of the employee's salary or bonus.

Mutual Agency.   Each partner is an agent of the partnership while acting within the scope of the partnership business. As an agent of the partnership he can bind the partnership to any contract that is within the apparent scope of the business. For example, a partner in a trading business can enter into contracts in the name of the partnership to borrow

money, buy merchandise, and hire employees. These are within the scope
of the business of a trading firm. On the other hand, a partner in a law firm
acting alone cannot bind his partners to a contract to buy merchandise or
to borrow money. These are not within the scope of the normal business
of a law firm. An outsider may not assume that a partner in a law firm
has these rights.

Partners among themselves may agree to limit the right of any one or
more of the partners to negotiate certain contracts for the partnership.
While such an agreement is binding upon the partners and upon outsiders
who know of the agreement, it is not binding upon outsiders who are unaware of its existence. Outsiders who are unaware of anything to the contrary have a right to assume that each of the partners has the normal
agency rights of a partner. For example, Adams, Brown, and Chase enter
into a partnership contract. Their agreement specifies that only Brown
may negotiate contracts to buy merchandise for the firm. Chase violates
this agreement and signs a contract with Wilson Company to supply the
firm with merchandise. Wilson Company is unaware of the special agreement among the partners. The partnership is bound by Chase's contract
with Wilson Company. However, Chase is liable to Adams and Brown for
any loss they may incur that is due to his unauthorized contract.

Mutual agency is an important characteristic of the partnership form
of business organization. It offers an important reason for the need of
care in the selection of partners. Good partners benefit all; a poor partner
can do a lot of damage. Mutual agency plus unlimited liability are the
reasons most partnerships are small; two, three, or four are common numbers of partners.

Unlimited Liability. If a partnership suffers losses and the partnership assets become insufficient to pay the partnership liabilities, the
creditors may satisfy their claims from the personal property of the partners. Furthermore, if the personal property of one or more of the partners
is insufficient to pay his share of the excess losses, the creditors may satisfy their claims from the property of the remaining partners who are able
to pay. This means that if the partnership assets are insufficient to meet
creditor claims, the creditors may look to the personal property of any of
the partners for satisfaction. Thus a partner has unlimited liability for the
debts of the partnership.

Unlimited liability may be illustrated as follows: Albert and Bates
each invest $1,000 in a partnership to operate a store. They agree to share
losses and gains equally. Albert has no property other than the $1,000 he
invests. Bates owns his own home, a farm, and has a savings account in
addition to his investment in the partnership. The partners rent a store
building. They also buy $10,000 worth of merchandise and fixtures by
paying $2,000 in cash and promising to pay the $8,000 balance at a later
date. The store building with the merchandise and fixtures is destroyed
by fire before the partners begin business. There is no insurance, all the

partnership assets are lost, and Albert has no other assets. The creditors may collect the full $8,000 of their claims from the personal property of Bates. Bates may later look to Albert for the payment of one half of the claims, if Albert ever becomes able to pay.

Advantages and Disadvantages of a Partnership

Limited life, mutual agency, and unlimited liability may be considered disadvantages of the partnership form of business organization. Yet, notwithstanding these disadvantages, the partnership has advantages over both the single proprietorship and the corporation forms of business organization. A partnership has the advantage of being able to bring together more money, more abilities, and more skills than a single proprietorship. Too, like a single proprietorship, a partnership is much easier to organize than a corporation. Also, the partnership does not have the many formal reports, the public supervision, and the heavy taxation of a corporation. In addition, the partners may act more freely and without the necessity of the formal stockholders' meetings and board of director's meetings of a corporation.

Formation of a Partnership

A partnership is formed by a contract. While an oral or implied contract is binding on the partners, a written contract is to be preferred. A written partnership contract is called the "articles of co-partnership."

Many partnerships, successful in other respects, have dissolved for the lack of agreement among the partners. Consequently, individuals entering into a partnership should attempt to anticipate every possible point of future disagreement. They should resolve these points in advance and enter the solutions in their written and signed partnership contract. Among the many points to be resolved are:

1. The firm name.
2. Location of the principal place of business.
3. Nature, purpose, and scope of the business to be conducted.
4. When the partnership begins.
5. The duration of the partnership.
6. The names of the partners and the capital contribution of each. If anything other than cash is contributed, the agreed values of the items contributed.
7. Rights and duties of each partner.
8. Provision for accounting records.
9. Earnings—how calculated and how shared.
10. Provisions for arbitration of any dispute between the partners.
11. Provisions for dissolution.
12. Special provisions covering any point of possible future disagreement.

Partnership Accounting

Most of the accounting of a partnership is exactly like the accounting of a single proprietorship. The day-by-day transactions are recorded in the same types of journals and registers, and are posted to the same kinds of ledgers. Likewise, the adjustments, work sheets, and statements are in most respects the same. It is only in accounting for transactions affecting proprietorship that partnership accounting differs from single proprietorship accounting. Here, because the ownership rights are divided among the several partners, there must be:

1. A capital account for each partner.
2. A withdrawals account for each partner.
3. An accurate measurement and division of earnings among the partners.

The need for a separate capital account and a separate withdrawals account for each of the members of partnership is fairly obvious. Each partner's capital account is credited and asset accounts showing the nature of the assets invested are debited in recording the investment of each partner. Likewise, a partner's withdrawals of cash and other assets are debited to his withdrawals account; and the withdrawals account is credited for a partner's share of the net income when the Income Summary account is closed at the end of an accounting period. These points need no further discussion. However, the subject of dividing earnings among the partners does need additional discussion.

Nature of Partnership Earnings

In law and in custom a partnership is recognized as a personal association of individuals who have joined themselves together for profit. As a member of the association, an individual partner, although he works for the partnership, is not considered an employee. He is a partner and an associate in the partnership. Consequently, as a member of the partnership, he cannot enter into an employer-employee, contractual relationship with himself. A partner, like a single proprietor, cannot legally hire himself and pay himself a salary. Law and custom recognize this. Law and custom recognize that a partner works for partnership profits and not for a salary. Also, law and custom recognize that a partner invests his money in the partnership for earnings and not for interest.

Although partners have no legal right to salaries in payment for their services or to interest on their investments, partners should realize that their earnings have a threefold nature. Partnership earnings do include a return for services, even though the return is contained within the earnings and is not a salary in a legal sense. Likewise, partnership earnings include a return on invested capital, although the return is not interest in the legal sense of the term. In addition to a return for services and a return on capital invested, partnership earnings also include a payment for sharing risk, which is pure economic profit.

Often, if earnings are to be fairly shared, partners must recognize this threefold nature of their earnings. For example, if one partner contributes five times as much capital as another partner, the method of sharing earnings should take this into consideration. Likewise, if the services of one partner are much more valuable than the services of another partner, some provision in the sharing of earnings should be made for the unequal values.

Division of Earnings

Many methods of sharing partnership earnings are employed. All attempt in one way or another to recognize their threefold nature. Seven methods of sharing earnings will be discussed here. They are:

1. On a stated fractional basis.
2. On the basis of the ratio of capital investments.
3. On the basis of the ratio of average capital investments.
4. Interest on the capital investments and the remaining earnings on the basis of a fixed ratio.
5. Interest on the capital investment excess or deficiency and the remaining earnings in a fixed ratio.
6. Salaries to the partners and the remainder in a fixed ratio.
7. Salaries to the partners, interest on the capital investments, and the remainder in a fixed ratio.

Partnership law provides that in the absence of a contrary agreement, all partnership earnings are shared equally. This means that if partners do not agree in advance as to the method of sharing earnings, each partner receives an equal share. Partners may agree in advance to any method of sharing earnings; and if they agree as to the method of sharing earnings and say nothing of losses, losses are shared in the same manner as earnings.

Earnings Allocated on a Stated Fractional Basis

The easiest method of dividing partnership earnings is to give to each partner a stated fraction of the total. A division on a stated fractional basis may provide for an equal sharing if the service and capital contributions of the partners are equal. An equal sharing may also be provided when the greater capital contribution of one partner is equalized by a greater service contribution of another partner. Or, if the service contributions and capital contributions of the partners are unequal, a fixed ratio may easily provide for an unequal sharing. All that is necessary in any case is for the partners to agree as to the fractional share to be given to each partner.

For example, the partnership agreement of Morse and North may provide that each partner is to receive one half of the earnings; or the agreement may provide for two thirds of the earnings to Morse and one third to North; or it may provide for three fourths to Morse and one fourth to North. Any fractional basis may be agreed upon as long as the partners feel that earnings are thereby fairly shared. For example, assume that the partnership agreement of Morse and North provides for a two-thirds and one-third sharing and that the earnings for a year are $9,000. After all revenue and expense accounts are closed, if the earnings are $9,000, the partnership Income Summary account has a $9,000 credit balance. The Income Summary account is closed, and the earnings are allocated to the partners with the following general journal entry:

Dec.	31	Income Summary......................	9,000.00	
		A. P. Morse, Withdrawals...........		6,000.00
		R. G. North, Withdrawals..........		3,000.00
		To close the Income Summary account and to allocate the earnings to the partners.		

Division of Earnings on the Basis of the Ratio of Capital Investments

If the business of a partnership is of such a nature that the earnings are closely related to the total amount of money invested, as in the investment banking business, a division of earnings on the basis of the ratio of the capital investments of the partners offers a fair basis of allocation. For example, assume that Chase, Davis, and Fall agree to share earnings on the basis of the ratio of their beginning capital investments. If the beginning capital investments are Chase $50,000, Davis $30,000, and Fall $40,000, and if the earnings for the first year are $24,000, the respective shares of the partners are calculated as follows:

Step 1:
Chase, capital.......................... $ 50,000
Davis, capital.......................... 30,000
Fall, capital........................... 40,000
Total Invested..................... $120,000

Step 2:
Share of earnings to Chase $\frac{\$50,000}{\$120,000} \times \$24,000 = \$10,000$

Share of earnings to Davis $\frac{\$30,000}{\$120,000} \times \$24,000 = \$6,000$

Share of earnings to Fall $\frac{\$40,000}{\$120,000} \times \$24,000 = \$8,000$

The general journal entry to allocate the earnings to the partners is then:

Dec.	31	Income Summary......................	24,000.00	
		T. S. Chase, Withdrawals...........		10,000.00
		S. A. Davis, Withdrawals...........		6,000.00
		R. R. Fall, Withdrawals............		8,000.00
		To close the Income Summary account and to allocate the earnings to the partners.		

If disagreements are to be avoided, when earnings are divided on the basis of the ratio of capital investments, the partnership agreement must be specific on a number of points. Some of the points for specific agreement are: (1) Will withdrawals be permitted? (2) If withdrawals are permitted, how will they be treated in the accounts? (3) If withdrawals cause the amounts invested by the partners to fluctuate during an accounting period, how will capital investment ratios be calculated?

When earnings are allocated on the basis of capital investment ratios and capital investments fluctuate throughout the accounting period, the partnership agreement must specify the method of calculating the investment ratios. Capital ratios may be calculated on the basis of: (1) capital investments at the beginning of the partnership, (2) capital investments at the beginning of each accounting period, (3) capital investments at the end of each accounting period, or (4) average capital investments. Methods two and four are commonly used methods.

If the partnership agreement specifies an allocation of earnings based on the ratios of either end of the accounting period investments or average investments, the partners must agree as to the method of handling withdrawals. On this point many partnership agreements provide that each partner may withdraw a fixed amount each month for personal living expenses. These monthly withdrawals are considered to be made in anticipation of earnings and are in the nature of a salary. However, they are not a salary in the legal sense of the term. Furthermore, they are not an expense of the business, and they are usually debited to a partner's Withdrawals account. Withdrawals in excess of the fixed monthly maximum amount provided for personal living expenses are normally considered deductions from capital invested. These excess amounts are usually debited to a partner's Capital account.

Earnings Allocated on the Basis of Average Investments

When earnings are allocated on the basis of the ratio of capital investments and the investments of the partners fluctuate throughout the year, the partners may agree to allocate earnings on the basis of average investments. The average investment of a partner is calculated as follows:

The investment of a partner at the beginning of the fiscal year is multiplied by the number of months it remains unchanged. The result of this multiplication expresses the investment in month-dollars. A *month-dollar* is the equivalent of one dollar invested for one month. When the investment of the partner changes, the new investment is multiplied by the number of months that it remains unchanged. This expresses the new investment in month-dollars. This multiplication procedure is repeated for each time the amount of the investment is changed during the year. The changing investments expressed in month-dollars are then added together. This gives the total month-dollars invested during the year. The total month-dollars invested is then divided by twelve, the number of months in a year, to secure the average investment of the partner.

For example, assume that R. S. Holt and D. D. Good divide earnings on the basis of their average capital ratios and that on December 31 their Capital accounts appeared as follows:

R. S. Holt, Capital					D. D. Good, Capital			
Apr. 1	15,000	Jan. 1	90,000		July 1	20,000	Jan. 1	70,000
Dec. 1	30,000	Oct. 1	15,000					

If Holt and Good have a net income of $28,000 the average investments and the shares of each are calculated as follows:

If Holt's investment during the year was:
$90,000 for 3 months (Jan. 1 to Apr. 1)
75,000 for 6 months (Apr. 1 to Oct. 1)
90,000 for 2 months (Oct. 1 to Dec. 1)
60,000 for 1 month (Dec. 1 to Dec. 31)

Holt's average investment during the year was:
$90,000 × 3 = $270,000
75,000 × 6 = 450,000
90,000 × 2 = 180,000
60,000 × 1 = 60,000
Total $960,000 month-dollars

$ 80,000 average investment
12)$960,000 month-dollars

If Good's investment during the year was:
$70,000 for 6 months (Jan. 1 to July 1)
50,000 for 6 months (July 1 to Dec. 31)

Good's average investment during the year was:
$70,000 × 6 = $420,000
50,000 × 6 = 300,000
Total $720,000 month-dollars

$ 60,000 average investment
12)$720,000 month-dollars

And the allocation of the net income is:
Holt's average investment..........$ 80,000
Good's average investment.......... 60,000
$140,000

Holt's share $\dfrac{\$\ 80,000}{\$140,000}$ × $28,000 = $16,000

Good's share $\dfrac{\$\ 60,000}{\$140,000}$ × $28,000 = $12,000

The journal entry to allocate the net income to the partners is:

Dec.	31	Income Summary......................	28,000.00	
		R. S. Holt, Withdrawals............		16,000.00
		D. D. Good, Withdrawals..........		12,000.00
		To close the Income Summary account and to allocate the earnings.		

Interest on Capital Investments

When earnings are allocated in the ratio of the partners' Capital accounts, the entire earnings allocation is based upon investments. If earnings are closely related to the amount of money invested and other factors are unimportant, such a method of allocation may be fair. Often other factors are important, and partners may wish to share only a portion of the earnings in the capital ratio. In such cases a portion of the earnings may be allocated to the partners in the form of interest on their investments, and the balance may be allocated in some other manner such as a fixed ratio. Such a system recognizes that one of the factors in the production of earnings is the money invested; and it allocates to each partner a share of the earnings that is in proportion to the amount he has invested.

When interest is allowed on the investments of the partners, a portion of the earnings equal to a fixed percentage of the investments is allocated in the capital ratio. For example, assume that the partnership agreement of Adams and Brown, who have investments of $10,000 and $20,000, respectively, provides for 6 per cent interest on investments and an equal sharing of the remainder of all gains or losses. Under such an agreement the share of each of the partners in a $15,000 net income is calculated as follows:

Net Income..			$15,000.00
Allocated as interest:			
Adams (6 per cent on $10,000).....................	$ 600.00		
Brown (6 per cent on $20,000).....................	1,200.00	1,800.00	
Balance after interest.............................		$13,200.00	
Balance allocated equally:			
Adams...	$6,600.00		
Brown...	6,600.00	$13,200.00	

The Income Summary account of Adams and Brown may be closed, and the net income allocated to the partners with two journal entries. (The entries may be combined.) If two entries are used, the first allocates $1,800 to the partners in their capital ratios. It is:

Dec.	31	Income Summary......................	1,800.00	
		A. O. Adams, Withdrawals..........		600.00
		T. C. Brown, Withdrawals..........		1,200.00
		To allocate earnings to the partners equal to 6 per cent on their investments.		

The second entry closes the Income Summary account and shares the remaining earnings. It is:

Dec.	31	Income Summary......................	13,200.00	
		A. O. Adams, Withdrawals..........		6,600.00
		T. C. Brown, Withdrawals..........		6,600.00
		To close the Income Summary account and to share the remaining earnings equally.		

When a portion of the earnings are allocated in the form of interest on investments, the partnership agreement should specify whether the allocation is based on beginning investments, average investments, or ending investments.

Interest on Capital Excess or Deficiency

Partnership agreements are often so worded as to encourage each partner to maintain or increase his partnership investment. To do this the agreement may provide for a fixed investment by each partner and then provide further that interest be allowed on any excess amount invested and charged on any deficiency. For example, assume that the partnership agreement of Allen and Dale provides that each partner is to invest $10,-000. The agreement also provides that each partner is to be allowed interest at the rate of 8 per cent on his average investment in excess of the $10,000 and charged interest at 8 per cent on any deficiency. Then, after interest is allowed and charged, the agreement provides that remaining net income or loss is to be shared equally. If at the end of the first year of operation the partners have maintained average investments of Allen $8,000 and Dale $15,000, an income of $12,840 is shared as follows:

First, Allen is charged interest on an investment deficiency of $2,000, and Dale is allowed interest on an excess investment of $5,000. This is recorded with the following general journal entries:

Dec.	31	Allen, Withdrawals....................	160.00	
		Income Summary.................		160.00
		To charge Allen interest at 8 per cent on an investment deficiency of $2,000.		
	31	Income Summary.....................	400.00	
		Dale, Withdrawals................		400.00
		To allow Dale interest at 8 per cent on an excess investment of $5,000.		

After these entries are posted, the Income Summary account has a credit balance of $12,600 and appears as follows:

Income Summary

Dec. 31	(Expenses)	71,160	Dec. 31	(Sales)	84,000
	(Net income)	12,840			
		84,000			84,000
Dec. 31	(Dale interest)	400	Dec. 31	(Net income)	12,840
			31	(Allen interest)	160

The $12,600 balance in the Income Summary account is the balance after interest is allowed and charged. It is allocated to the partners, and the account is closed with the following entry:

Dec.	31	Income Summary...................... 12,600.00	
		Allen, Withdrawals.................	6,300.00
		Dale, Withdrawals.................	6,300.00
		To allocate equally the balance of income after interest at 8 per cent is allowed and charged.	

Under such an income-sharing agreement the shares of Allen and Dale in a $12,840 income are:

Allen:
One half the income after interest.................$6,300.00
    Less: Interest charged.......................... 160.00 $ 6,140.00

Dale:
One half the income after interest.................$6,300.00
    Add: Interest allowed.......................... 400.00   6,700.00
        Total Income............................. $12,840.00

Salaries as an Income-Sharing Basis

Often in a partnership one partner devotes full time to the partnership affairs and the other partner or partners devote only part time. Too, in partnerships in which all partners devote full time, the services of one partner may be more valuable than the services of the others. In such situations the partners may agree to reward the partner whose services are more valuable, or the partner who devotes more time to partnership affairs, with a larger share of the income. This may be accomplished by giving a larger fractional share of the income to the more valuable or longer working partner, or a portion of the income may be allocated to the more valuable or longer working partner in the form of a salary.

For example, assume that Robert and Owen form a partnership. Robert is to devote full time to partnership affairs. Owen who operates another business is to devote only a small amount of time to the partnership business. As a result, the partners agree to share income by allowing Robert an annual salary of $4,000 and allocating the remaining income or losses equally. If the income of the first year is $10,600, it is shared as follows:

Total Income... $10,600
Allocated to Robert as a salary......................   4,000
Balance after Robert's salary........................ $ 6,600
Balance allocated equally:
    Robert..$3,300
    Owen.. 3,300 $ 6,600

The Income Summary account is closed, and the income is shared with the following entries. They may be combined. The first entry allocates $4,000 of income to Robert as a salary; it is:

Dec.	31	Income Summary.....................	4,000.00	
		Robert, Withdrawals..............		4,000.00
		To allocate $4,000 of the income to Robert in the form of a salary.		

The second entry closes the Income Summary account and shares the remaining income equally; it is:

Dec.	31	Income Summary.....................	6,600.00	
		Robert, Withdrawals..............		3,300.00
		Owen, Withdrawals..............		3,300.00
		To close the Income Summary account and to share the remaining income.		

Income Allocated on a Basis of Salaries and Interest

In some instances in order to share income equitably, partners may agree to use both salaries and interest. In such cases the procedures already illustrated are combined. For example, assume that the partnership agreement of Johnson and Frank provides that income is to be shared as follows:

1. Interest at 8 per cent is to be allowed on the partners' initial investments.
2. Annual salaries of $3,000 to Johnson and $5,000 to Frank are to be allowed.
3. The remaining balance of the Income Summary account to be shared equally.

If the initial investments of the partners are Johnson $20,000 and Frank $8,000, the year's income of $14,000 is shared as follows:

Net Income...		$14,000
Allocated as interest:		
Johnson (8 per cent on $20,000)........................	$1,600	
Frank (8 per cent on $8,000)...........................	640	2,240
Balance after interest.....................................		$11,760
Allocated as salaries:		
Johnson...	$3,000	
Frank...	5,000	8,000
Balance after salaries and interest........................		$ 3,760
Balance shared equally:		
Johnson...	$1,880	
Frank...	1,880	$ 3,760

The following entries are used (they may be combined) to share the income of Johnson and Frank:

Dec.	31	Income Summary.....................	2,240.00	
		Johnson, Withdrawals.............		1,600.00
		Frank, Withdrawals...............		640.00
		To allocate income to the partners equal to 8 per cent on investments.		
	31	Income Summary.....................	8,000.00	
		Johnson, Withdrawals.............		3,000.00
		Frank, Withdrawals...............		5,000.00
		To allocate a portion of the income to the partners in the form of salaries.		
	31	Income Summary.....................	3,760.00	
		Johnson, Withdrawals.............		1,880.00
		Frank, Withdrawals...............		1,880.00
		To share the remaining income equally and to close the Income Summary account.		

In a legal sense, a partner does not work for a salary, nor does he invest in a partnership to earn interest; he invests and works for earnings. Yet, partnership agreements often provide that salaries and interest be allowed the partners. When a partnership agreement provides for salaries and interest, the partners should understand that both the salaries and interest are only methods of sharing losses and gains.

The previous illustration demonstrated the sharing of a $14,000 income by the use of salaries and interest. In this illustration the earnings of Johnson and Frank were greater than the salaries and interest allowed the partners. Johnson and Frank would use the same method to share earnings that were less than the salaries and interest, and they would use the same method to share a loss. For example, assume that the partnership has a net income of only $4,240 for a year. The income would be shared with the following journal entries:

Dec.	31	Income Summary.....................	2,240.00	
		Johnson, Withdrawals.............		1,600.00
		Frank, Withdrawals...............		640.00
		To allocate income to the partners equal to 8 per cent on investments.		
	31	Income Summary.....................	8,000.00	
		Johnson, Withdrawals.............		3,000.00
		Frank, Withdrawals...............		5,000.00
		To allocate a portion of the income to the partners in the form of salaries.		

At this stage in the sharing of the net income, if these entries are posted, the Income Summary account has a *debit* balance of $6,000. It appears as follows:

Income Summary

Dec. 31	(Expenses)	98,220	Dec. 31	(Sales)	102,460
	(Net income)	4,240			
		102,460			102,460
Dec. 31	(Interest)	2,240	Dec. 31	(Net income)	4,240
31	(Salaries)	8,000			

Since the loss-and-gain-sharing agreement of Johnson and Frank provides for an equal sharing of the balance of the Income Summary account after salaries and interest are allowed, the $6,000 debit balance is shared with the following journal entry:

Dec.	31	Johnson, Withdrawals.................	3,000.00	
		Frank, Withdrawals..................	3,000.00	
		Income Summary................		6,000.00
		To close the Income Summary account and to share equally the remaining debit balance.		

A net loss would be shared by Johnson and Frank in the same manner, the only difference being that the loss-and-gain-sharing procedure would begin with a debit balance in the Income Summary account and the final entry would share a larger debit balance.

Partnership Financial Statements

In most respects partnership financial statements are similar to single proprietorship statements. One common difference is that the income statement of a partnership often shows the allocation to the partners of the reported net income. This information is added to the statement following the reported net income. For example, an income statement prepared for Johnson and Frank may show in its last portion the allocation

Illustration 92—Method of Showing Allocation of Income on the Income Statement

```
Net Income . . . . . . . . . . . . . . . . . . . . . .                $4,240
    Allocation of the net income to the partners:
    S. S. Johnson:
        Interest at 8 per cent on investment . . . . . .    $1,600
        Salary . . . . . . . . . . . . . . . . . . . . .     3,000
            Total. . . . . . . . . . . . . . . . . . . .    $4,600
            Less: One half of the remaining debit balance    3,000
        Share of the net income. . . . . . . . . . . .               $1,600

    A. E. Frank:
        Interest at 8 per cent on investment . . . . . .    $  640
        Salary . . . . . . . . . . . . . . . . . . . . .     5,000
            Total. . . . . . . . . . . . . . . . . . . .    $5,640
            Less: One half of the remaining debit balance    3,000
        Share of the net income. . . . . . . . . . . .                2,640
Total Net Income . . . . . . . . . . . . . . . . . . .                $4,240
```

of the $4,240 net income of the last illustrated allocation (pp. 413 and 414) as in Illustration 92.

The balance sheet of a partnership may show for each partner the beginning investment, additions to and deductions from the beginning investment, withdrawals in anticipation of earnings, and the ending investment. More often, particularly if there are more than two partners, the balance sheet will show only the ending capital balance of each partner in somewhat the following manner:

PROPRIETORSHIP

```
S. S. Johnson, capital, December 31, 19-- . . . . . . .  $17,000
A. E. Frank, capital, December 31, 19-- . . . . . . . .    9,040
                                                                  $26,040
```

A supplementary schedule known as a *Schedule of Partners' Capital Accounts* is then attached to the balance sheet to show the details of each partner's Capital account. Such a schedule appears as in Illustration 93.

Illustration 93

JOHNSON AND FRANK
Schedule of Partners' Capital Accounts
For Year Ended December 31, 19--

	S. S. Johnson		A. E. Frank	
	Withdrawals	Capital	Withdrawals	Capital
Capital account balances, January 1, 19--		$20,000		$ 8,000
Additional investments				2,000
Withdrawal of investments.		1,000		
Net investments.		$19,000		$10,000
Withdrawals in anticipation of income. . .	$3,600		$3,600	
Share of the income.	1,600		2,640	
Net deduction from capital		2,000		960
Capital account balances, December 31, 19--		$17,000		$ 9,040

QUESTIONS FOR CLASS DISCUSSION

1. Frank Ringly cannot legally enter into a contract. May he become a partner?
2. James and Round are partners. James dies and his son claims the right to take his father's place in the partnership. Does he have this right? Why?
3. If a partnership agreement does not state the period of time that the partnership is to exist, when does the partnership end?
4. Frank and Boyd enter into a partnership. Frank invests a building worth $25,000, and Boyd invests $25,000 in cash. After several years they decide to dissolve the partnership. Frank claims the building as his property by right of investment. Is his claim valid? Why?
5. Small and Robert operate a store. Small manages the grocery department, and Robert manages the meat department. Small receives for his labor the gross profit of the grocery department less one half of the operating expense of the store. Robert receives for his labor the gross profit of the meat department less one half the operating expenses of the store. Are the men partners?
6. Williams has operated a store for many years, and Dean has worked for him. Two years ago Williams, with the consent of Dean, began to pay Dean 25 per cent of the net income in place of a fixed salary. Dean now claims that this makes him a partner in the business. Do you agree?

7. What is the meaning of the term "mutual agency" as it is applied to a partnership?

8. Brook and Moyer are partners in the operation of a store. Brook without the knowledge of Moyer enters into a contract for the purchase of merchandise to be sold by the partners. Moyer contends that the order was not authorized and refuses to take delivery. The vendor sues Brook and Moyer for the contract price of the merchandise. Will the firm have to pay? Why?

9. Would your answer to Question 8 be different if Brook and Moyer were partners in a public accounting firm?

10. May the members of a partnership limit the right of one of their members to bind the partnership to contracts? Is such an agreement binding (a) on the members of the partnership, and (b) on outsiders?

11. What is the meaning of the term "unlimited liability" when it is applied to the members of a partnership?

12. Kennedy, Porter, and Foulke have been partners for three years. The partnership is dissolving, Kennedy is leaving the firm, and Porter and Foulke plan to carry on the business. In the final settlement Kennedy places a $15,000 salary claim against the partnership. His contention is that since he devoted all of his time for three years to the affairs of the partnership, he has a claim for a salary of $5,000 for each year. Is his claim valid? Why?

13. The partnership agreement of Martin and Tritt provides for a two-thirds, one-third sharing of income but says nothing of losses. The operations for a year result in a loss. Martin claims that the loss should be shared equally since the partnership agreement said nothing of the method of sharing losses. Do you agree?

14. If income is to be shared on the basis of capital investments, what additional points affecting the sharing should be covered in the income-sharing agreement?

15. The Capital account of Ben Kreick appears as follows:

Ben Kreick, Capital

| July 1 | 3,000 | Jan. 1 | 8,000 |
| Aug. 1 | 1,000 | Nov. 1 | 5,500 |

What was Kreick's (a) beginning capital, (b) ending capital, and (c) average capital?

Problem 17–1

Allen, Beale, and Curtis invested $10,000, $8,000, and $6,000, respectively, in a partnership. During its first year the partnership earned $21,000.

Required:

Prepare general journal entries to close the Income Summary account and to allocate the net income to the partners under each of the following assumptions:

a) The partnership agreement did not provide a method of sharing income.

b) The partners had agreed to share income in the ratio of their beginning investments.

c) The partners had agreed to share income by allowing salaries of $4,000 to Allen, $6,000 to Beale, and $8,000 to Curtis; allowing interest of 8 per cent on the beginning investments; and sharing the remaining balance of the Income Summary account equally.

Problem 17–2

The Capital accounts of Dunn, Evans, and Gregg had balances of $12,000, $6,000, and $9,000 at the beginning of the current year. The partnership's income-sharing agreement provides that income be shared by allowing the partners salaries of $5,000, $8,000, and $6,000, respectively; allowing interest on the partners' beginning of the year investments at the rate of 6 per cent; and dividing the remaining balance of the Income Summary account equally.

Assume in turn that the current year's operations produced the following net incomes and loss:

  a) A net income of $23,800.
  b) A net income of $13,000.
  c) A net loss of $5,300.

Required:

Prepare a schedule that shows the shares of each of the assumed incomes and loss that would be received by each of the partners.

Problem 17–3

At the end of the past year the Capital account balances of Gary Cook and Melvin Dailey appeared as follows:

Gary Cook, Capital				Melvin Dailey, Capital			
Apr. 1	2,000	Jan. 2	40,000	July 1	10,000	Jan. 2	50,000
		July 1	6,000			Nov. 1	12,000

During the past year the partnership of Cook and Dailey earned $28,480. Their income-sharing agreement provides that income be shared by allowing salary allowances of $8,000 to Cook and $6,000 to Dailey, interest at 8 per cent on average investments, and dividing the remaining balance of the Income Summary account equally.

Required:

Prepare the income allocation section of the firm's income statement as of the end of the past year showing the allocaton of the income to the partners.

Problem 17–4

At the end of the past year's operations the condensed adjusted trial balance of Ottis and Payne appeared as follows:

OTTIS AND PAYNE
Adjusted Trial Balance, December 31, 19—

Cash.	$ 4,000	
Other assets.	16,900	
Other liabilities.		$ 2,200
Dale Ottis, capital.		9,500
Dale Ottis, withdrawals.	6,000	
Roy Payne, capital.		8,000
Roy Payne, withdrawals.	4,800	
Revenue from services.		32,000
Operating expenses.	20,000	
	$51,700	$51,700

At the beginning of the year the balance of the capital account of Dale Ottis was $8,000. On May 1 he had invested an additional $1,500 in the business. Also, at the beginning of the year the balance of the Capital account of Roy Payne was $9,000. On July 1 Payne had withdrawn $1,000 of his investment.

The income-sharing agreement of the partners provides that income be shared by allowing salary allowances of $500 per month to Ottis and $400 a month to Payne, interest on average investments at 8 per cent, and sharing the remaining balance of the Income Summary account equally.

Required:

1. Prepare general journal entries to close the Income Summary account and the partners' Withdrawals accounts.
2. Prepare an income statement showing the allocation of the net income to the partners.
3. Prepare the proprietorship section of the firm's balance sheet and a schedule of the partners' Capital accounts.

CLASS EXERCISES

Exercise 17-1

The partnership agreement of Burns and Carlson provides that income be shared by allowing the partners salaries of $7,000 and $5,000, respectively, and then sharing the remaining balance of the Income Summary account equally. At the end of their first year in business the firm had a net income of $5.00. Carlson suggested that the partners give the $5.00 to the office boy as a bonus and forget the sharing of income for the first year. If Burns agrees, who gains most from the decision and how much does he gain?

Exercise 17-2

The partnership of A & B earned $5,000 during its first year. Compute the share of each partner under each of the methods of sharing listed below:

A, Capital				B, Capital			
July 1	1,000	Jan. 1	5,000	June 1	500	Jan. 1	6,000
Sept. 1	500	Nov. 1	1,000			Sept. 1	2,375

1. Gains and losses are shared in the ratio of capital investments at the beginning of the year.
2. Gains and losses are shared on the basis of average investments.
3. Salaries of $150 a month for each to be allowed, and remaining balance to be allocated equally.
4. Interest at 6 per cent to be allowed on average capital investments, and remaining balance to be allocated equally.
5. Salaries of $150 a month for each to be allowed, interest at 6 per cent to be allowed on average capital investment, and the remaining balance to be allocated equally.

SUPPLEMENTARY PROBLEMS

Problem 17-A

The partnership agreement of Shields and Thorne provides that each partner is to invest $20,000 in the partnership. The agreement also provides that for any period of time that a partner's investment exceeds $20,000, he is to be allowed interest on the excess at the rate of 8 per cent per annum; and that for any period that a partner's investment is less than $20,000, he is to be charged interest on the deficiency at the rate of 8 per cent per annum. Furthermore, the agreement provides that after interest is allowed and charged, the remaining balance of the Income Summary account is to be shared by first allowing salaries of $8,000 to Shields and $6,000 to Thorne, and then sharing the remaining balance of the Income Summary account equally.

During its first year the partnership earned $23,400 before interest on investments was allowed and charged; and at the end of the first year the partners' Capital accounts appeared as follows:

Walter Shields, Capital				Robert Thorne, Capital		
Sept. 1	8,000	Jan. 1	20,000		Jan. 1	18,000
		Mar. 1	5,000		July 1	6,000

Required:

Prepare general journal entries to allow and charge interest on the partners' investments and to close the Income Summary account.

Problem 17–B

Dean Ross and Lewis Sears are about to form a partnership, and they are trying to decide how they will share gains and losses. They have discussed three ways:
1. In the ratio of their investments which they have agreed to maintain at $15,000 for Ross and $10,000 for Sears.
2. Salary allowances of $6,000 to Ross and $5,000 to Sears and the balance of the Income Summary account equally.
3. Salary allowances of $6,000 to Ross and $5,000 to Sears and the balance of the Income Summary account in ratio to their investments.

Required:

Prepare a schedule that will show under each of the methods of sharing profits the share of each partner in (1) a net income of $30,000, (2) a net income of $10,000, and (3) a net loss of $15,000.

Problem 17–C

M. J. Harris, who has operated a store called The Toggery for a number of years, has decided to expand by forming a partnership with E. E. Dahl. The men agree that after the revaluation of certain of his assets, Harris is to invest the assets of his business in the partnership and the partnership is to assume his liabilities. Dahl is to invest a building valued at $22,000, land valued at $3,500, and sufficient cash to make his total investment equal to the investment of Harris.

A post-closing trial balance of The Toggery ledger just prior to the revaluation of the assets carried the account balances shown on the following page.

Harris and Dahl agree that the amount shown as the allowance for bad debts is not sufficient to take care of all accounts that might not be collected. Consequently, they agree that the allowance should be increased to $500 before the assets are taken over by the partnership. They also agree that some of the inventory is not salable and that the inventory should be revalued at $16,500. Furthermore, they agree that sufficient depreciation has not been provided on the store equipment and that the balance of the Accumulated Depreciation, Store Equipment account should be increased to $2,000.

THE TOGGERY

Post-Closing Trial Balance, February 28, 19—

Cash.	$ 1,675	
Accounts receivable.	8,650	
Allowance for bad debts.		$ 175
Merchandise inventory.	17,200	
Store equipment.	4,500	
Accumulated depreciation, store equipment.		1,700
Accounts payable.		2,300
M. J. Harris, capital.		27,850
	$32,025	$32,025

Required:

Assume that the accounting records of The Toggery are to be continued and used by the new firm.

1. Prepare general journal entries to revalue the assets prior to the formation of the partnership.
2. Prepare a general journal entry to record the investment of Dahl in the business.
3. Prepare a balance sheet for the partnership reflecting the investments of the partners.

Chapter

18

PARTNERSHIPS: DISSOLUTIONS AND LIQUIDATIONS

A PARTNERSHIP is a personal association based upon a contract between specific individuals. Anything that causes a change in the personnel of the association ends the original contract and causes the original partnership to end and dissolve. Partnerships are dissolved in several ways; the more common are:

1. *The Substitution of a New Partner for One or More of the Old.* A, B, and C enter into a partnership. Later C, with the consent of A and B, sells his interest to D. When A and B take D into the partnership in the place of C, a new partnership is formed, and a new contract between A, B, and D is substituted for the old contract between A, B, and C.
2. *The Withdrawal of a Partner.* E, F, and G enter into a partnership. Later, F withdraws. The withdrawal of F ends the partnership of E, F, and G. If E and G continue the business, a new partnership contract is drawn, and a new partnership between E and G is formed.
3. *The Addition of a New Partner.* H, I, and J form a partnership. Later, K is admitted to the partnership. When K is admitted, a new partnership of H, I, J, and K takes the place of the old partnership.
4. *A Mutual Agreement to Dissolve and Liquidate.* Partners may agree to dissolve and end their association. In such cases the assets are normally converted into cash, the liabilities are paid, and the remaining cash is returned to the individual partners.

Dissolutions and Liquidations

A partnership may dissolve, and a new partnership may be organized to continue the business, or a partnership may dissolve and liquidate. When a new partner is added to an old partnership or an old partner withdraws and the remaining partners continue the business, a new partnership is created and takes the place of the old partnership. In such cases, when the business of an old partnership continues under a new partnership, a *dissolution* is said to occur. A *liquidation* goes beyond a simple dissolution. In a liquidation the partnership is dissolved, the business ends, the assets are sold, the creditors are paid, and the remaining cash is distributed to the partners.

Both simple dissolutions and dissolutions in which a partnership business is liquidated are discussed in the pages that follow.

Sale of a Partnership Interest

All double-entry accounting is based on the equation: *Assets = Liabilities + Proprietorship.* In this equation the assets are the property of the business, the liabilities are the claims of the creditors, and the proprietorship is the equity or ownership right of the business owner or owners. The fundamental accounting equation is restated at this point because many partnership problems are easier to understand if they are examined with the fundamental accounting equation in mind. The sale of a partnership interest is a good illustration of this point.

For example, assume that Abbott, Burns, and Camp are equal partners in a $15,000 partnership that has no liabilities. The accounting equation that shows the ownership rights of the partners is as follows:

ASSETS		=	PROPRIETORSHIP	
Cash......................	$ 3,000		Abbot, capital..............	$ 5,000
Merchandise...............	8,000		Burns, capital..............	5,000
Store equipment............	4,000		Camp, capital..............	5,000
Total.................	$15,000		Total.................	$15,000

Camp's equity in this partnership is $5,000. If Camp sells his equity to Davis for $7,000, he is selling his $5,000 interest in the partnership assets. The entry on the partnership books to transfer the equity is:

Feb.	4	Camp, Capital.........................		5,000.00	
		Davis, Capital.....................			5,000.00
		To transfer Camp's equity in the partnership assets to Davis.			

After this entry is posted, the accounting equation that shows the assets and equities of the new partnership is as follows:

ASSETS		=	PROPRIETORSHIP	
Cash......................	$ 3,000		Abbot, capital..............	$ 5,000
Merchandise...............	8,000		Burns, capital..............	5,000
Store equipment............	4,000		Davis, capital..............	5,000
Total.................	$15,000		Total.................	$15,000

Two points should be noted in regard to this transaction. First, the $7,000 that Davis paid to Camp is not recorded in the partnership books. Camp sold and transferred his $5,000 equity in the assets to Davis. The entry that records the transfer is a debit to Camp, Capital for $5,000 and a credit to Davis, Capital for $5,000. Furthermore, the entry is the same whether Davis pays Camp $7,000 or $70,000. The amount is paid directly to Camp. It is a side transaction between Camp and Davis and does not affect the amount of the partnership assets.

The second point to be noted is that Abbott and Burns must agree to the sale and transfer if Davis is to become a member of the partnership. Abbott and Burns cannot prevent Camp from selling his interest in the assets to Davis. On the other hand, Camp cannot force Abbott and

Burns to accept Davis as a partner. If Abbott and Burns agree to accept Davis as a partner, a new partnership is formed and a new contract with a new loss-and-gain-sharing ratio must be drawn. If Camp sells his interest to Davis, and either Abbott or Burns refuses to accept Davis as a partner, the old partnership must be liquidated. In such a situation, Davis acquires only the liquidation rights of Camp.

Retirement and Withdrawal of a Partner

Often a partnership is terminated by the retirement of a partner. When a partner retires, he may sell his partnership interest to an outsider or to one or more of his old partners; or he may withdraw his equity in the form of cash or other partnership assets. When a partner retires and withdraws his equity in cash or other assets, his withdrawal reduces in equal amounts both the net assets and the proprietorship. The reduction in net assets may be (a) equal to the book value of the retiring partner's equity, (b) less than the book value of the retiring partner's equity, or (c) greater than the book value of the retiring partner's equity. Likewise, in settlement of his claim against the assets, the retiring partner may take cash, other assets, or a note payable of the new partnership. If the partners agree, the retiring partner may take a combination of assets, or he may take a combination of assets and a note. In every case the amount and nature of the items taken by the retiring partner are matters on which the partners must agree.

Whenever possible, the best practice is for the partners to provide in advance, in their partnership contract, the exact procedure to be followed when a partner retires and withdraws from the partnership. When a procedure is agreed upon in advance, the procedure commonly provides for an audit of the accounting records and a revaluation of the assets. The revaluation of the assets just prior to the retirement of a partner is very desirable because it places all of the assets on the books at their current values and causes the retiring partner's Capital account to reflect the current value of his equity. Often, if a partnership agreement provides for an audit and revaluation of the partnership assets when a partner retires, it also provides that the retiring partner is to withdraw assets equal to the book value of his revalued equity.

For example, assume that Blue is retiring from the partnership of Smith, Blue, and Short. The partners have operated a successful hardware business for a number of years; and they have always shared losses and gains in the ratio of Smith, one half; Blue, one fourth; and Short, one fourth. Their partnership agreement provides for an audit and revaluation of the assets upon the retirement of a partner. Their balance sheet just prior to the audit and revaluation follows in Illustration 94.

The audit and appraisal indicates that the merchandise inventory is overvalued by $4,000. It also indicates that due to market changes the

Illustration 94

SMITH, BLUE, AND SHORT
Balance Sheet, October 31, 19--

ASSETS			PROPRIETORSHIP	
Cash		$11,000	Smith, capital	$22,000
Merchandise inventory.		16,000	Blue, capital.	10,000
Fixed assets	$20,000		Short, capital	10,000
Less: Accum. depr. .	5,000	15,000		
Total Assets . . .		$42,000	Total Proprietorship . .	$42,000

fixed assets should be valued at $25,000 with accumulated depreciation of $8,000. The entries to record these revaluations are:

Oct.	31	Smith, Capital.	2,000.00	
		Blue, Capital.	1,000.00	
		Short, Capital.	1,000.00	
		Merchandise Inventory.		4,000.00
		To reduce the value of the merchandise inventory.		
	31	Building.	5,000.00	
		Accumulated Depreciation, Building.		3,000.00
		Smith, Capital.		1,000.00
		Blue, Capital.		500.00
		Short, Capital.		500.00
		To increase the value of the fixed assets.		

Losses and gains from the revaluation of assets are always shared by the partners in their loss-and-gain-sharing ratio. The fairness of this is easy to see when it is remembered that if the partnership did not terminate, such losses or gains would sooner or later be reflected on the income statement.

In the case of Smith, Blue, and Short, after the entries revaluing the partnership assets are recorded, a balance sheet showing the new asset values and the new equities appears as in Illustration 95.

Illustration 95

SMITH, BLUE, AND SHORT
Balance Sheet, October 31, 19--

ASSETS			PROPRIETORSHIP	
Cash		$11,000	Smith, capital	$21,000
Merchandise inventory.		12,000	Blue, capital.	9,500
Fixed assets	$25,000		Short, capital	9,500
Less: Accum. depr. .	8,000	17,000		
Total Assets . . .		$40,000	Total Proprietorship . .	$40,000

After the revaluation of the assets, if Blue withdraws from the partnership and takes assets equal to his equity, the entry to record his withdrawal is as follows:

Oct.	31	Blue, Capital.........................	9,500.00	
		Cash.............................		9,500.00
		To record the withdrawal of Blue from the partnership of Smith, Blue, and Short.		

In withdrawing, Blue does not have to take cash in settlement of his equity. He may take any combination of assets to which the partners agree, or he may take the note of the new partnership. If, in this illustration, Smith and Short need cash with which to continue the business, they may induce Blue to take a note of the new partnership in part settlement. If Blue takes cash in the amount of $4,500 and the new partnership's note for the balance, the transaction is recorded as follows:

Oct.	31	Blue, Capital.........................	9,500.00	
		Cash.............................		4,500.00
		Notes Payable...................		5,000.00
		To record the withdrawal of Blue from the partnership of Smith, Blue, and Short.		

Needless to say, the withdrawal of Blue creates a new partnership. Consequently, a new partnership agreement and a new loss-and-gain-sharing ratio is required. If the new partners, Smith and Short, do not agree to a new ratio, the law provides that they will share losses and gains equally.

Partner Withdraws Taking Assets of Less Value than His Book Equity

Sometimes when a partner retires, the remaining partners may not wish to have the assets revalued and the new asset values recorded. In such cases the partners may agree that the assets are overvalued. Also in such cases the partners may agree that, due to the overvalued assets, the retiring partner should, in settlement of his equity, take assets of less value than the book value of his equity. Sometimes, too, when the assets are not overvalued, the retiring partner may be so anxious to retire that he is willing to take less than the current value of his equity just to get out of the partnership or out of the business.

When a partner retires taking assets of less value than the book value of his equity, he is in effect leaving a portion of his book equity in the business. In such cases, the remaining partners divide the unwithdrawn portion of the retiring partner's book equity in their loss-and-gain-sharing ratio. For example, assume that Black, Brown, and White are partners sharing gains and losses in the ratio of 2:2:1. Their assets and equities are as follows:

ASSETS		PROPRIETORSHIP	
Cash.....................	$ 5,000	Black, capital..............	$ 6,000
Merchandise..............	9,000	Brown, capital.............	6,000
Store equipment...........	4,000	White, capital.............	6,000
Total Assets...........	$18,000	Total Proprietorship.....	$18,000

Brown is so anxious to withdraw from the partnership that he is willing to retire if he is permitted to take $4,500 in cash in settlement of his equity. Black and White agree to the $4,500 withdrawal, and Brown retires. The entry to record the retirement of Brown is:

Mar.	4	Brown, Capital.........................	6,000.00	
		Cash...........................		4,500.00
		Black, Capital....................		1,000.00
		White, Capital...................		500.00
		To record the withdrawal of Brown.		

In retiring, Brown did not withdraw $1,500 of the book value of his equity. This is divided between Black and White in their loss-and-gain-sharing ratio. The loss-and-gain-sharing ratio of the original partnership was Black, 2; Brown, 2; and White, 1. Therefore in the original partnership, Black and White shared gains and losses in the ratio of 2 to 1. The unwithdrawn book equity of Brown is shared by Black and White in this 2 to 1 ratio.

Partner Withdraws Taking Assets of Greater Value than His Book Equity

There are two common reasons for a partner receiving upon retirement assets of greater value than his book equity. First, the partnership may have unrecorded goodwill, or certain of the partnership assets may be undervalued. Second, the partners continuing the partnership may be so anxious for the retiring partner to withdraw that they are willing for him to take assets of greater value than his book equity.

When assets are undervalued or unrecorded and the partners do not wish to change the recorded values, the partners may agree to permit a retiring member to withdraw assets of greater value than his book equity. In such cases the retiring partner is, in effect, withdrawing his own book equity and a portion of the book equities of his partners. For example, assume that Jones, Thomas, and Finch are partners sharing gains and losses in the ratio of 3:2:1. Their assets and equities are as follows:

ASSETS		PROPRIETORSHIP	
Cash.....................	$ 5,000	Jones, capital..............	$ 9,000
Merchandise..............	10,000	Thomas, capital............	6,000
Fixed assets..............	3,000	Finch, capital.............	3,000
Total Assets...........	$18,000	Total Proprietorship.....	$18,000

Finch wishes to withdraw from the partnership; Jones and Thomas plan to continue the business. The partners agree that certain of the assets are undervalued, but they do not wish to increase the recorded values of the assets. The partners further agree that if the current values of the assets were recorded, the total of the assets would be increased by $6,000. If the assets were increased in the accounting records by $6,000, the equity of Finch would increase $1,000. Therefore, the partners agree that $4,000 is the proper value for the equity of Finch, and that Finch may withdraw this amount in cash. The entry to record the withdrawal of Finch is:

May	7	Finch, Capital..........................	3,000.00	
		Jones, Capital..........................	600.00	
		Thomas, Capital......................	400.00	
		Cash............................		4,000.00
		To record the withdrawal of Finch who takes assets of greater value than his book equity.		

Death of a Partner

The death of a partner automatically dissolves and ends a partnership. The estate of the deceased partner is entitled to receive the value of the deceased partner's equity. The articles of co-partnership should contain provisions for settlement in case a partner dies. One of the purposes of these provisions should be to provide a method for determining the current value of the deceased partner's equity. This requires at least: (a) an immediate closing of the books to determine the earnings since the end of the previous accounting period, and (b) a method for determining and recording the current value of the assets on the date of a partner's death. Upon the death of a partner and after the current value of the deceased partner's equity is determined, the remaining partners and the administrators of the deceased partner's estate must agree to a disposition of the deceased partner's equity. They may agree to a sale of the equity to the remaining partners or to an outsider, or they may agree to the withdrawal of assets in settlement of the equity. Entries for both of these procedures have already been presented.

Admission of a Partner by Investment

A new partner may join an existing partnership by the purchase of an interest from one or more of the old partners, or a new partner may be admitted upon the investment of additional funds in the partnership. When a new partner purchases an interest from one or more of the old partners, a share of the existing proprietorship is transferred to the new partner, and the total assets and equities of the partnership remain unchanged. This was illustrated on pages 421 and 422. Although the assets and equities remain unchanged when a new partner purchases an interest from one or more of the old partners, when a new partner is admitted to an existing partnership upon the investment of additional funds, both the assets and equities of the business are increased. This may be illustrated as follows:

Bates and Cross are partners with the following assets and equities:

ASSETS		PROPRIETORSHIP	
Cash......................	$2,000	Bates, capital................	$4,000
Merchandise................	3,000	Cross, capital................	2,000
Other assets................	1,000		
Total Assets............	$6,000	Total Proprietorship......	$6,000

Davis is to become a member of the firm upon the investment of $4,000. For his investment, Davis is to receive a 40 per cent equity in the assets of the firm. The investment of Davis is recorded as follows:

Apr.	8	Cash..................................	4,000.00	
		Davis, Capital.....................		4,000.00
		To record the investment of Davis.		

After this entry is recorded, the total of the assets of the firm of Bates, Cross, and Davis is $10,000; and Davis, at this time, has an equity in the assets of $4,000, or 40 per cent. It should be noted that while Davis receives a 40 per cent equity in the assets, he does not necessarily receive 40 per cent of the earnings. When a partnership is formed, partners must agree as to the equity that each partner is to have in the assets and, in addition, as to the method in which they will share gains and losses. If Bates, Cross, and Davis share gains and losses in proportion to their investment, Davis will receive 40 per cent. If the partners do not agree to a loss-and-gain-sharing ratio, all share equally.

Admission of a Partner by Investment, Bonus to the Old Partners

In the previous illustration Davis invested $4,000 and received an equity in the new partnership that was equal to his investment. Sometimes a partner invests in a going business and receives an equity in the assets of the business that is less than the amount of his investment. Usually when a new partner is willing to accept an equity in a going business that is less than his investment (1) either the assets of the going business are undervalued, or (2) the business is unusually profitable.

For example, Payne and Robert operate a very successful and profitable business in which they share the net income equally. The assets and equities of the partners are as follows:

ASSETS		PROPRIETORSHIP	
Cash.....................	$ 1,000	Payne, capital..............	$10,000
Merchandise...............	15,000	Robert, capital.............	10,000
Fixed assets...............	4,000		
Total Assets...........	$20,000	Total Proprietorship.....	$20,000

Owen wishes to become a member of the firm. He is willing to invest $12,000 for a one-fourth share of the assets and a one-fourth share of the net income. Payne and Robert agree that Owen may become a member of the firm under these terms. The investment of Owen is recorded by the bonus method as follows:

Jan.	3	Cash..................................	12,000.00	
		Owen, Capital.....................		8,000.00
		Payne, Capital....................		2,000.00
		Robert, Capital...................		2,000.00
		To record the $12,000 investment of Owen in the partnership of Payne, Robert, and Owen.		

Owen invests $12,000 cash in the firm and receives an equity of only $8,000 in the firm's assets. The equities of Payne and Robert are increased $2,000 each by the investment of Owen. The equities of all of the partners are calculated as follows:

EQUITY OF THE NEW PARTNER:

Step 1: Investment of the old partners.......................... $20,000
Investment of the new partner.......................... 12,000
Total Investment.................................... $32,000

Step 2: One fourth of the total proprietorship to the new partner as per
the partnership agreement............................. $32,000
×¼
$ 8,000

EQUITIES OF THE OLD PARTNERS:

Step 3: Cash invested by new partner........................... $12,000
Equity of the new partner............................. 8,000
Bonus to old partners................................. $ 4,000

Step 4: Payne, capital (original)............................... $10,000
One half of the $4,000 bonus.......................... 2,000
Payne, capital (new).................................. $12,000

Robert, capital (original)............................. $10,000
One half of the $4,000 bonus.......................... 2,000
Robert, capital (new)................................. $12,000

Owen invests $12,000 in the partnership and receives an equity of $8,000. The difference between Owen's investment and the amount of his equity is called a *bonus*. Owen is willing to give this $4,000 bonus to Payne and Robert for the privilege of sharing in the expected large earnings of the firm. The bonus is shared by the original partners in their loss-

and-gain-sharing ratio. This is logical; the bonus compensates Payne and Robert for the expected extra earnings that will now go to Owen.

Admission of a Partner by Investment, Goodwill to the Old Partners

Often under circumstances similar to the previous illustration a new partner may object to receiving an equity in the assets that is less than the amount he invests. For example, in the previous illustration Owen may be willing to invest $12,000 for a one-fourth interest in the new firm's assets and earnings, but he may object to having his equity shown at $8,000. He may wish the transaction handled in such a manner that for a one-fourth interest in the firm he invests $12,000 and receives a $12,000 credit in his Capital account. This can be accomplished if goodwill is recorded.

A business is said to possess goodwill when, because of its reputation, location, or some other factor, it has above-average earnings for a business in its field. In this example, if Owen is willing to pay $12,000 for a one-fourth interest in the firm of Payne, Robert, and Owen, the firm is assumed to possess goodwill. (The subject of goodwill is discussed in more detail later in this chapter.) The amount of the goodwill in this case is calculated:

Step 1: If Owen will invest $12,000 for a one-fourth interest, the firm is assumed to be worth $48,000. This is calculated:

$$\$12,000 = \tfrac{1}{4} \text{ of } \$48,000$$

Step 2: If the value of the firm is $48,000, then the value of the equities of the old partners is $36,000. This is calculated:

Total equity of the new firm.	$48,000
Less: Investment of new partner.	12,000
Value of the old partners' equities.	$36,000

Step 3: And the value of the goodwill to be placed on the books is $16,000. This is calculated as follows:

Total value of the equity of the old partners.	$36,000
Less: Book value of the physical assets of the old partnership.	20,000
Value of the goodwill.	$16,000

After the goodwill of Payne and Robert is calculated, the following entry is made to record the goodwill:

Jan.	3	Goodwill.	16,000.00		
		Payne, Capital.			8,000.00
		Robert, Capital.			8,000.00
		To record the goodwill of Payne and Robert.			

When a business possesses goodwill and that goodwill is being recorded in preparation for the admission of a new partner, the goodwill is divided among the old partners in their loss-and-gain-sharing ratio. The reasoning behind this is somewhat as follows. When goodwill is recorded, it is an indication that the business is worth more than the book value of its physical assets. If the business having goodwill were sold, it would be sold for more than the book value of its physical assets, and the gain would be divided in the loss-and-gain-sharing ratio. Therefore, since goodwill measures the value of a business in excess of the book value of its physical assets, an increase in proprietorship resulting from recording goodwill is divided in the loss-and-gain-sharing ratio.

If Owen invests $12,000, after the $16,000 of goodwill is recorded, he may receive a $12,000 credit in his Capital account, a one-fourth interest in the assets, and one fourth of the earnings in return for his investment. His investment under these circumstances is recorded as follows:

Jan.	3	Cash.................................	12,000.00	
		Owen, Capital.....................		12,000.00
		To record the investment of Owen.		

After the entry recording the investment of Owen is posted, the assets and equities of the new partnership are as follows:

ASSETS		PROPRIETORSHIP	
Cash......................	$13,000	Payne, capital..............	$18,000
Merchandise..............	15,000	Robert, capital.............	18,000
Fixed assets..............	4,000	Owen, capital..............	12,000
Goodwill..................	16,000		
Total Assets...........	$48,000	Total Proprietorship.....	$48,000

Admission of a Partner by Investment, Bonus to the New Partner

Sometimes a partner invests in a going business and receives an equity that is greater than the amount of his investment. When this occurs, normally one or more of three things is responsible: (1) Either the assets are overvalued and the partners do not wish to revalue the assets and record their current values, (2) the old partners are having difficulty raising new capital, or (3) the old partners feel that the new partner, because of his special abilities or other factors, will contribute more to the partnership than the money he invests.

For example, Boone, Crocket, and David, who share gains and losses in the ratio of 2:2:1, have been in business as partners for a number of years. The assets and equities of the partners are as follows:

ASSETS		PROPRIETORSHIP	
Cash......................	$ 1,000	Boone, capital..............	$ 8,000
Merchandise..............	14,000	Crocket, capital............	8,000
Fixed assets..............	5,000	David, capital..............	4,000
Total Assets...........	$20,000	Total Proprietorship.....	$20,000

Frank is a young man with much ability and wide experience in the business field of the partnership. Boone, Crocket, and David are so desirous of having Frank join their firm that they are willing to give him a one-third interest for an investment of $7,000. Frank agrees to join the firm, and his investment is recorded by the bonus method as follows:

Feb.	5	Cash....................................	7,000.00	
		Boone, Capital........................	800.00	
		Crocket, Capital......................	800.00	
		David, Capital........................	400.00	
		Frank, Capital....................		9,000.00
		To record the $7,000 investment of Frank.		

Frank invests $7,000 and receives a bonus of $2,000, which together give him a one-third equity in the firm. The $2,000 bonus is contributed to the new partner by the old partners. They contribute in their loss-and-gain-sharing ratio.

The equities of the partners are calculated as follows:

EQUITY OF THE NEW PARTNER:

Step 1: Investment of the old partners..........................$20,000
Investment of the new partner.......................... 7,000
Total Investment....................................$27,000

Step 2: One third of the total proprietorship to the new partner as per
the partnership agreement.............................$27,000
$\times \frac{1}{3}$
$ 9,000

EQUITIES OF THE OLD PARTNERS:

Step 3: Equity of the new partner...............................$ 9,000
Cash invested by the new partner........................ 7,000
Bonus paid by old partners.............................$ 2,000

Step 4: Boone, capital (original)................................$ 8,000
Less: Two fifths of bonus............................. 800
Boone, capital (new).....................................$ 7,200

Crocket, capital (original)...............................$ 8,000
Less: Two fifths of bonus............................. 800
Crocket, capital (new)...................................$ 7,200

David, capital (original)................................$ 4,000
Less: One fifth of bonus.............................. 400
David, capital (new).....................................$ 3,600

Admission of a Partner by Investment, Goodwill to the New Partner

When a new partner is admitted to a partnership with an equity that is larger than his investment, the old partners may object to having their equities reduced to provide the bonus. They may be willing for the new partner to receive an equity that is larger than his investment, but they may want the transaction recorded in such a manner that their own equities are not reduced. This may be accomplished if goodwill is recorded and an amount equal to the goodwill is credited to the Capital account of the new partner.

For example, Boone, Crocket, and David may wish to admit Frank to their firm with a one-third equity in the assets and earnings. They may also want the transaction recorded in such a manner as to not reduce the recorded amounts of their equities. To do this goodwill is recorded and the Capital account of Frank is credited with an amount that is equal to both his cash investment and the goodwill. The amount of the goodwill is calculated as follows:

Step 1: If the equity of the old partners is to remain at $20,000 and this equity is to be two thirds of the total proprietorship, then the total proprietorship will be $30,000.

$$\$20,000 = \tfrac{2}{3} \text{ of } \$30,000$$

Step 2: If the total proprietorship is $30,000, then the equity of the new partner is $10,000. This is calculated:

Total equities of the firm.............................$30,000
Less: Equities of the old partners.................. 20,000
Equity of the new partner..........................$10,000

Step 3: And the value of the goodwill to be placed on the books is $3,000. This is calculated:

Equity to be received by the new partner..............$10,000
Less: Cash investment of the new partner...........   7,000
Goodwill to be recorded.............................$ 3,000

The entry that gives Frank an equity of $10,000 upon the investment of $7,000 in the firm of Boone, Crocket, David, and Frank is as follows:

Feb.	5	Cash................................	7,000.00	
		Goodwill...........................	3,000.00	
		Frank, Capital....................		10,000.00
		To record the $7,000 investment of Frank.		

Recording Goodwill

When it exists, goodwill is a very valuable asset. Goodwill may result from a favorable reputation, a convenient location, an efficient, fair, and courteous method of treating customers, or from some other reason. However, because of its intangible nature and the difficulty with which it is measured, goodwill is recorded on numerous occasions when it does not exist. This sometimes occurs when goodwill is recorded upon the admission of a new partner to a going business. In such cases goodwill is sometimes recorded when actually the assets should be revalued. For this reason, accountants prefer not to record goodwill when a new partner is admitted to a going business with an equity that differs from his investment. They prefer to either revalue the assets, if they are incorrectly valued; or to record a bonus, if the assets are properly valued.

Even though goodwill is sometimes recorded when it does not exist, goodwill is a valuable asset that very often does exist. When it exists and is being purchased or sold, goodwill may be recorded. If it is not being bought or sold, accountants feel that goodwill should not be recorded because of the difficulty of placing a fair value on it. They feel that only a sale fairly values goodwill. When goodwill is bought or sold, accountants are of the opinion that a buyer and a seller dealing at arms' length place a fair value on the goodwill.

Above-average earnings are considered the best evidence of the existence of goodwill. The value to be placed on goodwill at the time of its sale is often determined by capitalizing the extra earnings. For example, a business in a field in which the normal return is 10 per cent has a capital investment of $100,000 and earns an average return of $12,000 yearly. If the business earned a return equal to the average for this type of business, it would earn an average of $10,000 yearly. Therefore, the business has above-average earnings amounting to $2,000 yearly. Capitalizing these above-average earnings at 10 per cent indicates that in this type of business it takes an investment of $20,000 to earn $2,000 ($2,000 ÷ 10 per cent = $20,000). The $20,000 capitalized value of the extra earnings may be taken as a measure of the value of the goodwill of this firm.

Capitalizing above-average earnings is one method that may be used in placing a value on goodwill. Other methods are commonly used. However, a discussion of other methods of valuing goodwill is deferred to a more advanced accounting course.

Liquidations

Numerous circumstances may cause the dissolution of a partnership. Likewise, a partnership may dissolve and its business may be continued by a newly organized partnership, or a partnership may dissolve and its business may be terminated. So far this chapter has presented several cases in which a change in personnel caused the dissolution of a partnership. In each case, the business was continued by a newly organized partnership. The remainder of the dissolutions discussed in this chapter differ from the ones previously discussed in that in each case the partnership business is terminated. Dissolutions in which the business of a partnership is terminated are often called "liquidations." Technically there are two steps involved in the termination of a business: they are a *realization* and a *liquidation*. A realization is the process of converting assets into cash; and a liquidation is the distribution of the realized cash to the proper parties. In actual practice the combined steps are commonly referred to as a "liquidation."

Although many situations occur in liquidations, all liquidations may be divided into two general types. These are: (1) liquidations in which all of the assets are realized before a distribution of cash is made, and (2) liquidations by installments. Three examples of liquidations in which all of the assets are realized before a distribution is made are discussed in the remainder of this chapter. For the student who wishes to go deeper into the subject of liquidations, installment liquidations are discussed in the advanced text of this series.

All of the Assets Realized before a Distribution, Assets Are Sold at a Profit. The liquidation of a partnership under this assumption may be illustrated with the following example. Ottis, Skinner, and Parr have operated a partnership for a number of years; they have always shared losses and gains in the ratio of 3:2:1. Due to a number of unsatisfactory conditions, the partners decide to liquidate the business as of December 31, 19—. On that date the books are closed, the income from operations is transferred to the partners' Capital accounts, and the condensed balance sheet shown in Illustration 96 is prepared.

Illustration 96

OTTIS, SKINNER, AND PARR
Balance Sheet, December 31, 19--

ASSETS		LIABILITIES	
Cash	$10,000	Accounts payable	$ 5,000
Merchandise inventory.	15,000		
Other assets	25,000	PROPRIETORSHIP	
		Ottis, capital	15,000
		Skinner, capital	15,000
		Parr, capital.	15,000
Total Assets	$50,000	Total Liab. and Prop.. .	$50,000

In any liquidation the business always ends and the assets are sold. Normally, either a gain or a loss results from the sale of each group of assets. These losses and gains are called "losses and gains from realization" and shared by the partners in their loss-and-gain-sharing ratio. If Ottis, Skinner, and Parr sell their merchandise inventory for $12,000 and their other assets for $34,000, the asset sales and the allocation of the net gain from realization are recorded as follows:

Jan.	12	Cash.	12,000.00	
		Loss or Gain from Realization.	3,000.00	
		Merchandise Inventory.		15,000.00
		To record the sale of the merchandise inventory at a loss.		
	12	Cash.	34,000.00	
		Other Assets.		25,000.00
		Loss or Gain from Realization.		9,000.00
		To record the sale of the other assets at a profit.		
	12	Loss or Gain from Realization.	6,000.00	
		Ottis, Capital.		3,000.00
		Skinner, Capital.		2,000.00
		Parr, Capital.		1,000.00
		To allocate the net gain from realization to the partners in their loss-and-gain-sharing ratio of 3:2:1.		

Careful notice should be taken of the last of the three journal entries just shown. In the termination of a partnership, when the assets are sold at a loss or a gain, the loss or gain from realization is allocated to the partners in their loss-or-gain-sharing ratio. Often students, in solving liquidation problems, attempt to allocate and distribute the assets to the partners in their loss-and-gain-sharing ratio. Obviously this is not correct; it is not assets but losses and gains that are shared in the loss-and-gain-sharing ratio.

After the assets of a partnership are sold and the gain or loss from realization is allocated to the partners, the partnership cash exactly equals the combined equities of the partners and creditors. This point is illustrated for Ottis, Skinner, and Parr in the balance sheet shown in Illustration 97.

After the assets of a partnership are realized and the gains or losses from realization are shared by the partners, entries are made to distribute the realized cash to the proper parties. Since the creditors have

Illustration 97

OTTIS, SKINNER, AND PARR
Balance Sheet, January 15, 19--

ASSETS		LIABILITIES	
Cash	$56,000	Accounts payable	$ 5,000
		PROPRIETORSHIP	
		Ottis, capital	18,000
		Skinner, capital	17,000
		Parr, capital	16,000
Total Assets	$56,000	Total Liab. and Prop..	$56,000

first claim against the assets, they are paid first. After the creditors are paid, the remaining cash is divided among the partners. Each partner has the right to cash equal to his equity or, in other words, cash equal to the balance of his Capital account. The entries to distribute the cash of Ottis, Skinner, and Parr are as follows:

Jan.	15	Accounts Payable....................	5,000.00	
		Cash...........................		5,000.00
		To pay the claims of the partnership creditors.		
	15	Ottis, Capital........................	18,000.00	
		Skinner, Capital.....................	17,000.00	
		Parr, Capital........................	16,000.00	
		Cash...........................		51,000.00
		To distribute the remaining cash to the partners according to the balances of their Capital accounts.		

Notice that after losses and gains from realization are shared and the creditors are paid, each partner receives liquidation cash equal to the balance remaining in his Capital account. This is because the balance of a partner's Capital account shows his equity in the partnership assets.

All Assets Are Realized before a Distribution, Assets Are Sold at a Loss, Each Partner's Capital Account Is Sufficient to Absorb His Share of the Loss. In a partnership liquidation, the assets sometimes are sold at a net loss. In such cases the loss from realization is allocated to the partners in their loss-and-gain-sharing ratio. For example, if contrary to the assumptions of the previous illustration, the merchandise inventory of Ottis, Skinner, and Parr is sold for $9,000 and the other assets for $13,-000, the entries to record the sales and the allocation of the losses are:

Jan.	12	Cash...................................	9,000.00	
		Loss or Gain from Realization...........	6,000.00	
		Merchandise Inventory.............		15,000.00
		To record the sale of the merchandise inventory at a loss.		
	12	Cash...................................	13,000.00	
		Loss or Gain from Realization...........	12,000.00	
		Other Assets.....................		25,000.00
		To record the sale of the other assets at a loss.		
	12	Ottis, Capital.........................	9,000.00	
		Skinner, Capital.......................	6,000.00	
		Parr, Capital..........................	3,000.00	
		Loss or Gain from Realization.......		18,000.00
		To allocate the net loss from realization to the partners in their loss-or-gain-sharing ratio.		

After the entries for the sale of the assets and the allocation of the losses are recorded, a balance sheet of the partnership appears as in Illustration 98. The balance sheet shows the equities of both the creditors

Illustration 98

OTTIS, SKINNER, AND PARR
Balance Sheet, January 15, 19--

ASSETS		LIABILITIES	
Cash	$32,000	Accounts payable	$ 5,000
		PROPRIETORSHIP	
		Ottis, capital	6,000
		Skinner, capital	9,000
		Parr, capital.	12,000
Total Assets	$32,000	Total Liab. and Prop.. .	$32,000

and the partners in the partnership cash. The following entries are required to distribute the cash to the proper parties:

Jan.	15	Accounts Payable....................	5,000.00	
		Cash............................		5,000.00
		To pay the partnership creditors.		
	15	Ottis, Capital.......................	6,000.00	
		Skinner, Capital....................	9,000.00	
		Parr, Capital.......................	12,000.00	
		Cash...........................		27,000.00
		To distribute the remaining cash to the partners according to the balances of their Capital accounts.		

Notice that after realization losses are shared and the creditors are paid, each partner receives cash equal to the balance of his Capital account.

All Assets Are Realized before a Distribution, Assets Are Sold at a Loss, a Partner's Capital Account Is Not Sufficient to Cover His Share of the Loss. Sometimes a partner's share of realization losses is greater than the balance of his Capital account. In such cases the partner whose share of losses is greater than his capital balance must cover the deficit by paying cash into the partnership. If he is unable to pay, the remaining partners must share this additional loss among themselves in their loss-and-gain-sharing ratio. For example, assume contrary to the previous two illustrations that Ottis, Skinner, and Parr sell the partnership merchandise for $3,000 and the other assets for $4,000. The entries to record the sales and the allocation of the losses are as follows:

Jan.	12	Cash...............................	3,000.00	
		Loss or Gain from Realization...........	12,000.00	
		Merchandise Inventory............		15,000.00
		To record the sale of the merchandise inventory at a loss.		
	12	Cash...............................	4,000.00	
		Loss or Gain from Realization...........	21,000.00	
		Other Assets.....................		25,000.00
		To record the sale of the other assets at a loss.		
	12	Ottis, Capital.......................	16,500.00	
		Skinner, Capital....................	11,000.00	
		Parr, Capital.......................	5,500.00	
		Loss or Gain from Realization.......		33,000.00
		To record the allocation of the loss from realization to the partners in their loss-or-gain-sharing ratio.		

After the entry allocating the loss from realization is posted, the Capital account of Ottis has a debit balance of $1,500 and appears as follows:

Ottis, Capital

Jan. 12	(Realization loss)	16,500	Dec. 31	Balance	15,000

Since the partnership agreement provides that Ottis is to share one half of the losses or gains, and since his Capital account is not large enough to absorb his share of the losses in this case, he must pay $1,500 into the partnership to cover his full share of the losses. If he is able to pay, the following entry is made:

Jan.	13	Cash.................................	1,500.00	
		Ottis, Capital....................		1,500.00
		To record the additional investment of Ottis to cover his share of the realization losses.		

After the $1,500 is received from Ottis, the partnership has cash amounting to $18,500. The following entries are then made to distribute the cash to the proper parties:

Jan.	15	Accounts Payable.....................	5,000.00	
		Cash.............................		5,000.00
		To pay the creditors of the partnership.		
	15	Skinner, Capital......................	4,000.00	
		Parr, Capital........................	9,500.00	
		Cash.............................		13,500.00
		To distribute the remaining cash to the partners according to the balances of their Capital accounts.		

Often when a partner's share of partnership losses exceeds the balance of his Capital account, the partner is unable to make up the deficit. In such cases, since each member of a partnership has unlimited liability, the deficit must be borne by the remaining partner or partners. For example, assume that, contrary to the previous illustration, Ottis is unable to pay in the $1,500 necessary to cover the deficit in his Capital account. If Ottis is unable to pay in an amount sufficient to cover his deficit, the $1,500 of losses that he is unable to pay must be shared by Skinner and Parr in their loss-or-gain-sharing ratio. In the original loss-or-gain-sharing agreement, the partners shared losses and gains in the ratio of Ottis, 3; Skinner, 2; and Parr, 1. Therefore, Skinner and Parr shared losses and gains in the ratio of 2 to 1; and Ottis's $1,500 loss in excess of his capital account balance is apportioned between Skinner and Parr in this ratio. Normally the defaulting partner's deficit is transferred to the Capital accounts of the remaining partners. This is accomplished for Ottis, Skinner, and Parr with the following entry:

Jan.	15	Skinner, Capital....................	1,000.00	
		Parr, Capital.....................	500.00	
		Ottis, Capital.................		1,500.00
		To transfer the deficit of Ottis to Skinner and Parr.		

After the deficit of Ottis is transferred to Skinner and Parr, the Capital accounts of the partners appear as follows:

Ottis, Capital

Jan. 15	(Loss from realization)	16,500	Dec. 31	Balance	15,000
			Jan. 15	(Deficit to Skinner and Parr)	1,500

Skinner, Capital

Jan. 15	(Loss from realization)	11,000	Dec. 31	Balance	15,000
15	(Share of Ottis's deficit)	1,000			

Parr, Capital

Jan. 15	(Loss from realization)	5,500	Dec. 31	Balance	15,000
15	(Share of Ottis's deficit)	500			

After the deficit of Ottis is transferred to Skinner and Parr, the $17,000 of liquidation cash is distributed with the following entries:

Jan.	15	Accounts Payable....................	5,000.00	
		Cash...........................		5,000.00
		To pay the partnership creditors.		
	15	Skinner, Capital....................	3,000.00	
		Parr, Capital.....................	9,000.00	
		Cash...........................		12,000.00
		To distribute the remaining cash to the partners according to the balances of their Capital accounts.		

It should be understood that the inability of Ottis to meet his share of the partnership losses at this time does not relieve him of liability. If at any time in the future Ottis becomes able to pay, Skinner and Parr may collect from him the full $1,500. Skinner may collect $1,000 and Parr, $500.

Installment Liquidations

Often at the time of a liquidation the realization of partnership assets requires a considerable period of time. Often, too, in such cases the partners may not wish to wait until all assets are realized before they begin to receive their portions of the realized cash. In other words, the partners may wish to liquidate their partnership in installments. For a further discussion of this subject the student is referred to the advanced text of this series.

QUESTIONS FOR CLASS DISCUSSION

1. What is the difference between a partnership dissolution and a partnership liquidation?

2. Abbot has a one-half interest in the partnership of Abbot, Burns, and Crawford and receives one half of the net income. Davis buys Abbot's one-half interest in the partnership assets. The new partnership makes no agreement as to the method of sharing income. At the end of the first year Davis claims one half of the income on the grounds that he purchased Abbot's interest. Burns and Crawford object and say that since there was no agreement, income should be shared equally. In case of legal action, who will probably win?

3. Green wishes to sell to Johnson his interest in the partnership of Green and Horn. Horn refuses to have Johnson as a partner. Can Green force Horn to accept Johnson as a partner? Can Horn prevent Green from selling his interest to Johnson? What happens if Green sells to Johnson and Horn will not accept Johnson as a partner?

4. Mason, Nash, and Parr are equal partners in a $15,000 partnership. Mason with the consent of Nash and Parr sells his $5,000 interest to Robert. Give the entry to record the sale of the interest if: (a) Robert pays Mason $5,000 for the interest, (b) Robert pays Mason $7,000 for the interest, and (c) Robert pays Mason $4,600 for the interest.

5. Rienhardt, Richard, and Roblee are partners with Capital accounts of $5,000 each. French gives Roblee $8,000 for his one-third interest in the partnership. The bookkeeper debits Roblee and credits French for $5,000. French objects. He wants his Capital account to show a balance of $8,000, the amount he paid for his interest. Explain why French's Capital account is credited for $5,000.

6. When partnership assets are revalued just prior to the retirement of a partner, the losses and gains from revaluation are shared by the partners in the same ratio as that in which they share income from operations. Why?

7. What is the effect on the net assets of (a) the retirement of a partner, (b) the sale of a partnership interest, and (c) the admission of a new partner by investment?

8. Middleton invests in a partnership and receives a one-third interest in the partnership assets. Does this also mean that he receives a one-third interest in the partnership income?

9. Why would a man investing in a partnership be willing to take an equity that is less than his investment? Why would a man investing in a partnership demand an equity greater than his investment?

10. When a new partner is admitted to a going partnership with a bonus or goodwill to the old partners, the bonus or goodwill is shared by the old partners in their loss-and-gain-sharing ratio. Why?

11. A firm possesses goodwill. Give several reasons that may account for the existence of the goodwill.

12. A firm that earns $25,000 a year on an investment of $200,000 is said to have goodwill. If a return of 10 per cent is normal in the industry of the firm and the firm's excess income is capitalized at 10 per cent as a measure of the value of the firm's goodwill, what value is placed on the goodwill?

13. When a business is terminated, a realization and a liquidation occur. What is a realization? What is a liquidation?

14. After all partnership assets are realized and all creditor claims are paid, the remaining cash should exactly equal the sum of the balances of the partners' Capital accounts. Why?

15. Small, Robert, and Block are partners. In a liquidation, Block's share of the partnership losses exceeds his Capital account balance. He is unable to meet the deficit from his personal assets, and the excess losses are shared by his partners. Does this relieve Block of liability?

PROBLEMS

Problem 18–1

Duggan, Early, and Hale each have a $7,000 interest in a partnership and share losses and gains equally. (a) Duggan is willing to retire if permitted to take assets having a book value of $7,000. (b) Early is willing to retire if permitted to take assets having a book value of $6,000. (c) Hale is willing to retire if permitted to take assets having a book value of $8,000.

Required:

1. Assume that each partner retires. Give the journal entries to record in turn the retirements.
2. Assume that rather than sharing losses and gains equally the partners share in the ratio of 3:2:1. Give the entries to record the retirement of Early, and then give the entries to record the retirement of Hale.

Problem 18–2

Reed, Scott, and Taylor are partners sharing losses and gains in their capital ratio. Their Capital account balances are: $18,000, $12,000, and $6,000. Urie is to be admitted to the partnership upon the investment of $6,000. Give the entries to record the admission of Urie if:
1. Urie receives an equity equal to his investment.
2. Urie receives a one-eighth interest, and a bonus is recorded.
3. Urie receives a one-eighth interest, and goodwill is recorded.
4. Urie receives a one-sixth interest, and a bonus is recorded.
5. Urie receives a one-sixth interest, and goodwill is recorded.

Problem 18–3

Jensen, Kirby, the Landon are partners sharing losses and gains in the ratio of 2:2:1. Kirby plans to withdraw from the partnership. On the date of Kirby's withdrawal the equities of the partners in the assets of the partnership are as follows: Jensen, $12,000; Kirby, $10,000; and Landon, $6,000. Give the entries for the withdrawal of Kirby under each of the following assumptions:
1. Kirby sells his interest to Morse and takes Morse's note for $12,000.
2. Kirby withdraws taking partnership cash in the amount of $10,000 for his interest.
3. Kirby withdraws taking cash in the amount of $10,750.
4. Kirby withdraws taking $6,000 in cash and delivery equipment carried on the books at $3,000 less accumulated depreciation of $500.

5. Kirby withdraws taking $1,200 in cash and the note of the new partnership in the amount of $10,000.
6. Kirby transfers his interest to Jensen and Landon taking Jensen's $7,200 personal note for three fifths of his interest and Landon's $4,800 personal note for two fifths of his interest.

Problem 18–4

Folsom, Gibson, and Hess are partners having investments of $9,000, $6,000, and $9,000 and sharing income in their capital ratio. The partners are about to take Irving into their partnership. Give the entries for the admission of Irving under each of the following assumptions:

1. Irving purchases a one-fourth interest in the partnership from Folsom, Gibson, and Hess in such a manner that the ratio of the investments of the original partners remains unchanged.
2. Irving pays Folsom $7,000 for two thirds of Folsom's interest in the partnership.
3. Irving invests $8,000 and receives a one-fourth interest in the partnership.
4. Irving invests $8,000, receives a one-fifth interest, and a bonus is recorded.
5. Irving invests $8,000, receives a one-fifth interest, and goodwill is recorded.
6. Irving invests $9,000, receives a one-third interest, and a bonus is recorded.
7. Irving invests $9,000, receives a one-third interest, and goodwill is recorded.

Problem 18–5

Mason, Nelson, and Ottis have decided to liquidate their partnership. As partners they have always shared losses and gains in the ratio of 2:1:1. Before liquidation their balance sheet appeared as follows:

MASON, NELSON, AND OTTIS

Balance Sheet, October 31, 19—

Cash	$ 2,500	Accounts payable	$ 5,000
Accounts receivable	7,500	Mason, capital	10,000
Merchandise inventory	17,000	Nelson, capital	10,000
Equipment	8,000	Ottis, capital	10,000
	$35,000		$35,000

In the realization the accounts receivable were sold for $6,200, the merchandise was sold for $18,500, and the equipment was sold for $5,800. After all sales were completed, the cash was distributed to the proper parties.

Required:

Give in general journal form the entries to record the realization and liquidation.

Problem 18–6

Darby, Ewing, and Fox are partners who have always shared losses and gains in the ratio of 5:3:2. They plan to liquidate their partnership. Just prior to the liquidation their balance sheet appeared as follows:

DARBY, EWING, AND FOX

Balance Sheet, March 31, 19—

Cash	$ 3,500	Accounts payable	$13,500
Other assets	45,000	Darby, capital	10,000
		Ewing, capital	20,000
		Fox, capital	5,000
	$48,500		$48,500

Required:

Prepare general journal entries to record the realization and liquidation of the partnership under each of the following assumptions:

1. The other assets are sold for $50,500.
2. The other assets are sold for $30,000.
3. The other assets are sold for $22,000, and the partner with the deficit is able to pay in the amount of his deficit.
4. The other assets are sold for $20,000, and the partners have no assets other than those invested in the business.

CLASS EXERCISES

Exercise 18–1

Abbot, Birch, and Collins formed a partnership to operate a business. Abbot invested $6,000, Birch invested $4,000, and Collins invested $2,000. They agreed to share losses and gains equally. Their business lost heavily, and after six months they decided to liquidate. After converting all of the partnership assets to cash and paying all creditor claims, $3,000 of partnership cash remained.

Required:

Prepare a general journal entry to distribute the cash to the partners.

Exercise 18–2

Moss, Newton, and Olson formed a partnership to carry out a real estate venture. Moss invested two acres of land valued at $4,000; Newton invested $4,000 in cash; and Olson invested $2,000 in cash. The partners installed street and water mains at a cost of $6,000 and divided the land into ten lots of equal value. Newton and Olson, with the consent of Moss, each took two of the lots at cost for their personal use. The remaining six lots were sold for $15,000, and the partnership was dissolved.

Required:

Prepare a general journal entry to distribute the partnership cash to the partners.

SUPPLEMENTARY PROBLEMS

Problem 18–A

The partnership of Buttler and Calvert shares losses and gains equally. On February 28 of the current year their balance sheet appears as follows:

BUTTLER AND CALVERT

Balance Sheet, February 28, 19—

Cash....................	$ 1,500	Buttler, capital............	$30,000
Other assets...............	46,500	Calvert, capital............	30,000
Goodwill..................	12,000		
	$60,000		$60,000

Dixon wishes to join the firm with a one-third equity. He is willing to invest an amount sufficient to secure a one-third equity and a one-third share of the income; however, he insists that his investment remain in the partnership and that the goodwill be removed from the books. Nevertheless, he admits that the partnership possesses goodwill and that its fair value is $12,000.

Required:

1. If everyone is treated fairly, how much should Dixon pay for his interest?
2. Give the entries in general journal form to record the admission of Dixon and the removal of the goodwill.

Problem 18–B

Until March 3 of the current year Adams, Baxter, and Cuttle were partners sharing losses and gains in their capital ratio. On that date Baxter suffered a heart attack and died. Adams and Cuttle immediately ended the operations of the business and prepared the following adjusted trial balance:

ADAMS, BAXTER, AND CUTTLE

Adjusted Trial Balance, March 3, 19—

Cash...	$ 6,500	
Accounts receivable..	10,000	
Allowance for bad debts....................................		$ 500
Merchandise inventory......................................	24,000	
Store equipment..	12,000	
Accumulated depreciation, store equipment..............		4,000
Land..	5,000	
Building..	45,000	
Accumulated depreciation, building.....................		8,000
Accounts payable...		4,500
Adams, capital...		30,000
Baxter, capital..		30,000
Cuttle, capital..		15,000
Adams, withdrawals...	1,500	
Baxter, withdrawals..	1,500	
Cuttle, withdrawals..	1,500	
Revenues..		45,000
Expenses..	30,000	
	$137,000	$137,000

Required:

1. Prepare entries in general journal form to close the revenue, expense, income summary, and withdrawal accounts of the partnership.
2. Assume that the estate of Baxter agreed to accept the land and building in full settlement of its claim against the partnership assets, and that Adams and Cuttle planned to continue the business and to rent the building from the estate. Give the entry to transfer the land and building and to settle with the estate.
3. Assume in the place of the foregoing that the estate of Baxter demanded a cash settlement and that the business had to be sold to a competitor who gave $70,000 for the noncash assets. Give in general journal form the entries to transfer the noncash assets to the competitor and to distribute the cash to the proper parties.

Problem 18–C

For a number of years Nash and Owen have been partners in a real estate firm specializing in developing subdivisions. The partners shared losses and gains equally. On March 1 of the current year a balance sheet of the firm appeared as follows:

NASH AND OWEN

Balance Sheet, March 1, 19—

Cash....................	$ 2,000	Nash, capital.............	$ 50,000
Subdivision land..........	98,000	Owen, capital.............	50,000
	$100,000		$100,000

On the date of the balance sheet Nash and Owen, in need of cash to develop a subdivision, induced Potter to invest $35,000 and to become a member of their partnership with a one-third interest in its assets and income. However, the new partners could not agree on policies, and before incurring any expenses they decided to sell their subdivision land and to liquidate. The highest bid for the land was $66,500. The partners accepted the bid and divided the partnership cash.

Required:

1. Under the assumption that a bonus was recorded at the time Potter joined the firm, give the entries to record the admission of Potter and to record the firm's liquidation.
2. Under the assumption that goodwill was recorded at the time Potter joined the firm, give the entries to record the admission of Potter and to record the firm's liquidation.

Chapter
19

CORPORATIONS: ORGANIZATION
AND OPERATION

THE THREE common types of business organizations are single proprietorships, partnerships, and corporations. Of the three, corporations are fewer in number than either single proprietorships or partnerships. Yet, in dollar volume, corporations transact much more business than do both single proprietorships and partnerships combined. Corporations are said to account for over 90 per cent of all business transacted in the United States. Consequently, because of the amount of business transacted and also because almost every person reading this paragraph will at some time either work for or own an interest in a corporation, an understanding of the nature of corporations and their accounting is important.

Corporation Defined

Almost one hundred and fifty years ago, Chief Justice Marshall of the United States Supreme Court defined a corporation as "an artificial being, invisible, intangible, and existing only in the contemplation of the law. Being a creature of the law, it possesses only those properties which the charter of its creation confers upon it, either expressly or as incidental to its very existence." This definition implies that (1) a corporation is a legal entity, or legal person, separate and distinct from the natural persons who are its owners; (2) a corporation is created by an act of a sovereign state; and (3) a corporation has only those powers given it by the state and either expressed or implied in its charter. While this famous definition points out some of the important characteristics of corporations, a better understanding of corporations and their popularity as a form of business organization may be gained from an examination of some of the advantages and disadvantages of the corporation as a form of business organization.

Advantages of the Corporation

Among the more important advantages of the corporate form of business organization are the following:

Separate Legal Entity. From the definition of a corporation by Chief Justice Marshall has grown the doctrine that a corporation is a legal entity separate and distinct from the natural persons who own it. The owners of a corporation are called *stockholders;* the stockholders own the corporation, but they are not the corporation. The corporation, in a legal sense, is an artificial person, separate and distinct from its stockholders. While this doctrine is an admitted legal fiction, courts will uphold it in all but those cases where justice requires that it be denied.

Also, although the doctrine of separate existence is an admitted legal fiction, its recognition gives a corporation all the rights and responsibilities of a natural person excepting those rights and responsibilities that only a natural person may exercise, such as the right to marry or to vote. A corporation may buy, own, and sell property in its own name. It may sue in its own name, and it may be sued in the courts just like a natural person. It may enter into contracts with both outsiders and its own stockholders. In short, through its agents, a corporation may conduct its business affairs as a legal person with the rights, duties, and responsibilities of a person.

Lack of Liability of Its Stockholders. As a separate legal entity a corporation is responsible for its own acts and its own debts, and its stockholders have no liability for either. From the viewpoint of an investor this is perhaps the most important advantage of a corporation.

Ease of Transferring Ownership Rights. The transfer of an interest in a corporation is very easy when compared to the transfer of an interest in a partnership. To transfer an interest in a partnership requires the unanimous consent of all partners, the dissolution of the old partnership, and the organization of a new partnership. To transfer an interest in a corporation requires only a transfer of the ownership of the stock that represents the interest.

Since a corporation is a separate legal entity, the transfer of an interest in a corporation has no effect on the corporation. Furthermore, a stockholder may transfer and dispose of his stock in a corporation at will; he need not ask the permission of anyone. Stock exchanges such as the New York Stock Exchange have been organized to facilitate the sale and exchange of shares of stock by bringing together buyers and sellers.

Continuity of Life. The death, incapacity, or withdrawal of a stockholder does not affect the life of a corporation. The life of a corporation depends upon its charter. A corporation may continue to exist for the period of time stated in its charter, which may be any length of time permitted by the laws of the state in which it is organized. At the expiration of the time stated, the charter may normally be renewed. This makes possible a perpetual life for a successful corporation.

No Mutual Agency. Mutual agency does not exist in a corporation. A corporation stockholder acting as an individual stockholder does not have the power to bind the corporation to contracts. His participation in the affairs of the corporation is limited to the right to vote in the stockholders' meetings. Consequently, stockholders need not exercise the care of partners in selecting the people with whom they associate themselves in the ownership of a corporation.

Ease of Capital Assembly.   Corporations find it much easier to raise large amounts of capital than do partnerships. This is because of the limited liability of stockholders, their lack of mutual agency, and the ease with which an interest in a corporation as represented by shares of its stock can be bought and sold. Limited liability, lack of mutual agency, and the ease with which stock can be transferred make it possible for corporations to raise large sums of money from the combined investments of many small stockholders. For example, Standard Oil of New Jersey has in excess of a quarter of a million stockholders, and the American Telephone and Telegraph Company has in excess of a million stockholders. A corporation's capital-raising ability is normally limited only by the profitableness with which it can employ the funds of its stockholders. This is very different from a partnership. The capital-raising ability of a partnership is always limited by the number of its partners and their individual wealth. The number of partners in a partnership in turn is usually limited by mutual agency and unlimited liability.

Disadvantages of the Corporation

Among the more important disadvantages of the corporation as a form of business organization are:

Governmental Control and Supervision.   Corporations are created by fulfilling the requirements of the corporation laws of a state. Because of this corporations are said to be "creatures of the state." As "creatures of the state" corporations are subject to much closer state control and supervision than are single proprietorships and partnerships. This supervision and control usually involves long and complicated reports to various state and federal agencies.

In addition, all the rights, powers, and duties of corporations, their stockholders, and officials are derived from corporation laws. There would be no objection to this if corporation laws were simple and easy to understand. Unfortunately, the corporation laws of the various states are notoriously diverse, complicated, and in some cases vague. As a result the exact rights, duties, and responsibilities of corporations, their directors, and stockholders vary from state to state and are often difficult to define precisely.

Taxation.   The greatest disadvantage of the corporate form of business organization is usually considered to be its extra burden of taxation. Corporations as business units are subject to all of the taxes to which single proprietorships and partnerships are subject. In addition, corporations are subject to several taxes not levied on either single proprietorships or partnerships. The most important of these are state and federal income taxes which exceed 50 per cent of a corporation's income. However, insofar as the owners of a corporation are concerned, the burden does not end here. The income of a corporation is taxed twice. It is taxed first as corporation income and again as personal income when distributed to the stockholders in the form of dividends. This differs from single proprietorships and partnerships. Single proprietorships and partnerships, as business units, are not subject to income taxes. Their income is taxed only as the personal income of their owners.

Lack of Liability of the Stockholders. Lack of liability of the stockholders was listed as an advantage of the corporate form of business organization. In a small corporation, when an attempt is made to borrow money or secure credit, it may also be a disadvantage. Lack of stockholders' liability reduces the credit of a corporation. This is because, when the stockholders have no liability, a creditor may look only to the assets of the corporation for the satisfaction of his claims. Consequently, credit is normally limited to an amount for which the assets of the corporation furnish adequate security. For example, other things being equal, a partnership with a capital of $50,000 can often borrow more money than can a corporation with an equal capital. This is because of the unlimited liability of the partners. When a partnership becomes bankrupt, if its assets are not sufficient to meet the claims of its creditors, the creditors may look to the personal assets of the partners for satisfaction. The creditors of the corporation may look only to the assets of the corporation.

Of course the effect of lack of liability of its stockholders on a small corporation's credit can be and often is overcome by having one of its stockholders of means endorse its notes or agree to make good its obligations to creditors. However, the stockholder of means must be willing to stand back of the corporation, because the effect of his endorsement or his agreement to make good the corporation's debts is to remove the limitation on his liability.

Organizing a Corporation

A corporation is created by securing a charter from one of the forty-nine states or the federal government. To secure a charter from one of the states it is necessary to fulfill the requirements of the corporation laws of that state. Federal charters are limited to certain types of businesses such as national banks and savings and loan associations and to quasi-government corporations such as the Federal Deposit Insurance Corporation.

At one time corporation charters were granted by special acts of state legislatures. Today, in the various states, this power has been delegated to the secretary of state or some other state official. In delegating the power to issue corporation charters, the various state legislatures pass laws setting forth the requirements to be met by persons desiring such a charter. These requirements vary with the states, but in general they call for filing several copies of an application for a corporation charter. Normally, the application must be signed by three or more subscribers to the prospective corporation's stock who are called the "incorporators." The application usually must include the following:

1. The name of the corporation and the address of its principal office within the state.
2. The purpose for which the corporation is organized.
3. The period of time during which the proposed corporation is to exist.
4. The amount of stock authorized and its par value. If the stock is to have no par value, a statement must usually be made to that effect.
5. If there is to be more than one kind or class of stock, the amount of each class of stock authorized.
6. If the stock is to be divided into different kinds or classes, a statement must be made as to the preferences, qualifications, limitations, restrictions, and rights of each of the various classes.
7. The names and addresses of the subscribers to shares of stock and the amount of stock subscribed by each.

Normally the secretary of state or other designated state officer is required to examine the application for a charter to see that it complies with the law. If the application is in order and all fees, taxes, and charges have been paid, the charter is issued. In many states a copy of the application is approved and returned to the incorporators as the corporation charter. In any case, the corporation is created and comes into existence with the issuance of its charter.

After the corporation comes into existence, usually at the first meeting of its stockholders, bylaws to govern the conduct of the corporation affairs are adopted. Bylaws normally include among other things:

1. The time, place, manner of calling, and rules for conducting meetings of the stockholders and the board of directors.
2. The number, qualifications, duties, powers, and length of office of the members of the board of directors.
3. The appointment, duties, powers, compensations, and length of office of the corporation officers other than directors.
4. Any proper rules and regulations to govern the acts of the board of directors and corporation officers.

The bylaws together with the charter give the basic rules for the conduct of the affairs of the corporation. It is important that all acts of the stockholders, board of directors, and officers conform with the regulations of both the charter and the bylaws.

Management of a Corporation

The stockholders are the owners of a corporation. Seldom are they equal owners because usually stockholders own different numbers of shares of stock. Each share of stock represents one ownership right in the corporation and gives its owner one vote in the meetings of the stockholders. Theoretically, stockholders controlling the votes of 50 per cent of the stock plus one share control a corporation. Actually, because many stockholders do not vote or participate, a much smaller percentage of votes is frequently sufficient for control.

Normally the stockholders of a corporation meet once each year. At their annual meeting they elect members of the board of directors and transact such other business as is provided in their bylaws. In most large corporations many of the stockholders do not attend the annual meeting. Often such stockholders delegate their right to vote at the stockholders' meeting to an agent. This is accomplished by signing a legal document known as a power of attorney or a *proxy.*

Although the ultimate control of a corporation rests with its stockholders, this control is exercised only indirectly through the election of the members of the board of directors. The individual stockholder, as a stockholder, does not actively participate in the management of a corporation. His right as a stockholder to participate in management begins and ends with his vote in the meetings of the stockholders.

The board of directors is responsible for the direction of the business affairs of the corporation. The directors are trustees of both the stockholders and the creditors and must faithfully serve both. The directors may act only as a board of directors, they have no power as individual directors to transact corporation business. As a collective body, the board of directors has final authority in the management of the corporation. They select and elect the administrative officers to whom they delegate the active management of the business affairs of the corporation. The board of directors may bind the corporation to contracts, and they may delegate to selected officers and employees the power to enter into contracts in the name of the corporation. The kind of contracts that may be negotiated by each officer and employee is usually limited by the board of directors. For example, the sales manager may be given power to enter into sales contracts. As a result he may negotiate sales contracts but has no power to bind the corporation to other kinds of contracts.

The administrative officers of a corporation are headed by a president who is the chief executive officer. He is normally responsible for the appointment of all officers and employees other than those appointed by the board of directors. The president is normally responsible directly to the board of directors for controlling and supervising the business affairs of the corporation.

Most corporations have one or more vice-presidents who are vested with specific managerial powers and duties by the president and the board of directors. In addition, the corporation secretary normally has charge of the corporation records, and the treasurer is custodian of the corporation funds.

Corporation Accounting

The majority of all transactions completed by a corporation are recorded in the same manner and in the same types of journals and ledgers as are the transactions of a single proprietorship or a partnership of equal size. Generally, a corporation's accounts and accounting differ only for the transactions that directly affect its stockholders' equity. For example, it will be recalled that in a business owned by a single individual, the owner's equity and changes in that equity resulting from earnings are recorded in the owner's Capital account. Likewise, in a partnership the ownership rights plus changes resulting from earnings are recorded in the Capital accounts of the several partners. In both types of companies no distinction is made between invested capital and retained earnings; and, consequently, the amounts invested by each owner plus increases and decreases in each owner's equity resulting from gains and losses are recorded in the same account, the owner's Capital account. However, in a corporation this is different. In a corporation a distinction is made between proprietorship resulting from stockholders' investments and proprietorship resulting from earnings retained in the business. Furthermore, this distinction is carried into the accounts and onto the balance sheet. In the accounts the distinction results in two separate classes of proprietary accounts: (1) *contributed capital accounts,* and (2) *retained earnings accounts.* The contributed capital accounts show the amounts originally invested in the corporation by its stockholders; and the retained earnings accounts show the earnings retained in the business.

It is important to note that there is a very good reason for the two distinct classes of accounts. The reason is that in many states a corporation may not pay dividends or distribute any of its assets to its stockholders if the dividends or other distributions reduce the corporation proprietorship to an amount less than the amount paid to the corporation by its stockholders for their stock. Separate contributed capital and retained earnings accounts help preserve a historical record in the accounts of the amounts paid to the corporation by its stockholders for their stock.

State laws that prohibit the payment of dividends by a corporation when the proprietorship of the corporation is less than the amount originally paid to the corporation by its stockholders for their stock were written to protect corporation creditors. The reasoning behind these laws is as follows:

1. A corporation is a legal entity, and its creditors may look only to the corporation's assets for the satisfaction of their claims.
2. When a corporation pays cash or other assets to its stockholders in the form of dividends, the corporation is reducing in like amounts both its assets and its proprietorship.
3. If dividends may not be paid when to do so would reduce the proprietorship to a point below the amount originally paid to the corporation by its stockholders for their stock, then a fund of assets equal in amount to the investments of the original stockholders is maintained in the business for the protection of the creditors.

Corporation Proprietorship Accounts Illustrated

To demonstrate the use of separate accounts for contributed capital and retained earnings as found in corporation accounting, and to contrast their use with the use of a single capital account in a sole proprietorship, assume that on January 5, 1959, a single proprietorship and a corporation having five stockholders were formed. Assume further that $25,000 was invested in each business. In the sole proprietorship the owner, John Ohm, invested the entire amount; and in the corporation five stockholders each bought 500 shares of its $10 par value common stock at $10 per share. After the investments were recorded, the owner-equity accounts of the two companies appeared as follows:

SINGLE PROPRIETORSHIP John Ohm, Capital	CORPORATION Common Stock
1959 Jan. 5 25,000	1959 Jan. 5 25,000

To continue the illustration, it will be recalled that in a single proprietorship or a partnership, when the Income Summary account is closed, the amount of the gains or losses is transferred from the Income Summary account to the Capital account or accounts of the owner or owners. In a corporation this differs; in a corporation the amount of the gains or losses is transferred to the Retained Earnings account. For example, if in the two firms under discussion, each earned $8,000 during the first year and retained the earnings for use in carrying on their operations, after the Income Summary accounts were closed, the proprietorship of each appeared in its accounts as follows:

SINGLE PROPRIETORSHIP John Ohm, Capital	CORPORATION Common Stock
1959 Jan. 1 25,000 Dec. 31 8,000	1959 Jan. 1 25,000
	Retained Earnings
	1959 Dec. 31 8,000

And the proprietorship of each appeared on its balance sheet prepared at that time as follows:

SINGLE PROPRIETORSHIP	CORPORATION
PROPRIETORSHIP	STOCKHOLDERS' EQUITY
John Ohm, capital, January 1, 1959....................$25,000	Common stock, $10 par value, authorized and issued 2,500 shares...................$25,000
Add: Net income........... 8,000	Retained earnings............. 8,000
John Ohm, Capital, December 31, 1959.................$33,000	Stockholders' Equity..........$33,000

Note in the illustration of the stockholders' equity section of the corporation balance sheet just shown how the original investments of its five stockholders are added together and are shown as one amount, "Common stock, $25,000." The sum of the original investments of the several stockholders of a corporation having but one type of stock, as in the corporation of this illustration, is always shown as a single amount on the corporation's balance sheet. Listing the sum of the original investments of the stockholders of a corporation in a single amount on the balance sheet emphasizes the separate legal entity of a corporation. It also emphasizes the lack of liability of the stockholders. Since the stockholders of a corporation are often numerous, change daily, and have no liability for the corporation's debts, there is no need for listing the name of each. The identity of the individual stockholders of a corporation is normally of little importance to a reader of a corporation balance sheet. This is quite different from a single proprietorship or a partnership. The names of the single proprietor or the partners are usually very important to the reader of a partnership or single proprietorship balance sheet because, for instance, if the reader is a creditor, he knows that he may look to the personal assets of the individual proprietor of partners for the satisfaction of his claims.

To continue the illustration of the use of corporation proprietorship accounts, assume that the two companies under discussion each lost $11,000 during their second year. If there were no withdrawals in the single proprietorship or additional investments in either firm, the proprietorship accounts of the firms appeared as follows at the end of the second year:

SINGLE PROPRIETORSHIP				CORPORATION			
John Ohm, Capital				**Common Stock**			
1959		1959					
Dec. 31	33,000	Jan. 5	25,000			1959	
		Dec. 31	8,000			Jan. 5	25,000
	33,000		33,000				
1960		1960			**Retained Earnings**		
Dec. 31	11,000	Jan. 1	33,000				
				1960		1959	
				Dec. 31	11,000	Dec. 31	8,000

Observe that the Retained Earnings account of the corporation has a debit of $11,000 and a credit of $8,000. This causes the account to have a debit balance of $3,000. A corporation is said to have a *deficit* when it has a debit balance in its Retained Earnings account as in this illustration. A deficit is in effect a negative amount of retained earnings.

At the end of the second year the proprietorship sections from the balance sheets of the two companies appeared as follows:

SINGLE PROPRIETORSHIP		CORPORATION	
PROPRIETORSHIP		STOCKHOLDERS' EQUITY	
John Ohm, capital, January 1,		Common stock, $10 par value	
1960	$33,000	2,500 shares authorized and	
Deduct: Net loss	11,000	issued	$25,000
John Ohm, Capital, December		Deduct: Deficit	3,000
31, 1960	$22,000	Stockholders' Equity	$22,000

During their second year both the corporation and the proprietorship suffered losses of $11,000, which in each case reduced the equities of their owners to $22,000. Notice in the illustration just given how the $22,000 equity of the stockholders in the corporation is shown by listing the amount of the corporation's stock and deducting therefrom the $3,000 deficit.

The corporation of the preceding simplified illustrations had only one kind of stock and only one contributed capital account, its Common Stock account. It should be noted that a corporation may have several contributed capital accounts; for example, if a corporation issues more than one kind or class of stock, it will have a separate account for recording the transactions in each class. Likewise, for reasons of law or management, a corporation may use more than one retained earnings account. If it does so, it will divide the amount of its stockholders' equity that results from retaining earnings in the business and it will place portions in each of the several retained earnings accounts. These points will be discussed in more detail later.

Cash Dividends and Retained Earnings

A dividend is a distribution made to the stockholders of a corporation. Dividends are declared or voted by the board of directors. Courts have generally held that the board of directors is the sole judge of when a dividend should be paid. Therefore, the stockholders have no right to dividends until declared by the board of directors. Dividends may be paid in cash, other assets, or in a corporation's own stock. Cash dividends are the most common; and, unless otherwise stated, a dividend is assumed to be a cash dividend. A cash dividend is normally stated in terms of so many dollars per share of stock. For example, a corporation may declare and pay a cash dividend of two dollars per share on its outstanding common stock. This means the owner of ten shares of such stock will receive a dividend of ten times two dollars, or a total of twenty dollars.

In many states a dividend may be declared and paid only if earnings equal to or greater than the amount of the dividend have been accumulated. Earnings are credited to and are accumulated in the Retained Earnings account. For this reason, it is often said that dividends are paid from retained earnings. In a sense this statement is true. However, it should be realized that dividends are also usually paid in cash. Consequently, the payment of dividends reduces, in equal amount, both the cash and the retained earnings.

Since the ownership of shares of corporation stock is transferable, a corporation must be careful to whom it pays dividends. The corporation's stock owners of today may not be the stock owners of tomorrow. For this reason a corporation must keep accurate records of its changing stockholders. Also to be fair to its changing stockholders, dividends are normally declared on one date to be paid on a future date to the *stockholders of record* of a specified third date. Stockholders of record are stockholders as shown by the corporation's records. For example, a board of directors may declare a dividend on December 28, to be paid on January 15 to the stockholders of record of January 10. Three dates are involved in this declaration. December 28 is called the *date of declaration;* January 10 is called the *date of record;* and January 15 is called the *date of payment.* Declaring dividends on one date to be payable to the stockholders of record on a future date gives each new purchaser of stock an opportunity to have his ownership recorded by the corporation in time to receive the dividend.

A stockholder has no right to a dividend until a dividend is declared by the board of directors. However, as soon as a cash dividend is declared, the dividend is a liability of the corporation, normally a current liability, and must be paid. Furthermore, the stockholders have the right to sue and force the payment of a cash dividend once it is declared. Since dividends are usually declared on one date to be paid on a future date, two entries are used to record the declaration and payment of each dividend. The first entry, which is made at the time of the declaration, reduces the proprietorship and records the liability for the dividend. It is as follows:

Dec.	28	Retained Earnings......................
		     Common Dividend Payable.........
		     To record the declaration of a dividend
		     of $2.00 per share on the 1,000 shares of
		     common stock outstanding.
			2,000.00	2,000.00

The second entry records the actual payment of the dividend and is as follows:

Jan.	15	Common Dividend Payable.............
		     Cash............................
		     To record the payment of the dividend
		     declared on December 28.
			2,000.00	2,000.00

Stock Certificates

When an investor buys stock in a corporation, he receives a stock certificate as evidence of the number of shares purchased. Normally, only one certificate is issued for each block of stock purchased—the one certificate may be for any number of shares. For example, the certificate shown in Illustration 99 is for ten shares of stock.

Illustration 99

Number		Shares
98		-10-

Incorporated under the laws of the State of Illinois

WESTFIELD PUBLISHING COMPANY

This Certifies that, _____ Robert Wetzel _____

is the owner of _____ -ten- _____ fully paid and non-assessable $100.00 par value shares of the Common Capital Stock of the Westfield Publishing Company transferable on the books of the corporation in person or by duly authorized attorney upon surrender of this Certificate properly endorsed.

IN WITNESS WHEREOF the said company has caused this Certificate to be signed by its duly authorized officers and its corporate seal to be hereunto affixed this __10th__ day of __March__, A. D. 19.55.

WESTFIELD PUBLISHING COMPANY

ATTEST:

S. A. Small
Secretary

By *Perry A. Greenleaf*
President

Usually a corporation has a supply of blank stock certificates printed and numbered serially. Each blank certificate normally has printed on it: (1) the name of the corporation, (2) the number of the certificate, and (3) the par value of each share if the shares have a par value. When the certificate is issued: (1) the name of the owner, (2) the number of shares, and (3) the date of issuance are written in. The certificate is then signed by the proper corporation officers or their agents, and the certificate is delivered to its owner.

The owner of stock may transfer at will either part or all of his stock. To do so he completes the endorsement on the reverse side of his stock certificate and returns the certificate to the corporation. For example, assume that Robert Wetzel, who is the owner of the certificate for ten shares of stock shown in Illustration 99, sells three of his ten shares to William Morris. Wetzel completes the endorsement on the back of his stock certificate, as shown in Illustration 100, and signs his name to the

Illustration 100—Stock Certificate (Reverse Side) Showing Endorsement for Transferred Stock

For value received, I hereby sell, assign and transfer unto

William Morris

three (3) Shares of the Capital Stock represented by the within Certificate and do hereby irrevocably constitute and appoint Sylvia Wingard Attorney, to transfer the said stock on the books of the within-named Corporation, with full power of substitution in the premises.

DATED January 1, 1960

Robert Wetzel

In presence of:

Charles Blackburn

endorsement in the presence of a witness. He then returns the stock certificate to the corporation. The corporation cancels the old certificate, retains it, and issues two new certificates. The corporation issues and sends one new certificate for three shares to William Morris, and it issues and sends the other new certificate for seven shares to Wetzel.

Rights of Stockholders

If a corporation issues but one kind of stock, the stock is known as *common stock*. When individuals purchase the common stock of a corporation, they acquire all of the specific rights granted by the corporation's charter to its common stockholders. In addition, they acquire the general rights granted to stockholders by the laws of the state in which the corporation is organized. The laws of the various states differ, but in general all common stockholders have the following rights:

1. The right to share in management by voting in the stockholders' meetings.
2. The right to sell or otherwise dispose of their stock.
3. The right to have first opportunity to purchase any additional shares of common stock issued by the corporation. This is called the *pre-emptive right* of common stockholders. It gives a common stockholder the opportunity to protect his interest in the assets and earnings of the corporation and to protect his voting position in the stockholders' meetings. For example, if a stockholder owns one fourth of the common stock of a corporation, he has first opportunity to buy one fourth of any new common stock

issued by the corporation. This right enables the stockholder to maintain his one-fourth interest.

4. The right to share pro rata with other common stockholders in any dividends declared by the board of directors.
5. The right to share, if the corporation is liquidated, in any assets remaining after the creditors are paid.

Preferred Stock

A corporation may issue more than one kind or class of stock. If a corporation issues two classes of stock, one class is generally known as *common stock* and the other as *preferred stock*. Unless specifically denied by the preferred stock contract, preferred stockholders have all the rights of common stockholders. Often the preferred stock contract of a corporation denies the preferred stockholders the right to vote in the meetings of the stockholders. However, in return for the relinquished right to vote, preferred stockholders are granted a preference as to the payment of dividends and, in addition, are sometimes granted a preference as to the return of the par or other stated value of their stock in a liquidation. A preference as to dividends does not give the preferred stockholders an absolute right to dividends. The preference gives the preferred stockholders the right, if dividends are declared by the board of directors, to receive their preferred dividend before the common stockholders are given a dividend. In other words, if dividends are declared, a dividend must be declared and paid to the preferred stockholders before a dividend may be paid to the common stockholders. However, in any case, if the board of directors is of the opinion that no dividends should be paid, then neither the preferred stockholders nor the common stockholders have a right to a dividend.

On the majority of all preferred stocks issued, dividends are limited to a fixed maximum amount. For example, a share of $100 par value, 6 per cent, nonparticipating, preferred stock has a preference each year to a dividend of 6 per cent of its par value, or to a dividend of $6.00. The dividend on such a stock is limited each year to this amount. Although the dividends on the majority of preferred stocks are limited in amount, the dividends on common stocks are normally limited only by the earning power of the issuing corporation and the judgment of its board of directors.

While the dividends on the majority of preferred stocks are limited to a fixed basic percentage or amount, some preferred stock contracts grant the right, under certain circumstances, to dividends in excess of a fixed basic percentage or amount. Such preferred stocks are called *participating preferred stocks*. Participating preferred stocks may be fully participating, or their participation may be limited to a fixed maximum amount. The exact terms of participation depend in each case on the preferred stock contract. For example, if a corporation issues a fully participating, 6 per cent, $100 par value, preferred stock, the owners of such stock have a preference to dividends each year of $6.00 per share. Then, each year, after the common stockholders receive a 6 per cent dividend, the preferred stockholders have the right to participate with the common stockholders in any additional dividends declared.[1] The participation is usually on the basis of an equal additional percentage per share dividend to each group of stockholders.

Often when preferred stock is participating, the participation is limited. For example, a $100 par value, 5 per cent, preferred stock may be issued with the right of participation in dividends to the extent of 10 per cent of its par value. Such a stock has a preference to dividends of 5 per cent each year. It also has a right, after the common stockholders receive a 5 per cent dividend, to participate in additional dividends until it has received 10 per cent, or $10, per share. Its participation rights end at this point.

In addition to being participating or nonparticipating, preferred stocks are either *cumulative* or *noncumulative*. A cumulative preferred stock is one on which any undeclared dividends accumulate each year until they are paid. A noncumulative preferred stock is one on which the right to receive dividends is forfeited in any year in which dividends are not declared.

The accumulation of dividends on cumulative preferred stocks does not guarantee the payment of dividends. Dividends cannot be guaranteed because the earnings from which they are paid cannot be guaranteed. However, when a corporation issues cumulative preferred stock, it does agree to pay its cumulative preferred stockholders both their current dividends and any unpaid back dividends, called *dividends in arrears,* before it pays a dividend to its common stockholders. The effect of such an agreement may be demonstrated with an illustration. For example, assume that the Denver Corporation was organized in 1950 and that it issued $100,000 of 6 per cent, cumulative, nonparticipating, preferred stock and $100,000 of common stock. During the following ten years its earnings and dividends were as shown in Illustration 101.

Notice that the Denver Corporation incurred losses during its first two years, and it did not pay dividends during these years. During its third year it had earnings, but the earnings were not sufficient to make good the losses of the previous years. Consequently, it waited until its fourth year to begin dividend payments. During the fourth and fifth years, the current and back dividends of the cumulative preferred stockholders were paid in full. After this the preferred stockholders received only their current 6 per cent dividend. Common dividends began in the fifth year.

---

[1] Dividends on par value shares are frequently stated as a percentage of par value. Dividends on no-par shares (described later in this chapter) are in terms of dollars and cents per share.

Illustration 101

EARNINGS AND DIVIDENDS OF THE DENVER CORPORATION

Year	Income or Loss* to Retained Earnings	Balance of Retained Earnings before Dividends	Preferred Dividends Paid	Balance Due to Preferred Owners	Common Dividends Paid	Balance of Retained Earnings after Dividends
1950	$ 4,000*	$ 4,000*	–0–	$ 6,000	–0–	$ 4,000*
1951	5,000*	9,000*	–0–	12,000	–0–	9,000*
1952	7,000	2,000*	–0–	18,000	–0–	2,000*
1953	22,000	20,000	$20,000	4,000	–0–	–0–
1954	18,000	18,000	10,000	–0–	$ 4,000	4,000
1955	24,000	28,000	6,000	–0–	9,000	13,000
1956	32,000	45,000	6,000	–0–	13,000	26,000
1957	28,000	54,000	6,000	–0–	11,000	37,000
1958	26,000	63,000	6,000	–0–	15,000	42,000
1959	30,000	72,000	6,000	–0–	18,000	48,000

* Denotes a loss or a deficit.

Stock Values

Several values apply to a share of stock. For instance, stocks are said to have a par value, a market value, a book value, a redemption value, and an estimated liquidation value. These several values are discussed in the following paragraphs.

Par Value. Par value is the arbitrary value established for a share of stock in the charter of its issuing corporation. It is also the value printed on the face of each stock certificate. Par value does not necessarily measure the worth of a share of stock; it is only an arbitrary value placed on the stock by its issuing corporation. Under the laws of the majority of the states, corporations may not legally issue and sell their stock to the initial stockholders for less than par value. However, under the laws of some states, stock may be issued initially for less than par value, but the owners of the stock become contingently liable to the creditors of the corporation for the amount of the discount. Discount on stock is the difference between par value and the amount paid to the issuing corporation for the stock when the amount paid is less than par. The contingent liability of owners of stock issued at a discount is dependent upon the future inability of the issuing corporation to meet its own debts. The contingent liability is to future creditors; it is not a direct liability to the corporation.

Some stocks are issued without par value. Such stocks are called *no-par value stocks.*

Book Value. The book value of a share of stock is the amount of proprietary equity represented by one share of ownership as this is shown by the books of the corporation. The book value of a share of stock measures the equity of the owner of one share in the assets of the corporation. If only one kind of stock has been issued, its book value per share may be found by dividing the net assets of the corporation by the number of shares outstanding. Since net assets, or assets minus liabilities, are equal to the corporate proprietorship, which in turn is equal to contributed capital plus retained earnings, the book value of a share of stock is more easily computed by dividing corporate proprietorship by the number of shares outstanding (provided there is only one class of stock outstanding).

If a corporation issues both common and preferred stock, the book value of each depends upon the preferences granted to the preferred stockholders. The preferences granted the preferred stockholders determine the claims of the preferred stockholders to the corporation's net assets. To illustrate this, assume that a corporation has the following capitalization:

```
Common stock (1,000 shares, $100 par)....................$100,000
Preferred stock (1,000 shares, $100 par)...................  100,000
Retained earnings.........................................   50,000
     Total Stockholders' Equity...........................$250,000
```

If the preferred stock of this corporation is nonparticipating and there are no dividends in arrears, the book value of the preferred stock is equal to its par value of $100 per share. Under these circumstances all of the retained earnings are allotted to the common stock. This is because the preferred stockholders having received all of their dividends have no further claim on the past earnings of the corporation as represented by the balance of the Retained Earnings account. Under the circumstances just outlined, the book value of the common stock is $150,000 divided by 1,000 shares, or $150 per share. In cases where preferred dividends are in arrears, available retained earnings equal to the dividends in arrears are allotted to the preferred stock; any remaining retained earnings are then allotted to the common stock.

If the preferred stock of the corporation whose capitalization was just illustrated is fully participating, the retained earnings are allotted pro rata to each class of stock. Under such circumstances, if there are no preferred dividends in arrears, the book value of each kind of stock is $125. If dividends are in arrears, available retained earnings equal to the dividends in arrears is assigned to the preferred stock, and the balance of retained earnings is allotted pro rata to each class of stock.

If preferred stock is limited as to participation, available retained earnings equal in amount to the percentage or rate of participation are assigned to the preferred stock.

Market Value.   The market value of a share of stock is the price at which a share of stock can be sold. Market values are influenced by earnings, dividends, book value, and general market conditions.

Redemption Value.   Redemption values apply to preferred stocks. Often corporations issuing preferred stock reserve the right to redeem the stock by paying the preferred stockholders the par value of their stock plus a premium. The amount that a corporation agrees to pay to redeem a share of its preferred stock is called the "redemption value" of the stock. Normally, a corporation reserves the right to either redeem or to permit the stock to remain outstanding as it chooses.

Estimated Liquidation Value. The estimated liquidation value of a share of stock is the amount that would be received by the stockholder if the corporation were liquidated. It is determined by the preferences granted each class of stockholders and the estimated amounts to be received from the sale of the assets.

Incorporation of a Partnership

Often, in order to secure a lack of personal liability, a more permanent organization, or additional funds, partnerships are incorporated. When a partnership is reorganized into a corporation, if the partnership has been in existence long, the assets of the partnership commonly require revaluation before they are taken over by the corporation. This is because:

1. There may have been errors in keeping the books of the old business. Usually it is wise to call in a certified public accountant to audit the books in order that he may express an opinion as to the amounts shown for the assets and liabilities.
2. Fixed assets purchased several years previous to the reorganization may be grossly overvalued or undervalued on the books of the old business due to price changes and market fluctuations.
3. The old business may have unrecorded goodwill.

Incorporation of a Partnership Illustrated. To illustrate the reorganization of a partnership into a corporation, assume that Hill, Dale, and Knob, who have always shared earnings in the ratio of 2:2:1, decide to expand their business and to reorganize it into a corporation to be known as the Apex Corporation. A condensed balance sheet of the partnership just prior to the reorganization is shown in Illustration 102.

Illustration 102
HILL, DALE, AND KNOB
Balance Sheet, May 30, 19--

ASSETS			LIABILITIES		
Cash		$ 2,500	Accounts payable. . .	$ 9,300	
Accounts receivable.	$ 6,000		Mortgage payable. . .	7,000	
Allow. for bad debts	300	5,700	Total Liabilities .		$16,300
Merchandise inventory		25,000			
Store equipment. . .	$ 4,800			PROPRIETORSHIP	
Accumulated depr.. .	1,200	3,600			
Building	$18,000		Hill, capital	$13,500	
Accumulated depr.. .	6,000	12,000	Dale, capital	15,000	
Land		2,500	Knob, capital	6,500	
			Total Proprietorship		35,000
Total Assets . .		$51,300	Total Liab. and Prop.		$51,300

In planning the reorganization of the partnership into a corporation, the partners agree that:

1. The assets are to be revalued as follows: (a) The allowance for bad debts is to be increased to $500 in order to allow for certain doubtful accounts. (b) The merchandise inventory is to be written down $800 to allow for damaged and shopworn merchandise. (c) The building is to be written up to its present replacement cost of $30,000, and the accumulated depreciation is to be increased to show the building to be one-third depreciated.
2. The assets and liabilities are to be taken over by the new corporation; and each partner is to accept $100 par value stock of the corporation at par in exchange for his partnership equity.

The following journal entries are required to revalue the partnership assets and to allocate the losses and gains from revaluation to the partners:

May	30	Loss or Gain from Revaluation..........	200.00	
		Allowance for Bad Debts...........		200.00
		To increase the allowance for bad debts to allow for additional probable losses.		
	30	Loss or Gain from Revaluation..........	800.00	
		Merchandise Inventory............		800.00
		To revalue the merchandise inventory.		
	30	Building.............................	12,000.00	
		Accumulated Depreciation, Building..		4,000.00
		Loss or Gain from Revaluation.......		8,000.00
		To increase the value of the building to its replacement cost and to show the building to be one-third depreciated.		
	30	Loss or Gain from Revaluation..........	7,000.00	
		Hill, Capital.....................		2,800.00
		Dale, Capital.....................		2,800.00
		Knob, Capital....................		1,400.00
		To allocate the net gain from revaluation to the partners in their loss-and-gain-sharing ratio.		

Losses or gains from revaluation may be allocated to the partners as each asset is revalued. However, if there are many assets, it is easier to place the loss or gain from each revaluation in a loss or gain account and then to allocate the balance of the loss or gain account to the partners in their loss-and-gain-sharing ratio.

After the entries revaluing the assets of Hill, Dale, and Knob are posted, a trial balance of the partnership ledger gives the amounts for the revalued assets and proprietorship shown in Illustration 103.

After the assets of a partnership in the process of reorganization are revalued, the additional entries required by the reorganization depend upon whether the partnership books are to be retained and used by the corporation or new books are to be opened for the corporation. Commonly, if the partnership books have been well kept, they are retained. Consequently, in this illustration assume that the books of Hill, Dale, and Knob are to be retained for use by the corporation taking over the partnership.

Illustration 103

HILL, DALE, AND KNOB
Trial Balance, May 30, 19--

Cash	$ 2,500	
Accounts receivable.	6,000	
Allowance for bad debts.		$ 500
Merchandise inventory.	24,200	
Store equipment.	4,800	
Accumulated depreciation, store equipment.		1,200
Building	30,000	
Accumulated depreciation, building .		10,000
Land	2,500	
Accounts payable		9,300
Mortgage payable		7,000
Hill, capital.		16,300
Dale, capital.		17,800
Knob, capital.		7,900
	$70,000	$70,000

If the partnership books are to be retained, after the assets of Hill, Dale, and Knob are revalued and the gain from the revaluation is transferred to the partners' Capital accounts, only one additional entry is required to change the partnership books into the books of the corporation. The entry is an entry to close the partners' Capital accounts and to open the corporation's Common Stock account. It appears as follows:

May	30	Hill, Capital........................	16,300.00	
		Dale, Capital........................	17,800.00	
		Knob, Capital........................	7,900.00	
		Common Stock..................		42,000.00
		To record the distribution of common stock to the partners in exchange for their partnership equities.		

After the foregoing entry is posted, the books of Hill, Dale, and Knob are the records of the Apex Corporation. Of course, at the time the entry is prepared and posted, the shares of stock representing the interest in the new corporation of each of the former partners should be delivered to him.

Organization Costs

The cost of organizing a corporation such as the costs of printing stock certificates, legal fees, promoters' fees, and amounts paid to the state to secure a charter are called organization costs. When a corporation is organized, the amounts paid to secure its organization are commonly debited to an account called Organization Costs. Theoretically, the balance of the account represents an intangible asset from which the corporation will benefit throughout its entire life; and, theoretically, the balance of the account should be written off as an expense proportionally over the life of the corporation. However, since organization costs have no value in a liquidation, and since the exact life of a corporation is never known in advance, many accountants favor the write-off of organization costs during the early years of a corporation's life. There is no good reason for this other than to be conservative. Being organized and operating is of as much value to a corporation in its twentieth year as in its first. Nevertheless, to be conservative, organization costs are commonly written off to an expense account or directly to the Retained Earnings account over, for example, the first five years of a corporation's life.

Before 1954, when organization costs were written off during the early years of a corporation's life, the expense resulting from the write-off could normally not be deducted as an expense in calculating income subject to federal income taxes. However, since 1954, the Internal Revenue Code has provided that certain organization costs can be deducted proportionally over the first five or more years of a corporation's life.

QUESTIONS FOR CLASS DISCUSSION

1. List (a) the advantages, and (b) the disadvantages of the corporation as a form of business organization.
2. A corporation is said to be a legal entity. What is meant by this?
3. What effect does the doctrine of a separate legal existence have upon the ability of a corporation to enter into contracts with its stockholders? What effect does this doctrine have upon the liability of stockholders for the debts of a corporation in which they own stock?
4. How may lack of liability of its stockholders be (a) an advantage, and (b) a disadvantage to a small corporation?
5. A small corporation wishes to borrow money from a bank. The bank agrees to loan the money if S. L. French, a large stockholder in the corporation, will personally endorse the corporation's note. Why does the bank ask for the endorsement of French on the corporation's note? Would the bank demand the endorsement of French if the business were organized as a partnership and French were a partner?
6. What is a power of attorney? What is a proxy?
7. What are the two kinds of accounts in which are recorded the equities of the stockholders in a corporation? Why are these equities recorded in two different kinds of accounts?
8. In corporation accounting, what is a deficit?
9. Why are the names of the individual stockholders of a corporation normally of little importance to the creditors of the corporation?
10. The Income Summary account of a corporation shows a net income of $50,000. (a) Give the entry to close the Income Summary account. How does the

entry differ from the entry to close the Income Summary account of a single proprietorship or a partnership?

11. What is the reasoning behind laws that prohibit the payment of dividends by a corporation when to do so would reduce the corporation's proprietorship to a point below the amount originally invested in the corporation by its stockholders?

12. What are the three dates involved in the declaration and payment of a cash dividend?

13. Laws place no limit on the amounts partners may withdraw from a partnership. On the other hand, laws regulating corporations place definite limits on the amounts that may be withdrawn by the owners of corporations in the form of dividends. Why is there a difference?

14. At the annual meeting of the stockholders of a corporation the president reported that the corporation had earned during the year $450,000 after taxes. Then he told the stockholders that the board of directors were of the opinion that the corporation could pay only $90,000 in cash dividends. Can you offer a reason for this corporation's ability to pay only $90,000 in dividends when it has earned five times that amount?

15. On December 21 the Green Corporation declared a cash dividend of $3.00 per share on its 1,000 shares of outstanding common stock. The dividend was to be paid on January 20 to stockholders of record of January 15. Give the entries for the declaration and payment of the dividend.

16. How is the ownership of stock transferred?

17. List the rights of common stockholders.

18. What is the pre-emptive right of common stockholders?

19. What are the meanings of the following words when applied to stock: (a) preferred, (b) participating, (c) nonparticipating, (d) cumulative, and (e) noncumulative?

20. What are the meanings of the following terms when applied to stock: (a) par value, (b) book value, (c) market value, (d) redemption value, and (e) estimated liquidation value?

21. What are organization costs?

PROBLEMS

Problem 19–1

On January 12, 1958, James Bush, John Carr, and Robert Dean associated themselves together in the operation of a business. Each invested $15,000. During 1958 their company lost $4,500, and during 1959 it earned $18,000. On January 5, 1960, the three men agreed to pay out to themselves $12,000 of the accumulated earnings of the business. On January 10, 1960, the $12,000 was paid out.

Required:

1. Under the assumption that the business is organized as a partnership, prepare journal entries (1) to record the investments of the men, (2) to close the Income Summary account at the end of 1958 and again at the end of 1959, and (3) to record the distribution of the earnings.

2. Under the assumption that the business is organized as a corporation and that $100 par value common stock is issued at par, prepare journal entries (1) to record the investments, (2) to close the Income Summary account at the end of 1958 and again at the end of 1959, and (3) to record the distribution of the earnings.

Problem 19–2

Dodds Corporation has outstanding 2,000 shares of $100 par value, 6 per cent preferred stock and 1,000 shares of $100 par value common stock. The preferred stock is cumulative and nonparticipating. During a seven-year period the Dodds Corporation paid out the following amounts in dividends:

1954	$24,000
1955	–0–
1956	–0–
1957	32,000
1958	20,000
1959	30,000
1960	21,000

Required:

1. *a*) Prepare a form with column headings as follows:

Year	Amount Distributed in Dividends	Total to Preferred	Balance Due Preferred	Total to Common	Dividend per share Preferred	Dividend per Share Common

    b) In the first column of the form copy the years, and in the second column opposite the proper years copy the amounts distributed in dividends.

    c) Then fill in the information opposite each year in the remaining columns.

2. Prepare and complete a second form according to the foregoing directions under the assumption that rather than being cumulative and nonparticipating, the preferred stock of Dodds Corporation is noncumulative and nonparticipating.

3. Prepare and complete a third form according to the foregoing directions under the assumption that the preferred stock of Dodds Corporation is cumulative and fully participating.

Problem 19–3

On March 31 of the current year the balance sheet of Southlake Supply Company appeared as follows:

SOUTHLAKE SUPPLY COMPANY

Balance Sheet, March 31, 19—

ASSETS			LIABILITIES		
Cash		$ 4,110	Accounts payable		$ 6,370
Accounts receivable	$18,300		Mortgage payable		12,000
Allowance for bad debts	350	17,950	Total Liabilities		$18,370
Merchandise inventory		37,280			
Store equipment	$10,000		PROPRIETORSHIP		
Accumulated depreciation	2,000	8,000			
Office equipment	$ 2,300		James Burns, capital	$48,170	
Accumulated depreciation	950	1,350	Paul Cain, capital	32,150	
Building	$32,000		Total Proprietorship		80,320
Accumulated depreciation	8,000	24,000			
Land		6,000			
Total Assets		$98,690	Total Liab. and Prop.		$98,690

Burns and Cain have operated the Southlake Supply Company for a number of years as partners sharing losses and gains in the ratio of 3 to 2. The partners have entered into an agreement with Dean Noyes to reorganize their firm into a corporation to be known as Southlake Corporation. The agreement has these provisions:

1. The corporation is to issue 1,000 shares of $100 par value common stock.
2. The partnership books are to be retained and used by the corporation.
3. The assets of the partnership as shown by its March 31 balance sheet are to be revalued as follows:
   a) The allowance for bad debts is to be increased $500 to allow for additional doubtful accounts.
   b) The recorded value of the store equipment is to be increased to $12,-000; and the balance of the Accumulated Depreciation, Store Equipment account is to be increased to show the store equipment to be 20 per cent depreciated.
   c) The recorded value of the building is to be increased to the building's replacement cost of $40,000. The amount of accumulated depreciation on the building is to be increased to show the building one-fourth depreciated.

4. After the assets are revalued, any partner whose Capital account balance is not an equal multiple of $100 is to withdraw sufficient cash so as to reduce his account balance to the nearest $100 multiple.
5. After the Capital accounts of the partners are reduced to the nearest $100 multiple, the partners are to accept in exchange for their partnership equities, shares of stock in the corporation equal in par value to their equities.
6. The remaining stock is to be sold to Dean Noyes at par for cash.

Required:

1. Prepare journal entries that will change the partnership to a corporation and that will give effect to the foregoing provisions.
2. Prepare a balance sheet for the corporation.

CLASS EXERCISES

Exercise 19–1
Corporations A, B, and C each have outstanding 10,000 shares of common stock. Following is additional information as to the assets, liabilities, and stockholders' equity in each of the corporations:

	Corporation A	*Corporation B*	*Corporation C*
Assets..................	$309,000	$227,000	?
Liabilities...............	?	45,000	$ 71,000
Common stock............	250,000	100,000	50,000
Retained earnings or deficit.	?	?	?

Required:

Under the assumption that the book value per share of the stock of Corporation A is the same as the book value per share of the stock of Corporation B and also of Corporation C, present the calculations necessary to determine the missing amounts indicated by the question marks.

Exercise 19–2

On December 31 of the current year the common stock of the Standard Corporation sold on the stock exchange at $10.50 per share. On that date the stockholder equity section of the company's balance sheet appeared as follows:

STOCKHOLDERS' EQUITY

Preferred stock, 7 per cent, cumulative and nonparticipating, $10 par
  value, 10,000 shares issued and outstanding........................$100,000
Common stock, $5.00 par value, 50,000 shares issued and outstanding.... 250,000
Retained earnings.. 210,000
    Total Stockholders' Equity................................$560,000

Required:

1. What is the market value of a share of the corporation's common stock?
2. What are the par values of the corporation's (a) preferred stock, and (b) common stock?
3. If there are no dividends in arrears, what are the book values of the corporation's (a) preferred stock, and (b) common stock?
4. If there are no dividends in arrears and if the preferred stock of the corporation were fully participating rather than nonparticipating, what would be the book value of (a) the corporation's preferred stock, and (b) its common stock?

SUPPLEMENTARY PROBLEMS

Problem 19–A

Bain Corporation has had outstanding since its organization 10,000 shares of $10 par value, 6 per cent, preferred stock and 10,000 shares of $25 par value common stock. During a six-year period the company paid out the following amounts in dividends: 1955, $3,000; 1956, nothing; 1957, $10,000; 1958, $25,-000; 1959, $28,000; and 1960, $35,000.

Required:

1. Prepare three schedules with columnar headings as follows:

Year	Total to Preferred Stockholders	Balance Due Preferred Stockholders	Total to Common Stockholders	Dollars per Share Preferred	Dollars per Share Common	Per Cent per Share Preferred	Per Cent per Share Common

2. Complete a schedule under each of the following assumptions showing for each year the total dollars paid to the preferred stockholders, the balance due the preferred stockholders, total dollars to the common stockholders, etc.:
   a) The preferred stock is noncumulative and nonparticipating.
   b) The preferred stock is cumulative and nonparticipating.
   c) The preferred stock is cumulative and participating to 9 per cent of its par value.

Problem 19–B

Following are the stockholders' equity sections from the balance sheets of five corporations:

1. STOCKHOLDERS' EQUITY:

Cumulative and nonparticipating, $100 par value, 6 per cent, preferred stock, authorized and issued 1,000 shares .... $ 100,000
Common stock, $25 par value, 10,000 shares authorized and issued 250,000
Retained earnings 64,000
Total Stockholders' Equity .... $ 414,000

2. CAPITAL STOCK AND RETAINED EARNINGS:

Preferred stock, 6 per cent, $100 par value, cumulative and fully participating, 1,000 shares authorized and issued .... $ 100,000
Common stock, $100 par value, 1,000 shares authorized and issued 100,000
Total Contributed Capital .... $ 200,000
Retained earnings 38,000
Total Capital Stock and Retained Earnings .... $ 238,000

3. PROPRIETORSHIP:

Five per cent preferred stock, $50 par value, cumulative and fully participating, 5,000 shares authorized and issued .... $ 250,000
Common stock, $100 par value, 5,000 shares authorized and issued 500,000
Total Capital Stock Authorized and Issued .... $ 750,000
Retained earnings 210,000
Total Capital Stock and Retained Earnings .... $ 960,000

4. STOCKHOLDERS' INTEREST:

Preferred stock, $100 par value, 7 per cent cumulative and nonparticipating, 500 shares authorized and issued .... $ 50,000*
Common stock, $100 par value, 500 shares authorized and issued 50,000
Retained earnings 6,000
Total Stockholders' Interest .... $ 106,000

* The current year's dividend is unpaid on the preferred stock.

5. STOCKHOLDERS' EQUITY:

Cumulative and nonparticipating, $10 par value, 7 per cent preferred stock, 100,000 shares authorized and issued $1,000,000*
Common stock, $25 par value, 100,000 shares authorized and issued 2,500,000
Total Contributed Capital $3,500,000
Deficit 540,000
Stockholders' Equity $2,960,000

* Three years' dividends are in arrears on the preferred stock.

Required:

Prepare a schedule showing the book value per share of the preferred and common stock of each corporation.

Problem 19–C

Fern Ridge Corporation has had outstanding since it was organized 100,000 shares of $5.00 par value common stock and 1,000 shares of $100 par value, 6 per cent preferred stock. The current year's and two prior years' dividends have not been paid on the preferred stock. However, the company has recently prospered, and the board of directors wants to know how much cash will be required for dividends if a $0.60 per share dividend is paid on the common stock.

Required:

Prepare a schedule for the board of directors showing the total amount of cash required for dividends to both the common and preferred stockholders under each of the following assumptions:

  a) The preferred stock is noncumulative and nonparticipating.
  b) The preferred stock is cumulative and nonparticipating.
  c) The preferred stock is cumulative and fully participating.
  d) The preferred stock is cumulative and participating to 10 per cent.

Chapter

20

CORPORATIONS: STOCK
TRANSACTIONS

THE REORGANIZATION of the partnership of Hill, Dale, and Knob into the Apex Corporation was used in Chapter 19 to illustrate the formation of a corporation by the reorganization of a partnership. The situation presented in this illustration was a simple one, and a minimum of entries were used in recording it. This chapter will present additional situations and entries commonly encountered when corporations are organized and their stock is sold.

The Authorization of Stock

A corporation comes into existence when its charter is granted. The charter of a newly organized corporation authorizes it to issue a fixed amount of stock. This stock may be of one kind and be known as "common stock," or both common and preferred stock may be authorized. Whether a corporation secures the right to issue only common stock or it secures the right to issue both common and preferred stock, it may issue only the amount of each authorized by its charter. Often a corporation will secure an authorization to issue more stock than it plans to sell at the time of its organization. This enables the corporation, at any time in its future, to expand through the sale of the additional stock without the need to apply to the state for the right to issue more stock. For example, a corporation that needs $100,000 to begin its operations secures the right to issue stock in the amount of $150,000 but then issues only $100,000 of the authorized stock. At any time in its future it may issue the additional $50,000 of stock without applying to the state for the right to issue more stock.

When a corporation receives its charter, the amount of preferred stock and the amount of common stock it is authorized to issue may be recorded in its General Journal with a memorandum entry similar to the one shown below:

June	10	On this date the Eastlake Corporation received a charter which authorized it to issue 1,000 shares of $100 par value preferred stock and 1,000 shares of $100 par value common stock.

When authorized stock is recorded with such a memorandum entry, the entry cannot be posted in the sense that debits and credits are entered in the accounts. However, when such an authorization entry is made, a

474

memorandum of the amount of each class of stock authorized is also entered in each of the stock accounts in somewhat the manner shown in Illustration 104.

Illustration 104

Common Stock

Date	Explanation	F	Debit	Date	Explanation	F	Credit
	Authorized on June 10, 19—, to issue 1,000 shares of $100 par value common stock.						

Preferred Stock

Date	Explanation	F	Debit	Date	Explanation	F	Credit
	Authorized on June 10, 19—, to issue 1,000 shares of $100 par value preferred stock.						

Selling Stock for Cash

When stock is sold for cash and the stock is immediately issued, a single entry may be used to record the sale and issuance of the stock. For example, the Eastlake Corporation may use an entry similar to the following to record the sale and issuance of 200 shares of the stock, the authorization of which is recorded above:

June	15	Cash...............................	20,000.00		
		Common Stock....................		20,000.00	
		Sold and issued 200 shares of $100 par value common stock.			

After the entry is posted, the Common Stock account of the corporation appears as follows:

Common Stock

Date	Explanation	F	Debit	Date	Explanation	F	Credit
	Authorized on June 10, 19—, to issue 1,000 shares of $100 par value common stock.			19— June 15			20,000.00

Authorized Stock on the Balance Sheet

The amounts of each class of stock authorized should always be shown in the capital stock accounts. In addition, after a corporation issues a portion of its stock, both its stock authorized and its stock issued should be shown on its balance sheet. Stock authorized and stock issued are often shown on a balance sheet in the following manner:

```
                STOCKHOLDERS' EQUITY

Preferred stock, $100 par value per
   share, authorized 1,000 shares, is-
   sued 650 shares . . . . . . . . . .     $65,000
Common stock, $100 par value per share,
   authorized 1,000 shares, issued 750
   shares. . . . . . . . . . . . . . .      75,000
        Total Stock Issued. . . . . .               $140,000
```

Stock Subscriptions

Often corporations sell their stock for cash and immediately issue the stock. Often, too, when stock is first sold, especially in the organization of a new corporation, it is sold by means of *subscriptions*. When stock is sold by means of subscriptions, a person wishing to become a stockholder signs a subscription blank or a subscriptions list on which he subscribes to a certain number of shares of stock and agrees to pay for the stock either in one amount or in installments. When the subscription is accepted by the corporation, it becomes a contract. Subscription contracts are commonly entered into long before payments are due on the subscribed stock and long before the subscribed stock is to be issued.

When a prospective stockholder signs a corporation's subscription list or one of its subscription blanks, and the corporation accepts the subscription, the corporation acquires an asset. The asset is the right to receive payment from the subscriber. At the same time, the proprietorship of the corporation is increased by the amount the subscriber agrees to pay. The increase in assets is recorded in an account called, for common stock, *Subscriptions Receivable Common Stock;* and the increase in proprietorship is recorded in an account called, for common stock, *Common Stock Subscribed*. Both of these accounts are of a temporary nature. The subscriptions receivable will be converted into cash or other assets when the subscriber pays for his stock. Likewise, when payment is completed, the stock subscribed will be issued and will become outstanding stock. Normally subscribed stock is not issued until paid for because a subscriber might sell and transfer his stock to a third party and then refuse to pay.

If a corporation receives subscriptions to both common and preferred stock, separate subscriptions receivable and stock subscribed accounts must be kept for each class of stock. If the number of subscribers becomes large, the subscriptions receivable accounts often become controlling accounts that control subsidiary Subscribers' Ledgers. The controlling account for each class of subscriptions receivable and its Subscribers' Ledger operate in the same manner as, for example, the Accounts Receivable controlling account and the Accounts Receivable Ledger discussed in a previous chapter.

Entries for the Sale of Stock through Subscriptions

To illustrate the entries required when a corporation sells its stock through subscriptions, assume that the Northgate Corporation receives a charter on July 2, 19—, that authorizes it to issue 1,000 shares of $100 par value common stock. On the same day it receives subscriptions to 500 shares of the stock at par. Later the subscriptions are paid and the stock is issued. When the charter is received, the following entry is made to record the stock authorized:

| July | 2 | On this date the Northgate Corporation received a charter granting it the right to issue 1,000 shares of $100 par value common stock. | | |

The subscriptions to 500 shares of the stock at par are recorded with an entry similar to the following:

July	2	Subscriptions Receivable Common Stock..........................	50,000.00	
		Common Stock Subscribed........		50,000.00
		Received subscriptions to 500 shares of stock at par.		

If the subscribers pay for their stock in one payment, the payment is recorded as follows:

July	15	Cash...............................	50,000.00	
		Subscriptions Receivable Common Stock.......................		50,000.00
		Received payment of subscriptions to 500 shares of common stock.		

When stock is sold through subscriptions, the stock is paid for in full as soon as the subscriptions are paid in full. When stock is sold through subscriptions, as soon as the subscriptions are paid, the subscribed stock is issued. The entry to record the issuance of the 500 shares of Northgate Corporation Stock appears as follows:

July	15	Common Stock Subscribed............	50,000.00	
		Common Stock.................		50,000.00
		Issued 500 shares of common stock previously subscribed and paid for.		

Subscriptions Receivable and Stock Subscribed on the Balance Sheet

Under the laws of many states a subscriber to stock legally becomes a stockholder upon the acceptance of his signed subscription contract by a corporation. Under the laws of these states a subscriber receives all the rights and privileges of a stockholder as soon as his signed subscription contract is accepted. This is true even though the stock is not paid for and a stock certificate is not issued until a later date. Consequently, if stock is subscribed but unissued on the balance sheet date, the amount of unissued subscribed stock should be disclosed on the balance sheet. For example, assume that a corporation which is authorized to issue $100,000 of $100 par value common stock has issued $60,000 of its authorized stock and has accepted subscriptions to an additional $25,000 of the unissued stock. This situation may be disclosed on the balance sheet as follows:

STOCKHOLDERS' EQUITY

```
Common stock, $100 par value per share,
  authorized 1,000 shares, issued 600
  shares . . . . . . . . . . . . . . . .   $60,000
Unissued common stock subscribed, 250
  shares . . . . . . . . . . . . . . . .    25,000
     Total Common Stock Issued and Sub-
       scribed. . . . . . . . . . . .             $85,000
```

When uncollected subscriptions receivable exist on the balance sheet date, the intention is normally to collect the amounts due within a relatively short period of time. Therefore, unpaid subscriptions normally appear on the balance sheet as current assets under the title of "Subscriptions Receivable Common Stock" or "Subscriptions Receivable Preferred Stock."

Subscriptions Collected in Installments

Often subscription contracts provide that subscribers may pay for their stock in installments. In such cases, when the subscriptions are accepted, the subscriptions receivable account is debited and the stock subscribed account is credited for the amount the subscribers agree to pay. Then as each installment is collected, Cash is debited and the subscriptions receivable account is credited for the amount collected. After the last installment is collected, the stock is issued. For example, assume that on August 2, the Northgate Corporation accepts subscriptions for twenty-five shares of its $100 par value common stock at par. Assume further that the subscription contracts provide that 10 per cent of the subscription price is to be paid upon acceptance of the subscriptions and that the balance is to be paid in two equal installments due September 30 and October 30. The entries to record the sale of the stock are:

Aug.	2	Subscriptions Receivable Common Stock. .	2,500.00	
		Common Stock Subscribed.		2,500.00
		Received subscriptions to twenty-five shares of $100 par value stock.		

Aug.	2	Cash...................................	250.00	
		Subscriptions Receivable Common		
		Stock.........................		250.00
		Ten per cent cash received with subscrip-		
		tions.		
Sept.	30	Cash...................................	1,125.00	
		Subscriptions Receivable Common		
		Stock.........................		1,125.00
		Received cash in payment of subscrip-		
		tions.		
Oct.	30	Cash...................................	1,125.00	
		Subscriptions Receivable Common		
		Stock.........................		1,125.00
		Received final payment from sub-		
		scribers.		
	30	Common Stock Subscribed..............	2,500.00	
		Common Stock....................		2,500.00
		Issued stock to fully paid subscribers.		

Subscriptions in Default

It sometimes happens that a subscriber to stock fails to complete his subscription payments. In such cases a corporation may sue and collect the amount of the unpaid subscription. However, it is usually easier to declare the subscribed stock forfeited and to sell the forfeited stock to a new purchaser.

When the board of directors of a corporation declares subscribed stock forfeited, after a subscription installment has remained unpaid for a certain length of time, a problem arises as to what to do with the amount already paid in by the defaulting subscriber. The decision in each case depends upon the laws of the state of incorporation and the wishes of the board of directors. In some states a corporation is permitted by law to retain the amount paid in by a defaulting subscriber. In other states a corporation must return to the defaulting subscriber the amount of his payments less any selling expenses and losses on the resale of the forfeited stock.

To illustrate the entries for forfeited stock, assume that Melvin Klope subscribes at par to ten shares of the Northgate Corporation's $100 par value common stock. His subscription contract calls for a down payment of 10 per cent and two equal installment payments. After paying the down payment, Klope defaults. Later his stock is declared forfeited and is sold at $96 per share. If the Northgate Corporation is organized in a state that requires the return of a defaulting subscriber's payments less losses and expenses on the resale of his forfeited stock, the following entries are required to record the transactions growing out of Klope's default:

Nov.	1	Subscriptions Receivable Common Stock.. Common Stock Subscribed......... To record the subscription of Melvin Klope.	1,000.00	1,000.00
	1	Cash............................... Subscriptions Receivable Common Stock......................... To record the 10 per cent subscription payment.	100.00	100.00
Dec.	15	Common Stock Subscribed............. Subscriptions Receivable Common Stock......................... Melvin Klope, Defaulted Subscriptions......................... To record the forfeit of ten shares of common stock.	1,000.00	900.00 100.00
	21	Cash............................... Melvin Klope, Defaulted Subscriptions.... Common Stock.................. To record the sale of forfeited stock at $96 per share and to charge the loss to Klope.	960.00 40.00	1,000.00
	21	Melvin Klope, Defaulted Subscriptions.... Cash......................... To charge the defaulted subscriptions account of Klope with expenses resulting from the sale of his forfeited stock.	25.00	25.00
	21	Melvin Klope, Defaulted Subscriptions.... Cash......................... To refund the subscription payment less expenses and loss on the resale of forfeited stock.	35.00	35.00

If the Northgate Corporation is incorporated in a state that does not require the return of payments of defaulting subscribers and the board of directors chooses not to return the balance of Klope's payment, the following series of entries are required to record the transactions growing out of the default:

Nov.	1	Subscriptions Receivable Common Stock.. Common Stock Subscribed......... To record the subscription of Klope.	1,000.00	1,000.00
	1	Cash............................... Subscriptions Receivable Common Stock......................... To record the 10 per cent subscription payment.	100.00	100.00

Dec.	15	Common Stock Subscribed............	1,000.00	
		Subscriptions Receivable Common		
		Stock........................		900.00
		Contributed Capital from Forfeited		
		Stock........................		100.00
		To record the forfeit of ten shares of		
		stock.		
	21	Cash...............................	960.00	
		Contributed Capital from Forfeited Stock.	40.00	
		Common Stock..................		1,000.00
		To record the sale of the forfeited stock		
		at $96.		
	21	Contributed Capital from Forfeited Stock.	25.00	
		Cash..........................		25.00
		To record the payment of expenses re-		
		sulting from the sale of forfeited stock.		

Klope's initial payment of $100 exceeds the loss and expenses on the re-sale of his forfeited stock by $35. If the corporation retains this amount, both its assets and proprietorship are increased by $35. The increase in proprietorship is recorded in the account "Contributed Capital from Forfeited Stock," as the foregoing entries show.

Stock Premiums and Discounts

Par value is an arbitrary value that a corporation places on a share of its stock at the time of its organization. Normally a corporation may choose any amount as par value for its stock; but stocks with par values of $100, $50, $25, $10, $5, and $1 are common. Early corporation laws required all stocks to have a par value. Today, most states permit corporations to issue stock having no par value.

When a corporation issues stock having a par value, the par value is printed on each stock certificate and is used by the corporation in ac-counting for the stock. Also, in many states, when a corporation issues par value stock, it establishes for itself a *minimum legal capital* equal to the par value of the issued stock. For example, if a corporation issues 1,000 shares of $100 par value stock, it establishes for itself a minimum legal capital of $100,000.

When corporation laws establish a minimum legal capital for a corpora-tion, they also normally require a corporation's stockholders to invest in the corporation, assets equal in value to the minimum legal capital or to be liable to the corporation's creditors for the deficiency. In other words, these corporation laws require stockholders to give a corporation par value for its stock or to be liable for the deficiency. In addition, when corpora-tion laws establish a minimum legal capital for a corporation, they nor-mally also make illegal any payments to stockholders of dividends or their equivalent when these payments reduce the corporation's proprietorship below its minimum legal capital. Corporation laws governing minimum legal capital were written in an effort to protect corporation creditors. The authors of these laws reasoned somewhat as follows: The creditors of a corporation may look only to the assets of the corporation for the satisfaction of their claims. Consequently, when a corporation is organized, its stockholders should provide it with a fund of assets equal to its minimum legal capital. Thereafter, this fund of assets should remain with the corporation and should not be returned to its stockholders in any form until all creditor claims are paid.

Although par value helps to establish minimum legal capital and is used in accounting for par value stock, it does not establish a stock's worth or the price at which a corporation must issue its stock. If purchasers of stock are willing to pay more than par value, a corporation may sell and issue its stock at a price above par. Likewise, in some states, if purchasers of stock will not pay par value, a corporation may issue its stock at a price below par. Normally a corporation's potential earning power and the supply of investment funds determine whether purchasers of stock will pay par, less than par, or more than par for the corporation's stock.

When a corporation sells and issues its stock at a price above the stock's par value, the stock is said to be issued at a *premium*. A premium is an amount in excess of par paid by the purchasers of newly issued stock. For example, if a corporation sells and issues its $100 par value stock for $109 per share, the $9.00 in excess of par is called a "premium." Although a premium is an amount in excess of par paid by the purchasers of newly issued stock, it is not considered a profit of the issuing corporation. A premium is considered a part of the investment of the stockholder who pays more than par for his stock. When a corporation issues its stock at a premium, its stockholders invest more than the legal minimum of capital. Since premiums are amounts invested by stockholders in excess of minimum legal capital, they should be accounted for separately from the par value of the stock to which they apply.

In a great many states it is illegal for a corporation to sell and issue its stock for less than par value. However, in some states, stock may be sold and issued for less than par. When a corporation sells and issues its stock at a price below the stock's par value, the stock is said to be issued at a *discount*. For example, a corporation that sells and issues its $100 par value stock at $89 per share is said to issue the stock at a discount. In this case the discount is $11 per share. A discount is the difference between par value and the price paid for stock when the price paid is less than par. When stock is sold at a discount, the discount is not considered a loss to the issuing corporation. When a corporation issues its stock at a discount, its stockholders are investing less than the minimum legal capital. In such cases, in most states, the stockholders are contingently liable for the investment deficiency. This contingent liability is called a *dis-*

count liability. Careful notice should be taken that stockholders owning stock issued at a discount are not contingently liable to the issuing corporation; they are contingently liable to the corporation's creditors. Insofar as the issuing corporation is concerned, stock issued at a discount is paid for in full. However, if at any time after stock is issued at a discount the issuing corporation becomes bankrupt, its creditors may in many states, if the current owners of the stock originally issued at a discount knew at the time they purchased the stock that it was originally issued at a discount, force the current owners of the stock to pay in the amount of the discount. The money paid in is then used for the satisfaction of the creditor claims. It should be noted from the foregoing that if the ownership of specific shares of stock originally issued at a discount can be traced from one owner to the next, and the owners knew of the discount, then the discount liability follows the stock from owner to owner.

Since a stock discount represents a deficiency in the investment of the stockholders who buy stock at a discount, it should be accounted for separately from the par value of the stock to which it applies.

Entries for Stock Sold at a Premium

When, for example, common stock is sold at a premium and the stock is immediately issued, the transaction may be recorded as follows:

Dec.	1	Cash...............................	110,000.00	
		Common Stock....................		100,000.00
		Premium on Common Stock........		10,000.00
		To record the sale of 1,000 shares of $100 par value common stock at $110 per share.		

If subscriptions are taken for stock at a premium, the subscriptions collected, and the stock issued, the following entries are used to record the transactions:

Dec.	2	Subscriptions Receivable Common Stock..	10,250.00	
		Common Stock Subscribed.........		10,000.00
		Premium on Common Stock........		250.00
		Received subscriptions for 100 shares of $100 par value common stock at $102.50 per share.		
Jan.	2	Cash...............................	10,250.00	
		Subscriptions Receivable Common Stock.........................		10,250.00
		Collected subscriptions in full.		
	2	Common Stock Subscribed.............	10,000.00	
		Common Stock....................		10,000.00
		Issued stock to fully paid subscribers.		

Notice that the subscriptions receivable account is debited at the time the subscription is taken for the sum of the par value of the stock and the premium; this is the amount the subscribers agree to pay. Notice, too, that the stock subscribed account is credited for the par value of the stock and that the premium is credited to a premium account at the time the subscriptions are taken.

Entries for Stock Sold at a Discount

Although in many states it is illegal to sell and issue stock at a discount and in those states in which stock may be sold and issued at a discount a discount liability attaches to such stock, corporations do occasionally sell and issue their stock at a discount. When stock is sold for cash at a discount and immediately issued, the transaction may be recorded with an entry similar to the following:

Mar.	5	Cash.......................................	8,900.00	
		Discount on Common Stock.............	1,100.00	
		Common Stock....................		10,000.00
		Sold and issued 100 shares of $100 par value common stock at $89 per share.		

When stock is subscribed at a discount and later paid for and issued, the following series of entries are required to record the transactions:

Mar.	10	Subscriptions Receivable Common Stock..	950.00	
		Discount on Common Stock.............	50.00	
		Common Stock Subscribed..........		1,000.00
		Received subscriptions for ten shares of $100 par value common stock at $95 per share.		
Apr.	10	Cash......................................	950.00	
		Subscriptions Receivable Common Stock		950.00
		Collected subscriptions in full.		
	10	Common Stock Subscribed.............	1,000.00	
		Common Stock....................		1,000.00
		Issued stock to fully paid subscribers.		

Premiums and Discounts in the Accounts

The amounts shown in a corporation's stock premium and discount accounts together with the balances of its stock accounts measure the capital contributions of the corporation's stockholders. If a corporation has issued both common and preferred stocks at other than their par values, separate premium and discount accounts should be maintained for each. If part of an authorization of one kind of stock, for example, common stock, has been sold at a discount and later another block of the same authorization of stock has been sold at a premium, both a common stock premium account and a common stock discount account should be maintained. The premium on one sale and the discount on another sale should not be entered in the same account and thereby be offset. This is because the stockholders who purchased their stock at a discount are subject to discount liability, and the discount liability should not be lost in the accounts and concealed from the creditors.

As previously stated, when stock is sold at a discount, the discount should not be offset in the accounts against a premium. Likewise, until legally removed, a discount should remain in the accounts and should appear on the balance sheet as notice to the creditors of a possible additional source of funds. In a few states a discount may be legally removed from the accounts by transferring earnings from a retained earnings account to a discount account. In other states a discount may be legally removed from the accounts only by the receipt of funds equal to the discount from the stockholders who own the stock purchased at a discount.

A stock premium is an amount in excess of par paid by stockholders for newly issued stock. When a corporation sells its stock at a premium, its stockholders invest in the corporation more than the minimum legal capital. Some states permit corporations to return as dividends to their stockholders such investments in excess of minimum legal capital; other states prohibit such returns. In other words, some states permit corporations to pay out as dividends amounts received as stock premiums, and other states prohibit such payments. Although it has nothing to do with the legality of such payments, many leading accountants think dividends should not be paid from amounts received as stock premiums. They feel that the rights of both stockholders and creditors are better protected if stock premiums are considered a part of the permanent capital of a corporation and, therefore, not subject to dividend charges. In other words, they feel that the balance of a premium account should not be reduced by dividend payments and that the balance of a premium account should remain on the books throughout the life of a corporation.

Premiums and Discounts on the Balance Sheet

Stock premiums and discounts help measure the capital contributions of stockholders. They are a part of the proprietorship of a corporation, and on a balance sheet are commonly added to or are deducted from the stock to which they relate. For example, premiums and discounts may appear on a balance sheet as in Illustration 105 on the next page.

No-Par Stock

As previously stated, par value is the arbitrary value that a corporation places on a share of its stock at the time of its organization. Par value has a legal significance in that it helps to establish minimum legal capital. However, since stock may be issued at a premium or at a discount, even in a newly organized corporation a stock's par value may have little relation to its book value or its market value. In an older corporation, after earnings or losses, a stock's par value may have still less relation to

Illustration 105
SHAREHOLDERS' EQUITY

```
Preferred stock, 6 per cent, $100 par value,
    authorized 2,500 shares, issued 1,500
    shares . . . . . . . . . . . . . . . . .    $150,000
    Add: Premium on preferred stock. . . . . .    10,000
        Amount paid in . . . . . . . . . . .               $160,000
Common stock, $100 par value, authorized
    2,500 shares, issued 2,000 shares. . . .    $200,000
    Add: Premium on common stock . . . . . . .     5,000
    Deduct: Discount on common stock . . . . .     3,000
        Amount paid in . . . . . . . . . . .                202,000
            Total Contributed Capital. . . . . .                        $362,000
Retained earnings. . . . . . . . . . . . .                               127,000
            Total Shareholders' Equity . . . .                          $489,000
```

book value or market value. The lack of relation between par value and book value may be easily demonstrated with the stockholders' equity sections from the balance sheets of corporations A and B, which follows:

CORPORATION A

Common stock, par value $100, authorized and issued 1,000 shares.	$100,000	
Retained earnings.	50,000	
Total Capital Stock and Retained Earnings.		$150,000

CORPORATION B

Common stock, par value $100, authorized and issued 1,000 shares.	$100,000	
Deficit.	30,000	
Total Capital Stock and Deficit.		$70,000

Notice that the common stocks of both Corporation A and Corporation B have a par value of $100 per share. However, Corporation A has retained earnings of $50,000, and the book value of a share of its stock is $150. At the same time, Corporation B has a deficit of $30,000, and the book value of a share of its stock is only $70. This is a difference in book values of $80 per share for stocks, the par values of which are the same.

Although it cannot be so easily demonstrated, the difference in the market values of these stocks is probably much more than $80 per share. This is because earnings affect the market value of a stock, and obviously the earnings of these two corporations have not been equal. Corporation A has retained earnings of $50,000; its operations have apparently been profitable. On the other hand, Corporation B's operations have apparently been unprofitable because it has a deficit of $30,000.

Although the par value of a stock may have little relation to its book value or its market value, par value does establish the minimum price below which stock may not be issued if a discount liability is to be avoided. Prior to 1912 all stocks issued by corporations in the United States were required to have a par value and were thus subject to discount liability. However, in that year the state of New York passed a law making legal the issuance of so-called no-par stock or stock without par value. Since then all states have passed similar laws.

When no-par stock laws were first passed, their advocates claimed a number of advantages for no-par stock. Of the several advantages claimed, the following were among the more important:

1. Since a no-par stock cannot have a par value engraved upon its certificates, an investor must investigate its worth before investing. Many uninformed investors have difficulty realizing that a par value does not establish a stock's worth. In the past, a par value beautifully engraved across the face of a stock certificate often made it easy for unscrupulous promoters to sell near worthless stock to unsuspecting and uninformed investors. The unsuspecting and uninformed investors had difficulty resisting near worthless "$100 par value stock on sale at a special price of $50 per share."

2. Assets other than cash are sometimes accepted by a corporation in exchange for its stock. In such cases, if the stock given is par value stock and the assets accepted have a fair market value that is less than the exchanged stock's par value, the board of directors may be tempted to place an inflated value on the assets accepted. If the assets accepted in the exchange are given an inflated value equal to the exchanged stock's par value, the stock is issued at par and a discount liability does not attach. Since no-par stock is without par value, no such temptation exists.

3. Since no-par stock does not have a par value, it cannot be issued at a discount. Therefore, no-par stock may be issued at any price without a discount liability attaching.

Accounting for No-Par Stock

When a corporation is authorized to issue no-par stock, the authorization is recorded in the same manner as that for par value stock. For example, the Porter Corporation which is authorized to issue 5,000 shares of no-par common stock records the authorization with an entry similar to the following:

Sept.	17	On this date a charter was granted to the Porter Corporation which authorized it to issue 5,000 shares of no-par-value common stock.		

When no-par-value stock is issued, the issuance may be recorded in one of two ways. The choice between the two methods depends upon the laws of the state of incorporation and the wishes of the board of directors. Some state laws require that a corporation must credit the entire proceeds from the sale of no-par stock to the no-par stock account. In other states, when no-par stock is issued, the board of directors may choose to place a *stated value* upon the no-par stock. When a stated value is placed on no-par stock and the stock is sold for more than the stated value, the no-par stock account is credited for the stated value and the remainder is credited to a contributed capital account called, for instance, "Contributed Capital in Excess of Stated Value of No-Par Stock." To illustrate the two methods of recording no-par stock, assume that the Porter Corporation, whose stock authorization was previously illustrated, sells and issues 1,000 shares of its authorized stock at $42 per share.

If the Porter Corporation is organized in a state in which the entire amount received from the sale of no-par stock must be credited to the no-par stock account, it will record the sale as follows:

Sept.	20	Cash..............................	42,000.00	
		No-Par Common Stock............		42,000.00
		To record the sale and issuance of 1,000 shares of no-par common stock at $42 per share.		

If the Porter Corporation is organized in a state in which the board of directors may place a stated value on no-par stock, accounting for the sale of the no-par stock is similar to accounting for par value stock. For example, if the board of directors places a stated value of $25 per share on the stock, the sale and issuance of the stock is recorded as follows:

Sept.	20	Cash..............................	42,000.00	
		No-Par Common Stock............		25,000.00
		Contributed Capital in Excess of Stated Value of No-Par Stock......		17,000.00
		To record the sale at $42 per share of 1,000 shares of no-par stock having a stated value of $25 per share.		

Although the account title "Contributed Capital in Excess of Stated Value of No-Par Stock" is long and unwieldly, and the title "Premium on No-Par Stock" is sometimes used, the longer title is the better. Normally, premiums are associated with par values, and if the word "premium" is used to denote an excess over stated value, the fact that a stated value is involved should be made clear. For example, if the word "premium" is used in the title of an account in which the excess over stated value of no-par stock is recorded, the title should be, for instance, "Premium Over Stated Value of No-Par Stock."

From the foregoing it is obvious that when a stated value is placed on no-par stock, the accounting treatment for such stock is similar to that for par value stock. However, a sharp distinction should be made between a par value and a stated value; they are not synonymous. A par value is a more formal value than a stated value. A par value is established by a corporation at the time of its organization. It appears in the corporation's charter and normally can be changed only by an application to the state.

A stated value is more flexible. The board of directors of a corporation establishes a stock's stated value by resolution. Normally, at any time, they may also change the stated value of a stock by passing an additional resolution. Often, if the stated value of a stock is first set too high and the stock cannot be sold at the established stated value, the board of directors will reduce the stated value in order that the stock can be sold for its stated value.

No-Par Stock and Legal Capital

State laws permitting the issuance of no-par stock vary as to their minimum legal capital requirements for corporations issuing such stock. Most states require that the entire amount received by a corporation from the sale of its no-par stock be considered minimum legal capital and as such be made unavailable for dividend payments. A few states permit a corporation issuing no-par stock to establish its minimum legal capital at the stated value of such stock and to pay out as dividends any amount above stated value received from the sale of such stock. In other words, these states permit dividends to be paid from contributed capital. Although in each case the laws of the state of incorporation are the final authority on the legality of dividends from contributed capital, accountants are almost uniformly opposed to calling such distributions "dividends." Their opposition stems from the fact that calling such distributions "dividends" may mislead an uninformed person as to the prosperity being enjoyed by the corporation paying such "dividends."

Exchanging Stock for Assets Other than Cash

Corporations often accept assets other than cash in exchange for their stock. When they do so, the transaction is recorded in somewhat the following manner:

Apr.	3	Machinery............................	10,000.00	
		Buildings............................	25,000.00	
		Land................................	5,000.00	
		Common Stock....................		40,000.00
		Exchanged 400 shares of common stock at par for machinery, building, and land.		

When a corporation accepts assets other than cash in exchange for its stock, it is the duty of the board of directors to place a fair market value on the accepted assets. If the assets are fairly valued, such transactions are perfectly proper. Nevertheless, when par value stock is exchanged for assets other than cash and a discount is not recorded, outsiders may question the value placed on the assets. They may question whether the assets accepted are really worth the par value of the stock given. If the value of the assets is not equal to the par value of the stock exchanged, a discount should be recorded. However, such discounts are seldom ever recorded.

This is because as a rule, unless fraud is evident, courts will accept the judgment of a board of directors as to the value placed on assets taken in exchange for stock. Consequently, boards of directors are prone to inflate the value of assets accepted in exchange for par value stock in order, when necessary, to avoid the recording of a discount. Such inflation is unnecessary when no-par stock is exchanged for assets other than cash. This is considered a point in favor of no-par stock.

Special Records of a Corporation

A corporation records the majority of its transactions in the same manner and in the same types of journals and ledgers as those of a single proprietorship or a partnership. However, because of its special nature a corporation does use certain special records. The more important of these are the: (1) Minute Book, (2) Subscribers' Ledger, (3) Stock Certificate Book, and (4) Stockholders' Ledger.

The Minute Book. The Minute Book of a corporation contains the official record of the proceedings of the meetings of its stockholders and its board of directors. In addition, it normally contains copies of the corporation charter and bylaws.

Because of the nature of a corporation, certain of its acts must be authorized by either its stockholders or its board of directors. For example, the declaration of dividends, the purchase or construction of major assets, and the borrowing of money must be authorized by a corporation's board of directors. Acts such as these are authorized by resolutions passed at a meeting of the board of directors. The Minute Book contains a copy of each such resolution and the action taken thereon.

The Subscribers' Ledger. If the subscriptions to a corporation's stock are numerous, and especially if they are collected in installments, an account is opened for each subscriber in a subsidiary Subscribers' Ledger. When a Subscribers' Ledger is maintained, a subscriptions receivable account in the General Ledger acts as a controlling account for the subscribers' accounts in the Subscribers' Ledger. Collections from subscribers may be recorded in the Cash Receipts Journal, or a special Subscribers' Journal may be designed and used. Regardless of the journal used, the total of all subscriptions collected is debited to the Cash account and credited to a subscriptions receivable account in the General Ledger. In addition, when a Subscribers' Ledger is maintained, the amounts collected from each subscriber are credited to his account in the Subscribers' Ledger.

If a corporation has numerous subscribers to both its common stock and to its preferred stock, it normally maintains separate subscribers' ledgers for the subscribers to each class of stock. The Subscriptions Receivable Common Stock account then controls the accounts of the Common Stock Subscribers' Ledger, and the Subscriptions Receivable Preferred Stock account controls the Preferred Stock Subscribers' Ledger.

The Stock Certificate Book.   A Stock Certificate Book contains a
number of blank, preprinted stock certificates attached to stubs. The certificates and stubs are bound in the Stock Certificate Book in the manner
of a checkbook. As each stock certificate is issued, the name of its owner,
the number of shares, and the date of issuance are entered on a blank
certificate, and the certificate is signed by the proper corporation officials.
At the same time, the name and address of the stock owner, the number
of shares, and the date are entered on the certificate stub. The certificate
is then removed and delivered to its owner.

When stock is transferred, the old certificate is returned to the corporation, marked canceled, and attached to its stub in the Stock Certificate
Book. One or more new certificates are then issued in its place. As a result of these procedures, the Stock Certificate Book contains a current
record of the shares of stock owned by each stockholder.

Since the stubs of the Stock Certificate Book show the number of shares
of stock owned by each stockholder, the total number of shares of stock
outstanding as shown by these stubs should agree with the number of
shares outstanding as shown by the stock account in the General Ledger.
Because of this, the Stock Certificate Book acts in the manner of a subsidiary ledger controlled by the stock account. The control is on the basis
of shares of stock rather than dollars.

When a corporation issues both common and preferred stock, it uses
separate Stock Certificate Books as well as separate stock accounts for
each.

Stockholders' Ledgers.   In a small corporation having but a few
stockholders, the stubs of a Stock Certificate Book are often a sufficient
record of the shares of stock owned by each stockholder. However, in a
corporation with more than a very few stockholders such a record is not
sufficient. In a corporation with more than a few stockholders, additional
records of the stock owned by each stockholder are needed. These additional records usually take the form of stockholder accounts, a separate
account for each stockholder, each account showing the number of shares
owned. These accounts are kept in ledgers called *Stockholders' Ledgers.*
If a corporation issues but one kind of stock, only one ledger is needed.
However, if a corporation issues both common and preferred stock, a
separate ledger is maintained for the stockholders owning each class of
stock. Furthermore, when a corporation issues both common and preferred
stock and a stockholder owns a portion of only one of the classes of stock,
only one stockholder account is required for the stockholder. However,
two accounts are needed for a stockholder owning portions of both classes
of stock. One account is maintained in the Common Stockholders' Ledger
to show the number of shares of common stock owned by the stockholder,
and another account is maintained in the Preferred Stockholders' Ledger
to show the number of shares of preferred stock owned.

Like a Stock Certificate Book, a Stockholders' Ledger is also a supplementary record of the stock outstanding and is controlled by a stock account in the General Ledger. Also, like a Stock Certificate Book, the control is on a basis of shares of stock rather than dollars.

The stockholder accounts in a Stockholders' Ledger are always kept in terms of shares of stock rather than in dollars and cents. Each stockholder's account shows the number of shares of stock issued to him, the number of shares returned for transfer, and the balance of shares held. This is shown in Illustration 106 with the account of G. C. West from the Stockholders' Ledger of the Northgate Corporation. An examination of the stockholder's account shows that on July 10, West was issued 100 shares of original issue stock. On August 15, the certificate for these 100 shares was returned, and 20 of the shares were transferred to John Davis. This transfer is indicated by the return of certificate No. 3 and the issuance in its place of certificates No. 27 for 20 shares and No. 28 for 80 shares. On October 3, the account shows the purchase and transfer of 50 shares of stock from John Soha.

Illustration 106

Stockholder's Name		G. C. West		Address	118 N. Bridgeton St. Portland, Oregon		
Date		No. of Certificate Returned	From Whom Transferred To Whom Transferred	No. of Certificate Issued	Shares Returned and Transferred	Shares Issued	Shares Held
July	10		Original Issue	3		100	100
Aug.	15	3	John Davis	27	20		
		3	Reissue	28		80	80
Oct.	3	19	John Soha	56		50	130

When stock is transferred from one owner to another, insofar as the issuing corporation is concerned, the total number of shares outstanding remains unchanged. Consequently, no entries are needed in the general ledger accounts to record the transfer. However, the transfer must be recorded in the Stockholders' Ledger. Often the entries in the Stockholders' Ledger are made directly from the stock certificates involved in the transfer.

Transfer Agent and Registrar

In a small corporation the Stock Certificate Book, the Stockholders' Ledger, and any other stock records, as well as the duty of transferring shares of stock from one owner to another, are the responsibility of the corporation secretary. In a large corporation whose stock is listed on a major stock exchange, the transfer of stock and the stockholders' records are the responsibility of a *transfer agent* and a *registrar*. Assigning the duty of transferring stock and the keeping of stockholders' records to a transfer agent and to a registrar helps to insure that only the proper amount of stock is issued and that the stock records are honestly and accurately kept. Usually registrars and transfer agents are large banks or trust companies.

When the owner of stock in a corporation having a registrar and a transfer agent wishes to transfer his stock to a new owner, he completes the endorsement on the back of his certificate and sends the certificate to the transfer agent. The transfer agent cancels the old certificate and issues one or more new certificates which he sends to the registrar. The registrar records the transfer in the Stockholders' Ledger and sends the new certificate or certificates to the proper owners.

In addition to maintaining the Stockholders' Ledger, the registrar is also assigned the duty of preparing the official lists of stockholders for stockholders' meetings and for the payment of dividends.

QUESTIONS FOR CLASS DISCUSSION

1. What are the balance sheet classifications of the accounts: (a) Subscriptions Receivable Common Stock, and (b) Common Stock Subscribed?
2. Southdale Corporation received a charter on March 15 that granted it the right to issue 1,000 shares of $100 par value common stock. On March 20 the corporation issued the stock at par for cash. Give the entries to record these transactions.
3. What is a stock premium? What is a stock discount?
4. Differentiate between discount on stock and discount on a note given to a bank in order to borrow money.
5. Does a corporation earn a profit by selling its stock at a premium? Does a corporation incur a loss by selling its stock at a discount?
6. Why do corporation laws make purchasers of stock at a discount contingently liable for the discount? To whom are purchasers of stock at a discount contingently liable?
7. Discounts on stock and premiums on the same stock should not be recorded in a single account. Why?
8. On May 1 the Renolds Corporation received subscriptions to 100 shares of its $100 par value common stock at $105 per share. The subscription contract called for a 10 per cent down payment to accompany the contract and the payment of the balance in two equal installments due in thirty and sixty days. Give the entries to record (a) the receipt of the subscription, (b) the receipt of the down payment, (c) the receipt of the installment payments, and (d) the issuance of the stock.
9. On April 3 the Morgan Corporation received subscriptions to 1,000 shares of its $100 par value common stock at $98 per share. The subscriptions contracts called for a 20 per cent down payment to accompany the subscriptions contracts and the payment of the balance thirty days thereafter. Give the entries to record (a) the receipt of the subscriptions, (b) the receipt of the down payment, (c) the receipt of the balance due, and (d) the issuance of the stock.
10. If a subscriber to stock pays a portion of his subscription and then defaults, what happens to the amount he has paid?
11. On April 12 the Reed Corporation received from Paul Wood a subscription

at par to 100 shares of its $100 par value common stock. The subscription contract called for a 10 per cent down payment with the balance to be paid in thirty days. Wood paid the down payment and then defaulted. On May 10 the board of directors declared the stock forfeited, and on May 20 the stock was sold at $98 per share. There were sale expenses of $60. Give the entries to record the transactions under the assumption that the corporation is organized in a state that requires the return to a defaulting subscriber of his payments less the loss on the sale of his forfeited stock and less the expenses of selling the stock.

12. Give the entries for the transactions of Question 11 under the assumption that the Reed Corporation is organized in a state that permits a corporation to retain the payments of a defaulting subscriber and that the board of directors so votes.

13. What advantages are claimed for no-par stock?

14. On April 1 the Mason Corporation sold and issued 1,000 shares of its no-par common stock for $78,000. No stated value was placed on the stock. Give the entry for the sale of the stock.

15. Assume that the Mason Corporation (Question 14) placed a stated value of $50 per share on its no-par stock. Give the entry for the sale of the stock.

16. What is the nature of each of the following corporation records: (1) Minute Book, (2) Subscribers' Ledger, (3) Stock Certificate Book, and (4) Stockholders' Ledger?

17. What are the duties and responsibilities of a corporation's registrar and transfer agent?

18. Wetzel, who owns twenty shares of Pine Corporation common stock, sells five of the shares to Davis. Describe the entries that are required in the records of the Pine Corporation to record the transfer.

PROBLEMS

Problem 20–1

On March 22 of the current year the Malone Corporation received a charter granting it the right to issue 4,000 shares of $25, 6 per cent, cumulative and nonparticipating, preferred stock and 10,000 shares of $10 par value common stock. It then completed these additional transactions involving stock.

Mar. 23 Accepted subscription contracts and $2,100 in down payments on 2,000 shares of common stock at $10.50 per share. The subscription contracts called for a 10 per cent down payment with the balance in two installments due in thirty and sixty days.

28 Accepted down payments of $5,400 and subscription contracts for 1,000 shares of preferred stock at $27 per share. The subscription contracts called for a 20 per cent down payment with the balance due in thirty days.

Apr. 22 Received payment of the first installment on the common stock subscriptions of March 23.

27 Received the balance due on the preferred stock subscriptions of March 28. Issued the stock.

May 2 Accepted a 10 per cent down payment and subscription contracts for 1,000 shares of common stock at $9.75 per share. The subscription contracts called for a 10 per cent down payment and the balance in two equal installments due in thirty and sixty days.

> 22   Received the final installment on the common stock subscriptions of March 23. Issued the stock.

Required:

1. Prepare general journal entries to record the foregoing transactions.
2. Prepare the stockholders' equity section of the corporation's balance sheet as of the close of business on May 22.

Problem 20–2

On March 1 of the current year Atlas Corporation received a charter granting it the right to issue 1,500 shares of $100 par value, 5 per cent, cumulative and nonparticipating, preferred stock and 10,000 shares of $10 par value common stock. The corporation then completed the following transactions:

Mar.   1   Accepted subscriptions to 1,000 shares of preferred stock at $96 per share and to 6,000 shares of common stock at $11 per share.

      5   Gave the company's lawyers 100 shares of common stock, valued at $1,100, in full settlement for their services in securing the corporation charter and for their advice on organization matters. The board of directors voted to charge the $1,100 to the Organization Costs account and to write off the balance of the account over the next five years.

    10   Collected the preferred subscriptions in full and issued the stock.

    10   Collected in full the subscriptions to 5,000 of the common shares subscribed on March 1, and collected $5.50 per share on the remaining 1,000 shares subscribed on that date. Issued the stock to to the fully paid subscribers.

    12   Exchanged 2,000 shares of common stock for factory land on which the board of directors placed a value of $22,000.

Required:

1. Open T-accounts for Cash, Subscriptions Receivable Preferred Stock, Subscriptions Receivable Common Stock, Land, Organization Costs, Preferred Stock, Discount on Preferred Stock, Preferred Stock Subscribed, Common Stock, Premium on Common Stock, and Common Stock Subscribed. Enter the transactions in the T-accounts.
2. Prepare a balance sheet for the Atlas Corporation as of March 12.

Problem 20–3

On April 1 of the current year the Rexus Corporation received a charter granting it the right to issue 2,500 shares of $100 par value common stock. It then completed the following additional stock transactions:

Apr.   2   Received $15,000 in cash and subscriptions to 1,500 shares of common stock at par. The subscription contracts called for a 10 per cent down payment with the balance in two equal installments due in thirty and sixty days.

May   2   Received payment in full on the first installment on the subscriptions of April 2.

June   1   Received $63,000 from the common stock subscribers in payment of the second installment on their subscriptions of April 2. John Burke, a subscriber to 100 shares of stock, failed to pay his second installment.

     1   Issued the stock of the fully paid subscribers.

   28   The board of directors declared the 100 shares of stock subscribed by John Burke to be forfeited and ordered it sold to the highest

bidder. (The Rexus Corporation is organized in a state in which payments of defaulting subscribers less losses and expenses resulting from the sale of their forfeited stock must be returned.)

July   7   Sold the forfeited stock of John Burke for $9,800.

8   Paid $65 of advertising and other sale costs resulting from the sale of John Burke's forfeited stock.

8   Returned to John Burke the balance remaining from his subscription payments.

Required:

Prepare journal entries to record the foregoing transactions.

Problem 20–4

On March 28 of the current year Timberline Corporation received a charter granting it the right to issue 2,500 shares of $10 par value common stock. During the remainder of the year the corporation completed the following transactions in stock:

Apr.   3   Issued at par for cash:

Certificate No. 1 for 600 shares to L. D. Ross.

Certificate No. 2 for 600 shares to W. C. Payne.

Certificate No. 3 for 800 shares to J. A. Kepner.

24   Issued certificate No. 4 to L. D. Kell for 500 shares in exchange for $5,500 cash.

May 10   Transferred W. C. Payne's stock to L. D. Ross.

22   Transferred 200 shares of J. A. Kepner's stock to L. D. Ross.

Required:

1. Prepare general journal entries to record the stock transactions of the Timberline Corporation. Post the entries to T-accounts.
2. Prepare a subsidiary Stockholders' Ledger. Record the transactions in the accounts of this ledger.

CLASS EXERCISES

Exercise 20–1

J. E. Baxter Corporation was organized in 1955 to take over the going business of J. E. Baxter, a single proprietorship. On March 1 of the current year the president of the corporation, J. E. Baxter, owned 9,000 of the 10,000 shares of the corporation's outstanding $10 par value common stock. On that date, in order to provide the corporation with additional capital, the president secured an authorization to issue 5,000 additional shares of common stock. He then purchased the additional stock at $12 per share. After the authorization and sale were recorded, the bookkeeper of the company prepared the following statement showing the equity of the stockholders' in the assets of the corporation:

J. E. BAXTER CORPORATION

Statement of Stockholders' Equity

Common stock, $10 par value, authorized and outstanding 15,000 shares.	$150,000
Premium on common stock	10,000
Total Contributed Capital	$160,000
Retained earnings	93,500
Total Stockholders' Equity	$253,500

After the additional stock was sold to the president, the minority stockholders protested that their rights had been ignored and that they had suffered a loss as a result of the transaction. The president acknowledged their protest and agreed to pay them the book value of their loss.

Required:

1. Name the right of the minority stockholders that was ignored.
2. Prepare a statement showing the calculation of the book value of the loss suffered by the minority stockholders.

Exercise 20–2

The Flying Giant Engine Company was organized with an authorization to issue 2,000 shares of $100 par value common stock. It then completed in chronological order the following transactions in stock. Give in general journal form the entry to record each.

1. The promoters purchased 200 shares of stock at par for cash.
2. Three hundred shares were sold at $98 per share for cash.
3. Two hundred and forty shares were sold at $102 per share for cash.
4. Five hundred shares were issued in exchange for real estate.
5. Subscriptions were accepted to one hundred and fifty shares at $102 per share; terms were 50 per cent cash with the subscriptions and 50 per cent in thirty days. The 50 per cent down payments accompanied the subscriptions.
6. Paid the cost of printing the stock certificates, $150.
7. Issued twenty shares at $102 per share to pay a lawyer for his services in organizing the corporation.
8. Received cash in payment of the second 50 per cent on the subscriptions of Transaction 5; issued the stock.

SUPPLEMENTARY PROBLEMS

Problem 20–A

Empire Corporation received a charter on April 8 of the current year. The charter granted it the right to issue 2,500 shares of $100 par value, 5 per cent cumulative and nonparticipating preferred stock and 50,000 shares of $10 par value common stock. During its first day of existence the corporation completed a number of stock transactions, and at the end of the first day the bookkeeper of the company prepared the following trial balance:

EMPIRE CORPORATION

Trial Balance, April 8, 19—

Cash	$513,000	
Subscriptions receivable preferred stock	48,500	
Subscriptions receivable common stock	52,500	
Discount on preferred stock	6,000	
Preferred stock		$100,000
Preferred stock subscribed		100,000
Common stock		300,000
Common stock subscribed		100,000
Premium on common stock		20,000
	$620,000	$620,000

Required:

Reproduce in general journal form the entries that resulted in the April 8 trial balance of the Empire Corporation. (Assume that all stock subscribed and issued was originally subscribed and recorded in the subscription receivable accounts. Assume also that all transactions in each class of stock were at the same price per share and were recorded in the same manner.)

Problem 20–B

The following accounts with their amounts appeared in the ledger of the Cascade Corporation on March 31 of the current year:

Cash

Feb. 15	7,500
Mar. 17	21,750
22	2,400

Common Stock, $5.00 Par Value

Feb. 15	Authorized to issue 10,000 shares
	Mar. 17 29,000

Subscriptions Receivable Common Stock

Feb. 15	30,000	Feb. 15	7,500
22	9,600	Mar. 17	21,750
		22	2,400
		31	750

Common Stock Subscribed

Mar. 17	29,000	Feb. 15	30,000
31	1,000	Mar. 22	10,000

T. A. Stone Defaulted Subscriptions

Mar. 31	250

Discount on Common Stock

Mar. 22	400

Required:

1. Reproduce from the foregoing accounts in chronological order the entries in general journal form that were made by the Cascade Corporation.
2. Prepare a balance sheet for the corporation as of March 31.
3. Prepare general journal entries to record these additional transactions of the Cascade Corporation:
   - Apr. 15 The corporation sold the defaulted stock of T. A. Stone for $4.50 per share.
   - 17 Paid expenses amounting to $35 that resulted from the sale of T. A. Stone's defaulted stock.
   - 17 Returned to T. A. Stone the amount of his subscription payment remaining after losses and expenses were deducted.

Problem 20–C

On January 28 of the current year Hollyfield Corporation received a charter granting it the right to issue 10,000 shares of $25 par value common stock. The corporation then completed the following transactions:

- Jan. 28 Accepted $35,000 and subscriptions to 5,000 shares of common stock at $28 per share. The subscription contracts called for a 25 per cent down payment and the balance in thirty days.
- Feb. 5 The board of directors voted to give the company's lawyers 100 shares of common stock in full settlement for their services in obtaining the corporation charter and for their advice on other organization matters. The certificates were issued.

Feb. 10   Exchanged 3,000 shares of common stock for factory land valued at $4,000 and a factory building valued at $80,000.

27   Received payment in full from the common stock subscribers of January 28. Issued the stock.

Required:

Prepare general journal entries to record the foregoing transactions.

Chapter

21

CORPORATIONS: CONTRIBUTED AND RETAINED CAPITAL

ACCOUNTING is not static. On the contrary, although the changes are slow, as such changes should be, accounting is constantly changing and advancing as accountants strive for better ways of accomplishing their tasks and better means of expressing ideas. Nowhere is this easier to see than in accounting terminology; for example, in the use of the term "surplus."

Surplus

A few years back accounting textbooks sometimes carried the statement, "A corporation's proprietorship is represented by its capital stock and surplus." In these texts "surplus" was defined as "that part of a corporation's proprietorship not represented by the par or stated value of its capital stock." Surplus was also divided into "earned surplus," which was defined as surplus resulting from earnings retained in the business, and "capital surplus" which was surplus from all sources other than earnings. And each of these was in turn divided and subdivided to show the sources of the capital surplus and the intended use of the earned surplus. These divisions, as they were commonly given, are graphically illustrated in the outline of Illustration 107.

The student should examine carefully the outline of Illustration 107; and he should add an understanding of the terms "surplus," "capital surplus," "paid-in surplus," and "earned surplus" to his fund of accounting knowledge. An understanding of these terms is important because although their use is being discontinued, they are still found in the literature of accounting and in some published financial statements.

It is well that the use of the term "surplus" is being abandoned in accounting and business circles. Actually the term has a general connotation of an "excess" of something; however, this is not the meaning of the term in accounting. Certainly in accounting the use of the term "surplus" was and is not meant to convey the idea that there was or is an excess of corporate capital, or cash, or assets of any kind. The term, properly qualified with descriptive adjectives, did and does purport to show the source or sources of some of the corporate assets. Fortunately, to avoid any misunderstanding, new and more meaningful terminology is being developed.

More than twenty years ago leading accountants recognized the possibilities for misunderstandings resulting from the use in published balance sheets of the word "surplus"; and in 1941 the Committee on Accounting Procedure of the American Institute of Certified Public Accountants suggested a general discontinuance of its use. The committee suggested that in the place of the word "surplus," designations be used that would emphasize the distinction between (a) legal capital, (b) capital in excess of

Illustration 107—Outline from a Previous Edition of This Text Showing Sources of Capital Surplus and the Divisions of Earned Surplus

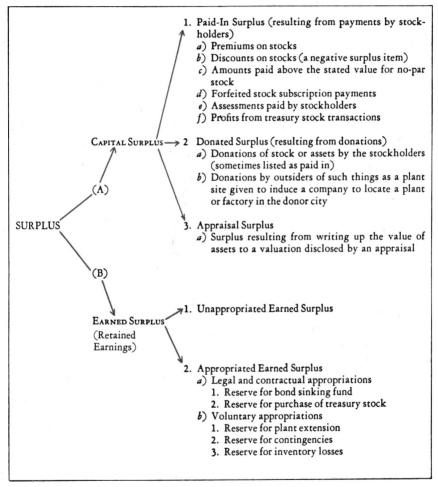

1. Paid-In Surplus (resulting from payments by stockholders)
   a) Premiums on stocks
   b) Discounts on stocks (a negative surplus item)
   c) Amounts paid above the stated value for no-par stock
   d) Forfeited stock subscription payments
   e) Assessments paid by stockholders
   f) Profits from treasury stock transactions

CAPITAL SURPLUS → 2 Donated Surplus (resulting from donations)
   a) Donations of stock or assets by the stockholders (sometimes listed as paid in)
   b) Donations by outsiders of such things as a plant site given to induce a company to locate a plant or factory in the donor city

(A)

SURPLUS

3. Appraisal Surplus
   a) Surplus resulting from writing up the value of assets to a valuation disclosed by an appraisal

(B)

EARNED SURPLUS
(Retained
Earnings)

1. Unappropriated Earned Surplus

2. Appropriated Earned Surplus
   a) Legal and contractual appropriations
      1. Reserve for bond sinking fund
      2. Reserve for purchase of treasury stock
   b) Voluntary appropriations
      1. Reserve for plant extension
      2. Reserve for contingencies
      3. Reserve for inventory losses

legal capital, and (c) undivided profits.[1] Extensive discussions of this proposal followed, and in 1949 the Committee recommended that in the balance sheet presentation of stockholders' equity:

(1) The use of the term *surplus* (whether standing alone or in such combinations as *capital surplus, paid-in surplus, earned surplus,* etc.) be discontinued.

---

[1] *Accounting Terminology Bulletins No. 1,* "Review and Résumé" (New York, American Institute of Certified Public Accountants, 1953), p. 28.

(2) The contributed portion of proprietary capital be shown as:
  (a) Capital contributed for, or assigned to, shares, to the extent of the par or stated value of each class of shares presently outstanding.
  (b) (i) Capital contributed for, or assigned to, shares in excess of such par or stated value (whether as a result of original issue of shares at amounts in excess of their then par or stated value, or of a reduction in par or stated value of shares after issuance, or of transactions by the corporation in its own shares) ; and
  (ii) Capital received other than for shares, whether from shareholders or from others.
(3) The term *earned surplus* be replaced by terms which will indicate source, such as *retained income, retained earnings, accumulated earnings,* or *earnings retained for use in the business.* In the case of a deficit, the amount should be shown as a deduction from contributed capital with appropriate description.[2]

From the foregoing it can be seen that if the recommendations of the Committee on Accounting Procedure are followed, stockholders' equity will be shown on published balance sheets under two main headings: (1) contributed capital, and (2) retained earnings (or some other such designation that indicates source). Furthermore, under the contributed capital heading should appear: (*a*) the par or stated value of the outstanding stock; (*b*) capital contributed for, or assigned to, shares of stock in excess of their par or stated value; and (*c*) capital contributed other than for shares.

It is of interest to note that on present-day published balance sheets of most large corporations the recommendations of the Committee are generally followed.

Outline Showing the Divisions of Stockholders' Equity. Illustration 108 graphically shows and makes possible a comparison of the divisions of stockholders' equity when both old and new terminology are used. Observe that two important differences result from the use of the new terminology: (1) the word "surplus" is eliminated, and (2) the items formerly classified as "capital surplus" or "paid-in surplus" are shown under the new terminology as part of the contributed capital.

Illustration 108 is reproduced at this point because, as previously stated, it is important that accounting students and others who read corporation balance sheets understand the source and nature of each portion of stockholders' equity whether it appears under an old or a new terminology heading.

Contributed Capital

The issuance of stock is the primary source of a corporation's contributed capital. The original sale of a corporation's par value stock results in contributed capital equal to the par value of the stock plus the premium, or less the discount allowed, on the sale. The issuance of stock at par, at a premium, and at a discount, and the issuance of no-par stock were sub-

---

[2] *Ibid.,* pp. 30 and 31.

jects of the previous chapter and need no further discussion here.

In addition to the original sale of its stock, a corporation may secure contributed capital from: (1) transactions in its own stock, called treasury stock transactions; and (2) sources other than transactions involving its stock, for example, gifts and donations. Each of these sources of contributed capital will be discussed in more detail later in this chapter.

Illustration 108

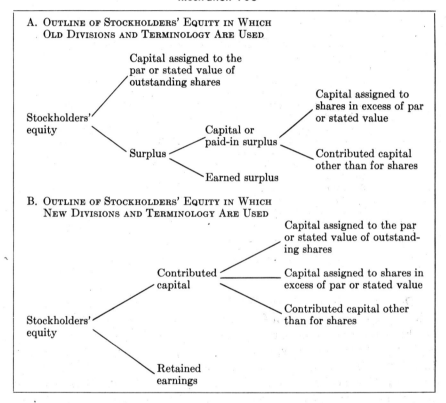

A. OUTLINE OF STOCKHOLDERS' EQUITY IN WHICH OLD DIVISIONS AND TERMINOLOGY ARE USED

Stockholders' equity
  Capital assigned to the par or stated value of outstanding shares
  Surplus
    Capital or paid-in surplus
      Capital assigned to shares in excess of par or stated value
      Contributed capital other than for shares
    Earned surplus

B. OUTLINE OF STOCKHOLDERS' EQUITY IN WHICH NEW DIVISIONS AND TERMINOLOGY ARE USED

Stockholders' equity
  Contributed capital
    Capital assigned to the par or stated value of outstanding shares
    Capital assigned to shares in excess of par or stated value
    Contributed capital other than for shares
  Retained earnings

Contributed Capital in the Accounts and on the Statements. Formerly, and when that portion of a corporation's contributed capital in excess of the par or stated value of its stock was commonly called "capital surplus," or "paid-in surplus," it was not an uncommon practice to place all capital or paid-in surplus items in a single ledger account called Capital Surplus or Paid-In Surplus. Today, this is not considered good accounting. Today, accountants generally open in the ledger, in the place of one capital or paid-in surplus account, the number of contributed capital accounts needed. Usually an account is opened as required for each of the various sources of contributed capital. Furthermore, in addition to the separate accounts, it is considered good practice to list separately on the balance sheet the amount of each different kind of contributed capital, as is shown in Illustration 109.

In Illustration 109, the second item is "Capital contributed by stock-holders in excess of the par value of their stock, $11,500." This item resulted from premiums paid by the original common stockholders. At the time the amounts originated they were probably credited to an account called "Premium on Common Stock." However, as in Illustration 109, it is a common practice to show an item such as this on the balance sheet under a more descriptive caption than the name of the account in which it is recorded.

Illustration 109
CONTRIBUTED CAPITAL AND RETAINED EARNINGS

Common stock, $10 par value, 10,000 shares authorized, issued, and outstanding . . .	$100,000
Capital contributed by stockholders in excess of the par value of their shares.	11,500
Contributed capital, treasury stock transactions	3,000
Total Capital Contributed by Stockholders	$114,500
Other contributed capital:	
Contributed capital resulting from the donation of a plant site by the Tri-City Chamber of Commerce	22,000
Contributed capital from forfeited stock subscriptions	200
Total Contributed Capital	$136,700
Retained earnings	56,100
Total Contributed Capital and Retained Earnings.	$192,800

Donations of Capital by Outsiders. Sometimes a corporation will receive a gift or a donation from some person or persons other than its stockholders. For example, a corporation may, as an inducement to locate a plant in a particular city, receive a plant site as a gift. Such a donation increases both the assets and the stockholders' equity by the fair market value of the contributed asset. The increase in the stockholders' equity is contributed capital, capital contributed by others than the stockholders. The fourth item in Illustration 109 represents such a donation.

Contributed Capital and Dividends. Under the laws of some states, dividends may be charged only to the Retained Earnings account and may not be debited to a contributed capital account. In other words, in those states, contributed capital may not be returned to the stockholders as dividends. However, one of the reasons for separate contributed capital accounts and a separate listing of contributed capital items on the balance sheet is that, under the laws of some states, dividends may be debited or charged to certain of the contributed capital accounts. Seldom may dividends be charged against the par or stated value of the outstanding stock; however, the exact contributed capital accounts to which a corporation may charge dividends depend upon the laws of the state of its incorporation. For this reason it is usually wise for the board of directors of a corporation to secure competent legal advice before charging dividends to any contributed capital account.

Treasury Stock

Corporations often reacquire shares of their own stock. Sometimes a corporation will purchase shares of its own stock on the open market to be given to its employees in the form of bonuses. Sometimes a corporation will buy shares of its own stock in order to maintain a favorable market for the stock. Occasionally a corporation in a poor financial position will receive shares of its own stock as a gift from its own stockholders. Regardless, when a corporation reacquires shares of its own stock, such stock is known as *treasury stock*. Treasury stock is a corporation's own stock that has been issued and then reacquired either by purchase or gift. Notice that the stock must be the corporation's own stock; the acquisition of the stock of an outside corporation does not create treasury stock. Furthermore, the stock must have been once issued and then reacquired; only stock issued and then reacquired qualifies as treasury stock. This latter characteristic is important. It is the characteristic that distinguishes treasury stock from unissued stock. It is important because stock once issued at par value and then reacquired as treasury stock may be legally reissued at a discount without a discount liability attaching thereto.

As just pointed out, treasury stock differs from unissued stock in that it may be sold at a discount without discount liability. However, in other respects treasury stock has the same status as unissued stock. Both are considered proprietorship items rather than assets. Both are subtracted from authorized stock to secure outstanding stock when such things as book values are calculated. Neither receives dividends nor has a vote in the meetings of stockholders.

Purchase of Treasury Stock[3]

When a corporation purchases shares of its own stock, it reduces in equal amounts both its assets and its stockholders' equity. To illustrate this, assume that on May 1 of the current year the condensed balance sheet of the Curry Corporation appears as in Illustration 110.

Illustration 110

CURRY CORPORATION
Balance Sheet, May 1, 19--

ASSETS		CAPITAL	
Cash	$ 30,000	Common stock, $100 par value,	
Other assets	95,000	authorized and issued 1,000	
		shares	$100,000
		Retained earnings.	25,000
Total Assets	$125,000	Total Capital.	$125,000

---

[3] There are several ways of accounting for treasury stock transactions. This text will discuss the so-called cost basis, which seems to be the most widely used, and it will leave a discussion of other methods to a more advanced text.

If on May 1 the Curry Corporation purchases 100 shares of its outstanding common stock on the open market at $115 per share, the transaction is recorded as follows:

May	1	Treasury Stock, Common...............	11,500.00	
		Cash............................		11,500.00
		Purchased 100 shares of treasury stock at $115 per share.		

The debit of the foregoing entry to the Treasury Stock, Common account records a reduction in the equity of the stockholders of the Curry Corporation; and the credit to Cash records a reduction in its assets. Both reductions are equal to the cost of the treasury stock purchased. After the entry is posted, a new balance sheet of the corporation will show the reductions in assets and stockholders' equity as in Illustration 111.

Illustration 111

CURRY CORPORATION
Balance Sheet, May 1, 19--

ASSETS		CAPITAL	
Cash	$ 18,500	Common stock, $100 par value, authorized and issued 1,000 shares of which 100 are in the treasury. . . .	$100,000
Other assets	95,000		
		Retained earnings of which $11,500 is restricted by the purchase of treasury stock.	25,000
		Total.	$125,000
		Less: Cost of treasury stock	11,500
Total Assets	$113,500	Total Capital.	$113,500

Notice in the second balance sheet of the Curry Corporation that the balance of its Treasury Stock, Common account appears in the stockholders' equity section as a deduction from the total of the common stock and retained earnings. In comparing the two balance sheets, notice that the purchase of the treasury stock reduces the totals of both the assets and stockholders' equity by the $11,500 cost of the treasury stock.

Notice also in the capital section on the second balance sheet that the dollar value of the issued stock of the Curry Corporation remains unchanged at $100,000. The amount of *issued stock* of a corporation is not changed by the purchase of treasury stock. However, the purchase of treasury stock does reduce *outstanding stock*. In the case of the Curry Corporation, the purchase of the 100 shares of treasury stock reduced the outstanding stock from 1,000 to 900 shares.

There is a distinction between issued stock and outstanding stock. Issued stock is stock that has been issued; it may or may not be outstanding on the balance sheet date. Outstanding stock is stock that has been issued and is outstanding. Only outstanding stock is effective stock, receives dividends, is given a vote in the meetings of stockholders, and enters into such things as the calculation of book values.

Restricting Retained Earnings by the Purchase of Treasury Stock. When a corporation purchases treasury stock, the effect on the corporation's assets and proprietorship is the same a cash dividend. When a corporation purchases treasury stock or declares a cash dividend, it transfers corporation assets to its stockholders and thereby reduces both its assets and its proprietorship. Consequently, since the effect of the purchase of treasury stock is the same as a cash dividend, most states place limitations upon the purchase of treasury stock just as they place limitations upon the payment of dividends. These limitations usually provide that a corporation may purchase treasury stock only to the extent of its retained earnings available for dividend charges, after which the retained earnings become restricted and legally unavailable for further dividend charges. This means that (1) only a corporation with retained earnings available for dividend charges may purchase treasury stock; and (2) a corporation with retained earnings available for dividend charges may either purchase treasury stock to the extent of such retained earnings or it may use such retained earnings as a basis for the payment of dividends, but it may not do both. In other words, a corporation may not purchase treasury stock to the extent of its retained earnings available for dividend charges and then use the same retained earnings again as a basis for the declaration of dividends. It may not by the purchase of treasury stock transfer corporation assets to its stockholders to the extent of its retained earnings available for dividend charges and then transfer more assets by means of cash dividends.

In states where certain contributed capital items may be charged with dividends, these contributed capital items may normally also be used as a basis for the purchase of treasury stock and become restricted when so used.

Notice in Illustration 111 how the restriction of retained earnings is shown on the balance sheet. The restriction may also be shown by means of a footnote.

Treasury Stock as an Asset. In the past treasury stock has appeared on corporation balance sheets as an asset. This is an error. The acquisition of treasury stock reduces in equal amounts both the assets and the proprietorship of a corporation. Consequently, it is generally agreed that treasury stock should appear on the balance sheet as a deduction in the proprietorship section.

Reissuance of Treasury Stock

When treasury stock is reissued, it may be reissued at its cost price, it may be reissued at a price above its cost, or it may be reissued at a price below its cost.

Reissuance of Treasury Stock at Cost. When treasury stock is sold and reissued at its cost price, the entry to record the transaction is the reverse of the entry used to record the purchase of treasury stock. For example, assume that the Curry Corporation sells ten shares of the hundred shares of treasury stock, the purchase of which at $115 was previously illustrated. The entry to record the transaction appears as follows:

May	27	Cash...................................	1,150.00	
		Treasury Stock, Common...........		1,150.00
		Reissued ten shares of treasury stock at its cost price of $115 per share.		

Notice that the sale of the ten shares of treasury stock at cost restores to the corporation the exact amount of assets and proprietorship taken away when these ten shares were purchased.

Reissuance of Treasury Stock at a Price above Cost. Although treasury stock may be sold at its cost price, it is commonly sold at a price either above or below its cost. When treasury stock is sold at a price above its cost, the amount received in excess of cost is commonly credited to a contributed capital account called "Contributed Capital, Treasury Stock Transactions." For example, assume that the Curry Corporation sells for $120 per share an additional ten shares of the treasury stock purchased at $115 per share. The entry to record the transaction appears as follows:

June	3	Cash...................................	1,200.00	
		Treasury Stock Common...........		1,150.00
		Contributed Capital, Treasury Stock Transactions....................		50.00
		Sold at $120 per share treasury stock that cost $115 per share.		

Reissuance of Treasury Stock at a Price below Cost. When treasury stock is reissued at a price below its cost, the entry to record the sale normally depends upon whether the corporation selling the stock has contributed capital resulting from previous transactions in treasury stock. If a corporation has contributed capital resulting from previous sales of treasury stock, a loss on the sale of treasury stock may be debited to the account of such contributed capital. For example, assume that after having sold ten shares of its one hundred shares of treasury stock at $115 and ten shares at $120 per share, the Curry Corporation sells ten shares at $110. The entry to record the transaction appears as follows:

July	7	Cash...................................	1,100.00	
		Contributed Capital, Treasury Stock Transactions.......................	50.00	
		Treasury Stock, Common...........		1,150.00
		Sold ten shares of treasury stock purchased at $115 per share for $110 per share.		

If a corporation selling treasury stock at a price below its cost does not have contributed capital from previous treasury stock transactions, a loss on the sale of treasury stock is normally debited to retained earnings. For example, if the Curry Corporation sells its remaining seventy shares of treasury stock at $110 per share, the following entry is made to record the transaction:

July	10	Cash..................................	7,700.00	
		Retained Earnings.....................	350.00	
		Treasury Stock, Common...........		8,050.00
		Sold treasury stock purchased at $115 per share for $110 per share.		

Donated Treasury Stock

Stockholders sometimes return to a corporation as a gift a portion of their stockholdings. Such donations are common when a corporation is in need of additional assets and the donated stock is to be resold to provide the assets.

When the stockholders of a corporation donate a portion of their stock to the corporation, the corporation secures the stock without cost. Consequently, since the acquisition of donated treasury stock does not decrease a corporation's assets nor increase its liabilities, the acquisition has no effect upon its proprietorship. On the other hand, although the acquisition of donated treasury stock does not affect a corporation's proprietorship, the sale of donated treasury stock increases both its assets and its proprietorship. These points may be demonstrated as follows with the Bell Corporation.

On June 1 the Bell Corporation, having experienced a series of losses, finds itself in the need of additional assets to carry on its operations. In order to secure the assets the stockholders of the corporation decide to donate to the corporation a portion of their stockholdings which are to be sold to outsiders for cash. A balance sheet of the corporation before the donation appears as in Illustration 112.

Illustration 112
BELL CORPORATION
Balance Sheet, June 1, 19--

ASSETS		CAPITAL	
Cash	$ 1,000	Common stock, $100 par value,	
Other assets	103,000	authorized and issued 1,000	
		shares	$100,000
		Retained earnings.	4,000
Total Assets	$104,000	Total Capital.	$104,000

If the corporation's stockholders donate pro rata a hundred shares of stock to the corporation, the donation is recorded with a memorandum entry somewhat as follows:

| June | 1 | Received on this date from the stockholders as a donation one hundred shares of $100 par value common stock. | | | | |

Such an entry cannot be posted in the sense that dollar amounts are entered in the accounts. However, when treasury stock is received as a donation, a treasury stock account is opened in the ledger and the amount of treasury stock received is shown in the account by means of a memorandum. This memorandum in the treasury stock account is in effect a posting of the memorandum entry in the General Journal recording the receipt of the stock. It may appear as shown in Illustration 113.

Illustration 113
Treasury Stock, Common

Date	Explanation	F	Debit	Date	Explanation	F	Credit
June 1	One hundred shares of treasury stock received from the stockholders as a donation.						

After the Bell Corporation receives the hundred shares of treasury stock from its stockholders, a new balance sheet showing the financial position of the corporation appears as in Illustration 114.

Illustration 114
BELL CORPORATION
Balance Sheet, June 1, 19--

ASSETS

		CAPITAL	
Cash	$ 1,000	Common stock, $100 par value, authorized and issued 1,000 shares of which 100 are in the treasury	$100,000
Other assets	103,000	Retained earnings	4,000
Total Assets	$104,000	Total Capital	$104,000

A comparison of the balance sheets prepared before and after the donation of the treasury stock shows that the donation did not affect either the total assets or the total proprietorship of the corporation.

Although the receipt of donated treasury stock does not increase or decrease the assets and proprietorship of a corporation, the sale of donated treasury stock increases both. For example, if the Bell Corporation sells its hundred shares of donated treasury stock for $92 per share, both its assets and its proprietorship are increased by $9,200, and the transaction is recorded as follows:

June	7	Cash.................................	9,200.00	
		Contributed Capital, Sale of Donated		
		Treasury Stock...................		9,200.00
		Sold a hundred shares of donated treasury stock at $92 per share.		

After the treasury stock is sold and the transaction recorded, a balance sheet showing the new financial position of the Bell Corporation appears as in Illustration 115.

Observe in the Bell Corporation balance sheet prepared after the sale of the treasury stock that both the assets and proprietorship of the corporation are increased $9,200 by the sale of the donated treasury stock. The increase in assets is recorded in the Cash account; the increase in proprietorship is recorded in the Contributed Capital, Sale of Donated Treasury Stock account.

Illustration 115

BELL CORPORATION
Balance Sheet, June 7, 19--

ASSETS		CAPITAL	
Cash	$ 10,200	Common stock, $100 par value, authorized and issued 1,000 shares	$100,000
Other assets	103,000	Retained earnings.	4,000
		Contributed capital, sale of donated treasury stock . .	9,200
Total Assets	$113,200	Total Capital.	$113,200

Capital from the Write-Up of Fixed Assets

Before 1940 it was not uncommon for corporations to write up fixed assets values to amounts established by appraisals. Such write-ups increased both the amount of a corporation's assets and its proprietorship. The increase in proprietorship was commonly credited to an account called "Appraisal Surplus." However, in 1940 the American Institute's Committee on Accounting Procedure expressed the opinion that "Accounting for fixed assets should normally be based on cost, and any attempt to make property accounts reflect current values is both impracticable and inexpedient."[4] Since the expression of this opinion, such write-ups have been less common. However, a corporation with capital resulting from a previous write-up of fixed assets should show such capital in the "other contributed capital" section of its balance sheet as, for example, "Capital from the write-up of fixed assets."

---

[4] *Accounting Research Bulletin No. 5*, "Depreciation on Appreciation" (New York: American Institute of Certified Public Accountants, 1940), p. 1.

Retained Earnings

Retained earnings, as the name implies, is stockholder equity that has resulted from retaining income in the business. The retained income includes income from normal operations as well as gains from such transactions as the sale of fixed assets or investments.

Retained earnings may be free and unappropriated, or they may be "earmarked" or appropriated for some special purpose. Generally, only the amount of free or unappropriated retained earnings is considered immediately available for dividends. Of course, what is meant by the phrase "available for dividends" is that a credit balance exists in the Retained Earnings account and dividends may be debited thereto.

It should be remembered that dividends are normally paid in cash, and their payment reduces in like amounts both the cash and the stockholders' equity. The existence of accumulated earnings, as evidenced by a credit balance in the Retained Earnings account, makes the payment of dividends legally possible. However, whether dividends are paid also depends upon the availability of cash with which to pay them. If cash or assets that will become cash in a short period of time are not available, a board of directors may think it wise to forego the declaration of dividends, even though retained earnings exist. Often the board of directors of a corporation having a large balance in its Retained Earnings account will not declare a dividend because all of the corporation's current assets are needed in the operation of the business.

Appropriations of Retained Earnings

When a corporation earns income, the income increases both its net assets and its stockholders' equity. At the end of each accounting period, the increase in stockholders' equity is transferred from the Income Summary account to the Retained Earnings account. The credit balance of the Retained Earnings account is then available to absorb debits resulting from the declaration of dividends.

Although the entire balance of a corporation's Retained Earnings account is usually available to absorb debits resulting from the declaration of dividends, it is normally not wise to exhaust the balance for this purpose. Earnings are a source of assets. Some of the assets from earnings should be paid out in dividends; but some should be retained in the business for emergencies, for distribution as dividends in years in which earnings are not large enough to pay normal dividends, and for use in expanding the operations of the company. The last reason is an important one. If a corporation is to expand and grow, it may sell additional shares of its stock to secure the assets needed in the expansion; however, it may also expand by using assets acquired through earnings. The Ford Motor Company is a good example of a company that has made use of the latter method of expansion. Less than $100,000 was originally invested in the

Ford Motor Company, and the company has grown to its present size primarily from retaining in the business assets from earnings.

When a corporation expands by retaining assets from earnings, two things normally happen: (1) The funds acquired through earnings are invested in plant, equipment, merchandise, and other assets and are not available for dividends. And (2) through the retention of earnings, the Retained Earnings account often becomes large. These results may create a problem for the board of directors. The problem is that some stockholders who do not realize that the retained earnings are invested in plant and other assets used in the business, upon seeing a large amount of retained earnings reported on the balance sheet, agitate for more and bigger dividends that often cannot be paid.

Although the practice is not now as common as it once was, some corporations meet the foregoing problem by earmarking or appropriating retained earnings. Retained earnings are earmarked or appropriated by placing portions of the balance of the Retained Earnings account in various reserves of retained earnings. For example, a corporation may place portions of the balance of its Retained Earnings account in a reserve for working capital (current assets are known as working capital, and the excess of current assets over current liabilities is known as net working capital), a reserve for plant expansion, a reserve for inventory losses, a reserve for bond sinking fund, and/or a reserve for contingencies. Such reserves are known as special purpose reserves of retained earnings or special purpose surplus reserves. They are created to inform the stockholders that it is the intention of the board of directors to retain in the business assets equal in amount to the appropriated reserves.

Any special purpose reserve of retained earnings is created by transferring a portion of the balance of the Retained Earnings account to a reserve account. Some special purpose reserves are of a temporary nature; for example, the reserve for inventory losses which is created by a board of directors in anticipation of a large decline in inventory prices. Others are of a more or less permanent nature, such as the reserve for working capital, which is created when a corporation retains funds from its earnings to supply part of its current asset needs. Also, some reserves are created with a single appropriation and others are built up over a period of years. The reserve for plant expansion is perhaps the most common of the latter and will be used here to show how all reserves of retained earnings are created.

To illustrate the creation of a reserve for plant expansion, assume that the board of directors of the Deeplake Corporation recognizes that in five years their plant will need to be expanded by the construction of a $100,000 addition. To finance the expansion, the members of the board of directors discuss the possibility of waiting until the addition is needed and then securing the required funds through the sale of $100,000 of additional common stock. They also discuss the possibility of financing the expansion through the annual retention for each of the succeeding five years of $20,-000 of assets from earnings. Income in excess of this amount is being earned; and the board decides that this is the better plan.

In order to retain $20,000 of assets from earnings in the business each year, the board of directors of the Deeplake Corporation recognizes that it is only necessary for the board to refrain from paying this amount out in dividends. However, the board also recognizes that if earnings are retained, the Retained Earnings account and the amount reported on the balance sheet under the caption "Retained earnings" will grow each year, and that this will create a demand on the part of some of the stockholders for bigger dividends. Consequently, the board may decide that at the end of each of the succeeding five years it will vote an appropriation and transfer of $20,000 of retained earnings from the Retained Earnings account to the Reserve for Plant Expansion account.

If the board follows through on this plan and votes the appropriation each year, the entry to record each appropriation is as follows:

Dec.	28	Retained Earnings....................	20,000.00	
		Reserve for Plant Expansion........		20,000.00
		To record the appropriation and transfer of retained earnings to the reserve for plant expansion.		

It should be observed that the transfer of $20,000 of retained earnings each year from the Retained Earnings account to the Reserve for Plant Expansion account does not provide the funds for the expansion. On the contrary, earnings provide the funds; the appropriations do nothing more than inform the stockholders of the intention of the board to retain in the business assets acquired from earnings in an amount equal to the reserve.

Voluntary and Contractual Reserves. Appropriations of retained earnings may be voluntary or they may be required by contract. Voluntary reserves are reserves such as the reserve for plant expansion or the reserve for inventory losses. They are made at the discretion of the board of directors; and since they are created at the discretion of the board of directors, the board may reverse its judgment at any time and return a voluntary reserve to the Retained Earnings account.

Contractual reserves such as a reserve for bond sinking fund differ from voluntary reserves in that they are required by a contract. Often, when a corporation issues bonds, it enters into a contract with its bondholders to appropriate and set aside in a reserve for bond sinking fund, a portion of its earnings each year until the bonds are paid. The purpose of such appropriations is to prevent assets acquired from earnings in amounts equal to the appropriations from being disbursed in the form of dividends.

This tends to strengthen the security behind the bonds by causing the retention of assets in the business. Bond sinking fund reserves are discussed in more detail in the next chapter.

Reserves of Retained Earnings on the Balance Sheet. Special purpose reserves of retained earnings are created to reduce the balance of the Retained Earnings account and to inform the stockholders of the intentions of the board of directors in regard to retaining assets from earnings in the business. The stockholders are informed of the board's intentions when they read the stockholders' equity section of the corporation's balance sheet where the reserves are commonly shown as in Illustration 116.

Illustration 116
STOCKHOLDERS' EQUITY

Common stock, $1.00 par value, 500,000 shares authorized, issued, and outstanding . . .			$500,000
Retained earnings:			
Appropriated retained earnings:			
Reserve for plant expansion	$110,000		
Reserve for bond sinking fund	50,000		
Reserve for working capital	30,000		
Total		$190,000	
Unappropriated retained earnings.		105,000	
Total Retained Earnings			295,000
Total Contributed Capital and Retained Earnings.			$795,000

Disposing of Appropriations of Retained Earnings. Reserves of retained earnings are created by transferring a portion of the balance of the Retained Earnings account to a reserve account. Some reserves are of a temporary nature; and after the purpose for which they were created has been accomplished or has passed, such reserves should be removed from the accounts. A reserve is removed from the accounts by returning its balance to the Retained Earnings account.

American Accounting Association on Reserves. The American Accounting Association's Committee on Concepts and Standards Underlying Corporate Financial Statements has gone on record in favor of discontinuing in published balance sheets the use of the term "reserve" in reporting appropriations of retained earnings.[5] The Committee makes this recommendation because in general usage the word "reserve" has the connotation of "funds kept on hand to meet demands." Obviously, from the discussions of the foregoing pages, this is not the intended meaning of the term when it is used on published balance sheets. The Committee would favor calling a reserve for plant expansion, for example, "retained earnings appropriated for plant expansion." In addition to the recommenda-

---

[5] *Reserves and Retained Income, Supplementary Statement No. 1,* Committee on Concepts and Standards Underlying Corporate Financial Statements (Columbus, Ohio: American Accounting Association, 1950), p. 1.

tion on terminology, the Committee also favors showing the entire amount of retained earnings on the balance sheet as a single amount and of informing stockholders of appropriations by means of footnotes.

It is of interest to note that the Committee on Concepts and Standards in its discussion of reserves of retained income says:

> Appropriations of retained income which purport to reflect managerial policies relative to earnings retention are ineffective, and frequently misleading, unless all retained income which has in fact been committed to operating capital is earmarked. Partial appropriation fosters the implication that retained earnings not earmarked are available for distributions.[6]

In other words, the Committee feels that reserves that purport to reflect managerial policy toward income retention are both ineffective and often misleading. The Committee feels that such reserves are often misleading because readers of balance sheets are apt to think that the funds from the retained earnings that are not appropriated are in fact available for dividend distribution when often a major share of such funds are invested in assets used in the business.

In line with the Committee's thoughts, it is of interest to note that appropriations of retained income are not as common as they once were.

Stock Dividends

A corporation may distribute dividends in cash, in assets other than cash, in script (written promises to pay cash at a later date), or in shares of its own stock. Dividends in cash and in shares of a corporation's own stock are the most common; and since cash dividends have been previously discussed, this section will be devoted to dividends of a corporation's own stock.

The term "stock dividend" is commonly used to describe an issuance by a corporation of its own common shares to its common shareholders without consideration and under conditions indicating that such action is prompted mainly by a desire to give the recipient shareholders some evidence of their respective interests in retained earnings without the distribution of cash or other property which the board of directors deems it desirable to retain in the business.[7]

In previous sections it was pointed out that a cash dividend reduced in like amounts both the assets and the proprietorship of a corporation. A stock dividend differs in that it has no effect on either the assets or the total proprietorship of the corporation issuing it. Because of their lack of effect on assets, stock dividends are often declared by corporations that have used their funds from retained earnings in expansion and, consequently, do not feel that they have sufficient cash with which to pay a

---

[6] *Ibid.,* p. 1.

[7] *Accounting Research Bulletin No. 43,* "Restatement and Revision of Accounting Research Bulletins" (New York: American Institute of Certified Public Accountants, 1953), p. 49.

cash dividend. A stock dividend gives such an expanding corporation an opportunity to distribute to its stockholders some evidence of earnings but at the same time to keep for use in the business the actual assets obtained through the earnings.

Actually the effect of a stock dividend is a transfer of retained earnings to contributed capital. To illustrate, assume that at the end of the current year the Northwest Corporation has the following capital stock and retained earnings, but that it has no funds which the board of directors feels can be spared for dividends:

```
                 CAPITAL STOCK AND RETAINED INCOME

Common stock, $100 par value, authorized 1,500
    shares, issued and outstanding 1,000 shares    $100,000
Capital contributed by stockholders in excess
    of the par value of their shares . . . . . .      8,000
         Total Contributed Capital. . . . . . . .  $108,000
Retained earnings. . . . . . . . . . . . . .         35,000
         Total Contributed and Retained Capital .  $143,000
```

Assume further that on December 28 the board of directors of the Northwest Corporation declared a 10 per cent or 100-share stock dividend distributable on January 20 to stockholders of record of January 15.

If the fair market value of the stock of the Northwestern Corporation on December 28 is $150 per share, the following entries are required to record the declaration and distribution of the dividend:

Dec.	28	Retained Earnings......................	15,000.00	
		Common Stock Dividend Distributable............................		10,000.00
		Premium on Common Stock.........		5,000.00
		To record the declaration of a 100-share common stock dividend.		
Jan.	20	Common Stock Dividend Distributable....	10,000.00	
		Common Stock....................		10,000.00
		To record the distribution of a 100-share common stock dividend.		

Note that the foregoing entry merely changes the form of $15,000 of the stockholders' equity from retained earnings to contributed capital. Note also that the amount of retained earnings transferred is equal to the fair market value of the 100 shares of stock issued ($150 × 100 shares = $15,-000).

When a stock dividend of less than 20 to 25 per cent is declared and paid, the Committee on Accounting Procedure recommends,[8] as in the foregoing illustration, that retained earnings equal to the fair market value of the issued stock be transferred from retained earnings to contributed capital. Their reason for this recommendation grows out of the fact

---

[8] *Ibid.,* p. 51.

that many stockholders upon receipt of a stock dividend feel that they have actually received retained earnings equal to the market value of the stock issued to them. Of course this is not at all true. However, since this is the belief of many stockholders, the Committee is of the opinion that in a stock dividend such as this, retained earnings equal to the fair market value of the issued stock should be transferred to contributed capital. This, the Committee points out, removes retained earnings equal to the dividend from the Retained Earnings account and makes these retained earnings unavailable for either further stock or cash dividends.

As previously pointed out, a stock dividend does not distribute funds from retained earnings to the stockholders, nor does it affect in any way the assets of the corporation. Likewise, it has no effect on the corporation's total capital and no effect on the individual equities of its stockholders. To illustrate these last points, assume that Johnson owned ten shares of the Northwest Corporation's stock prior to the stock dividend recorded in previous paragraphs. The total contributed and retained capital of the corporation before the dividend and the book value of Johnson's ten shares were as follows:

Common stock (1,000 shares)	$100,000
Premium on common stock	8,000
Retained earnings	35,000
Total Contributed and Retained Capital	$143,000

$143,000 ÷ 1,000 SHARES OUTSTANDING = $143 PER SHARE BOOK VALUE
$143 × 10 = $1,430 FOR THE BOOK VALUE OF JOHNSON'S TEN SHARES

A 10 per cent stock dividend gives a stockholder one new share for each ten shares previously held. Consequently, Johnson received one new share; and after the dividend, the contributed and retained capital of the corporation and the book value of Johnson's holdings are as follows:

Common stock (1,100 shares)	$110,000
Premium on common stock	13,000
Retained earnings	20,000
Total Contributed and Retained Capital	$143,000

$143,000 ÷ 1,100 SHARES OUTSTANDING = $130 PER SHARE BOOK VALUE
$130 × 11 = $1,430 FOR THE BOOK VALUE OF JOHNSON'S ELEVEN SHARES

Before the stock dividend, Johnson owned 10/1,000 or 1/100 of the stock of the Northwest Corporation and his holdings had a book value of $1,430. After the stock dividend, he owned 11/1,100 or 1/100 of the corporation and his holdings still had a book value of $1,430. In other words, there was no effect on his equity other than that it was repackaged from ten units into eleven units. Likewise, the only effect on the proprietorship of the corporation was a permanent appropriation and transfer to contributed capital of $15,000 of retained earnings. Consequently, insofar as both the corporation and Johnson are concerned, there was no shift in equities or corporation assets.

However, although a stock dividend does not have any effect on corporation assets and does not cause a shift in equities, a small stock dividend normally does have an effect on the total market value of the shares involved and on the holdings of any one stockholder. This effect can be described as follows: Observe that the stock of the Northwest Corporation had a book value of $143 per share before the stock dividend but a market value of $150. In other words, the stock was selling at approximately 5 per cent above its book value. Consequently, other things being equal, since after the dividend all stockholder rights are divided 1,100 ways rather than 1,000 ways, the stock should decline after the dividend to where it sells at a price which is approximately 5 per cent in excess of its new book value of $130, or at a price of approximately $136.50 ($130 + (5% of $130) = $136.50) per share. However, if the stock of Northwest Corporation reacts as do the stocks of most corporations in such situations, it may decline in market value but not to $136.50. Obviously, then, if this happens, Johnson will have an increase in the market value of all of his shares. Consequently, he will have from the stock dividend a gain in the total market value of his holdings.

Since a stock dividend is payable in stock rather than in assets, it is not a liability. Consequently, if a balance sheet is prepared between the dates of declaration and payment of a stock dividend, the par value of the dividend stock and the applicable premium should be separately listed and described in the contributed capital section of the balance sheet.

Stock Splits

Sometimes, when a corporation's stock is selling on the stock exchanges at a very high price, the corporation will call in the stock and issue two, three, four, five, or more new shares in the place of each old share previously outstanding. For example, a corporation having outstanding $100 par value stock that is selling for $375 a share may call in the old shares and issue to the stockholders two shares of $50 par value, or four shares of $25 par value, or ten shares of $10 par value, or any number of shares of no-par value stock in exchange for each $100 share formerly held. This is known as a *stock split* or a *stock split-up*, and its usual purpose is to effect a reduction in the market price of the stock and, consequently, to facilitate trading in the stock.

A stock split has no effect on the total proprietorship of a corporation, the equities of the individual stockholders, or on the balances of any of the contributed or retained capital accounts. Consequently, all that is required in recording a stock split is a memorandum entry reciting the facts of the split.

Corporation Income Taxes

Of the three common types of business organizations, the corporation alone as a business unit is subject to federal income taxes. Single proprietorships and partnerships as business units are not required to pay federal income taxes and normally are not required to pay state income taxes. Insofar as federal income tax laws are concerned and the laws of most states, the income of single proprietorships and partnerships is taxed as the personal income of the single proprietor or the partners.

Federal, and where applicable, state income taxes are now generally recognized as one of a corporation's expenses of doing business. However, no attempt is normally made to classify the expense on the income statement; rather it is commonly listed at the end of the statement as in Illustration 117.

Illustration 117—Section of the Income Statement Showing Treatment of Income Taxes

```
                    NORTHGATE CORPORATION
         Income Statement for Year Ended December 31, 19--

    Revenue from sales:
      Sales . . . . . . . . . . . . . . . . . . .   $1,449,000
    ─────────────────────────────────────────────────────────

    Income before state and federal income taxes $   100,000
      Less: Provision for state and federal in-
            come taxes. . . . . . . . . . . . . .      55,000
    Net Income. . . . . . . . . . . . . . . . .   $   45,000
```

On the work sheet prepared for a corporation, state and federal income taxes may be treated in the nature of an adjustment in the Adjustments columns. However, they are also treated as in Illustration 118, where "income before taxes" is divided into "Provision for State and Federal Income Taxes" and "Net Income."

When income taxes are handled on the work sheet as in Illustration 118, the revenue and expense accounts are closed to the Income Summary account in the usual manner. Then the Income Summary account is closed with two entries as follows:

Dec.	31	Income Summary......................	55,000.00	
		State and Federal Income Taxes Payable.........................		55,000.00
		To record the liability for state and federal income taxes payable.		
	31	Income Summary......................	45,000.00	
		Retained Earnings................		45,000.00
		To close the Income Summary account.		

The first of the foregoing entries sets up the liability for the state and federal income taxes payable; the second closes the Income Summary account and transfers the amount of the net income to Retained Earnings.

Illustration 118—Section of Work Sheet Showing Treatment of Income Taxes

Account Titles			Income Statement		Balance Sheet	
			Debit	Credit	Debit	Credit
			1,352,000	1,452,000	878,000	778,000
Provision for state and federal income taxes			55,000			55,000
Net income after taxes			45,000			45,000
			1,452,000	1,452,000	878,000	878,000

Statement of Retained Earnings

At the end of each accounting period, in addition to a balance sheet and an income statement, it is customary to prepare for a corporation a statement of retained earnings or, if old terminology is used, a statement of earned surplus. A statement of retained earnings is prepared to show the changes that have occurred in retained earnings during an accounting period. Such a statement may be simple or complex, as the following pages will show.

Illustration 119 is a reasonably simple statement of retained earnings and is prepared from the information shown in the following two accounts from the ledger of the Westwood Corporation:

Retained Earnings

1959				1959			
Mar. 24	Quarterly dividend		3,000	Jan. 1	Balance		180,250
June 21	Quarterly dividend		3,000	Dec. 31	Net income after taxes		53,400
Sept. 27	Quarterly dividend		3,000				
Dec. 20	Quarterly dividend		3,000				
20	Stock dividend		20,000				
20	Reserve for plant expansion		25,000				
31	Balance		176,650				
			233,650				233,650
				1960			
				Jan. 1	Balance		176,650

Reserve for Plant Expansion

			1958	
			Dec. 22	25,000
			1959	
			Dec. 20	25,000

When the statement of retained earnings of the Westwood Corporation as shown in Illustration 119 is compared with the information shown in the corporation's Retained Earnings and Reserve for Plant Expansion accounts, it is apparent that the statement is nothing more than a report of the changes recorded in the accounts.

Illustration 119

WESTWOOD CORPORATION
Statement of Retained Earnings
For Year Ended December 31, 1959

Unappropriated Retained Earnings:		
Balance of unappropriated retained earnings, January 1, 1959 . . .		$180,250
Additions:		
Net income after state and federal income taxes		53,400
Total		$233,650
Deductions and appropriations:		
Quarterly cash dividends. . . .	$12,000	
Dividend paid in common stock .	20,000	
Retained earnings appropriated for plant expansion	25,000	
Total Deductions and Appropriations		57,000
Balance of unappropriated retained earnings, December 31, 1959 . .		$176,650
Appropriated Retained Earnings:		
Reserve for plant expansion, January 1, 1959	$25,000	
Appropriated during 1959	25,000	
Reserve for plant expansion, December 31, 1959		50,000
Total Retained Earnings Appropriated and Unappropriated.		$226,650

Correction of Errors and the Recording of Nonrecurring Items

Sometimes an error affecting income is made in one accounting period and is not discovered until a later period. Since the income of each period is closed to the Retained Earnings account, such errors cause either an overstatement or an understatement of retained earnings. Once such errors were corrected almost exclusively by direct debits or credits to the Retained Earnings account. Today, there are two schools of thought on the corrections of such errors, as well as on the handling of such extraneous and nonrecurring items as material gains and losses on the sale of fixed assets and losses resulting from catastrophes not ordinarily covered by insurance such as wars, riots, floods, and earthquakes.

Of the two schools of thought on the handling of prior period errors and extraneous items, one would handle such transactions and corrections by direct debits and credits to the Retained Earnings account. Under this treatment the items would appear only on the statement of retained earnings. The other school of thought insists that such corrections and items should be taken through the Income Summary account and that they should appear on the income statement of the period in which they occur or are discovered. The two schools of thought are the opposing sides of a debate as to whether the income statement should report *only the results of the regular operations of the current period* or should be an *all-inclusive statement.*

To illustrate the positions of the opposing sides, assume that on December 28, 1958, the bookkeeper of the Dale Corporation in error recorded as machinery repairs the purchase of a $5,000 machine. The error caused a $5,000 overstatement of expenses and a $5,000 understatement of the 1958 income carried to retained earnings and was not discovered until February 23, 1959. In addition to the foregoing, during the last week of February, Green Creek overflowed its banks and swept away a small building carried in the accounts at $8,000. The company had no flood insurance.

Current Operating Performance Income Statement. Accountants who think the income statement should report only the results of current operations would record the correction of the foregoing error and the flood loss as follows:

Feb.	23	Machinery............................	5,000.00	
		Retained Earnings................		5,000.00
		To correct an error of the previous accounting period in which the purchase of machinery was recorded as machinery repairs.		
	28	Retained Earnings.....................	8,000.00	
		Accumulated Depreciation, Building.....	2,000.00	
		Building........................		10,000.00
		To record the destruction of a building by a flood.		

The items of the entries just given are extraneous and nonrecurring. When they are handled in the manner shown, they do not appear on any income statement. However, they would appear on the 1959 statement of retained earnings as shown in Illustration 120 on the next page.

All-Inclusive Income Statement. Accountants who favor an all-inclusive income statement would record the correction of the error discussed in previous paragraphs and the flood loss as follows:

Feb.	23	Machinery............................	5,000.00	
		Correction of Prior Years' Income....		5,000.00
		To correct an error of the previous accounting period in which the purchase of machinery was recorded as machinery repairs.		

Illustration 120

DALE CORPORATION
Statement of Retained Earnings
For Year Ended December 31, 1959

Retained earnings, January 1, 1959	$117,800
Correction of errors of prior years:	
Add:	
Understatement of 1959 income resulting from charging the purchase of machinery to machinery repairs	5,000
Corrected balance of retained earnings, January 1, 1959	$122,800
Current operations:	
Add:	
Net income after state and federal income taxes	43,000
Total	$165,800
Deduct:	
Loss resulting from the destruction of a building by flood . $ 8,000	
Cash dividends. 20,000	28,000
Retained Earnings, December 31, 1959.	$137,800

Feb.	28	Loss from Flood........................	8,000.00	
		Accumulated Depreciation, Building......	2,000.00	
		Building........................		10,000.00
		To record the destruction of a building by a flood.		

When extraneous and nonrecurring items are handled in the manner just shown, the accounts Loss from Flood and Corrections of Prior Years' Income are closed to the Income Summary account and the items appear on the income statement as in Illustration 121.

Illustration 121

DALE CORPORATION
Income Statement for Year Ended December 31, 1959

Revenue from sales	$600,000
Less: Cost of goods sold	350,000
Gross profit from sales.	$250,000
Operating expenses	165,000
Income from operations	$ 85,000
Add: Correction of understatement of 1959 income resulting from recording the purchase of a machine as machinery repairs.	5,000
Total.	$ 90,000
Deduct: Loss from flood.	8,000
Income before state and federal income taxes	$ 82,000
Provision for state and federal income taxes	42,000
Net Income Carried to Retained Earnings. . .	$ 40,000

When an income statement is prepared, as in Illustration 121, under the all-inclusive concept, all corrections of errors affecting prior years' income and all extraneous items are reported on the income statement. Likewise, only the amount of the net income plus deductions for dividends and changes resulting from appropriations of retained earnings appear on the retained earnings statement.

Proponents of the all-inclusive income statement argue that all items of income and all losses should appear on the income statement of the period in which they occur and that at no time should the income statement be bypassed and items affecting either current or prior years' income be taken directly to retained earnings. They point out that as a result of this procedure, if the net incomes reported on all of the income statements prepared by a corporation during its life are added, the sum will exactly equal the income that the corporation has earned during its life. They also claim that this procedure gives a better and more complete picture of a corporation's earnings.

Accountants who favor the current operating performance income statement point out that stockholders and investors are primarily interested in the item reported on the income statement as "net income," and that these people do not always carefully note the items added and deducted in arriving at the reported "net income" figure. Consequently, if extraneous and nonrecurring items are carried to the income statement, some stockholders and investors may be misled as to a corporation's earning power. They feel that when extraneous and nonrecurring items are carried directly to retained earnings, the income statement gives a better picture of a corporation's earning capacity.

The Committee on Accounting Procedure of the American Institute of Certified Public Accountants seems to favor the current operating performance concept of the income statement. The Committee has recommended that where such items are material in amount and would tend to impair the significance of reported net income, the recording of nonrecurring items and error corrections be by direct debits and credits to retained earnings.[9]

Of course the recommendation of the Committee does not settle the argument, and until such time as authoritative opinions are more in agreement, a student or an instructor is justified in accepting either view.

Write-Off of Intangible Assets

An intangible asset is an asset that has no physical existence, and its value results from the rights that its possession confers on its owner. Intangible assets are classified into two groups: (1) those having a term of existence limited by law such as patents which have a legal life of seventeen years and copyrights which have a renewable legal life of twenty-

---

[9] *Accounting Research Bulletin No. 43*, "Restatement and Revision of Accounting Research Bulletins" (New York: American Institute of Certified Public Accountants, 1953), p. 63.

eight years; and (2) those having no such limited term of existence such as goodwill and organization costs.

During the life of an intangible of the first type, it is customary to write off its cost by means of periodic charges to an expense account. If it becomes apparent during the life of such an asset that its period of usefulness will be longer or shorter than the original estimate, the amount of the periodic charge may be increased or decreased.

The costs of intangibles of the second type may be kept on the books throughout the life of a corporation. However, if it should become evident that the term of existence of an intangible of this type has become limited, its cost should also be written off by means of periodic charges to an expense account.

If it should become apparent that an intangible of either type has become worthless, its remaining cost should be charged at once to an expense account or directly to retained earnings, if a current operating performance income statement is preferred and the amount is sufficiently large as to distort the reported net income.[10]

QUESTIONS FOR CLASS DISCUSSION

1. Give the accounting meanings of the terms: (a) surplus, (b) earned surplus, (c) capital surplus, and (d) paid-in surplus.
2. Why do accountants feel that the word "surplus" should not be used in published balance sheets as a term to describe a portion of the stockholders' equity?
3. Under what descriptive headings and subheadings is the equity of the stockholders in a corporation shown on most present-day balance sheets?
4. What is treasury stock? How is it like unissued stock? How does it differ from unissued stock? What is the legal significance of this difference?
5. The General Plastics Corporation bought 100 shares of the stock of Capital Steel Corporation and turned it over to its treasurer for safekeeping. Is this treasury stock? Why or why not?
6. What is the effect of the purchase of treasury stock in terms of assets and stockholders' equity? What is the effect on a corporation's assets and stockholders' equity of the donation to it of treasury stock?
7. Distinguish between issued stock and outstanding stock.
8. Why do state laws place limitations on the purchase of treasury stock?
9. What is appraisal surplus?
10. Why are retained earnings sometimes appropriated and placed in special reserves of retained earnings?
11. Does the appropriation and transfer of retained earnings to a reserve for plant expansion provide funds for the expansion? How does a reserve for plant expansion aid in the accumulation of funds for a plant expansion?
12. How does a corporation dispose of an appropriation of retained earnings such as a reserve for plant expansion?
13. Explain why the American Accounting Association's Committee on Concepts and Standards Underlying Corporate Financial Statements does not favor the showing of appropriations of retained earnings on published balance sheets.

---

[10] *Ibid.*, pp. 38 and 39.

14. What is the effect in terms of assets and stockholders' equity of the distribution of (a) a cash dividend, and (b) a stock dividend?
15. What is the difference between a stock dividend and a stock split?
16. Courts have held that dividends paid in the stock of the paying corporation are not income to their recipients. Why?
17. If a balance sheet is prepared between the date of declaration and the date of distribution of a dividend, how should the dividend be shown if it is distributable in (a) cash, and (b) stock?
18. How may an "all-inclusive income statement" differ from a "current operating performance income statement"?

PROBLEMS

Problem 21–1

Following is the section of Benard Corporation's balance sheet showing the equity of its stockholders:

CAPITAL STOCK AND SURPLUS

Preferred stock, $100 par value, 6 per cent cumulative and nonparticipating, 2,500 shares authorized and issued..................		$250,000	
Common stock, $10 par value, authorized 50,000 shares, issued 40,000 shares.........		400,000	
Total Stock Issued....................			$ 650,000
Capital surplus:			
Premium on preferred stock...............	$ 37,500		
Premium on common stock...............	14,300		
Treasury stock surplus..................	6,200		
Donated surplus........................	15,000		
Total............................	$ 73,000		
Less: Discount on common stock........	1,600		
Total Capital Surplus...............		$ 71,400	
Earned surplus:			
Appropriated:			
Reserve for plant expansion.............	$100,000		
Reserve for working capital.............	50,000		
Total.............................	$150,000		
Unappropriated earned surplus............	174,100		
Total Earned Surplus...............		324,100	
Total Surplus......................			395,500
Total Capital Stock and Surplus.......			$1,045,500

Required:

Rearrange and restate the stockholders' equity section of this balance sheet so that it will conform with the proposals of the American Institute of Certified Public Accountants. (The donated surplus on the balance sheet arose from the donation of a plant site by the Eastburg Chamber of Commerce, and the treasury stock surplus from the purchase and sale of treasury stock.)

Problem 21–2

On March 15 of the current year Dunaham Corporation received a charter granting it the right to issue 25,000 shares of $10 par value common stock. During the next two years the company completed the following transactions:
  a) Received subscriptions to 10,000 of its shares of common stock at $10.75 per share.

b) Collected the subscriptions in full and issued the stock.
c) Exchanged 10,000 shares of stock for the following assets of Diamond Corporation: machinery and equipment, $40,000; building, $55,000; and land, $13,000.
d) Earned net income before taxes of $60,000. Although the transactions resulting in earnings affect numerous accounts, the sum total of their effect is always an increase in net assets. Consequently, to simplify the situation of this problem, record the net income by debiting Cash for $65,000 and crediting Accumulated Depreciation of Machinery and Equipment for $4,000, Accumulated Depreciation of Building for $1,000, and Income Summary for $60,000.
e) Recorded a $30,000 liability for state and federal income taxes.
f) Closed the Income Summary account.
g) Declared a $0.75 per share cash dividend.
h) Paid the dividend previously declared.
i) Paid the state and federal income taxes of transaction (*e*).
j) Purchased 2,000 shares of treasury stock at $11.25 per share.
k) Sold 800 shares of treasury stock at $12 per share.
l) Sold 400 shares of treasury stock at $11 per share.
m) Earned net income before taxes of $72,000. Debit Cash for $80,000. Credit Accumulated Depreciation of Machinery and Equipment for $6,500, Accumulated Depreciation of Building for $1,500, and Income Summary for $72,000.
n) Recorded a $37,000 liability for state and federal income taxes.
o) Closed the Income Summary account.
p) Appropriated $10,000 of retained earnings and placed in a reserve for plant expansion.
q) Declared a $0.75 per share cash dividend.

Required:

1. Open the following T-accounts: Cash, Subscriptions Receivable Common Stock, Machinery and Equipment, Accumulated Depreciation of Machinery and Equipment, Building, Accumulated Depreciation of Building, Land, State and Federal Income Taxes Payable, Dividends Payable, Common Stock, Common Stock Subscribed, Premium on Common Stock, Treasury Stock Common, Contributed Capital from Treasury Stock Transactions, Retained Earnings, Reserve for Plant Expansion, and Income Summary.
2. Record the transactions directly in the T-accounts.
3. Prepare the stockholders' equity section of the company's balance sheet as it would appear after the foregoing transactions were recorded.

Problem 21–3

Northwood Corporation has outstanding 1,000 shares of $100 par value common stock. At the end of several unprofitable years ending last December 31, the corporation found itself with a deficit of $20,500 and in need of additional working capital. To supply the working capital the corporation's stockholders agreed to donate pro rata 25 per cent of their shares to be sold by the corporation for cash. On January 28 the stock was donated, and on February 10 it was sold at $92 per share.

Required:

1. Give the entries to record the donation and the sale of the stock.
2. Calculate the book value per share of the corporation's stock: (*a*) before

the donation; (b) after the donation but before the treasury stock was sold; and (c) after the treasury stock was sold.

Problem 21-4

On January 10 of the current year the board of directors of Stonehill Corporation voted to appropriate $35,000 of retained earnings and to place it in a reserve for plant expansion. After the appropriation was recorded, the company had the following amounts of contributed and retained capital:

Common stock, $100 par value, 12,000 shares authorized, 10,000
    shares issued $1,000,000
Reserve for plant expansion. 175,000
Unappropriated retained earnings. 65,000
      Total. $1,240,000

On January 20 the board of directors signed a contract for the construction of the addition to the plant for which the reserve for plant expansion was created, and on October 12, upon completion of the addition, the contractor was paid the contract price, $169,750.

At their November 15 meeting the board of directors voted to return the balance of the Reserve for Plant Expansion account to unappropriated retained earnings. They also voted a 1,400 share stock dividend distributable on December 15 to stockholders of record on December 10. The market value of a share of the company's stock on November 15 was $125.

Required:

1. Prepare entries to record the January 10 appropriation, the payment of the contractor, the return of the reserve for plant expansion to unappropriated retained earnings, the declaration of the stock dividend, and the distribution of the dividend.
2. Prepare the stockholder equity section of the company's balance sheet as it would appear after the foregoing transactions.

Problem 21-5

Following are the condensed Income Summary and Retained Earnings accounts of Gem Corporation as of the end of the 1960 accounting period:

Income Summary

1960			1960		
Dec. 31	Cost of goods sold	300,000	Dec. 31	Revenue from sales	540,000
31	Operating expenses	~~180,000~~			
Add		6000			
		30000			
		158000			

Retained Earnings

1960			1960		
Mar. 29	Cash dividend	4,000	Jan. 2	Balance	86,500
June 26	Cash dividend	4,000			
Sept. 29	Cash dividend	4,000			
Dec. 27	Cash dividend	4,000			
27	Stock dividend	12,000			
		58000			

All events and transactions affecting the two accounts are reflected therein with the following exceptions:

a) On January 26, 1960, the company's auditor discovered that on December 24, 1959, a $2,200 check in payment for extraordinary repairs to the building had been debited in error to the Building Repairs account.

b) On March 22, 1960, the company's building suffered $6,000 of damage to its roof as the result of a windstorm. Repairs were made and paid for in cash on April 4. The company is located in a section of the country where such storms are most unusual, and there was no insurance.

c) The 1960 state and federal income taxes amount to $30,000.

Required:

1. Under the assumption that the management of the company thinks the company's income statement should reflect only current operating performance, prepare:
   a) Entries to record the three foregoing unrecorded events and transactions and to close the Income Summary account.
   b) A condensed 1960 income statement.
   c) A 1960 statement of retained earnings.
2. Under the assumption that the management of the company thinks the company's income statement should be an all-inclusive statement, prepare:
   a) Entries to record the foregoing unrecorded events and transactions and to close the Income Summary account.
   b) A condensed 1960 income statement.
   c) A 1960 statement of retained earnings.

CLASS EXERCISES

Exercise 21–1

The bookkeeper of Abar Inc., prepared the following statement of retained earnings for the year ended December 31, 1959:

ABAR, INC.

Statement of Retained Earnings
For Year Ended December 31, 1959

Retained earnings, January 1, 1959	$32,400
Net income	8,200
Total	$40,600
Dividends paid	4,200
Retained Earnings, December 31, 1959	$36,400

An examination of the corporation's records disclosed the following:

a) The December 31, 1958, inventory was understated by $2,300. The error was not corrected during 1959 because, according to the bookkeeper, "it would correct itself by the end of 1959."

b) During the last week of December, 1958, $2,800 of store equipment having a life of ten years was purchased and debited in error to the Purchases account. The error had not previously been discovered or corrected.

c) The minutes of the meetings of the board of directors and the Cash Disbursements Journal disclosed the following dividend record. All dividend transactions had been properly recorded.

Dividend	Declared	Paid
$1,000	Dec. 28, 1958	Jan. 15, 1959
$1,000	Mar. 27, 1959	Apr. 15, 1959
$1,000	June 27, 1959	July 15, 1959
$1,200	Sept. 28, 1959	Oct. 15, 1959
$1,200	Dec. 27, 1959	Unpaid

Required:

1. If you had been engaged by Abar, Inc., during January, 1959, to audit its books and had discovered, at that time, the errors listed, what correcting entries would you have asked the bookkeeper to make. Assume that the management of Abar, Inc., favors an income statement that shows only the effects of current operations.
2. Assuming that the correcting entries suggested by you were made by the bookkeeper during January of 1959, prepare a corrected 1959 statement of retained earnings for Abar, Inc. Ignore the effects of income taxes.

SUPPLEMENTARY PROBLEMS

Problem 21–A

Following are the contributed capital and retained earnings sections from Corkwood Corporation's 1959 and 1960 balance sheets.

CONTRIBUTED CAPITAL AND RETAINED EARNINGS (as of December 31, 1959):

Common stock, $10 par value, 50,000 shares authorized, 40,000 shares issued...	$400,000
Premium on common stock.....................................	16,000
Total Contributed Capital...............................	$416,000
Retained earnings..	309,500
Total Contributed Capital and Retained Earnings............	$725,500

CONTRIBUTED CAPITAL AND RETAINED EARNINGS (as of December 31, 1960):

Common stock, $10 par value, 50,000 shares authorized, 47,800 shares issued of which 1,000 are in the treasury.......................	$478,000
Premium on common stock.....................................	82,300
Total Contributed Capital...............................	$560,300
Retained earnings..	189,150
Total...	$749,450
Less: Cost of treasury stock................................	18,000
Total Contributed Capital and Retained Earnings...........	$731,450

On March 28, June 25, September 27, and again on December 29, 1960, the board of directors declared $0.25 per share dividends on the outstanding stock. On October 25, while the stock was selling at $18.50 per share, the corporation declared a 20 per cent dividend payable in stock. The new shares were issued on November 10. The treasury stock was purchased on August 7.

Required:

Under the assumption that there were no transactions effecting retained earnings other than the ones given, determine the 1960 net income of Corkwood Corporation. Present calculations to prove your net income figure.

Problem 21–B

The December 31, 1959, balance sheet of Mercury Corporation showed the corporation's retained earnings as follows:

Retained earnings:
Reserve for plant expansion............................$ 40,000
Unappropriated retained earnings........................ 132,500
Total Retained Earnings.............................$172,500

The management of Mercury Corporation believes that their company's income statement should reflect current operating performance and that unusual and nonrecurring transactions should be carried directly to the Unappropriated Retained Earnings account. Consequently, at the end of 1960 the Unappropriated Retained Earnings account of the company appeared as follows:

Unappropriated Retained Earnings

1960				1960			
Mar.	5	Cost of a lawsuit lost	11,200	Jan.	1	Balance	132,500
	27	Quarterly cash dividend	5,000		27	Understatement of 1959	
June	28	Quarterly cash dividend	5,000			income due to an over-	
	28	Stock dividend	28,400			statement of deprecia-	
Sept.	26	Quarterly cash dividend	5,500			tion on machinery	2,400
Dec.	29	Quarterly cash dividend	5,500	Dec.	31	Net income after state	
	29	Reserve for plant ex-				and federal taxes	67,450
		pansion	10,000				
	31	Balance	131,750				
			202,350				202,350
				1961			
				Jan.	1	Balance	131,750

Required:

1. Prepare a statement of retained earnings for Mercury Corporation that reflects the entries in the foregoing account.
2. Prepare a second statement of retained earnings for Mercury Corporation as it would appear if the management of the company preferred an all-inclusive income statement rather than a current operating performance income statement.

Chapter

22

WHEN A business borrows money that is not to be repaid for a relatively long period of time, it may borrow by means of a mortgage, by means of bonds, or by issuing long-term notes.

Borrowing Money by Means of a Mortgage

A business may borrow by placing a mortgage on some or all of its fixed assets. A mortgage actually involves two legal documents. The first is a kind of promissory note called a *mortgage note*. This is secured by a second legal document called a *mortgage* or a *mortgage contract*. In the mortgage note the one who mortgages property promises to repay the money borrowed. The mortgage or mortgage contract requires a number of things of the one who mortgages property. Normally, among other things, he must keep the mortgaged property in a good state of repair, carry adequate insurance, pay the interest on the mortgage note, and, often, make payments to reduce the amount of the mortgage liability. These duties and responsibilities are always set forth in the mortgage contract. In addition to setting forth the duties and obligations of the one who mortgages property, the mortgage contract also grants the mortgage holder certain rights. Among these rights is the right to foreclose the mortgage in case the mortgagor fails in any of his duties, such as paying the interest, keeping the property in repair, or carrying adequate insurance. In a foreclosure a court takes possession of the mortgaged property for the mortgage holder. The court may order the sale of the mortgaged property. If the mortgaged property is sold, the proceeds of the sale go first to pay the claims of the mortgage holder. After the claims of the mortgage holder are satisfied, any money remaining is paid to the former owner of the mortgaged property.

When a business borrows by means of a mortgage, the transaction commonly involves the business and a single bank or insurance company. Because banks and insurance companies may normally loan to a single borrower no more than an amount equal to 10 per cent of their net worth, this always places a limitation on the size of a mortgage loan. Consequently, large companies often cannot find a single lender who wishes to lend and may legally lend to one borrower the amount of money they wish to borrow. In such cases, in the place of a mortgage loan, bonds are often issued. Bonds make possible the division of a large loan into portions that may be sold to many small investors.

Borrowing Money by Issuing Bonds

Borrowing money by issuing bonds is quite similar to borrowing by issuing a mortgage note and a mortgage. Actually in many cases the greatest difference it that when bonds are issued, a number of bonds, often in denominations of $1,000, are issued in the place of a single mortgage note. For all practical purposes each of the bonds issued is a promissory note. Each is a promise in writing to pay a definite sum of money to its holder, or owner of record, at a fixed future date. Like promissory notes, bonds bear interest; and like a mortgage note, bonds are often secured by a mortgage on certain assets. However, since bonds may be owned and transferred during their lives by a number of people, they differ from promissory notes in that they do not name the lender.

When a company issues bonds secured by a mortgage, it normally selects an investment firm to which it turns over the bonds for sale to the general public. Usually the investment firm, known as the *underwriter*, buys the bonds outright from the issuing company and then resells them to investors. In addition to the underwriter, the company issuing bonds secured by a mortgage selects a trustee to represent the bondholders. In most cases the trustee is a large bank or trust company. The company issuing the bonds executes and delivers to the trustee the mortgage which acts as security for the bonds. It is the duty of the trustee to see that the company fulfills all the pledged responsibilities of the mortgage contract, or as it is often called, the *deed of trust*. It is also the duty of the trustee to foreclose if the company does not fulfill all of the pledges of the deed of trust.

Who May Issue Bonds

Most large companies are organized as corporations, and corporations have made extensive use of bonds as a means of financing. However, the sale of bonds is not a privilege limited to businesses organized as corporations. The federal government issues bonds, and most state and local governmental units make wide use of bonds in financing projects. Likewise partnerships and single proprietorships may issue bonds. However, since governmental accounting is a special field and since the issuance of bonds by single proprietorships and partnerships is not at all common, this text, as do most accounting texts, will limit its consideration of bonds to corporate bonds.

Classification of Bonds

Over the years corporation lawyers and financiers have created and issued a wide variety of bonds each with slightly different combinations of characteristics. Consequently, a single method of classifying bonds is impossible, and bonds are classified in a number of ways. Two common ways in which bonds are classified are: (1) as to the methods of payment of principal and interest, and (2) as to the type of security.

Bonds Classified as to the Methods of Payment of Principal and Interest. When bonds are classified as to the methods of payment of principal, they may be either *serial bonds* or *sinking fund bonds*. When serial or term bonds are issued, portions of the bonds become due and are paid in installments over a period of years. For example, a corporation may issue $1,000,000 of serial bonds with the provision that $100,000 of the bonds become due and are to be paid each year until all are paid.

When sinking fund bonds are issued, the deed of trust provides that a sinking fund be created to pay the bonds at maturity. Sinking funds are discussed in more detail later in this chapter.

Bonds may be issued without provision for either installment payments or a sinking fund. Such bonds are normally payable in one amount at maturity and are often to be paid with funds from the sale of a new bond issue.

When bonds are classified as to the method of interest payment, they are either *registered bonds* or *coupon bonds*. The ownership of registered bonds is registered or recorded with the issuing corporation. Registration offers some protection from loss or theft. Title to such bonds is transferred in much the same manner as title to stock is transferred. Interest payments on registered bonds are usually made by checks mailed to the registered owners.

Coupon bonds secure their name from the interest coupons attached to each bond. Each coupon calls for the payment on the interest payment date of the amount of interest due on the bond to which it is attached. The coupons are detached as they become due and are deposited with a bank for collection in much the same manner as an out-of-town note is deposited for collection. Often the ownership of a coupon bond is not registered with the issuing corporation. Such unregistered coupon bonds are bearer paper, and ownership is transferred by delivery. Sometimes bonds are registered as to principal only with interest payments by coupons.

Bonds Classified as to Security. Bonds may be secured bonds or unsecured bonds. Unsecured bonds are called *debentures*. They depend for their security upon the general credit standing of their issuing corporation. Only financially strong corporations are able to sell unsecured bonds. Most corporations must issue secured bonds. When bonds are secured, they are normally secured by mortgages or liens on assets. Such bonds are often classified according to the type of assets pledged for their security. Some of the more common classifications of secured bonds are *real estate mortgage bonds, equipment trust bonds,* and *collateral trust bonds.* An issue of real estate mortgage bonds is normally secured by a mortgage on a portion or all of the issuing corporation's plant and equipment. Equipment trust bonds are commonly issued by railroads and are secured by a mortgage on rolling stock and equipment. Collateral trust bonds are commonly issued by corporations that own the stocks and bonds of other corporations. They are secured by these stocks, bonds, and other negotiable instruments which are deposited with a trustee.

Why a Corporation Issues Bonds

When a corporation is in need of long-term funds, it may secure these funds by issuing either additional common stock, preferred stock, or bonds. Each has its advantages and disadvantages.

Stockholders are corporation owners, and bondholders are creditors. Issuing additional common stock spreads control of management over a larger number of stockholders and spreads earnings over a larger number of shares of stock. Since bondholders are creditors, they do not share in either management or earnings. Furthermore, since bonds are usually secured by a mortgage or lien and interest payments are fixed in amount, the rate of interest paid on bonds is usually less than the dividend rates on either common or preferred stocks.

The stockholders of a corporation are its owners and as such receive dividends only when income sufficient to pay the dividends has been earned. Whenever sufficient income has not been earned, the stockholders receive no dividends. They must wait for dividends until sufficient income is earned. This is not true of bondholders. Bondholders are creditors, and payments of interest to bondholders must be made when due whether any income is earned or not. If interest payments are not made when due, the bondholders of a corporation may foreclose and take the corporation's assets pledged for their security.

In this age of high corporation income taxes, taxes are also always a factor in a decision between issuing stocks or bonds. Bond interest is a deductible expense in the calculation of income subject to income taxes, while dividends are a sharing of income and are not a deductible expense. Because of this the federal income tax is often one of the most important factors in a decision between issuing preferred stock or bonds. The importance of this factor is demonstrated in the table shown in Illustration 122. The table shows the results of three methods a corporation may use in securing additional funds.

Often the deciding factor in a decision between issuing additional stocks or issuing bonds is the estimated amount of future earnings and their probable stability. If the rate of earnings per dollar invested is expected to be greater than the bond interest rate or the rate of dividends on preferred stock, and is also expected to be stable, it is usually to the advantage of the common stockholders to issue either bonds or preferred stock. On the other hand, if the expected rate of earnings is less than the bond interest rate or the rate of dividends on preferred stock, the common stockholders receive a greater return if additional common stock rather than either bonds or preferred stock is issued. For example, assume that the Apex Corporation which has $2,000,000 of common stock outstanding wishes to raise an additional $2,000,000 for the expansion of its business. The results of three methods of securing the additional funds are shown in Illustration 122. This table shows the results first with an assumed op-

Illustration 122

	Operating Income of $400,000			Operating Income of $70,000		
	Plan No. 1	Plan No. 2	Plan No. 3	Plan No. 1	Plan No. 2	Plan No. 3
Common stock, $100 par...............	$4,000,000	$2,000,000	$2,000,000	$4,000,000	$2,000,000	$2,000,000
Preferred stock, 6 per cent cumulative......		2,000,000			2,000,000	
4 per cent bonds...................			2,000,000			2,000,000
Total Capitalization........	$4,000,000	$4,000,000	$4,000,000	$4,000,000	$4,000,000	$4,000,000
Operating income before federal income tax...	$ 400,000	$ 400,000	$ 400,000	$ 70,000	$ 70,000	$ 70,000
Deduct: Bond interest expense............			80,000			80,000
Income (or deficit*) after bond interest expense..	$ 400,000	$ 400,000	$ 320,000	$ 70,000	$ 70,000	$ 10,000*
Deduct: Federal income taxes of 50 per cent...	200,000	200,000	160,000	35,000	35,000	–0–
Net income (or deficit*) after federal taxes......	$ 200,000	$ 200,000	$ 160,000	$ 35,000	$ 35,000	$ 10,000*
Preferred dividends.................		120,000			120,000	
Income (or deficit*) after taxes and preferred dividends or bond interest..................	$ 200,000	$ 80,000	$ 160,000	$ 35,000	$ 85,000*	$ 10,000*
Income (or deficit*) per share of common stock.......	$5.00	$4.00	$8.00	$0.875	$4.25*	$0.50*

erating income of $400,000 and then with an assumed operating income of $70,000 per year. Plan No. 1 assumes that the Apex Corporation issues an additional $2,000,000 of common stock which brings its common stock outstanding to a total of $4,000,000. Plan No. 2 assumes that the additional funds are raised by issuing $2,000,000 of 6 per cent preferred stock. Plan No. 3 assumes that $2,000,000 of 4 per cent bonds are sold. Obviously, Plan No. 3 is to the advantage of the original common stockholders if earnings are large. However, when earnings are less than the interest on the bonds, Plan No. 1 offers the greatest return to the original stockholders. Notice the effect on the three methods of financing of the assumed federal corporation income tax rate of 50 per cent. Actually, since corporation tax rates have reached the 50 per cent level, a corporation's choice between issuing stock and issuing bonds is normally a choice between common stock and bonds. Today, because of federal income taxes, new preferred stock issues are not common.

Recording Bond Transactions

A decision to issue bonds rests with the board of directors of a corporation. However, many corporations provide in their charters that a decision by the board of directors to issue bonds must be approved by the stockholders.

When bonds are to be issued, after the resolution to issue bonds is passed by the board of directors and approved by the stockholders, the bonds are printed, and the deed of trust is drawn. The deed of trust always states the total amount of bonds that is secured by it and that may be issued. Only the amount of bonds authorized in the deed of trust may be sold. After bonds are printed and the deed of trust is drawn, the deed of trust is deposited with the trustee of the bondholders. When the deed of trust is deposited with the trustee of the bondholders, an entry is made to record the authorization of the bond issue. The entry is usually a memorandum entry and appears somewhat as follows:

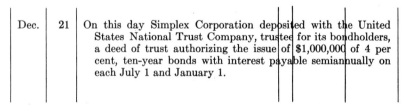

| Dec. | 21 | On this day Simplex Corporation deposited with the United States National Trust Company, trustee for its bondholders, a deed of trust authorizing the issue of $1,000,000 of 4 per cent, ten-year bonds with interest payable semiannually on each July 1 and January 1. | | |

In addition to the memorandum entry in the General Journal, a memorandum as to the amount of bonds authorized is also placed in the Bonds Payable account in the ledger.

Often when an issue of bonds is authorized, more bonds are authorized than are to be immediately issued. For example, often if a corporation has an immediate need for only $750,000 but the property it is mortgaging is ample to secure a $1,000,000 bond issue, a deed of trust is drawn for the larger amount, and $1,000,000 of bonds are authorized. Then only $750,-000 of bonds, the amount necessary to cover immediate needs, is sold. The remaining bonds are held in reserve to be sold when additional funds are needed. In such a situation where only $750,000 is presently needed but the property being mortgaged is sufficient to secure a $1,000,000 bond issue, if the deed of trust were drawn for only the $750,000 immediately needed, it would be necessary to use a second mortgage as security if an additional loan of $250,000 were later needed. Issuing a second mortgage would be undesirable because the claims of the first mortgage would take priority over those of the second mortgage. This would cause the second mortgage to be less desirable, and it would normally make a higher rate of interest necessary on the second mortgage.

After the deed of trust is deposited with the trustee of the bondholders, a corporation may sell its bonds. For example, if on January 1 Simplex Corporation sells $750,000 of the $1,000,000 of bonds, the authorization of which was previously illustrated, the entry to record the sale appears as follows:

Jan.	1	Cash...............................	750,000.00	
		Bonds Payable...................		750,000.00
		Sold $750,000 of the 4 per cent bonds authorized.		

When a corporation with bonds payable outstanding prepares a balance sheet, it should show both the amount of its authorized bonds payable and the amount of bonds issued and outstanding. For example, if Simplex Corporation prepares a balance sheet immediately after the sale of the $750,000 of bonds just recorded, it may show the liability for its bonds as follows:

Long-Term Liabilities:

```
First-mortgage, 4 per cent bonds pay-
    able, due December 31, 1970:
  Authorized . . . . . . . . . . . . .   $1,000,000
  Unissued . . . . . . . . . . . . .        250,000
  Issued and outstanding . . . . . .                   $750,000
```

When both the amount of bonds authorized and the amount issued and outstanding are shown on the balance sheet, owners of the bonds are in a better position to judge whether the assets pledged as security for the bonds are ample to cover the entire issue.

Authorized but unissued bonds may be sold and issued whenever funds are needed. For example, if after issuing $750,000 of its $1,000,000 of authorized bonds Simplex Corporation finds itself in need of additional funds, it may issue the remainder of its authorized bonds. When it does so, it will make the following entry:

July	1	Cash...............................	250,000.00	
		Bonds Payable..................		250,000.00
		Issued the remainder of the authorized 4 per cent bonds.		

On each July 1 and January 1 thereafter, when Simplex Corporation pays the semiannual interest on its $1,000,000 of outstanding 4 per cent bonds, the following entry is made:

Jan.	1	Bond Interest Expense...............	20,000.00	
		Cash...........................		20,000.00
		Made the semiannual payment of interest on the $1,000,000 of 4 per cent bonds outstanding.		

In 1970, when the Simplex bonds are paid and retired, the entry to record their retirement is as follows:

Dec.	31	Bonds Payable....................	1,000,000.00	
		Cash..........................		1,000,000.00
		To record the retirement of $1,000,000 of 4 per cent, first-mortgage bonds.		

Bonds Sold between Interest Dates

When bond certificates are printed, they promise to pay a specified amount of interest on each specified interest date. Sometimes bonds are sold on their interest dates; more often they are sold between interest dates. When bonds are sold between interest dates, it is customary to charge the bond purchasers for the amount of interest accrued since the previous interest payment date and to return the accrued interest thus collected to the purchasers on the next interest payment date. For example, assume that on March 1, a corporation sells $100,000 of 4 per cent bonds on which interest is payable semiannually on each January 1 and July 1. The entry to record the sale between interest dates is as follows:

Mar.	1	Cash...............................	100,666.67	
		Bond Interest Expense.............		666.67
		Bonds Payable...................		100,000.00
		To record the sale of $100,000 of bonds on which two months' interest has accrued.		

At the end of four months, on the July 1 semiannual interest payment date, the purchasers of these bonds are paid a full six months' interest. This interest payment includes four months of interest earned by the bondholders after March 1 and the two months of accrued interest collected from the bondholders at the time the bonds were sold. The entry to record the interest payment is:

July	1	Bond Interest Expense.................	2,000.00	
		Cash............................		2,000.00
		To record the payment of the semiannual interest on the bonds.		

After this entry is posted, the Bond Interest Expense account has a $1,-333.33 debit balance and appears as follows:

Bond Interest Expense

July 1 (Payment)	2,000.00	Mar. 1 (Accrued interest)	666.67

The $1,333.33 debit balance in the Bond Interest Expense account is the interest expense on the $100,000 of bonds at 4 per cent for the four months from March 1 to July 1.

Bond Interest Rates

When a corporation borrows by issuing bonds, the rate of interest it must pay depends upon its credit standing, the security offered, and upon the current *market rate for bond interest*. The market rate for bond interest is the rate of interest that borrowers are willing to pay and lenders are willing to take for the use of money. The market rate fluctuates from day to day as the supply and demand of investment funds fluctuate.

When a corporation issues bonds, it specifies in the deed of trust and on each bond the rate of interest it will pay. This rate is called the *contract rate*. Normally, when a board of directors authorizes a bond issue, it estimates the rate of interest the market will demand and offers a contract rate equal to its estimate. However, a period of time always elapses between the authorization of a bond issue and its sale, and during this period bond interest rates fluctuate. Consequently, when bonds are finally sold, their contract rate seldom coincides with the market rate.

Bonds Sold at a Discount

When a corporation offers a bond issue with a contract rate of interest that is below the prevailing market rate, the bonds can be sold only at a discount. For example, assume that a corporation offers $100,000 of 4 per cent, ten-year bonds on which interest is payable semiannually. Assume further that on the day the bonds are offered the prevailing interest rate for like bonds is slightly in excess of 4 per cent, and as a result the highest bid for the offered bonds is $99,000. If the corporation accepts this bid and sells the bonds, the entry to record the sale is:

Jan.	1	Cash.................................	99,000.00	
		Discount on Bonds Payable............	1,000.00	
		Bonds Payable...................		100,000.00
		Sold bonds at a discount.		

The corporation of this illustration receives $99,000 that it may use for ten years. For the use of the $99,000 the corporation agrees to repay $100,000 and to pay $4,000 in interest during each of the ten years, or a total of $40,000. Or, in other words, to the corporation the cost of the use of $99,000 for ten years is the difference between the amount received and the amounts to be paid, or is:

```
Amounts to be paid:
    Face of the bonds.......................................$100,000
    Interest (4 per cent annually for ten years)................  40,000
        Total to Be Paid....................................$140,000
Amount received:
    Bid price of the bonds.................................  99,000
        Cost of the $99,000 for Ten Years.....................$ 41,000
```

If the $41,000 cost of the use of the $99,000 is divided equally over each of the ten years in the life of the bond issue, the annual cost is $4,100. Furthermore, if the $4,100 annual cost is expressed as a percentage of the $99,000, the annual rate of interest is in effect 4.14+% ($4,100 ÷ $99,000 = 0.0414+). Obviously, then, a discount has the effect of adjusting and increasing an offered contract rate.

The corporation of this illustration receives $99,000 for its bonds; but in ten years it must repay $100,000. The $1,000 discount is one of the costs of using the $99,000. This additional cost must be paid at the maturity of the bond issue. However, since each year in the life of the bond issue benefits from the use of the $99,000, it is only fair that each should bear a fair share of the $1,000 discount.

The accounting procedure of dividing a discount and charging a fair share to each accounting period in the life of the applicable bond issue is called *amortizing* a discount. There are several methods of amortizing a discount, one common method is the straight-line method. In the straight-line method, a discount is divided equally and an equal portion is charged to each accounting period in the life of the bond issue to which it applies. For example, if the $1,000 discount on the $100,000 of 4 per cent, ten-year bonds of this illustration is amortized by the straight-line method, each of the ten years in the life of the issue must bear $100 of the discount. Furthermore, if each of the ten years bears $100 of discount, then each semiannual interest period of six months must bear $50 of discount. Consequently, if the $1,000 of discount is amortized by the straight-line method, the following entry is made on each semiannual interest payment date to record the payment of $2,000 of interest to the bondholders and the amortization of $50 of discount:

July	1	Bond Interest Expense..................	2,050.00	
		Cash.............................		2,000.00
		Discount on Bonds Payable........		50.00
		To record the payment of six months' interest and the amortization of one twentieth of the discount.		

The amortization of $50 of discount at the time of each interest payment increases the recorded bond interest expense by $50 each six months, or by $100 each year. The amortization of the $50 of discount each six months also completely writes off the $1,000 of discount by the end of the ten-year life of the bond issue.

Bonds Sold at a Premium

When a corporation offers a bond issue with a contract rate that is higher than the market rate, purchasers of the bonds will normally pay more than par, and the bonds will be sold at a premium. For example, assume that a corporation offers $100,000 of 5 per cent, ten-year bonds on which the interest is payable semiannually. Assume further that the market rate of interest on similar bonds is below 5 per cent on the day the bonds are offered and as a result they are sold at a premium for $102,000. The entry to record the sale is:

Jan.	1	Cash................................	102,000.00	
		Premium on Bonds Payable........		2,000.00
		Bonds Payable...................		100,000.00
		Sold bonds at a premium.		

The corporation of this illustration received $102,000 that it may use. To this corporation, like the one of the previous illustration, the cost of using the $102,000 is the difference between the amount received and the amounts to be paid, or is:

```
Amounts to be paid:
  Face of the bonds.......................................$100,000
  Interest (5 per cent annually for ten years)................  50,000
    Total to Be Paid......................................$150,000
  Amount received.........................................  102,000
    Cost of the $102,000 for Ten Years....................$ 48,000
```

And, if the $48,000 cost is divided equally over the ten years of the bond issue, the annual cost is $4,800, or in effect 4.70+% ($4,800 ÷ $102,-000 = 0.0470+) per year. Obviously, then, a premium like a discount is also an adjustment of an offered contract rate. However, a premium has the effect of decreasing an offered contract rate.

When bonds are sold at a premium, since the premium is in effect an adjustment of the offered contract rate, the premium should be amortized if each accounting period in the life of the bond issue is to bear its fair

544 · FUNDAMENTAL ACCOUNTING PRINCIPLES [Ch. 22

share of the cost of the borrowed money. If a premium is amortized on a straight-line basis, an equal amount is written off each accounting period. For example, if the $2,000 premium on the bond issue of this illustration is amortized on a straight-line basis, $200 must be written off each year or $100 must be written off at the time of each interest payment. If $100 of premium is written off at the time of each interest payment, the entry to record the payment and the amortization of the premium is:

July	1	Bond Interest Expense................	2,400.00	
		Bond Premium.......................	100.00	
		Cash............................		2,500.00
		To record the payment of six months' interest and the amortization of one twentieth of the premium.		

Observe in the foregoing entry that the amortization of the premium has the effect of reducing the recorded interest expense from the $2,500 paid the bond holders to $2,400.

Accrued Bond Interest Expense

Often when bonds are sold, the interest periods of the bond issue do not coincide with the issuing company's accounting periods. In such cases it is necessary at the end of each accounting period to make an adjustment for the bond interest accrued. For example, on March 1, 1960, a corporation having a yearly accounting period which ends on December 31, sells $100,000 of 4½ per cent, twenty-year bonds for $101,200. The interest on the bonds is to be paid semiannually on each March 1 and September 1. The entry to record the September 1 semiannual interest payment is as follows:

Sept.	1	Bond Interest Expense................	2,220.00	
		Premium on Bonds Payable............	30.00	
		Cash............................		2,250.00
		To record the payment of the interest on the bonds and the amortization of the premium.		

On December 31, 1960, and on each December 31 thereafter throughout the life of this bond issue, there are always four months' accrued interest on these bonds. The interest will not be paid until the following March 1; therefore, at the end of each accounting year, an adjusting entry like the following is required:

Dec.	31	Bond Interest Expense................	1,480.00	
		Premium on Bonds Payable............	20.00	
		Bond Interest Payable.............		1,500.00
		To record four months' accrued interest on the bonds.		

This adjusting entry may be reversed at the beginning of the new accounting period. If the entry is reversed, the normal interest payment and premium amortization entry is made when the interest is paid on March 1.

Premiums and Discounts on Bonds Outstanding Less than Their Full Term

The bonds of the previous illustrations were either ten-year bonds or twenty-year bonds and were assumed to be outstanding in each case a full ten or twenty years. Often bonds are not outstanding the full ten, twenty, or other term of years in their authorized lives. For example, assume that in November, 1959, a $1,000,000 twenty-year bond issue dated January 1, 1960, and due January 1, 1980, was authorized. Assume further that interest is payable semiannually on the issue on each January 1 and July 1 and that the issue was sold on March 1, 1960, at a discount of $47,600.

Between January 1, 1960, and January 1, 1980, is a period of twenty years, or 240 months; but between March 1, 1960, and January 1, 1980, is a period of only 238 months. Consequently, since the bonds are outstanding only 238 months, the discount must be amortized over this shorter period. Therefore, when the interest is paid on July 1, 1960, four months' discount, or $800 ($47,600 $\times$ $\frac{4}{238}$ = $800) of discount, should be written off; and on January 1, 1961, and at the end of each six months thereafter, six months' discount, or $1,200 ($47,600 $\times$ $\frac{6}{238}$ = $1,200), should be amortized.

Discounts and Premiums on the Balance Sheet

The trend in balance sheet presentation is to show bond premiums and discounts somewhat as follows:

Long-Term Liabilities:
    First 5 per cent real estate mortgage
        bonds, due in 1978. . . . . . . $2,500,000
        Add: Unamortized premium. 30,000 $2,530,000
    Collateral trust 4 per cent bonds,
        due in 1980 . . . . $1,000,000
        Deduct: Unamortized discount. . .   22,000   978,000

It is not uncommon for bond discount to be placed on the balance sheet as an asset under a long-term prepaid expense classification called "Deferred charges" and for bond premium to be shown as a "Deferred credit." However, general opinion now rejects the idea that bond discount is a prepaid expense; rather this opinion holds that bond discount is an "unpaid interest expense" and will not be payable until the bonds mature. This expense accrues over the life of the bonds. Therefore bond discount should be deducted from the maturity value of the bonds on the balance sheet to reduce the maturity value for the discount not yet earned by investors and not yet an actual liability to the issuing corporation. Similarly premium on bonds should be added to the maturity value of the bond liability since the premium represents the liability of the corporation to pay interest in excess of the market rate over the remaining life of the bonds.

Costs of a Bond Issue

When bonds are issued, there are certain costs such as attorneys' fees, printing, and so on. Often the sum of these costs is material in relation to the bond issue. Theoretically, the costs of issuing bonds is a prepaid expense that should be set up in a separate account and written off over the life of the issue. However, as a practical measure such costs are commonly added to the discount, if the bonds are sold at a discount, or are deducted from the premium, if they are sold at a premium, and are then written off with the premium or discount. This treatment is not theoretically accurate; however, it is long established and has the same effect as the more accurate treatment of such costs as a separate prepaid item.

Redemption of Bonds

Bonds are commonly issued with the provision that they may be redeemed at the option of the issuing corporation, usually upon the payment of a premium. Such bonds are known as *callable bonds*. Corporations commonly insert redemption clauses in deeds of trust because if interest rates decline, it may be advantageous to call and redeem outstanding bonds and to issue in their place new bonds paying a lower rate of interest.

Not all bond issues have a provision giving their issuing company the right to call. However, even though the right to call is not provided in the deed of trust, a company may secure the same effect by purchasing its bonds on the open market. Often such an action is wise when a company has available funds and its bonds are selling on the market at a price below the par value of the bonds plus their unamortized premium or at a price below the par value of the bonds minus their unamortized discount. For example a company has outstanding on their interest date $1,000,000 of bonds upon which there is unamortized premium of $12,000. The bonds are selling at 98.5 per cent of their par value, and the company decides to buy and retire one tenth of the issue. The entry to record the purchase and retirement is:

Apr.	1	Bonds Payable........................	100,000.00	
		Premium on Bonds Payable.............	1,200.00	
		Gain on the Retirement of Bonds....		2,700.00
		Cash.............................		98,500.00

The retirement of the bonds results in a gain of $2,700. This gain is the difference between the cash given and the par value of the bonds retired plus the amount of premium applicable to them.

Convertible Bonds

In order to make a bond issue more attractive, the deed of trust may give owners of the bonds the right to exchange each bond for a fixed number of shares of the issuing company's common stock. Such bonds are known as convertible bonds. They offer investors initial security of investment and, if the issuing company prospers, an opportunity to share in the prosperity by converting their bonds to stock. Conversion is always at the option of the bondholder and is not exercised except when to do so is to the advantage of the bondholder.

When bonds payable are converted into capital stock, the conversion results in the change of creditor equity into ownership equity. The generally accepted rule for determining the accounting measure of the amount contributed for the shares issued to the bondholders is that the book value of the liability becomes the book value of the capital contributed for the new shares. For example, assume that (1) a company has outstanding $1,000,000 of bonds upon which there is unamortized discount of $8,000; (2) the bonds are convertible at the rate of a $1,000 bond for eighteen shares of the company's $50 par value common stock; and (3) $100,000 of the bonds have been presented on their interest date for conversion. The entry to record the conversion is:

May	1	Bonds Payable........................	100,000.00	
		Discount on Bonds Payable.........		800.00
		Common Stock....................		90,000.00
		Premium on Common Stock........		9,200.00
		To record the conversion of bonds.		

Note in the foregoing entry that the book value of the bonds, $99,200, sets the accounting value of the capital contributed. Usually when bonds have a conversion privilege, the privilege is not exercised until the market value of the stock and the normal dividend payments are sufficiently high to make the conversion profitable to the bondholders.

Bond Sinking Fund

Although bonds normally offer a smaller return than do either common or preferred stocks, they appeal to a portion of the investing public. Normally the appeal of bonds results from their fixed return in the form of interest and their greater security. Security is very important to bond investors. A corporation issuing bonds may offer bond investors a measure of security by placing a mortgage on certain of its assets. Often a corporation will offer additional security by agreeing in its deed of trust to create a *bond sinking fund*. A bond sinking fund is a fund of assets accumulated to pay the bondholders when an issue of bonds becomes due.

When a corporation issuing bonds agrees in its deed of trust to create a bond sinking fund, it normally agrees to create the fund by periodically making deposits of cash with a sinking fund trustee. It is the duty of the sinking fund trustee to safeguard the cash deposited, to invest it in good sound securities, and to add the interest or dividends earned on these securities to the sinking fund. Generally, when the bonds become due, it is also the duty of the sinking fund trustee to sell the securities in the sinking fund and to use the proceeds to pay the bondholders. The sinking fund trustee may or may not be the trustee with whom the deed of trust is deposited.

When a sinking fund is created, the amount that must be deposited periodically in the fund in order to provide a sum of money sufficiently large to retire a bond issue at maturity will depend upon the net rate of compound interest that can be earned on the invested funds. The net rate of interest that is earned is a compound rate because the earnings of the fund are continually reinvested by the sinking fund trustee to earn an additional return. The rate is a net rate because the sinking fund trustee commonly deducts the fee for his services from the earnings.

To illustrate the operation of a bond sinking fund, assume that a corporation issues $1,000,000 of ten-year bonds. In its deed of trust the corporation agrees to deposit with a sinking fund trustee at the end of each year in the life of the bond issue a sufficient amount of cash so as to create a fund large enough to retire the bonds at maturity. If the bond sinking fund trustee is able to invest the funds in such a manner as to earn a 3 per cent net return, $87,230.50 must be deposited each year. If $87,230.50 is deposited each year and a 3 per cent return earned, the fund will grow to maturity as shown in Illustration 123.

Illustration 123

End of Year	Amount Deposited	Interest Earned on Fund Balance	Balance in Fund after Deposit and Interest
1	$87,230.50	–0–	$ 87,230.50
2	87,230.50	$ 2,616.90	177,077.90
3	87,230.50	5,312.30	269,620.70
4	87,230.50	8,088.60	364,939.80
5	87,230.50	10,948.20	463,118.50
6	87,230.50	13,893.60	564,242.60
7	87,230.50	16,927.30	668.400.40
8	87,230.50	20,052.00	775,682.90
9	87,230.50	23,270.50	886,183.90
10	87,230.50	26,585.60	1,000,000.00

Calculating the amount that must be deposited in a sinking fund each year in order that the sums deposited and the compound interest earned on these amounts will produce a fund of a required size is a problem reserved for a course in mathematics of finance or advanced accounting. It is deemed sufficient here that the student understand how such a fund operates.

When a sinking fund is created, by periodic deposits, the entry to record the amount deposited with the sinking fund trustee each year appears as follows:

Dec.	31	Bond Sinking Fund..................... 87,230.50	
		Cash.............................	87,230.50
		Deposited cash with the sinking fund trustee.	

Each year the sinking fund trustee invests the amount deposited in the fund, and each year he collects and reports the amount earned on the investments. His sinking fund earnings report results in a journal entry to record the sinking fund income. For example, if $87,230.50 is deposited at the end of the first year in the sinking fund, the accumulation of which is shown in Illustration 123, and 3 per cent net is earned on the amount deposited, the entry to record the sinking fund earnings at the end of the second year appears as follows:

Dec.	31	Bond Sinking Fund.................... 2,616.90	
		Sinking Fund Earnings.............	2,616.90
		To record the earnings of the sinking fund.	

The balance of the Sinking Fund Earnings account appears on the income statement as financial revenue in the other revenues and expenses section.

When bonds mature, it is usually the duty of the sinking fund trustee to convert the investments of the fund into cash and to pay the bondholders. Normally if the sinking fund securities, when sold, produce the amount needed to pay the bondholders, the sinking fund trustee pays the bondholders and notifies the corporation. When the corporation receives notice that its bonds have been paid by the sinking fund trustee, it makes the following entry:

Jan.	3	Bonds Payable.................... 1,000,000.00	
		Bond Sinking Fund.............	1,000,000.00
		To record the payment of our bonds by the sinking fund trustee.	

Sinking fund investments normally earn slightly more or slightly less than anticipated. Consequently, when a sinking fund is liquidated, there is always either a little more or a little less cash in the fund than is needed to pay the bondholders. If there is more cash in a sinking fund than is needed to pay the bondholders, after the bondholders are paid, the excess cash is returned to the corporation by the sinking fund trustee. The entry to record the receipt of returned sinking fund cash is as follows:

Jan.	3	Cash................................	3,105.00	
		Bond Sinking Fund................		3,105.00
		Unused balance of sinking fund returned by the sinking fund trustee.		

If there is an insufficient amount of cash in a sinking fund with which to pay the bondholders when bonds become due, the debtor corporation must pay the amount of the shortage into the fund. The entry to record this is:

Jan.	3	Bond Sinking Fund..................	1,382.20	
		Cash.............................		1,382.20
		To record the payment of cash to the sinking fund trustee to cover the deficit in the fund.		

Bond Sinking Fund Reserve

If a corporation disburses in dividends all the net assets acquired each year through current earnings and in addition transfers still more assets to a sinking fund trustee in the form of sinking fund deposits, the corporation may within a period of a very few years find itself without sufficient assets, particularly current assets, to operate. It may find itself in a position where it can neither pay dividends nor make sinking fund deposits. To prevent this, a corporation required by a deed of trust to make sinking fund deposits may also be required to create a bond sinking fund reserve. The purpose of the reserve is to reduce dividend payments by reducing the balance of the Retained Earnings account available to receive dividend charges.

To illustrate the creation of a bond sinking fund reserve, assume that the deed of trust of the corporation whose bond fund accumulations are shown in Illustration 123 provides for the creation of such a reserve. Assume further that the corporation is required by the deed of trust to appropriate and transfer from its Retained Earnings account to its Bond Sinking Fund Reserve account an amount each year equal to the sum of its sinking fund deposit plus the earnings that year of its sinking fund investments. If the corporation creates the bond sinking fund reserve, it will make the following entry at the end of the first year in the life of the bond issue:

Dec.	31	Retained Earnings....................	87,230.50	
		Bond Sinking Fund Reserve.........		87,230.50
		To record the appropriation of retained earnings equal to the deposit in the bond sinking fund.		

Only $87,230.50 of the balance of the Retained Earnings account is transferred to the bond sinking fund reserve at the end of the first year because the deposit in the sinking fund is made at the end of the year and, consequently, there are no sinking fund earnings. However, at the end of the second year, if the sinking fund deposit earns a net return of 3 per cent, the corporation of the illustration will transfer $89,847.40 of the balance of its Retained Earnings account to the reserve for bond sinking fund. The foregoing amount is determined by adding the amount of the sinking fund deposit, $87,230.50, and the amount of the sinking fund earnings, $2,616.90, as reported by the sinking fund trustee. Likewise, the appropriations will continue to increase throughout the life of the bond issue as the earnings of the bond fund investments increase.

If a bond sinking fund reserve agreement provides only that a corporation must create such a reserve out of retained earnings, it is possible for a corporation having a large balance in its Retained Earnings account at the time it enters into such an agreement to defeat the purpose of the agreement. The corporation can pay out all of its current earnings in dividends and make its appropriations from the balance of the Retained Earnings account accumulated prior to the agreement. To prevent this a sinking fund reserve agreement may provide that a corporation may pay dividends only out of current earnings and only to the extent that such earnings exceed the sinking fund reserve agreement.

After a bond issue matures and is paid, the balance of the bond sinking fund reserve created during the life of the issue can be disposed of only by returning it to the Retained Earnings account. The entry to accomplish this is:

Jan.	15	Bond Sinking Fund Reserve..........	1,000,000.00	
		Retained Earnings..............		1,000,000.00
		To return the balance of the Reserve for Bond Sinking Fund account to the Retained Earnings account.		

A balance in the Retained Earnings account resulting from the return of a bond sinking fund reserve is available for dividend charges. However, cash with which to pay the dividends often is not available because assets equal in amount to the returned retained earnings were accumulated in the bond sinking fund, were used to pay off the bond issue, and, after the bond issue is paid, are in effect invested in the building or other fixed assets acquired through the proceeds of the bond issue.

Long-Term Notes

When bond interest rates are temporarily unfavorable and funds are available from four or five large banks or insurance companies, often long-term notes maturing in two, three, or five years are issued in the place of bonds. Also, in some instances, in order to avoid the costs of issuing bonds and dealing with several thousand bondholders, when funds are available from four or five large banks and insurance companies, long-term notes maturing in ten, twenty, or more years are issued in the place of bonds.

Long-term notes whether maturing in two or three years or in ten or more years are often secured by mortgages. Too, those maturing in ten or more years often provide for sinking funds. Consequently, long-term notes take on the characteristics of both mortgages and bonds. Ordinarily they differ from both only in that they are placed with a few lenders, usually at par. Insofar as accounting is concerned, long-term notes receive the same treatment as mortgages or bonds.

Stocks and Bonds as Investments

A business may buy stocks and bonds as investments. When a company invests in stocks and bonds, the investments are classified as either *temporary investments* or *long-term investments*. The classification depends in each case upon whether the securities are readily marketable and upon the intention of the investing company. If readily marketable stocks and bonds are purchased as an investment and it is the intention of the investing company to keep the securities for only a short period of time, the investment is classified as a temporary investment, a current asset. If the intention is to keep the stocks and bonds for a long period of time, usually more than a year, the investment is classified as a long-term investment.

Temporary investments or short-term investments are often made by a company whose business is of a seasonal nature. Normally, in such a company during the busy season, much of the current assets is invested in inventories and accounts receivable. During the slack or off season these inventories and accounts receivable are turned into cash through sales and collections. Often during the slack season, in order to earn additional income, this temporarily idle cash is invested in high-grade securities. At the beginning of the next busy season these securities are converted back to cash.

Long-term investments are investments of a more or less permanent nature. They differ from temporary investments in that they are to be kept for a long period of time. Long-term investments include funds earmarked for special purposes, such as bond funds and building funds, as well as real estate and other long-term assets owned but not employed in the regular operations of the business. Long-term investments appear on the balance sheet in a classification of their own under the title of "Long-term investments." The long-term investments section appears on the balance sheet immediately following the current asset section.

Stocks and bonds purchased as investments are normally bought through brokers who charge a commission for their services. Brokers acting as agents for their customers buy and sell stocks and bonds on stock exchanges such as the New York Stock Exchange. Hundreds of thousands of shares of stock and thousands of bonds are bought and sold each day on stock exchanges. Each day the prices at which stocks and bonds are sold are published on the financial pages of many newspapers. Prices of stocks are quoted on the basis of dollars and ⅛ dollars per share. For example, a stock quoted at 46⅛ sold for $46.125 per share, and stock quoted at 25½ sold for $25.50 per share. Bonds are normally issued in $1,000 denominations, but their prices are quoted on the basis of $100. For example, a $1,000 bond quoted at 98⅛ sold at $981.25, and a $1,000 bond quoted at 86¼ sold for $862.50.

Temporary Investments.   When stocks and bonds are bought as temporary investments, they are recorded at their total cost, which includes the commission paid to the broker. For example, 1,000 shares of American Sales Corporation common stock are purchased as a temporary investment at 23¼ plus the broker's commission of $200. The entry to record the transaction is as follows:

Sept.	10	American Sales Corporation Stock.......	23,450.00	
		Cash............................		23,450.00
		Purchased 1,000 shares of stock at a cost of $23,250 plus the broker's commission of $200.		

If either dividends or interest are received while stocks and bonds are held as investments, the amount received is classified as financial revenue and appears on the income statement in the financial revenue section. When dividends are received on stocks held as either temporary or long-term investments and interest is received on bonds held as short-term investments, an entry similar to the following is made:

Oct.	5	Cash...............................	1,000.00	
		Investment Earnings...............		1,000.00
		Received a dividend of $1.00 per share on American Sales Corporation common stock.		

When interest is received on bonds held as long-term investments, a different method is commonly used in recording the earnings. This method is discussed later in this chapter under long-term investments.

When stocks and bonds purchased as temporary investments are sold, normally a gain or a loss is incurred. If the amount received from the sale of stocks and bonds held as investments is greater than the original total cost of the investments plus the commission on the sale and other costs, there is a gain. For example, if the 1,000 shares of American Sales Corporation common stock, the purchase of which at a total cost of $23,450 was recorded above, are sold at 25¾ less a commission and taxes on the sale of $205, there is a gain of $2,095, and the transaction is recorded as follows:

Jan.	7	Cash............................	25,545.00	
		American Sales Corporation Stock....		23,450.00
		Gain on the Sale of Investments......		2,095.00
		Sold 1,000 shares of stock for $25,750 less		
		a commission and other costs of $205.		

When stocks and bonds purchased as temporary investments are sold at a price that is less than their total cost plus the sale costs, a loss is incurred. For example, if the shares of American Sales Corporation stock of the previous illustrations are sold for 22½ less a commission and taxes of $196, a loss of $1,146 is incurred, and the transaction is recorded as follows:

Jan.	7	Cash............................	22,304.00	
		Loss on the Sale of Investments..........	1,146.00	
		American Sales Corporation Stock....		23,450.00
		Sold 1,000 shares of stock for $22,500 less		
		a commission and other costs of $196.		

When an income statement is prepared at the end of an accounting period, interest and dividends earned on stocks and bonds plus any gains or losses on the sale of investments are listed at the end of the income statement in the other revenues and expenses section.

If a balance sheet is prepared while temporary investments are held, the amount of such investments should appear as a current asset immediately following the cash. Since temporary investments are current assets, they are normally valued on the balance sheet at the lower of cost or market. Both the cost and present market prices should be shown as follows:

```
Current Assets:
  Cash . . . . . . . . . . . . . . . . . .      $23,000
  Temporary investments, at cost (present
    market price, $14,700) . . . . . . . . .     13,250
  Notes receivable . . . . . . . . . . . .        2,500
```

Long-Term Investments. Stocks purchased as a long-term investment are accounted for in the same manner as stocks purchased as a temporary investment. Likewise, the entry to record the acquisition of bonds purchased as a long-term investment is similar to the entry for stocks purchased as a temporary investment. However, since bonds purchased as a long-term investment are normally purchased at either a premium or at a discount and are often held to maturity, the entry to record the interest earned on bonds held as a long-term investment differs from the entry for interest earned on bonds held as a temporary investment.

To illustrate the entries for bonds purchased as a long-term investment, assume that ten $1,000, 4 per cent, twenty-year bonds on which the interest is paid semiannually are purchased on their interest date fifteen years before maturity at 98¼. The brokerage commission on the purchase is $25, which brings the total cost of the ten bonds to $9,850. The entry to record the purchase of these bonds is as follows:

Jan.	1	Zest Corporation Bonds................ Cash........................... Purchased ten bonds for $9,825 plus a commission of $25.	9,850.00	9,850.00

Bonds differ from stocks in that sooner or later they mature and are normally redeemed at their face value. For example, if the Zest Corporation bonds just illustrated are held to maturity and are redeemed at face value, they will be redeemed at $1,000 each. Consequently, if these bonds are held to maturity, they produce interest at 4 per cent each year they are held plus a gain, at the end of fifteen years, of the $150 difference between their cost and their maturity value. This $150 difference between total cost and maturity value, although it is a combination of discount and commission, is called a discount. A discount on bonds purchased as a long-term investment is treated as an adjustment of the bond interest earned. Normally a portion is amortized on each interest payment date. If a portion of the $150 discount on the Zest Corporation bonds is amortized on each semiannual interest payment date, the entry to record the semiannual receipt of the interest and the amortization of the discount is as follows:

July	1	Cash................................. Zest Corporation Bonds.............. Bond Interest Earned............. Received the interest on the Zest Corporation bonds and amortized one thirtieth of the discount.	200.00 5.00	205.00

In the entry just given, the $5.00 debit to the bond investment account increases the recorded book value of the Zest Corporation bonds. After the entry is posted, the bond investment account appears as follows:

Zest Corporation Bonds

(Cost)	9,850.00	
(Amortization)	5.00	

If these bonds are held to maturity, and the balance of the account is increased $5.00 on each semiannual interest date, when the bonds mature, they will be shown in the account at their full maturity value of $10,000.

Bonds purchased as long-term investments may be sold before maturity. If the Zest Corporation bonds are held three years and then sold, the bond investment account just prior to the sale will show a value of $9,880 for these bonds and will appear as follows:

Zest Corporation Bonds

1960	
Jan. 1	9,850.00
July 1	5.00
1961	
Jan. 1	5.00
July 1	5.00
1962	
Jan. 1	5.00
July 1	5.00
1963	
Jan. 1	5.00

If the bonds are sold after three years for $9,975 less a commission of $25, the entry to record the sale is as follows:

Jan.	1	Cash..................................	9,950.00	
		Zest Corporation Bonds............		9,880.00
		Gain on the Sale of Investments.....		70.00
		Sold Zest Corporation bonds for $9,975 less a commission of $25.		

Bonds may be purchased as long-term investments at a cost greater than their maturity value. In such cases the bonds are recorded at their total cost. The difference between total cost and maturity value is called a premium and is treated as an adjustment of the interest rate. Normally the premium is amortized over the remaining life of the bonds. For example, twenty $1,000, 4 per cent bonds are purchased ten years before maturity at a total cost of $20,250. The entry to record the purchase is:

Jan.	1	Able Corporation Bonds................	20,250.00	
		Cash............................		20,250.00
		Purchased twenty bonds at a premium.		

If the interest on these bonds is paid semiannually, the entry to record the receipt of the interest and to record the amortization of the premium is:

July	1	Cash..................................	400.00	
		Able Corporation Bonds............		12.50
		Bond Interest Earned.............		387.50
		Received interest and amortized one twentieth of the premium.		

Unless there is a material decline in market prices, long-term investments in stocks are shown in the accounts and on the balance sheet at cost, and long-term investments in bonds are shown at cost adjusted for any amortization of premiums or discounts. Since these investments are not for sale, minor fluctuations in market prices are normally ignored.

Bonds Purchased between Interest Dates.   Often bonds are purchased between interest dates. In such cases the purchaser pays for any interest accrued since the last interest payment. For example, if a $1,000, 4½ per cent bond on which interest is paid semiannually on January 1 and July 1 is purchased on March 1, at par, the entry to record the purchase is.

Mar.	1	Best Corporation Bonds................	1,000.00	
		Bond Interest Earned..................	7.50	
		Cash.............................		1,007.50
		Purchased a bond with two months' accrued interest.		

On July 1, the semiannual receipt of interest on this bond is recorded.

July	1	Cash.................................	22.50	
		Bond Interest Earned..............		22.50
		Received interest on the Best Corporation bond.		

The net effect of these two entries on the Bond Interest Earned account is a credit of $15. This is the equivalent of four months' interest, March 1 to July 1, on $1,000 at 4½ per cent.

The Corporation Balance Sheet

Corporation balance sheets are normally longer and more complicated than the balance sheets of either single proprietorships or partnerships. In this and the three previous chapters a number of isolated corporation balance sheet sections have been illustrated. In order to bring all of these illustrations together, the balance sheet of the Best Corporation is shown in Illustration 124 on the next page.

The Corporation Earnings Statement

The detail presented in the income statement or earnings statement, as well as in the balance sheet, depends upon the use for which the statement is prepared, or upon the class of readers to which the statement is to be presented. Statements to management must contain considerably more detail than those presented to stockholders and the general public. Actually, the basic statements to all groups should be compact and concise. Where considerable amount of detail must be reported, this should be done in supplementary schedules. The principal statements should be

Illustration 124
BEST CORPORATION
Balance Sheet, December 31, 1959

ASSETS

Current Assets:			
Cash			$ 15,000
Able Corporation common stock			5,000
Accounts receivable		$ 50,000	
Less: Allowance for bad debts		1,000	49,000
Merchandise inventory			115,000
Subscriptions receivable common stock			15,000
Prepaid expenses			1,000
Total Current Assets			$200,000
Long-Term Investments:			
Bond sinking fund			$ 15,000
Toledo Corporation common stock			5,000
Total Long-Term Investments			20,000
Fixed Assets:			
Land			$ 28,000
Buildings		$190,000	
Less: Accumulated depreciation		30,000	160,000
Store equipment		$ 85,000	
Less: Accumulated depreciation		20,000	65,000
Total Fixed Assets			253,000
Intangible Assets:			
Goodwill			23,000
Deferred Charges:			
Unamortized moving costs			4,000
Total Assets			$500,000

LIABILITIES

Current Liabilities:			
Notes payable		$ 10,000	
Accounts payable		24,000	
State and federal income taxes payable		16,000	
Total Current Liabilities			$ 50,000
Long-Term Liabilities:			
First 5% real estate mortgage bonds, due in 1979		$100,000	
Deduct: Unamortized discount		2,000	98,000
Total Liabilities			$148,000

CONTRIBUTED CAPITAL AND RETAINED EARNINGS

Contributed Capital:			
Common stock, $100 par value per share, author-ized 2,500 shares, issued 2,000 shares		$200,000	
Unissued common stock subscribed, 250 shares		25,000	
Capital contributed by the stockholders in excess of the par value of their shares		33,000	
Total Contributed Capital			$258,000
Retained Earnings:			
Unappropriated retained earnings		$ 69,000	
Appropriated retained earnings:			
Bond sinking fund reserve	$15,000		
Building fund reserve	10,000	25,000	
Total Retained Earnings			94,000
Contributed Capital and Retained Earnings			352,000
Total Liabilities and Capital			$500,000

reasonably short, each being contained on a single page, or in the case of the balance sheet, on not more than two facing pages (arranged for the account form statement).

Statements of earnings illustrated so far in this text have been multiple-step statements; i.e., cost of goods sold is deducted in one step, then operating expenses, then provision for income taxes, etc. This implies a preferential order for the recovery of the costs and expenses. Actually, in theory, there is no such preferential order for there can be no net income from the business unless all costs and expenses are recovered.

To avoid some of the implications of the multiple-step income statement, the single-step form of income statement is being used more and more in published reports. This form of statement may be in considerable detail, but generally when employed for the published statement, it is condensed, as in Illustration 125. Illustration 125 is adapted from a recent annual report to stockholders by the National Dairy Products Corporation (amounts and footnotes are omitted as not being essential to illustration of form).

Illustration 125

NATIONAL DAIRY PRODUCTS CORPORATION
Statement of Earnings for the Year Ended December 31, 19—

Revenue:

Sales less discounts allowed . . . . $ . . . . .
Dividends, interest, and other income . . . .
 Total . . . . $ . . . . .

Revenue Deductions:

Cost of products . . . . $ . . . . .
Delivery expenses . . . .
Selling expenses . . . .
General and administrative expenses . . . .
Miscellaneous charges—net . . . .
Interest on long-term debt . . . .
Provision for federal and Canadian taxes on income . . . .
 Total . . . . $ . . . . .
Net Earnings for the Year . . . . $ . . . . .

QUESTIONS FOR CLASS DISCUSSION

1. What two legal documents are involved when a company borrows by giving a mortgage? What is the purpose of each?
2. What is the primary difference between a share of stock and a bond?
3. What is a deed of trust? What are some of the provisions that are commonly contained in a deed of trust?
4. Define or describe: (a) registered bonds; (b) coupon bonds; (c) serial bonds; (d) sinking fund bonds; (e) redeemable bonds; (f) convertible bonds; and (g) debenture bonds.
5. Company A issued $1,000,000 of 5 per cent, ten-year bonds and sold them at 105; Company B issued $1,000,000 of 4 per cent, ten-year bonds and sold them at 95. Which company paid the higher rate of interest for the use of its borrowed funds?
6. On December 9, 1960, Lock Corporation authorized a $1,000,000, 4 per cent, ten-year bond issue dated January 1, 1961, and with interest payable each January 1 and July 1. On January 1, 1961, $400,000 of the bonds were sold at par. On the following March 1 the remaining $600,000 of bonds were sold

for $582,300 plus accrued interest. On July 1 the first semiannual interest payment was made. Give the entries to record these transactions.

7. On January 1, on their date of issue, Brown Corporation sold and issued at 104 $100,000 of 4½ per cent, ten-year bonds on which the interest is payable on each January 1 and July 1. Give the entries for (a) the sale of the bonds, (b) the semiannual payment of interest and amortization of the premium, and (c) the retirement of the bonds at maturity.

8. On April 1, on their date of issue, Green Corporation sold and issued at 97 $100,000 of 4 per cent, twenty-year bonds on which the interest is payable semiannually on each April 1 and October 1. (a) Give the entries for the sale of the bonds and the first interest payment and discount amortization. (b) Give the adjusting entry that is required each December 31 to record the accrued bond interest expense. (c) Give the entry to reverse the accrued bond interest adjusting entry. (d) Give the entry to record the April 1 bond interest payment and discount amortization.

9. What are the balance sheet classifications of (a) a bond sinking fund, and (b) a reserve for bond sinking fund?

10. On January 1, on their date of issue, Standard Corporation issued at par $1,000,000 of 4 per cent, ten-year bonds. In its deed of trust the corporation agreed to create a bond sinking fund by making annual deposits with a trustee of sums that with the interest earned would create a fund sufficient to retire the bonds at maturity. Assume that the trustee can invest the funds so as to earn 3 per cent, that $87,230.50 is deposited at the end of each year, and that the fund grows to maturity as shown in Illustration 123. (a) Give the entry to record the deposit made at the end of the first year of the life of the bond issue. (b) Give the entry to record the second-year earnings of the sinking fund. (c) Give the entry to record the deposit made at the end of the fifth year. (d) Give the entry to record the fifth-year earnings of the fund.

11. Assume that the bond sinking fund of Question 10 earns slightly more than 3 per cent and at the end of the tenth year has a balance of $1,002,460. Give the entries (a) to record the payment of the bonds by the sinking fund trustee, and (b) to record the return of the balance of the fund to the Standard Corporation.

12. What purposes are served by the creation of (a) a bond sinking fund, and (b) a reserve for bond sinking fund?

13. Assume that in addition to the bond sinking fund the Standard Corporation (Question 10) also agreed to create a reserve for bond sinking fund. The corporation agreed to create the reserve for bond sinking fund by appropriating at the end of each year during the life of its bond issue an amount of retained earnings equal to the sum of its deposit with the sinking fund trustee and the earnings of the sinking fund during that year. If the sinking fund earns a return each year equal to the assumed earnings of the table in Illustration 123, give the entries for the appropriations at the ends of the (a) second, and (b) fifth years in the life of the bond issue.

14. A company purchased 1,000 shares of American Manufacturing Corporation common stock at 42¼ plus a brokerage commission of $450. Later the company sold the stock at 52½ less a brokerage commission of $520. Give the entries to record the transactions.

15. On March 1, a firm purchased ten $1,000, 4 per cent, twenty-year bonds of the Daul Corporation as a temporary investment at 97¼ plus accrued interest and a commission of $25. Interest is payable on the bonds semiannually

on each July 1 and January 1. Give the entries for (a) the purchase of the bonds, and (b) the July 1 semiannual receipt of interest.

16. On October 1, the firm of Question 15 sold the ten $1,000 bonds at 99½ plus accrued interest and less a commission of $25. Give the entry to record the sale.

17. The Hite Corporation purchased as a long-term investment on their interest payment date, ten years before maturity, ten $1,000, 4 per cent bonds of the Blue Company at 104¼ plus a commission of $25. The corporation held the bonds for five years and sold them on their next interest payment date at 101¾ less a commission of $25. Give the entries to record (a) the purchase, (b) the receipt of a semiannual interest payment, and (c) the sale of the bonds.

18. How does the single-step income statement differ from the multiple-step form?

PROBLEMS

Problem 22–1

Stillson Corporation has outstanding 10,000 shares of $100 par value common stock which was issued when the corporation was organized ten years ago. During the ten years of its organization the corporation has grown and now needs additional capital. The corporation's board of directors estimates that with an additional $1,000,000 the company can expect to earn an average of $250,000 per year before bond interest and income taxes. Income taxes are expected to continue at 50 per cent. Three methods of securing the additional $1,000,000 have been suggested to the board of directors. They are 10,000 additional shares of $100 par value common stock; 10,000 shares of $100 par value, 5 per cent preferred stock; and $1,000,000 of 4 per cent, twenty-year bonds.

Required:

Calculate the earnings per share that will accrue to the original common stockholders of Stillson Corporation if (a) additional common stock is issued; (b) preferred stock is issued; and (c) bonds are issued to secure the additional capital. (Assume that the security in each case can be issued at par.)

Problem 22–2

On April 10 of the current year Reed Corporation deposited a deed of trust with the United Trust Company which authorized it to issue $1,000,000 of 5 per cent, twenty-year bonds dated May 1 of the current year and on which the interest is payable on each May 1 and November 1. It then completed during the current and the succeeding year the following transactions:

July   1   Sold the entire issue of bonds for $1,035,700 plus accrued interest.
Nov.   1   Paid the semiannual interest on the bonds.
Dec. 31   Recorded the accrued interest on the bonds.
Jan.   1   Reversed the accrued interest adjusting entry.
May   1   Paid the semiannual interest on the bonds.

Required:

Prepare general journal entries to record the foregoing transactions.

Problem 22–3

On March 15, 1955, Pacific Corporation deposited a deed of trust with Oregon Trust Company which authorized the issue of $1,000,000 of 4 per cent, twenty-year bonds dated April 1, 1955, and paying interest on each April 1 and

October 1. After depositing the deed of trust the corporation completed the following transactions:

1955
Apr. 1 Sold the entire issue of bonds at 97.%
Oct. 1 Paid the semiannual interest on the bonds.
Dec. 31 Recorded the accrued interest on the bonds.
1956
Jan. 1 Reversed the accrued interest adjusting entry.
Apr. 1 Paid the semiannual interest on the bonds.
1960
Apr. 1 Paid the semiannual interest on the bonds.
Apr. 1 Purchased on the open market and retired $100,000 of the bonds. The purchase price, including commissions, was $96,850.

Required:

Prepare general journal entries to record the foregoing transactions.

Problem 22–4

On December 14, 1955, Sudan Corporation deposited a deed of trust with Southeast Trust Company which authorized it to issue $1,000,000 of 4 per cent, four-year bonds. (Four years are an unrealistically small number of years for a bond issue. However, by using such a small number, all of the entries for a bond sinking fund and a bond sinking fund reserve may be required without requiring many repetitive entries.)

In its deed of trust Sudan Corporation agreed to create a bond sinking fund by depositing with a trustee $239,027 at the end of each year in the life of its bond issue. It was assumed that the investments of the sinking fund would earn 3 per cent net and that the fund would grow to maturity as follows:

End of Year	Amount Deposited	Interest Earned on Fund Balance	Balance in Fund after Deposit and Interest
1	$239,027.00	$ 0.00	$ 239,027.00
2	239,027.00	7,170.90	485,224.90
3	239,027.00	14,556.80	738,808.70
4	239,027.00	22,164.30	1,000,000.00

In addition to the bond sinking fund, the Sudan Corporation agreed in its deed of trust to create a bond sinking fund reserve by appropriating retained earnings each year equal to the sum of the sinking fund deposit and the sinking fund earnings of that year.

After depositing the deed of trust, the corporation completed the following transactions:

1956
Jan. 1 Sold the $1,000,000 of bonds at par.
Dec. 31 Deposited $239,027 with the sinking fund trustee.
     31 Transferred $239,027 of retained earnings to the sinking fund reserve.
1957
Dec. 31 Deposited $239,027 with the sinking fund trustee.
     31 Received the sinking fund trustee's report which showed earnings of $7,170.90.

31 Transferred retained earnings to the sinking fund reserve equal to the sum of the sinking fund deposit and the sinking fund earnings.

1958
Dec. 31 Deposited $239,027 with the sinking fund trustee.

31 Received the sinking fund trustee's report which showed earnings of $14,220.50. (This is $336.30 less than was anticipated when the fund was planned. However, it is not sufficient to necessitate a change in the deposits required of the Sudan Corporation.)

31 Appropriated and placed in the reserve for bond sinking fund retained earnings equal to the sum of the sinking fund deposit and the sinking fund earnings.

1959
Dec. 31 Deposited $239,027 with the sinking fund trustee.

31 Received the sinking fund trustee's report which showed sinking fund earnings of $23,695.

31 Appropriated and placed in the reserve for bond sinking fund retained earnings equal to the sum of the sinking fund deposit and the sinking fund earnings.

1960
Jan. 12 Received a report from the sinking fund trustee which showed that the bonds had been paid in full. Attached to the report was a check for the excess of earnings in the bond sinking fund.

15 Returned the balance of the bond sinking fund reserve to unappropriated retained earnings.

Required:

Prepare general journal entries to record the foregoing transactions.

Problem 22–5

A firm completed the following investment transactions during the current year:

Feb. 1 Purchased as a long-term investment ten Bethel Corporation, $1,000, 5 per cent, ten-year bonds on their interest date seven years before maturity. The purchase price was 101½ plus a commission of $25.

Mar. 14 Purchased as a temporary investment 1,000 shares of Lane Corporation common stock at 23¼ plus a commission of $260.

Apr. 1 Purchased as a temporary investment ten Irving Corporation, $1,000. 4 per cent, twenty-year bonds on which interest is payable semiannually on each February 1 and August 1. The purchase price was 97½ plus two months' accrued interest and a commission of $25.

June 5 Received a $0.50 per share dividend on the Lane Corporation stock.

Aug. 3 Received a check for the semiannual interest on the Bethel Corporation bonds. Amortized a portion of the premium paid when these bonds were purchased.

4 Received a check for the semiannual interest on the Irving Corporation bonds.

Oct. 12 Sold the Lane Corporation stock at 27 less a commission and other sale costs of $265.

15 Purchased as a long-term investment 600 shares of Holmes Corporation common stock at 48½ plus a commission of $300.

Nov. 1 Sold the Irving Corporation bonds at 99¼ plus three months' accrued interest and less a commission of $25.

Dec. 15 Received a $0.75 per share dividend on the Holmes Corporation common stock.

Required:

Prepare general journal entries to record the foregoing transactions.

CLASS EXERCISES

Exercise 22–1

Company A sold $100,000 of twenty-year, 5 per cent bonds on their date of issue for $109,600. Company B sold $100,000 of twenty-year, 4 per cent bonds for $89,600 on their date of issue.

Required:

1. Prepare entries for each company to record the sale of the bonds and the payment of the semiannual interest and amortization of the premium or discount.
2. Which company showed the higher interest cost on its income statement?
3. What was the rate of interest expense on the money received in each case?

Exercise 22–2

On May 12 of the current year a firm purchased 100 shares of the $10 par value common stock of Ronald Corporation at 25¼ plus a commission of $25. On July 6 the firm received a 50 per cent stock dividend; and on August 10 it sold 100 of the shares at 20½ less a commission of $20.

Required:

Prepare the entry to record the foregoing transactions.

SUPPLEMENTARY PROBLEMS

Problem 22–A

On July 1 of the current year Westwood Corporation sold $600,000 face value, 4 per cent, twenty-year bonds which were dated March 1 of the current year and upon which the company agreed to pay interest on each March 1 and September 1. The total cash received from the issue by Westwood Corporation was $602,100.

Required:

Prepare general journal entries to record: (*a*) the sale of the bonds; (*b*) the payment of interest on September 1; (*c*) the accrued interest of December 31; (*d*) the reversal of the accrued interest adjusting entry; and (*e*) the payment of interest on March 1 of the following year.

Problem 22–B

During December of the past year Steel Corporation deposited a deed of trust with the trustee of its bondholders that authorized it to issue $1,000,000 of 4 per cent, ten-year bonds dated January 1 of the current year and with interest payable on each July 1 and January 1. On March 1 of the current year, after two months' interest had accrued, the company sold $900,000 of the bonds.

Required:

1. Under the assumption that the company received $923,700 for the bonds and their accrued interest, give the entries for: (*a*) the sale of the bonds; (*b*) the first semiannual interest payment; and (*c*) the second semiannual interest payment.
2. Under the assumption that the company received $882,400 for the bonds and their accrued interest, give the same series of entries.

Problem 22–C

On December 3, 1955, Bronson Corporation deposited a deed of trust with the trustee of its bondholders which authorized the issue of $5,000,000 of 4½ per cent, twenty-year, convertable bonds, dated January 1, 1956, and upon which the interest is payable on each July 1 and January 1. The conversion clause of the deed of trust granted the bondholders the right to convert the bonds before January 1, 1966, into shares of the company's common stock at the rate of eighty shares of $10 par value common stock for each $1,000 bond.

Required:

Give the general journal entries to record the following transactions:

a) On February 1, 1956, sold $4,000,000 of the bonds receiving a total of $4,134,500.
b) Made the first interest payment on July 1, 1956.
c) Made the second interest payment on January 1, 1957.
d) Purchased on the open market on January 1, 1958, and retired one fourth, $1,000,000 par value, of the outstanding bonds. The total cash outlay was $995,000.
e) At the option of the bondholders, on January 1, 1960, converted bonds having a par value of $1,000,000 to common stock.

Chapter

23

MANUFACTURING ACCOUNTING

In previous chapters, this text has given consideration to the accounting problems of service-type companies and merchandising companies. In this and the next two chapters consideration is given to some of the accounting problems of manufacturing enterprises.

Manufacturing and merchandising companies are alike in that both depend for revenue upon the sale of one or more commodities or products. However, they differ in that a merchandising company buys the products it sells in the finished state in which they are sold, while a manufacturing company buys raw materials which it changes by a process of manufacture into the finished products it sells. For example, a shoe store buys shoes and sells them in the same form in which they are purchased; but a manufacturer of shoes buys leather, cloth, glue, nails, and dye and manufactures these items into the shoes he sells.

Some of the similarities and differences of merchandising and manufacturing companies are readily apparent when their income statements are compared. For example, compare the income statement of the Nelson Hardware Company, Illustration 18, on page 108, with that of the Excel Manufacturing Company, Illustration 127, on page 574. Notice that the revenue, selling expense, and general and administrative expense sections of the two statements are quite similar. However, when the cost of goods sold sections are compared, a difference readily becomes apparent. To emphasize this difference, the cost of goods sold section from the income statement of a merchandising company is condensed and reproduced in Illustration 126 below beside that of a manufacturing company.

Illustration 126

MERCHANDISING COMPANY	MANUFACTURING COMPANY
Cost of goods sold:	Cost of goods sold:
Merchandise inventory......$14,200.00	Finished goods inventory...$ 11,200.00
Purchases................. 34,150.00	Cost of goods manufactured
Goods available for sale.....$48,350.00	(see Schedule B-1)..... 170,500.00
Merchandise inventory...... 12,100.00	Goods available for sale....$181,700.00
Cost of Goods Sold.......$36,250.00	Finished goods inventory... 10,300.00
	Cost of Goods Sold.....$171,400.00

Notice in the cost of goods sold section from the income statement of the manufacturing company that the inventories of goods for sale are called *finished goods inventories* rather than merchandise inventories. Notice too that the "Purchases" element on the statement of the merchandising company becomes "Cost of goods manufactured (see Schedule B–1") on the statement of the manufacturing company. These differences grow out of the fact that the merchandising company buys its goods ready for sale, while the manufacturing company creates its salable products from raw materials.

The words "see Schedule B–1" refer the reader of the income statement of the manufacturing company to a separate schedule called a "Schedule of the Cost of Goods Manufactured." This manufacturing schedule or manufacturing statement (see page 575) presents the cost of manufacturing the products created by the manufacturing company. The records and techniques that are used in accounting for the cost of goods manufactured as reported on the manufacturing statement are the distinguishing characteristics of manufacturing accounting.

Systems of Accounting in Manufacturing Companies

The accounting system used by a manufacturing company may be either a so-called general accounting system or it may be a cost accounting system. A general accounting system is a noncost accounting system. It makes use of periodic physical inventories of raw materials, goods in the process of manufacture, and finished goods; and it has as its goal the determination of the total cost of the goods manufactured during each accounting period. A cost accounting system differs from a noncost system in that it makes use of perpetual inventories in accounting for raw materials, goods in process, and finished goods, and has as its goal the determination of the unit cost to manufacture a product or perform a service. General accounting or noncost accounting systems are the subject of this chapter; cost accounting systems are discussed in the next two chapters.

Elements of Manufacturing Costs

A manufacturing company takes *raw materials* and by the application of *direct labor* and *overhead costs* converts these raw materials into finished products. Raw materials, direct labor, and overhead costs are called the "elements of manufacturing costs."

Raw Materials. The raw materials of a manufacturing company are the commodities that enter directly into and become a part of its finished products. Such items as leather, dye, cloth, nails, and glue are raw materials of a shoe manufacturer. Raw materials are often called *direct materials*. Direct materials are materials the costs of which are chargeable directly to the product or products manufactured, and are distinguished from *indirect materials* or factory supplies which are such items as grease and oil for the machinery, cleaning fluids, etc. Indirect materials are accounted for as overhead costs.

The raw materials of a manufacturer are called "raw materials," even though they may not necessarily be in their natural raw state. For example, leather is manufactured from hides, nails are manufactured from iron ore, and cloth is manufactured from cotton. Nevertheless, leather, nails, and cloth are the raw materials of a shoe manufacturer even though they are the finished goods of a previous manufacturer.

Direct Labor. Direct labor is labor, the cost of which is chargeable directly to the product or products manufactured. It is often described as the work of those people who work, either with machines or hand tools, directly on the materials that are converted into the finished product. In manufacturing, direct labor is distinguished from *indirect labor*. Indirect labor is the labor of superintendents, foremen, millwrights, engineers, janitors, and others who do not work directly on the finished products. Indirect labor aids in production; often it makes production possible; but it does not enter directly into the finished product. Indirect labor is accounted for as an overhead cost.

In noncost manufacturing accounting, an account called *Direct Labor* is debited each payday for the sum of the wages of those workers who work directly on the product. Likewise, each payday, the wages of superintendents, foremen, janitors, and other indirect workers are debited to one or more indirect labor accounts. Also, at the end of each accounting period, the amounts of accrued direct labor and accrued indirect labor are recorded in the direct and indirect labor accounts by means of adjusting entries. From this it can be seen that the payroll accounting of a manufacturing company is similar to that of a merchandising company. When a cost accounting system is not involved, no new techniques are required, and only the new direct and indirect labor accounts distinguish the payroll accounting of a manufacturing company from the payroll accounting of a merchandising company.

Overhead Costs. Overhead costs, often called *manufacturing overhead* or *factory burden,* include all of the manufacturing costs incurred in the manufacturing operations other than direct materials and direct labor. Overhead costs may include:

Indirect labor.	Heat, lights, and power.
Factory supplies.	Depreciation of plant and equipment.
Repairs to buildings and equipment.	Patents written off.
Insurance on plant and equipment.	Small tools written off.
Taxes on plant and equipment.	Workmen's compensation insurance.
Taxes on raw materials and work in process.	Payroll taxes on the wages of the factory workers.

Overhead costs do not include selling and administrative expenses. Selling and administrative expenses are not a part of factory overhead costs because they are not incurred in the manufacturing operations. They are not incurred in order to produce the manufactured products.

Payroll taxes on the wages of factory workers are given in the list of overhead cost items, and they are an important item in manufacturing accounting. However, no new techniques in addition to those presented in Chapter 16 are required in accounting for these taxes; consequently, in order to simplify the situations of this and the next two chapters, payroll taxes are omitted in the illustrations.

All overhead costs are recorded in overhead cost accounts in the ledger. The overhead accounts in the ledgers of manufacturing companies vary from company to company. The exact accounts used depend in each case upon the nature of the company and the amount of information desired. For example, one indirect labor account may be used or several accounts, such as Indirect Labor—Superintendence, Indirect Labor—Engineering, Indirect Labor—Building Maintenance, may be opened in the ledger. Or, to illustrate further, one account called "Expired Insurance on Plant Equipment" may be maintained, or an expired insurance account each for buildings and the different kinds of equipment may be used. Regardless of the exact accounts used, the overhead costs are recorded in the accounts in the same manner and with the same types of journals as are selling and administrative expenses. Some, such as indirect labor and light and power, are recorded in a Voucher Register or a Cash Payments Journal as they are paid and are then posted to the ledger accounts. Other overhead costs, such as depreciation and expired insurance, reach the ledger accounts from the General Journal where they are first recorded by means of adjusting entries. Two of the overhead costs mentioned in the list previously given require special attention at this point. They are *patents written off* and *small tools written off*.

Patents

Patents are granted by the federal government to encourage the invention of new machines and mechanical devices. A patent gives its owner the exclusive right to manufacture the patented machine or mechanical device for a period of seventeen years. All of the costs of developing a patented machine or mechanical device, or the costs of acquiring the patent rights to a machine or device developed by someone else, are debited to an asset account called "Patents." The Patents account is classified for balance sheet purposes as an *intangible asset*. An intangible asset is an asset, the value of which results solely from the rights it gives its owner. Other intangible assets are trade-marks, copyrights, and franchises.

Although a patent gives its owner the exclusive right to manufacture a patented device for a period of seventeen years, the cost of the patent should be written off over a shorter period of time if its useful life is estimated to be less than seventeen years. For example, if a patented device costing $20,000 has an estimated useful life of only ten years, the following adjusting entry is made at the end of each full accounting year during its useful life:

Dec.	31	Patents Written Off......................	2,000.00	
		Patents............................		2,000.00
		To write off one tenth of the expired patent cost.		

The debit of this entry causes the $2,000 of patents cost to appear on the manufacturing statement as one of the manufacturing costs. The credit of the entry directly reduces the balance sheet value of the Patents account. Normally, patents are written off directly to the Patents account as in this entry.

Small Tools

In all factories the cost of an asset such as a large item of machinery or equipment is debited to a fixed asset account when the asset is acquired. This cost is then charged to manufacturing overhead throughout the life of the asset by means of depreciation adjusting entries. The recording of depreciation is a very satisfactory method for charging to manufacturing overhead the cost of a large machine. However, the recording of depreciation is normally not a satisfactory way to charge the cost of small hand tools to overhead.

The small hand tools of a factory are normally of little individual value. Yet, because of their great number, their total value is often large. The great number of small tools in a factory along with their small individual value and the ease with which they are lost and broken make the recording of depreciation on small hand tools somewhat impractical. Consequently, in many factories small hand tools are accounted for on an inventory basis. The cost of the small tools on hand at the beginning of an accounting period is shown by the debit balance of an account called "Small Tools." As wrenches, hammers, drills, and other small tools are purchased throughout each accounting period, their cost is debited to the Small Tools account. At the end of each accounting period, the small tools on hand in the factory are inventoried. Often, since the lives of all small tools are short, all usable tools are listed on the inventory at cost. Normally the cost of the tools remaining at the end of an accounting period is less than the cost of the tools on hand at the beginning plus the cost of the tools purchased during the period. The difference represents the cost of the tools broken, lost, and stolen. At the end of each accounting period an adjusting entry is made to reduce the balance of the Small Tools account to the cost of the tools remaining on hand. This entry appears as follows:

Dec.	31	Small Tools Written Off................	200.00	
		Small Tools.....................		200.00
		To adjust the balance of the Small Tools account to the cost of the tools on hand.		

The debit of the entry just given records as an overhead item the cost of the tools lost, broken, and stolen. The credit of the entry reduces the balance sheet value of the Small Tools account to the cost of the tools remaining on hand.

Accounts Peculiar to a Manufacturing Company

Because of its manufacturing operations, the ledger of a manufacturing company normally contains more accounts than the ledger of a merchandising company. Some of the accounts are the same as those found in the ledger of a merchandising company. For example, accounts such as Cash, Accounts Receivable, Sales, and many selling and administrative expenses are found in the ledgers of both manufacturing and merchandising companies. However, many accounts are peculiar to a manufacturing company. For instance, accounts such as Machinery and Equipment, Accumulated Depreciation of Machinery and Equipment, Factory Supplies, Factory Supplies Used, Raw Materials Inventory, Raw Material Purchases, Goods in Process Inventory, Finished Goods Inventory, and Manufacturing Summary are normally found only in the ledgers of manufacturing companies. Some of these accounts require special attention.

Raw Material Purchases Account.   When a general accounting system is in use, the costs of all raw materials purchased by a manufacturing company for use in the manufacture of its products are debited to an account called "Raw Material Purchases." Normally, when raw materials are purchased, each purchase is first recorded in a Voucher Register or a Raw Material Purchases Journal. Usually a special column is provided in either the Voucher Register or the journal to receive all the debits resulting from the individual purchases. This makes it possible to post all of the individual raw material purchases to the Raw Material Purchases account in one amount at the end of the month. After all posting is completed, the balance of the Raw Material Purchases account shows the amount of raw materials purchased. At the end of the accounting period, the balance of the Raw Material Purchases account is transferred by a closing entry to the Manufacturing Summary account. This is similar to the way the balance of the Purchases account of a merchandising company is transferred to a Cost of Goods Sold account.

Raw Materials Inventory Account.   The raw material inventories of a manufacturing company are treated in much the same manner as the merchandise inventories of a merchandising company. When a perpetual inventory system is not in use, the debit balance of the Raw Materials Inventory account shows the cost of the raw materials on hand at the beginning of the accounting period. Also when a perpetual inventory system is not in use, the cost of the raw materials on hand at the end of each accounting period is found by taking a physical inventory. Then, in the closing procedure at the end of each accounting period, the amount of the beginning inventory of raw materials is transferred from the Raw Materials Inventory account to the debit side of the Manufacturing Summary account by debiting the Manufacturing Summary account and crediting Raw Materials Inventory. After this, the amount of the ending raw materials inventory is credited to the Manufacturing Summary account and debited to the Raw Materials Inventory account. This is similar to the treatment given to the merchandise inventories of a merchandising company. The procedures are the same; only the accounts differ.

Goods in Process Inventory Account. Normally, at any time, all manufacturing companies, excepting those in which the process of manufacture consists of a single operation, have on hand partially completed products. These are products that have received a portion or all of their raw materials and have had some direct labor and overhead costs applied but that are not completed. These unfinished products in the process of manufacture are called *goods in process* or *work in process*. In a company in which a cost accounting system is not in use the cost of the goods in process at the end of an accounting period is found by taking a physical inventory. (Physical inventories of goods in process are discussed in more detail beginning on page 581.) The physical inventory of goods in process is recorded at the end of each accounting period in an account called "Goods in Process Inventory" or "Work in Process Inventory."

The treatment of the Goods in Process Inventory account is similar to the treatment of the Raw Materials Inventory account. At the end of each accounting period, before closing entries are made, the balance of the Goods in Process Inventory account shows the cost of the goods in process at the beginning of the accounting period. This beginning balance is transferred to the Manufacturing Summary account with a closing entry that has a debit to the Manufacturing Summary account and a credit to Goods in Process Inventory. The amount of the ending inventory of goods in process is then debited to the Goods in Process Inventory account and credited to the Manufacturing Summary account.

Manufacturing Summary Account. At the end of each accounting period, all of the accounts the balances of which enter into the calculation of the cost of goods manufactured are closed to and their balances are summarized in an account called "Manufacturing Summary." After all of the accounts the balances of which enter into the calculation of the cost of goods manufactured are closed to the Manufacturing Summary account, the balance of the Manufacturing Summary account is equal to the cost of the goods manufactured. This balance is then in turn closed and transferred to the Income Summary account. Notice that this is the identical treatment given to the Cost of Goods Sold account as described in Chapter 6.

Finished Goods Inventory Account. The finished goods of a manufacturing company are its manufactured products in their completed state ready for sale. The finished goods on hand at the end of an accounting period, when a cost accounting system is not in use, are determined by a physical inventory. (Physical inventories of finished goods are discussed in more detail beginning on page 381.) The finished goods inventory of a manufacturing company is similar to the merchandise inventory of a merchandising company in that both are goods ready for sale. Actually, the only difference is that the manufacturing company creates its finished goods from raw materials, while the merchandising company purchases its goods in their finished state.

As just stated, the finished goods inventory of a manufacturing company is similar to the merchandise inventory of a merchandising company in that both are goods in their finished state ready for sale. Furthermore, they are also alike in that they both receive the same treatment in the accounts and on the work sheet. At the end of each accounting period, the debit balance of the Finished Goods Inventory account shows the amount of finished goods that was on hand at the beginning of the period. This balance is transferred to the Income Summary account with a closing entry that has a debit to Income Summary and a credit to Finished Goods Inventory. Also, the Income Summary account is credited and the Finished Goods Inventory account is debited for the amount of the ending finished goods inventory. This is the identical treatment given to the merchandise inventory of a merchandising company when a Cost of Goods Sold account is not used.

The three inventories, raw materials, goods in process, and finished goods are a distinguishing characteristic of manufacturing. All three are classified as current assets for balance sheet purposes.

Income Statement of a Manufacturing Company

As previously stated, the income statement of a manufacturing company normally differs from that of a merchandising company only in the cost of goods sold section. On the income statement of a manufacturing company, in this section, the item "Cost of goods manufactured" replaces the item "Purchases." Also, finished goods inventories are substituted for merchandise inventories. In all other respects the statements are alike. To illustrate these points, the income statement of the Excel Manufacturing Company is shown in Illustration 127 on the following page.

Notice in the income statement of the Excel Manufacturing Company that only the total of the cost of goods manufactured is shown in the cost of goods sold section. The total of the cost of goods manufactured is an important item. Yet, this total alone does not show a sufficient amount of information for managerial purposes. While it is possible to expand the cost of goods sold section of the income statement in order to show the details of the cost of goods manufactured, to do so is not a common practice. The common practice is to give only the total of the cost of goods manufactured in the cost of goods sold section and to attach a supporting schedule showing the details of the cost of the goods manufactured. This supporting schedule is called a "schedule of the cost of goods manufactured" or a "manufacturing statement."

Manufacturing Statement

The three cost elements of a manufacturing process are raw materials, direct labor, and overhead costs. A manufacturing statement is normally so constructed as to emphasize these elements. Notice in the manufacturing statement shown in Illustration 128 that the first section of the statement presents the cost of the raw materials used. Also observe that the manner of presentation is the same as that used on the income statement of a merchandising company to present the cost of the goods purchased and sold.

Illustration 127

THE EXCEL MANUFACTURING COMPANY
Income Statement for Year Ended December 31, 19--

Revenue:			
Sales			$310,000
Cost of goods sold:			
Finished goods inventory, January 1, 19--		$ 11,200	
Cost of goods manufactured (see Schedule			
B-1).		170,500	
Goods available for sale.		$181,700	
Finished goods inventory, December 31, 19--		10,300	
Cost of goods sold.			171,400
Gross profit.			$138,600
Operating expenses:			
Selling expenses:			
Sales salaries.	$18,000		
Advertising expense	5,500		
Delivery salaries	12,000		
Shipping supplies used.	250		
Delivery equipment insurance expired. .	300		
Depreciation of delivery equipment. . .	2,100		
Total Selling Expenses.		$ 38,150	
General and administrative expenses:			
Office salaries	$ 3,700		
Officers' salaries.	12,000		
Miscellaneous general expense	200		
Bad debts expense	1,550		
Office supplies used.	100		
Depreciation of office equipment. . . .	200		
Total General and Administrative			
Expenses.		17,750	
Total Operating Expenses.			55,900
Operating income.			$ 82,700
Financial expense:			
Bond interest expense			4,000
Net income before state and federal income			
taxes			$ 78,700
Provision for state and federal income taxes			39,600
Net Income.			$ 39,100

The so-called second section of a manufacturing statement shows the cost of the direct labor applied to production. Direct labor is the labor of employees, the cost of which is chargeable directly to the manufactured products.

The third section of the manufacturing statement shows the overhead costs applied to production during the period. If the overhead accounts are not too numerous, the balance of each account is often listed in this section. If the overhead accounts are numerous, only the total of all may be shown. In such cases the total is supported by a separate attached schedule showing the amount of each individual overhead cost.

In the last section of the manufacturing statement the calculation of the cost of goods manufactured is completed. Here the beginning goods in process inventory is added to the sum of the direct materials, direct labor, and the sum of the manufacturing overhead costs to secure the cost of all of the goods in process during the period. Then, from the cost of all the goods in process during the period, the cost of the goods still in process at the end of the period is subtracted to secure the cost of the goods manufactured.

Illustration 128

THE EXCEL MANUFACTURING COMPANY　　　　　Schedule B-1
Schedule of the Cost of Goods Manufactured
For Year Ended December 31, 19--

Raw materials:			
Raw materials inventory, January 1, 19--		$ 8,000	
Raw materials purchased.	$85,000		
Freight on raw materials purchased	1,500		
Delivered cost of raw materials purchased. . . .		86,500	
Raw materials available for use.		$94,500	
Raw materials inventory, December 31, 19--		9,000	
Raw materials used			$ 85,500
Direct labor			60,000
Overhead costs:			
Indirect labor		$ 9,000	
Supervision		6,000	
Power		2,600	
Repairs and maintenance.		2,500	
Factory taxes.		1,900	
Factory supplies used.		500	
Factory insurance expired.		1,200	
Small tools written off.		200	
Depreciation of machinery and equipment.		3,500	
Depreciation of building		1,800	
Patents written off		800	
Total Overhead Costs			30,000
Total Manufacturing Costs.			$175,500
Add: Goods in process inventory, January 1, 19--			2,500
Total Goods in Process during the Year . . .			$178,000
Deduct: Goods in process inventory, December 31, 19--			7,500
Cost of Goods Manufactured			$170,500

The manufacturing statement is prepared from the Manufacturing Statement columns of the manufacturing work sheet. All of the items that appear on the manufacturing statement are summarized in these Manufacturing Statement columns. All that is required in the construction of the manufacturing statement from the Manufacturing Statement columns of the work sheet is a rearrangement of the items into the proper manufacturing statement order. The manufacturing work sheet is shown in Illustration 129 on pages 578 and 579.

Work Sheet for a Manufacturing Company

The primary difference between the work sheet of a merchandising company and the work sheet of a manufacturing company using a noncost system is that in the work sheet of the manufacturing company two additional columns called the "Manufacturing Statement columns" are added. Normally, Manufacturing Statement columns are placed between the Adjustments columns and the Income Statement columns. In such cases the Adjusted Trial Balance and Cost of Goods Sold columns are omitted. When the Adjusted Trial Balance columns are omitted, the items of the Trial Balance columns are combined with the items of the Adjustments columns and sorted to the proper Manufacturing Statement, Income Statement, or Balance Sheet columns in a single operation. When the Cost of Goods Sold columns are omitted, the items entering into the calculation of the cost of goods sold are summarized in the Income Statement columns. Adjusted Trial Balance and Cost of Goods Sold columns may be placed on the work sheet of a manufacturing company. If Adjusted Trial Balance and Cost of Goods Sold columns are used, the Manufacturing Statement columns are placed between the Adjusted Trial Balance columns and the Cost of Goods Sold columns.

The work sheet of a manufacturing company is prepared in the same manner as the work sheet of a merchandising company. First a trial balance is prepared in the Trial Balance columns in the usual manner. The information for the adjustments is assembled, and the adjustments are made in the Adjustments columns. The work sheet adjustments of a manufacturing company are made in the same way as those of a merchandising company. The adjustments information for the work sheet shown in Illustration 129 is as follows:

a) Estimated bad debt losses ½ per cent of sales, or $1,550.
b) Office supplies used, $100.
c) Shipping supplies used, $250.
d) Factory supplies used, $500.
e) Expired insurance on factory, $1,200; and expired insurance on the delivery equipment, $300.
f) The inventory of small tools reveals that only $1,100 of small tools remain on hand in a usable state.
g) Depreciation of delivery equipment, $2,100.
h) Depreciation of office equipment, $200.
i) Depreciation of factory machinery and equipment, $3,500.
j) Depreciation of factory building, $1,800.
k) Yearly write-off of one seventeenth of the development cost of patents, $800.
l) Accrued wages: direct labor, $400; indirect labor, $60; delivery salaries, $80. All other employees paid on a monthly basis on the last day of each month.
m) One-half year of bond interest expense accrued, $2,000.

After the adjustments are completed on the manufacturing work sheet, the items in the Trial Balance columns are combined with the items of the Adjustments columns and are sorted to the proper Manufacturing Statement, Income Statement, or Balance Sheet columns. No new techniques are required here. However, certain of the trial balance items merit special attention.

Notice that the beginning raw materials and goods in process inventories are placed in the Manufacturing Statement debit column. Then at the bottom of the work sheet the ending raw materials inventory of $9,000 and the ending goods in process inventory of $7,500 are entered in the Manufacturing Statement credit column and in the Balance Sheet debit column. These procedures have the effect of adding the beginning raw materials and goods in process inventories to the costs of manufacturing and of deducting the ending inventories of raw materials and goods in process. Notice also that the beginning finished goods inventory is entered in the Income Statement debit column and that the $10,300 ending inventory of finished goods is entered in the Income Statement credit column and in the Balance Sheet debit column. This is the identical treatment given the merchandise inventories of a merchandising company when Cost of Goods Sold columns are not used. Many beginning accounting students have difficulty sorting the inventories of a manufacturing company to the proper columns on the manufacturing work sheet. This difficulty will not arise if it is remembered that the raw materials and goods in process have to do with manufacturing and go into the Manufacturing Statement columns, and that the finished goods inventory is the equivalent of the merchandise inventory of a merchandising company and is treated in the same manner.

Notice that in addition to the raw materials and goods in process inventories, the direct labor and manufacturing overhead costs are also summarized in the Manufacturing Statement columns. After the raw materials, goods in process, direct labor, and overhead costs are summarized in the manufacturing columns, the difference between the debit and credit Manufacturing Statement columns is the cost of the goods manufactured. This cost of goods manufactured is entered in the Manufacturing Statement credit column in order to make the debit and credit columns equal. It is also carried into the Income Statement debit column in the same debit position as the Purchases account of a merchandising company.

The Income Statement columns and Balance Sheet columns of a manufacturing work sheet, as well as the items in these columns, are treated in the same manner as they are treated on the work sheet of a merchandising company. Consequently, these columns need no further attention here.

Adjusting Entries

The adjusting entries of a manufacturing company are prepared in the same way as those of a merchandising company. An adjusting entry is prepared in the General Journal for each adjustment appearing in the Adjustments columns of the work sheet. No new techniques are required here.

Illustration 129

THE EXCEL MANUFACTURING COMPANY

Manufacturing Work Sheet for Year Ended December 31, 19—

Account Titles	Trial Balance Dr.	Trial Balance Cr.	Adjustments Dr.	Adjustments Cr.	Mfg. Statement Dr.	Mfg. Statement Cr.	Income Statement Dr.	Income Statement Cr.	Balance Sheet Dr.	Balance Sheet Cr.
Cash	11,000								11,000	
Accounts receivable	32,000								32,000	
Allowance for bad debts		300		(a) 1,550						1,850
Raw materials inventory	8,000				8,000					
Goods in process inventory	2,500				2,500					
Finished goods inventory	11,200						11,200			
Office supplies	150			(b) 100					50	
Shipping supplies	300			(c) 250					50	
Factory supplies	750			(d) 500					250	
Prepaid insurance	1,800			(e) 1,500					300	
Small tools	1,300			(f) 200					1,100	
Delivery equipment	9,000								9,000	
Accumulated depreciation of delivery equipment		2,400		(g) 2,100						4,500
Office equipment	1,700								1,700	
Accumulated depreciation of office equipment		1,200		(h) 200						1,400
Machinery and equipment	132,000								132,000	
Accumulated depreciation of machinery and equipment		15,000		(i) 3,500						18,500
Factory building	190,000								190,000	
Accumulated depreciation of factory building		18,000		(j) 1,800						19,800
Land	9,500								9,500	
Patents	12,000			(k) 800					11,200	
Accounts payable		14,000								14,000
First-mortgage bonds payable		100,000								100,000
Common stock		150,000								150,000
Retained earnings		33,660								33,660
Sales		310,000						310,000		
Raw material purchases	85,000				85,000					
Freight on raw materials	1,500				1,500					
Direct labor	59,600		(l) 400		60,000					
Indirect labor	8,940		(l) 60		9,000					

	Col 1	Col 2	Col 3	Col 4	Col 5	Col 6	Col 7	Col 8	Col 9	Col 10
Supervision	6,000				6,000					
Power expense	2,600				2,600					
Repairs and maintenance	2,500				2,500					
Factory taxes	1,900				1,900					
Sales salaries	18,000						18,000			
Advertising expense	5,500						5,500			
Delivery salaries	11,920		(l) 80				12,000			
Office salaries	3,700						3,700			
Officers' salaries	12,000						12,000			
Miscellaneous general expense	200						200			
Bond interest expense	2,000		(m) 2,000				4,000			
	644,560	644,560								
Bad debts expense			(a) 1,550				1,550			
Office supplies used			(b) 100				100			
Shipping supplies used			(c) 250				250			
Factory supplies used			(d) 500		500					
Factory insurance expired			(e) 1,200		1,200					
Delivery equipment insurance expired			(e) 300				300			
Small tools written off			(f) 200		200					
Depreciation of delivery equipment			(g) 2,100				2,100			
Depreciation of office equipment			(h) 200				200			
Depreciation of machinery and equipment			(i) 3,500		3,500					
Depreciation of building			(j) 1,800		1,800					
Patents written off			(k) 800		1,800					
Accrued wages payable				(l) 540						540
Bond interest payable				(m) 2,000						2,000
			15,040	15,040						
Raw materials inventory to Balance Sheet columns						9,000			9,000	
Goods in process inventory to Balance Sheet columns						7,500			7,500	
Finished goods inventory to Balance Sheet columns								10,300	10,300	
Cost of goods manufactured to Income Statement columns					170,500	170,500				
					187,000	187,000	241,600	320,300	424,950	346,250
State and federal income taxes							39,600			39,600
Net Income							39,100			39,100
							320,300	320,300	424,950	424,950

Closing Entries

When the accounts of a manufacturing company are closed, those showing manufacturing costs are closed to and are summarized in the Manufacturing Summary account. The entries to close the manufacturing accounts of Excel Manufacturing Company are as follows:

Dec.	31	Manufacturing Summary...............	187,000.00	
		Raw Materials Inventory...........		8,000.00
		Goods in Process Inventory........		2,500.00
		Raw Material Purchases...........		85,000.00
		Freight on Raw Material Purchases...		1,500.00
		Direct Labor.....................		60,000.00
		Indirect Labor...................		9,000.00
		Supervision......................		6,000.00
		Power Expense....................		2,600.00
		Repairs and Maintenance...........		2,500.00
		Factory Taxes....................		1,900.00
		Factory Supplies Used.............		500.00
		Factory Insurance Expired.........		1,200.00
		Small Tools Written Off...........		200.00
		Depreciation of Machinery and Equipment...........................		3,500.00
		Depreciation of Building...........		1,800.00
		Patents Written Off...............		800.00
		To close those manufacturing accounts having debit balances.		
	31	Raw Materials Inventory..............	9,000.00	
		Goods in Process Inventory...........	7,500.00	
		Manufacturing Summary..........		16,500.00
		To set up the ending raw materials and goods in process inventories and to remove their balances from the Manufacturing Summary account.		

The foregoing entries are taken from the information in the Manufacturing Statement columns of the work sheet of Illustration 129. Compare the first entry with the information shown in the Manufacturing Statement debit column. Observe that the second entry has the effect of subtracting the ending inventories of raw materials and goods in process from the manufacturing costs shown in the debit column.

The effect of the foregoing entries is to cause the Manufacturing Summary account to have a debit balance equal to the $170,500 cost of goods manufactured. This $170,500 debit balance of the Manufacturing Summary account is closed to the Income Summary account along with the cost and expense accounts, the balance of which appear in the Income Statement debit column. Observe the last credit in the following entry which is used to close the debit balance accounts, the balances of which appear in the Income Statement column of the work sheet of Illustration 129.

Dec.	31	Income Summary......................	241,600.00	
		Finished Goods Inventory..........		11,200.00
		Sales Salaries.....................		18,000.00
		Advertising Expense...............		5,500.00
		Delivery Salaries..................		12,000.00
		Office Salaries....................		3,700.00
		Officers' Salaries.................		12,000.00
		Miscellaneous General Expense......		200.00
		Bond Interest Expense.............		4,000.00
		Bad Debts Expense...............		1,550.00
		Office Supplies Used..............		100.00
		Shipping Supplies Used............		250.00
		Delivery Equipment Insurance Expired......		300.00
		Depreciation of Delivery Equipment..		2,100.00
		Depreciation of Office Equipment.....		200.00
		Manufacturing Summary..........		170,500.00
		To close the income statement accounts having debit balances.		

After the foregoing entry, the remainder of the income statement accounts of Illustration 129 are closed as follows:

Dec.	31	Finished Goods Inventory.............	10,300.00	
		Sales............................	310,000.00	
		Income Summary.................		320,300.00
		To close the Sales account and to bring the ending finished goods inventory on the books.		
	31	Income Summary......................	39,600.00	
		State and Federal Income Taxes Payable.........................		39,600.00
		To provide for state and federal income taxes.		
	31	Income Summary......................	39,100.00	
		Retained Earnings................		39,100.00
		To close the Income Summary account.		

Inventory Valuation Problems of a Manufacturing Company

In a manufacturing company using a noncost system, at the end of each accounting period, a value must be placed on the inventories of raw materials, goods in process, and finished goods. No particular problems are encountered in valuing raw materials. This is because the items of the raw materials inventory are in the same form in which they were purchased from a previous producer and a cost or market price may be applied. All that is required is that the items of raw materials be counted, weighed, or measured and a cost or market price applied. This seldom creates a problem. However, placing a value on the goods in process and finished goods inventories is generally not so easy. This is because items of goods in process and finished goods consist of raw materials to which a certain amount of labor and overhead costs have been applied in the process of manufacture. They are not items in the same form in which they were purchased. Consequently, a price paid to a previous producer cannot be used to measure their inventory value. Instead, the inventory value placed on each item of goods in process and finished goods must be built up by adding together estimates of the raw materials, direct labor, and overhead costs applicable to the item.

Estimating the raw materials applicable to an item of goods in process or finished goods is usually not too difficult. Likewise, from its state of completion, a foreman or other responsible plant official can normally make a reasonably accurate estimate of the direct labor applicable to an item of goods in process or finished goods. Usually these estimates do not present a difficult problem. However, estimating the overhead costs that are applicable to an item of goods in process or finished goods presents more of a problem. Often this problem is solved by assuming that overhead costs are closely related to direct labor. This is often a fair assumption. Often there is a close relationship between direct labor and items of overhead such as supervision, power, repairs, depreciation, etc. When this relationship is used to apply overhead to items of goods in process and finished goods, it is assumed that the relationship of the overhead to the direct labor in each item of goods in process and finished goods is the same as the relationship between the total overhead of the factory and the total direct labor of the factory.

For example, an examination of the manufacturing statement of the Excel Manufacturing Company in Illustration 128 will show that the total direct labor of the company was $60,000 and the overhead costs were $30,000. Or, an examination of the manufacturing statement will show that during the year the company applied in the production of all of its products $2.00 of direct labor for each $1.00 of overhead costs. Or, during the year the overhead costs in all of the production of the company was 50 per cent of the direct labor cost.

OVERHEAD COSTS $30,000 ÷ DIRECT LABOR, $60,000 = 50 PER CENT

Consequently, in estimating the overhead costs applicable to an item of its goods in process or finished goods, the Excel Manufacturing Company may assume that this 50 per cent overhead rate is applicable. It may assume that if in all of its production the overhead costs applied were 50 per cent of the direct labor, then in each item of the goods in process and finished goods inventories this relationship also exists.

If the Excel Manufacturing Company makes this assumption and its goods in process inventory consists of 1,000 units of Item X with each unit containing $3.75 of raw material and having $2.50 of applicable direct labor, then the goods in process inventory is valued as shown in Illustration 130.

Illustration 130

Product	Raw Materials Contained	Direct Labor Applicable	Overhead (50 Per Cent of Direct Labor)	Estimated Total Unit Cost	No. of Units	Total Inventory Valuation
Item X	$3.75	$2.50	$1.25	$7.50	1,000	$7,500.00

The Excel Manufacturing Company may use the same procedure in valuing the items of its finished goods inventory.

QUESTIONS FOR CLASS DISCUSSION

1. How does the income statement of a manufacturing company differ from the income statement of a merchandising company?
2. What are the three elements of manufacturing costs?
3. What are: (a) direct labor, (b) indirect labor, (c) direct material, (d) indirect material, and (e) overhead costs?
4. Name several items that are accounted for as overhead costs by a manufacturing company.
5. What is a patent? What is the legal life of a patent? Is the legal life of a patent the same as its useful or economic life?
6. Standard Company has a patented device that cost $51,000 to develop. Give the entry to record the yearly expiration of the patent on this device under the assumption that the patent will have a useful or economic life of ten years.
7. Explain why small tools are often accounted for on an inventory basis.
8. Name several accounts that are often found in the ledgers of both manufacturing and merchandising companies. Name several accounts that are found only in the ledgers of manufacturing companies.
9. What three new inventory accounts appear in the ledger of a manufacturing company?
10. How are the raw material inventories handled on the work sheet of a manufacturing company? How are the goods in process inventories handled? How are the finished goods inventories handled?
11. Which inventories of a manufacturing company receive the same work sheet treatment as the merchandise inventories of a merchandising company?
12. Which inventories of a manufacturing company appear on its manufacturing statement? Which appear on the income statement?
13. What accounts are summarized in the Manufacturing Summary account? What accounts are summarized in the Income Summary account?
14. What are the three manufacturing cost elements emphasized on the manufacturing statement?

15. What items are carried into the Manufacturing Statement columns of the manufacturing work sheet? What items are carried into the Income Statement columns? What items are carried into the Balance Sheet columns?

16. Why is the cost of the goods manufactured entered in the Manufacturing Statement credit column of the manufacturing work sheet and again in the Income Statement debit column?

17. May prices paid to a previous manufacturer for items of raw materials determine the balance sheet value of the items of the raw materials inventory? Why? May such prices also determine the balance sheet values of the goods in process and finished goods inventories? Why?

18. Standard Company used an overhead rate of 80 per cent of direct labor cost to apply overhead to the items of its goods in process inventory. If the manufacturing statement of the company showed total overhead costs of $45,000, how much direct labor did it show?

19. The manufacturing statement of a company showed the following costs: materials, $52,000; direct labor, $27,000; and overhead costs, $40,500. (a) If the company's overhead rate was based upon direct labor cost, what was the overhead rate? (b) If the company's $13,500 ending goods in process inventory had direct labor costs of $3,000, what was its direct material costs?

PROBLEMS

Problem 23–1

Following are the Manufacturing Statement columns from the work sheet of Symplex Company as of the end of the current year:

	Manufacturing Statement	
	Debit	Credit
Raw materials inventory.........................	11,500	
Good in process inventory.......................	15,700	
Raw material purchases.........................	22,200	
Direct labor...................................	24,000	
Indirect labor.................................	4,700	
Supervision...................................	8,000	
Power..	6,200	
Repairs to machinery...........................	1,700	
Rent of factory building........................	12,000	
Miscellaneous manufacturing costs...............	700	
Raw materials inventory to balance sheet..........		8,400
Goods in process inventory to balance sheet........		12,200
Cost of goods manufactured to income statement...		86,100
	106,700	106,700

Required:

Prepare a manufacturing statement for the firm.

Problem 23–2

The manufacturing work sheet of Barnhart Company is reproduced on the opposite page.

BARNHART COMPANY
Manufacturing Work Sheet for Year Ended December 31, 19—

Account Titles	Trial Balance Dr.	Trial Balance Cr.	Adjustments Dr.	Adjustments Cr.	Mfg. Statement Dr.	Mfg. Statement Cr.	Income Statement Dr.	Income Statement Cr.	Balance Sheet Dr.	Balance Sheet Cr.
Cash	15,500								15,500	
Accounts receivable	17,500								17,500	
Allowance for bad debts		200		(a) 350						550
Raw materials inventory	17,800				17,800					
Goods in process inventory	6,100				6,100					
Finished goods inventory	11,200						11,200			
Factory supplies	1,450			(b) 1,200					250	
Prepaid factory insurance	800			(c) 650					150	
Small tools	3,250			(d) 550					2,700	
Machinery and equipment	72,400								72,400	
Accumulated depreciation, machinery and equipment		18,700		(e) 3,600						22,300
Patents	10,200			(f) 800					9,400	
Accounts payable		3,700								3,700
Common stock		100,000								100,000
Retained earnings		14,900								14,900
Sales		138,000						138,000		
Raw material purchases	47,200				47,200					
Direct labor	26,700		(g) 600		27,300					
Factory rent	6,000				6,000					
Indirect labor	4,700		(g) 150		4,850					
Supervision	6,000				6,000					
Power	2,400				2,400					
Repairs to machinery	1,600				1,600					
Selling expenses	14,300						14,300			
General and administrative expenses	10,400		(a) 350				10,750			
	275,500	275,500								
Factory supplies used			(b) 1,200		1,200					
Factory insurance expired			(c) 650		650					
Small tools written off			(d) 550		550					
Depreciation of machinery and equipment			(e) 3,600		3,600					
Patents written off			(f) 800		800					
Wages payable				(g) 750						750
			7,900	7,900						
Raw materials inventory to Balance Sheet						18,800			18,800	
Goods in process inventory to Balance Sheet						8,700			8,700	
Finished goods inventory to Balance Sheet								11,000	11,000	
Cost of goods manufactured to Income Statement						98,550	98,550			
					126,050	126,050	134,800	149,000	156,400	142,200
State and federal taxes							4,400			4,400
Net Income to Retained Earnings							9,800			9,800
							149,000	149,000	156,400	156,400

Required:

1. From the work sheet prepare an income statement supported by a manufacturing statement.
2. Prepare closing entries.

Problem 23-3

Following are the items from the Manufacturing Statement columns of the incompleted work sheet prepared by Sparkman Manufacturing Company at the end of the current year. The illustration shows the items as they appeared after all adjustments were completed but before the ending work in process inventory was calculated and entered and before the cost of goods manufactured was calculated.

Sparkman Manufacturing Company manufactures a single product called Rockstone. On December 31, at the end of the current year, the goods in process inventory consisted of 1,000 units of Rockstone, each unit of which contained an estimated $6.00 of raw materials and had an estimated $1.60 of direct labor applied to it.

	Manufacturing Statement	
	Debit	Credit
Raw materials inventory........................	16,900	17,300
Goods in process inventory.....................	8,400	?
Raw material purchases.........................	170,500	
Raw material purchases returns.................		2,200
Discounts on raw material purchases............		3,400
Freight on raw material purchases..............	4,500	
Direct labor...................................	100,000	
Indirect labor.................................	27,500	
Supervision....................................	10,000	
Heat, light, and power.........................	5,400	
Repairs to machinery...........................	3,700	
Factory taxes..................................	2,600	
Small tools written off........................	1,100	
Depreciation of machinery......................	5,300	
Depreciation of factory building...............	4,900	
Patents written off............................	1,600	
Factory insurance expired......................	1,500	
Factory supplies used..........................	1,400	
Cost of goods manufactured.....................		
	365,300	365,300

Required:

1. Calculate the relationship between direct labor and overhead costs, and then use this relationship to determine the value of the ending goods in process inventory.

2. After placing a value on the ending goods in process inventory, determine the cost of goods manufactured.
3. Prepare a manufacturing statement for Sparkman Manufacturing Company.
4. Prepare entries to close the manufacturing accounts and to summarize their balances in the Manufacturing Summary account.
5. Prepare the entry to close the Manufacturing Summary account.

Problem 23–4

A trial balance taken from the ledger of Northgate Manufacturing Company on December 31, at the end of its current accounting period, appeared as follows:

NORTHGATE MANUFACTURING COMPANY
Trial Balance, December 31, 19—

Cash	$ 23,500	
Raw materials inventory	21,200	
Goods in process inventory	18,700	
Finished goods inventory	33,600	
Prepaid factory insurance	4,300	
Factory supplies	8,500	
Factory machinery	185,400	
Accumulated depreciation, factory machinery		$ 36,500
Accounts payable		14,200
Common stock		100,000
Retained earnings		39,500
Sales		418,600
Sales returns	1,200	
Raw materials purchased	81,400	
Direct labor	97,800	
Factory supervision	11,400	
Indirect labor	16,500	
Heat, light, and power	16,200	
Machinery repairs	5,100	
Rent of factory	12,000	
Property taxes, machinery	1,800	
Sales salaries	31,200	
Advertising	4,600	
Office rent	2,400	
Officers' salaries	20,500	
Office salaries	11,500	
	$608,800	$608,800

Additional information:
1. End of the accounting period inventories:
   a) Raw materials, $18,600.
   b) Goods in process consisted of 5,000 units of product with each unit containing an estimated $1.50 of raw materials and having had an estimated $2.00 of direct labor applied.
   c) Finished goods consisted of 4,000 units of product with each unit containing an estimated $2.55 of raw materials and having had an estimated $3.00 of direct labor applied.
   d) Factory supplies inventory, $900.

2. Expired factory insurance, $3,200.
3. Depreciation of factory machinery, $15,200.
4. Accrued wages payable:
    a) Direct labor, $2,200.
    b) Factory supervision, $600.
    c) Indirect labor, $400.
    d) Sales salaries, $1,200.
    e) Office salaries, $300.
5. Provision for state and federal income taxes payable, $40,600.

Required:

1. Enter the trial balance on a ten-column work sheet. Make the adjustments from the information given. Sort the items to the proper Manufacturing Statement, Income Statement, or Balance Sheet columns.
2. After the Direct Labor account and the overhead costs accounts have been adjusted and carried to the Manufacturing Statement columns, determine the relationship between the direct labor and overhead costs. Use this relationship to determine the overhead applicable to the goods in process and finished goods inventories. After the amounts of overhead applicable to the goods in process and finished goods inventories are determined, calculate the inventory values of the goods in process and finished goods inventories. Enter these inventory values on the work sheet and complete the work sheet.
3. From the work sheet prepare a manufacturing statement and an income statement.
4. Prepare closing entries.

CLASS EXERCISE

Exercise 23–1
An end-of-the-accounting-period trial balance of a manufacturing company follows. To simplify the problem and to save time the trial balance is in numbers of not more than two integers.

Required:

1. Prepare a manufacturing work sheet form on ordinary notebook paper.
2. Copy the trial balance on to the work sheet form and complete the work sheet using the following information:
    a) Inventories:
        Raw materials, $3.00.
        Goods in process, $5.00.
        Finished goods, $2.00.
        Factory supplies, $1.00.
    b) Allowance for bad debts an additional $2.00.
    c) Expired factory insurance, $1.00.
    d) Depreciation of factory machinery, $3.00.
    e) Accrued payroll:
        Direct labor, $4.00.
        Indirect labor, $2.00.
        Office salaries, $1.00.

SOUTHERN MANUFACTURING COMPANY

Trial Balance, December 31, 19—

Cash...	$ 4	
Accounts receivable..	5	
Allowance for bad debts.....................................		$ 1
Raw materials inventory.....................................	2	
Goods in process inventory..................................	4	
Finished goods inventory....................................	3	
Factory supplies..	3	
Prepaid factory insurance...................................	4	
Factory machinery..	23	
Accumulated depreciation, factory machinery.................		2
Common stock..		20
Retained earnings...		5
Sales...		81
Raw material purchases.....................................	15	
Freight on raw material.....................................	1	
Direct labor...	12	
Indirect labor..	3	
Power..	5	
Repairs..	2	
Rent of factory..	8	
Selling expense control.....................................	9	
General and administrative expense control..................	6	
	$109	$109

SUPPLEMENTARY PROBLEMS

Problem 23–A

The following information appears on the records of a manufacturing firm:

Inventories	Beginning	Ending
Finished goods................................	$10,500	$11,200
Goods in process..............................	6,500	5,700
Raw materials................................	16,000	18,000

Cost of goods sold............................	$56,000
Direct labor..................................	10,000
Factory overhead costs........................	5,800

Required:

On the basis of the information just given determine for the accounting period:

1. Cost of goods manufactured.
2. Total manufacturing costs incurred.
3. Cost of raw materials used.
4. Cost of raw materials purchased.

(Hint: It may be helpful to set up the manufacturing statement and the cost of goods sold section of the income statement.)

Problem 23–B

At the end of the current year a trial balance of the ledger of Brockton Manufacturing Company appeared as follows:

BROCKTON MANUFACTURING COMPANY

Trial Balance, December 31, 19—

Cash...	$ 19,200	
Accounts receivable.................................	32,500	
Allowance for bad debts.............................		$ 300
Raw materials inventory.............................	12,600	
Goods in process inventory..........................	14,800	
Finished goods inventory............................	21,100	
Prepaid insurance...................................	4,700	
Factory supplies....................................	6,900	
Office supplies.....................................	1,800	
Office equipment....................................	9,800	
Accumulated depreciation, office equipment...........		1,300
Factory machinery...................................	176,000	
Accumulated depreciation, factory machinery..........		29,300
Accounts payable....................................		11,900
Mortgage payable, machinery.........................		25,000
Common stock.......................................		100,000
Retained earnings...................................		43,500
Sales...		361,500
Sales returns.......................................	1,100	
Raw material purchases..............................	62,400	
Discounts on raw material purchases.................		1,200
Direct labor..	88,200	
Factory supervision.................................	11,600	
Indirect labor......................................	13,200	
Heat, light, and power..............................	18,700	
Machinery repairs...................................	5,400	
Rent of factory.....................................	12,000	
Property taxes, machinery...........................	1,900	
Sales salaries......................................	21,300	
Advertising...	4,500	
Office rent...	2,400	
Officers' salaries..................................	20,000	
Office salaries.....................................	11,000	
Interest expense....................................	900	
	$574,000	$574,000

Additional end-of-the-accounting-period information:
   1. Ending inventories:
      a) Raw materials, $11,900.
      b) Goods in process consisted of 2,500 units of product with each unit containing an estimated $1.30 of raw materials and having had an estimated $2.00 of direct labor applied. (Use the relationship of direct labor cost, after adjustment, to overhead costs, after adjustments, to determine the amount of overhead applicable to each unit of goods in process and to each unit of finished goods.
      c) Finished goods consisted of 2,000 units of product with each unit containing an estimated $2.79 of raw materials and having had an estimated $3.80 of direct labor applied.
      d) Factory supplies, $800.
      e) Office supplies, $600.
   2. Allowance for bad debts an additional 2 per cent of accounts receivable.
   3. Total expired insurance, $4,100, of which $3,800 is chargeable to the factory and $300 is chargeable to the office.

4. Depreciation:
   a) Office equipment, $900.
   b) Factory machinery, $11,800.
5. Accrued interest payable, $350.
6. Accrued wages payable:
   a) Direct labor, $1,800.
   b) Factory supervision, $400.
   c) Indirect labor, $600.
   d) Sales salaries, $1,100.
   e) Office salaries, $200.
7. Estimated state and federal income taxes payable, $28,200.

Required:

Prepare a work sheet, manufacturing statement, income statement, and closing entries.

Problem 23–C

A trial balance of the ledger of Dolphin Manufacturing Company as of the beginning of the current year appeared as follows:

DOLPHIN MANUFACTURING COMPANY
Trial Balance, January 1, 19—

Cash...	$ 18,600	
Accounts receivable.................................	36,400	
Raw materials inventory.............................	19,300	
Goods in process inventory..........................	17,100	
Finished goods inventory............................	24,500	
Prepaid factory insurance...........................	600	
Factory supplies....................................	1,100	
Machinery...	162,900	
Accumulated depreciation, machinery.................		$ 39,300
Accounts payable...................................		15,800
Common stock......................................		200,000
Retained earnings..................................		25,400
	$280,500	$280,500

During the year the company completed the following condensed transactions:
1. Sold $346,500 of finished goods on account.
2. Collected $344,700 of accounts receivable.
3. Purchased on account:

a) Factory supplies......................................	$ 5,400	
b) Machinery...	31,000	
c) Raw materials.......................................	92,100	
	$128,500	

4. Made cash disbursements in payment of:

a) Factory insurance premiums...........................	$ 3,000	
b) Accounts payable....................................	131,400	
c) Direct labor..	79,400	
d) Indirect labor.......................................	18,300	
e) Heat, light, and power...............................	6,800	
f) Machinery repairs...................................	4,700	
g) Selling expenses....................................	40,100	
h) General and administrative expenses..................	36,500	
	$320,200	

At the end of the accounting year the following inventory and adjustment information was available:

1. Inventories:
   a) Raw materials, $18,400.
   b) Goods in process consisted of 800 units of product with each unit containing an estimated $7.75 of materials and having had an estimated $7.50 of direct labor applied. (Use the relationship of direct labor cost, after adjustment, to overhead costs, after adjustments, to determine the amount of overhead costs applicable to each unit of goods in process and finished goods.)
   c) Finished goods inventory consisted of 1,000 units of product with each unit containing an estimated $9.50 of materials and having had an estimated $9.00 of direct labor applied.
   d) Factory supplies inventory, $600.
2. Expired factory insurance, $3,200.
3. Estimated depreciation of machinery, $16,900.
4. Accrued wages:
   a) Direct labor, $600.
   b) Indirect labor, $200.
5. State and federal income taxes payable, $20,900.

Required:

1. Open T-accounts and enter the January 1 trial balance amounts.
2. Record the condensed transactions directly in the T-accounts.
3. Prepare a trial balance of the T-accounts on a work sheet form. Complete the work sheet.
4. From the work sheet prepare a manufacturing statement, an income statement, and a balance sheet.
5. Enter the adjusting and closing entries directly in the T-accounts and prepare a post-closing trial balance.

Chapter

24

BASIC JOB ORDER COST
ACCOUNTING

Cost accounting has been described as that phase of accounting that has to do with the collection, summarization, analysis, and interpretation of the costs of a given product, process, or service. Cost accounting is not something distinct and entirely different from the so-called *general accounting* presented in the previous chapters. It differs from general accounting primarily in the matter of emphasis. In cost accounting, emphasis is upon the *unit cost* to produce a given product, process, or service. Actually cost accounting represents only an adaptation and expansion of general accounting. The adaptation and expansion is made in such a manner as to aid in the collection and segregation of data having to do with unit costs.

Once cost accounting was considered to apply primarily to manufacturing enterprises. This is no longer true. Cost accounting is now commonly found in many fields, such as merchandising, banking, transportation, and government service. Stores commonly use cost accounting to measure and control such things as the cost of advertising per dollar of sales and the cost of delivery service per dollar of sales. Banks commonly used cost accounting to measure the cost of providing certain types of checking accounts and other services. Transportation companies and government units use cost accounting to measure the costs of the services they perform. However, from a teaching standpoint, manufacturing enterprises offer some of the best examples of the application of cost accounting. Consequently, cost accounting for manufacturing enterprises will be used for purposes of illustration in this and the following chapter.

Cost Accounting Systems

There are two general types of cost accounting systems: (1) job order cost systems, and (2) process cost systems. However, of the two general types there are an infinite number of variations and combinations.

In cost accounting a *job* is often a single airplane, electric generator, or other machine manufactured to the specifications of a customer. A *job lot* is a quantity of identical items, such as five hundred identical typewriters manufactured as a job or a single order. A *job order cost system* is one that collects costs by jobs or by job lots. Such a system generally fits the needs of a company whose products are individually different in the sense that each lot or each unit of product is sufficiently unique to be

593

identifiable. For example, a job order cost system generally fits the needs of a company manufacturing to the individual order and specifications of its customers such items as large electric turbines. In such a company each unit of product is sufficiently different to make the collection of costs more practicable by a job order cost system. Likewise, a job order cost system often best fits the needs of a manufacturer of such items as typewriters. Such a manufacturer can break production into job lots of identical units of product and collect costs by the job lots.

A process cost system is one that collects costs by processes. Such a system generally fits the needs of a company whose production is characterized by a steady flow of raw materials into and through a series of processes to produce a uniform product. For example, a process cost system generally best fits the needs of a manufacturer of flour, paint, or gasoline.

Many businesses use a combination or a variation of both systems. For example, a company may use a process cost system within a larger over-all job order system. The manufacturer of large electric turbines just described may use a job order system to collect and control the costs of each special turbine produced. However, if such a manufacturer produces his own copper wire, he may also use a process cost system to gather and control the costs of producing copper wire.

The techniques of job order cost accounting are discussed in this chapter. A discussion of process cost accounting is reserved for the next chapter.

Cost Accounting and Perpetual Inventories

Two important characteristics distinguish a manufacturing cost accounting system from a general accounting system for a manufacturing firm such as that described in the previous chapter. These characteristics are: (1) the wide use of perpetual inventory controlling accounts in a cost accounting system, and (2) the flow of costs in a cost accounting system from the *Raw Materials, Accrued Factory Payroll,* and *Overhead Cost* accounts to and through the *Goods in Process* and *Finished Goods* accounts and on to the *Cost of Goods Sold* account.

Cost accounting is distinguished by the wide use of perpetual inventory controlling accounts. In a cost accounting system the purchase and use of all materials is recorded in a perpetual inventory account called the "Materials account." Also, in cost accounting, the Goods in Process and Finished Goods accounts become perpetual inventory accounts. The operation of perpetual inventory accounts and the operation of controlling accounts have been discussed in previous chapters. However, both subjects will be discussed again in this chapter.

In addition to the many perpetual inventory accounts, cost accounting is also distinguished by the flow of manufacturing costs from the Materials account, Accrued Factory Payroll account, and Overhead Costs controlling account to and through the Goods in Process and Finished Goods accounts and on to the Cost of Goods Sold account. This flow of costs is diagramed in Illustration 131 on the next page. This diagram shows that the Materials account, Accrued Factory Payroll account, and Overhead Costs controlling account are debited for the cost of materials, labor, and overhead items purchased and expired. It also shows that the Materials account, Accrued Factory Payroll account, and Overhead Costs account are credited and the Goods in Process account is debited for the cost of materials, labor, and overhead placed in production. These procedures flow or transfer the cost of materials, labor, and overhead from the Materials account, Accrued Factory Payroll account, and Overhead Costs account where their acquisition is first recorded to the Goods in Process account where their use in production is recorded.

In the diagram in Illustration 131, the Goods in Process account receives debits for the amounts of direct materials, direct labor, and overhead costs placed in production. Likewise, the Goods in Process account is credited for the jobs completed and transferred to the Finished Goods account as finished goods. As a result of these procedures the Goods in Process account is a perpetual inventory account, the balance of which shows the cost of the unfinished goods in the process of manufacture.

In the diagram showing the flow of costs in a cost accounting system, the Finished Goods account is debited and Goods in Process is credited for the cost of jobs completed. This flows or transfers the cost of these jobs as they are completed from the Goods in Process account to the Finished Goods account. Also in the diagram the Finished Goods account is credited and Cost of Goods Sold is debited for the cost of goods sold. This flows the cost of goods sold to the Cost of Goods Sold account. As a result of these procedures the Finished Goods account is a perpetual inventory account, the balance of which shows the cost of the unsold finished goods on hand at any time.

In a job order cost accounting system the cost to manufacture each job or product is known as soon as each job or product is completed. Consequently, as each job is completed its cost may be transferred from Goods in Process to Finished Goods. Likewise, when a job or an order of products is sold, its cost may be transferred at once from the Finished Goods account and charged to the Cost of Goods Sold account. Charging the cost of each job or lot of products sold to the Cost of Goods Sold account at the time of each sale is a worthwhile improvement over a general accounting system where the cost of goods sold cannot be charged or calculated until the end of the accounting period after a physical inventory is taken.

The Goods in Process Account

The Goods in Process account with the subsidiary ledger of job cost sheets which it controls is the predominating feature of a job order cost system.

In a general accounting system for a manufacturing company such as

Illustration 131—Diagram Showing the Flow of Costs in a Cost Accounting System

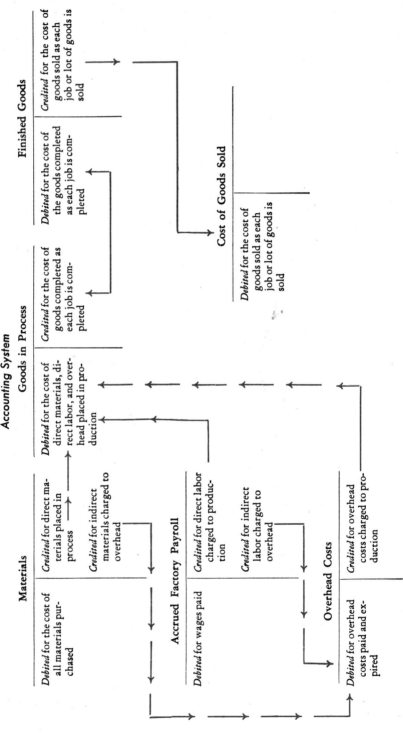

that described in the previous chapter, the unfinished work in process is determined at the end of each accounting period by means of a physical inventory. In making this physical inventory the goods in process are counted, and an estimate is made of the cost of the materials, labor, and overhead applicable to these goods. The need for this physical inventory and the opportunity for errors in estimating the materials, labor, and overhead applicable to it are weaknesses of a noncost system. These weaknesses are eliminated in a job order cost system by making the Goods in Process account a perpetual inventory account, the balance of which shows the cost of the work in process.

When a cost accounting system is in operation, the cost of the unfinished work in process at the beginning of an accounting period is shown by the debit balance of the Goods in Process account. Throughout the accounting period, materials, labor, and overhead costs are applied in the factory to the production of goods. The costs of the materials, labor, and overhead placed in production are periodically debited to the Goods in Process account. Also, throughout the accounting period, the cost of each job completed (the sum of the materials, labor, and overhead applicable to each job) is credited to the Goods in Process account as each job is completed. As a result of these procedures the Goods in Process account is a perpetual inventory account, the debit balance of which shows the cost of the material, labor, and overhead applicable to the incomplete jobs in process. This is shown in the following Goods in Process account:

Goods in Process

Mar.	1	Balance of goods in		Mar. 10	Job completed	8,000
		process	3,000	18	Job completed	11,000
	31	Materials used	17,000	24	Job completed	7,000
	31	Labor applied	10,000	30	Job completed	10,000
	31	Overhead applied (150 per		31	Balance of goods in	
		cent of direct labor)	15,000		process	9,000
			45,000			45,000
Apr.	1	Balance of goods in				
		process	9,000			

Job Cost Sheets. Not only is the Goods in Process account a perpetual inventory account, it is also a controlling account. The Goods in Process account is a controlling account for a subsidiary ledger of *job cost sheets* known as a *Job Cost Ledger*. The Goods in Process account in the General Ledger shows the total cost of the materials, labor, and overhead of all jobs placed in process. The individual job cost sheets in the subsidiary Job Cost Ledger, one for each job in process, show the costs of materials, labor, and overhead applicable to each individual job in process. A job cost sheet is shown in Illustration 132.

The job cost sheet shown in Illustration 132 has lines for the name and address of the customer for whom the product or products are being manufactured; a place for the job number; lines for a description of the product or products being manufactured; and places for the date on which

Illustration 132

JOB COST SHEET							
Customer's Name *Cone Lumber Company*						Job No. *7452*	
Address *Eugene, Oregon*							
Job Description *10 H.P. electric motor to customer's specifications*							
Date Promised *4/1*		Date Started *3/23*			Date Completed *3/29*		
	MATERIALS		**LABOR**		**OVERHEAD COSTS APPLIED**		
Date	Requisition No.	Amount	Time Ticket No.	Amount	Date	Rate	Amount
19___ Mar. 23	1-003	53.00	C-3422	8.00	3/29	150 per cent of the direct labor	$123.00
24			C-3478	16.00			
			C-3479	6.00			
25	1-079	21.00	C-4002	16.00	**SUMMARY OF COSTS**		
26			C-4015	16.00	Materials		$ 74.00
27			C-4032	12.00	Labor		82.00
28			C-4044	8.00	Overhead		123.00
					Total Cost of the job		279.00
					Remarks: *Completed and shipped* 3/29		
	Total	74.00	Total	82.00			

completion of the job is promised, the date it is started, and the date it is actually completed. It also has columns in which are charged the materials, labor, and overhead costs used to complete the job. These columns are all debit columns. All jobs are debited for the materials, labor, and overhead costs required to complete them. Credits to a job are sometimes made when materials are charged to the job but are unused and are later returned. Sometimes credits are also necessary to correct errors. However, credits to job cost sheets are so uncommon that no special place is provided for them. When it is necessary to credit a job, the credit may be shown as a subtraction item in a debit column, either in red ink or in black ink and encircled.

As a controlling account controlling a subsidiary ledger, the Goods in Process account and its subsidiary ledger of job cost sheets operate in the usual manner of controlling accounts and subsidiary ledgers. All materials, labor, and overhead debited to each individual job on its job cost sheet must be debited individually or in totals to the Goods in Process account. Likewise, all individual credits to job sheets must be credited to the Goods in Process controlling account either individually or in totals. Because of these requirements the balance of the Goods in Process account, after all posting is completed, should equal the sum of the balances of the individual job cost sheets in the Job Cost Ledger.

The Use of a Job Cost Sheet Illustrated.   The 10 H.P. electric motor manufactured for the Cone Lumber Company as a special order, and for which the job cost sheet is reproduced in Illustration 132, may be used to show the manner in which the Goods in Process account and its subsidiary ledger of job cost sheets operate. When this job is started on March 23, information as to the customer, job number, and job description is filled in on a blank job cost sheet, and the cost sheet is placed in the Job Cost Ledger. The job number identifies the job and makes easier the charges to it for materials and labor. As materials are required for this job, they are transferred from the materials storeroom to the factory and used to complete the job. At the time of their transfer the costs of the materials used on this job are charged to the job in the Materials column of the job cost sheet. At the same time the costs of the materials transferred and used on the job are recorded on a *materials used summary* from where they are charged in total at the end of the month to the Goods in Process account. At the end of each day the wages of the workmen who work directly on this electric motor are charged to the job in the Labor column of the job's cost sheet. The amount of these wages is also entered daily on a *labor cost summary* from where it is charged in total at the end of the month to the Goods in Process account. When this electric motor is finished on March 29, overhead is charged to the job in the Overhead column of the job cost sheet. The amount of overhead charged is based upon the cost of the direct labor applied to the job as shown by the total of the Labor column of the cost sheet. The amount of this overhead is entered on both the job cost sheet and on a *summary of overhead costs applied*. From the summary of overhead costs applied the overhead is charged in total at the end of the month to the Goods in Process account. It can be seen from these procedures that the Goods in Process account receives debits at the end of the month from the materials used summary, the labor cost summary, and the summary of overhead costs applied. These debits are equal to the individual debits on the several job cost sheets for the materials, labor, and overhead individually charged to the various jobs.

At any time a job is completed, it becomes finished goods. Its completion is shown in the records by marking its job cost sheet "completed" and removing the cost sheet from the Job Cost Ledger. Since this reduces the jobs in the ledger, it has the effect of crediting the cost of the job and substracting it from the sum of the accounts in the Job Cost Ledger. At the same time the job is completed and its cost sheet removed from the Job Cost Ledger, an entry is made to transfer the cost of the job from the Goods in Process account to the Finished Goods account. This entry credits the cost of the job to Goods in Process and debits it to Finished Goods. The entry appears as follows:

Mar.	29	Finished Goods........................	279.00	
		Goods in Process...................		279.00
		To transfer the cost of one 10 H.P. motor to Finished Goods.		

Proof of the Goods in Process Account. As previously stated, when a job order cost system is in use, each individual job in process is charged or debited on its job order cost sheet in the subsidiary Job Cost Ledger with the costs of the materials, labor, and overhead used in its manufacture. Likewise, the Goods in Process controlling account receives debits periodically for the sums of the individual amounts charged or debited on the several job cost sheets. When a job is completed, its cost sheet is removed from the Job Cost Ledger. Likewise, an entry is made that credits, removes, and transfers its cost from the Goods in Process account to the Finished Goods account. As a result of these procedures, when all posting is completed, the balance of the Goods in Process account should equal the sum of the material, labor, and overhead charged to those unfinished jobs, the job cost sheets of which are still in the Job Cost Ledger. Periodically a schedule of the jobs in process is made. This schedule shows the cost of the materials, labor, and overhead charged to the unfinished jobs, the cost sheets of which are still in the Job Cost Ledger. The sum of the materials, labor, and overhead shown on this schedule is compared with the balance of the Goods in Process account. They should be equal.

Accounting for Materials under a Job Cost System

Accounting for materials under a job cost system may be divided for purposes of study into two phases: (1) the acquisition of materials, and (2) the use of materials.

Acquisition of Materials. In a general accounting system for a manufacturer such as that described in Chapter 23, material transactions are recorded in three different accounts: Materials Inventory account, Material Purchases account, and Freight on Materials account. In a cost accounting system the transactions of these three accounts are recorded in a single account called the *Materials account*. The Materials account is a perpetual inventory account in which the purchase and use of both direct and indirect materials are recorded. It is also normally a controlling account controlling a subsidiary *Materials Ledger*. The Materials Ledger is a ledger having a separate account for each kind of materials purchased and used.

When a cost accounting system is in use, in order to properly control the purchase and use of materials, all materials are placed in a *materials storeroom* as they are purchased and received. The storeroom is the responsibility of a storeroom keeper. It is the duty of this storeroom keeper to store and care for all materials until they are needed in production, to issue materials to the factory for use in production as needed, and to inform the purchasing department by means of a *purchase requisition* when the supply of an item of materials is low and an order for a new supply should be placed.

Normally, when a good system of internal control is in use, the purchasing of all materials is the duty of the purchasing department. (See the discussion of the control of purchases in Chapter 7.) Normally, the purchasing department places orders for the purchase of materials only upon the receipt of properly prepared purchase requisitions. Upon receipt of a purchase requisition from the storeroom, the purchasing department prepares a *purchase order* which it sends to a vendor. Upon receipt of the purchase order, the vendor ships the items of materials ordered and sends an *invoice* to the purchasing department.

When the materials are received from the vendor, they are normally received by a receiving department. A receiving clerk in the receiving department counts and inspects the items of materials received. He then prepares with carbon paper several copies of a *receiving report*. The receiving report shows the nature and amount of each kind of materials received. The materials received and one copy of the receiving report are sent to the storeroom where the materials are stored until needed in production. Two additional copies of the receiving report are sent to the purchasing department.

In the purchasing department the receiving report is compared with the invoice. One copy of the receiving report is attached to the invoice along with a copy of the purchase requisition and a copy of the purchase order. If the invoice and its supporting documents are in order, a voucher is prepared, and the invoice and its supporting documents are attached to the voucher. The voucher is then sent to the accounting department where it is recorded in the Voucher Register with the following entry:

Mar.	5	Materials..............................	687.00	
		Vouchers Payable..................		687.00
		Purchased materials.		

The second of the two copies of the receiving report sent to the purchasing department is normally also forwarded to the accounting department at the time the voucher is forwarded. In the accounting department the unit prices and the total prices for the materials purchased are calculated and are entered on this second copy of the receiving report. The priced second copy of the receiving report is then used in the accounting department for entries in the subsidiary Materials Ledger.

Materials Ledger. In a cost accounting system the Materials account is a perpetual inventory account in which are recorded the purchase and use of all materials. It is also a controlling account controlling a subsidiary Materials Ledger. The subsidiary Materials Ledger is a ledger

Illustration 133

MATERIALS LEDGER CARD

Item __Armature core__   Stock No. __C-347__   Location in Storeroom __Bin 137__

Maximum __400__   Minimum __150__   Number to Reorder __200__

	RECEIVED				ISSUED				BALANCE		
Date	Receiving Report No.	Units	Unit Price	Total Price	Requi-sition No.	Units	Unit Price	Total Price	Units	Unit Price	Total Price
3/1									180	1.00	180.00
3/5					4345	20	1.00	20.00	160	1.00	160.00
3/11					4416	10	1.00	10.00	150	1.00	150.00
3/12	C-114	200	1.00	200.00					350	1.00	350.00

having a separate card for each kind, size, style, or grade of materials used in the factory. Each separate materials ledger card shows for the kind of material recorded on it the amounts of that material received, the amounts issued, and the balance of the material on hand. A subsidiary materials ledger card is shown in Illustration 133.

Use of Materials. As stated earlier, when a cost accounting system is in operation, all materials are placed in a materials storeroom as they are received from vendors. A storeroom keeper is in charge of the storeroom. It is the duty of the storeroom keeper to care for all of the materials in the storeroom and to issue materials only on a properly prepared and signed *materials requisition*. A materials requisition is shown in Illustration 134.

When materials are needed in the factory for production, a materials requisition is prepared and signed by a factory superintendent, foreman, or other responsible person. To prepare a materials requisition, information as to the quantity, description, and stock numbers of the materials desired is entered on a materials requisition blank. Since the people in charge of production do not normally know the unit prices or total prices of the materials needed, these columns are left blank until the requisition reaches the accounting department. However, the people in charge of production do know the particular job or overhead cost for which the materials are to be used. Therefore, they are responsible for filling in the number of the job or the number of the overhead cost account to which the materials are to be charged. These numbers are very important since

Illustration 134

MATERIALS REQUISITION			Requisition No. 45673	
To the Storeroom Keeper:				
Please deliver the following materials:				
Quantity	Description	Stock No.	Unit Price	Total

Charge to: Overhead Cost
                    Job. No. _____   Account No. _____

Date _____   Signed _____

they enable the accounting department to charge the materials to the proper job or overhead cost account. When a good system of internal control is in operation, only superintendents, foremen, and other responsible persons are permitted to sign and issue materials requisitions.

When a materials requisition is prepared and presented to the storeroom keeper, the storeroom keeper examines the requisition to see that it is properly prepared. He makes certain that the number of the job or the number of the overhead cost account to which the materials are to be charged is shown and that the requisition is signed by a person with the authority to sign requisitions. If the requisition is in order, he delivers the materials requested to the factory and forwards the requisition on to the accounting department.

In the accounting department, each requisition is first priced. The price of a material listed on a requisition is found by examining the materials inventory card of the material. This is the card shown in Illustration 133 which gives for a particular kind of material the amounts received, issued, and the balance on hand. Normally, at the time a requisition is priced, the materials requisitioned and issued are recorded as being issued in the issued columns of the proper materials ledger cards.

After a requisition is priced and the materials requisitioned on it are recorded in the Materials Ledger as having been issued, the materials requisition is then recorded on the proper job cost sheet or in the proper overhead cost account. If the materials requisitioned are direct materials, the requisition is recorded on the proper job cost sheet. If the materials are indirect materials, the requisition is recorded as a debit in an overhead account. After a requisition is charged to the proper job order cost sheet or to the proper overhead account, it is entered on a materials used summary. A materials used summary is shown in Illustration 135.

Illustration 135

MATERIALS USED SUMMARY			
Date	Requisition Number	Direct Materials	Indirect Materials
Mar. 1	45675	653 00	
1	45676	210 00	
1	45677		21 50
31	45797	156 50	
31	45798		8 60
		17,000 00	320 45

Since each materials requisition passes through a number of hands and is recorded in a number of places, it might be wise to summarize its travels as follows:

A materials requisition is:

1. Prepared in the plant or factory.
2. Exchanged in the storeroom for materials.
3. Forwarded to the accounting department where it is:
    a) Priced.
    b) Entered as materials issued in the Materials Ledger.
    c) Charged to a particular job or overhead account.
    d) Entered on the materials used summary.

A materials used summary is used to summarize the amounts of direct and indirect materials issued. Its use was discussed briefly on page 599.

At the end of a cost period, after all materials requisitions have been recorded on the materials used summary, the total of the Direct Materials column of the summary shows the amount of materials charged to jobs. Likewise, the total of the Indirect Materials column shows the amount of indirect materials charged to overhead accounts. The materials used summary is the source of the following entry which is made at the end of a cost period to record in the ledger accounts the cost of the materials used:

Mar.	31	Goods in Process.......................	17,000.00	
		Overhead Costs Control...............	320.45	
		Materials........................		17,320.45
		To record the amount of materials used.		

Proof of the Materials Account. As previously explained, all materials purchased and received are debited to the Materials account through entries in the Voucher Register. All materials received are also debited in the Received columns of individual materials inventory cards in the Materials Ledger. All materials issued are credited in the Issued columns of the individual materials cards in the Materials Ledger. All materials issued are also entered on a materials used summary from where they are credited at the end of the month to the Materials account. As a result of these procedures, after all posting is completed, the balance of the Materials account in the General Ledger should equal the sum of the balances of the individual cards in the Materials Ledger. This equality is proved periodically by totaling the balances of the inventory cards in the Materials Ledger and comparing the total with the balance of the Materials account.

Accounting for Labor under a Job Cost System

Like accounting for materials, accounting for labor under a job cost system may be divided for purposes of study into two phases: (1) acquisition of labor, and (2) use of labor.

Acquisition of Labor. Generally the hours of labor purchased from each factory employee are recorded daily by the use of time clocks and clock cards as explained in Chapter 16. Normally each employee is required each day to record the time he enters and the time he leaves the factory by means of a clock card stamped by a time clock. This applies to those employees whose work is classified as indirect labor as well as those whose work is classified as direct labor. The clock cards are summarized daily in a Payroll Register as was explained in Chapter 16. At the end of each payroll period, the Payroll Register is recorded with a general journal entry. Without the complications of payroll taxes, income taxes, and other deductions, the entries to record the Payroll Register and the payment of factory wages are as follows:

Mar.	7	Accrued Factory Payroll................	2,900.00	
		Vouchers Payable..................		2,900.00
		To record the factory payroll as shown in the Payroll Register.		
	7	Vouchers Payable.....................	2,900.00	
		Cash........................		2,900.00
		Paid the factory payroll for the week ending March 7.		

This series of entries is repeated at the end of each pay period. Consequently, at the end of each month, the Accrued Factory Payroll account has a series of entries on its debit side. (See the Accrued Factory Payroll account shown on page 608.) Each of the debit entries represents the amounts paid to the employees for both direct and indirect labor at the end of a pay period. The sum of the debits is the amount paid during the month to all employees for both direct and indirect labor.

Use of Labor. Clock cards serve as a record of the hours worked each day by each employee. However, they do not show the manner in which the employees spent their time while at work. They do not show the particular jobs on which the employees worked or the overhead cost tasks which the employees performed. Consequently, additional records of each employee's work must be made. These additional records are called *labor time tickets.* Labor time tickets tell how an employee spent his time while at work. A labor time ticket is shown in Illustration 136.

Illustration 136—A Time Ticket

Throughout each day, a labor time ticket like the one in Illustration 136 is prepared each time an employee is changed from one job to another. It may be prepared by either the worker or the foreman; it is commonly signed by both. If an employee works on only one job all day, only one time ticket is prepared. If an employee works on more than one job in a day, a ticket is made for each job. The time tickets serve as a basis for charging the proper jobs or overhead accounts for the employee's wages.

After the employees "clock out" and go home at the end of each day, the time tickets of each employee of that day are assembled in the time-keeping department. Here the time tickets of each employee are compared with his clock card to see that both agree as to the hours worked. The clock cards are then returned to the racks beside the time clocks, and the time tickets are sent to the accounting department.

In the accounting department, the time tickets are sorted into direct labor time tickets and indirect labor time tickets. The cost of the labor shown on the direct labor time tickets is charged to the proper jobs on their job cost sheets. The cost of the labor shown on the indirect labor time tickets is charged to the proper overhead accounts. Then both the sum of the direct labor time tickets and the sum of the indirect labor time tickets are entered on a labor cost summary. The use of the labor cost summary was briefly discussed on page 599. The labor cost summary is a form having a column for direct labor and a column for indirect labor. It may appear somewhat as shown in Illustration 137.

Illustration 137

LABOR COST SUMMARY		
Date	Direct Labor	Indirect Labor
3/1	$ 495.00	$ 110.00
3/2	515.00	105.00
3/3	525.00	115.00
Total	$10,000.00	$2,500.00

At the end of the month, after all labor time tickets have been summarized on the labor cost summary, the columns of the summary show the cost of the labor used during the month. The total of the Direct Labor column shows the cost of the direct labor applied to jobs; the total of the Indirect Labor column shows the cost of the indirect labor charged to overhead accounts. These totals are the basis of a general journal entry recording the labor used. The entry has a debit to the Goods in Process account for the total of the Direct Labor column of the summary and a debit to the Overhead Costs controlling account for the sum of the Indirect Labor column. The entry appears as follows:

Mar.	31	Goods in Process......................	10,000.00	
		Overhead Costs......................	2,500.00	
		Accrued Factory Payroll............		12,500.00
		To record the labor used as shown by the labor cost summary.		

Accrued Wages. When time tickets and a labor cost summary are used in recording the wages of factory workers, an accrued payroll adjusting entry at the end of the month is unnecessary. This is because the time tickets of all the days of the month, including those after the last full pay period at the end of the month, are summarized on the labor cost summary. Consequently, the journal entry which records the labor cost summary records both the wages earned and paid during the month and the wages earned but unpaid at the end of the month. This is illustrated in the Accrued Factory Payroll account shown in Illustration 138.

Illustration 138

Accrued Factory Payroll

Date		Explanation	F	Debit	Date		Explanation	F	Credit
Mar.	7	Payroll payment		2,900.00	Mar.	31	Labor cost summary		12,500.00
	14	Payroll payment		2,950.00					
	21	Payroll payment		3,105.00					
	28	Payroll payment		3,040.00					
	31	Balance (accrued payroll)		505.00					
				12,500.00					12,500.00
					Mar.	31	Balance (accrued payroll)		505.00

In the Accrued Factory Payroll account shown in Illustration 138, the first four items on the debit side are the amounts paid to the employees at the ends of the four weekly pay periods of the month. These amounts show the cost of the labor which has been purchased and for which payment has been made. The one item on the credit side shows the cost of the labor used. When all posting is completed at the end of the month, the account almost always has a credit balance. This is because the credit to the account comes from the labor cost summary, and all the time tickets of the month, including those after the last full pay period at the end of the month, are recorded on the labor cost summary.

Accounting for Overhead Costs under a Job Cost System

Accounting for overhead costs may also be divided into two phases for purposes of study: (1) the incurrence of overhead, and (2) the application of overhead.

Incurrence of Overhead Costs. Overhead costs include all manufacturing costs other than direct materials and direct labor. All overhead costs are recorded in an account called "Overhead Costs." This account is normally a controlling account controlling a subsidiary ledger called the *Overhead Costs Ledger.* The Overhead Costs Ledger contains an account for each different kind of overhead cost incurred.

Entries recording the incurrence of overhead items normally arise from four sources:

1. *Materials Requisitions and the Materials Used Summary.* All indirect materials used are an overhead item. Each day the materials requisitions for indirect materials are recorded in the proper account in the Overhead Costs Ledger and are summarized on the materials used summary. At the end of the month the total amount of indirect materials used as shown on the materials used summary is debited to the Overhead Costs controlling account.
2. *Labor Time Tickets and the Labor Cost Summary.* Indirect labor is also an overhead item. Each day the time tickets for labor classified as overhead cost are recorded in the proper overhead cost account in the subsidiary Overhead Costs Ledger and are summarized on the labor cost summary. At the end of the month the amount of indirect labor used as shown by the labor cost summary is debited to the Overhead Costs controlling account.
3. *Vouchers.* Throughout the month vouchers are prepared for miscellaneous items of overhead such as repairs completed by outsiders or telephone, light, and power. Normally a special column in the Voucher Register headed "Overhead Costs debit" is provided to collect the debits resulting from these items. The individual items in the column are posted to the proper account in the subsidiary Overhead Costs Ledger. The column total is posted at the end of the month to the debit side of the Overhead Costs controlling account.
4. *Adjusting Entries.* At the end of each month adjusting entries must be made in the General Journal to record such overhead items as depreciation, expired insurance, and taxes. These entries are posted to both subsidiary overhead costs ledger accounts and the Overhead Costs controlling account.

At the end of each month after posting, the debit side of the Overhead Costs account and its subsidiary Overhead Costs Ledger show the total overhead incurred.

Application of Overhead Costs. In a job cost system the cost of each job completed is computed as soon as the job is finished. In order to compute the cost of each job as soon as it is finished, it is necessary to identify with each job the costs of the materials, labor, and overhead that were used in its manufacture. No difficulties arise in identifying materials and labor costs with particular jobs. Material costs are identified with jobs by means of materials requisitions, and labor costs are identified with jobs by means of labor time tickets. However, identifying and charging overhead to jobs is not so easy. In the first place, items of overhead apply to all jobs and cannot be definitely identified with any particular job. In the second place, the exact cost of certain items of overhead, such as repairs to machinery, cannot be known until the end of an accounting period or at some other future date, which is usually days, weeks, or even months after many jobs are completed. Consequently, because of the impossibility of definitely identifying overhead with particular jobs and because the exact cost of certain overhead items cannot be known until some future date, overhead is normally applied by means of a *predetermined overhead rate* to each job as the job is finished.

A predetermined overhead rate for applying overhead to jobs as they are finished is established by (1) estimating the total amount of overhead that will be incurred during a future period of time, usually a year; (2) estimating, for example, the cost of the direct labor that will be applied to production during the same period of time; then (3) calculating the ratio of the estimated overhead to the estimated direct labor cost. This calculation may be expressed in equation form as follows:

$$\frac{\text{ESTIMATED FUTURE OVERHEAD COSTS}}{\text{ESTIMATED FUTURE DIRECT LABOR COST}} = \text{PREDETERMINED OVERHEAD RATE}$$

The ratio or predetermined overhead rate thus calculated is usually expressed as a percentage. It is called a "predetermined rate" because both elements of the ratio are predetermined by means of estimates.

To illustrate the calculation of a predetermined overhead rate based on direct labor cost, assume that in December, 1959, the cost accountant of a firm estimates that his firm's factory will incur overhead costs in the amount of $180,000 during 1960. He further estimates that $120,000 of direct labor will be used in production during the same period of time. If these estimates are used to establish the predetermined overhead rate for 1960, the overhead rate established is 150 per cent. This is calculated:

$$\frac{\text{ESTIMATED OVERHEAD COSTS } \$180,000}{\text{ESTIMATED DIRECT LABOR COST } \$120,000} = 150 \text{ PER CENT}$$

After this predetermined overhead rate is established for 1960, it is used throughout 1960 to assign overhead to jobs as they are completed. Overhead is assigned to each job, and the cost of each job is calculated in the following manner: (1) As each job is completed, the cost of materials used on the job is found by adding the amounts in the Materials column of the job's cost sheet. Then (2) the cost of the labor applicable to the job is found by adding the amounts in the Labor column of the cost sheet. After this, (3) the overhead applicable to the job is calculated by multiplying the cost of the direct labor used on the job, as shown by the total of the Labor column of the job cost sheet, by the predetermined overhead rate. The amount of overhead thus calculated is then (4) entered in the Overhead Costs Applied column of the job cost sheet. After this, (5) the materials used and the labor and overhead applied are entered in the summary section of the cost sheet and totaled.

When overhead is assigned to jobs on the basis of a predetermined overhead rate based upon direct labor cost, it is assumed that the overhead applicable to a particular job bears the same relation to the direct labor cost of that job as the total estimated overhead of the factory bears to the total estimated direct labor cost. This assumption may not be accurate in every case. However, when the ratio of overhead to direct labor cost is approximately the same for all jobs, an overhead rate based upon direct labor cost offers an easily calculated and fair basis for assigning overhead to jobs. In those cases in which the ratio of overhead to direct labor cost does not remain the same for all jobs, some other relationship must be used. Often overhead rates based upon the ratio of overhead to direct labor hours or overhead to machine hours are used. A discussion of these methods of applying overhead is reserved for an advanced course in cost accounting.

Recording Overhead Applied.   When a job cost system is in use, as each job is completed the overhead applicable to it is calculated and entered on its job cost sheet. At the same time, the amount of overhead applied to the completed job is entered on a summary of overhead costs applied. The use of the summary of overhead costs applied was previously discussed on page 599. At the end of each cost period overhead based upon direct labor cost is also applied to the unfinished jobs in process. The overhead applied to the unfinished jobs is entered on the cost sheets of these jobs and on the summary of overhead costs applied. As a result of these procedures the summary of overhead costs applied shows at the end of each cost period the total cost of overhead applied to all jobs. As stated earlier, the job cost sheets are the accounts of a subsidiary Goods in Process Ledger that is controlled by the Goods in Process account. Entering the amount of overhead applicable to a job on its job cost sheet charges overhead to an account in the subsidiary Goods in Process Ledger. Consequently, if the balance of the Goods in Process account in the General Ledger is to equal the sum of the balances of the job cost sheets, overhead charged to individual jobs must also be charged to the Goods in Process account. This is accomplished at the end of each month when the total overhead costs applied during the month, as shown by the summary of overhead costs applied, is recorded with a general journal entry. For example, if the total of the summary of overhead costs applied for the month of March is $15,000, the following entry is made:

Mar.	31	Goods in Process......................	15,000.00	
		Overhead Costs....................		15,000.00
		To record the overhead applied to jobs as shown by the summary of overhead costs applied.		

After the month-end entry recording the overhead applied to jobs is posted and after the several entries from the General Journal and the Voucher Register recording the actual overhead costs incurred are posted, the Overhead Costs controlling account appears as in Illustration 139.

Illustration 139

Overhead Costs

Date	Explanation	F	Debit	Date	Explanation	F	Credit
Mar. 31		V89	2,256.40	Mar. 31		G24	15,000.00
31		G24	2,500.00				
31		G24	320.45				
31		G24	9,856.40				
31	Balance	√	66.75				
			15,000.00				15,000.00
				Mar. 31	Balance	√	66.75

Overapplied and Underapplied Overhead. When a job cost system is in use, the actual overhead costs incurred each month are debited to the Overhead Costs account and the estimated amount of overhead applied to jobs is credited. In the Overhead Costs account shown in Illustration 139, the actual overhead costs incurred are represented by four debits. The first debit represents the amounts of overhead for which vouchers were prepared during the month. The second and third debits represent indirect materials and indirect labor as accumulated on the materials used summary and the labor cost summary. The last debit, normally there would be more than one, represents the many expired overhead items, such as depreciation, expired insurance, and taxes. The sum of the four debits is, as nearly as it can be measured, the overhead incurred. The one credit to the account is the estimated amount of overhead that was applied to all jobs. It resulted from recording the information of the summary of overhead costs applied.

Obviously, when the Overhead Costs controlling account is debited for the overhead costs actually incurred each month and credited for the overhead applied to jobs on the basis of an estimated predetermined overhead application rate, the Overhead Costs controlling account will seldom be in balance at the end of a month. Some months overhead costs actually incurred and debited to the account will exceed overhead applied to jobs and credited to the account. Other months the overhead costs applied to jobs and credited to the account will exceed the overhead actually incurred and debited to the account. When the Overhead Costs account has a debit balance at the end of the month (actual overhead greater than overhead applied), the balance of the account is known as *underapplied overhead.* When the balance of the Overhead Costs account is a credit balance (actual overhead less than overhead applied), the balance of the account is called *overapplied overhead.* The under- or overapplied balance is usually left in the Overhead Costs controlling account until the end of the year. If the balance of the Overhead Costs controlling account is small and fluctuates from debit to credit throughout the year, it is an indication that the predetermined overhead rate is very nearly accurate. However, if a large debit balance builds up in the account, it is an indication that the rate is too low and should be increased. If a large credit balance builds up, it is an indication that the rate is too high.

At the end of each year the balance of the Overhead Costs controlling account is closed to the Cost of Goods Sold account as an adjustment of the cost of the goods manufactured and sold during the year.

Finished Goods Account

When a job is finished in the factory, it is normally transferred from the factory to the finished goods warehouse where it is kept until it is sold and delivered to a customer. At the same time a job is completed and transferred to the finished goods warehouse, its cost sheet is removed from the Job Cost Ledger, marked "completed," and filed away. Also, at this time the cost of the completed job is transferred by means of a general journal entry from the Goods in Process account to the Finished Goods account. The Finished Goods account is usually a controlling account controlling a subsidiary Finished Goods Ledger. The Finished Goods account and its subsidiary Finished Goods Ledger are operated in the same manner as the Materials account and its subsidiary ledger. As goods are completed and transferred from the factory, the Finished Goods controlling account and the proper finished goods account in the subsidiary ledger are debited for their cost. As goods are sold, the Finished Goods controlling account and the proper finished goods account in the subsidiary ledger are credited for their cost. As a result of these procedures the Finished Goods account is a perpetual inventory account, the balance of which shows the amount of unsold finished goods on hand.

Cost of Goods Sold Account

When a job cost system is in use, the cost to manufacture an order or a job lot of goods is known as soon as the order or job lot is completed.

This cost is transferred at once from the Goods in Process account to the Finished Goods account. Likewise, when an order of goods is sold, since its cost is known, the cost of the goods sold is recorded at the time of the sale. For example, if goods costing $279.00 to manufacture are sold for $450.00, the sale and the cost of the goods sold are recorded as follows:

Mar.	29	Accounts Receivable/Cone Lumber Company.....................................	450.00	
		Sales..............................		450.00
		Delivered a 10 H.P. electric motor.		
	29	Cost of Goods Sold.....................	279.00	
		Finished Goods....................		279.00
		To record the cost of the motor sold to the Cone Lumber Company.		

The first entry just given records in the usual manner the sale of the 10 H.P. electric motor. The second entry transfers the cost of manufacturing the motor from the Finished Goods account to the Cost of Goods Sold account. The two entries may be combined into a single entry.

As a result of the procedures just outlined, the balance of the Cost of Goods Sold account shows at the end of each accounting period the cost of all goods sold.

When the cost of all goods sold is recorded in a Cost of Goods Sold account as sales are made, taking a physical inventory of finished goods in order to calculate the cost of goods sold is unnecessary. However, an occasional physical inventory of finished goods is still required in order to check the accuracy of the book inventory of finished goods.

Financial Statements under a Job Cost System

The balance sheet of a manufacturing company operating a job cost system does not differ from that of a company with a general accounting system, and it is prepared in the same manner. Likewise, the income statement of a manufacturing company operating a job cost system and its schedule of cost of goods manufactured are similar to those of a company operating a general accounting system. However, their preparation differs. This is because the trial balance of a company operating a job cost system shows the ending inventories rather than the beginning inventories of materials, goods in process, and finished goods. Furthermore, the cost of goods sold is shown on the trial balance as the balance of the Cost of Goods Sold account. As a result much of the information for the income statement and the schedule of cost of goods manufactured of a company operating a job cost system is secured from an analysis of its Finished Goods and Goods in Process accounts.

When an income statement is prepared for a company operating a job cost system, the sales as shown by the balance of the Sales account are listed first on the statement in the usual manner. After this, information for the cost of goods sold section is secured from an analysis of the Finished Goods account. The beginning balance of the Finished Goods account is the cost of the beginning inventory of finished goods. The debits transferring finished goods to the account show the cost of the goods manufactured. The ending balance of the account is the ending inventory of finished goods. After the Finished Goods account is analyzed and the cost of goods sold section of the income statement prepared, the remainder of the income statement is prepared in the usual manner from information secured from the balances of the selling, administrative, and financial expense accounts.

The schedule of cost of goods manufactured or the manufacturing statement of a company operating a job cost system is usually much less complicated than that of a company operating a general accounting system. It is normally prepared from an analysis of the Goods in Process account and may be prepared monthly. Such a monthly statement appears as in Illustration 140.

Illustration 140
APEX MANUFACTURING COMPANY
Manufacturing Statement for the Month Ended March 31, 19--

Direct materials requisitioned	$17,000
Direct labor applied to production	10,000
Overhead costs applied to production at a predetermined rate of 150 per cent.	15,000
Total.	$42,000
Add: Beginning inventory of goods in process .	3,000
Total.	$45,000
Deduct: Ending inventory of goods in process .	9,000
Cost of Goods Manufactured Using a Predetermined Overhead Application Rate.	$36,000

The ease with which a manufacturing statement may be constructed from an analysis of the Goods in Process account becomes apparent when the statement shown in Illustration 140 is compared with the Goods in Process account on page 597.

The manufacturing statement shown in Illustration 140 is for a period of one month. The manufacturing statement for a year is similar excepting that the cost of goods manufactured is adjusted at the end of the statement for the over- or underapplied overhead in the following manner:

Cost of goods manufactured using a predetermined overhead rate	$430,000
Add: Underapplied overhead.	1,340
Cost of Goods Manufactured at Actual Cost . . .	$431,340

QUESTIONS FOR CLASS DISCUSSION

1. The emphasis of cost accounting differs from the emphasis of general accounting. What is emphasized in cost accounting?

2. What are the two main types of cost accounting systems? Which system generally best fits the needs of a manufacturer (a) who manufactures machinery to his customers' specifications, (b) who manufactures adding machines in lots of 500 adding machines, and (c) who manufactures paint?

3. Give the cost accounting meanings of the following:
   a) Job order cost system.
   b) Process cost system.
   c) Job.
   d) Job lot.
   e) Job cost sheet.
   f) Labor time ticket.
   g) Materials requisition.
   h) Materials used summary.
   i) Labor cost summary.
   j) Summary of overhead costs applied.

4. What two important characteristics distinguish a manufacturing cost accounting system from a general accounting system for a manufacturer?

5. What are the subsidiary ledgers controlled by each of the following accounts: (a) Materials, (b) Goods in Process, and (c) Finished Goods?

6. How is the inventory of goods in process determined in a general accounting system? How may the inventory of goods in process be determined in a job cost system?

7. What is the purpose of a job cost sheet? What is the name of the ledger that is made up of the job cost sheets of the unfinished jobs in process? What controlling account controls this ledger?

8. What are the sources of the entries on the job cost sheets for (a) materials, and (b) for labor?

9. Refer to the job cost sheet shown in Illustration 132. How was the amount of overhead charged to this job determined?

10. Outline a procedure that may be used in a job cost system to account for the acquisition of materials.

11. Outline a procedure that may be used in a job cost system to account for the use of materials.

12. In a job cost system, what is the purpose of the materials used summary?

13. At the end of a cost period the Direct Materials column of a materials used summary totaled $36,742 and the Indirect Materials column totaled $3,297. (a) What amount of materials was charged to jobs during the cost period? (b) What amount of materials was charged to overhead cost accounts? (c) Give the general journal entry to record the materials used during the cost period.

14. Outline a procedure that may be used in a job cost system to account for the use of labor.

15. At the end of a cost period the Direct Labor column of a labor cost summary totaled $41,776 and the Indirect Labor column totaled $8,321. (a) How much labor was charged directly to jobs during this cost period? (b) How much labor was charged to overhead cost accounts? (c) Give the general journal entry to record the amount of labor used during the cost period.

16. When a cost accounting system is in use, why is it unnecessary to make an end-of-the-period adjusting entry to record the accrued factory wages?

17. What are the four common sources of entries recording overhead cost items?

18. At the end of a cost period after all entries have been posted: (*a*) What does the sum of the items recorded on the debit side of the Overhead Costs controlling account represent? (*b*) What is recorded on the credit side of the Overhead Costs controlling account? (*c*) What does the balance of the account represent?

19. How is a predetermined overhead rate established? Why is a predetermined overhead rate used in a job cost system to charge overhead to jobs?

20. In December of 1960 the accountant of the Universal Company estimated that his company would incur overhead in the amount of $300,000 during 1961. He also estimated that during 1961 his company would use $240,000 of direct labor. If these estimates were used to establish an overhead rate based upon direct labor cost, what was the overhead rate?

21. Assume that the Universal Company of Question 20 established its overhead rate based upon the estimates of $300,000 of overhead costs and $240,000 of direct labor. Assume further that during 1961, Job 2147 was completed by the company. The job cost sheet of the job showed $2,625 of direct materials used and $3,200 of direct labor charged. What was the cost of Job 2147?

22. What does the total of the summary of overhead costs applied show at the end of a cost period?

23. Why does a company using a job cost system normally have either overapplied or underapplied overhead at the end of each cost period?

24. At the end of a cost period the Overhead Costs controlling account has a debit balance. Is this overapplied or underapplied overhead?

25. The Universal Company sold for $3,000 a job, the cost sheet of which showed a total cost of $1,963. Give the entries to record the sale and the cost of the goods sold.

PROBLEMS

Problem 24–1

The following summarized transactions are a portion of those completed by Troy Manufacturing Company during a cost period:

a) Purchased materials on account, $145,000.
b) Paid freight on materials, $2,100.
c) Paid factory wages, $109,000.
d) Paid $4,700 for repairs to factory machinery.
e) Made adjusting entries to record: depreciation of factory building, $18,500; depreciation of machinery, $29,000; expired insurance, $2,400; and accrued factory taxes, $3,700.
f) Recorded the materials used summary. The column totals were:

Direct materials	$128,000
Indirect materials	7,000
	$135,000

g) Recorded the labor cost summary. The column totals were:

Direct labor	$102,000
Indirect labor	11,500
	$113,500

h) Recorded the summary of overhead costs applied. Overhead was applied to jobs during the cost period on the basis of direct labor cost. The rate was 75 per cent.

i) Recorded jobs finished and transferred to finished goods, $254,000.

j) Recorded the sale at $302,000 of jobs that cost $223,000.

Required:

1. Prepare general journal entries to record the summarized transactions.
2. Open T-accounts for Materials, Goods in Process, Finished Goods, Accrued Factory Payroll, Overhead Costs, and Cost of Goods Sold. Post those portions of the general journal entries that affect the T-accounts.
3. After posting the entries, list each of the T-accounts and tell what its balance represents.

Problem 24–2

Stonevalley Manufacturing Company uses a job order cost accounting system. On September 30 of the current year, after all entries had been posted, the firm's Goods in Process account appeared as follows:

Goods in Process

Date		Explanation	F	Debit	Date		Explanation	F	Credit
Sept.	1	Balance		16,500.00	Sept.	12	Job 785		31,600.00
	30	Materials		61,400.00		18	Job 783		35,400.00
	30	Labor		83,000.00		19	Job 784		53,300.00
	30	Overhead		74,700.00		24	Job 786		46,500.00
						28	Job 782		43,600.00
						30	Balance		25,200.00
				235,600.00					235,600.00

Required:

1. From the information in the Goods in Process account, prepare a manufacturing statement for Stonevalley Manufacturing Company for the month of September.
2. Under the assumption that the direct labor cost of Job 782 was $16,500, determine the cost of its materials.

Problem 24–3

Crawford Manufacturing Company manufactures on special order a small machine called a "solidifier." During a cost period the following jobs were in process:

Job	Product	Customer
872	8 H.P. Solidifier	D. S. Troy Company
873	3 H.P. Solidifier	Wade and Tyler
874	5 H.P. Solidifier	Eastport Mfg. Company

Materials were delivered by the storeroom keeper to the factory on the following materials requisitions:

[handwritten: bal. Good in Process $ 245.00]
[handwritten: bal. Finish goods 486]

Requisition No.	Amount	Charge to Job	Charge to Subsidiary Overhead Account
1521	82.00	872	
1522	60.00	872	
1523	64.00	873	
1524	68.00	874	
1525	12.00		Machinery lubricants
1526	16.00	872	
1527	47.00	874	
1528	8.00	872	
1529	52.00	873	
1530	14.00	873	
1531	10.00	874	
1532	24.00		Building repairs

The following labor time tickets were received in the accounting department:

Time Ticket No.	Amount	Charge to Job	Charge to Subsidiary Overhead Account
2112	16.00	872	
2113	18.00	872	
2114	16.00	873	
2115	8.00		Machinery repairs
2116	12.00	874	
2117	20.00	874	
2118	20.00	872	
2119	18.00	873	
2120	16.00	872	
2121	20.00	873	
2122	16.00	874	
2123	12.00	872	
2124	20.00	873	
2125	6.00		Building repairs
2126	12.00		Building repairs

Jobs 872 and 873 were completed during the cost period. Overhead was assigned to each job upon completion. The overhead rate used was 150 per cent of direct labor cost.

Overhead was also assigned to Job 874 which was still in process at the end of the cost period.

Required:

1. Prepare job cost sheets for Jobs 872, 873, and 874.
2. Prepare a materials used summary, a labor cost summary, and a summary of overhead costs applied. The summary of overhead costs applied should have a column for job numbers and a column for amounts of overhead applied to each job.

3. Enter the materials requisitions for direct materials in the materials columns of the proper job cost sheets. Enter all materials requisitions on the materials used summary. (Normally, materials requisitions for indirect materials are debited to the Indirect Materials account in the subsidiary Overhead Costs Ledger. This step is omitted here in order to shorten and simplify the problem.)

4. Enter the time tickets for direct labor in the labor columns of the proper job cost sheet. Enter all labor time tickets on the labor cost summary. (Normally, labor time tickets for indirect labor are debited to the Indirect Labor account in the subsidiary Overhead Costs Ledger. This step is omitted here in order to shorten and simplify the problem.)

5. Calculate the amount of overhead applicable to each job. Enter the overhead on the job cost sheets and on the summary of overhead costs applied.

6. Prepare general journal entries to record the (a) materials used summary, (b) labor cost summary, (c) summary of overhead costs applied, and (d) the jobs completed.

7. Open T-accounts for Goods in Process and Finished Goods. Post the portions of the journal entries applicable to these accounts. Prove the balances of the accounts.

CLASS EXERCISE

Exercise 24–1

The Goods in Process account of a firm using a job order cost system had a debit balance of $4,200 at the beginning of a cost period. During the period the cost accountant of the firm prepared and posted the following four entries:

Goods in Process......................	62,100.00		
Overhead Costs.......................	5,800.00		
Materials........................		67,900.00
To record the materials used.		
Goods in Process......................	50,500.00		
Overhead Costs.......................	12,700.00		
Accrued Factory Payroll............		63,200.00
To record the labor used.		
Goods in Process......................	40,400.00		
Overhead Costs....................		40,400.00
To record the overhead applied to jobs.		
Finished Goods.......................	142,100.00		
Goods in Process..................		142,100.00
To transfer to Finished Goods the costs of all jobs finished.		

Required:

Under the assumption that there was only one job in process at the end of the cost period and that it had $6,100 of material charged to it, determine the amount of labor and of overhead charged to the job.

SUPPLEMENTARY PROBLEMS

Problem 24–A

Westlake Manufacturing Company uses a job order cost system. During its first year in operation the firm completed the following condensed transactions:

a) Purchased materials on account, $183,800.
b) Returned $1,700 of materials purchased.
c) Paid freight on materials, $2,100.
d) Paid factory wages, $168,000.
e) Paid for repairs to factory machinery, $8,000.
f) Made year-end adjusting entries to record: depreciation of factory building, $18,000; depreciation of machinery, $28,000; expired factory insurance, $3,500; accrued factory taxes, $10,500.
g) Recorded the labor cost summary. The column totals were:

Direct labor	$141,000
Indirect labor	33,000
	$174,000

h) Recorded the materials used summary. The column totals were:

Direct materials	$154,500
Indirect materials	11,000
	$165,500

i) Recorded the summary of overhead costs applied. Overhead was applied to jobs during the cost period on the basis of direct labor cost. The rate was 80 per cent.
j) Recorded the costs of the jobs finished and transferred to finished goods, $312,000.
k) Recorded the sale at $405,000 of jobs that cost $270,000.
l) At the end of the year, closed the Overhead Costs account.

Required:

1. Prepare general journal entries to record the foregoing transactions.
2. Open T-accounts for Materials, Goods in Process, Finished Goods, Accrued Factory Payroll, Overhead Costs, and Cost of Goods Sold. Post the portions of the general journal entries that affect the accounts.
3. Prepare a manufacturing statement for the firm.
4. List the balance of each T-account and tell what the balance represents.
5. Give, also, the balance of the Overhead Costs account before it was closed, and tell what this balance represented.

Problem 24–B

A portion of the transactions completed by Midway Manufacturing Company during its first cost period are summarized as follows:

a) Purchased materials from vendors on account, $13,000.
b) Paid factory wages, $12,400.
c) Paid miscellaneous overhead cost items, $800.
d) Materials requisitions were used during the cost period to charge jobs with materials. The requisitions were then entered on a materials used summary. (Instructions for recording the summary are given in Item j.) An abstract of the requisitions showed the following amounts of materials

charged to jobs. (Charge the materials to the jobs by making entries directly in the job T-accounts in the subsidiary Job Cost Ledger.)

Job No. 1	$ 2,600
Job No. 2	1,300
Job No. 3	2,800
Job No. 4	3,000
Job No. 5	600
	$10,300

e) Labor time tickets were used to charge jobs with direct labor. The time tickets were then entered on a labor cost summary. (Instructions for recording the summary are given under Item k.) An abstract of the tickets showed the following amounts of labor charged to the several jobs. (Charge the labor to the several jobs by making entries directly in the job T-accounts in the Job Cost Ledger.)

Job No. 1	$2,400
Job No. 2	1,400
Job No. 3	2,600
Job No. 4	2,800
Job No. 5	400
	$9,600

f) Jobs Nos. 1, 3, and 4 were completed and transferred to finished goods. A predetermined overhead application rate of 150 per cent of direct labor cost was used to apply overhead to each job upon its completion. (Enter the overhead in the job T-accounts; mark the jobs "completed"; and make a general journal entry to transfer their costs to the Finished Goods account.)

g) Job Nos. 1 and 3 were sold on account for a total of $24,000.

h) At the end of the cost period, charged overhead to the uncompleted jobs at the rate of 150 per cent of direct labor cost. (Enter the overhead in the job T-accounts.)

i) At the end of the cost period, made entries to record: depreciation on the factory building, $2,300; depreciation on the machinery, $4,100; expired factory insurance, $600; and accrued taxes payable, $1,200.

j) Recorded the information of the materials used summary. The column totals were:

Direct materials	$10,300
Indirect materials	2,000
	$12,300

k) Recorded the information of the labor cost summary. The column totals were:

Direct labor	$ 9,600
Indirect labor	3,100
	$12,700

l) Recorded the information of the summary of overhead applied. (See Items f and h for the amount of overhead applied.)

Required:

1. Open the following general ledger T-accounts: Materials, Goods in Process, Finished Goods, Accrued Factory Payroll, Overhead Costs, and Cost of Goods Sold.

2. Open an additional T-account for each of the five jobs. Assume that each job's T-account is a job cost sheet in a subsidiary Job Cost Ledger.
3. Prepare general journal entries to record the applicable information of Items *a, b, c, f, g, i, j, k,* and *l.* Post the portions of the entries that affect the general ledger accounts opened.
4. Enter the applicable information of Items *d, e, f,* and *h* directly in the T-accounts that represent job cost sheets.
5. Present statistics to prove the balances of the Goods in Process and Finished Goods accounts.
6. List the general ledger accounts and tell what is represented by the balance of each account.

Chapter

25

BASIC PROCESS COST
ACCOUNTING

PROCESS COST accounting is a type of cost accounting used by continuous production industries, such as flour mills, sugar refineries, cement plants, and brickyards. In such industries the finished product results from the completion of a series of processes, each process advancing the product one step toward completion. For example, in a brickyard clay is mined from clay pits, ground and mixed with other ingredients, cut into bricks, and burned (baked) in kilns. In a brickyard finished bricks result from the mining, grinding and mixing, cutting, and burning processes.

The term *process* is used in continuous production industries to denote a manufacturing operation. The term is also used interchangeably with the phrase *processing department* to mean a physical grouping of the men and machines required to complete a stage or a step in the manufacture of a product. For example, in the brickyard just described each of the following processes or processing departments completes a step in the manufacture of bricks: mining department, grinding and mixing department, cutting department, and burning department.

Characteristics of Process Cost Accounting

A process cost accounting system is one in which costs are assembled in terms of processing departments. A number of characteristics are common to all process cost systems. Some of the more important are: (1) Costs are assembled in terms of departments. (2) The number of units of product processed as well as processing costs are recorded. (3) As an aid in controlling costs, per unit product costs for materials, for labor, and for overhead are usually calculated for each processing department. (4) Since a processing department will normally begin and end a cost account-period with inventories of unfinished goods in process, costs are calculated on the basis of *equivalent finished units* processed. (5) Costs are transferred and advanced from one processing department to the next. Each of these characteristics will be discussed in turn in the pages that follow.

Costs Assembled in Terms of Departments

The primary difference between job order cost accounting and process cost accounting is in the assembling of costs. In a job order system costs are assembled on job cost sheets by jobs or job lots of product. In a process system job cost sheets are not used, and costs are assembled by departments rather than by jobs. This difference is the result of differences in the manufacturing procedures and in the products of companies to which the two kinds of cost systems are applicable. A company to which a job cost system is applicable produces indentifiably different jobs or job lots of product, while a company to which a process cost system is applicable produces a continuous flow of standardized units of finished product.

The production of a continuous flow of standardized units of product makes it possible in a continuous production industry to assemble production costs and to calculate unit costs by departments. In such an industry, because of standardization, it is assumed that each like unit of product contains the same amounts of materials, labor, and overhead and is processed in the same manner in each department through which it passes. As a result, in such an industry the unit cost of completing a particular process in the manufacture of a product may be secured as follows: (1) The costs of the materials, labor, and overhead used in completing the process are charged for a cost accounting period of a day, week, or month to the goods in process account of the department responsible for the completion of the process. (2) The number of units of product processed in the department during the cost period are recorded. (3) At the end of the cost period, the sum of the costs of the materials, labor, and overhead charged to the department is divided by the number of units of product processed to secure the cost per unit processed. For example, if during a cost period the clay mining department of a brickyard is charged with $12,000 of materials, labor, and overhead and if during the same period it mines 20,000 yards of clay, the cost of mining clay during the cost period is $0.60 per yard. Costs of $12,000 divided by 20,-000 yards of clay gives a per unit cost of $0.60 per yard.

Charging Materials to Departments. Accounting for the purchase and receipt of materials under a process cost system is the same as under a job cost system. Materials are ordered by a purchasing department and received by a receiving department where they are counted, inspected, and forwarded on to a storeroom. Receiving reports are prepared and forwarded to the purchasing department and on to the accounting department where entries are made in the Voucher Register and on subsidiary materials ledger cards.

Although accounting for the acquisition of materials is the same under both job cost and process cost systems, accounting for the use of materials differs. Normally, in a process cost system no distinction is made between direct and indirect materials. Furthermore, since there are no jobs or job cost sheets, materials are not charged to jobs. Rather, both direct and indirect materials are charged directly to the goods in process accounts of the departments that consume the materials.

Material requisitions which are summarized on a materials used summary having a column for each department are often used to charge materials to the departments. Sometimes, when only a few kinds of materials are issued, material requisitions are not used. In such cases a record of the materials issued to each department is kept in the storeroom, and the amount issued to each department is reported at the end of each cost accounting period by means of a *consumption report*. At the end of each cost accounting period, the materials issued to each department as shown by the materials used summary or by the consumption report are charged to the departments by means of a general journal entry. For example, at the end of a cost accounting period the materials used summary of the Delta Processing Company, a firm having three processing departments, shows the following materials requisitioned and issued during the period:

```
Grinding department.....................................$ 9,900.00
Mixing department.......................................  2,040.00
Packaging department....................................  1,515.00
        Total Materials Issued..........................$13,455.00
```

The information of this summary is recorded with the following general journal entry:

Apr.	30	Goods in Process, Grinding Department...	9,900.00	
		Goods in Process, Mixing Department.....	2,040.00	
		Goods in Process, Packaging Department..	1,515.00	
		Materials........................		13,455.00
		To record the materials issued to the processing departments.		

In a process cost system unit processing costs are calculated for each processing department. Consequently, a separate goods in process account is required for each processing department. In the entry just given the materials charged to the goods in process accounts of the grinding, mixing, and packaging departments include both the direct and the indirect materials issued to the departments.

Charging Labor to Departments. Accounting for labor is in many respects very similar in both job cost and process cost accounting. Usually there are only three important differences. In the first place, normally no distinction is made in a process cost system between direct and indirect labor. In the second place, in a process cost system the labor time tickets are summarized each day by departments on a labor cost summary having a column for each department. And in the third place, since job cost sheets are not used, the time tickets are not recorded by jobs.

When a process cost system is in use, the amount of labor chargeable to each department is determined by labor time tickets that are summarized on a labor cost summary having a column for each department. At the end of each cost accounting period, the several column totals of the labor cost summary show the amounts of labor consumed in each of the departments. The cost of this labor is charged to the departments with a general journal entry as follows:

Apr.	30	Goods in Process, Grinding Department...	5,700.00	
		Goods in Process, Mixing Department.....	3,570.00	
		Goods in Process, Packaging Department..	909.00	
		Accrued Factory Payroll............		10,179.00
		To charge the departments with the labor applied to production.		

Charging Overhead to Departments. In those processing industries in which the rate of production fluctuates greatly from month to month, as in industries of a seasonal nature, a predetermined overhead rate may be used to charge overhead to the processing departments. Such a method of charging overhead tends to equalize the overhead charged to each unit of product in the different months. However, in processing industries where production is at a uniform rate, charging overhead by means of a predetermined rate is unnecessary. In such industries actual overhead incurred is charged to the departments and to the units of product processed.

In processing industries in which the rate of production is uniform, the methods and techniques of departmental accounting are commonly used to charge and allocate overhead costs to the departments. (It might be wise at this point for the student to review the portions of Chapter 10 having to do with departmental accounting.) Different combinations of methods and techniques are used by different companies. However, in one commonly used system all items of overhead are charged to undepartmentalized overhead cost accounts as they are paid and recorded. Then, at the end of the cost period, a *departmental overhead costs analysis sheet* is prepared to determine the portion of the total overhead that is applicable to each department. Such a departmental overhead costs analysis sheet may appear somewhat like that of the Delta Processing Company which is shown in Illustration 141. Such a departmental overhead costs analysis sheet is prepared by placing the balances of the undepartmentalized over-

Illustration 141

DELTA PROCESSING COMPANY
Departmental Overhead Costs Analysis Sheet
For Month Ended April 30, 19—

Undepartmentalized Cost Accounts	Basis of Allocation	Cost Account Balance	Allocations of Costs		
			Grinding Dept.	Mixing Dept.	Packaging Dept.
Superintendent's salary	Number of employees	$1,000	$ 595	$ 265	$ 140
Expired insurance	Value of equipment	522	348	79	95
Property taxes	Value of equipment	816	544	123	149
Depreciation of machinery	Value of equipment	1,920	1,280	288	352
Depreciation of building	Floor space	1,845	1,220	204	421
Power costs	Meters	404	288	61	55
Totals		$6,507	$4,275	$1,020	$1,212

head accounts in the first money column on the analysis sheet form and then allocating these balances to the columns of the processing departments according to the bases shcwn in the Basis of Allocation column.

When a departmental overhead analysis sheet such as that of the Delta Company is prepared, the information shown on the completed analysis sheet becomes the basis of a journal entry. This journal entry closes the undepartmentalized overhead cost accounts and transfers the overhead recorded in these accounts to the goods in process accounts of the processing departments. For example, the entry that closes the undepartmentalized overhead cost accounts of the Delta Processing Company and transfers the overhead recorded in these accounts to the several department goods in process accounts appears as follows:

Apr.	30	Goods in Process, Grinding Department...	4,275.00	
		Goods in Process, Mixing Department.....	1,020.00	
		Goods in Process, Packaging Department..	1,212.00	
		Superintendent's Salary.............		1,000.00
		Expired Insurance..................		522.00
		Property Taxes.....................		816.00
		Depreciation of Machinery..........		1,920.00
		Depreciation of Building...........		1,845.00
		Power Costs.......................		404.00
		To close the overhead cost accounts and to transfer the overhead recorded therein to the goods in process accounts of the departments.		

The debits of the illustrated entry were secured from the totals of the allocation columns of the Delta Company's departmental overhead costs analysis sheet. The credits are the balances of the company's undepartmentalized cost accounts which are shown in the first money column of the company's overhead costs analysis sheet.

Recording the Number of Units of Product Produced

In a factory using a process cost system, daily production records are maintained in each processing department. In some processing departments meters are attached to machines, and the meter readings are used as the basis of the daily production records. In other processing departments the foreman is made responsible for a daily count of production. The records of a department's daily production are summarized at the end of each month or other cost period on a department report called a *production report*. The production report of each department shows (1) the number of units of product that were in process in the department at the beginning of the cost accounting period. It also shows (2) the number of units finished in the department and transferred to the next department or to finished goods, and (3) the inventory of units still in process in the department at the end of the period. In addition, it shows the stages of completion of the beginning and ending inventories of goods in process. A production report for the grinding department of the Delta Processing Company is shown in Illustration 142.

Illustration 142

DEPARTMENT PRODUCTION REPORT		
Department *Grinding*	Month *April* , 19 __	
QUANTITY TO BE ACCOUNTED FOR:		
Units in process at the beginning of month	30,000	
Units placed in process during month	90,000	
Total to be accounted for		120,000
ACCOUNTED FOR AS FOLLOWS:		
Units completed and transferred to Mixing Department	100,000	
Units completed and on hand in department	0	
Unfinished units in process at end of month	20,000	
Total units accounted for		120,000

Stage of completion of the units in process at the beginning of the month as to:		Stage of completion of the unfinished units in process at the end of the month as to:	
Materials	Completed	Materials	Completed
Labor	1/3	Labor	1/4
Overhead	1/3	Overhead	1/4

Calculating Unit Processing Costs

In order to better control costs, companies using a process cost system normally calculate for each processing department the cost of materials, the cost of labor, and the cost of overhead per unit of product processed. Calculating the costs of materials, labor, and overhead per unit of product processed is not difficult in a department in which there are no beginning and ending inventories of work in process. All that is required in such cases is a division of the cost of the materials, the cost of the labor, and the cost of the overhead charged to the department by the number of units processed. For example, during a cost period the clay mining department of a brickyard was charged with $1,200 of materials, $6,000 of labor, and $4,800 of overhead. During the same period the department mined 20,000 yards of clay. As a result, the $1,200 of materials, $6,000 of labor, and $4,800 of overhead are each divided by 20,000 to secure a materials cost of $0.06, a labor cost of $0.30, and an overhead cost of $0.24 per yard of clay mined. In this case the calculations are easy. However, a depart-

ment often begins and ends a cost period with goods in a partially processed state of manufacture. In such cases the calculation of unit processing costs is not so simple.

When a processing department begins and ends a cost accounting period with inventories of work in process, the calculation of unit processing
costs is more difficult because the materials, labor, and overhead charged
to the department are used on three distinct tasks. (1) Portions of each
are used *to complete* the beginning inventory of goods in process. (2)
Portions of each are used *to start and finish* the processing of a number
of units of product. And (3) portions of each are used *to start* the processing of the unfinished ending inventory of goods in process. In such cases
a problem arises as to how much of the materials, how much of the labor,
and how much of the overhead charged to the department should be assigned to each of the inventories and to the goods started and finished.
Until a decision is made as to the portions of the materials, labor, and
overhead of a department that are applicable to each of the inventories
and to the goods started and finished, unit processing costs for material,
labor, and overhead, as well as the total cost of the units processed in a
department, cannot be calculated.

Calculating Equivalent Units

If the costs of the materials, labor, and overhead charged to a department are to be fairly apportioned among its beginning goods in process,
its goods started and finished, and its ending inventory of goods in process, the amounts of material, labor, and overhead assigned to each must be
expressed in *common denominators*. These common denominators are
called *equivalent finished units*. In assigning the costs of a department to
its inventories, and to its goods started and finished, equivalent finished
units of material, equivalent finished units of labor, and equivalent finished units of overhead are calculated.

The idea of equivalent finished units is based on the assumption that
the same amount of material is required to give each of four units of product one fourth of their material as is required to give a single unit of product all of its material, or that it takes the same amounts of labor and overhead to one-third complete each of three units of product as it takes to
completely finish a single unit.

The apportioning of the cost of labor charged to a department between
the department's inventories and its goods started and finished may be
used to illustrate the application of the idea of equivalent finished units
in apportioning all of a department's costs. For example, assume that:

   a) The grinding department of the Delta Processing Company is charged
   with $5,700 of labor during a cost period.
   b) Labor is added to the product evenly throughout the process of the
   grinding department.
   c) The goods in process in the department at the beginning of the cost
   period consisted of 30,000 units of product that were one-third completed
   when the period began.

d) The goods finished in the department consisted of 100,000 units. These in turn consisted of the 30,000 units in process at the beginning of the cost period plus 70,000 units started and finished during the period.

e) The ending inventory of goods in process in the department consisted of 20,000 units that were one-fourth finished when the period ended.

In arriving at the portions of the $5,700 of labor that are to be assigned to each of the inventories and to the goods started and finished, three calculations are made. Under the assumptions just listed these calculations are as follows:

CALCULATION ONE: The equivalent finished units of labor and the sum of the equivalent finished units of labor assigned to each of the inventories and to the goods started and finished are calculated as follows:

	Units Involved	Fraction of a Unit of Labor Added during This Period	Equivalent Units of Labor Added in This Department
Inventory of 30,000 units one-third completed at the beginning.........	30,000	⅔	20,000
Units started and finished............	70,000	1	70,000
Inventory of 20,000 units one-fourth completed at the end.............	20,000	¼	5,000
Total Equivalent Units..........			95,000

CALCULATION TWO: The total cost of the labor charged to the department is divided by the sum of the equivalent units of labor added to each of the inventories and to the goods started and finished. This gives the cost of an equivalent unit of labor.

$5,700 OF LABOR ÷ 95,000 EQUIVALENT UNITS = $0.06 PER EQUIVALENT UNIT

CALCULATION THREE: The equivalent units of labor added to each of the inventories and to the goods in process are then multiplied by the cost of an equivalent unit of labor to secure the share of the total labor cost that is chargeable to each of the inventories and to the goods started and finished.

Beginning inventory (20,000 equivalent units at $0.06)................$1,200
Units started and finished (70,000 equivalent units at $0.06)............ 4,200
Ending inventory (5,000 equivalent units at $0.06).................... 300
   Total Labor Charged to the Department.....................$5,700

The 30,000 units of the beginning goods in process inventory of this department were one-third completed when the cost period began. Consequently, they received two thirds of their labor and were two-thirds completed during this cost period. If it is assumed that it takes *one unit* of labor to begin and complete a unit of product, then these 30,000 units of product should each be charged with two thirds of a unit of labor. Each received two thirds of a unit of labor in this department during this cost period. Notice in the calculation of equivalent finished units that each of these units are assigned two thirds of a unit of labor. Observe also that the 70,000 units that were started and finished are each assigned a full unit of labor and that the 20,000 units that were started but only one-fourth finished are charged with one fourth of a unit. Notice in the calculation of equivalent finished units that the units involved in each of the inventories and the goods started and finished are multiplied by the fraction of a unit of labor applied to each. The results of these multiplications indicate the portions of the total labor cost of the department, measured in equivalent finished units of labor, that are applicable to each of the inventories and to the work started and finished.

The three calculations just illustrated show the use of the idea of equivalent finished units in assigning a department's labor to its inventories and to its goods started and finished. Calculations similar to these are also used in assigning a department's materials and overhead to its inventories and to its goods started and finished.

Transferring Costs from One Department to the Next

The manufacturing procedure of a continuous production company is carried on in one or more processing departments. In such a company the product is transferred and advanced from one processing department to the next as the steps in its manufacture are completed. As a result of this transfer of the product from one department to the next, when a process cost system is applied to such a company, the manufacturing costs of the product are also transferred and advanced from the goods in process account of one department to the goods in process account of the next until the last department is reached. The last department produces finished goods; consequently, the accumulated costs of the finished goods are transferred from the goods in process account of the last department to the finished goods account. For example, in the brickyard of previous illustrations it was assumed that during a cost period $12,000 of materials, labor, and overhead were charged to the goods in process account of the clay mining department. It was further assumed that this expenditure resulted in the production of 20,000 yards of clay which were delivered to the grinding and mixing department. As a result, at the end of the cost period the following entry is made by the cost accountant of the brickyard to transfer the mining costs of the 20,000 yards of clay from the goods in process account of the clay mining department to the goods in process account of the grinding and mixing department:

Mar.	31	Goods in Process, Grinding and Mixing Department.......................	12,000.00	
		Goods in Process, Clay Mining Department.......................		12,000.00
		To transfer to the grinding and mixing department the clay mining costs of 20,000 yards of clay.		

To continue the illustration, assume that during the same cost period $2,500 of material, labor, and overhead was charged to the grinding and mixing department; and that all of this $2,500 was expended in grinding and mixing the 20,000 yards of clay. Also, that after the clay was ground and mixed, all 20,000 yards were transferred to the cutting department to be cut into bricks. As a result of these assumptions, by the time the clay was ground and mixed and transferred to the cutting department, its accumulated costs amounted to $14,500 ($12,000 of clay mining costs plus $2,500 of grinding and mixing costs equal $14,500). At the end of the cost period these accumulated costs are transferred from the goods in process account of the grinding and mixing department to the goods in process account of the cutting department with the following entry:

| Mar. | 31 | Goods in Process, Cutting Department.... Goods in Process, Grinding and Mix ing Department............. To transfer to the cutting department the accumulated costs of mining, grind ing, and mixing 20,000 yards of clay. | 14,500.00 | 14,500.00 |

To continue the illustration still further, assume that in the same cost period $5,500 of material, labor, and overhead were charged to the cutting department. Assume further that all of this $5,500 was expended in cutting the 20,000 yards of clay into bricks and that all of the bricks were transferred to the burning department. As a result of these assumptions, by the time the cut bricks reached the burning department, their accumulated costs amounted to $20,000 ($12,000 of clay mining costs, $2,500 of grinding and mixing costs, and $5,500 of cutting costs). Consequently, at the end of the cost period, the following entry is made by the cost accountant to transfer the accumulated cost of the cut bricks from the Goods in Process, Cutting Department account to the Goods in Process, Burning Department account:

| Mar. | 31 | Goods in Process, Burning Department.... Goods in Process, Cutting Department To transfer to the burning department the accumulated cost of mining, grinding and mixing, and cutting 20,000 yards of clay into bricks. | 20,000.00 | 20,000.00 |

In a company using a process cost system, this accumulation and transfer of costs from one department to the next is continued until the last processing department is reached. The last processing department produces finished goods. Consequently, the accumulated costs of the goods processed in the last department and finished during a cost period are transferred from the goods in process account of the last department to the Finished Goods account. To illustrate this assume that $4,000 of material, labor, and overhead were charged to the burning department of the illustrative brickyard and that these costs were used to burn all the bricks transferred from the cutting department. If this assumption is made, the accumulated costs of the bricks finished and transferred to Finished Goods are $24,000 ($12,000, clay mining; $2,500, grinding and mixing; $5,500, cutting; and $4,000, burning). If the accumulated cost of the bricks finished amounts to $24,000, the entry to transfer the accumulated cost of the finished bricks to the Finished Goods account is:

Mar.	31	Finished Goods.......................	24,000.00	
		Goods in Process, Burning Depart- ment...........................		24,000.00
		To transfer to Finished Goods the ac- cumulated mining, grinding and mixing, cutting, and burning costs of the finished bricks.		

Department Processing Cost Summary

A continuous production company using a process cost system, just as any other manufacturing company, prepares a balance sheet, an income statement, and a manufacturing statement. The balance sheet and the income statement are prepared in the usual manner. However, the manufacturing statement of such a company is usually prepared by combining the information shown in the *process cost summaries* of the several processing departments of the company. A process cost summary is shown in Illustration 143. A process cost summary is a report peculiar to a company using a process cost system. In such a company a separate process cost summary is prepared for each processing department. The process cost summary of a department is prepared from information in the department's production report, see Illustration 142 (p. 629), and from information in its goods in process account. A process cost summary of a department shows: (1) the costs charged to the department, (2) the department's equivalent unit processing costs for materials, labor, and overhead, and (3) the cost applicable to each of the department's inventories and to its goods started and finished. Observe how the process cost summary of the Delta Company shown in Illustration 143 emphasizes these three points. This process cost summary is explained in more detail in the illustration of process cost accounting that follows.

Process Cost Accounting Illustrated

Several of the characteristics of process cost systems have been individually illustrated and discussed in the previous pages of this chapter. On this and the next few pages, the subject matter of these individual illustrations is brought together and expanded into a more complete illus-

Illustration 143

DELTA PROCESSING COMPANY
Process Cost Summary, Grinding Department
For Month Ended April 30, 19--

COSTS CHARGED TO THE DEPARTMENT:

Material requisitioned	$ 9,900
Labor charged.	5,700
Overhead costs incurred.	4,275
	$19,875
Goods in process at the beginning of the month	4,250
Total Costs to Be Accounted for.	$24,125

EQUIVALENT UNIT PROCESSING COSTS:

Material:	Units Involved	Fraction of a Unit Added	Equivalent Units Added
Beginning inventory	30,000	-0-	-0-
Units started and finished	70,000	1	70,000
Ending inventory	20,000	1	20,000
			90,000

Unit processing cost for material: $9,900 ÷ 90,000 = $0.11

Labor and Overhead:	Units Involved	Fraction of a Unit Added	Equivalent Units Added
Beginning inventory	30,000	2/3	20,000
Units started and finished	70,000	1	70,000
Ending inventory	20,000	1/4	5,000
			95,000

Unit processing cost for labor: $5,700 ÷ 95,000 = $0.06
Unit processing cost for overhead: $4,275 ÷ 95,000 = $0.045

COSTS APPLICABLE TO THE WORK OF THE DEPARTMENT:

Goods in Process, One-third Processed at the Beginning of April:

Costs charged to the beginning inventory of goods in process during previous month	$4,250	
Material added (all added during March).	-0-	
Labor applied (20,000 x $0.06)	1,200	
Overhead applied (20,000 x $0.045)	900	
Cost to Process.		$ 6,350

Goods Started and Finished in the Department during April:

Material added (70,000 x $0.11).	$7,700	
Labor applied (70,000 x $0.06)	4,200	
Overhead applied (70,000 x $0.045)	3,150	
Cost to Process.		15,050
Total Cost of the Goods Processed in the Department and transferred to the Mixing Department (100,000 Units at $0.214 Each)		$21,400

Goods in Process, One-fourth Processed at the End of April:

Material added (20,000 x $0.11).	$2,200	
Labor applied (5,000 x $0.06).	300	
Overhead applied (5,000 x $0.045).	225	
Cost to One-fourth Process		2,725
Total Costs Accounted for.		$24,125

tration of a process cost accounting system. This more complete illustration is the process cost system of the Delta Processing Company, a company which is assumed to manufacture a patented home remedy called "Noxall."

It is assumed in the illustration of process cost accounting that:

The manufacturing procedure of the Delta Processing Company is carried on in three processing departments. They are the grinding department, the mixing department, and the packaging department. In the manufacturing process of the Delta Company material AAA is finely ground in the grinding department, after which it is transferred to the mixing department where materials BBB and CCC are added, and the resulting mixture is thoroughly mixed. This mixing process results in the product Noxall, which is transferred upon completion to the packaging department. In the packaging department the Noxall is packaged in paper boxes and packed in cartons. The cartons of Noxall are then transferred to the finished goods warehouse, where they are stored until sold.

The Delta Company assumes:

a) That all of the material AAA that is placed in process in the grinding department is placed in process at the very beginning of the process.
b) That all of the materials BBB and CCC that are placed in process in the mixing department are placed in process evenly throughout the process. In other words, the company assumes that when the product is one-third processed in this department, it has received one third of its materials BBB and CCC, and that when the product is three-fourths processed, it has received three-fourths of its materials BBB and CCC.
c) That three fifths of the materials of the packaging department are used at the beginning of the process and that two fifths are used at the end of the process. However, this has no effect because the company follows the practice of completing the packaging of all Noxall finished each day. As a result of this policy, there is never an inventory of partially processed product in the packaging department.
d) That the labor and overhead applied in each process are applied evenly throughout the process.

During the month of April, the Delta Company completed the following transactions affecting its processing operations:

a) Prepared vouchers as follows:
Material purchases, $12,900.
Factory payroll, $9,500.
Superintendent's salary, $1,000.
Power costs, $404.
b) Paid $23,000 of vouchers payable.

The effect of these transactions on the accounts is shown with the following general journal entries:

Apr.	...	Materials............................	12,900.00	
		Accrued Factory Payroll................	9,500.00	
		Superintendent's Salary.................	1,000.00	
		Power Costs..........................	404.00	
		Vouchers Payable.................		23,804.00
		Recorded Vouchers Payable.		
	...	Vouchers Payable......................	23,000.00	
		First National Bank................		23,000.00
		Paid Vouchers Payable.		

On April 30, at the end of the monthly cost period, the following adjusting journal entry was made to record the overhead costs accrued and expired:

Apr.	30	Expired Insurance..........................	522.00	
		Property Taxes..........................	816.00	
		Depreciation of Machinery..............	1,920.00	
		Depreciation of Building................	1,845.00	
		Prepaid Insurance...................		522.00
		Property Taxes Payable.............		816.00
		Accumulated Depreciation, Machinery		1,920.00
		Accumulated Depreciation, Building..		1,845.00
		To record overhead costs accrued and expired.		

On April 30, at the end of the monthly cost period, the materials used summary showed the following amounts of materials requisitioned by the departments:

Grinding department.....................................	$ 9,900.00
Mixing department.....................................	2,040.00
Packaging department..................................	1,515.00
Total..	$13,455.00

The information of the materials used summary was recorded with the following general journal entry:

Apr.	30	Goods in Process, Grinding Department...	9,900.00	
		Goods in Process, Mixing Department.....	2,040.00	
		Goods in Process, Packaging Department..	1,515.00	
		Materials.......................		13,455.00
		To charge the departments for materials requisitioned.		

At the end of the cost period the labor cost summary indicated that the following amounts of labor were applied to production in the several departments during the period:

Grinding department.....................................	$ 5,700.00
Mixing department.....................................	3,570.00
Packaging department..................................	909.00
Total..	$10,179.00

The following general journal entry was made to charge this labor to the goods in process accounts of the several departments:

Apr.	30	Goods in Process, Grinding Department...	5,700.00	
		Goods in Process, Mixing Department.....	3,570.00	
		Goods in Process, Packaging Department..	909.00	
		Accrued Factory Payroll............		10,179.00
		To charge the departments with the labor applied to production.		

On April 30, after all journal entries recording overhead costs were posted, a departmental overhead costs analysis sheet was prepared. The overhead costs analysis sheet appeared as in Illustration 144.

Illustration 144

DELTA PROCESSING COMPANY

Departmental Overhead Costs Analysis Sheet
For Month Ended April 30, 19—

Undepartmentalized Cost Accounts	Basis of Allocation	Cost Account Balance	Allocations of Costs		
			Grinding Dept.	Mixing Dept.	Packaging Dept.
Superintendent's salary	Number of employees	$1,000	$ 595	$ 265	$ 140
Expired insurance	Value of equipment	522	348	79	95
Property taxes	Value of equipment	816	544	123	149
Depreciation of machinery	Value of equipment	1,920	1,280	288	352
Depreciation of building	Floor space	1,845	1,220	204	421
Power costs	Meters	404	288	61	55
		$6,507	$4,275	$1,020	$1,212

After the departmental overhead costs analysis sheet was prepared, the following general journal entry was made to close the overhead costs accounts and to transfer and charge their balances to the goods in process accounts of the several departments:

Apr.	30	Goods in Process, Grinding Department....	4,275.00	
		Goods in Process, Mixing Department.....	1,020.00	
		Goods in Process, Packaging Department..	1,212.00	
		Superintendent's Salary............		1,000.00
		Expired Insurance................		522.00
		Property Taxes....................		816.00
		Depreciation of Machinery..........		1,920.00
		Depreciation of Building............		1,845.00
		Power Costs......................		404.00
		To close the overhead cost accounts and to transfer the overhead recorded therein to the goods in process accounts of the departments.		

After all of the illustrated entries were posted, the goods in process accounts of the three processing departments appeared as follows:

Goods in Process, Grinding Department

Apr.	1	Beginning inventory	4,250	
	30	Materials	9,900	
	30	Labor	5,700	
	30	Overhead	4,275	
			24,125	

Goods in Process, Mixing Department

Apr. 1	Beginning Inventory	3,785
30	Materials	2,040
30	Labor	3,570
30	Overhead	1,020

Goods in Process, Packaging Department

Apr. 30	Materials	1,515
30	Labor	909
30	Overhead	1,212

On April 30, the production reports prepared by the department foremen gave the following information in regard to the inventories of work in process and the goods started and finished in each of the departments during the month:

	Grinding Department	Mixing Department	Packaging Department
Units in the beginning inventories of goods in process..............	30,000	16,000	–0–
Stage of completion at beginning of the period of the beginning inventories of goods in process........	$\frac{1}{3}$	$\frac{1}{4}$	
Units started in process and finished during period.............	70,000	85,000	101,000
Total units finished and transferred to next department or to finished goods........................	100,000	101,000	101,000
Units in the ending inventories of goods in process	20,000	15,000	–0–
Stage of completion of ending inventories of goods in process.....	$\frac{1}{4}$	$\frac{1}{3}$	

After receiving the production reports of each of the three departments, the cost accountant prepared a process cost summary for the grinding department. This process cost summary was prepared from information in the goods in process account and the production report of the grinding department. It appeared as in Illustration 145 on the next page.

Several points should be noted in regard to the process cost summary of the grinding department of the Delta Company. In the first place, notice that the report is divided into three sections. The first section, headed *Costs Charged to the Department,* reports the costs charged to the grinding department. The second section, headed *Equivalent Unit Processing Costs,* consists of the calculation of equivalent finished units and equivalent finished unit costs. The third section, headed *Costs Applicable to the Work of the Department,* accounts for the portions of the material, labor, and overhead costs applicable to each of the inventories and to the work started and finished. Notice at the end of the third section of the summary

Illustration 145

DELTA PROCESSING COMPANY
Process Cost Summary, Grinding Department
For Month Ended April 30, 19--

COSTS CHARGED TO THE DEPARTMENT:

Material requisitioned	$ 9,900
Labor charged.	5,700
Overhead costs incurred. . . . . . '.	4,275
	$19,875
Goods in process at the beginning of the month	4,250
Total Costs to Be Accounted for.	$24,125

EQUIVALENT UNIT PROCESSING COSTS:

Material:

	Units Involved	Fraction of a Unit Added	Equivalent Units Added
Beginning inventory	30,000	-0-	-0-
Units started and finished	70,000	1	70,000
Ending inventory	20,000	1	20,000
			90,000

Unit processing cost for material: $9,900 + 90,000 = $0.11

Labor and Overhead:

	Units Involved	Fraction of a Unit Added	Equivalent Units Added
Beginning inventory	30,000	2/3	20,000
Units started and finished	70,000	1	70,000
Ending inventory	20,000	1/4	5,000
			95,000

Unit processing cost for labor: $5,700 + 95,000 = $0.06
Unit processing cost for overhead: $4,275 + 95,000 = $0.045

COSTS APPLICABLE TO THE WORK OF THE DEPARTMENT:

Goods in Process, One-third Processed at the Beginning of April:

Costs charged to the beginning inventory of goods in process during previous month	$4,250	
Material added (all added during March).	-0-	
Labor applied (20,000 x $0.06)	1,200	
Overhead applied (20,000 x $0.045)	900	
Cost to Process.		$ 6,350

Goods Started and Finished in the Department during April:

Material added (70,000 x $0.11).	$7,700	
Labor applied (70,000 x $0.06)	4,200	
Overhead applied (70,000 x $0.045)	3,150	
Cost to Process.		15,050
Total Cost of the Goods Processed in the Department and transferred to the Mixing Department (100,000 Units at $0.214 Each)		$21,400

Goods in Process, One-fourth Processed at the End of April:

Material added (20,000 x $0.11).	$2,200	
Labor applied (5,000 x $0.06).	300	
Overhead applied (5,000 x $0.045).	225	
Cost to One-fourth Process		2,725
Total Costs Accounted for.		$24,125

that the total of the costs assigned to the inventories and to the units started and finished is exactly equal to the total costs charged to the department as shown by the first section of the summary.

The first section of a department's process cost summary summarizes the costs charged to the department. Notice how the first section of the process cost summary of the grinding department summarizes the costs charged to the department as shown in the department's goods in process account. Compare this first section with the goods in process account of the department as illustrated at the bottom of page 638.

The second section of a department's process cost summary shows the calculation of equivalent finished unit processing costs. It is prepared from information given in the department's production report and goods in process account. The information as to the units involved and the amount of material, labor, and overhead applicable to the inventories and to the goods started and finished comes from the department's production report (see Illustration 142). Information as to the costs of the material, labor, and overhead applicable to the units of the inventories and the goods started and finished comes from the department's goods in process account.

Notice in the second section of the process cost summary of the grinding department that two separate calculations of equivalent finished units are made. Two separate calculations of equivalent finished units are required in this department because the material added to the product and the labor and overhead added to the product are not added in the same proportions and at the same stages in the processing procedure of the department. All material is added *at the beginning* of the process, and labor and overhead are added *evenly throughout* the process. Consequently, the number of equivalent finished units of material added to the inventories of the department and to its goods started and finished is not the same as the number of equivalent finished units of labor and overhead added.

Observe in the second section of the grinding department's process cost summary, in the calculation of equivalent finished units for materials, that the beginning inventory is assigned no material. In the grinding department all of the material placed in process is placed in process at the beginning of the process. The 30,000 units of the beginning inventory were one-third completed at the beginning of the April cost period. Consequently, these 30,000 units of product received all of their grinding department material during March when their processing was first started. They should bear none of the $9,900 of material costs charged to the department during April because they received no material in the department during April. Consequently, in the calculation of equivalent finished units for material these units are assigned no material. Also, in the third section of the process cost summary where an accounting is made of the costs applicable to each of the inventories and the goods started and finished, no material costs are assigned to the beginning goods in process inventory.

Notice in the calculation of equivalent finished units for labor and overhead that the beginning inventory units which were one-third completed at the beginning of the cost period are each assigned two thirds of a unit of labor and overhead. If these units were one-third completed at the beginning of April, then they were two-thirds completed during the April cost period. Beginning accounting students often have difficulty at this point. In a situation such as this, beginning accounting students are apt to assign only an additional one-third unit of labor and overhead when two thirds of a unit is required.

The third section of a department's process cost summary shows how the material, labor, and overhead costs charged to the department are assigned to the inventories and to the goods started and finished. Notice, for example, how costs are assigned to the beginning work in process inventory. The first amount charged to the beginning inventory is the $4,250 of beginning inventory costs. This amount represents the cost of the material, labor, and overhead used to one-third complete the inventory during March, the previous cost period. Normally, the second charge to a beginning inventory of work in process is for the additional material assigned to it. However, in the grinding department no additional material costs are assigned during April to the beginning inventory of work in process because these units received all of their material when their processing was first begun during the previous month. The second charge to the beginning inventory is for labor. The $1,200 portion of the $5,700 of grinding department April labor costs that is applicable to the beginning inventory is calculated by multiplying the number of equivalent finished units of labor used in completing the beginning inventory by the cost of an equivalent finished unit of labor (20,000 equivalent finished units of labor at $0.06 each). The third charge to the beginning inventory is for overhead. The $900 portion of the $4,275 of April overhead costs that is applicable to the beginning inventory is found by multiplying the equivalent finished units of overhead used in completing the beginning inventory by the cost of an equivalent finished unit of overhead (20,000 × $0.045).

After costs are assigned to the beginning inventory of work in process, the procedures used in assigning costs to the beginning inventory are repeated in the third section in assigning costs to the work started and finished and to the ending inventory of work in process.

Notice in the second section of the grinding department's process cost summary that the equivalent finished unit cost for material is $0.11 and that the equivalent finished unit cost for labor is $0.06 and for overhead is $0.045. The total of these three finished unit costs is $0.215. Notice, however, in the third section of the summary that the unit cost of the 100,-000 units finished and transferred is $0.214. The cost of the units finished and transferred is $0.214, which is less than $0.215, because unit costs were less in the department during the previous month, and 30,000 of the 100,000 units processed and transferred from the department were one-third processed at these lower costs during the previous month. A division of the $6,350 of costs assigned to the 30,000 beginning inventory units indicates that they cost $0.21167 each to process ($6350 ÷ 30,000 = $0.21167).

After completing the process cost summary of the grinding department, the cost accountant of the Delta Processing Company prepared and posted the following general journal entry. The entry transferred to the mixing department the costs assigned to the 100,000 units of product that were processed in the grinding department and transferred to the mixing department during the cost period. Information as to the costs assigned to the 100,000 units was taken from the third section of the process cost summary of the grinding department.

Apr.	30	Goods in Process, Mixing Department.....	21,400.00	
		Goods in Process, Grinding Department.........................		21,400.00
		To transfer the costs of the 100,000 units of product transferred to the mixing department.		

After the cost accountant posted the entry transferring the costs of the 100,000 units of product from the grinding department to the mixing department, the goods in process account of the grinding department appeared as follows:

Goods in Process, Grinding Department

Apr.	1	Beginning inventory	4,250	Apr.	30	Costs of 100,000 units	
	30	Materials	9,900			transferred to the mix-	
	30	Labor	5,700			ing department	21,400
	30	Overhead	4,275		30	Ending inventory	2,725
			24,125				24,125
May	1	Beginning inventory	2,725				

Notice that after the goods in process account of the grinding department is credited for the cost of the 100,000 units transferred to the mixing department, the balance of the account shows the value placed on the grinding department's ending inventory of goods in process. This $2,725 grinding department ending inventory of goods in process for the month of April becomes its beginning inventory for the month of May.

After the cost accountant posted the entry transferring the grinding department costs of the 100,000 units of product to the mixing department, the goods in process account of the mixing department appeared as follows:

Goods in Process, Mixing Department

Apr.	1	Beginning inventory	3,785	
	30	Materials	2,040	
	30	Labor	3,570	
	30	Overhead	1,020	
	30	Grinding department		
		costs transferred	21,400	
			31,815	

After posting the entry transferring the grinding department costs of the 100,000 units transferred to the mixing department, the cost accountant prepared a process cost summary for the mixing department. Information required in the process cost summary was taken from the mixing department's production report and from its goods in process account. The process cost summary appeared as in Illustration 146.

Two points in the process cost summary of the mixing department require special attention. The first is the calculation of equivalent finished

Illustration 146

DELTA PROCESSING COMPANY
Process Cost Summary, Mixing Department
For Month Ended April 30, 19--

COSTS CHARGED TO THE DEPARTMENT:

Materials requisitioned	$ 2,040
Labor charged	3,570
Overhead costs incurred	1,020
Total Processing Costs.	$ 6,630
Goods in process at the beginning of the month.	3,785
Costs transferred from the grinding department (100,000 units at $0.214 each)	21,400
Total Costs to Be Accounted for	$31,815

EQUIVALENT UNIT PROCESSING COSTS:

	Units Involved	Fraction of a Unit Added	Equivalent Units Added
Materials, Labor, and Overhead:			
Beginning inventory	16,000	3/4	12,000
Units started and finished.	85,000	1	85,000
Ending inventory.	15,000	1/3	5,000
Total Equivalent Units.			102,000

Unit processing cost for materials: $2,040 + 102,000 = $0.02
Unit processing cost for labor: $3,570 + 102,000 = $0.035
Unit processing cost for overhead: $1,020 + 102,000 = $0.01

COSTS APPLICABLE TO THE WORK OF THE DEPARTMENT:

Goods in Process, One-fourth Completed at the Beginning of April:

Costs charged to the beginning inventory of goods in process during previous month	$ 3,785	
Materials added (12,000 x $0.02).	240	
Labor applied (12,000 x $0.035)	420	
Overhead applied (12,000 x $0.01)	120	
Cost to Process		$ 4,565

Goods Started and Finished in the Department during April:

Costs in the grinding department (85,000 x $0.214).	$18,190	
Materials added (85,000 x $0.02).	1,700	
Labor applied (85,000 x $0.035)	2,975	
Overhead applied (85,000 x $0.01)	850	
Cost to Process		23,715
Total Accumulated Cost of Goods Transferred to the Packaging Department (101,000 units at $0.28)		$28,280

Goods in Process, One-third Processed at the End of April:

Costs in the grinding department (15,000 x $0.214).	$ 3,210	
Materials added (5,000 x $0.02)	100	
Labor applied (5,000 x $0.035).	175	
Overhead applied (5,000 x $0.01).	50	
Cost to One-third Process		3,535
Total Costs Accounted for		$31,815

units. Since the materials, labor, and overhead of the mixing department are all added to the product evenly throughout the process of the department, only a single calculation of equivalent units processed is required. This differs from the grinding department, the previous department of this illustrative problem. It will be recalled that two calculations of equivalent units processed were required for the grinding department. This was because the material placed in process and the labor and overhead placed in process in the grinding department were not placed in process in the same proportions and at the same stages in the processing procedure.

The second point needing special attention in the mixing department process cost summary is the method of handling the grinding department costs transferred to this department. During April, 100,000 units of product with accumulated grinding department costs of $21,400 were transferred to the mixing department. Of these 100,000 units, 85,000 were started in process in the mixing department, finished, and transferred to the packaging department. The remaining 15,000 units were still in process in the department at the end of the cost period.

Notice in the first section of the process cost summary of the mixing department how the $21,400 of grinding department costs transferred to the mixing department are added to the other costs charged to the department. Compare the information in this first section with the goods in process account of the mixing department as it is illustrated on page 639 and again as it is illustrated at the bottom of page 643.

Notice again in the third section of the process cost summary of the mixing department how the $21,400 of grinding department costs are apportioned between the 85,000 units started and finished and the 15,000 units started but still in process in the department. The 16,000 units of the beginning goods in process inventory of the department received none of this $21,400 charge. The units of the beginning inventory received none of this charge because they were transferred from the grinding department during the previous month. Their grinding department costs are included in the $3,785 of costs charged to the beginning inventory during March, the previous cost period.

The third section of the process cost summary of the mixing department shows that 101,000 units of product with accumulated costs of $28,280.00 were completed in the mixing department during April and transferred to the packaging department. After completing the process cost summary of the mixing department, the cost accountant prepared the following entry to transfer the accumulated cost of these 101,000 units from the mixing department to the packaging department.

Apr.	30	Goods in Process, Packaging Department..	28,280.00	
		Goods in Process, Mixing Department		28,280.00
		To transfer the accumulated grinding department and mixing department costs of the 101,000 units transferred to the packaging department.		

After the cost accountant posted the entry transferring the costs of the 101,000 units from the goods in process account of the mixing department to the goods in process account of the packaging department, the goods in process account of the mixing department appeared as follows:

Goods in Process, Mixing Department

Apr. 1	Beginning inventory	3,785	Apr. 30	Costs of 101,000 units	
30	Materials	2,040		transferred to the pack-	
30	Labor	3,570		aging department	28,280
30	Overhead	1,020	30	Ending inventory	3,535
30	Grinding department				
	costs transferred	21,400			
		31,815			31,815
May 1	Beginning inventory	3,535			

Notice that after the goods in process account of the mixing department is credited for the costs of the 101,000 units of product transferred to the packaging department, the balance of the account is $3,535.00. This is the value placed on the ending inventory of goods in process in the department.

After the entry transferring the accumulated costs of the 101,000 units of product from the mixing department to the packaging department was posted, the Goods in Process, Packaging Department account appeared as follows:

Goods in Process, Packaging Department

Apr. 30	Materials	1,515	
30	Labor	909	
30	Overhead	1,212	
30	Grinding and mixing		
	costs transferred to		
	department	28,280	
		31,916	

After posting the entry transferring the $28,280.00 of grinding department and mixing department costs to the packaging department, the cost accountant prepared a process cost summary for the packaging department. The process cost summary appeared as in Illustration 147.

Since there are no beginning or ending goods in process inventories in the packaging department, its process cost summary is much simplified. Because there are no beginning and ending inventories of goods in process, all units processed in the department are finished and a calculation of equivalent finished units is unnecessary. Also, because there are no inventories of goods in process in the department, all of the costs charged to the department are applicable to the 101,000 units of product received in the department, packaged, and transferred to finished goods. This last point makes it possible to omit the so-called third section from the department's process cost summary. The so-called third section may be omitted because the first section of the report shows the amount of materials, the amount of labor, and the amount of overhead applicable to the 101,000 units processed.

Illustration 147

DELTA PROCESSING COMPANY
Process Cost Summary, Packaging Department
For Month Ended April 31, 19--

```
Costs Charged to the Department:
  Materials requisitioned . . . . . . . . .        $ 1,515
  Labor charged . . . . . . . . . . . . .              909
  Overhead expenses incurred. . . . . . . .          1,212
    Total Processing Costs. . . . . . . . .        $ 3,636
  Costs transferred from the mixing depart-
    ment  (101,000  units at $0.28 each). .         28,280
    Total Costs Charged to the 101,000
      Units Received in the Department,
      Packaged and Transferred to Finished
      Goods (101,000 Units at $0.316 Each)         $31,916

Unit Processing Costs:
  101,000 units of product were received in
    this department, processed and trans-
    verred to finished goods. There were no
    inventories of goods in process.
      Unit processing cost for materials: $1,515 +
        101,000 = $0.015
      Unit processing cost for labor: $909 + 101,000 =
        $0.009
      Unit processing cost for overhead: $1,212 +
        101,000 = $0.012
```

After completing the process cost summary for the packaging department, the cost accountant of the Delta Processing Company prepared and posted the following general journal entry to transfer from the goods in process account of the packaging department to the Finished Goods account the $31,916.00 accumulated costs of the goods completed by the company in April.

Apr.	30	Finished Goods........................	31,916.00	
		Goods in Process, Packaging Depart-		
		ment.........................		31,916.00
		To transfer to Finished Goods the ac-		
		cumulated costs of the goods completed		
		during April.		

After the cost accountant posted the entry transferring the costs of the 101,000 units from the goods in process account of the packaging department to the Finished Goods account, the goods in process account of the packaging department appeared as follows:

Goods in Process, Packaging Department

Apr. 30	Materials	1,515	Apr. 30	Costs of 101,000 units transferred to finished goods	31,916
30	Labor	909			
30	Overhead	1,212			
30	Grinding and mixing costs transferred to department	28,280			
		31,916			31,916

Notice that the Goods in Process, Packaging Department account does not have a balance after the costs of the finished goods are transferred to the Finished Goods account. The account has no balance because the packaging department has no goods in process at the end of the month.

After posting the entry transferring to Finished Goods the accumulated costs of the 101,000 units of product finished during April, the cost accountant prepared from the process cost summaries of the three processing departments the manufacturing statement shown in Illustration 148. The $13,455 shown on the

Illustration 148

DELTA PROCESSING COMPANY
Manufacturing Statement for Month Ended April 30, 19--

Materials requisitioned	$13,455
Labor applied	10,179
Overhead costs incurred	6,507
Total Processing Costs.	$30,141
Add: Goods in process at the beginning of April	8,035
Total Goods in Process.	$38,176
Deduct: Goods in process at the end of April	6,260
Cost of Goods Manufactured.	$31,916

manufacturing statement of the Delta Company for materials requisitioned was secured by combining the amounts shown for materials requisitioned on the individual process cost summaries of its three departments. The amounts shown for labor, overhead, and the inventories were secured in the same manner.

Other Cost Accounting Problems

Obviously, it is impossible in two chapters of an elementary accounting text to discuss all of the many interesting problems of cost accounting. Such problems as joint-products, by-products, units lost or spoiled in process, and the application of cost accounting to merchandising and service-type companies must be deferred to a more advanced course. Likewise, such variations of job order and process cost systems as are found in standard cost systems and estimated cost systems must also be deferred.

QUESTIONS FOR CLASS DISCUSSION

1. Characterize the manufacturing methods of a company to which a process cost accounting system is applicable.
2. Give the cost accounting meanings of the term "process."
3. What are the common characteristics of a process cost accounting system?
4. During a cost accounting period the molding department of a manufacturing firm using a process cost system had charged to it $2,100 of materials, $4,130 of labor, and $1,750 of overhead. During the period the department produced 50,000 units of finished product. What was the cost per unit for materials, labor, and overhead?
5. How does accounting for the use of materials differ under a process cost system from accounting for the use of materials under a job cost system?
6. The materials used summary of a company using a process cost system shows the following amounts of materials issued to its three processing departments during a cost period:

Melting department...........................$2,350
Molding department........................... 1,875
Finishing department.......................... 600
$4,825

Give the general journal entry to record the information of the materials used summary.

7. How does accounting for the use of labor under a process cost system differ from accounting for the use of labor under a job cost system?
8. The labor cost summary of a company using a process cost system shows the following amounts of labor applicable to each of its departments:

Melting department...........................$ 3,400
Molding department........................... 2,150
Finishing department.......................... 4,725
$10,275

Give the general journal entry to record the information of the labor cost summary.

9. Outline a system for charging overhead to the departments of a firm using a process cost system.
10. The Gamma Company operates a process cost accounting system. The company follows the practice of charging all overhead items to undepartmental-

DEPARTMENTAL OVERHEAD COSTS ANALYSIS SHEET
For Period Ended May 31, 19—

Undepartmentalized Cost Accounts	Basis of Allocation	Cost Account Balance	Allocation of Costs		
			Melting Dept.	Molding Dept.	Finishing Dept.
Factory supervision	Number of employees	$3,800	$1,000	$1,000	$1,800
Personal property taxes	Value of property	900	200	300	400
Expired insurance	Value of property	450	100	150	200
Depreciation of machinery	Value of property	1,350	300	450	600
Light and power	Meters	750	50	100	600
Rent of building	Floor space	1,009	200	300	500
		$8,250	$1,850	$2,300	$4,100

ized cost accounts. At the end of each cost accounting period the company prepares a departmental overhead costs analysis sheet to determine the overhead applicable to each of its departments. The analysis sheet for the cost period ending May 31 is given on the previous page. Prepare a general journal entry to close the undepartmentalized cost accounts and to charge the overhead to the processing departments.

11. What is a production report? What information is commonly shown on a production report?

12. What is an equivalent finished unit of (a) labor, (b) materials, and (c) overhead? Why are equivalent finished units calculated for a processing department?

13. Compute the output of a department measured in equivalent finished units under the following assumptions:
   a) Beginning inventory of goods in process, 12,000 units, one-fourth completed at the beginning of the cost period.
   b) Goods started and finished during the period, 63,000 units.
   c) Ending inventory of goods in process, 9,000 units, one-third completed.

14. A department of a processing firm had charged to it during a cost period $87,000 of labor. At the beginning of the cost period the department had in process 21,000 units of product that were two-thirds finished. During the cost period the department started and finished an additional 18,000 units of product. At the end of the cost period the department had 8,000 units of product that were one-half finished. How much of the $87,000 of labor should be charged to each of the inventories and to the goods started and finished? (Assume that labor is added to the product evenly throughout the process.)

15. How many equivalent finished unit calculations are required in the preparation of a process cost summary for each of the following departments?
   Department A In Department A all materials, labor, and overhead are added to the product of the department evenly throughout the process of the department.
   Department B In Department B all materials are added at the beginning of the process, and labor and overhead are added evenly throughout the process.
   Department C In Department C all materials are added at the beginning of the process. One half of the labor added to the product of this department is added evenly throughout the first one third of the process, and the other one half is added evenly throughout the last two thirds of the process. Overhead is added evenly throughout the entire process.

16. Differentiate between a department production report and a department process cost summary.

17. The process cost summary of a department normally has three sections. What is shown in each section?

18. What is the normal source of the information shown on the manufacturing statement of a firm using department process cost summaries?

PROBLEMS

Problem 25–1
The product of Durham Processing Company is manufactured on a continuous basis in two processing departments. The product is begun in Department A

and is transferred and completed in Department B. During a cost period $20,125 of labor was charged to the product in process in Department A. During this same period the company finished in Department A and transferred to Department B a total of 23,800 units of product, of which 8,000 were in process at the beginning of the cost period and 15,800 were begun and finished during the period. The 8,000 that were in process at the beginning were two-fifths complete as to labor when the period began. In addition to the foregoing units, 7,200 units were in process in Department A and were one-third complete as to labor when the period ended.

Required:

Calculate the equivalent units of labor applied to the product of Department A and determine the amounts of labor that are applicable to the goods started and finished and to the beginning and ending inventories of the department.

Problem 25–2

The product of Morton Processing Company is produced on a continuous basis in a single processing department in which material, labor, and overhead are added to the product evenly throughout the manufacturing process.

At the end of the current May cost period, after the costs of the material, labor, and overhead used were charged to the Goods in Process account of the single processing department, the Goods in Process account appeared as follows:

Goods in Process

May 1	Balance	1,362	
31	Materials	5,325	
31	Labor	10,863	
31	Overhead	15,194	
		32,744	

During the cost period the company finished and transferred to finished goods a total of 72,000 units of the product, of which 9,000 were in process at the beginning of the cost period and 63,000 were begun and finished during the period. The 9,000 that were in process were one-third processed when the period began. In addition to the foregoing units, 8,000 additional units were in process and were one-fourth completed at the end of the cost period.

Required:

1. Prepare a process cost summary for the department.
2. Draft the general journal entry to transfer to Finished Goods the cost of the product finished in the department during the month.

Problem 25–3

Two operations, mixing and finishing, and two departments are used in the manufacturing procedure of Alpha Processing Company. The manufacturing procedure is begun in the mixing department and completed in the finishing department.

At the beginning of the May cost period there were in the mixing department 5,000 units of product which were three-fifths processed. These units were completed during the cost period and transferred to the finishing department. Also, the processing of 31,000 additional units was begun in the mixing department during the cost period. Of these 31,000 units, 23,000 were finished and transferred to the finishing department during the period. The remaining 8,000 units were in the department in a one-half processed state at the end of the period.

It is assumed that the material, labor, and overhead applied in the mixing department are applied evenly throughout the process of the department.

At the end of the cost period, after entries recording the materials used summary, the labor cost summary, and the overhead cost analysis sheet were posted, the Goods in Process, Mixing Department account of the Alpha Processing Company appeared as follows:

Goods in Process, Mixing Department

May 1	Balance	2,901	
31	Materials	9,280	
31	Labor	12,209	
31	Overhead	6,090	
		30,480	

Required:

1. Prepare a process cost summary for the mixing department of Alpha Processing Company.
2. Prepare the general journal entry to transfer to the finishing department the cost of the goods completed in the mixing department and transferred to the finishing department.

CLASS EXERCISE

Exercise 25–1

During a cost period the processing of 48,000 units of product was completed in Department A of a processing firm and the units were transferred to the firm's Department B for further processing. Of these 48,000 units, 12,000 were in process and were one-third completed at the beginning of the period. The processing of the remaining 36,000 units was begun and completed during the period. In addition to the foregoing 48,000 units, there were 10,000 units in process in Department A which were three-fifths processed at the end of the period.

Required:

Calculate the equivalent units of material added to the product of Department A under each of the following separate assumptions:

a) That all the materials added to the product of the department are added when the process of the department is first begun.

b) That the materials added to the product of the department are added evenly throughout the process of the department.

c) That one half the materials added in the department are added when the process of the department is first begun and that the other one half is added when the process of the department is three-fourths completed.

SUPPLEMENTARY PROBLEMS

Problem 25–A

Crane Processing Company manufactures a simple product on a continuous basis in a single department. All materials are added in the manufacturing process of this product when the process is first begun. Labor and overhead are added evenly throughout the process.

During the current April cost period the company completed and transferred to finished goods a total of 43,000 units of the product. These consisted of 5,000 units that were in process at the beginning of the cost period and 38,000 units that were begun and finished during the period. The 5,000 units of the beginning goods in process inventory were complete as to materials and four-fifths complete as to labor and overhead when the period began.

In addition to the foregoing units, 6,000 units were in process at the end of the period, complete as to materials and one-half complete as to labor and overhead.

Since the company has but one processing department, it has only one Goods in Process account in its ledger. At the end of the period, after entries recording material, labor, and overhead had been posted, the Goods in Process account appeared as follows:

Goods in Process

Apr.	1	Balance	5,333
	30	Materials	27,060
	30	Labor	9,744
	30	Overhead	14,868
			57,005

Required:

Prepare a process cost summary and the general journal entry to transfer to Finished Goods the cost of the product completed in the department during April.

Problem 25–B

Southhill Processing Company manufactures on a continuous basis a product that is processed in two departments, Department A and Department B. At the end of the monthly, May cost period, after the entries recording the materials used summary, the labor cost summary, and the departmental overhead costs analysis sheet were posted, the goods in process accounts of the two departments appeared as follows:

Goods in Process, Department A

May	1	Balance	3,095
	31	Materials	7,500
	31	Labor	6,050
	31	Overhead	3,850

Goods in Process, Department B

May	1	Balance	5,950
	31	Materials	17,700
	31	Labor	16,320
	31	Overhead	6,720

The May production reports of the departments gave the following information:

	Department A	Department B
May 1 inventory of goods in process.......	15,000 units	12,000 units
State of completion on May 1............	⅓	¼
Product started and finished.............	40,000 units	47,000 units
May 31 inventory of goods in process.....	10,000 units	8,000 units
Stage of completion on May 31	½	½

Southhill Processing Company assumes that all material placed in process in Department A is placed in process when the process of the department is first begun. It further assumes that the labor and overhead applied to the product of the department are applied to the product evenly throughout the process of the department.

The company also assumes that all material, labor, and overhead added to the product in Department B are added evenly throughout the process of the department.

At the end of the May cost period, after charging each department in its goods in process account with its share of the materials, labor, and overhead costs, and after receiving the department production reports, the cost accountant of Southhill Processing Company prepared the following process cost summary for the company's Department A.

SOUTHHILL PROCESSING COMPANY

Process Cost Summary, Department A
For Month Ended May 31, 19—

COSTS CHARGED TO THE DEPARTMENT:

Materials requisitioned................................	$ 7,500.00
Labor charged.......................................	6,050.00
Overhead costs incurred.............................	3,850.00
	$17,400.00
Goods in process at the beginning of the month............	3,095.00
Total Costs to Be Accounted for........................	$20,495.00

EQUIVALENT UNIT PROCESSING COSTS:

Material:	Units Involved	Fraction of a Unit Added	Equivalent Units Added
Beginning inventory............	15,000	–0–	–0–
Units started and finished.......	40,000	1	40,000
Ending inventory..............	10,000	1	10,000
			50,000

Unit processing cost for material: $7,500 ÷ 50,000 = $0.15

Labor and Overhead:	Units Involved	Fraction of a Unit Added	Equivalent Units Added
Beginning inventory............	15,000	⅔	10,000
Units started and finished.......	40,000	1	40,000
Ending inventory..............	10,000	½	5,000
			55,000

Unit processing cost for labor: $6,050 ÷ 55,000 = $0.11
Unit processing cost for overhead: $3,850 ÷ 55,000 = $0.07

COSTS APPLICABLE TO THE WORK OF THE DEPARTMENT:

Goods in Process, One-third Processed at the Beginning of May:

Cost charged to beginning inventory of goods in process during the previous month..................	$3,095.00	
Materials added (all added during April)..........	–0–	
Labor applied (10,000 × $0.11)....................	1,100.00	
Overhead applied (10,000 × $0.07)...............	700.00	
Cost to process (carried forward)............		$ 4,895.00

Goods Started and Finished in the Department during May:

Materials added (40,000 × $0.15).................	$6,000.00	
Labor applied (40,000 × $0.11)...................	4,400.00	
Overhead applied (40,000 × $0.07)...............	2,800.00	
Cost to process...........................		13,200.00
Total Cost of the Goods Processed in the Department and Transferred to Department B (55,000 Units at $0.329 Each)................................		$18,095.00

Goods in Process, One-half Processed at the End of May:

Materials added (10,000 × $0.15).................	$1,500.00	
Labor applied (5,000 × $0.11)....................	550.00	
Overhead applied (5,000 × $0.07)................	350.00	
Cost to one-half process.....................		2,400.00
Total Costs Accounted for........................		$20,495.00

Required:

1. Prepare the general journal entry to transfer to Department B the costs of the goods processed in Department A and transferred to Department B.
2. After completing Requirement 1, prepare a process cost summary for Department B.
3. Prepare the general journal entry to transfer to the Finished Goods account the costs of the product finished in Department B.

Chapter

26

MANAGEMENT'S USE OF
ACCOUNTING DATA

ALTHOUGH management uses in many ways information gathered by means of accounting; most of the uses may be grouped under three main headings: (1) reporting the effects of past decisions; (2) controlling operations; and (3) planning.

The balance sheet, the income statement, and their related schedules, such as the manufacturing statement, are formal reports used by management to show the effects of past decisions. The collection of data for and the preparation and use of these reports were the subjects of several of the earlier chapters of this text, and their analysis and interpretation is the subject of Chapter 29. Likewise, the use of accounting as a tool in controlling operations was illustrated through the discussion of controlling sales and purchases in Chapter 7 and controlling cash receipts and cash disbursements in Chapters 10 and 15. Consequently, these phases of management's use of accounting data will be passed over for now and this and the next chapter will be devoted to a discussion of the uses of accounting data in planning.

Planning

A plan is a procedure or a course of action; and planning is the process of examining several alternative courses of action and deciding which is best. Planning always requires decisions as to future actions.

Planning may involve one small part of a business, or it may involve the entire enterprise; consequently, in studying management's use of accounting data in planning, it is best to consider as separate subjects: (1) period planning, and (2) project planning.

Period planning is better known as budgeting. It is the process of planning the entire activity of a business for a future period of time, usually one year, although many companies project their plans in a general way for from five to ten years ahead. Period planning is of vital interest to businessmen and is the subject of the next chapter.

Although period planning and project planning tend to merge into one another and period planning always involves project plans, project planning has to do primarily with decisions about small segments of a business or about individual projects such as buying or building new fixed assets, increasing the volume of business by entering new markets, increasing or decreasing the sales price of a product, and numerous others.

656

Purchase of Fixed Assets

Plans involving the acquisition of fixed assets are among the most important faced by management. They are important not only because large sums of money are often involved but also because fixed assets, once acquired, may affect business operations for a long period of time.

Normally, when management is considering the purchase of a new fixed asset, it is interested in: (1) How long will it take the asset to pay for itself? And (2) what will be the return on the investment? Calculations called *the payback period* and *the rate of return on the average investment* are commonly made to shed light on these questions.

To illustrate these calculations assume that Murray Company is considering the purchase of a machine to be used in manufacturing a new product called Product 2XY. The new machine will cost $16,000, have a service life of eight years, and no salvage value. The management of the company estimates that 10,000 units of Product 2XY will be sold each year and the sales will result in an annual profit of $1,800, as shown in Illustration 149.

Illustration 149
PROFIT FROM ANNUAL SALES OF PRODUCT 2XY

Annual sales of Product 2XY		$30,000
Deduct:		
Cost of materials, labor, and overhead other than depreciation on the new machine	$15,500	
Depreciation on new machine	2,000	
Additional selling and administrative expenses	8,900	26,400
Annual before taxes profit from sale of product		$ 3,600
Income taxes (assumed rate 50%)		1,800
Annual after Taxes Profit from Sale of Product		$ 1,800

Payback Period. Through the annual sale of 10,000 units of Product 2XY, the Murray company expects to gain $30,000 of revenue. The $30,000 is sufficient to recover all of the cost of producing and selling the 10,000 units of product and to leave a profit of $1,800. Among the costs recovered each year in the $30,000 of revenue is $2,000 depreciation on the new machine. Consequently, $3,800 ($2,000 depreciation plus $1,800 of profit) is available each year to "pay back" the cost of the machine. Therefore the payback period on the $16,000 investment in this new machine is 4.21+ years and is calculated:

$$\$16,000 \div \$3,800 = 4.21+ \text{ YEARS TO RECOVER COST}$$

Making a payback period calculation requires judgment in estimating sales, cost of sales, and expenses. Using a payback period calculation also requires judgment as to the length of a proper payback period. What is a desirable payback period in the case of any asset is related to the total estimated life of the asset. For example, a payback period of ten years on a typewriter is normally too long; in the average business a typewriter will wear out in a shorter period. Likewise, a required payback period of eight years for a building is too short; most buildings are useful for a period five times that long.

The Rate of Return on the Average Investment. Depreciation will reduce by $2,000 each year the book value of the machine, the purchase of which is proposed by the Murray Company. Consequently, the average amount that will be invested in this machine can be calculated by adding the machine's book values as they will be at the beginning of each of the eight years of the machine's life and then dividing the sum by eight. However, an easier calculation that gives the same result is to add the book values at the beginning of the first and last years of the machine's life and divide the sum by two. When this calculation is made, the average amount that will be invested in the machine is:

$$\frac{\$16,000 + \$2,000}{2} = \$9,000$$

And the rate of return on this average investment is then found by dividing the estimated annual profit from the sale of the product, after taxes, by the average investment as follows:

$$\$1,800 \div \$9,000 = 20\%$$

In deciding whether the 20 per cent return is good or bad, the Murray Company must measure the return against the risks involved and against other possible uses of the funds.

Often in calculating the average investment in a machine that will have no salvage value, the cost of the machine is simply divided by two. This is usually sufficiently accurate for most calculations. After all, the cost of the machine is the amount that is invested on the first day of the machine's life, and if there is a profit from the sale of the product and if depreciation is accurately estimated, all of this cost is recovered by the last day of the machine's estimated life.

Replacement of Fixed Assets

Improvements in equipment often give management some of its most difficult problems. For example, Allen W. Oakes Company has a machine which it has used for two years. The machine cost $36,000, and its life was estimated new at twelve years with no salvage value. An equipment salesman has offered the company a $5,000 trade-in allowance for this machine on a new semiautomatic machine having a list price of $40,000. The life of the new machine is estimated at ten years with no salvage value. The capacities of both the old and the new machines are the same; however, the equipment salesman offers the following statistics to show the annual savings that will result from the purchase of the new equipment:

Operating Costs	Keep Old Machine	Buy New Machine
Labor to operate machine.............................	$ 5,400	$1,800
Supplies..	450	600
Repairs..	200	300
Taxes..	350	400
Power..	1,200	1,500
Depreciation.......................................	3,000	4,000
Total Operating Costs..........................	$10,600	$8,600

Apparently the new semiautomatic machine offers a large saving in operating labor and over-all savings of $2,000 each year. However, the merits and demerits of the situation are easier to see if it is recognized that the cost of the old equipment is a "sunk" cost and that the "out-of-pocket" costs of the two alternatives are more important. A comparison of the estimated out-of-pocket costs is as follows:

Out-of-Pocket Operating Costs	Keep Old Machine	Buy New Machine
Labor to operate machine.............................	$5,400	$1,800
Supplies..	450	600
Repairs..	200	300
Taxes..	350	400
Power..	1,200	1,500
For recovery of additional capital.....................		3,500
Total Out-of-Pocket Operating Costs..............	$7,600	$8,100

The new machine sells for $40,000 less a trade-in allowance of $5,000, or it requires a cash outlay of $35,000. In the table of out-of-pocket costs, this $35,000 is spread over the life of the new machine by the annual $3,500 charge for the recovery of additional capital.

An examination of the table of out-of-pocket costs will show that the purchase of the new machine will require an additional $500 in out-of-pocket costs each year, or a total of $5,000 over the life of the machine. Consequently, other things being equal, the company will be better off if it continues to use the old equipment.

In the place of the foregoing, management may approach this asset replacement problem in another manner. It may calculate the savings other than for depreciation and capital outlay that will result from the purchase of the new machine and then determine the length of time required for these savings to pay back the capital outlay. For example, in the previous illustration, the costs other than for depreciation and capital outlay are:

Costs Other than Depreciation and Capital Outlay	Keep Old Machine	Buy New Machine
Labor to operate machine.............................	$5,400	$1,800
Supplies..	450	600
Repairs..	200	300
Taxes..	350	400
Power..	1,200	1,500
Totals..	$7,600	$4,600

From the table just given, it is obvious that when depreciation and capital outlay are not considered, there is a **$3,000** savings in favor of the new machine. However, it would require 11⅔ years for this savings to return the capital outlay ($35,000 ÷ $3,000 = 11⅔); and, consequently, since the life of the new machine is only ten years, the capital outlay would not be fully recovered.

It should be noted that the foregoing discussions are not all of the picture. If the company purchases the new machine, it will have an average of $17,500 ($35,000 ÷ 2 = $17,500) invested in the machine during its ten-year life. Regardless of where these funds are secured, the purchase of the machine results in a sacrifice of interest. Consequently, if, say, 4 per cent is the going rate of interest, an additional $700 ($17,500 × 4 per cent) should be added to the costs of the new machine.

Product Pricing

Prices are commonly not determined entirely by competition; most companies, as a rule, have some control over the prices at which they sell their products. This is true because, with the exception of certain raw materials, few similar products are exactly alike. Quality and style often differ. Also, the amounts of services furnished by the sellers of like products commonly vary. Consequently, similar products often sell at different prices.

Similar products can be sold at different prices because they are not exactly alike. And because similar products are not exactly alike, many companies in pricing a product can and do add a fair profit to the costs of the product's materials, labor, and overhead at the normal rate of production, and then by aggressive advertising and selling get the price asked.

In setting the sales price of a product, many factors are usually involved. Two factors that are commonly involved are: (1) if the demand for a product is elastic, the number of units that will be sold will vary with the price; and (2) when production volume varies, some expenses vary with the volume and some remain fixed.

The first factor stated in another way is: When the demand for a product is elastic, if the price of the product is lowered, at each successive lower price more units of the product will be sold; and if the price is increased, at each successive higher price fewer units will be sold.

For a better understanding of the second of the factors just given, consider the following lists of expenses incurred in driving an automobile 8,000 miles per year:

Expenses That Vary with Mileage		*Annual Fixed Expenses*	
Gasoline and oil	$210	Depreciation	$400
Tires	28	Insurance	72
Lubrication	16	License fee	10
Repairs	20		$482
	$274		

The lists show the expenses incurred in driving a car 8,000 miles per year. If the car were driven 12,000 miles in a year rather than 8,000, the expenses incurred for gasoline, oil, tires, lubrication, and repairs would increase in proportion to the increase in miles. However, the annual fixed expenses would remain more or less fixed and unchanged.

Just as there are expenses that remain fixed and expenses that vary with the number of miles that a car is driven, there are also expenses that remain fixed and expenses that vary with the number of units of product that are manufactured in a factory. And, as will be shown, these fixed and variable expenses are often a factor in setting the price of a product.

In setting the price of a product, management normally tries to set the price at an amount that will result in the greatest reasonable profit. The profit must be within reason or new competition and, sometimes, government intervention are invited. Normally, the greatest profit results from the price that produces the greatest amount of *marginal revenue*. Marginal revenue is revenue from sales less variable expenses or the expenses that vary with sales. For example, in setting the price for a new portable radio on which the variable expenses are $10 per set, the management of Electronics, Inc., prepared the estimates of Illustration 150.

Illustration 150

Suggested Sales Price per Set	Units That Can Be Sold	Sales Revenue	Variable Expenses	Marginal Revenue
$20.00	10,000	$200,000	$100,000	$100,000
17.50	30,000	525,000	300,000	225,000
15.00	36,000	540,000	360,000	180,000
12.00	48,000	576,000	480,000	96,000
11.00	60,000	660,000	600,000	60,000

Obviously, from the information of Illustration 150, the price that will produce the greatest amount of marginal revenue is $17.50. At this price 30,000 sets can be sold and $225,000 of marginal revenue earned. The price of $17.50 pays all of the variable expenses of its volume and leaves $225,000 of marginal revenue to cover the fixed expenses and provide a profit.

If a company manufactures more than one product, its pricing problems become more complicated and are often affected by capacity to produce. For example, Taplett and Company manufactures two products, Product M having variable expenses of $12 per unit and Product S having variable expenses of $16 per unit. The products are similar but noncompetitive; and although the materials from which they are manufactured differ, the machines and methods used in their manufacture are almost identical. Taplett and Company has the capacity to produce either 10,000 units of Product M, or 10,000 units of Product S, or a number of units of product M plus a number of units of Product S, the sum of which is 10,000. In setting prices, Taplett and Company prepared the estimates of Illustration 151.

Illustration 151

Suggested Sales Price per Unit	Units That Can Be Sold	Sales Revenue	Variable Expenses	Marginal Revenue
Product M				
$25.00	3,000	$ 75,000	$ 36,000	$ 39,000
20.00	5,000	100,000	60,000	40,000
18.00	6,000	108,000	72,000	36,000
16.00	8,000	128,000	96,000	32,000
15.00	10,000	150,000	120,000	30,000
Product S				
$30.00	2,000	$ 60,000	$ 32,000	$ 28,000
25.00	5,000	125,000	80,000	45,000
23.00	7,000	161,000	112,000	49,000
22.00	8,000	176,000	128,000	48,000
21.00	9,500	199,500	152,000	47,500

An examination of Illustration 151 shows that Taplett and Company could gain the greatest amount of marginal revenue from each product at prices of $20 for Product M and $23 for Product S. However, these prices require production of 5,000 units of Product M and 7,000 units of Product S, a total of 12,000 units. Consequently, since Taplett and Company can produce only 10,000 units, the greatest amount of revenue, within its capacity to produce, will be gained at prices of $25 for product M and $23 for Product S.

Obviously pricing problems are usually more complicated than the ones given in the foregoing simplified situations. For example, in the foregoing situations the fact that some expenses are neither fixed nor variable is ignored. Nevertheless, and regardless of this, the factors of demand and of fixed and variable expenses are present in almost all pricing situations; and if management is to maximize profits, it must know as much as possible about the fixed, the semifixed, and the variable expenses of manufacturing and marketing each of its products.

Cost of an Additional Volume of Business

When a cost accounting system is in use, the per unit costs obtained from the system are average costs. Cost systems are designed to give average costs; and these average costs are useful in pricing a product and for many other purposes. However, when there are decisions as to the wisdom of obtaining an additional volume of business, average costs are not necessarily the important costs. Often, the important costs are the added costs, called *incremental costs* or *differential costs*. For example, a firm operating at its normal capacity, which is approximately 80 per cent of its full capacity, has annually been producing and selling approximately 100,000 units of product with the results of Illustration 152.

Illustration 152

Sales (100,000 units @ $10.00)		$1,000,000
Materials (100,000 units @ $3.50)	$350,000	
Labor (100,000 units @ $2.20)	220,000	
Overhead (100,000 units @ $1.10)	110,000	
Selling expenses (100,000 units @ $1.40)	140,000	
Administrative expenses (100,000 units @ $0.80)	80,000	900,000
Operating Profit		$ 100,000

The sales department of the firm reports that it has a customer who has offered to buy 10,000 units of product at $8.50 per unit. The sale to the new customer is several times larger than any one previous sale made by the company, and it would not affect other business since it is in an entirely new territory. In considering the wisdom of accepting the new order, the management of the company asked its accounting department to prepare statistics to show the probable profit or loss that would result from the sale. The accounting department prepared the estimates of Illustration 153 based upon the average costs previously given.

Illustration 153

Sales (10,000 units @ $8.50)		$85,000
Materials (10,000 units @ $3.50)	$35,000	
Labor (10,000 units @ $2.20)	22,000	
Overhead (10,000 units @ $1.10)	11,000	
Selling expenses (10,000 units @ $1.40)	14,000	
Administrative expenses (10,000 units @ $0.80)	8,000	90,000
Operating Loss		$ 5,000

If a decision were based solely on the estimates of Illustration 153, the new business would likely be rejected. However, before rejecting the order, the costs of the new business were examined more closely and the following additional information obtained. (1) Manufacturing 10,000 additional units of product would require materials and labor at $3.50 and $2.20 per unit just as with normal production. (2) However, the 10,000 units could be manufactured with overhead costs in addition to those already incurred of only $5,000 for power, packing, and handling labor. (3) Commissions and other selling expenses resulting from the sale would amount to $2,000 in addition to the selling expenses already incurred. And (4) $1,000 of additional administrative expenses in the form of clerical work would be required if the order were accepted. On the basis of this added information, the statement of Illustration 154 showing the effect of the additional business on the normal business of the company was prepared.

It is obvious from Illustration 154 that when the present business is charged with all of the present costs and the additional business is charged only with its incremental or differential costs, accepting the additional business at $8.50 per unit will apparently result in an additional profit of $20,000.

Illustration 154

	Present Business		Additional Business		Present Plus the Additional Business
Sales....................		$1,000,000		$85,000	$1,085,000
Materials..............	$350,000		$35,000		$385,000
Labor..................	220,000		22,000		242,000
Overhead..............	110,000		5,000		115,000
Selling expenses........	140,000		2,000		142,000
Administrative expenses..	80,000		1,000		81,000
Totals..............		900,000		65,000	965,000
Operating Profit.....		$ 100,000		$20,000	$ 120,000

Incremental or differential costs always apply to a particular situation at a particular time. For example, adding units of product to a given volume of production might or might not increase depreciation expense. If the additional production requires more machines and more space, depreciation expense is increased. Likewise, if present machines are used but the additional units shorten their life, more depreciation expense results. However, if present machines are used and their depreciation depends more upon time or obsolescence, rather than upon use, additional depreciation expense might not result from the added units of product.

Buy or Make

Incremental or differential costs are often a factor in a decision as to whether a given part or product should be bought or made. For example, a manufacturer has idle machines upon which he can make Part 417 of his product. This part is presently purchased at a delivered cost of $1.20 per unit. The manufacturer estimates that to make Part 417 would cost $0.45 for materials, $0.50 for labor, and an amount of overhead. At this point a question arises as to how much overhead should be charged. If the normal overhead rate of the department in which the part would be manufactured is 100 per cent of direct labor cost, and this amount is charged against Part 417, then the unit cost of making Part 417 would be $0.45 for materials, $0.50 for labor, and $0.50 for overhead, a total of $1.45. At this cost, the manufacturer would be better off to buy the part at $1.20 each.

However, on a short-run basis the manufacturer might be justified in ignoring the normal overhead rate and in charging Part 417 for only the added overhead costs resulting from its manufacture. Among these added overhead costs might be, for example, power to operate the machines that would otherwise be idle, depreciation on the machines if the manufacture of the part resulted in additional depreciation, and any other overhead items that would be added to the overhead already incurred. Furthermore, if these added overhead items total less than $0.25, the manufacturer might be justified on a short-run basis in manufacturing the part. However, on a long-term basis, Part 417 should be charged a full share of all overhead.

Any amount of overhead less than $0.25 per unit results in a total cost for Part 417 that is less than the purchase price of $1.20 per unit. Nevertheless, in making a final decision as to whether the part should be bought or made, the manufacturer should consider in addition to costs such things as quality, the reactions of customers and suppliers, and other intangible factors. When these additional factors are considered, small cost differences may become a minor factor.

As a final note it should be observed that while the situations described in this chapter are only a sample of situations encountered and are in many cases oversimplified, they serve their purpose when they bring some of the factors involved in period planning to the attention of the student.

QUESTIONS FOR CLASS DISCUSSION

1. If depreciation is an expense, explain why, when the product of a machine is sold at a profit, the amount of the machine's cost that is recovered each year through the sale of its product includes both the profit from the sale of the product and the year's depreciation.

2. During its life, what is the average amount that will be invested in a machine that cost $10,000 and has an estimated service life of four years and an estimated trade-in value of $1,600?

3. Differentiate between a "sunk cost" and an "out-of-pocket cost."

4. When a company is contemplating the purchase of a new fixed asset to replace an obsolete fixed asset, which is usually the more significant the costs "sunk" in the obsolete asset or the out-of-pocket costs necessary to acquire and operate the new asset?

5. Differentiate between fixed costs, semifixed costs, and variable costs.

6. A company manufactures and sells in the United States 500,000 units of a product at $5.00 per unit. Its manufacturing costs are $3.00 per unit, and its selling expenses are $1.50 per unit. Can you describe a situation under which the company may be willing to sell an additional 100,000 of the units abroad at $2.90 per unit?

7. Within a given marketing area, is the demand for gasoline elastic or inelastic? Should a service station operator who is about to start a price war by cutting his pump price for gasoline, give some consideration to the elasticity of the demand for gasoline? Why?

8. Six years ago a company purchased for $1,000,000 the mineral rights to an ore body containing 1,000,000 tons of ore. The company invested an additional $1,000,000 in mining machinery designed to exhaust the mine in ten years. During its first five years the mine produced 500,000 tons of ore that were sold at a profit. During its sixth year 100,000 tons of ore were mined; but due to technological changes in the manufacturing processes of the customers to whom the ore was normally sold, there was little demand for the ore and it was sold at a loss of $1.00 per ton. If during the next four years the remain-

ing 400,000 tons of ore could be mined and sold at a loss of $1.00 per ton, and and there was no prospect of ever doing better, would you recommend that the ore be mined and sold at a loss or would you recommend that the mine be closed so that there would be no loss from mining and selling the remaining ore?

9. A lumber mill buys logs at $30 per thousand board feet and manufactures them into a line of lumber products including packing crates that are made from lumber that would be burned as waste if the crates were not manufactured. The cost accountant of the firm has produced statistics to show that the crates are manufactured and sold at a loss. In his statistics he charges the crates with the lumber used in their manufacture at the rate of $30 per thousand board feet. If you were the manager of this firm, what information would you want before discontinuing the manufacture of the crates?

10. A company that normally manufactures 100,000 units of a product annually is considering the manufacture and sales of an additional 20,000 units annually. In discussing the costs of manufacturing the additional units, the term "differential costs" is used. What is meant by this term?

PROBLEMS

Problem 26–1

Voltz Company is considering the addition of a new product to its line. The new product will require the use of factory space not presently used, and its manufacture will require additional machinery costing $40,000 and having a ten-year life with no salvage value. The following additional information is available:

Estimated sales of new product	$80,000
Estimated costs:	
Material	27,000
Labor	10,000
Overhead including depreciation of new machinery	16,000
Selling and administrative expenses	12,000
State and federal income taxes	60%

Required:

Calculate (a) the payback period on the investment in new machinery, and (b) the rate of return on the average investment in new machinery.

Problem 26–2

Three years ago Walton Company purchased at a total cost of $30,000 a stamping machine for use in its factory. Since that time a new semiautomatic machine that does the same work at a considerable saving in operating costs has come on the market. Walton Company has received a trade-in offer of $3,000 for its old machine on one of the new semiautomatic ones. The following statistics comparing the machines are available:

	Old Machine	New Machine
Listed selling price	$30,000	$45,000
Estimated life new	15 years	12 years
Estimated salvage value	None	None
Capacity in units per hour	1,800 units	1,800 units
Maintenance, supplies, etc., per year	$1,500	$1,200
Power costs per year	$ 400	$ 450
Operating labor costs per year	$5,000	$1,200

At the moment Walton Company is negotiating a $100,000 to $150,000, 4 per cent, long-term loan. The funds are to be used in modernizing and expanding the plant. The larger loan of $150,000 is sufficient to cover the cost of the new machine; consequently, funds to purchase the machine are no problem.

Required:

Prepare statistics to show whether or not it would be wise for Walton Company to trade in its old stamping machine on the new semiautomatic one.

Problem 26–3

Because of patents, Roxbury Company has a monopoly on the manufacture and sale of a product it calls Roxtone. Variable costs in the manufacture and sale of Roxtone are $12 per unit for any number of units up to 15,000. When more than 15,000 units are produced, because of the economies of volume purchasing, the variable costs are reduced to $10 per unit. Fixed costs are $100,000 for the production of up to 15,000 units. Then because more machines, employees, and supervision are required, fixed costs are increased to $175,000 for production of between 15,000 to 30,000 units; and they are increased to $240,000 for production of between 30,000 to 45,000 units. Estimated sales at various prices are as follows:

Estimated Salable Units	Selling Price
2,000	$50
5,000	40
10,000	30
20,000	25
35,000	20
45,000	15

Required:

Prepare statistics to show the profit at each selling price.

Problem 26–4

Sampson Company manufactures a wrench that it sells to wholesalers at $1.15 each. During a normal year the firm manufactures and sells approximately 100,000 wrenches. Data on a normal year's costs of manufacturing and selling 100,000 wrenches are as follows:

Materials	$ 24,400
Direct labor	25,100
Overhead	20,000
Selling costs	16,900
Administrative costs	15,800
	$102,200

A mail-order firm has offered to buy from Sampson Company 10,000 wrenches at $0.95 each to be marketed under the mail-order firm's trade name. If accepted, the order would not be expected to affect sales through present channels.

A study of a normal year's costs and their relation to the new business reveals that: (1) Material costs in the production of the wrenches is 100 per cent variable. (2) Of a normal year's overhead costs, one half would remain fixed at any level of production from zero to 125,000 units and one half would vary directly with production. (3) The per unit direct labor costs for the additional business would be 50 per cent greater than the per unit costs of a normal year because the additional business would require overtime at time and one half. (4) There would be no additional selling costs resulting from the new business. (5) Acceptance of the new business would increase administrative costs by $1,000.

Required:

Prepare a comparative income statement for the Sampson Company that shows (1) in one set of columns the operating profit of a normal year, (2) in a second set of columns the operating profit that may be expected from the new business, and (3) in a third set of columns the combined operating profit that may be expected from the normal and the new business.

CLASS EXERCISE

Exercise 26–1

Black Ink Printing Company has a request from the Rio Theatre for price quotations on the printing of either 1,000, 2,000, or 5,000 show cards. The following information is available:

Cost of setting type and press setup for running the
    job...$20.00
Paper and ink per 500 copies.................... 5.00
Direct labor for operating press per 500 copies...... 2.00
Variable plant overhead chargeable to the job...... 80% of direct labor
Profit....................................... 10% on job cost

Required:

1. Prepare a schedule showing the costs for each quantity of show cards, the price to be quoted for each quantity, and the price per show card for each quantity.
2. Point out the fixed costs in the printing of the show cards, and discuss the effect of these fixed costs on the unit cost of a show card when either 1,000, 2,000, or 5,000 cards are printed.

SUPPLEMENTARY PROBLEMS

Problem 26–A

Hampton Company operates at an average annual capacity of 20,000 units of a product which it produces on two 10,000-unit capacity, five-year-old machines that cost $5,000 each and which have been depreciated under the assumption that they would have no salvage value at the end of an expected ten-year life. The company has an opportunity to expand its scale of operations from 20,000 units to 30,000 units annually. However, to do so it must either: (1) purchase a new and larger machine having an annual capacity of 35,000 units, an expected life of ten years with no salvage value, and costing $32,000, less a trade-in allowance of $1,000 each on the two old machines; or (2) purchase for $1,000 a secondhand machine of the same age and 10,000-unit capacity and having the same remaining expected useful life as their old machines. Material costs would be the same whether three old machines or one new machine is used. However, since each of the old machines and also the new machine requires an operator, the new machine offers an annual saving of the wages of two operators. This saving and other savings are evident from an examination of the following table in which are given the costs of operating a single old machine producing 10,000 units of product annually and of operating one of the new larger machines at an annual rate of 30,000 units of product annually:

	Old 10,000 Unit Machine	New 35,000 Unit Machine
Labor (one man)	$4,200	$4,200
Maintenance	75	300
Power	150	250
Insurance, taxes, and etc.	100	1,200

Required:

Prepare statistics to aid the management of Hampton Company in its decision between the purchase of the secondhand 10,000-unit capacity machine and the new 35,000-unit capacity machine. Assume that Hampton Company must pay 4 per cent for the use of long-term capital.

Problem 26–B

The Rheta Rose Manufacturing Company produces an item which it sells direct to consumers under its own brand. The item sells at $12.50 per unit, which is a long-established price. Owing to a general decline in business activity, sales are currently being made at the rate of 5,000 units per month, which is only 40 per cent of the normal productive capacity of the plant of the company.

An analysis of the costs of the company for a recent month, during which only 4,000 units were produced and 5,000 units sold, shows the following:

MANUFACTURING COSTS

Direct labor	$ 9,900.00
Superintendent's salary	1,000.00
Assistant superintendent's salary	750.00
Power purchased	560.00
Direct materials	4,000.00
Purchased parts	2,400.00
Depreciation of building	1,420.00
Maintenance of building	206.00
Heat and light	348.00
Indirect labor	2,240.00
Miscellaneous supplies	800.00
Depreciation of machinery	3,640.00
Repairs to machinery	480.00
Property taxes	600.00
Insurance (fire)	80.00
Social security taxes	456.00
Miscellaneous	1,120.00
	$30,000.00

SELLING COSTS

Manager's salary	$ 833.33
Salesmen's commissions	18,750.00
Travel	247.05
Advertising	500.00
Clerical salaries	300.00
Packing and shipping	2,108.43
Miscellaneous	1,203.79
	$23,942.60

ADMINISTRATIVE AND GENERAL COSTS

Officer's salaries	$ 1,525.00
Office salaries	975.50
Telephone and telegraph	217.73
Supplies	486.21
Bad debts	625.00
Miscellaneous	392.86
	$ 4,222.30

An offer has been received from a chain store by the treasurer of the company to purchase 5,000 units a month of the products with only immaterial modifications, to be shipped and billed to the individual stores. The items would be sold under the store's label and would be packed and shipped as directed by the chain at their expense. They offer $7.00 per unit unpacked on the basis of a one-year contract. The management of the Rheta Rose Company does not expect that there will be an improvement in the business within the next year, and there is no fear that the sale of the items to the chain would reduce the present volume of sales to consumers. The company does not believe it can afford to accept the offer as it is losing on its present price of $12.50; therefore, it appears that losses would be substantially increased by entering into the sales contract with the chain.

The treasurer calls you in to prepare an analysis which will show the result of accepting the order in comparison with the result if the order is not accepted. In preparing your analysis you are to assume that all items of cost are either completely fixed or completely variable, depending upon the usual dominant characteristic of each item and the data given herein. (The foregoing problem is reproduced with the permission of the American Institute of Certified Public Accountants from its Uniform Certified Public Accountant Examination, Part II, No. 1, May, 1949.)

Chapter

27

THE MANAGEMENT of any business plans. It is impossible to conceive of a business in which objectives have not been set and plans made to reach the objectives. For example, with an act so simple as the purchasing of an item of supplies, there must be a plan to use the supplies.

Although the management of any company plans, the ways in which managements plan vary. Some managements are very informal in their planning; all of their planning is done on scraps of paper or in the heads of management and remains there. Other managements commit their plans to paper in an orderly manner and are said to prepare *budgets*. A budget is a *plan* of future action, and budgeting is the process of *planning* future action. The key words in the foregoing sentence are "plan" and "planning."

Budgets and Their Objectives

Why do managements plan? It is easy to say that the purpose of planning is to maximize profits. This is true; but the benefits of planning or budgeting reach beyond this and may be grouped under several headings as follows:

Planning. When a firm plans, it may be assumed that its actions are based upon thorough investigations, study, and research. Not only should this result in the best conceivable plans but it should also instill in executives the habit of basing decisions upon investigations and study.

Co-ordinating. Co-ordination requires that a business be operated as a whole rather than as a group of separate departments. When a budget plan is prepared, the objectives of each department are determined in advance; these objectives are co-ordinated; and, for example, the production department is scheduled to produce what the selling department can sell.

Communicating. When a budget is prepared, the budget becomes a means of informing the organization not only of the plans that have been approved by management but also of the budgeted actions that management wishes the organization to take during the budget period.

Motivating. When obtainable budgeted objectives are set, all persons responsible can normally be depended upon to make every effort to attain or exceed the objectives for which they are personally responsible.

The Budget Period

Budget periods normally coincide with accounting periods. This means that in most companies the budget period is one year in length. However, in addition to their annual budgets, many companies prepare long-range budgets setting forth their major objectives for from three to five or ten years in advance. Such long-range budgets are often used as the framework into which each annual budget is fitted.

Although most budgets are prepared for a year, yearly budgets are commonly broken down into quarterly or monthly budgets. Short-term budgets of a quarter or a month are useful yardsticks for measuring the degree of accomplishment toward the total results desired.

Illustration 155

CONSOLIDATED STORES, INC.
Income Statement with Variations from Budget
For Month Ended April 30, 19--

	Actual	Budget	Variations
Sales	$63,500	$60,000	$+ 3,500
Less: Sales returns and allowances.	1,800	1,700	+ 100
Sales discounts	1,200	1,150	+ 50
Net sales	$60,500	$57,150	$+ 3,350
Cost of goods sold:			
Merchandise inventory, April 1, 19--.	$42,000	$44,000	$- 2,000
Purchases, net.	39,100	38,000	+ 1,100
Freight-in.	1,250	1,200	+ 50
Goods for sale.	$82,350	$83,200	$- 850
Merchandise inventory, April 30, 19--	41,000	44,100	- 3,100
Cost of goods sold.	$41,350	$39,100	$+ 2,250
Gross profit.	$19,150	$18,050	$+ 1,100
Operating expenses:			
Selling expenses:			
Sales salaries.	$ 6,250	$ 6,000	$+ 250
Advertising expense	900	800	+ 100
Store supplies used	550	500	+ 50
Depreciation of store equipment	1,600	1,600	
Total Selling Expenses.	$ 9,300	$ 8,900	$+ 400
General and administrative expenses:			
Office salaries	$ 2,000	$ 2,000	
Office supplies used.	165	150	$+ 15
Rent.	1,100	1,100	
Expired insurance	200	200	
Depreciation of office equipment.	100	100	
Total General and Administrative Expenses .	$ 3,565	$ 3,550	$+ 15
Total Operating Expenses.	$12,865	$12,450	$+ 415
Income from Operations.	$ 6,285	$ 5,600	$+ 685

When an annual budget is broken down into monthly budgets, monthly budget reports like that of Illustration 155 are normally prepared to compare actual achievements with the budgeted plan.

Preparing a Budget

A company's budget is commonly the work of a budget committee which may be made up of the president who acts as chairman, the sales manager, the production manager, and other department heads, depending upon the nature of the company.

Sales Budget. The budget committee's first major task is the sales budget. An estimate of the quantity of goods to be sold and the revenue to be derived from sales is the starting point in the preparation of most budgets. This is because the plans of all departments are related to sales and expected revenues.

The sales budget commonly grows out of a reconciliation of forecasted business conditions, plant capacity, proposed selling expenses, such as advertising, and estimates of expected sales as submitted by the salesmen through their sales manager. The gain from having sales estimates prepared by salesmen is that they are familiar with their territories; and, also, they normally feel a greater responsibility for reaching goals they have had a hand in setting.

Expense Budget. As soon as a tentative sales estimate can be made, it is communicated to department heads such as the sales manager and office manager who are asked to make estimates of the expenses of their departments. The department heads normally make their estimates on a basis of the previous year's expenses, adjusted for increases or decreases in the amount of expected service required of them, changes in salary and wage scales, changes in supply costs, and other pertinent data. The estimates must meet with the approval of the budget committee or they are increased or decreased; however, asking for estimates from department heads helps to secure the co-operation of the department heads in carrying out the final budget.

Production Budget. The volume of goods to be produced is computed by adding the desired end-of-the-budget-period inventory to budgeted sales and deducting the beginning inventory. The calculation may be made on the basis of either dollars or units. If units are used, and for example, sales of an item are estimated at 2,500 units and the desired ending inventory is 200 units, a total of 2,700 units must be in stock during the year. If the beginning inventory is 250 units, 2,450 units must be produced.

If there are dull and busy seasons, production and employment may be kept at a uniform level by increasing the inventory during dull seasons and decreasing it during busy seasons.

Plant and Equipment Budget. The plant and equipment budget lists the equipment to be scrapped and additional equipment that must be purchased if the proposed production program is carried out. The purchase of additional equipment requires funds; anticipating equipment additions in advance of needs normally makes it easier to provide the required funds.

At times estimated production may exceed the capacity of the plant to produce. Budgeting makes it possible to anticipate such situations and to either revise the production schedule or increase the capacity of the plant.

Cash Budget. After tentative sales, expenses, production, and equipment budgets have been set, the cash budget is prepared. The cash budget is important. A company should have at all times enough cash to meet its needs but not too much. Too much cash is undesirable because extra cash often cannot be profitably invested.

A cash budget requires that management forecast its cash receipts and disbursements. This usually results in better cash management. Also, a cash budget enables management to arrange well in advance for loans to cover any anticipated inadequacies.

In preparing the cash budget, anticipated receipts are added to the beginning balance of cash, and anticipated expenditures are deducted. Annual cash budgets are usually broken down into monthly cash budgets. Illustration 156 shows a monthly cash budget for Consolidated Stores, Inc.

Illustration 156
CONSOLIDATED STORES, INC.
Cash Budget for January, 19--

Cash balance, January 1, 19-- . . .		$32,500
Add estimated cash receipts:		
Cash sales	$43,200	
Collections of accounts receivable	18,650	
Interest on investments.	750	
Property rentals	1,800	64,400
Available cash		$96,900
Deduct estimated disbursements:		
Accounts payable	$41,300	
State and federal taxes.	2,750	
Payrolls	8,250	
Building repairs	15,300	
Dividends.	4,000	
Miscellaneous items.	1,200	72,800
Estimated Cash Balance, January 31, 19--		$24,100

Master Budget. After the sales, expenses, production, equipment, and cash budgets are co-ordinated and completed, they are combined into a master budget. The master budget is then approved by the board of directors and transmitted to the organization as the approved objectives of the budget period.

Accounting and Budgeting

The preparation and carrying out of a budget involves all departments of a business; consequently, it is not primarily an accounting function. However, the task of assembling data and translating it into financial terms often falls to the accounting department. The accounting department, since it is in charge of the accounting records and is constantly dealing with actual transactions, is well qualified to deal with budget data.

One of the budget tasks that the accounting department is commonly called upon to perform is the preparation from the budget of an estimated income statement for the budget year and an estimated balance sheet as it will appear at the end of the budget year, if the plans of the budget are carried out. This task is, in a sense, actually one of accounting for events before they happen. It differs but little from accounting for events after they happen.

Preparing Estimated Statements

Normally, when the accounting department is called on to prepare an estimated balance sheet and an estimated income statement as the statements will appear at the end of the budget period if the budgeted plans are followed, it is called upon to do so a month or more before the budget period begins. For example, the accounting department may be given during the last week of November a copy of the budget and a request for estimated statements for the year beginning on the following January 1.

During the last week in November, the accounting department does not know what the following December 31 post-closing or January 1 opening trial balance amounts will be. Consequently, its first task is to project the company's account balances ahead and arrive at the December 31, estimated, post-closing trial balance for the current year.

After arriving at this December 31, estimated, post-closing trial balance, the estimated, post-closing trial balance is commonly entered in the first two money columns of a work sheet. Next the proposed transactions of the budget are entered in the second pair of work sheet columns in the same manner as adjustments are entered on an ordinary work sheet. For example, if the budget plans sales on account of $250,000, the name of the Sales account is entered on the work sheet in the Account Titles column below the names of the estimated trial balance accounts; and then Sales is credited and Accounts Receivable is debited for $250,000 in the second pair of money columns in the same manner that an adjustment is entered on an ordinary work sheet.

After all of the budgeted transactions are entered on the work sheet, the estimated trial balance amounts in the first pair of money columns are combined with the budget amounts in the second pair of columns and are sorted to the proper Income Statement and Balance Sheet columns of the work sheet. After this, the estimated income statement and estimated balance sheet are prepared from the information in the Income Statement and Balance Sheet columns in the same manner as an ordinary income statement or balance sheet.

Fixed and Variable Budgets

Some companies prepare each year what are known as fixed budgets; other companies prepare so-called variable budgets.

When a fixed budget is prepared, it is assumed by the company preparing it that sales can be estimated with a sufficient degree of accuracy so that only one plan is needed. Consequently, the one plan is a fixed or static plan. Actually, the plan is fixed only to the extent that a serious effort is made to achieve it. If this is found to be impossible, the plan is changed.

Variable budgets are based on the assumption that sales cannot be estimated with a sufficient degree of accuracy for the adoption of only a single plan. When a variable budget is prepared, maximum and minimum amounts of sales are estimated and several plans are prepared based upon the maximum, the minimum, and several amounts between. For example, if the maximum sales are estimated to be $240,000 and the minimum to be $210,000, plans for $210,000, $220,000, $230,000, and $240,000 may be prepared. Then, during the budget period sales are carefully watched; and if, for example, sales are running at the $210,000 rate, department heads are expected to adjust their expenses to the $210,000 plan.

Fixed and Variable Expenses and Break-Even Points

Companies that prepare variable budgets normally make studies of the relationship of their costs, expenses, and sales at various levels of production. One of the studies commonly made is a break-even point analysis. The break-even point for a company is the point at which revenue from sales exactly equals cost of goods sold plus expenses. It is the point where there is neither a profit nor a loss.

To better understand something of the nature of expenses, visualize a company in which the sum of the cost of goods sold and expenses is always less than sales and at all volumes varies exactly in proportion to sales. In such a company there is always a profit no matter if one unit or a hundred thousand units of a product are sold. For example, assume that in this imaginary company each unit of product sells for $1.00 and the cost of goods sold and expenses of each unit sold total $0.90. Under these assumptions there is a profit of $0.10 if one unit is sold and a profit of $10,000 if one hundred thousand units are sold.

Actually, a company such as that described in the previous paragraph seldom exists because although some expenses vary in proportion to sales, other expenses are fixed. For example, expenses such as sales commissions, shipping and delivery expenses, and, perhaps, advertising may vary almost directly with sales; while such expenses as depreciation, taxes, rent, and heat remain more or less fixed regardless of the volume of sales.

When a company has both fixed and variable expenses, it also has a point or volume of sales at which it breaks even. For example, assume that a company selling a single product at $100 per unit has fixed expenses that total $30,000 and its cost of goods sold and variable expenses are 75 per cent of the selling price of each unit sold. The break-even point for this company may be calculated as follows:

Let S = the volume of sales at the break-even point.

Then:

$$S = \$30,000 + 0.75S$$
$$S - 0.75S = \$30,000$$
$$0.25S = \$30,000$$
$$S = \frac{\$30,000}{0.25}$$
$$S = \$120,000$$

The company breaks even at a sales volume of $120,000. At this volume the 25 per cent of each sales dollar that is available to cover fixed expenses and provide a profit exactly provides the $30,000 of fixed expenses and leaves nothing over for a profit.

A break-even chart that shows the break-even point for the firm just described appears as in Illustration 157. Observe in the chart that the curve showing total costs and expenses begins at $30,000 and extends upward, and that the curve showing sales begins at zero and intersects the

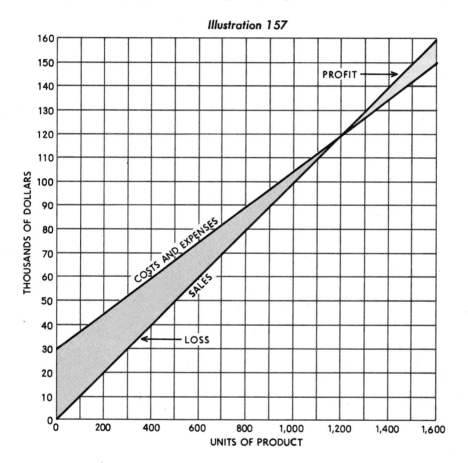

Illustration 157

cost and expense curve at $120,000. This is the break-even point. When sales go above this point, increasing profits are earned as shown by the spread between the two lines; and when sales go below the break-even point, increasing losses are incurred.

The illustrated situation just described, in which a company has $30,-000 of fixed expenses and its cost of goods sold and variable expenses are 75 per cent of sales, represents an oversimplification of the normal fixed and variable expense situation. The company of the illustrated situation has only one product; most companies have many products, the sales of which result in different amounts of fixed and variable expenses. Too, in the illustrated situation it is assumed that expenses are either fixed or variable. Some expenses are fixed; some vary directly with sales; and others vary with sales but not in the same proportion as sales.

Nevertheless, break-even calculations and charts for a business are of value because they call the attention of management to the volume, cost, and profit relationships of the business. This will almost always result in better management decisions.

QUESTIONS FOR CLASS DISCUSSION

1. What is gained by the preparation of budgets?
2. What is the normal length of a budget period?
3. What are some of the advantages of having a budget prepared by a budget committee made up of department heads?
4. What is a sales budget? An expense budget? A production budget? An equipment budget? A cash budget? A master budget?
5. A manufacturing firm plans to begin a budget year with 1,680 units of its product on hand; it plans to sell 48,000 units during the year; and it plans to end the year with an inventory of 1,200 units. If production is to be at a uniform rate throughout the year, how many units of product should the firm plan to produce each month?
6. Differentiate between a fixed budget and a variable budget.
7. What happens at the break-even point in terms of fixed expenses, variable expenses, and profits?
8. A firm's cost of goods sold and variable expenses are 60 per cent of each sales dollar, and its fixed expenses are $80,000. What is its break-even point?
9. Often several months before a budget year begins, an accounting department is asked to prepare an estimated income statement for the budget year and an estimated balance sheet to show the effect of carrying out the budget plans. Describe how such estimated statements can be prepared.
10. The president of a company expressed the opinion that he thought his company benefited from having its department heads meet before the beginning of a new year to discuss the prospects of the new year but that any time spent preparing a formal budget was wasted. Express your opinion on this subject.

PROBLEMS

Problem 27–1

During each of the past several years Haddox Company has operated at 70 per cent of capacity and has manufactured and sold 100,000 units of its one product with the following average results:

Sales..		$1,000,000
Cost of goods sold.............................		650,000
Gross profit from sales........................		$ 350,000
Selling expenses..............................	$150,000	
Administrative expenses........................	100,000	250,000
Net Income before Taxes.......................		$ 100,000

The sales manager of the company has suggested that a 10 per cent reduction in the sales price of the product would result in a 25 per cent increase in the number of units sold.

A breakdown of the $6.50 per unit average cost of goods manufactured and sold shows the following costs:

Direct material.............................	$1.00
Direct labor................................	2.00
Variable overhead...........................	1.00
Fixed overhead.............................	2.50
	$6.50

For any volume up to 100 per cent of capacity, the direct material, direct labor, and variable overhead costs would vary directly with the volume and the fixed overhead would remain fixed.

An analysis of the selling expenses indicates that for any volume up to 100 per cent of capacity, one third of the average selling expenses of the past several years would remain fixed and two thirds would vary with the dollar volume of sales. Likewise, one half of the administrative expenses would remain fixed and one half would vary with the number of units sold.

Required:

Prepared an estimated income statement that shows the results of decreasing the sales price of the product 10 per cent and increasing the number of units sold by 25 per cent.

Problem 27–2

On December 31 of the current year Central Sales Company expects to have a cash balance of $5,800, accounts receivable balance of $35,500, and an accounts payable balance of $21,400. Its budgeted sales, purchases, and cash expenditures for the following three months are as follows:

	January	February	March
Sales.....................................	$24,000	$18,000	$27,000
Purchases................................	14,000	17,300	18,000
Payroll..................................	2,400	2,400	2,800
Rent.....................................	1,000	1,000	1,000
Other cash expenses......................	1,200	1,600	1,400
Purchase of store equipment..............	...	5,000	...
Payment of quarterly dividend............	...	...	4,000

All sales are on account; and past experience indicates that 85 per cent is collected in the month following the sale, 10 per cent in the next month, and 4 per cent in the third month. Application of the experience to the December 31 balance of accounts receivable indicates that $28,000 of the $35,500 will be collected in January, $5,200 in February, and $1,600 in March.

Purchases on account are paid for in the month following each purchase.

Required:

Prepare cash budgets for each of the months in the first quarter of the new year.

Problem 27–3

Assume that it is the first week in December of the current year and the accounting department of Eastgate Manufacturing Company has been asked to prepare a set of estimated statements as the statements will appear at the end of the year beginning next January 1. The accounting department has projected ahead the account balances of November 30 of the current year and has arrived at the following estimated December 31 post-closing trial balance:

EASTGATE MANUFACTURING COMPANY

Estimated Post-Closing Trial Balance, December 31, 19—

Cash	$ 29,500	
Accounts receivable	35,000	
Allowance for bad debts		$ 3,100
Raw materials inventory	19,800	
Goods in process inventory	15,200	
Finished goods inventory	22,700	
Prepaid factory insurance	1,200	
Factory supplies	2,900	
Factory machinery	182,000	
Accumulated depreciation, factory machinery		50,600
Accounts payable		16,500
State and federal income taxes payable		21,000
Dividends payable		3,000
Common stock, $100 par value		150,000
Premium on common stock		15,000
Retained earnings		49,100
	$308,300	$308,300

The budget plans of Eastgate Manufacturing Company call for the following condensed transactions to be completed during the coming year:

1. Sales (all on account)		$360,000
2. Purchases (all on account):		
Raw materials	$ 62,000	
Factory supplies	5,000	
Factory machinery (on October 1)	85,000	152,000
3. Cash receipts:		
Collection of accounts receivable	$355,000	
($3,100 of accounts receivable will be written off as bad debts.)		
Sale during October of 500 shares of $100 par value common stock at $140 per share	70,000	425,000
4. Cash disbursements:		
Payment of accounts payable	$153,500	
Payment of insurance premiums (debit prepaid factory insurance)	3,600	
Payment of dividends	12,000	
State and federal income taxes payable	21,000	
Direct labor	90,000	
Factory supervision	12,000	
Indirect Labor	9,500	
Heat, light, and power	18,700	
Machinery repairs	5,400	
Rent of factory building	12,000	
Property taxes, machinery	1,600	
Sales salaries	28,200	
Advertising	4,200	
Officers' salaries	20,000	
Office salaries	11,000	402,700

5. End of the budget year adjustments will be required for:
    a) Expired factory insurance...................... $ 3,800
    b) Factory supplies used.........................   5,400
    c) Bad debts expense.............................   3,600
    d) Depreciation of factory machinery..............   18,200
6. End of the budget year inventories are expected to be:
    Raw materials..................................   20,800
    Goods in process...............................   14,900
    Finished goods.................................   21,200
7. Quarterly dividends of $2.00 per share are expected to be declared on the stock outstanding on March 31, on June 30, on September 30, and on December 31.
8. A combined state and federal income tax rate of 60 per cent is expected.

Required:

Enter the December 31, estimated trial balance amounts in the Trial Balance columns of a manufacturing work sheet. Then enter the budgeted transactions in the Adjustments columns in the same manner that adjustments are entered. Next, enter the budgeted adjustments and complete the work sheet.

Problem 27–4

From the work sheet of Problem 27–3 prepare an estimated manufacturing statement, an estimated income statement, and an estimated balance sheet for the budget year.

Problem 27–5

Walton Company manufactures a single product called a Pingtopper which it sells for $50 per unit. The company's annual fixed costs are $42,000, and the variable costs of manufacturing and selling Pingtoppers are $35 per unit.

Required:

1. Calculate the break-even point of the Walton Company.
2. Prepare a break-even chart for the company.

CLASS EXERCISE

Exercise 27–1

During the past year Newport Company incurred a loss in selling 10,000 units of its product at $30 per unit. The company's annual fixed costs were $120,000, and the variable costs per unit of product sold were $21. In order to increase sales, the management of the company is considering the wisdom of spending $15,000 on advertising during the coming year.

Required:

Under the assumptions that the company will continue to sell its product at $30 per unit and that its foregoing fixed costs will remain fixed and its variable costs will continue to be $21 per unit, determine the break-even points:
    a) If the $15,000 is spent for advertising.
    b) If the $15,000 is not spent.

SUPPLEMENTARY PROBLEMS

Problem 27-A

Following are average revenue and expense data for Companies A and B:

	Company A		Company B	
Sales........................		$1,200,000		$1,200,000
Fixed expenses...............	$240,000		$600,000	
Variable expenses............	720,000	960,000	360,000	960,000
Income before Taxes.........		$ 240,000		$ 240,000

Company A and Company B each sell a single product. Both products sell for $1,000 per unit. However, beyond this the products have nothing in common.

Required:

1. Under the assumptions that at any volume of sales the foregoing fixed expenses of each company will remain fixed and the variable expenses will vary exactly with sales, prepare break-even charts for each company.
2. Assume that with no change in sales price the sales volume of each company declines one third. Explain the difference in the effect of the decline on each company's income before taxes.
3. Beyond their break-even points, what is the difference in the effect of an increasing sales volume in each company?

Problem 27-B

During the first six months of the current year Milford Stamping Company produced 100,000 units of its one product with the following costs:

MILFORD STAMPING COMPANY

Schedule of Cost of Goods Manufactured
For the Six-Month Period Ended June 30, 19—

Raw materials:			
Raw materials inventory, January 1, 19—................			$ 9,300
Raw materials purchased.............................			20,000
Raw materials available for use.......................			$38,900
Raw materials inventory, June 30, 19—................			10,500
Raw materials used.................................			$28,400
Direct labor.......................................			25,000
Overhead costs:			
Indirect labor.....................................		$6,500	
Supervision.......................................		3,200	
Power...		6,000	
Factory rent......................................		2,400	
Depreciation of machinery..........................		2,700	
Factory supplies used..............................		1,000	
Insurance and taxes, machinery......................		800	22,600
Cost of Goods Manufactured........................			$76,000

On June 30 the company completed the replacement of much of its old machinery with new high-speed, semiautomatic machinery which is expected to increase the output by 50 per cent. However, it is expected that the new machinery will cause a 10 per cent decrease in total direct labor costs, a 10 per cent increase in total power costs, a 100 per cent increase in depreciation costs and in insurance and taxes, a 30 per cent increase in factory supplies used, and no change in other overhead costs. Because of the more rapid use of raw materials, the company expects to increase the size of its raw materials inventory and to reach the end of the year with $12,000 of raw materials on hand.

Required:

1. Prepare an estimated schedule of costs of goods manufactured for the six months beginning July 1 that will reflect the foregoing expectations.
2. Prepare a schedule comparing the unit costs for material, labor, and overhead for the six months ended June 30 with the unit costs expected during the six months beginning July 1.

Chapter
28

ANALYSIS AND INTERPRETA-
TION OF FINANCIAL
STATEMENTS

ACCORDING to the dictionary, to analyze is to separate the parts of a whole so as to see the relationship of the parts to the whole and to each other. Also, according to the dictionary, to interpret something is to explain it or to tell its meaning. Consequently, to analyze and interpret financial statements is to separate financial statements into their parts so as to see the relationship of the parts to the whole and to each other, and to tell the meaning of what is seen. Numerous books have been written on the subject of financial statement analysis and interpretation. Obviously, an introductory accounting text can examine only some of the more fundamental techniques of statement analysis and interpretation.

Comparative Statements

A commonly used technique in the analysis and interpretation of financial statements is the preparation of comparative financial statements. A single balance sheet shows the assets, liabilities, and proprietorship of a business as of a specific date. A comparative balance sheet shows the assets, liabilities, and proprietorship of the business on two or more dates and, consequently, shows the changes that have taken place. The changes are normally the results of past operating policies. An interpretation of these changes offers management a guide to future policies.

In its most simple form a comparative balance sheet consists of the item amounts from two of a company's successive balance sheets arranged side by side in a single statement. When item amounts from successive balance sheets are arranged side by side, changes in item amounts may be seen. However, in examining such a comparative balance sheet the average person often has difficulty in grasping significant changes. Consequently, a comparative balance sheet showing only dollar amounts may be improved by also showing in both dollar amounts and in percentages the changes that have occurred. To accomplish this, two additional columns are added to a simple comparative balance sheet. In the first of the additional columns is shown in dollars the amount of increase or decrease for each statement item. In the second column is shown the percentage of increase or decrease for each item. (See Illustrations 158 and 159.) When changes in items are shown in both dollar amounts and

Illustration 158

ANCHOR SUPPLY COMPANY
Comparative Balance Sheet
December 31, 1958, and December 31, 1959

	Years Ended December 31		Amount of Increase or Decrease* during	Percentage of Increase or De- crease*
	1959	1958	1959	during 1959
ASSETS				
Current Assets:				
Cash	$ 14,000	$ 89,000	$ 75,000*	84.3*
Notes receivable	4,000	1,500	2,500	166.7
Accounts receivable, net	68,000	64,000	4,000	6.3
Merchandise inventory.	190,000	184,000	6,000	3.3
Prepaid expenses	5,800	6,000	200*	3.3*
Total Current Assets	$281,800	$344,500	$ 62,700*	18.2*
Investments:				
Real estate.	-0-	$ 30,000	$ 30,000*	100.0*
Apex Company 4 per cent bonds. . .	-0-	50,000	50,000*	100.0*
Total Investments.	-0-	$ 80,000	$ 80,000*	100.0*
Fixed Assets:				
Office equipment	$ 5,000	$ 5,000		
Less: Accumulated depreciation .	1,500	1,200		
	$ 3,500	$ 3,800	$ 300*	7.9*
Store equipment.	$ 24,000	$ 11,000		
Less: Accumulated depreciation .	6,200	4,300		
	$ 17,800	$ 6,700	11,100	165.7
Buildings.	$210,000	$ 60,000		
Less: Accumulated depreciation .	33,200	32,000		
	$176,800	$ 28,000	148,800	531.4
Land	$ 50,000	$ 20,000	30,000	150.0
Total Fixed Assets	$248,100	$ 58,500	$189,600	324.1
Total Assets	$529,900	$483,000	$ 46,900	9.7
LIABILITIES				
Current Liabilities:				
Notes payable	-0-	$ 10,000	$ 10,000*	100.0*
Accounts payable	$ 53,400	60,000	6,600*	11.0*
Wages payable	800	1,200	400*	33.3*
Total Current Liabilities. . .	$ 54,200	$ 71,200	$ 17,000*	23.9*
Fixed Liabilities:				
Mortgage payable	$ 60,000	$ 10,000	$ 50,000	500.0
Total Liabilities.	$114,200	$ 81,200	$ 33,000	40.6
CAPITAL				
Common stock	$250,000	$250,000		
Retained earnings.	165,700	151,800	$ 13,900	9.2
Total Capital.	$415,700	$401,800	$ 13,900	3.5
Total Liabilities and Capital	$529,900	$483,000	$ 46,900	9.7

in percentages, items showing either a large dollar change or a large percentage change stand out and are readily seen by the person examining the comparative balance sheet. For example, in the comparative balance sheet of the Anchor Supply Company shown in Illustration 158, the item "Cash" shows a large dollar change and the item "Notes receivable" shows a large percentage change. The large dollar change in "Cash" stands out in the column showing increases and decreases in dollar amounts. Likewise, although the dollar amount is small, the large percentage change in "Notes receivable" stands out in the column showing percentage changes.

Illustration 159

ANCHOR SUPPLY COMPANY
Comparative Income Statement
Years Ended December 31, 1958, and December 31, 1959

	Years Ended December 31		Amount of Increase or Decrease* during 1959	Percentage of Increase or De- crease* during 1959
	1959	1958		
Gross sales	$973,500	$853,000	$120,500	14.1
Sales returns	13,500	10,200	3,300	32.4
Net sales	$960,000	$842,800	$117,200	13.9
Cost of goods sold.	715,000	622,500	92,500	14.9
Gross profit from sales	$245,000	$220,300	$ 24,700	11.2
Operating expenses:				
Selling expenses:				
Advertising	$ 10,000	$ 5,000	$ 5,000	100.0
Sales salaries.	113,500	98,000	15,500	15.8
Store supplies used	3,200	2,800	400	14.3
Depreciation of store equipment .	1,900	1,700	200	11.8
Delivery expense.	12,800	14,000	1,200*	8.6*
Total Selling Expenses.	$141,400	$121,500	$ 19,900	16.4
General and administrative expenses:				
Office salaries	$ 32,500	$ 31,000	$ 1,500	4.8
Officers' salaries.	24,000	24,000		
Office supplies used.	1,300	1,250	50	4.0
Expired insurance	1,600	1,200	400	33.3
Depreciation of office equipment.	300	300		
Depreciation of buildings	1,200	950	250	26.3
Bad debts	2,400	2,200	200	9.1
Total Gen. and Admin. Expenses	$ 63,300	$ 60,900	$ 2,400	3.9
Total Operating Expenses. . .	$204,700	$182,400	$ 22,300	12.2
Operating income.	$ 40,300	$ 37,900	$ 2,400	6.3
Financial revenue and expense:				
Interest earned	1,300	2,050	750	36.6*
	$ 41,600	$ 39,950		
Interest expense	2,300	1,100	$ 1,200	109.1
Net Income before Taxes	$ 39,300	$ 38,850	$ 450	1.2

A comparative income statement is prepared in the same manner as a comparative balance sheet. Normally, the item amounts from a company's income statements of two successive periods are placed side by side, with dollar changes and percentage changes shown in additional columns. A comparative income statement of the Anchor Supply Company is shown in Illustration 159.

Analyzing and Interpreting Comparative Statements. In analyzing and interpreting the data of comparative statements, it is necessary for the analyst to select for study the items showing significant dollar changes or significant percentage changes. The analyst normally considers the changes individually and jointly to determine the reasons for each and to determine if possible whether the changes are favorable or unfavorable. For example, in the comparative balance sheet of the Anchor Supply Company in Illustration 158, the first item showing a significant change is

"Cash." Cash shows a large decrease. At first glance this appears unfavorable. However, when the decrease in "Cash" is considered with the decrease in "Investments" and the increase in "Store equipment," "Buildings," and "Land," plus the increase in "Mortgage payable," it becomes apparent the company has materially increased its fixed assets between the two balance sheet dates. Further study reveals that the company has apparently constructed a new building on land that it had previously held as an investment until needed in this expansion. Also, it seems that the company has paid for its new fixed assets by reducing its cash, selling its Apex Company bonds, and issuing a $50,000 mortgage.

The second item showing a significant change on the Anchor Supply Company comparative balance sheet is "Notes receivable." The item "Notes receivable" shows a large percentage increase. From the balance sheet itself there is no ready explanation of this increase. However, the increase warrants further investigation by the analyst, even though the total dollar amount involved is comparatively small.

As a tool of management for controlling operations, the comparative income statement is usually more valuable than a comparative balance sheet. For example in the comparative income statement of the Anchor Supply Company (Illustration 159), "Gross sales" increased 14.1 per cent and "Net sales" increased 13.9 per cent. At the same time, "Sales returns" increased 32.4 per cent. The rate of increase for returned sales is more than twice that of gross sales. Returned sales represent wasted sales effort, and they indicate dissatisfied customers. Such an increase in sales returns should be investigated, and the reason for the increase determined if at all possible.

In addition to the large increase in the percentage of "Sales returns" on the income statement of the Anchor Supply Company, it is significant that the rate of increase of "Cost of goods sold" is greater than the rate of increase of "net sales." This is an unfavorable trend and should be remedied if at all possible.

In attempting to account for the Anchor Supply Company's increase in sales, the increase in advertising and the large increase in fixed assets merit attention. It is reasonable to expect a large expenditure for advertising to result in an increase in sales. It is also reasonable to expect an increase in fixed assets to result in an increase in the sales of a merchandising company or to result either in an increase in sales or in a decrease in the cost of goods sold of a manufacturing company.

Calculating Percentages of Increase or Decrease.   When percentages of increase or decrease are calculated for comparative statements, the amount of increase or decrease in an item is divided by the amount shown for the item in the base year. No problems arise in these calculations when positive amounts are shown for items in the base year. For example, in Illustration 160 all items show positive amounts in the 1958 base year. However, when there is no amount shown for an item in the base year or there

Illustration 160

	1959	(Base Year) 1958	Amount of Increase or Decrease*	Per Cent of Increase or Decrease*
Item one........................	$15,000	$10,000	$ 5,000	50
Item two........................	5,000	10,000	5,000*	50*
Item three.......................	–0–	10,000	10,000*	100*
Item four (a negative* amount in the second year)....................	5,000*	10,000	15,000*	150*

is a negative amount shown in the base year, percentages of increase or decrease are not calculated. For example, in Illustration 161 the items have no amounts or negative amounts in the 1958 base year, and percentages are not calculated.

Illustration 161

	1959	(Base Year) 1958	Amount of Increase or Decrease*	Per Cent of Increase or Decrease*
Item one..........................	$1,200	–0–	$1,200	
Item two (negative* amount in 1958)....	3,500	$500*	4,000	
Item three (negative* amounts in both years)............................	500*	250*	250*	
Item four (negative* amounts in both years)............................	100*	400*	300	

Comparing Data of More than Two Accounting Periods. When a comparative statement is constructed using the data from statements of more than two accounting periods, there are two ways of showing increases and decreases. (1) The data of each accounting period after the first may be compared with the data of the immediately preceding accounting period as shown in Illustration 162. Or (2) the data of each accounting pe-

Illustration 162

	Year Ended			Amount of Increase—Decrease*		Per Cent of Increase—Decrease*	
	1959	1958	1957	1959–58	1958–57	1959–58	1958–57
Advertising	$99,000	$110,000	$100,000	$11,000*	$10,000	10*	10

riod after the first may be compared with the data of the first accounting period as shown in Illustration 163.

Both methods of presentation are used. However, when percentages of increase and decrease are shown by the first method, the percentage results are subject to misinterpretation. For example, as shown in Illustration 162, 1958 advertising increased 10 per cent over 1957 advertising, and 1959 advertising decreased 10 per cent from 1958 advertising. As a result, it would appear that the 10 per cent increase should exactly offset the

Illustration 163

	Year Ended			Amount of Increase—Decrease*		Per Cent of Increase—Decrease*	
	1959	1958	1957	1959–57	1958–57	1959–57	1958–57
Advertising	$99,000	$110,000	$100,000	$1,000*	$10,000	1*	10

10 per cent decrease. However, this is not true. The confusion results from using two different bases in the calculation of the percentages.

Trend Percentages.   Trend percentages or index numbers are a useful tool in the comparison of data from several of a company's financial statements. Trend percentages emphasize the changes in financial statement items that occur with the passage of time. They are calculated as follows:

1. A base year is selected; it should be a representative year for all items.
2. The amount of each item on the statements of the base year is assigned a weight of 100 per cent.
3. Then each item from the statements of the years after the base year is expressed as a percentage of its base year amount. To find these percentages, the amounts of an item in each year after the base year are divided by the amount of the item in the base year.

For example, the Illustration 164 amounts were shown on the income statements for sales, cost of goods sold, and gross profit. If 1954 is made

Illustration 164

	1954	1955	1956	1957	1958	1959
Sales................	$210,000	$204,000	$292,000	$284,000	$310,000	$324,000
Cost of goods sold......	145,000	139,000	204,000	198,000	218,000	229,000
Gross Profit............	$ 65,000	$ 65,000	$ 88,000	$ 86,000	$ 92,000	$ 95,000

the base year for the data of Illustration 164, the trend percentages for "Sales" are calculated by dividing by $210,000 the amounts shown for "Sales" in each of the years after the first. The trend percentages for "Cost of goods sold" are found by dividing by $145,000 the amounts shown for "Cost of goods sold" in each of the years after the first. And, the trend percentages for "Gross profit" are found by dividing the amounts shown for "Gross profit" by $65,000. When these divisions are made, the trends for these three items appear as in Illustration 165.

Illustration 165

	1954	1955	1956	1957	1958	1959
Sales.............................	100	97	139	135	148	154
Cost of goods sold...............	100	96	141	137	150	158
Gross profit.....................	100	100	135	132	142	146

It is of interest to note in the trends of these items that while after the second year the trend of sales is upward, the trend of cost of goods sold is upward at a slightly more rapid rate. This indicates a contracting rate of gross profit, and it should receive the attention of management.

It should be pointed out in a discussion of trends that the trend of a single balance sheet or income statement item is seldom too informative. However, a comparison of the trends of related balance sheet and income statement items often tells the analyst a great deal. For example, a downward trend of sales with an upward trend of merchandise inventory, accounts receivable, and loss on bad debts would generally indicate an unfavorable situation. Likewise, a downward trend of sales accompanied by an upward trend of cost of goods sold and selling expenses would also appear unfavorable. Also, an upward trend of sales with a higher upward trend of accounts receivable, merchandise inventory, bad debts, and selling expense might indicate that the greater amount of sales is being achieved at too great a cost. On the other hand, an upward trend of sales with a downward trend or a slower upward trend of accounts receivable, merchandise inventory, and selling expenses would indicate an increase in operating efficiency.

Common-Size Statements. The comparative financial statements illustrated thus far do not, except in a casual manner, show proportional changes in balance sheet or income statement items. Changes in proportions are often presented and emphasized by means of common-size statements.

A common-size statement is so called because of the manner in which it presents items. For example, on a common-size balance sheet (1) the total of the assets is assigned a value of 100 per cent; (2) the total of the liabilities and proprietorship is also assigned a value of 100 per cent; and then (3) each individual asset, liability, and proprietorship item is presented as a fraction of one of the 100 per cent totals. When several balance sheets are presented in this manner as a means of analysis, the items of each balance sheet are expressed in common-size figures. They are expressed as fractions of 100 per cent. A common-size comparative balance sheet for the Anchor Supply Company is shown in Illustration 166.

A common-size income statement is constructed in much the same manner as a common-size balance sheet. Net sales are assigned a value of 100 per cent, and then each individual income statement item is shown as a percentage of net sales.

Illustration 166

ANCHOR SUPPLY COMPANY
Comparative Balance Sheet
December 31, 1958, and December 31, 1959

	Years Ended December 31		Common-Size Percentages	
	1959	1958	1959	1958
ASSETS				
Current Assets:				
Cash	$ 14,000	$ 89,000	2.64	18.43
Notes receivable	4,000	1,500	0.76	0.31
Accounts receivable, net	68,000	64,000	12.83	13.25
Merchandise inventory.	190,000	184,000	35.86	38.10
Prepaid expenses	5,800	6,000	1.09	1.24
Total Current Assets	$281,800	$344,500	53.18	71.33
Investments:				
Real estate	-0-	$ 30,000	-0-	6.21
Apex Company 4 per cent bonds.	-0-	50,000	-0-	10.35
Total Investments.	-0-	$ 80,000	-0-	16.56
Fixed Assets:				
Office equipment	$ 5,000	$ 5,000		
Less: Accumulated depreciation	1,500	1,200		
	$ 3,500	$ 3,800	0.66	0.78
Store equipment.	$ 24,000	$ 11,000		
Less: Accumulated depreciation	6,200	4,300		
	$ 17,800	$ 6,700	3.36	1.39
Buildings.	$210,000	$ 60,000		
Less: Accumulated depreciation	33,200	32,000		
	$176,800	$ 28,000	33.36	5.80
Land	$ 50,000	$ 20,000	9.44	4.14
Total Fixed Assets	$248,100	$ 58,500	46.82	12.11
Total Assets	$529,900	$483,000	100.00	100.00
LIABILITIES				
Current Liabilities:				
Notes payable.	-0-	$ 10,000	-0-	2.07
Accounts payable	$ 53,400	60,000	10.08	12.42
Wages payable.	800	1,200	0.15	0.25
Total Current Liabilities.	$ 54,200	$ 71,200	10.23	14.74
Long-Term Liabilities:				
Mortgage payable	60,000	10,000	11.32	2.07
Total Liabilities.	$114,200	$ 81,200	21.55	16.81
CAPITAL				
Common stock	$250,000	$250,000	47.18	51.76
Retained earnings.	165,700	151,800	31.27	31.43
Total Capital.	$415,700	$401,800	78.45	83.19
Total Liabilities and Capital. . . .	$529,900	$483,000	100.00	100.00

Common-size income statements are very informative and are a useful tool of management. This is because when the common-size 100 per cent amount shown for sales is assumed to represent one sales dollar, then the common-size amounts for each of the remaining income statement items show how each sales dollar was distributed to costs, to expenses, and to profit. For example, on the comparative income statement shown in Illustration 167, the 1958 cost of goods sold consumed 73.86 cents of each sales dollar. In 1959, cost of goods sold consumed 74.48 cents from each sales dollar. While the amount of increase is apparently small, if in 1959 the proportion of cost of goods sold had remained at the 1958 level, more than $6,000 of additional gross profit would have been earned. When this $6,000 of additional gross profit is viewed with the $39,300 of 1959 net income in mind, it becomes important.

Comparative common-size percentages point out efficiencies and inefficiencies that are otherwise difficult to see, and for this reason are a valu-

Illustration 167

ANCHOR SUPPLY COMPANY
Comparative Income Statement
Years Ended December 31, 1958, and December 31, 1959

	Years Ended December 31		Common-Size Percentages	
	1959	1958	1959	1958
Gross sales	$973,500	$853,000	101.41	101.21
Sales returns	13,500	10,200	1.41	1.21
Net sales	$960,000	$842,800	100.00	100.00
Cost of goods sold	715,000	622,500	74.48	73.86
Gross profit from sales	$245,000	$220,300	25.52	26.14
Operating expenses:				
Selling expenses:				
Advertising	$ 10,000	$ 5,000	1.04	0.59
Sales salaries	113,500	98,000	11.82	11.63
Store supplies used	3,200	2,800	0.33	0.33
Depreciation of store equipment	1,900	1,700	0.20	0.20
Delivery expense	12,800	14,000	1.33	1.66
Total Selling Expenses	$141,400	$121,500	14.72	14.41
General and administrative expenses:				
Office salaries	$ 32,500	$ 31,000	3.38	3.68
Officers' salaries	24,000	24,000	2.50	2.85
Office supplies used	1,300	1,250	0.14	0.15
Expired insurance	1,600	1,200	0.17	0.14
Depreciation of office equipment	300	300	0.03	0.04
Depreciation of buildings	1,200	950	0.13	0.11
Bad debts	2,400	2,200	0.25	0.26
Total General and Administrative Expenses	$ 63,300	$ 60,900	6.60	7.23
Total Operating Expenses	$204,700	$182,400	21.32	21.64
Operating income	$ 40,300	$ 37,900	4.20	4.50
Financial revenue and expense:				
Interest earned	1,300	2,050	0.14	0.24
	$ 41,600	$ 39,950		
Interest expense	2,300	1,100	0.24	0.13
Net Income before Taxes	$39,300	$38,850	4.09	4.61

able tool of management. To illustrate, sales salaries of the Anchor Supply Company took a higher percentage of each sales dollar in 1959 than in 1958. On the other hand, office salaries took a smaller percentage of each 1959 sales dollar. Furthermore, although the loss from bad debts was greater in 1959 than in 1958, loss from bad debts took a smaller proportion of each sales dollar in 1959 than in 1958.

Analysis of Working Capital

The term *working capital* is often used to denote the excess of a company's current assets over its current liabilities. Likewise, the term "working capital" is commonly used as a synonym for total current assets. When working capital is used as a synonym for total current assets, the term *net working capital* is used to denote the excess of current assets over current liabilities. Accountants are not in agreement on the use of these terms. However, for purposes of discussion this text will use the term "working capital" to mean total current assets, and it will refer to the excess of current assets over current liabilities as net working capital.

When balance sheets are analyzed, working capital (total current assets) and net working capital (the excess of current assets over current liabilities) always receive close attention. This is as it should be. An adequate amount of working capital and net working capital enables a company to carry sufficient inventories, to meet current debts, to take advantage of cash discounts, and to extend favorable terms to customers. These are desirable. A company that is deficient in working capital and is unable to do these things is in a poor competitive position. Its chances of survival are normally small, unless its working capital position is improved. Inadequacy of working capital has ended the business lives of many companies whose total assets were far in excess of their liabilities.

Many factors affect working capital requirements. The type of business in which a particular company is engaged is one factor. For example, railroads, public utilities, and other companies in which inventories consist only of supplies used in making repairs, need proportionately less working capital than do manufacturing or merchandising companies. Likewise, merchandising companies selling on a cash basis need less working capital than companies granting credit. Consequently, when the adequacy of working capital is studied, consideration must be given to the type of business under review.

Current Ratio. The net working capital of a company should be sufficient to enable it to pay its current debts as they become due. However, neither working capital nor net working capital is a measure of debt-paying ability. This may be demonstrated by the following example:

	Company A	Company B
Current assets (working capital)...............	$100,000	$20,000
Current liabilities.........................	90,000	10,000
Net Working Capital........................	$ 10,000	$10,000

In the illustration, Company A's current assets are five times as large as Company B's current assets, and both have the same amount of net working capital. However, Company B's current assets are twice the amount of its current liabilities, while Company A's current assets are only a little more than once the amount of its current liabilities. Company B's current assets may shrink in half when they are turned into cash and still be adequate to meet its current debts. On the other hand, Company A's current assets may shrink only 10 per cent and still be adequate to meet current debts. Obviously, as the example shows, the relationship of current assets to current liabilities is more important as a measure of debt-paying ability than is either the amount of working capital or net working capital.

The relationship of a company's current assets to its current liabilities is known as its *current ratio*. A company's current ratio is considered a measure of its debt-paying ability. The current ratio of Company B of the illustration just given is calculated as follows:

$$\frac{\text{CURRENT ASSETS, \$20,000}}{\text{CURRENT LIABILITIES, \$10,000}} = 2$$

A firm's current ratio is calculated by dividing its current assets by its current liabilities. After the division is made, the relationship is expressed as, for example, Company B's current assets are two times its current liabilities, or Company B has $2.00 of current assets for each $1.00 of current liabilities, or simply the current ratio of Company B is 2 to 1.

A ratio is the relationship of items expressed mathematically. The current ratio is the relationship of the current assets and current liabilities expressed mathematically. A high current ratio indicates a high ratio of current assets to current liabilities. The higher the ratio, the more liquid is a company's current position, and normally the better it can meet its current obligations.

For many years bankers and other grantors of credit measured a credit-seeking company's debt-paying ability by whether or not it had a current ratio of 2 to 1. Today most grantors of credit realize that the rule-of-thumb of a 2 to 1 current ratio is not an adequate test of debt-paying ability. They realize that whether or not a particular company's current ratio is good or bad depends upon at least three factors. These factors are:

1. The nature of the company's business.
2. The distribution of its current assets.
3. The turnover of certain of its current assets.

The nature of a company's business has much to do with its working capital requirements. A public utility or a railroad which normally has no inventories other than supplies, and which grants little or no credit, can often operate on a current ratio of less than 1 to 1. On the other hand, a manufacturer of articles in which style is the important sales factor may find a current ratio of more than 2 to 1 to be inadequate. In such a company, a misjudgment of style can make an inventory of finished goods almost worthless. Perhaps the best test of the adequacy of a company's current ratio is a comparison with the current ratios of a number of its close competitors. However, these are often unavailable.

Distribution of Current Assets. In an analysis of debt-paying ability, the distribution of current assets is important. Normally, a company with a high proportion of cash to accounts receivable, merchandise inventory, and other current assets is in a better position to meet quickly its current debts than is a company with most of its current assets tied up in accounts receivable and merchandise. The company with cash may pay its current debts at once. The company with accounts receivable and merchandise normally must turn these items into cash before it can pay its debts. In turning accounts receivable and merchandise into cash there is always a possibility of shrinkage. However, when current assets are analyzed, the fact that merchandise is normally sold for more than its balance sheet value and consequently produces more than its balance sheet value of cash should not be ignored.

The distribution of current assets may be examined in two ways. A schedule showing the percentage of each current asset to the total of current assets may be constructed, and the *acid-test ratio* may be calculated. A schedule showing the distribution of the current assets of the Anchor Supply Company appears as in Illustration 168.

Illustration 168

	December 31, 1959		December 31, 1958	
	Amount	Per Cent	Amount	Per Cent
Current Assets:				
Cash....................	$ 14,000	4.97	$ 89,000	25.83
Notes receivable..........	4,000	1.42	1,500	0.44
Accounts receivable, net...	68,000	24.13	64,000	18.58
Merchandise inventory....	190,000	67.42	184,000	53.41
Prepaid expenses........	5,800	2.06	6,000	1.74
Totals................	$281,800	100.00	$344,500	100.00

The acid-test ratio offers an easily calculated check on the distribution of the current assets. The acid-test ratio is often called the *quick ratio* because it is the ratio of "quick assets" to current liabilities. The "quick assets" are cash, notes receivable, accounts receivable, and marketable securities. They are the current assets that can quickly be turned into cash. An acid-test ratio of 1 to 1 is normally considered to be satisfactory. However, this is a rule-of-thumb and should be applied with care. The acid-test ratio of the Anchor Supply Company on December 31, 1959, is calculated as follows:

Quick Assets:		*Current Liabilities:*	
Cash....................	$14,000	Accounts payable........	$53,400
Notes receivable..........	4,000	Wages payable............	800
Accounts receivable.......	68,000	Total.................	$54,200
Total.................	$86,000		

ACID-TEST RATIO = $86,000 ÷ $54,200 = 1.59, OR ACID-TEST RATIO = 1.59 TO 1

Turnover of Accounts Receivable. The turnover of certain current assets affect working capital requirements. For example, companies AAA and BBB sell the same amounts of merchandise on account each month. However, company AAA grants terms of thirty days to its customers, while company BBB grants sixty days. Both collect their accounts at the end of the credit periods granted. But, as a result of the difference in terms, AAA turns over or collects its accounts twice as rapidly as does BBB. Also, as a result of the more rapid turnover, AAA requires only one half the investment in accounts receivable that is required of BBB.

The turnover of accounts receivable is calculated by dividing net sales for a particular year by end-of-the-year accounts receivable. Illustration 169 shows the calculation of the turnover of accounts receivable of the Anchor Supply Company for 1958 and 1959. The turnover of accounts receivable of 14.12 times in 1959 in comparison with 13.16 times in 1958

Illustration 169

	1959	1958
Net sales for year..............................	$960,000	$842,200
Year-end accounts receivable....................	68,000	64,000
Times accounts receivable were turned over (sales ÷ accounts receivable)...........................	14.12	13.16

indicates that the accounts receivable of the Anchor Supply Company were collected more rapidly in 1959.

Theoretically, only charge sales rather than the sum of charge and cash sales should be used in calculating the turnover of accounts receivable. Likewise, the amount of accounts receivable before the subtraction of the allowance for bad debts should be used. However, information as to the amount of charge sales is seldom available in a published balance sheet, and many published balance sheets report accounts receivable at their net amount. Consequently, total charge and cash sales and net accounts receivable must often be used in the calculation.

Likewise, as in the calculation of merchandise turnover, if the year's end accounts receivable are not representative, an average of the year's accounts receivable may be used in the calculation of the turnover of accounts receivable.

Days' Sales Uncollected. The turnover of accounts receivable is one indication of the speed with which a company collects its accounts receivable. *Days' sales uncollected* is another indication of the same thing. To illustrate the calculation of days' sales uncollected, assume that a company has charge sales during 1959 of $250,000 and that it has accounts receivable at the end of the year of $25,000. If a company has charge sales of $250,000 and year-end accounts receivable of $25,000, then one tenth of its charge sales are uncollected at the end of the year. These uncollected sales are equal to the charge sales made during one tenth of a year, or they are equal to the charge sales of 36.5 days ($\frac{1}{10} \times 365$ days in a year = 36.5 days). The calculation of days' sales uncollected in equation form appears as follows:

$$\frac{\text{ACCOUNTS RECEIVABLE, \$25,000}}{\text{CHARGE SALES, \$250,000}} \times 365 = 36.5 \text{ DAYS' SALES UNCOLLECTED}$$

Days' sales uncollected takes on more meaning when credit terms are known. According to a rule-of-thumb, a company's accounts receivable should not exceed one and one-third times the days in the credit period it grants. If the company whose days' sales uncollected is calculated in the illustration just given offers terms of thirty days, then 36.5 days is within the rule-of-thumb amount. However, if the terms are 2/10, n/30, days' sales uncollected of 36.5 days would seem excessive.

Days' sales uncollected is sometimes used as a test of a company's accounts receivable. If days' sales uncollected are excessive, it is assumed that some of the accounts are probably old and uncollectible.

Turnover of Merchandise Inventory.   The turnover of a company's merchandise inventory is the number of times its average merchandise inventory is sold during an accounting period. Merchandise turnover is considered a test of merchandising efficiency. A high turnover is considered a mark of good merchandising. Also, from a working capital point of view, a company with a high turnover requires a smaller investment in inventory than one producing the same amount of sales with a low turnover. Turnover of merchandise inventory is calculated by dividing cost of goods sold by average merchandise inventory. Cost of goods sold is the amount of merchandise at its cost price that was sold during an accounting period; average merchandise inventory is the average amount of merchandise at its cost price that was on hand during the period. The 1959 merchandise turnover of the Anchor Supply Company is calculated as follows:

$$\frac{\text{COST OF GOODS SOLD, \$715,000}}{\text{AVERAGE MERCHANDISE INVENTORY, \$187,000}} = \begin{array}{l} \text{MERCHANDISE TURNOVER OF} \\ \text{3.82 TIMES} \end{array}$$

The cost of goods sold is taken from the company's 1959 income statement. The average inventory is found by dividing by two the sum of the January 1, 1959, inventory of $190,000 and the December 31, 1959, inventory of $184,000. In a company in which the beginning and ending inventories are not representative of the amount of inventory normally on hand, a more accurate turnover may be secured by using the average of all the twelve month-end inventories rather than just the beginning and ending inventories.

Standards of Comparison

When financial statements are analyzed by the computation of ratios and turnovers, the analyst must determine whether the ratios and turnovers obtained are good, bad, or just average. In a decision as to whether ratios are good, bad, or just average, the analyst must have some basis of comparison. The following bases of comparison are available:

1. A trained analyst of long experience may compare the ratios and turn-overs of the company under review with his own mental standards built up as the result of past experiences.
2. An analyst may calculate for purposes of comparison the ratios and turn-overs of a selected group of competitive companies in the same industry as the one whose statements are under review.
3. Published ratios and turnovers such as those put out by Dun & Bradstreet or those found in Moody's and Poor's manuals may be secured for purposes of comparison.
4. Some local and national trade associations gather financial statement data from their members and publish standard or average ratios for their trade or industry. These offer the analyst a very good basis of comparison when they are available.
5. Rule-of-thumb standards may be used as a basis of comparison.

Of the five types of standards upon which comparisons may be based, the ratios and turnovers of a selected group of competitive companies normally offer the best standards of comparison. Rule-of-thumb stand-ards should be applied with care if erroneous conclusions are to be avoided.

Other Balance Sheet and Income Statement Relationships

Several balance sheet and income statement relationships in addition to those having to do with working capital are important to the analyst of financial statements. Some of the more important are discussed in the fol-lowing pages.

Capital Contributions of Owners and Creditors. The share of the assets of a company contributed by its owners and the share contributed by its creditors are always of interest to the analyst. The contributions of the owners and the creditors of the Anchor Supply Company are calcu-lated as in Illustration 170.

Illustration 170

	1959	1958
Total liabilities.....................................	$114,200	$ 81,200
Total proprietorship.............................	415,700	401,800
Total liabilities and proprietorship................	$529,900	$483,000
Creditors' equity (line 1 divided by line 3).........	21.55%	16.81%
Owner's equity (line 2 divided by line 3)...........	78.45%	83.19%

Creditors like to see a high proportion of ownership equity. This is be-cause the equity of the owners acts as a cushion in the absorption of losses. The greater the equity of the owners in proportion to that of the creditors, the greater the losses that can be absorbed by the owners before the creditors begin to suffer a loss.

From the standpoint of the creditors a high percentage of owner equity is desirable. However, if an enterprise can earn a return on borrowed capital that is in excess of the cost of the borrowed capital, then an increase in creditor equity is often desirable from the standpoint of the owners. When a company operates on borrowed capital, it trades or operates on capital supplied by its creditors. For this reason, when a company operates on borrowed capital, it is said to be *trading on the equity*. It is trading on the equity of its creditors. When returns are in excess of the cost of borrowed capital, trading on the equity is often desirable from the viewpoint of the owners of a business. However, if earnings are unstable, it may be dangerous.

Net Income to Proprietorship. One of the more important objectives of a business enterprise is to earn a profit for its owners. The ratio of net income to proprietorship measures success in accomplishing this objective. It is calculated for the Anchor Supply Company for the year of 1959 as follows:

$$\frac{\text{Net Income, \$39,300}}{\text{Proprietorship, \$401,800}} = \text{Net Income Ratio of 9.78 Per Cent}$$

Net income after taxes and normally the amount of beginning proprietorship are used in the calculation of this ratio. However, if during the period, proprietorship fluctuated greatly, an average proprietorship may give a more nearly accurate picture.

Pledged Fixed Assets to Long-Term Liabilities. Companies commonly borrow money by issuing a note or bonds secured by a mortgage on certain of their fixed assets. The ratio of pledged fixed assets to long-term liabilities is often calculated to measure the security granted to mortgage or bondholders by the pledged assets. This ratio is calculated by dividing the book value of the pledged assets by the liabilities for which they are pledged. It is calculated for the Anchor Supply Company in 1958 and 1959 as in Illustration 171.

Illustration 171

	1959	1958
Buildings..	$210,000	$60,000
Less: Accumulated depreciation....................	33,200	32,000
Buildings, net.......................................	$176,800	$28,000
Land...	50,000	20,000
Book value of pledged fixed assets.................	$226,800	$48,000
Mortgage payable...................................	$ 60,000	$10,000
Ratio of pledged assets to secured liabilities........	3.78 to 1	4.8 to 1

The usual rule-of-thumb minimum standard for this ratio is 2–1. However, this is a ratio that needs careful interpretation. This is because the ratio shows the relationship of the *book value* of the pledged fixed assets to the long-term liabilities. Even when depreciation is accurately estimated and recorded, book values do not measure the amount that would be secured in a foreclosure or a liquidation. Estimated liquidation values or foreclosure values are a better measure of the protection offered bondholders or mortgage holders by the pledged fixed assets. Often, in situations in which fixed assets are pledged to secure long-term liabilities, the long-term income earning ability of the company whose assets are pledged is more important to the long-term creditors than the book value of the pledged assets.

Times Fixed Interest Charges Earned. The number of times that fixed interest charges are earned is often calculated to measure the security of the return offered to bondholders or a mortgage holder. The number of times fixed interest charges are earned is found by dividing the amount of income before the deduction of income taxes and fixed interest charges by the amount of the fixed interest charges. Since fixed interest charges are an expense that take precedence over income taxes, income before the deduction of income taxes is used in the calculation. Likewise, since the calculation is the number of times the fixed interest charges are earned, fixed interest charges are not deducted in determining the income used in the calculation. Often the return of a company's long-term creditors is considered secure if the company consistently earns its fixed interest charges two or more times each year.

The Effect of Price Level Changes

When financial statements for a period of several years are analyzed, the analyst must keep in mind the effect on the statements of *price level changes*. Price level changes are changes in the purchasing power of money. Often, if price level changes are ignored, incorrect conclusions may be drawn. For example, during the period of 1945 through 1959 many companies showed a large dollar increase in sales when their physical volume of sales actually remained unchanged or increased only a small amount. In these companies the increase in dollar volume of sales was caused by the decrease in the purchasing power of the dollar. During these years, 1945–59, a dollar purchased a smaller amount of goods each year; or, in other words, during each of these years it required an increasing number of dollars to buy the same amount of goods.

Price level changes affect the items of the income statement, but their effect is not limited to income statement items. Price level changes also affect balance sheet items. For example, many companies are operating today with fixed assets, the replacement costs of which are several times their reported balance sheet values. This is particularly true of buildings purchased or constructed prior to 1942.

No effort will be made here to enter into an exhaustive discussion of the effect of price level changes on financial statements. Such a discussion is reserved for a more advanced course. However, the student should be aware of this phenomenon.

Other Analytical Devices

Many analytical devices are available to aid the analyst in separating the parts of financial statements so as to see the relationship of the parts to the whole and to each other. Several kinds of comparative statements, ratios, and turnovers have been discussed in this chapter; break-even analysis was discussed in a previous chapter; and the statement of sources and applications of funds is the subject of the next chapter. All are valuable tools of the analyst. However, they do not replace the good judgment of the analyst. They are only tools that aid in bringing the data under review into a sharper focus.

QUESTIONS FOR CLASS DISCUSSION

1. Why does a comparative balance sheet often have columns showing increases and decreases in both dollar amounts and in percentages?
2. Where possible calculate percentages of increase and decrease for the following unrelated items. (The asterisk following an amount indicates a deficit.)

	1960	1959
Buildings, net	$78,000	$60,000
Investments	-0-	68,000
Notes payable	10,000	-0-
Retained earnings	3,000*	12,000
Cash	12,000	2,500*

3. Calculate trend percentages for the following items:

	1956	1957	1958	1959	1960
Sales	$150,000	$168,000	$180,000	$186,000	$192,000
Merchandise inventory	30,000	35,700	39,600	42,600	46,200
Accounts receivable	18,000	23,040	24,300	25,200	27,360

Is the situation presented by the trends of the items favorable or is it unfavorable?

4. When trends are calculated and compared, what item trends should be compared with the trend of sales?
5. Why are common-size statements so called?
6. What items are assigned a value of 100 per cent (a) on a common-size balance sheet, and (b) on a common-size income statement?
7. Define the terms (a) working capital, and (b) net working capital.

8. For the following transactions tell which increase net working capital, which decrease net working capital, and which have no effect on net working capital:
   a) Collected accounts receivable.
   b) Borrowed money from the bank by giving an interest-bearing note.
   c) Declared a cash dividend.
   d) Paid a cash dividend.
   e) Sold fixed assets at their book value.
   f) Sold merchandise at a profit.

9. Which of the transactions of Question 8 results in an increase in working capital but does not result in an increase in net working capital?

10. Why are adequate amounts of working capital and net working capital of importance to a business?

11. List several factors that have an effect on working capital requirements.

12. The Abbot Company has a current ratio of 2 to 1. List several reasons why this ratio may not be adequate.

13. Tell the significance of each of the following ratios and turnovers and tell how each is calculated:
   a) Current ratio.
   b) Acid-test ratio.
   c) Turnover of accounts receivable.
   d) Turnover of merchandise inventory.
   e) Net income to proprietorship ratio.
   f) Ratio of pledged fixed assets to long-term liabilities.

14. How are days' sales uncollected calculated? What is the significance of the number of days' sales uncollected?

15. Why do creditors like to see a high proportion of ownership equity?

16. What is meant by the phrase "trading on the equity"?

17. What are price level changes? Why must the effect of price level changes often be considered when statements covering a period of several years are analyzed?

PROBLEMS

Problem 28–1

The following data was taken from the year-end statements prepared by a merchandising company:

Cash	$ 12,000
Notes receivable (due in ninety days)	3,000
Accounts receivable	45,000
Beginning-of-the-year merchandise inventory	82,000
End-of-the-year merchandise inventory	80,000
Notes payable (due in sixty days)	8,000
Accounts payable	42,000
Sales	450,000
Purchases	358,000

Required:

Calculate: (a) current ratio, (b) acid-test ratio, (c) turnover of accounts receivable, (d) days' sales uncollected, and (e) merchandise turnover.

Problem 28–2

A condensed income statement and a balance sheet of Eastern Supply Company follow:

EASTERN SUPPLY COMPANY

Income Statement for Year Ended December 31, 19—

Sales...		$300,000
Cost of goods sold:		
Merchandise inventory, January 1, 19—..............	$ 44,000	
Purchases.......................................	206,000	
Goods for sale...................................	$250,000	
Merchandise inventory, December 31, 19—............	40,000	
Cost of goods sold...............................		210,000
Gross profit from sales.............................		$ 90,000
Operating expenses................................		70,000
Income before Taxes..............................		$ 20,000

EASTERN SUPPLY COMPANY

Balance Sheet, December 31, 19—

Cash.....................	$ 6,000	Accounts payable.........		$ 25,000
Accounts receivable, net....	24,000	Mortgage payable (secured		
Merchandise inventory.....	40,000	by a mortgage on land and		
Equipment, net...........	15,000	buildings................		16,000
Building, net.............	35,000	Common stock............		50,000
Land....................	5,000	Retained earnings.........		34,000
	$125,000			$125,000

Required:

Calculate for the Eastern Supply Company:

a) Current ratio.
b) Acid-test ratio.
c) Days' sales uncollected.
d) Merchandise turnover.

e) Owners' equity.
f) Creditors' equity.
g) Ratio of pledged fixed assets to long-term liabilities.

Problem 28–3

Following are the condensed 1959 and 1960 statements of Westfield Sales Company, a wholesale firm:

WESTFIELD SALES COMPANY

Comparative Income Statements

Years Ended December 31, 1959–60

	1960	1959
Sales..	$476,000	$451,000
Cost of goods sold:		
Merchandise inventory, January 1....................	43,000	41,000
Purchases.......................................	305,600	273,800
Goods for sale....................................	$348,600	$314,800
Merchandise inventory, December 31.................	56,000	43,000
Cost of goods sold................................	$292,600	$271,800
Gross profit from sales.............................	$183,400	$179,200
Operating expenses................................	163,400	156,600
Income before Taxes..............................	$ 20,000	$ 22,600

WESTFIELD SALES COMPANY
Comparative Balance Sheets
December 31, 1959–60

	1960	1959
Assets:		
Cash	$ 14,000	$ 12,000
Accounts receivable	38,000	44,000
Merchandise inventory	56,000	43,000
Fixed assets, net	104,000	102,000
Total Assets	$212,000	$201,000
Liabilities and stockholders' equity:		
Accounts payable	$ 26,000	$ 28,000
Notes payable	10,000	6,000
Mortgage payable (due in 1970)	40,000	40,000
Common stock	100,000	100,000
Retained earnings	36,000	27,000
Total Liabilities and Stockholders' Equity	$212,000	$201,000

Required:

1. Calculate common-size percentages for sales, cost of goods sold, gross profit from sales, operating expenses, and income before taxes; and calculate the current ratio, acid-test ratio, merchandise turnover, and days' sales uncollected for each of the two years.
2. Comment on the situation shown by your calculations.

Problem 28–4

KENDALL SALES COMPANY
Comparative Balance Sheets, December 31, 1954–60

	1954	1955	1956	1957	1958	1959	1960
Assets:							
Current assets:							
Cash	$ 24,000	$ 32,000	$ 50,000	$ 66,000	$ 42,000	$ 28,000	$ 26,000
Accounts receivable, net	100,000	108,000	122,000	172,000	240,000	304,000	328,000
Inventories	120,000	130,000	132,000	156,000	270,000	310,000	340,000
Other current assets	16,000	18,000	14,000	16,000	12,000	10,000	10,000
Total Current Assets	$260,000	$288,000	$318,000	$370,000	$ 564,000	$ 652,000	$ 704,000
Fixed assets, net	280,000	284,000	290,000	292,000	600,000	616,000	612,000
Total Assets	$540,000	$572,000	$608,000	$662,000	$1,164,000	$1,268,000	$1,316,000
Equities:							
Current liabilities	$ 80,000	$ 84,000	$ 88,000	$104,000	$ 248,000	$ 380,000	$ 480,000
Long-term liabilities	60,000	60,000	60,000	60,000	240,000	240,000	240,000
Total Liabilities	$140,000	$144,000	$148,000	$164,000	$ 488,000	$ 620,000	$ 720,000
Common stock	$200,000	$200,000	$200,000	$200,000	$ 400,000	$ 400,000	$ 400,000
Retained earnings	200,000	228,000	260,000	298,000	276,000	248,000	196,000
Total Stockholders' Equity	$400,000	$428,000	$460,000	$498,000	$ 676,000	$ 648,000	$ 596,000
Total Liabilities and Stockholders' Equity	$540,000	$572,000	$608,000	$662,000	$1,164,000	$1,268,000	$1,316,000

KENDALL SALES COMPANY

Comparative Income Statements for Years Ended December 31, 1954–60

	1954	1955	1956	1957	1958	1959	1960
Sales....................	$400,000	$500,000	$572,000	$680,000	$760,000	$840,000	$870,000
Cost of goods sold..........	260,000	326,000	372,000	460,000	536,000	608,000	630,000
Gross profits from sales	$140,000	$174,000	$200,000	$220,000	$224,000	$232,000	$240,000
Operating expenses.........	100,000	110,000	120,000	130,000	196,000	220,000	232,000
Net Income before Taxes.....	$ 40,000	$ 64,000	$ 80,000	$ 90,000	$ 28,000	$ 12,000	$ 8,000

Required:

From the condensed comparative balance sheets and income statements of Kendall Sales Company just given:

1. Calculate trend percentages for the items.
2. Analyze and comment on the situation shown by the statements.

CLASS EXERCISES

Exercise 28–1

Common-size and trend percentages for the sales, cost of goods sold, and expenses of a company follow:

COMMON-SIZE PERCENTAGES				TREND PERCENTAGES		
	1958	1959	1960	1958	1959	1960
Sales............	100	100	100	Sales............ 100	103	105
Cost of goods sold..	70	72	74	Cost of goods sold.. 100	103	106
Expenses.........	20	19	18	Expenses......... 100	95	90

Required:

Present statistics to prove whether the net income increased, decreased, or remained unchanged during the period covered by the percentages.

Exercise 28–2

Sales of Company A during 1960 were $200,000. Its cost of goods sold during the same year was $150,000, its selling expenses were $20,000, and its administrative expenses were $10,000. From this data construct an income statement for Company A that shows both dollar amounts and common-size percentages.

SUPPLEMENTARY PROBLEMS

Problem 28–A

Following are data taken from the current statements of two wholesale companies selling similar lines of products:

DATA FROM THE CURRENT DECEMBER 31 BALANCE SHEETS:

	Company A	Company B
Cash	$ 6,000	$ 5,000
Notes receivable	2,400	4,400
Accounts receivable	32,000	54,800
Merchandise inventory	34,000	46,400
Prepaid expenses	1,100	600
Total Current Assets	$ 75,500	$111,200
Fixed assets, net	81,300	94,200
Total Assets	$156,800	$205,400
Accounts payable	$ 33,000	$ 49,700
Notes payable	5,000	7,500
Accrued payables	600	1,200
Total Liabilities	$ 38,600	$ 58,400
Common stock	100,000	100,000
Retained earnings	18,200	47,000
Total Liabilities and Capital	$156,800	$205,400

DATA FROM THE CURRENT YEARLY INCOME STATEMENTS:

	Company A	Company B
Sales	$256,000	$493,200
Cost of goods sold	179,300	345,400
Net income before taxes	10,700	23,700
Inventory on January 1	36,000	45,600

Required:

Calculate the ratios, turnovers, and percentages you think are appropriate in order to determine which of the foregoing companies is the better short-term credit risk.

Chapter

29

STATEMENT OF SOURCES AND APPLICATIONS OF FUNDS

A STATEMENT of sources and applications of funds, often called a statement of changes in net working capital, is a statement designed to summarize the financial activities of a business and to present the reasons for the changes in its current financial position. It is sometimes called a "where got, where gone statement." Although this last title is a little vague and sounds somewhat crude, it does emphasize the purpose of such a statement, which is to show the sources or where a business got funds and where it applied or used the funds.

A statement of sources and applications of funds is especially valuable to the businessman whose knowledge of accounting is limited and who upon examination of his income statement observes and asks himself the question, "My income statement shows ample net income, but I am having difficulty finding sufficient funds with which to pay my bills. Have I actually earned any income; and if I have, what has happened to it?" The statement of sources and application of funds answers the question of what happened to the income; it also shows what happened to funds received from other sources.

Nature of Funds

When the word "funds" is used in connection with a funds statement, the term has reference to more than the "cash" of a business. The term as it is used actually means net working capital or, in other words, current assets minus current liabilities.

When the term "funds" is used in the broad sense of net working capital, it is easy to see why current assets are considered "funds." The more important of the current assets are cash, accounts receivable, and merchandise inventory, and are often called "circulating assets." They are so called because, in a sense, they circulate; the cash is used to buy merchandise, which is sold and turned into accounts receivable, which are collected and turned back into cash, which is used to buy more merchandise, and so on. Actually, the accounts receivable are only one step away from cash and the merchandise is only two steps away.

Although it is easy to see where cash, accounts receivable, and merchandise inventory fit into the picture of a company's funds, it is sometimes a little difficult to see the place of the current liabilities. However, when it is remembered that in addition to having sufficient cash and an adequate supply of merchandise, a company must also pay its debts when due, the place of the current liabilities becomes more clear—the current liabilities must be paid from the circulating assets. Consequently, when a company's current position is examined, the examination is not complete without a look at the current liabilities that soon must be paid from the current assets.

The Funds Statement

Illustration 172 shows a statement of sources and applications of funds prepared for the Moss Corporation. Observe that the statement, like an income statement, covers a period of time; its purpose is to show the changes that have taken place in net working capital during the period for which it is prepared. Notice also that the statement really has two parts. In the first part or section is shown the amount of increase or decrease in net working capital; and the second part or section accounts for the increase or decrease.

Illustration 172

MOSS CORPORATION
Statement of Sources and Applications of Funds
For Year Ended December 31, 1960

	Dec. 31, 1959	Dec. 31, 1960	Net Working Capital Increase	Net Working Capital Decrease
CHANGES IN NET WORKING CAPITAL				
Current Assets:				
Cash	$ 8,000	$ 5,000		$ 3,000
Notes receivable	500	1,200	$ 700	
Accounts receivable, net	12,000	18,000	6,000	
Merchandise inventory.	16,000	21,000	5,000	
Prepaid expenses	1,000	800		200
Current Liabilities:				
Accounts payable	9,000	12,500		3,500
Dividends payable.	700	1,000		300
			$11,700	$ 7,000
Net Increase in Net Working Capital. . . .				4,700
			$11,700	$11,700

SOURCES AND APPLICATIONS OF NET WORKING CAPITAL

Sources of net working capital:			
From current operations:			
Net income per income statement		$11,600	
Add: Depreciation of equipment.		800	
Depreciation of buildings.		900	$13,300
From sale of stock:			
Par value of stock sold		$15,000	
Premium		1,500	16,500
Total Sources of Net Working Capital. . . .			$29,800
Applications of net working capital:			
Purchase of buildings		$14,000	
Purchase of land		3,000	
Payment of mortgage		5,000	
Payment of dividends.		3,100	
Total Applications of Net Working Capital .			25,100
Net Increase in Net Working Capital			$ 4,700

In the first part, headed "Changes in Net Working Capital," each net working capital item is listed, the dollar amounts of each item at the beginning and end of the period are given, and the increase or decrease in each item is shown. Also, at the end of the first part or section the net amount of the increase or decrease in net working capital is given. The net amount of the increase or decrease in net working capital is the difference between the sum of the net working capital increases and the sum of the net working capital decreases. In this case, the increases exceeded the decreases and there was a net increase. If the decreases had exceeded the increases, there would have been a net decrease.

The second part of a funds statement accounts for the increase or decrease in net working capital by listing the sources and applications of funds. Sources of funds increase net working capital; applications of funds decrease net working capital; and the amount that net working capital is increased or decreased is the difference between the two. Observe that the last items in both sections of the Moss Corporation's funds statement are the amount of its increase in net working capital.

The sources and applications of net working capital shown on the Moss Corporation's funds statement are illustrative of possible sources and applications. A more complete list of sources would include: (1) additional investments on the part of the owner or owners of a company; (2) sales of noncurrent assets; (3) long-term borrowings, and (4) income from operations. A more complete list of applications would include: (1) purchases of noncurrent assets; (2) payments of long-term debts; (3) payments of dividends; (4) reductions in the amounts invested in the business by the owner or owners; and (5) losses from operations.

Working Papers

As an aid in their work, accountants prepare numerous memoranda, analysis, notes, and informal papers that serve as a basis for the more formal reports presented to management or to their clients. These analysis, notes, and memoranda are known as "working papers" and are invaluable tools of the accountant.

In previous chapters working papers used in the preparation of income statements and balance sheets and called "work sheets" were discussed. In this chapter an additional "work sheet" or working paper that is used in the preparation of the funds statement is introduced. The new working paper is like the familiar work sheet of previous chapters in that it has columns for adjustments and columns for sorting items. However, it differs in that its adjustments are used solely in the preparation of the funds statement and are never entered in the accounts.

Preparing a Funds Statement

When a statement of sources and applications of funds is prepared, normally the information for the statement is first assembled on a working

Illustration 173

MOSS CORPORATION

Working Paper for Statement of Sources and Applications of Funds
For Year Ended December 31, 1960

Accounts and Explanations	Balance Sheet Data for December 31 1959	Balance Sheet Data for December 31 1960	Changes Resulting from an Excess of Debits	Changes Resulting from an Excess of Credits	Adjustments Debits	Adjustments Credits	Changes in Net Working Capital Increases	Changes in Net Working Capital Decreases	Sources and Applications of Funds Applications	Sources and Applications of Funds Sources
Debits:										
Cash	8,000	5,000		3,000				3,000		
Notes receivable	500	1,200	700				700			
Accounts receivable, net	12,000	18,000	6,000				6,000			
Merchandise inventory	16,000	21,000	5,000				5,000			
Prepaid expenses	1,000	800		200				200		
Equipment	8,000	7,500		500	(g) 500					
Buildings	31,000	45,000	14,000			(d) 14,000				
Land	8,000	11,000	3,000			(d) 3,000				
	84,500	109,500								
Credits:										
Accumulated depreciation, equipment	2,100	2,400		300	(b) 800	(g) 500				
Accumulated depreciation, buildings	8,800	9,700		900	(b) 900					
Accounts payable	9,000	12,500		3,500				3,500		
Dividends payable	700	1,000		300				300		
Mortgage payable	5,000		5,000			(e) 5,000				
Common stock	35,000	50,000		15,000	(c) 15,000					
Premium on common stock		1,500		1,500	(c) 1,500					
Retained earnings	15,900	20,400		4,500	(a) 11,600	(h) 4,000 / (f) 3,100				
Reserve for plant expansion	8,000	12,000		4,000	(h) 4,000					
	84,500	109,500	33,700	33,700						
Funds provided by net income						(a) 11,600	11,600			11,600
Add: Depreciation of equipment						(b) 800				800
Depreciation of buildings						(b) 900				900
Funds provided by sale of stock						(c) 16,500				16,500
Funds applied to purchase of buildings					(d) 14,000				14,000	
Funds applied to purchase of land					(d) 3,000				3,000	
Funds applied to payment of mortgage					(e) 5,000				5,000	
Funds applied to payment of dividends					(f) 3,100				3,100	
					59,400	59,400	11,700	7,000	25,100	29,800
Increase in Net Working Capital								4,700	4,700	
							11,700	11,700	29,800	29,800

paper like that of Illustration 173, and the funds statement is then prepared from the working paper.

A working paper like that of Illustration 173 is prepared in the following manner:

1. The dollar amounts from the balance sheets of the beginning and the end of the period covered by the funds statement under construction are copied into the first two columns of the working paper. Observe in Illustration 173 that debit balance items are listed first and are followed by credit balance items. This arrangement is a convenience and places the accumulated depreciation with the liabilities and proprietorship.
2. Then each item change between the two dates is entered in the second pair of columns according to whether the change resulted from an excess of debits or an excess of credits to the item. For example, in Illustration 173 Cash decreased $3,000 between the two balance sheet dates. If Cash decreased, there was an excess of credits to Cash. Likewise, an excess of debits resulted in the $700 increase in Notes Receivable.
3. Next, after the charges are entered, adjustments to the noncurrent items as required are entered in the Adjustments columns of the working paper. These adjustments are discussed in more detail later in this chapter.
4. After the adjustments are entered and completed, (a) the changes in the noncurrent items on the working paper have either been eliminated because they had no effect on net working capital, or (b) they have been canceled out and carried to the bottom of the working paper under an appropriate source or application title. Consequently, next after the adjustments are completed, the changes in current asset and current liability items are sorted to the columns headed "Changes in Net Working Capital"; and the adjustment items at the bottom of the working paper showing sources and applications of funds are carried into the "Sources and Applications" columns.
5. The working paper is then completed by adding the columns.

After the working paper is completed, the statement of sources and applications of funds is prepared from the information in the last four columns of the working paper.

Adjustments in the Preparation of a Funds Statement

When a working paper for the preparation of a funds statement is constructed, the "changes" shown in its second pair of columns represent one of three things: (1) increases or decreases in net working capital; (2) sources or applications of funds; or (3) bookkeeping transactions that did not affect net working capital.

In the preparation of a funds working paper, the first type of changes, increases or decreases in current asset and current liability items, may be sorted at once to the "Changes in Net Working Capital" columns. However, the second and third types of changes, changes in noncurrent items, normally require adjustments. The adjustments of these items on the working paper of Illustration 173 are as follows:

a) The 1960 income statement of the Moss Corporation showed net income after taxes of $11,600. In the 1960 closing entries these earnings were carried to the Retained Earnings account and are partially responsible for the $4,500 change in the balance of the Retained Earnings account. However, the $11,600 of earnings was a source of funds; consequently, the following adjustment is made to set out and make more clear the nature of the source:

Adjustments

	Debits	Credits
Retained earnings	(a) 11,600	
Funds provided by net income		(a) 11,600

b) The funds provided by the operations of a business are normally greater than the amount of the net income shown on the income statement. This can be best explained by the use of the following simple illustration of the scissors grinding and knife sharpening business of John Silva. John Silva goes about town sharpening scissors and knives. He has an old push cart in which he carries his tools; and he conducts his business entirely on a cash basis. At the end of the current year he prepared the following income statement showing the results of his year's operations:

JOHN SILVA
Income Statement for Year Ended December 31, 19—

Revenue from scissors grinding and knife sharpening..............$2,000
  Less: Depreciation of equipment............................ 100
Net Income from Operations.................................$1,900

Obviously, since the recording of $100 depreciation did not affect the amount of his funds, John Silva's business must have provided him with $2,000 of funds rather than the $1,900 shown on his income statement as his net income.

Therefore, as in the illustration of the previous paragraph, although depreciation is an expense, the charge for depreciation does not involve a current expenditure of funds; and, consequently, to determine the amount of funds provided by operations, it is necessary to add the depreciation charges to the net income. This is done on the working paper of the Moss Corporation with the following adjustment:

Adjustments

	Debits	Credits
Accumulated depreciation, equipment	(b) 800	
Accumulated depreciation, buildings	(b) 900	
Funds provided by net income:		
Add: Depreciation of equipment		(b) 800
Depreciation of buildings		(b) 900

Amortization of patents, depletion of wasting assets, and bond discount are additional expenses that, like depreciation, do not require current expenditures of funds and must be added to net income to determine the funds provided by operations.

c) During 1960 the Moss Corporation sold and issued 150 shares of its common stock at a premium. This is shown by the $15,000 increase in the balance of the Common Stock account and the $1,500 increase in the balance of the premium account. This sale of stock was a source of funds;

and the source is set out and made clear on the Company's working paper with the following adjustment:

	Debits	Credits
Common stock..............................	(c) 15,000	
Premium on common stock.....................	(c) 1,500	
Funds provided by the sale of stock..............		(c) 16,500

d) The Moss Corporation used $17,000 of its funds to purchase additional land and buildings. This is shown by the $14,000 increase in the Buildings account and the $3,000 increase in Land. This application of funds is set out on the working paper of Illustration 173 with the following adjustments:

	Debits	Credits
Funds applied to the purchase of buildings.........	(d) 14,000	
Funds applied to the purchase of land............	(d) 3,000	
Buildings..		(d) 14,000
Land..		(d) 3,000

e) A $5,000 mortgage was paid by the company as shown by the decrease in the balance of its Mortgage Payable account. This application of funds is set out on the working paper with the following adjustment:

	Debits	Credits
Funds applied to payment of mortgage.............	(e) 5,000	
Mortgage payable...............................		(e) 5,000

f) The Moss Corporation's statement of retained earnings showed that dividends amounting to $3,100 were paid during the year. This application of funds is set out on the working paper with the following adjustment:

	Debits	Credits
Funds applied to the payment of dividends.........	(f) 3,100	
Retained earnings...............................		(f) 3,100

g) Commonly, when a working paper for a funds statement is prepared, some of the changes in noncurrent items are the result of bookkeeping transactions that did not involve funds. These changes are eliminated with reversing entries that dispose of the changes. Adjustments (g) and (h) on the working paper of the Moss Corporation are of this nature.

During 1960, the Moss Corporation retired and scrapped fully depreciated equipment carried on the books at its cost of $500. The bookkeeping entry made early in 1960 to record the retirement of this equipment was as follows:

Jan.	12	Accumulated Depreciation, Equipment...	500.00	
		Equipment.......................		500.00
		To record the retirement of fully depreciated equipment.		

The posting of this entry resulted in the $500 decrease in the balances of the Equipment and Accumulated Depreciation, Equipment accounts, as shown on the working paper. The entry had no effect on the funds of the company; consequently, the resulting changes in the two accounts as they appear on the working paper are eliminated by the following reversing entry:

	Debits	Credits
Equipment....................................	(g) 500	
Accumulated depreciation, equipment.............		(g) 500

h) At the end of 1960, the board of directors of the company transferred $4,000 of retained earnings to the reserve for plant expansion. This did not involve funds; and, consequently, the resulting changes in the affected accounts as they appear on the working paper are eliminated by the following reversing entry:

	Debits	Credits
Reserve for plant expansion.....................	(h) 4,000	
Retained earnings...............................		(h) 4,000

After the adjustments are completed on the funds statement working paper of Illustration 173, all of the changes in noncurrent items are balanced out by the adjustments. For example, the $500 credit opposite Equipment in the "changes" columns is balanced out by a $500 debit in the Adjustments columns; and the $14,000 debit opposite Buildings in the "changes" columns is balanced out by a $14,000 credit in the Adjustments columns. Consequently, after the adjustments are completed, the changes in current asset and current liability items, as shown in the "changes" columns of the working paper, are transferred from the "changes" columns to the Changes in Net Working Capital columns, if they have not already been transferred; and the portions of the adjustments at the bottom of the working paper that set out the nature of the changes in noncurrent items are transferred from the Adjustments columns to the Sources and Applications columns. After this, the working paper is completed by totaling the amounts in the last four columns.

After the working paper for the preparation of a funds statement is completed, it is a simple matter to complete the formal sources and applications of funds statement. This can readily be seen if the information on the funds statement of Illustration 172 is compared with the information of the working paper of Illustration 173.

Nature of the Adjustments on a Funds Statement Working Paper

If the adjustments on the funds statement working paper of Illustration 173 are examined, it will be seen that these adjustments are of two different types. They are: (1) adjustments that cancel out bookkeeping entries that did not affect funds; and (2) adjustments that set out and more clearly indicate the nature of the charges representing sources and applications of funds.

Adjustments of the first type are necessary in order to eliminate from the working paper all of the changes that did not affect funds. After the adjustments of this first type are completed, the remaining "changes" in the "changes" column represent either increases or decreases in net working capital or sources or applications of funds; these remaining changes appear on the funds statement.

The adjustments of the second type, adjustments that make more clear the sources and applications of funds, are a convenience. In preparing funds statement working papers, accountants will vary as to the number of these adjustments that they make. On the working paper of Illustration 173, every change in a noncurrent item that represented a source or application of funds was canceled out with an adjustment that carried the item to the bottom of the statement under a title that clearly indicated the nature of the source or application. When a change such as the $4,500 increase in the Retained Earnings account (Illustration 173) results from a combination of sources or applications, it is necessary to make adjustments that will clearly set out the nature of each source or application. However, when a change represents a single source or application, such as the $14,000 increase in the Buildings account (Illustration 173), and the nature of the source or application is obvious, an adjustment is not necessary. In such a case, the amount of the change may be carried from the "changes" column to either the Sources or Applications column without adjustment. In Illustration 173 the $14,000 increase in buildings, the $3,000 increase in land, and the $5,000 decrease in mortgage payable could have been carried directly to the Sources and Applications columns without adjustments because the nature of these applications was obvious and clarifying adjustments were not absolutely necessary.

Sources of Information for a Funds Statement Working Paper

Although a funds statement can often be prepared from the information on a company's balance sheet, income statement, and statement of retained earnings, it is normally much easier to prepare such a statement if the accounts of the company can be examined.

QUESTIONS FOR CLASS DISCUSSION

1. What is a statement of sources and applications of funds designed to show?
2. When the word "funds" is used in connection with a funds statement, what are "funds"?
3. What are circulating assets and why are they so-called?
4. List several sources of funds. Where may a company apply funds?
5. What are working papers?

6. On December 12 a company borrowed $10,000 by giving its bank a sixty-day, interest-bearing note. Will this transaction appear on the year-end funds statement as a source of funds?

7. A company that began an accounting period with $45,000 of merchandise inventory, ended the period with $40,000 of inventory. Was this decrease in inventory a source of funds?

8. A company wrote off a fully depreciated fixed asset. What account balances appearing on the company's funds statement working paper were affected by the write-off? How was the write-off treated on the funds statement working paper? Why was it treated in this manner?

9. Explain why such expenses as depreciation, amortization of patents, and amortization of bond discount are added to the net income in order to determine the amount of funds provided by the operation of a business.

10. When a funds statement working paper is prepared, after the "changes" resulting from bookkeeping transactions that did not affect working capital are eliminated, (a) what do the remaining changes in current asset and current liability items represent? (b) What do the remaining changes in the noncurrent items represent?

PROBLEMS

Problem 29–1

Baker Company's comparative balance sheets of December 31, 1959, and 1960, carried the following debit and credit amounts:

	December 31	
Debits	*1959*	*1960*
Cash...	$ 4,300	$ 7,500
Accounts receivable, net.....................	10,000	12,000
Merchandise inventory.......................	32,000	31,500
Prepaid expenses............................	1,200	1,000
Store equipment.............................	14,000	20,100
	$61,500	$72,100
Credits		
Accumulated depreciation of store equipment..	$ 4,800	$ 6,100
Accounts payable............................	19,400	16,800
Common stock, $10 par value................	25,000	30,000
Premium on common stock....................	......	2,500
Retained earnings...........................	12,300	16,700
	$61,500	$72,100

An examination of Baker Company's 1960 income statement and accounting records revealed:

a) Net income for the year, $7,400.

b) The year's recorded depreciation on the store equipment amounted to $2,100.

c) Five hundred shares of common stock were issued at $15 per share.

d) Cash dividends paid, $3,000.

e) Store equipment costing $6,900 was purchased.

f) Fully depreciated store equipment that cost $800 was discarded, and its cost was removed from the accounts.

Required:

Prepare a funds statement working paper and a statement of sources and applications of funds.

Problem 29–2

The comparative balance sheets of Central Sales Company for the years ended December 31, 1959, and 1960 carried the following debit and credit amounts:

	December 31	
Debits	*1959*	*1960*
Cash	$ 22,300	$ 12,400
Accounts receivable, net	15,600	16,200
Merchandise inventory	51,400	50,200
Prepaid expenses	1,100	1,400
Long-term investments	18,900	
Store equipment	14,300	15,000
Office equipment	4,200	3,900
Land		20,000
Buildings		60,000
	$127,800	$179,100

Credits		
Accumulated depreciation, store equipment	$ 3,600	$ 4,300
Accumulated depreciation, office equipment	1,300	1,400
Accumulated depreciation, buildings		1,200
Accounts payable	12,700	11,300
Notes payable (due in 54 days)		5,000
Mortgage payable		40,000
Common stock	100,000	100,000
Retained earnings	10,200	15,900
	$127,800	$179,100

An examination of the company's 1960 income statement, statement of retained earnings, and accounting records revealed:

a) A net income for the year of $8,400.

b) The income statement showed depreciation of store equipment, $1,300; office equipment, $400; and buildings, $1,200.

c) The long-term investments on the 1959 balance sheet consisted of stocks and bonds which were sold during 1960 for $21,200. The gain was carried directly to retained earnings.

d) Store equipment on the books at the time of its sale at a cost of $800, less $600 of accumulated depreciation, was sold during the year for its book value.

e) Fully depreciated office equipment that cost $300 was discarded, and its cost and accumulated depreciation were removed from the books.

f) Store equipment costing $1,500 was purchased.

g) Cash dividends amounting to $5,000 were paid during the year.

Required:

Prepare a funds statement working paper for Central Sales Company and a statement of sources and applications of funds.

Problem 29–3

Brighter Homes Store is organized as a single proprietorship and is owned and operated by Dale Olsen. At the ends of 1959 and 1960 the company's balance sheets carried the following condensed debit and credit amounts:

	December 31	
Debits	*1959*	*1960*
Cash..	$ 6,400	$ 7,100
Accounts receivable, net................................	17,200	16,800
Merchandise inventory..................................	33,700	36,400
Other current assets....................................	800	500
Store equipment.......................................	8,400	13,100
	$66,500	$73,900

Credits		
Accumulated depreciation, store equipment.................	$ 3,200	$ 1,800
Accounts payable......................................	16,800	14,200
Dale Olsen, capital....................................	46,500	57,900
	$66,500	$73,900

Dale Olsen's 1960 statement of changes in the proprietor's Capital account carried the following information:

Dale Olsen, capital, January 1, 1960......................		$46,500
Add: Additional investment............................		5,000
Total Investment......................................		$51,500
Net income per income statement........................	$12,400	
Less: Withdrawals for living expenses...................	6,000	
Excess of net income over withdrawals....................		6,400
Dale Olsen, Capital, December 31, 1960..................		$57,900

An examination of the store equipment accounts revealed that: (1) There was $1,200 depreciation of store equipment expense charged during the year. (2) Store equipment costing $4,800 was purchased. (3) Store equipment carried on the books on the day of its exchange at its cost of $2,800, less $2,400 accumulated depreciation, was traded on like new equipment having a cash price of $3,100. A trade-in allowance of $600 was received. (4) Fully depreciated store equipment that cost $200 was junked and its cost and accumulated depreciation were removed from the accounts.

Required:

Prepare a funds statement working paper and a statement of sources and applications of funds for the Brighter Homes Store.

CLASS EXERCISES

Exercise 29–1

The following accounts appeared in the ledger of a firm at the end of its accounting year:

Machinery					
Jan. 1	Balance	41,700	Jan. 3	Fully depreciated ma-	
May 16	Machinery purchased	3,200		chinery	600
July 8	Extraordinary repairs	1,240	5	Machinery sold	1,750

Accumulated Depreciation, Machinery

Jan. 3	Fully depreciated machinery	600	Jan. 1	Balance	14,320
5	Machinery sold	1,400	Dec. 31	Year's depreciation	4,800

Retained Earnings

Jan. 5	Loss on machinery sold	200	Jan. 1	Balance	85,200
Dec. 22	Cash dividends	8,000	Dec. 31	Net income	18,600

Required:

Give in general journal form the funds statement working paper adjustments required by the entries in the foregoing accounts.

Exercise 29–2

From the following income statement information prepare a schedule showing the funds provided by current operations:

Sales		$680,000
Cost of goods sold (includes depreciation of plant, $46,000)		420,000
Gross profit		$260,000
Operating expenses:		
Salaries (including $2,000 accrued)	$110,000	
Advertising (after deducting $900 prepaid)	9,800	
Taxes (all accrued and unpaid)	8,700	
Depreciation of furniture and equipment	12,000	
Bond interest (including $200 discount amortization)	5,200	
Bad debts	1,800	
Total Expenses		$147,500
Net income before income taxes		$112,500
Less: Federal income taxes (unpaid)		56,000
Net Income for the Year		$ 56,500

SUPPLEMENTARY PROBLEM

Problem 29–A

The December 31, 1959, and 1960 balance sheets of Western Mercantile Company carried the following debit and credit amounts:

	December 31	
Debits	*1959*	*1960*
Cash	$ 12,600	$ 10,200
Accounts receivable, net	32,900	35,100
Merchandise inventory	86,400	85,200
Prepaid expenses	1,800	1,500
Office equipment	5,600	5,000
Store equipment	28,300	29,800
	$167,600	$166,800

	December 31	
Credits	*1959*	*1960*
Accumulated depreciation, office equipment..............$	2,400	$ 2,500
Accumulated depreciation, store equipment..............	6,500	7,500
Accounts payable......	23,500	22,400
Notes payable.......................................	5,000	10,000
Common stock, $10 par value........................	100,000	110,000
Premium on common stock..........................	5,500	6,500
Retained earnings..................................	24,700	7,900
	$167,600	$166,800

An examination of the company's income statement, statement of retained earnings, and accounts revealed the following:

a) A net loss for the year of $1,900.

b) Depreciation expense charged on office equipment, $500; and on store equipment, $1,700.

c) Office equipment that was carried at its cost of $600 with accumulated depreciation of $400 was sold for $300. The gain was carried directly to Retained Earnings.

d) Store equipment costing $2,200 was purchased.

e) Fully depreciated store equipment that cost $700 was discarded and its cost and accumulated depreciation were removed from the accounts.

f) Cash dividends of $4,000 were paid during the year.

g) A 1,000 share stock dividend was declared and paid. On the date of declaration the common stock of the company had a fair market value of $11 per share.

Required:

Prepare a funds statement working paper and a statement of sources and applications of funds.

Chapter

30

FUNDAMENTAL ACCOUNTING CONVENTIONS, CONCEPTS, AND STANDARDS

DATA GATHERED by means of accounting and summarized in financial statements are used by management as the basis for both routine operating and policy decisions. Such data also commonly become the basis for additional decisions by grantors of credit, governmental agencies, labor unions, stockholders, and investors. Obviously, if accounting data summarized in financial statements are to be both understood and relied upon by members of these diverse groups, such data and statements must be prepared in conformity with generally recognized and accepted accounting principles.

Thus far in this text an effort has been made to present the fundamentals of accounting cast in light of generally recognized and accepted accounting principles. However, it is deemed wise at this point to restate in a brief manner the more important of these principles both as a means of emphasis and review.

Generally Accepted Accounting Principles

What are the generally accepted principles of accounting? From where did they come? Do they exist in a codified form? What is the basis of their authority? These questions can perhaps best be answered in their reverse order.

The basis of the authority of any accounting principle rests solely on its acceptance by members of the accounting profession. Accounting principles are not laws in the sense of the laws of physics or chemistry, and they do not exist anywhere in codified form; rather they are to be found in the current literature of accounting, for example, in the published bulletins of the Committee on Accounting Procedure of the American Institute of Certified Public Accountants, in the pronouncements of committees of the American Accounting Association, and in the writings of scholars in accounting. Actually, some of what are commonly known as accounting principles are better described as good accounting practices and others are better described as *conventions, concepts,* and *standards.* In either case it should be emphasized that they are man-made and are not immutable like the natural laws of science.

From where have accounting principles come? Accounting principles have evolved (and are evolving today) from the combined thinking of the members of the accounting profession who were (and are) in turn influenced by the needs of business managements, governmental agencies. labor unions, stockholders, investors, and the general public. The aggregate of these influences gave (and give) rise to accounting theories. Some of the theories were (and are) accepted and some rejected. The general acceptance of a theory gave (and gives) it the status of an accounting principle.

What are the generally accepted principles of accounting? Short discussions of some of the more significant follow.

The Money Convention. One of the more important of what may best be called conventions is the "money convention." Briefly this convention holds that accounting should record "money invested" and "money borrowed," trace the various recommitments of this "money capital" as it is invested and reinvested in the business process, and finally measure out of gross "money revenue," resulting from business activity, the return or recapture of "money capital" with any residue being designated as "money income." Thus the balance sheet reports in effect the number of dollars received from every source (from creditors, from stockholders or proprietors, and from retained income) and over against this shows where these dollar funds are invested (in inventories, unused supplies or prepaid services, in fixed assets, etc., and a balance of uncommitted cash). It should be noted that this convention holds that it is not the function of accounting to account for value. In fact the value of the dollar itself is in a state of constant change. But the accountant is not deterred by these value changes from his primary purpose of "accounting for dollars." He continues to "count dollars" in spite of continuing and often material changes in their value (purchasing power), feeling that that count can be done with a high degree of accuracy and objectivity, while determination of "value" is both subjective and dependent upon future events. It is recognized, however, that supplementary analyses based on the reliable "dollar" reports and showing the effects of price level change on all the basic accounting statements are valuable and highly desirable, particularly during periods of abnormally high or abnormally low prices.[1] Nevertheless, conventional accounting reports prepared in compliance with the money convention are presently considered more useful for general business purposes since they are based on verifiable and objective evidence and contain a minimum of subjective speculation.

Thus it must be concluded from this convention that the reader of the balance sheet is not warranted in interpreting the asset amounts listed on the balance sheet as the values of those assets. Rather these are the commitments or investments made for business purpose. Their value depends on their earning power. And earning power of the future cannot be pre-

---

[1] The disturbing effects of rapidly changing prices and particularly of current abnormally high prices have received much attention in recent studies. It is beyond the scope of this text to discuss this problem fully. See Chapter 28 for a brief discussion of the problems involved.

cisely measured just as no other future event can be exactly foretold. Yet, past earnings history interpreted in the light of the conditions known at the time should be greatly revealing, of much help in charting the future course of business enterprise and in estimating the value of enterprise assets.

The Accounting Period Convention. In spite of the difficulties involved in allocating costs and expenses and in measuring revenue for the short period, it is considered essential to maximum usefulness for periodic reports to be prepared, usually on a calendar- or fiscal-year basis, often with many interim reports during the year. It is obvious that most business ventures cannot be completed within such a short period of time. Many transactions would overlap any series of short periods chosen. Yet, it is highly important for business to have test readings upon the progress being made; it needs reliable estimates of the gain or loss from operations; and it needs current costs of its most important activities. Where these readings are made by the consistent application of principles and procedures proved reliable in the laboratory of experience, confidence in the short-term reports is fully justified.

The calendar year is the most commonly chosen accounting period. This is in part due to long-established practice and in part to accommodate business reports to social and economic (including governmental) conventions. The selection of the "natural" business year as the formal accounting period has gained much headway in recent years. The natural year is that twelve months' period ending at the lowest point of business activity for the period. For example, the business which has its lowest volume of activity in the summer would select a summer month to end its fiscal year, since the closing process would be easiest then and would interfere less with the routines of business operation.

The Business Entity Convention. In accounting for businesses, each enterprise is considered to be a separate accounting entity, with the affairs of the business and those of the owners being kept entirely separate. The business unit is viewed as owning all resources committed to its purposes, subject, of course, to the equitable interests of creditors. Therefore, all reports and records are prepared with the viewpoint of this entity in mind. The analysis of all transactions and the test readings of cost and revenue are conditioned by this assumption.

The Going-Concern Convention. Accounting reports are prepared on the assumption that the business unit will continue to function in its usual manner, performing the same general business functions for which it has invested in present plant and equipment and obtaining therefrom a reasonable business success. In other words, continuity of business activity is the reasonable expectation. Should the business be faced with termination, loss of usefulness, or liquidation, the orthodox accounting statements would not satisfactorily report the true conditions to those interested.

It is on the basis of this convention that the accounting process can remain fixed on the objective of faithfully recording and tracing dollars invested in assets. If the normal expectation of the going concern is a valid assumption for the particular enterprise, then periodic recovery of the dollars committed to its assets seems fairly assured, even though some of these assets are usually unmarketable to such a degree that only a fraction of their unamortized cost might be recovered from a direct sale.

Consistency. As has been noted from time to time in this text, two or more methods or procedures may have been derived in accounting practice to accomplish a particular accounting objective. There are several methods for computing depreciation. More than one method has been found to be satisfactory in arriving at the cost of inventory. One method may be considered more useful for one enterprise, while another may be more satisfactory for a concern operating under different circumstances. Recognizing the validity of different methods used under the varying circumstances of business operations, it is therefore necessary to insure a high degree of comparability of accounting data from period to period for each individual concern. For this reason accountants insist on a consistent application of accounting methods in any one company, period after period, and that any departures from this doctrine of consistency must be fully stated and the effects thereof on the accounting statements must be fully disclosed.

The reader of a company's accounting statements should be able to assume, in the absence of clear indications to the contrary, that generally accepted principles of accounting have been followed in a consistent manner in the preparation of the statements. Only on the basis of this assumption can real confidence in accounting reports be maintained.

Materiality. Accounting must be practical. For this reason strict adherence to a "principle" is not required where the increase in the accuracy of accounting reports is not sufficient to justify the increased cost of compliance. For example, if a wastepaper basket is purchased at a cost of $1.29, that cost might better be charged to expenses in the period of purchase than be amortized over the five-year estimated life of the asset, because of the extra accounting cost involved in amortizing over the long period. A uniform policy should be adopted to govern such exceptions and should be followed consistently.

The Cost Principle. In line with the "money convention" previously discussed, a cost principle has developed and is applied with almost universal consistency in accounting practice. This principle may be outlined as follows:

1. All assets and services acquired by a business enterprise are measured at date of acquisition by the costs incurred to secure the asset (or service) and place it in position or condition for business use.
2. Costs incurred are measured by the amounts invested on a cash or cash-equivalent basis. If the consideration given for the particular asset is cash, the measure of cost incurred is the entire amount of the cash outlay made

to secure the asset and get it ready for use. If the consideration given was other than cash, the measure of the consideration is the cash-equivalent value of the consideration, or the fair value (on a cash-equivalent basis) of the thing received, whichever is the more clearly evident.[2]

3. Costs incurred should be so classified as to facilitate subsequent accounting for those costs. For example, if real estate consisting of land and a building is purchased, the total cost should be allocated in the accounts between Land and Buildings, for the cost of the latter must be amortized over the useful life of the asset.

4. For each accounting period the amount of costs absorbed in producing revenue, or otherwise expired, should be determined and deducted from revenue in the determination of net income for the period. (See the Income Principle section following.)

A deviation from the cost principle is required in the case of assets received by donation. Donated assets are recorded at their cash-equivalent value as of the date of the donation. This departure from the cost principle is considered necessary because every resource of a business enterprise, regardless of its origin, should be properly accounted for, and only by assigning all resources with their fair value at the time of acquisition can the earning power of the enterprise be accurately determined.

The Income Principle.   In general this principle holds that one of the major objectives of accounting is the proper determination of periodic income through the matching of appropriate costs against revenue. The net income of an enterprise is the measure of the increase in that enterprise's net assets (assets less liabilities) brought about through profitable exchanges of product and services or through sale of assets other than stock in trade.

Revenue Recognition.   The term "revenue" refers to the accounting measure of the amount of assets received in the sale of products and services. The amount of revenue is the cash or cash-equivalent value of the consideration received in exchange for goods and services sold. The term "revenue" also includes gain on the sale or exchanges of assets other than stock in trade (such as gain on the sale of fixed assets) and also gain from the advantageous settlement of liabilities. For example, if a business owes bonds payable with a book value of $100,000 and is able to pay these bonds before maturity by buying them in the open market for $98,000, the business gains $2,000.

The more common bases utilized in accounting for the recognition of revenue together with the circumstances under which each might be used follow:

Sales Basis.   Revenue is usually taken up in the records and reported when the transactions giving rise to it are completed. This is generally referred to as the "sales basis" for the recognition of revenue. Although revenue is earned throughout the whole business process, its amount is

---

[2] *Accounting Research Bulletin No. 43,* "Restatement and Revision of Accounting Research Bulletins" (New York: American Institute of Certified Public Accountants, 1953), p. 38.

not determinable until a price is agreed upon between a buyer and a seller and a legal sale is made. For example, a manufacturer earns a part of his revenue upon completing each of these necessary business steps: (1) manufacturing goods for sale; (2) securing orders from customers; and (3) delivering the goods to customers. Yet until all the steps are completed, there is no right to collect the sales price. The sales basis of accounting for revenue recognizes this, and revenue is not measured and reported as realized until a sale is completed. A sale is assumed to be completed when assets such as cash, accounts receivable, or the like are transferred from the buyer to the seller.

Under the sales basis of revenue recognition, revenue is reported in the period in which the sales are completed. This method is considered reliable when two conditions are satisfied:

1. When the ultimate collection of the sales price seems reasonably assured.
2. When most or all of the applicable costs and expenses of the sale can be determined with reasonable approximation in the period of the sale. Obviously, the accountant should not report a sale as revenue where there is considerable doubt as to the final outcome, or as to the *net income* derived from the sales transaction.

Since there are occasions when one or both of the foregoing conditions do not exist, revenue is also at times reported on a "cash basis" and sometimes on a "production basis."

Cash Basis. Under some business situations it may be desirable to defer the reporting of revenue until cash is actually collected. Certainly this would be the case where there is considerable doubt as to the amounts which will ultimately be collected under a sales contract. An illustration of the cash basis of revenue recognition is often seen in accounting for installment sales. Revenue from the sale of goods on an installment basis may either (1) be taken up in the period of sale (the sales basis just discussed), or (2) be reported only as cash is collected, if the collection period is relatively long and if experience shows that many of the goods are never fully paid for and must be repossessed (a right usually reserved to the seller in case of failure of payment by the buyer).

To illustrate the second of these methods, assume that the City Music Company accounts for its installment sales of pianos on a cash basis and that in May of this year it sold a piano for $800, terms 10 per cent cash with the balance to be paid in equal monthly installments of $30 each over the next two years. The entry in general journal form to record the sale on a cash basis is:

May	5	Cash..	80.00	
		Installment Accounts Receivable..........	720.00	
		Inventory of Pianos (at cost)........		480.00
		Deferred Gross Profit from Sales......		320.00
		To record the installment sale of a piano.		

Note in the foregoing entry that the gross profit on the sale of this piano is 40 per cent of the sales price ($320 ÷ $800 = 0.4, or 40 per cent) and that the amount of this gross profit is credited to the account Deferred Gross Profit from Sales.

It also should be noted that the foregoing entry is made under the assumption that a perpetual inventory system is in use. Otherwise the credit of the entry to the account "Inventory of Pianos" would be to an account commonly called "Cost of Installment Sales," which, if it were used, would be closed at the end of the accounting period as a reduction of the cost of goods sold.

To continue the illustration, as each monthly installment is collected, City Music Company records it as follows:

June	5	Cash....................................	30.00	
		Installment Accounts Receivable.....		30.00
		Collected monthly installment.		

If all installments due are collected during the year of the sale, City Music Company repeats the foregoing entry seven times (June through December) to record a total of $210 collected in monthly installments which together with the $80 downpayment add to a sum of $290 collected from this sale. Then, at the end of the accounting period as a result of the $290 collected, the company makes the following entries to take the amount of the realized gross profit onto their income statement:

Dec.	31	Deferred Gross Profit from Sales........	116.00	
		Realized Gross Profit..............		116.00
		To record the realized gross profit from the sale of a piano.		
	31	Realized Gross Profit...................	116.00	
		Income Summary.................		116.00
		To close the Realized Gross Profit account.		

In examining the foregoing entries recall that the company's rate of gross profit is 40 per cent. Then note that $116 is 40 per cent of the $290 collected and that the company has recognized its revenue from the sale of this piano only as it was collected in cash.

After the foregoing entries are made, the balance of the Deferred Gross Profit from Sales account is $204 and is carried to the liability side of the balance sheet as unearned revenue.

To continue the illustration, assume that after making his December payment the buyer of this piano defaults and that after several months of attempting to collect, City Music Company is forced to repossess the piano. The entry to record the repossession is:

Mar.	12	Used Pianos (for estimated fair value)....	275.00	
		Deferred Gross Profit from Sales.........	204.00	
		Losses on Repossessions...............	31.00	
		Installment Accounts Receivable.....		510.00
		To record a repossession.		

In the foregoing entry the unpaid $510 balance of the installment account receivable is greater than the sum of the fair market value of the repossessed piano and the remaining deferred gross profit on the sale; consequently, the resulting loss is charged to "Losses on Repossessions." Had there been a gain, it would have been credited to an account "Gains on Repossessions." Both of these accounts are closed to Income Summary at the end of the period.

The foregoing short discussion of the accounting treatment of installment sales is given only for the purpose of illustrating the cash basis of revenue recognition. A more complete discussion is deferred to an advanced text.

Production Basis. Sometimes the sales basis for taking up revenue fails even approximately to recognize revenue in the periods in which the revenue is earned. For example, a contractor specializing in large construction jobs often finds that the typical project requires two or more years for completion. If such a contractor has a three-year project and if he takes up revenue on a sales basis, he will recognize the revenue from this job and take up the profit in the year of completion. Yet portions of the revenue and profit are actually earned in each of the three years required for the job's completion. Furthermore, if the contractor has only a very few projects under construction at any one time, he may find that none or only a very few are completed in a single year in spite of the year being one of heavy activity. In such cases a contractor may elect to take up revenue and earnings on his projects on a percentage-of-completion basis or some other such basis that allocates earnings to the several periods in which they are earned.

To illustrate the production basis of recognizing revenue, assume that a contractor has under construction a large dam for which the total contract price is $80,000,000 and for which the estimated cost of construction is $75,000,000. As construction progresses the costs incurred are charged to a controlling account called "Construction in Progress." These costs include materials, labor, supplies, depreciation on all equipment, insurance, and all other expenses related to the project. If at the end of the first accounting period in which this dam is under construction the total of the costs charged to the dam is $15,000,000, the entry to take up the revenue on the basis of the partial performance and to set up the asset increment is:

Dec.	31	Unbilled Accounts Receivable......	16,000,000.00	
		Construction Revenue.........		16,000,000.00
		To take up revenue based on partial performance.		

The $15,000,000 of construction costs that have been incurred during the first year are used in determining the amount of revenue taken up in the foregoing entry. The $15,000,000 of costs are one fifth of the total estimated $75,000,000 of costs; consequently, the foregoing entry takes up one fifth ($80,000,000 × ⅕ = $16,000,000) of the total contract price as the amount of the year's revenue from this project.

The $16,000,000 of revenue and the construction costs are shown on the year's income statement as follows:

```
Construction revenue . . . . . . . . . . .  $16,000,000
Construction costs (details in a schedule)   15,000,000
Construction profit. . . . . . . . . . . .  $ 1,000,000
```

In the foregoing illustration the relation of costs incurred to total estimated costs is used to measure partial performance. Sometimes other means of judging partial performance must be used.

Matching Costs and Revenues.   The Committee on Accounting Procedure stated in *Accounting Research Bulletin No. 13* that "it is plainly desirable to provide, by charges in the current income statement, properly classified, for all foreseeable costs and losses applicable against current revenues, to the extent that they can be measured and allocated to fiscal periods with reasonable approximation." Thus in determining net income from business operations all costs which are *applicable* to the revenue of the period should be charged against that revenue. Costs are "applicable" if it is reasonably apparent that they represent an investment in resources and services consumed in the process of realizing that particular revenue.

Costs are applicable to the revenue of the period under each of the following circumstances:[3]

(1) If there is "a direct identification or association with the revenue of the period." As illustrations of costs directly associated with revenue of the period are cost of merchandise delivered to customers, sales commissions, etc.

(2) If there is "an indirect association with the revenue of the period, as in the case of office salaries or rent."

A commonly accepted axiom in accounting holds that no (money) income emerges until and unless (money) capital is preserved intact. This

---

[3] "Accounting Concepts and Standards Underlying Corporate Financial Statements (1948)," Committee on Concepts and Standards (Columbus, Ohio: American Accounting Association, 1948).

is to say that there can be no gain on investment where the investment is lost. For this reason other measurable expirations of asset costs even though not associated with the production of revenue for the period must be deducted from revenue before a final measurement of net income can be made. Thus losses from fire and storm, from the sale of capital assets, and from all other causes even though not related to the ordinary operations of the business must be deducted from revenue before any beneficial net increase in business assets can be reported.

The measurement of "expired" cost (or the cost that should be deducted from the period's revenue) is in part precise and in part estimated through consistent application of definite methods. With reference to the period of expiration, expired costs are accounted for as follows:

1. Cost of assets and services consumed in their entirety in one period—the measure of these costs is precisely recorded in the books in accordance with the cost principle. Part of these costs (of assets and services consumed) is applicable to the revenue of the period and is so charged; part is applicable to the future in that it is transformed into goods or services to be sold or used in the future. This latter portion of the cost is represented largely by inventories.

2. Cost of assets and services consumed more or less gradually over two or more periods—the total cost of this type of assets and services is also recorded in the books in accordance with the cost principle, but it is necessary to arrive at a rational allocation of the total as between the current and future periods. This is done through the consistent application of methods found most useful in the industry, the methods being based on experience and expert opinion. In general the cost division is made by determining first the portion of cost which seems reasonably beneficial to future periods, and then subtracting these deferred costs from the total to secure the amount to be matched against current revenue.

It is important to remember that only actual dollar costs are matched if the "money convention" is adhered to carefully. Errors in judgment in making an allocation of costs as between current and future periods will inevitably creep into short-term reports of income earned. Thus good accounting practice is continuously alert to improve the matching process. Careful selection and consistent application of methods is the best insurance of accuracy in this significant "test reading" (income statement) of the accountant.

"Applicable costs" are deducted from current revenue only when they are measurable "with reasonable approximation." It is important that all costs incurred in producing the revenue of the period be matched against that revenue. However, if accounting data are to be based on objective verifiable evidence, no guesswork can enter into the determination of the accounting amounts. For this reason, when, in the considered judgment of the accountant, material costs applicable to the current revenue cannot be determined in the period of the revenue with sufficient accuracy to satisfy the accountant, he should not include these costs in the current income statement. For example, a company introduces a new machine. In the first year it may be felt that imperfections may be found by the users which the company will feel obligated to remedy, perhaps at considerable cost. Yet, no experience background is available by which to estimate this applicable cost "with reasonable approximation." This cost should be referred to by footnote or parenthetical notation on the income statement pointing to the omission of the expected cost and thus emphasizing the provisional nature of the net income figure. These costs will be reported in later statements when their amounts are known. Of course, if the potential cost is so material as to make misleading any statement of net income, the revenue itself may have to be deferred until a more definite computation of applicable cost can be made.

Conclusion

Again it should be emphasized that *it is not the function of accounting to account for value,* but rather to account for "money invested" and "money borrowed," tracing this "money capital" through the often intricate series of commitments and recommitments in various facilities to be used for business purposes, and finally measuring out of "money revenue" the return or recapture of "money capital" with any residue being designated as "net income." In fundamental objective, the accountant's job is not dissimilar to that of the manager of a wheat storage elevator. The latter may store No. 1 Red Canadian wheat in a given elevator. He is concerned with the number of bushels of wheat received, with the number of bushels issued, and must account for the number of bushels remaining. He is also concerned with the change in the price (or value) of wheat, but he does not allow this concern to affect his accounting. He is accountable for a definite number of bushels of wheat, and that is what his primary statement of accountability must show. Similarly, the accountant must account for dollars. He, too, is concerned with the change in the value of his unit of accountability, the dollar, but his primary statements should make a precise accounting based on methodical count of dollars. After preparing statements based on the "money convention," analytical statements may be prepared to show changes in value.

QUESTIONS FOR CLASS DISCUSSION

1. What are "generally accepted accounting principles"?
2. Why is it important for accounting statements to be prepared in conformity with generally accepted accounting principles?
3. What is the basis of the authority of any accounting principle?
4. From where do accounting principles come?
5. Briefly explain the money convention of accounting.
6. A company's balance sheet shows assets of $1,000,000. Does this amount represent the value of the assets? Explain.
7. The Mason Iron Works has substantial investments in buildings, machinery, furnaces, and other depreciable assets. The general manager argues that no depreciation should be placed on the books for the current year, since prices have increased to such an extent that the assets are worth more at the end

of the year than at the start. Do you agree? Give reasons for your answers.

8. A company changed its method of inventory costing three times during the past five years, using in turn average cost, Fifo, and Lifo. Is each of these methods considered acceptable for inventory pricing? Criticize the practice of the company, pointing out the specific principle violated.

9. What is the cost principle?

10. What is revenue? What are three common bases for recognizing and reporting revenue? When is revenue recognized under each of the three bases? Under what circumstances should each of the bases be used?

11. What is meant by "matching costs and revenues"?

12. Name three "expired costs" or expenses which may be directly associated with the revenue of a retail furniture dealer. Name three expenses which may have indirect association with his revenue.

13. The Flood Company manufactured and sold a new type air conditioner during the past year. The air conditioners are sold under a six months' guarantee. It is felt that the cost of adjusting the conditioners sold during the first year will be rather heavy, but there is no basis for an accurate estimate of this cost. Against what revenue should this cost be matched? How would you treat this cost at the end of the first year?

14. An automobile dealer offers a customer $800 cash for his used car. However, if the customer will buy a new car for $3,600, he will allow the customer $1,000 trade-in on his old car. If the customer accepts the offer for trading in his old car, what is the cost of the new car to the customer? What is the amount of revenue to the dealer from the sale of the new car?

15. Why is the "net income" reported on the income statement sometimes referred to as a "test reading"?

16. Why is revenue on installment sales sometimes taken up on the cash basis?

17. Why is revenue on long-term contracts sometimes taken up on the production basis? If a contractor has a rather large number of construction contracts, even though of relative long term, is it important that he use the production basis of reporting revenue in order to secure periodic income measurements which reflect the approximate amounts earned each period?

PROBLEMS

Problem 30–1

On August 2 Marlin Electric Company sold for $300 on an installment basis an electric refrigerator that cost $180. The contract called for a $25 down payment and $25 on the first of each month until full payment was made. The customer failed to make his November 1 payment, and on December 12 the refrigerator was repossessed. The appraised value of the repossessed refrigerator was $120 and expenses of repossession were $5.00.

Required:

Under the assumption that the company closes its books on December 31 and that it takes up revenue on the basis of collections, give the entries necessary to account for the installment sale.

Problem 30–2

During January, 1960, while completing his initial audit of the accounts of Southshore Corporation, an auditor discovered that the company followed the practice of recognizing bad debt losses in the years in which bad accounts were written off. During 1957, 1958, and 1959 the company reported net incomes of $12,600, $14,200, and $13,800, respectively. In arriving at these income figures the company had written off to the Bad Debts Expense account the following amounts of uncollectible accounts:

	In 1957	In 1958	In 1959
Accounts from 1955 sales	$200		
Accounts from 1956 sales	650	$350	$ 50
Accounts from 1957 sales		550	700
Accounts from 1958 sales			800
Total Accounts Written Off	$850	$900	$1,550

From an examination of the December 31, 1959, accounts receivable it was estimated that the following additional amounts of accounts were uncollectible:

Accounts from 1958 sales	$ 650
Accounts from 1959 sales	1,350
Total	$2,000

Required:

1. Determine the company's 1957, 1958, and 1959 incomes under the principle of matching revenues and expenses.
2. Under the assumption that the company wishes its 1960 income statement to be prepared under the current operating performance concept, prepare a journal entry to correct the reported income of prior periods.

Problem 30–3

Potter Company sells on an installment basis for $900 a machine that costs $600. A $100 down payment is required at the time of each sale, with the balance payable over a period of from two to three years. On December 31 of the current year the following information in regard to the year's sales of this machine was available:

Sales (100 machines)	$90,000
Installment accounts receivable	72,000
Expenses	8,000
Income tax rate	52%

Required:

1. Prepare an income statement for the company under the assumption that it recognizes revenue on a sales basis.
2. Prepare another income statement under the assumption that the company recognizes revenue on a cash basis and that one half of the expenses are deferred.

Problem 30–4

On December 31 of the current year the Construction Costs controlling account in the ledger of Interstate Contractors had a balance of $6,880,000. This balance represented the year's costs on three long-term contracts as follows:

	Total Contract Prices	Total Estimated Costs	Costs for This Year
Mason Bridge Contract	$ 9,250,000	$8,750,000	$3,500,000
Mellon County Road	4,200,000	3,600,000	1,200,000
Falcolm Dam	10,000,000	8,600,000	2,180,000
			$6,880,000

The first two contracts were started this year. The Falcolm Dam was completed this year, and the revenue taken up on this contract for the two years prior to the current year totaled $7,300,000.

Required:

1. Using the production basis, prepare an entry to take up the year's revenue on these contracts.
2. Prepare a partial income statement showing the company's gross profit for the year.

CLASS EXERCISE

Exercise 30–1

On January 4 of the current year Southlake Sales Company paid $18,000 for land to be used as a warehouse site. In addition they paid an attorney $500 for a title search on the land, and they paid $1,100 of delinquent taxes on the property. During January old buildings on the land were razed at a cost of $1,200; however, $200 was realized from the sale of salvaged materials. During the five-month period beginning on February 1 a warehouse was erected on the site at a total construction cost of $120,000. On February 1, when the warehouse was begun, a $1,440 premium on a three-year fire insurance policy on the new building was paid. The warehouse was occupied on July 1. On August 5 an $800 payment was made to the city in full of an assessment for paving the street beside the warehouse. The life of the warehouse was estimated at forty years.

Required:

Determine the amounts at which the land and building should appear on the end of the year balance sheet.

SUPPLEMENTARY PROBLEMS

Problem 30–A

The sales and expenses of J. B. Stone Company for the current year, its first year in business, were as follows:

Cash sales..	$16,800
Sales on thirty-day accounts.................................	12,400
Installment sales (two years to pay; collections during the year, $12,000)...	36,000
Operating expenses..	12,800

Required:

Under the assumption that the gross profit on sales was 40 per cent of selling prices, prepare two income statements for the company. (a) In the first income statement assume that all revenue is recognized on the sales basis. (b) In the second income statement assume that the revenue from cash and thirty-day charge sales is recognized on a sales basis and that installment sales revenue is recognized on a cash basis.

Problem 30–B

Valley Construction Company began three jobs during 1958. Job No. 1 was completed during 1959, and Job Nos. 2 and 3 were completed during 1960. Following are the contract prices, estimated total costs, and yearly costs for the three jobs:

Job No.	Contract Prices	Estimated Costs	1958 Costs	1959 Costs	1960 Costs
1............	$2,500,000	$2,250,000	$1,800,000	$ 504,000	
2............	4,000,000	3,600,000	1,080,000	945,000	$1,610,000
3............	3,000,000	2,700,000	72,000	1,440,000	1,117,000
Totals.......	$9,500,000	$8,550,000	$2,952,000	$2,889,000	$2,727,000

Required:

Determine the amounts of revenue the company will recognize in each of the three years if: (*a*) it recognizes revenue on a sales basis, and (*b*) if it recognizes revenue on a production basis.

Bank—*Cont.*
draft, 216
loan, recording a, 240
reconciliation, statement of, 221
service charges, 220
statement, 218
Bills of exchange; *see* Drafts
Bills of lading
order, 253
order, used with sight draft, 253
straight, 253
Bonds
accrued interest expense on, 544
amortizing discount on, 542
amortizing premium on, 543
authorization of, 538
callable, 546
classification of, 534
collateral trust, 535
convertible, 546
costs of a bond issue, 546
coupon, 535
debentures, 535
deed of trust, 534
discounts and premiums on balance sheet, 545
equipment trust, 535
interest rates, 541
premiums and discounts on bonds outstanding less than a full year, 545
purchased between interest dates, 557
quotations, 553
real estate mortgage, 535
recording transactions in, 538
redemption of, 546
registered, 535
retirement of, 540
second mortgage, 539
secured, 535
serial, 535
as short-term investments, 553
sinking fund, 547
sinking fund reserve, 550
sold between interest dates, 540
sold at a discount, 541
sold at a premium, 543
and stocks as investments, 552
times interest earned, 700
U.S. savings, as a payroll deduction, 380
underwriter, 534
unsecured; *see* Debentures
who may issue, 534
why a corporation issues, 536
Bonus method of recording the admission of a partner, 428, 431
Book of final entry, 36; *see also* Ledgers
Book inventories; *see* Perpetual inventories
Book of original entry, 36; *see also* Journals

Book value
of fixed assets, 292
of stock, 462
Bookkeeping
mechanics of double entry, 22
relation to accounting, 2
techniques
dollar signs, 44
omission of zeros in cents column, 44
periods and commas, 44
Books of original entry, changes in for departmental accounting, 188
Borrowing money
by issuing bonds, 534
by means of long-term notes, 551
by means of a mortgage, 533
with notes, 240
Break-even chart, 676
Break-even points, 676
Budget
cash, 673
comparing actual achievement with budget plan, 672
expense, 673
fixed and variable, 675
master, 674
objectives of, 671
period, 671
plant and equipment, 673
preparing a, 672
preparing estimated statements, 675
sales, 672
Bulletin F, 289
Burden; *see* Overhead costs
Business entity convention, 7, 723
Business papers and procedures, need for, 126
Business papers used in purchasing, 131
Business transactions
and accounting values, 6
defined, 1
effect on the accounting equation, 7

C

C.P.A., 3
Calculating
cost of goods sold, 107
equivalent units, 630
interest, 237
interest by sixty-day, 6 per cent method, 238
unit process costs, 629
Callable bonds, 546
Canceled checks, 218
Capital
accounts, schedule of partners, 415
contributed; *see* Contributed capital
contributions of owners and creditors, 698

Exams Jan 25 8-10